To Asha, my beloved wife,
who left me in early 2008,
after being my life partner for twenty-five years

FOREWORD

Satheesh Kumar has written a comprehensive book on corporate governance in the Indian context. The book covers the subject from so many different angles that you can find something useful in it regardless of the nature of your interest in the field.

For those who are interested in a detailed understanding of the state of corporate governance in India, there is a lot of material in this book. Kumar tells us about how independent the independent directors really are, how much are they paid, how often they meet and how much time can they really devote to each company, given their other commitments.

There is a great deal to be said for a positive theory of corporate governance—not as it should be, nor as it is legally required to be, but as it is—and Kumar provides plenty of this positive theory in his book. Every chapter has small mini cases that provide examples of how corporate governance actually works in real life.

Apart from the obvious examples like Satyam, the book also discusses a number of lesser known ones, both of badly run companies and better run ones. While most of the examples are from India, there are a few interesting examples from other countries to provide an international perspective on the subject.

One of the strengths of the book is its ability to draw on press reports, articles, and interviews, providing valuable insights into the attitudes and beliefs of managers, directors, and investors. For investors and other stakeholders desiring a pragmatic description of how companies actually run, the book provides interesting information.

At the same time, Kumar provides a lot of material for those who desire a normative theory of how companies should be ideally governed. He provides a good introduction to the vast literature on this subject, with pointers for further reading for those who wish to pursue any of these topics in greater depth. He casts his net far and wide and cites a large number of academic and popular writers, both Indian and foreign.

Though Kumar does have a strong idealistic view on how corporate governance should work, he still succeeds in providing a balanced account of alternative theories and approaches. You do not have to necessarily agree with all his views to take advantage of the book. Even if you have a sceptical and cynical view of corporate governance—for example, the economists' agency theory view—you can still read the book with benefit.

The mini cases, in particular, invite the readers to think on their own and come to their own conclusions. Kumar leaves us in no doubt about what his views are on each of the examples, but he does not force the readers to accept those views.

Finally, for those who seek to understand corporate governance from a regulatory or compliance perspective, Kumar provides a detailed coverage of the various corporate governance codes, both in India and elsewhere in the world. Starting with the Cadbury code in the UK, he goes on to discuss the reports of the SEBI committees chaired by Kumar Mangalam Birla and Narayana Murthy, as well as the Naresh Chandra Committee of the Company Law Ministry. In between, he also mentions some of the key provisions of the Sarbanes–Oxley Act in the US.

All said, this is an interesting book that would appeal to many different types of readers.

In the interest of full disclosure, I must add that Satheesh Kumar is related to me, though he is not my relative for corporate governance purposes as defined in the Companies Act!

Prof. J.R. Varma
Professor at IIM, Ahmedabad

PREFACE

Corporate governance is a set of processes, customs, policies, and laws that affects the way a company is directed, administered, and controlled. It relates to decisions that define expectations, grant power, or verify performance in an organization. Even though the thrust on economic reforms by the government in 1991 pushed the Indian industry to reform its governance practices, the release of the Cadbury Report in 1992 prompted the industry to take a serious look at its practices. The first such effort happened in 1998 when CII decided to evolve a desirable code for corporate governance. SEBI, the market regulator, felt that opening up of the capital market would necessitate better and proper governance practices and so it appointed a committee under the chairmanship of Sri Kumar Mangalam Birla. After researching the prevailing governance practices, the committee recommended ways to improve upon them. SEBI accepted and included most of the recommendations in the listing agreement and formulated Clause 49.

The worldwide collapse of Enron in 2001 made the importance of corporate governance clear to the Indian industry, the polity, and the public. Later, incidents such as the collapse of WorldCom, Global Crossing, Tyco, etc. in the US, collapse of Parmalat and Barings in Europe, and the fall of GITIC in Asia had an impact on governance strategies. The latest casualty of poor governance due to lack of self-regulation has been our own Satyam Computers, which was not only regulated by the Clause 49 guidelines but also by the supposed-to-be-more-stringent Sarbanes–Oxley Act of the US. Occurrence of such corporate crises has reinforced the need to follow more appropriate governance practices by the corporates in India.

My own interest in this area was kindled after reading two well-known books: *Boards at Work* by Ram Charan and *The Board Book* by Susan F. Shultz. These books were written before the high-profile corporate failures in the US. I learnt more about the subject of corporate governance when I took up a full-time teaching assignment in which I even designed a course curriculum. My interaction with the working directors at the Masterclass for Directors, a programme conducted by the Institute of Directors (IOD), gave further impetus to write this book.

Corporate governance has again come into focus recently and the few textbooks that are available in this area deal with the external factors, trying to relate governance with the market capitalization of companies, laws, and regulations. However, time and again it has been proved that external factors cannot enforce good governance, and no real improvement is possible if the board does not want good governance to happen. This book, therefore, shifts the focus from governance by external regulation to self-regulation by boards and thus follows a unique approach.

ABOUT THE BOOK

The book has been planned specifically for students of management, and care has been taken to make the book equally insightful to the faculty and related professionals too.

The book covers the evolution of corporate governance practices, the structure of the board, and the board development process, along with analysing the future of governance. An entire chapter has been devoted to the conduct and actions of different types of directors. Since, governance depends on the nature and structure of ownership of a corporation and may vary from company to company and from county to country, the book throws light on the governance problems related to typical ownership patterns in companies too. For instance, the difference in the challenges faced by the companies in the US, where there is a typical scenario of wide dispersion among the ownership, finds a mention in the book.

Each chapter opens with a case study that introduces the student to the essence of the chapter. It is suggested that the faculty discuss the case before proceeding with the chapter. At the end of each chapter, critical thinking exercises and project assignments, besides concept review questions, have been included for readers to be able to appreciate, identify with, and learn ways to tackle various real-life related issues.

Students doing research in this area will also find this book useful as care has been taken to provide in-depth knowledge of the subject. Owing to its rich coverage and thought-provoking case studies, the book will be a valuable companion to experienced professionals as also practising managers.

KEY FEATURES

Expounds on issues and challenges faced by corporates in the application of governance in India as well as abroad

Includes detailed reports of some of the various committees constituted by SEBI, including the Kumar Mangalam Birla Committee Report, Narayana Murthy Committee Report, and Clause 49 guidelines

Contains extensive discussion on the European Union approach to corporate governance

Provides three real-life cases in each chapter, including well-known ones such as Satyam Computers, Bajaj Auto Ltd, Reliance Industries Ltd, and many more to aid readers in understanding and relating to the concepts better

COVERAGE AND STRUCTURE

The book is divided into four parts. An overview of the contents is provided below.

Part I traces the evolution of contemporary governance practices and the modern corporation.

Chapter 1, Governance on the Move, introduces the concept of corporate governance. It talks about the distinction between management and governance, and the concept of the modern corporation as a manifestation of capitalism. Concerns and anxieties arising out of ownership dispersion and agency-related issues are also discussed. The chapter also covers the roles played by the board of directors and regulators.

Chapter 2, Capitalism, Modern Corporation, and Governance, explores the rights, expectations, and interests of shareholders. It discusses the various theories and models of corporate governance.

Chapter 3, Evolution of Corporate Governance—Practices and Regulations, describes the events that led to the current thrust on corporate governance. It discusses the role of the government and the importance of the whistle-blowing mechanism, giving an overview of the difficulties faced in the implementation of corporate governance. The chapter also deals with the evolution of the various codes of governance, including the Cadbury Report in UK, Sarbanes–Oxley Act 2002, and the commitiees constituted by SEBI.

Part II is unique, in that it shifts the responsibility of ensuring good governance from external controls to internal controls.

Chapter 4, Structure of the Board—Directors, Types of Boards, and Committees, deals with the purpose of the board, its structure, types, styles of functioning, as well as stages of evolution. It also details the different types of directors and emphasizes the importance of independent directors in companies.

Chapter 5, The Board Development Process—Selection, Development, Compensation, and Performance Review, looks into how to select the right people. It enumerates on the processes of selection, development of directors, and the roles of CEO and the HR head. It also details the process of compensating the CEO and other executive and non-executive directors.

Chapter 6, Boards and Leadership, explores the strategic role the board of directors has to play. Other than describing the best practices of today, it also talks about the contradictions that exist. The chapter throws light on some of the strategy processes and tools used by the board, including the SWOT analysis, value chain analysis, and balanced scorecard. It also discusses the ethical principles for the board.

Part III takes the discussion on corporate governance further from the stakeholder perspective.

Chapter 7, Governance Problems Related to Typical Ownership Patterns, discusses some of the most common ownership structures in private sector and the typical issues associated with them. It explains how institutions enforce governance in companies that hold high stakes. Conflicts of interests in different types of ownership structures, along with their remedial actions, have been discussed too.

Chapter 8, Governance, Capital Market Institutions, and Government, discusses the importance of shareholder activism in enabling good governance. It also details the roles of the regulators, limitations of regulation, etc. and describes the different provisions in the company laws in India that have a direct bearing on the governance aspect. The chapter ends with a discussion on governance ratings and their merits and demerits.

Chapter 9, Directors in Action—Ground Rules for Performing Multitudes of Roles and Duties, discusses various actions practised by a non-executive director, independent director, lead independent director, committee member, committee chair, chairman of the board, executive director, and a CEO.

Part IV explores the future of corporate governance.

Chapter 10, Where Do We Go from Here? takes a critical look at the best practices of today, and assesses the innovative or preferred practices for the future. It narrates the characteristics of the board of the future and also discusses if a political approach to governance would be better.

Appendices contains some of the landmark reports in corporate governance.

I have immense pleasure in presenting this book to students, teachers, and others who are interested in the subject. While every attempt has been made to cover every aspect of governance, by no means do I claim or consider my work to be complete. I request each of my readers to evaluate the book from his or her own perspective and give suggestions for improvements.

ACKNOWLEDGEMENTS

I was not sure whether or not to accept the proposal to write this book as I was yet to recover from the shock and grief of my wife's untimely demise. After much thought I decided to take up the challenge as it would keep me fully engaged, without much time to ponder over the loss. However, I never imagined that it would be so rigorous and demanding. But now I feel happy that it is in print. While I had been publishing articles and papers on the subject, and even nurtured the ambition of writing a book, I never expected that it would be this soon.

I am grateful to my colleagues B. Harish, Anitha Kumari, and Sabu M. Nair at IBS, Kochi, who gave me unstinted support during this pressing period. Dialogues with Harish introduced me to some new thinking. I am also grateful to P.V. Ignatius, the Dean at IBS, for his encouragement and support. Librarians Sabu Antony and Sanoj Kumar also have been a wonderful help at all times.

I am also equally grateful to my erstwhile faculty colleagues at SCMS Business School, Kochi, who have been a constant encouragement for me. Dr Radhakrishnan Nair, Editor, *SCMS Journal of Indian Management*, deserves special mention for all the support and encouragement. Mrs Susan Babu, Librarian, needs to be lauded for her highly committed and proactive approach. Acknowledgement is also due to my close friends and immediate relatives who have always been supportive and tolerant of my long absences.

I am also indebted to the wisdom of experts, practitioners, and authors whose work I have referred to while writing this book.

Last but not the least, I acknowledge the support, patience, and love of my sons—Aravind and Aswin—who have shown great responsibility in times of need.

T.N. Satheesh Kumar

CONTENTS

PART II   BOARDS AND GOVERNANCE

4. Structure of the Board—Directors, Types of Boards, and Committees   155

5. The Board Development Process—Selection, Development, Compensation, and Performance Review   196

6. Boards and Leadership   264

PART III THE STAKEHOLDER PERSPECTIVE

PART IV   THE ROAD AHEAD—THE FUTURE OF GOVERNANCE

APPENDICES

PART I

CORPORATIONS AND THEIR GOVERNANCE

- Governance on the Move
- Capitalism, Modern Corporation, and Governance
- Evolution of Corporate Governance—Practices and Regulations

CHAPTER 1

GOVERNANCE ON THE MOVE

The corporate governance debate has done little to improve the constitution of many boards. If anything the attention has been switched from building larger and better corporate cakes to applying the boardroom icing to existing cakes in recommended ways.

– Prof. Colin Coulson-Thomas (2002), Member, Board of Examiners, IOD

LEARNING OBJECTIVES

After studying this chapter, you will be able to

- Describe the recurrent crises in corporate governance, the importance of good governance, and the early initiatives in the area
- Differentiate between managing and governing
- Define corporate governance
- Understand the present scenario of corporate governance
- Decipher the advantages and disadvantages of corporate governance
- Explain who has to play a major role in governance—boards of directors or regulators?

Opening Case

Where Were the Board and Its Independent Directors?

What happened in India's biggest private sector enterprise, Reliance Industries Ltd (RIL), during the years 2005 and 2006, owing to the rivalry between the two sons of the legendary Dhirubhai Ambani—Mukesh and Anil, led people to believe that everything was not right in the governance of the organization. Let us briefly discuss the issues that were thrown open by the episode.

Mrs Kokilaben, mother of Mukesh and Anil, reportedly issued a note to inform the media and public about the scheme of settlement after the demise of their father. How could a decision as important as the restructuring or demerger of companies all publicly held be taken by an individual? What role did the boards of different companies involved in the issue play? While the investors, the government, the capital market regulator, and the public were relieved that the spat between the brothers was amicably settled, what led Mrs Kokilaben as the head of the family, which at the time reportedly held only 34 per cent of the shares in RIL (without disclosing the details of holding), to assume that the demerger was in the interest of the remaining shareholders who accounted for 66 per cent of the holding? (The subsequent annual report put the promoter holding at 46.76 per cent, including the persons acting in concert.) Not even once when the entire episode was enacted did the board of RIL show any signs of exercising their power and authority as representing the interests of the larger group of shareholders. It seems unfortunate that no shareholder (including institutional holders) raised the question: 'Where was the board?' Anil Ambani might have become a worthy whistle-blower on governance practices of family-managed companies by writing to the Securities and Exchange Board of India (SEBI) on certain transactions that RIL and/or its board or Mukesh entered into and the governance shortfalls therein, but could we rightly say that he was passionate about corporate governance as he too failed to clear the fog over the issue of 34 per cent holding of the family? The board of directors of RIL had six independent directors (institutional nominees included) out of a total of twelve. Why did it not occur to them that they have a fiduciary duty to shareholders to ensure the future health of the company?

Discussion Questions
1. Do you think that the board of RIL played its fiduciary role?
2. In predominantly family-owned and managed companies, boards' roles are limited and the presence of independent directors is only for conformance to regulations. Comment.

Source: Taken from Indian Family-Managed Companies: The Corporate Governance Conundrum. Paper presented by T.N. Satheesh Kumar at The International Conference on Business and Finance 2005 at IBS, Hyderabad.

A BRIEF HISTORY OF CORPORATE GOVERNANCE

Corporate governance has been in vogue for many decades ever since the term was first used by Bob Tricker as the title of his book on the subject. However, a new emphasis emerged on the subject, thanks to the corporate and financial scandals of the early 2000s, starting with Enron. Every major government functionary, political party, industry association, and corporate captain has started advocating the need for better corporate governance practices, and many changes have evolved ever since. New standards of corporate governance, accounting, and reporting have been established. While many of the changes and new standards were welcome, most of them, however, related to the process of enforcement and compliance with external laws and regulations. In the US, the stringent Sarbanes–Oxley Act of 2002 had definitely helped in strengthening the internal processes of compliance. It had not, however, been found to be effective in curbing or preventing governance failures as most of the failures happened due to lack of character at the core of the company, which goes beyond just compliance with regulations. Governance issues have once again been pushed to the forefront in the years 2007 and 2008, and particularly more so in the year 2009, with the sub-prime crisis and financial turmoil that followed and the startling disclosures of the financial irregularity practised by the chairman of a global IT service provider from India.

In the US, the highly respected and century-old organization Lehman Brothers came to naught, insurance giant AIG had to be taken over by the US government, Goldman Sachs needed fresh injection of capital, and the US government had to announce a $700-billion bail-out package for banks and other financial institutions. The world seemed to be heading for a recession following the high inflation rates, high interest rates, liquidity crunch, and lower demand. What was initially perceived to be an isolated problem in the housing mortgages area soon spread over the entire spectrum of economy and presently, recession is still looming over the global economy. Acts initiated for maximizing profit and shareholder value actually have resulted in the drastic reduction of profits (even pushing firms to losses) and erosion of value for shareholders.

In India, the proposal of the hitherto IT bellwether Satyam Computer Services Ltd (popularly known as Satyam) to acquire two associate companies in totally unrelated areas was given a go by its eminent board. However, the uproar of the investors against the merger proposal led to its call off by the promoters. The subsequent revelation by the promoter chairman that the company has been reporting inflated profits and other financial parameters has stunned investors, the regulator, accounting bodies, and even the government, leading to the dismissal of the board and installing a board of government nominees. The Satyam episode has brought to light the deficiencies in the corporate governance system in the country, and the role of the board, independent directors, auditors, audit committees, and regulators are being put under the microscope.

If one analyses the failures from a framework of realism, one can identify that most of these failures squarely rest on poor corporate governance founded on a few factors namely, short-termism; greed of managers, corporates, and even investors; the laid-back attitude of the major investors including institutional investors; and the lack of a questioning culture in the boardroom.

The credit for providing a guideline for corporate governance among the US corporations goes to General Motors and that for enforcing the governance norms goes to the California Public Employees Retirement System (CalPERS) and the UK-based industry-constituted Cadbury Committee. In India, the Confederation of Indian Industry (CII) is to be given credit for kick-starting in 1998 the formal thinking process on the needs of corporate governance. However, there have been well-governed companies like Tata Iron & Steel Company Ltd (TISCO, rechristened as Tata Steel) because of the enlightened corporate behaviour of its founders.

While many countries have created regulations to see that organizations practise better governance processes, these mechanisms have not been found very encouraging. Even though legislating new laws such as the Sarbanes–Oxley Act can help in strengthening the internal processes, the market for corporate control, which is very essential for good governance to happen, cannot be made strong since the minority shareowners are too widely dispersed to show any strength of unity and solidarity, and the larger shareholders such as institutions and mutual funds or private equities have other vested interests on their investments. Governance failures and corporate/bank collapses have happened more in the US, which is home to governance-conscious institutions like CalPERS and TIAA-CREF (Teachers Insurance and Annuity Association-College Retirement Equities Fund) than anywhere else.

MANAGING VERSUS GOVERNING

Governance is essentially different from management. While managing refers to running an enterprise to meet operational and financial objectives, governing aims to ensure that the enterprise is being run well and being guided in the right direction, in the pursuit of the very purpose or goal of the enterprise. The responsibility of governance rests with the board of directors of the enterprise. But this governing body of the enterprise, the board of directors, very rarely appears in the organization chart. The organization chart usually depicts a management hierarchy with the chief executive (managing director) at the apex, heading the organizational pyramid, and various managerial levels working with the concept of delegation of authority and responsibility for management functions downwards while demanding accountability upwards.

The board, the body responsible for governance, doesn't have any hierarchy. Every director has equal responsibility and similar duties and powers. According to the Companies Act 1956 in India and company law worldwide, there is no boss for the board. While members of the management might find a place on the board (as is usually the case in a unitary board), their role as member of the board is different from their role as member of the management (Fig. 1.1).

The directors are so called because their primary task is to direct the enterprise towards its goal by overseeing the managers and the management process.

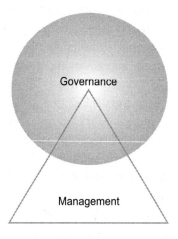

Source: Tricker 2001

Fig. 1.1   Unitary board

CORPORATE GOVERNANCE DEFINED

A definition for corporate governance is in order now. In 1988, two American scholars—Philip Cochran and Steven Wartick—defined corporate governance as 'an umbrella term that includes specific issues arising from interactions among senior management, shareholders, boards of directors, and other corporate stakeholders' (Tricker 2001). Bob Garratt has defined it in more clear terms in the context of the new century after the high profile corporate failures that shook the way the corporations are governed: 'Corporate governance deals with the appropriate board structures, processes, and values to cope with the rapidly changing demands of both shareholders and stakeholders in and around their enterprises' (Garratt 2003).

CORPORATE GOVERNANCE IN THE CURRENT ERA

The original conceivers of the corporate concept did not envisage such complex organizational structures of change as we see in today's dynamic scenario. Consequent to globalization, companies have gone and established entities by crossing the borders, and such operations can involve complex networks of subsidiary and associate companies, limited partnerships controlling listed public companies, public companies controlling privately held companies, and cross-holdings of shares and cross directorships. Such corporate frameworks may operate under multiple legal and regulatory systems, jurisdictions, organization structures, and cultures. Such complexities usually raise puzzling questions for issues related to corporate governance, accounting, and financial reporting. Such structural changes in the corporates are dynamic in nature and evolve very rapidly.

The legal and regulatory framework needs to keep pace with the dynamic nature of corporate structural evolutions. Hence, the challenge before businesses, boards, regulators, and the government of any country is to evolve governance practices and processes that are sensitive to these complex and dynamic organizational forms, and the equally complex, dynamic, and ever-evolving methods of financing in a dynamic capital market scenario.

Modern Corporation—The Poster Boy of Capitalism

The creation of the corporate form for running businesses or enterprises was a milestone in the advancement of capitalism. The corporate form or the joint stock company enabled businesses to sell stock to the public to raise the necessary capital, which was considered permanent unless the management consciously decided to change the course of the company. The investors, while being owners (part owners), had their liabilities limited to the extent of their investment itself, which meant that in case the corporation fails, creditors could not be in hot pursuit of the individual investors for the payment of dues beyond their stakes in the company. Over time, corporation has become the most sought after vehicle through which enterprises could be established and grown. If one reads business history, 'big business' can be found to be the result of the corporate form of enterprise not only in the US (the place where the 'firm' achieved enormous presence and clout), but also in other parts of the world.

As a corollary, or natural outcome, arose the scenario where the owners who did not have the necessary expertise or who did not want to be managing the affairs of the enterprise but were content with the fruits of ownership, entrusting the management of the enterprise with professional managers, who were not required to have any significant ownership in the enterprise. These professional managers were in effect acting as 'agents' on behalf of the owners. This invariably resulted in 'agency conflicts'—conflicts between corporate managers and their owners. With the managers trying to further their own individual interests, their acts at many times were in conflict with the interests of the owners. This has, more often than not, given rise to governance-related issues.

The majority of enterprises in most parts of the world have been promoted by families and a good percentage of them are also managed by family members. A large percentage of them become public companies in order to mobilize more resources for growth. While institutions and other shareholders hold stakes in them, the majority of the holding usually rests with the family and promoters, who sometimes act in total disregard to the interests of other shareholders who are a minority. Some of them even run companies as their private properties, using them as vehicles to further their own interests of aggrandizing personal wealth or other personal interests. For instance, the owners of Satyam wanted the company to acquire family-promoted companies in totally unrelated sectors and even pushed the board for the approval of the same, which the board did, even though the stakeholding value of the promoters was only a meager 8.6 per cent on record. The outside investors, especially the institutional investors who together held about 60 per cent of the stakes cried foul and forced the promoters to call the proposed deal off. Subsequently, the promoters confessed to having been responsible for inflating profits and disclosed that the company did not have the Rs 50 billion cash depicted in the balance sheet and that the revenue figures, profit figures, and collectibles were all fudged over a period of seven to eight years. The Satyam saga has been watched with intense interest in India as well as abroad not only because the company is listed on the major US stock exchange NYSE, but also due to the fact that it raises questions on the roles of the board, independent directors, audit firms, audit committees, regulators, and investors. The corporate form and the very professional management it envisages have once again been put under close scrutiny by all concerned.

CORPORATE FORM—BOON OR BANE?

While the corporate form had enormous advantages in the establishment and mobilization of resources, as well as the management of the productive enterprises, it is also beset with lots of discrepancies. The basic premise of the corporate structure was to maximize profits by competing in the marketplace, but many experts feel that while the structure has been proven to be successful in making profits, every single mechanism—shareholders, directors, regulators, and even the market itself—that has been set up as some kind of check to prevent the externalizing of costs has been neutralized, short-circuited, or co-opted (Monks and Minnow 2006).

In the corporate structure, the management acts as an agent for the owner but it may not be always right to assume that their interests are in alignment. The assumption is that the managers, as agents, will treat other people's (owners') property with such care as if it is their own. But does this happen? Legal systems have tried to solve this problem by designing the director board for a corporation, who is expected to exhibit the highest standard of behaviour by assigning them fiduciary responsibility. With fiduciary responsibility comes accountability. Shareholders delegate authority to directors in their fiduciary capacity, and this necessitates them to be accountable to shareholders.

According to Monks and Minnow (2006), 'accountability is what makes delegated authority legitimate; without accountability, there is nothing to prevent abuse.' This was what went wrong with Satyam. The board and the directors did not show accountability.

The concept of fiduciary duty, while being the fundamental premise on which the corporate structure functions, has been under attack because many of the corporate failures happened as a result of the directors not acting in a fiduciary manner.

Even people like Adam Smith and Karl Marx were skeptical about the very corporate form of organizations and rendered it unworkable and both questioned whether it is possible to create a structure that will operate effectively and fairly, despite the fact that there is a separation between ownership and control. They wanted to fetch an answer to the question: is there any system to make a manager care as much about the company's performance as a shareholder does? (Monks and Minnow 2006). The issue gets complicated when there is no separation between ownership and control as in the case of family-managed companies where major owners adorn the roles of agents and also act as fiduciaries for the entire owners, like in the case of Satyam.

DIRECTORS' ROLE

The directors' role is integral to the very concept of the corporation. While company law may vary from country to country, there are many points that are common across the countries. The directors as a legal body draw enormous power because of the very nature of joint stock companies that gives the corporation the status of a separate legal entity. Though this enables the corporation to be separate from the owners, and also is beneficiary for the corporation in owning assets and/or entering into transactions in assets, it can also act as a monster in an extreme scenario.

Consider the hypothetical example of a corporation who has grown big and the capital outstanding getting reduced through the process of buyback. Suppose the corporation buys every shareholder including the promoters (who wouldn't sell if they are offered very attractive prices?), the resulting scenario could be creation of a deadly monster who becomes a legal entity without any owners to enforce compliance and without accountability. Thus, while the corporate form has many advantages, taken to the extreme, the form can be dangerous. Thus, the directors as a body (the board) have to play a very constructive and meaningful role in shaping, directing, and controlling the character and behaviour of a corporation or a company as an economic entity. In today's competitive world, the board has to work and act in a highly informed and learned manner, raising the board functions to such a level that it becomes a competitive advantage.

REGULATOR'S ROLE

While most countries have regulations on corporate governance, the failure of regulations to prevent frequent governance-related disturbances and troubles in many corporates, and sometimes the eventual failures of some of them, have given rise to questions on the efficacy of regulations to perpetuate better governance. There are contradicting views as well as evidences on the issue. There are practitioners like Bill George (2003), former CEO and later chairman of Medtronic Inc., and currently professor of management practice at Harvard Business School and director on the boards of Goldman Sachs, Novartis, Target, etc., who feel that 'although some changes in regulations are appropriate and necessary, they do not address the deeper issues at stake here. It is impossible to legislate integrity, stewardship, and sound governance.

Some like Aparna Ravi (2009), a lawyer specializing in corporate and securities law, feel that regulation about processes and disclosure rather than board action is more essential for better governance. Still others like J.R. Varma, professor, IIM Ahmedabad, feel that investors 'becoming nasty and even barbaric' will lead to better governance (as they will not hesitate in attempting a hostile takeover) or in effect, the governance of a corporate shall be taken care of by the investors and markets (Varma 2008).

CONCLUSION

Keeping in mind that the corporate form is the most common, and by and large the most advantageous for businesses and firms to grow, the governance issues of corporates has been the most important puzzle for management practitioners, shareowners, firms, regulators, academics, and the public. The chapters that follow attempt to unravel the multitude of issues that affect governance of corporations. The book is intended to cover the major aspects of corporate governance not only in India but also in different parts of the world as in a rapidly globalizing world, firms operate out of many countries, making global exposure a necessity.

SUMMARY

The corporate and financial scandals in the US at the turn of the century, starting with Enron, led to massive corporate failures, resulting in investors losing their money and employees their jobs. This brought into the limelight the need for stringent regulations that ensure better governance of corporates, and the US government enacted a specific law—the Sarbanes–Oxley Act—in 2002. But the happenings in 2007 in highly respected corporates such as Lehman Brothers and AIG led to a global economic meltdown from which most economies are yet to recover, indicating a need to improve on the post-Enron regulations. The Satyam scandal in India in 2009 has raised further questions about the roles of directors, especially the independent directors, the audit committee and the statutory auditors, the regulators, and the government, resulting in India and other countries too strengthening their corporate governance regulations.

The necessity for corporate governance has arisen from the very concept of the corporate form of enterprise. While the corporate form has many advantages, it has many discrepancies too. Governance issues arise because ownership is dispersed, making control difficult. Professional managers or experts are appointed to manage the affairs of the enterprise, and this can lead to agency-related issues. Corporate laws have tried to overcome this problem by creating a board structure that will act as a fiduciary on behalf of the owners and be accountable to them. Though the board and its directors have definite roles and responsibilities, they enjoy enormous powers under most laws and hence regulators also have to play a definite role in ensuring that such powers are not misused and corporates are well governed.

KEY TERMS

Accountability Being responsible to somebody

Capitalism An economic system in which enterprises can be owned privately for profit

Corporate A company form of enterprise with limited liability

Corporation A business firm whose articles of incorporation have been approved in some state

Disclosure The process of making the happenings known

Integrity Being honest and upright in character

Regulations Laws or rules to make sure that the system works in a fair way

Short-termism Tendency to look at short-term benefits alone

CONCEPT REVIEW QUESTIONS

1. What is the importance of good governance?
2. Distinguish between management and governance.
3. Discuss the advantages and disadvantages of the corporate form of business entity.
4. Briefly explain the roles of the board and the regulator in furthering corporate governance.

CRITICAL THINKING QUESTIONS

1. You are the promoter of RQP Do-It-Yourself-Products Ltd based in India. You want to have a board of directors constituted, with you as the CEO. What will be the structure of the board? Explain the rationale behind your choice. Make suitable assumptions.

PROJECT WORK

You want to invest in a particular cpmpany of your choice. Before you commit, you would like to check whether the company is reasonably well-governed. Since you are concerned about the reputation of the company as well as the liquidity, you would choose one of the constituents of a stock exchange index like BSE Sensex or NSE Nifty. Analyse the company's governance practices critically to enable you to make investments.

REFERENCES

Garratt, Bob (2003), *Thin on Top*, Nicholas Brealey Publishing, London.

George, Bill (2003), *Authentic Leadership: Rediscovering the Secrets to Creating Lasting Value*, Jossey-Bass, San Francisco.

Monks, Robert and Nell Minow (2006), 'The director's new clothes', in *Corporate Governance at the Crossroads*, Donald H. Chew Jr. and L. Stuart Gillan (eds), Tata McGraw-Hill, New Delhi.

Ravi, Aparna, 'A question of independence', *The Hindu*, 30 January 2009.

Tricker, Bob (1984), *Corporate Governance*, Gower, Aldershot, Surrey, UK.

Tricker, Bob (2001), *Pocket Director*, Viva Books, New Delhi.

Varma, Jayanth R., 'The big question: Why is shareholder activism not taking off in India?' *The Economic Times*, 27 September 2008.

Closing Case

Satyam Computer Services Ltd

Satyam in Sanskrit and many Indian languages means truth. The recent unfolding of events at Satyam Computer Services Ltd is a story of how truth was distorted by the 'untruthful' conduct of the promoters who were in the management of the company.

Satyam's Philosophy on Corporate Governance

The following is the opening of Satyam's Corporate Governance Report for the years 2006–07 and 2007–08.

Corporate governance assumes a great deal of importance in the business life of Satyam. The driving force of corporate governance at Satyam are its core values—belief in people, entrepreneurship, customer orientation, and the pursuit of excellence. The company's goal is to find creative and productive ways of delighting its stakeholders, .i.e., investors, customers, and associates, while fulfilling the role of a responsible corporate representative committed to best practices.

Satyam believes that sound corporate governance practices provide an important framework to assist the board in fulfilling its responsibilities. The board of directors is elected by shareholders with a responsibility to set strategic objectives to the management and to ensure that the long-term interests of all stakeholders are served by adhering to and enforcing the principles of sound corporate governance. Thus, the management is responsible to establish and implement policies, procedures, and systems to enhance long-term value of the company and delight all its stakeholders (associates, investors, customers, and society). The principle of 'delighting the stakeholder' is imbibed in everything we do at Satyam and is depicted in our value emblem (depicted below) as a mark of our commitment towards this principle.

On 16 December 2008, Ramalinga Raju announced that the twenty-year-old company would 'derisk' itself by diversifying into the infrastructure and realty business by acquiring two family-run firms: (1) a listed Maytas Infra Ltd where the Rajus had a stake of 35 per cent and (2) an unlisted Maytas Properties Ltd where the family ownership was around 36 per cent (Maytas is Satyam spelt backwards), using the $1.6 billion cash reserve of Satyam. Maytas Infra had Teja Raju, elder son of Ramalinga Raju, as the vice-chairman of the board, and Maytas Properties had his younger son Rama Raju Junior as its chairman. 'These arrangements have the flavour of a managing agency—a family controlling a clutch of companies by means of financial engineering' (*Businessworld*, 5 January 2009). On 17 December 2009, Raju announced the withdrawal of the proposal following the outrage of institutional investors.

An unprecedented shareholders' revolt that crashed Satyam's American Depository Receipts by 55 per cent on 16 December on New York Stock Exchange and plunged the stock 27 per cent to Rs 165.5 in mid-session the next day on the BSE, forced the Rajus to beat a hasty retreat. Satyam had already been slapped with suits for fraud and breach of contract such as the one by UK-based Upaid. But, amidst several questions of ethics and corporate governance lies an exclamation about the long-term intent of Rajus to stay in the information technology business.

'A design to quit', *Businessworld*, 29 December 2008, pp. 22–24

The promoter holding in Satyam has been declining over the years as is evident from the following table.

Historically, family firms have been alleged to be siphoning funds from a publicly listed company where the public holding was more than that of the promoters in favour of privately owned (private limited companies or partnerships) organizations through various means even

Promoter holdings in Satyam

Period ended	Holding (%)
March 2001	25.60
March 2002	22.26
March 2003	20.74
March 2004	17.35
March 2005	15.67
March 2006	14.02
March 2007	8.80
March 2008	8.74

Source: 'The writing on the wall', *Businessworld*, 12 January 2009.

to the extent of bleeding it to further their private interests. SEBI, in its initial years, had insisted on the promoter, holding at least 25 per cent of the post-issue capital whenever a company wanted to raise public money, presumably for the promoters to be committed to the venture. However as time went by, this provision got diluted.

On the Satyam move to acquire the two family-promoted companies the following observation was made in a newspaper. 'There was a time when industrialists used to run companies in whose equity they had a minute share; they were called managing agents. The government thought it improper. In the mindless manner of governments, it banned managing agency in the Companies Act of 1956. Bans do not remove institutions. Managing agents stopped calling themselves by that name, and continued as before' ('New-style promoter', *Businessworld*, 5 January 2009).

Even the other key executives of the company had been selling the Satyam shares just before the takeover drama was unveiled. 'Top executives, including Director Vinod Dham and CFO S. Vadlamani, sold Satyam shares in bulk just two months ago' ('A design to quit?' *Businessworld*, 29 December 2008).

The board of directors of Satyam on 16 December 2008 is given below.

Name	Designation
B. Ramalinga Raju	chairman
B. Rama Raju	managing director
Ram Mynampati	whole-time director
Mangalam Srinivasan	non-executive, independent director
Krishna Palepu	non-executive director
Vinod Dham	non-executive, independent director
M. Ram Mohan Rao	non-executive, independent director
T.R. Prasad	non-executive, independent director
V.S. Raju	non-executive, independent director

Role of Independent Directors: Meaningless, Difficult, and Risky?
Prithvi Haldea, chairman and managing director, Prime Database, wrote in *Economic Times*:

Satyam is a watershed event for the institution of independent directors (IDs). It has demonstrated that even highly credible, qualified, and educated persons are no insurance for corporate governance, that they are no watchdogs of the minority shareholders whose interests they are supposed to serve. In fact IDs end up serving a negative purpose, that of providing a false sense of security to the minority shareholders.

The natural conflict between promoters, whose primary motivation would be to unduly enrich themselves, and the IDs who are supposed to prevent this from happening, is at the core of the problem. However, how this conflict is resolved in India? By allowing promoters themselves to get such persons on their boards who will not even recognize this conflict, leave aside resolving it.

Haldea classifies independent directors into four categories.

Home directors   These comprise persons known personally to the promoter's relatives, friends, neighbours, ex-employees, ex-teachers, etc. Several loopholes exist to get them on the board. For example, according to the Companies Act 1956 all persons from the wife's and mother's side are not considered as relatives.

Value directors   Value directors are those that either bring knowledge and expertise to the company, such as lawyers, finance professionals, technocrats, civil servants, and so on, or they provide networking to the company by opening doors to the government, politicians, and institutions. Such persons are also hired to give a sense of comfort to the investors. Many of these would be people of high integrity.

Celebrity directors   This is the category that comprises people whose main reason to be invited to become an independent director is to add an aura of respectability and new value to the company, as also to impress the retail investors. This category includes film stars, lyricists, sportsmen, defence personnel, fiction writers, and the like. Most people in this category also would be people of high integrity. However, they would have very little clue to the corporate world or of promoters' designs.

PSU directors   This is the category that comprises people who are appointed on the boards of listed PSUs, typically by the political high command or the minister concerned. These people either carry out the mandate of the respective ministries or simply pursue their personal agenda of benefiting from these PSUs, and are clearly not concerned about the minority shareholders....

Courtesy Satyam, many value and celebrity directors are now seriously worried. They are worried about the possibility of their life's reputation getting ruined overnight, media ridicule and government prosecution. Between 15 December 2008 and 1 March 2009, as many as 195 individuals had resigned from the position of independent directors, and the number is growing by the day ('Independent directors: The bare truth', *Economic Times*, 14 May 2009).

Thus, the role of independent directors has been hotly debated post the Satyam episode.

According to P.R. Agarwala, chairman, Rupa & Co, a Kolkota-based hosiery manufacturer, 'After the Satyam scandal, no one wants to take a risk as there may be some hidden skeletons. Besides you must understand that independent directors could be unaware of some promoter-driven initiatives as they attend only a few meetings a year.' ('The Omerta followers', *Business Today*, 8 March 2009). Agarwala quit as independent director from the board of Khaitan Electricals within a month of joining. *Business Today*, in the same article, mentions other high profile exits from the position of independent directors from a number of companies. P.R.S. Oberoi, chairman, East India Hotels, resigned from the board of Jet Airways; N.S. Raghavan, former joint MD and one of the founders of Infosys, and founder, Nadathur Holdings and Investments, a venture capital firm, resigned from the board of Sobha Developers; and Hemendra Kothari, chairman, DSP Merril Lynch from Peninsular Land of Ashok Piramal Group, and T.K.K. Bhagavat, left the board of D.S. Kulkarni Developers, the Pune-based real estate firm.

Does the policy of independent directorship lack punch?

According to *Business Today*, 'The policy for IDs-prescribed under the Act (The Companies Act) and by SEBI in Clause 49 of the Listing Agreement – is weak, feel most experts.'

According to these experts, there are three major policy lacunae: lack of norms, insiders as independent, and lack of stipulation of role or a code of conduct ('Ensuring independence', *Business Today*, 22 February 2009):

Lack of norms: Clause 49 stops at laying down a few disqualifications which do not include criminal backgrounds or illiteracy. There are no norms on qualifications or experience required for independent directors. Companies, therefore, often tap celebrities, especially just before hitting the market for funds through IPOs (initial public offers). Jet Airways, for instance, has Shah Rukh Khan, Yash Chopra, and Javed Akhtar on its board.

'It is important to have independent directors with strength of character, who are willing to blow the whistle and be assertive,' says Virendra Jain, founder, Midas Touch Investors Association. In reality, however, companies often induct retired bureaucrats as independent directors to take advantage of their lack of domain knowledge.

Insiders as independent: 'Independent directors more often than not tend to be insiders such as former employees,' says Prithvi Haldea, founder and managing director, Prime Database. Though regulations disallow promoters to appoint their relatives as independent directors, a 'relative' excludes cousins and other close relations from the wife's and mother's side.

Lack of stipulation of role or a code of conduct: The existing policy for independent directors doesn't stipulate the role or a code of conduct. Thus, even though minority shareholders at Satyam have plenty of reasons to blame its independent directors, it cannot be automatically said that they violated Clause 49. 'The concept of independent directors is a myth, offering false sense of security to small shareholders,' says Haldea. He says several independent directors have told him they think their role is to add value to a company or help it network better, while in reality, it is to protect small shareholders' interests.

On 7 January 2009, Ramalinga Raju, chairman, in his letter to the board of directors disclosed that

1. The balance sheet as on 30 September 2008 carried
   (a) inflated (non-existent) cash and bank balances of Rs 50.4 billion (as against Rs 53.61 billion reflected in the books)

(b) an accrued interest of Rs 3.76 billion, which is non-existent

(c) an understated liability of Rs 12.3 billion on account of funds arranged by me

(d) an over-stated debtors position of Rs 4.9 billion (as against Rs 26.51 billion reflected in the books)

2. For the September quarter (Q2), revenues of Rs 27 billion and an operating margin of Rs 6.49 billion (24 per cent of revenues) as against the actual revenues of Rs 21.12 billion and an actual operating margin of Rs 0.61 billion (3 per cent of revenues), which has resulted in artificial and cash bank balances going up by Rs 5.88 billion in Q2 alone.

He also stated that the gap in the balance sheet has arisen purely on account of inflated profits over a period of last several years (limited only to Satyam standalone, books of subsidiaries reflecting true performance).What started as a marginal gap between actual operating profit and the one reflected in the books of accounts continued to grow over the years. It attained unmanageable proportions as the size of the company operations grew significantly (annualized revenue run rate of Rs 112.76 billion in the September quarter, 2008, and official reserves of Rs 83.92 billion).The differential in the real profits and the one reflected in the books was further accentuated by the fact that the company had to carry additional resources and assets to justify higher level of operations—thereby significantly increasing the costs.

He confessed that every attempt made to eliminate the gap failed. As the promoters held a small percentage of equity, the concern was that poor performance would result in a take-over, thereby exposing the gap. It was like riding a tiger, not knowing how to get off without being eaten. The aborted Maytas' acquisition Deal was the last attempt to fill the fictitious assets with real ones. Maytas' investors were convinced that this is a good divestment opportunity and a strategic fit. Once Satyam's problem was solved, it was hoped that Maytas' payments can be delayed. But that was not to be. What followed in the last several days is common knowledge.

On 9 January 2009, the government superseded the Satyam board and appointed its nominees Deepak Parekh, Kiran Karnik, and C. Achuthan on 11 January 2009.

Discussion Questions

1. In the backdrop of the Satyam incident, comment on the state of corporate governance in India.

2. Could outside directors and/or the regulator have averted the crisis?

3. What do you think could have led to the crisis and what should be done to prevent such instances of corporate failures in future?

CHAPTER 2

CAPITALISM, MODERN CORPORATION, AND GOVERNANCE

The directors of companies, being managers rather of other people's money than their own, it cannot well be expected that they should watch over it with the same anxious vigilance with which the partners in a private copartnery (business) frequently watch their own.

– Adam Smith, *Wealth of Nations*, 1776

LEARNING OBJECTIVES

After studying this chapter, you will be able to
- Describe the modern corporation and its merits and demerits
- Enumerate and discuss the rights of shareholders
- Elucidate the fiduciary responsibilities of boards and directors
- State the various theories of corporate governance
- Understand why governance matters
- Discuss governance in the context of different types of ownership
- Explain the need for clarity of roles of management and board

Opening Case

Dominant Shareholder in Management Aided by Rubber Stamp Board?

Berle and Means, as early as 1932, had dealt with many concerns about the very concept of joint-stock companies in their seminal work *Modern Corporation and Private Property*. They had pointed out that the two attributes of ownership—risking collective wealth in profit-seeking enterprise and ultimate management of responsibility for that enterprise—had become divorced. In other words, while legally the shareholders enjoy the power of selecting the board of directors, the control over the corporation and its resources rests with the management. Weidenbaum and Jensen, in their introduction to the 1991 edition of the book, state that Berle and Means (1932) had even discussed that 'those who control the corporation, even if they own a large block of stock, "can serve their own pockets better by profiting at the expense of the company than by making profits for it", which is nothing but an early and earthy statement of the agency problem' which we attribute to most of the governance failures.

Berle and Means (1932) had also foreseen that the corporate form will become a social institution of prominence beyond the imagination of many: 'The corporation has, in fact, become both a method of property tenure and a means of organizing economic life. Grown to tremendous proportions, it may be said to have evolved into a corporate system—as there was once a feudal system—which has attracted to itself a combination of attributes and powers, and has attained a degree of prominence entitling it to be dealt with as a major social institution. Spectacular as its rise has been, every indication seems to be that the system will move forward to proportions which would stagger imagination today; just as corporate system of today was beyond the imagination of most statesmen and businessmen at the opening of the present century.' Berle and Means had also raised serious concerns about the concentration of economic power because of the potential for the corporation to grow in size. Back in 1930, in a list drawn of 200 largest non-banking corporations, 'nearly all of these companies had assets of over $100 million, and 15 had assets of over a billion dollars. Their combined assets amounted to $81 billion or, as we shall see, nearly half of all corporate wealth in the United States.' Berle and Means had also made their concerns explicit: 'Finally, a society in which production is governed by blind economic forces is being replaced by one in which production is carried on under the ultimate control of a handful of individuals. The economic power in the hands of the few persons who control a giant corporation is a tremendous force, which can harm or benefit a multitude of individuals, affect whole districts, shift the currents of trade, bring ruin to one community and prosperity to another. The organization which they control has passed the realm of private enterprise—they have become more nearly social institutions.' According to them, 'approximately 2000 men were directors of the 200 largest corporations in 1930. Since an important number of these are inactive, the ultimate control of nearly half of the industry was actually in the hands of a few hundred men.'

Berle and Means (1932) also discussed the way the ownership has undergone wider dispersion and how it has aided the concentration of economic power in a few hands. They said that a wider dispersion has led to a situation where 'In place of actual physical properties over which the owner could exercise direction and for which he was responsible, the owner now holds a piece of paper representing a set of rights and expectations with respect to an enterprise... It has often been said that the owner of a horse is responsible. If the horse lives, he must feed it. If the horse dies, he must bury it. No such responsibility attaches to a share of stock. The owner is practically powerless through his own efforts to affect the underlying property'.

While Berle and Means (1932) had, in talking about control as distinct from ownership, said that 'where all stock except that held by majority interest is widely scattered, on the other hand, majority ownership (in the absence of a legal device) means undiminished actual control', they had concluded that 'in a truly large corporation, the investment necessary for majority ownership is so considerable as to make such control extremely expensive. Among such corporations, majority control is conspicuous more by its absence than by its presence. More often control is maintained with relatively small portion of ownership.'

The Reliance Demerger Issue

On 23 November 2004, immediately after the sibling rivalry in the Ambani family became public, Mukesh Ambani, Chairman and Managing Director of Reliance Industries Ltd (RIL), in an e-mail sent to the employees stated that 'there is no ambiguity in his (Dhirubhai's) legacy that the Chairman and Managing Director is the final authority on all matters concerning Reliance.... Our founder Chairman, Shri Dhirubhai Ambani had taken all necessary steps to separate ownership from management and had settled all of them within his lifetime.'

When Dhirubhai was alive and operating as the chairman, the two brothers were given equal status (though Mukesh was VC & MD and Anil MD, their salaries and perks were the same). There was no confusion regarding the allocation of responsibilities and power. But the whole scenario changed after his death and Mukesh was named the Chairman. As per the rules of the game at RIL (if reports in the media are to be believed), the Chairman has all the powers including the power to control other subsidiary, associate and investment companies of the group. Hence, as Chairman, Mukesh became the sole decision-maker compared to the earlier scenario of two equal (understudy) decision-makers. He got the authority to control the stakeholding RIL had in all the subsidiary/associate companies. Anil owed even the position of the Chairman of Reliance Energy (now Reliance Infrastructure) to RIL (or Mukesh). In short, he has simply been reduced to the position of just a professional manager in the group like any other professional manager who could even be fired by the Chairman with the support of the board.

Ranjit Shastri, Director of Psi, an advisory and investment firm, wrote on 13 December 2004, 'Clearly it's (RIL's) board must either be too passive or just plain ignorant about what goes around them. An independent board would not tolerate this kind of fighting at the top. Power is not concentrated in the hands of the CEO, but is distributed among members of the board. A cursory glance at Reliance's board of directors indicates a heavy dependence on family members and those loyal to the family.'

While the settlement between the brothers 'has been a big relief to the corporate sector in general and financial markets in particular, it has given rise to many questions and has also helped to bring out a number of corporate governance issues to the forefront. What role the board of a company should play in such situations? Who will handle such issues whenever a crisis arises? Shall it be left to the promoters' families to settle issues when the majority of ownership lies outside the family? Or, is the board which represents the interests of the entire shareholders responsible for settling such issues? What is the role of the regulator and the government when interests of millions of shareholders are involved?'

Discussion Questions
1. Are Berle and Means's views applicable to Reliance Industries Ltd?
2. Comment on Mukesh Ambani's claim that his father had taken all necessary steps to separate ownership from management during his lifetime.
3. Did the board of directors act in such a way as to fulfill its fiduciary duties in its right sense?

Source: 'Getting it right on the board', *Businessworld*, 3 December 2004.
Satheesh Kumar, 'Anil Ambani Ko Gussa Kyon Aaya?' *The Effective Executive*, November 2005.

MODERN CORPORATION AND CAPITALISM

The invention of the joint-stock companies or the corporate form of organizing business was a landmark development in the area of business and industrialization. The corporate form or joint-stock company was created as an economic entity with unlimited ability to raise resources as the company could raise large amounts as capital by selling shares to the general public, and hence could grow sometimes to colossal sizes as we have been witnessing in the last and current century. Wal-Mart, over a period of about 46 years, has grown to a size at which its revenues might be more than the combined GDP of a few developing countries. The corporate form was welcomed by the public also as the people could participate in the growth of a business by buying shares of the company but with liability limited to share holding. Also, they could exit the business if they were in need of liquidity or not satisfied with the performance of the company or returns by selling their holdings in securities markets. The term 'corporation' has come to represent size and widespread ownership in contrast to small, privately held firms, though the latter are also incorporated. While corporate form was in existence even in the 17th century in England and Holland when merchant companies like the East India Company and the Dutch East India Company were established as joint-stock companies, the East India Company was incorporated in the year 1600 when Queen Elizabeth I accorded permission for a 21-year charter (what we refer today as incorporation) to the Company of Merchants of London, trading into East Indies (Mantle 2008). The Royal Charter enabled the Crown to retain the royalty interest while letting private money fund investments necessary to develop economic and financial activity (Smith and Walter 2006). Charters usually contained monopoly provisions. One of the first ever joint-stock companies with 125 shareholders and a capital of £72,000, the company in effect ruled India till 1857, when the dissatisfaction of the company's native troops led to the Indian Mutiny, the first revolt against the British. The India Bill of 1858 was proposed to abolish the powers of the company and the Board of Control and transfer all authority to the Crown (Mantle 2008). The company continued for a few more years but was finally dissolved in 1874. The Dutch East India Company, established in 1602, was the first company to issue stock to the public and is often referred to as the first multinational (Mantle 2008).

While historically, England and Holland stand out as the initial implementers of the corporate concept, the concept flourished in the US, which has since become the epicentre of capitalism and front runner of the capitalist policies. The US started using the corporate form of business organization exclusively in areas such as textiles, insurance, banking, transportation, and other public utilities. As we have seen, the charters were provided by individual states according to the Constitution. By 1800, there were 300 companies in total (Smith and Walter 2006). The establishment of the New York Stock Exchange (NYSE) had enormous impact in furthering the growth of corporations as it facilitated easy transactions in corporate securities. Corporations became popular in the US and in other parts of the world as they provided entrepreneurs with a means to secure the funds needed for their capital and also because they offered choice for investors in allocating their savings to different companies.

According to Berle and Means (1932), 'The corporate system had done more than evolve a norm by which business is carried on. Within it, there exists a centripetal attraction which draws wealth together into aggregations of constantly increasing size, at the same time throwing controls into the hands of fewer men.' As the corporation became the choice of entrepreneurs for conducting businesses, seven changes have occurred, according to Berle and Means (1932):

1. The ownership has changed from that of an active to a passive agent. In place of actual properties over which the owner could exercise direction and be responsible, the owner now holds a piece of paper representing a set of rights and expectations with respect to an enterprise. But over the enterprise and over the physical property—the instruments of

production—in which he has an interest, the owner has little control. At the same time he bears no responsibility with respect to the enterprise or its physical property. It has often been said that the owner of a horse is responsible. If the horse lives he must feed it. If the horse dies, he must bury it. No such responsibility attaches to a share of stock. The owner is practically powerless through his own efforts to affect the underlying property.

2. The spiritual values that formerly went with ownership have been separated from it. Physical property capable of being shaped by its owner could bring to him direct satisfaction apart from the income it yielded in more concrete form. It represented an extension of his own personality. With the corporate revolution, this quality has been lost to the property owner much as it has been lost to the worker through the industrial revolution.

3. The value of an individual's wealth is coming to depend on forces entirely outside himself and his own efforts. Instead, its value is determined on the one hand by the actions of the individuals in command of the enterprise—individuals over whom the typical owner has no control, and on the other hand, by the actions of others in a sensitive and often capricious market. The value is thus subject to the vagaries and manipulations characteristic of the marketplace. It is further subject to the great swings in society's appraisal of its own immediate future as reflected in the general level of values in the organized markets.

4. The value of the individual's wealth not only fluctuates constantly—the same may be said of most wealth—but it is subject to a constant appraisal. The individual can see the change in the appraised value of his estate from moment to moment, a fact which may markedly affect both the expenditure of his income and his enjoyment of that income.

5. Individual wealth has become extremely liquid through the organized markets. The individual owner can convert it into other forms of wealth at a moment's notice and, provided the market machinery is in working order, he may do so without serious loss due to forced sale.

6. Wealth is less and less in a form which can be employed directly by its owner. When wealth is in the form of land, for instance, it is capable of being used by the owner even though the value of land in the market is negligible. The physical quality of such wealth makes possible a subjective value to the owner quite apart from any market value it may have. The newer form of wealth is quite incapable of this direct use. Only through sale in the market can the owner obtain its direct use. He is thus tied to the market as never before.

7. In the corporate system, the 'owner' of industrial wealth is left with a mere symbol of ownership while the power, the responsibility and the substance which have been an integral part of ownership in the past are being transferred to a separate group in whose hands lies control.

The 'Control' Factor

As the corporate form advanced, ownership of wealth became widely dispersed and control over it ceased to be in the same hands. Under the corporate form, control over the business's wealth is carried out mostly by those with minimum of ownership interest. For example, in the eighties, Tatas used to control the country's largest private sector steel company, Tata Iron and Steel Company Ltd (rechristened as Tata Steel), with slightly over 4 per cent stake. Satyam promoters controlled the $2 billion company with barely 8.5 per cent ownership. In many professionally managed companies, the managers of the company control the company's wealth even without holding any ownership. As Berle and Means (1932) say, 'Ownership of wealth without appreciable ownership appear to be the logical outcome of corporate development. Control divorced from ownership is not, however, a familial concept. It is a characteristic of the corporate system.'

Thus, a major issue in the management and governance of a corporate entity is that control of the wealth of a corporation is divorced from ownership. With the dispersion of ownership, no shareholder had effective control over the firm. Thus, came the concept of directors and board of directors, who under the fiduciary responsibility accorded to them by the shareholders control the firm on behalf of the shareholders.

Berle and Means (1932) describe the legal position of the board, or management. According to them, 'management may be defined as the body of men who, in law, have formally assumed the duties of exercising domination over the corporate business and assets. It then derives its position from a legal title of some sort universally. Under the American system of law, managers consist of a board of directors and the senior officers of the corporation. The board of directors commonly secures its legal title to office thorough election by the stockholders or those of them who, under the corporate charter, are accorded a vote. And today, almost in every country, the board of directors is considered to be the body representing the shareholders through the fiduciary responsibility assigned on them.' But Berle and Means assert a very important aspect: 'The law holds management to certain standards of conduct. This is the legal link between ownership and management.' According to them, 'the three main rules of conduct which the law has developed are: (1) a decent amount of attention to business, (2) fidelity to the interests of the corporation and (3) at least reasonable business prudence. The law sums up the three rules mentioned above by saying that the management stands in a "fiduciary" capacity towards the corporation.'

Thus, the boards in effect become the fiduciary top of the company on behalf of the shareholders. An ethical behavior is expected of directors while they sit on the board. They should not be acting against the interests of the company while protecting the interests of the shareholders. In fact, there is no contract between the shareholders and directors requisitioning the directors to indulge in actions that will result in the protection of interest of the shareholders. Similarly, there is no contract for a director to act as a dummy of one or a few shareholders. As Berle and Means (1932) say: 'It needs no agreement to make a director who is dependent on the will of one or two shareholders into a dummy. He is a dummy not because of a contract but because of his nature. First rate men will never be dummies; third rate men can never be prevented from being dummies where they are in fact dependent on the will of a small group, even though no precaution is taken by contract to make them so.'

Berle and Means (1932) say that 'management thus becomes, in an odd sort of way, the uncontrolled administration of a kind of trust having the privilege of perpetual accumulation. The shareholder is the passive beneficiary, not only of the original 'trust' but of the compounded annual accretions to it.' While joint-stock companies or the corporate form of business has become the posterboy of capitalism and has been the reason for the emergence of many big businesses, the very structure depends a lot on a 'strong moral sentiment' as envisioned by Smith (1761). According to Monks and Minow (2005), 'The corporate structure was designed to maximize profits through competition in the marketplace, but it has proven to be more successful in making profits, whether maximum or not, by imposing costs on others. Every single mechanism that has been set up as some kind of check to prevent this externalizing of costs has neutralized, short-circuited, or co-opted. Shareholders, directors, state, and federal legislature—even the marketplace itself—all are part of the myth of corporate accountability, and all are part of the reality of corpocracy.'

Directors, in theory, are fiduciaries for the shareholders and according to Monks and Minow (2005), quoting Judge Benjamin N. Cardozo's verdict in the Meinbard V. Salmon suit of 1928 in New York, the directors' action must be 'held to something stricter than the morale of the marketplace.' While Smith was all praise for the 'radical intellectual breakthrough of the joint-stock company with a separate legal personality' (Garratt 2003), he was skeptical of its workability. According to Monks and Minow, while Smith and Marx 'did not agree on much, but they both thought that the corporate form of organization was unworkable and for remarkably similar reasons. They questioned whether it is possible to create a structure that will operate efficiently and fairly, despite the fact that there is a separation between ownership and control.' Smith even 'saw that it had the potential to create social upheaval in the long term because there were no social mechanisms for checking its unlimited size, unlimited license, unlimited life, and consequently unlimited power.'

Shareholders—Their Rights, Expectations, and Interests

Shareholders as owners of the corporation have rights over the corporation and its assets. While at individual shareholder level rarely does a possibility arise for action directed at exercising their rights, the shareholders still have their rights given by the laws and conventions. Wallace and Zinkin (2005) quote a study undertaken among 1500 companies between September 1990 and December 1999: 'companies can choose to be like democracies—granting great powers to the voters; or they can choose to be like dictatorships—protecting the management from being accountable to the voters' (refer to Fig. 2.1).

According to them, the study reveals that 'democracies' appear to have outperformed the 'dictatorships' by a statistically significant 8.5 per cent per year in firm valuation (Wallace and Zinkin 2005).

However, Berle and Means (1932) were forced to conclude that the 'shareholder in the modern corporate situation has surrendered a set of definite rights for a set of definite expectations.'

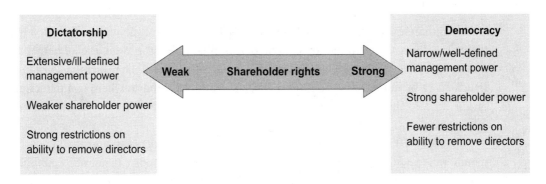

Fig. 2.1 Dictatorship–democracy relation

According to them, the effect of the growth of powers of directors and control has been to diminish the number of things on which a shareholder can count. The shareholder's position has been reduced to one with little more than loose expectations that a group of men acting as directors to run the enterprise for his and other shareholders' benefit will act out of obligation. But he is not in a position to demand that the board of directors do or refrain from doing any given thing.

According to the law prevailing everywhere with respect to joint-stock companies, the shareholders' position is not very encouraging. While they take the majority of the risk of establishing and running an enterprise, when it comes to rights their position is last. Shareholders have been pressured from both sides as providers of equity capital; they fall behind the providers of debt (bondholders or lenders) and providers of preference capital. The upside most people talk about is that while the benefits to lenders and preference shareholders are fixed, equity shareholders have potential for unlimited upside benefits. Very few appreciate the fact that the control of the upside benefits is entirely in the hands of the board of directors, who act as fiduciaries on behalf of equity holders (Wallace and Zinkin 2005).

According to the principles drawn up by International Corporate Governance Network (ICGN), there are five factors to be addressed while considering the rights of shareholders:

- Shareholders are entitled to be consulted before any major change is made to the corporation's strategic direction, as this will affect the risk profile of the business, and shareholders are entitled to have their risk profiles respected. In addition, the shareholders should approve anything that is likely to dilute shareholder equity or erode shareholder economic interests, before it is undertaken.
- Shareholders must have adequate access to be able to exercise the right to vote, and the ICGN goes so far as to suggest the adoption of secure telecommunication and electronic methods of voting to achieve this.
- Voting results should be disclosed in a timely manner for each resolution and there should be no difference between votes cast in person or in absentia.
- Divergences from a 'one share, one vote' are undesirable because they give certain shareholders disproportionate power, and any such divergence should be disclosed and justified.
- The duty to vote is a fiduciary obligation for institutional shareholders, subject to the costs of exercising a vote.

While shareholders have definite rights accorded by the law, the widely dispersed nature of the shareholders, the ignorance of shareholders of their rights, the lower level of activism among shareholders due to their bias for immediate very good returns alone rather than sustained good returns, lack of interest in exercising rights, etc. lead to a scenario where companies are more or less inert to the possibility of shareholders exercising their rights for improving corporate governance.

As Garratt (1996) says, 'With sufficient votes most shareholders can unseat a board, change a remuneration system, alter policies and strategies, and insist upon greater accountability. They rarely do. This is in part because small shareholders are so fragmented that the only viable option they have to show their feelings about the board is to buy or sell the shares. The modern major shareholders, the financial institutions, feel similarly. They have traditionally not been interested in corporate governance issues within a company and have expressed their opinions solely by buying or selling the shares.'

The same shareholders have definite expectations from boards having fiduciary duties and expect them to exercise the powers bestowed on them to meet those expectations. But the issue here is that the wants of the diverse set of shareholders are different. This is because the investment goals of the investors vary. Directors and boards in fact get confusing signals from the shareholders. Whereas mutual funds and institutional investors are more concerned about high returns over short and medium term, pension funds demand reasonable returns sustained over long periods of time. Individual investors will be concerned only about short-term returns. Venture capitalists will again have a target regarding returns than about long term sustainability of the firm. Corporate raiders will be more interested in the control of the enterprise paving way for acquiring and sometimes merging them with their companies. A socially responsible fund of the type Calvert Social Investment Fund will be more concerned about how the company conducts itself in a way as to enhance its triple bottom line. As Charan (1998) says, 'Shareholders are, after all, a diverse lot—the grandmother who owns ten shares as well as the activist pension fund. Some managers are in it to push a merger and make a quick gain, a move that might not be in the best interest of long term holders.' While in earlier days communication methods posed impediments to shareholder activism, the dawn of Internet has removed such impediments.

Conflict between Large and Minority Shareholders

In companies where a large shareholding is concentrated in the hands of one or a few shareholders, with the balance dispersed widely among a large number, usually there arise conflicts of interests between the controlling holders and the minority ones. The conflict usually arises from the use or diversion of earnings to the advantage of the controlling shareholder. While arguments are in favour of large investors so as to influence the managers to improve the efficiencies and force them to distribute more profits among shareholders as widely dispersed shareholders may not be able to do the same, this can lead to conflicts of interest and even to costs for the minority shareholders. In companies where large owners are also in the management, as is typical of many of the Indian companies, such substantial owners could exploit minority shareholders by rewarding themselves with higher salaries and benefits like commissions which can result in lesser distributable profits and consequently lesser distribution by way of dividend. And going by the 'one share, one vote' norm (which is widely accepted too), the minority holders will not be able to sway the decisions in their favour. Even if there are major shareholders outside the promoters or family numbers, like institutional investors, they again might not be able to force many decisions because their holding will still be smaller compared to those of the promoter-managers or they might be more keen to protect their own interests. The only avenue open to the minority holders is to resort to laws and regulations.

BOARDS AND THEIR FIDUCIARY DUTIES

According to Garratt (2003), the fiduciary duty of the directors (and boards) is 'to hold the company in trust for the future' which seems to be the most appropriate explanation for fiduciary duty. Phan (2000) says that the fiduciary duty of directors (and boards) essentially consists of two sub-duties namely, the duty of loyalty, and the duty of care. The duty of loyalty is a direct result of the agency theory of corporate governance. The second sub-duty, the duty of care, is related to the first, the duty of loyalty, and the duty of loyalty necessitates that a 'fiduciary shall not engage in practices that directly or indirectly harm the interests of his principal.' The duty of loyalty enables us to address issues related to conflicts of interest and those related to personal gains. Phan says that the duty of loyalty 'also implies that a fiduciary is in a monogamous relationship with the principal.' The duty of care of directors demands that they act in ways to protect and enhance the principal's position. Thus, boards and directors have to not only obey and act according to legal requirements but also have to develop a threshold of performance beyond the minimum to ensure that they make the best decision. Society may 'impose additional duty to the directors, for example to protect the environment, human rights, gender rights, etc. These are known as statutory duties' (Phan).

Garratt (2003) feels that post-Enron the three values of corporate governance namely accountability, probity, and ethics are receiving the righteous attention from the public. The Commonwealth Association of Corporate Governance (CACG) has suggested ten duties for directors. These ten duties require the board and the directors to behave within the following legal and ethical bounds.

The duty of legitimacy It emphasizes the importance of staying within national and international laws. While for a layman including this duty may look naive, the fact remains that many directors are ignorant of many aspects of company law and laws relating to capital markets in their country and international capital market regulations if they have chosen to raise capital internationally. Garratt (2003) suggests that the directors ask six simple questions to find out whether they are aware of the different implications when they accept an invitation to sit on a board:

1. If I have the word director on my business card but am not a member of the board of my organization, do I have the same liabilities as a board member?
2. If I am a director of a limited liability joint-stock company, am I covered as far as personal liabilities are concerned?
3. Do non-executive (independent) directors have fewer responsibilities than executive directors?
4. In a limited liability company, what is the prime duty of a director and the board to the shareholders?
5. If you are advising and working with the board, either as a senior manager or as a consultant, do you avoid directoral liability?
6. Are directors of state-owned organizations, including agencies and parastatals, exempt from normal directoral responsibilities?

Garratt (2003) says that almost 90 per cent board/director scores are incorrect going by the UK and Commonwealth laws. This is because according to these laws (which most other countries have adopted as laws or guidelines), the answers to the above questions will be:

1. Anyone 'purporting to be' or 'holding themselves out to be' a director will assume the same liabilities as a member of the board of directors. Using the title 'director of —' does not let you off the hook. It is, therefore, very unwise to give the title 'director' as part of a promotion if the person is not going to become a board member.
2. All directors have unlimited liability for their actions. The only limitation on the liability of a director of a company limited by share capital is on the paid-up shareholder capital.
3. There are no such terms as 'executive director' or 'non-executive director' in law. All directors are equal and each has a single vote.
4. The prime loyalty of a director is to the company as a separate legal entity. The argument is that if directors are ensuring the long-term health of their company, they are delivering their fiduciary duty.
5. Senior executives and external consultants who directly influence a particular decision with the board members having time and capacity to debate the decision among themselves can be considered to be 'shadow directors' and are therefore liable.
6. Nobody knows about it. There is no legal precedent or statute at present. The usual advice is to act as though the relevant company laws provide best-practice guidance, but that has not been tested in courts. In India if such companies are fully state-owned, company laws are applicable. If the government has diluted even a small portion of their holding in favour of the public, all regulations of the capital market regulator—SEBI—also become applicable in addition to the company laws. We have been witnessing an ongoing tussle between companies such as ONGC, NTPC, IOC, etc. and SEBI in respect of compliance with Clause 49 of the listing agreement.

Garratt (2003) says that knowing about laws and regulations is not enough. The board and directors also derive lot of power from the two basic documents of the company namely, the memorandum of association (MOA) and the articles of association (AOA). These will define how the company is going to be regulated internally, subject to the external laws that are applicable to every company. Another document that could be vital is the shareholders' agreement if it exists. Such an agreement may be prevalent in the case of closely held companies and are intended for owners specifying their rights and responsibilities. It should be noted that ignorance is not acceptable in the legal perspective. The directors have to be careful about the company or other directors on the board indulging in corrupt activities. Many countries have instituted laws against corruption and directors of companies which are operating across a number of countries have to be extremely careful.

The duty of upholding the three values of corporate governance   The three fundamental values generally accepted by everybody concerned with good governance are (Garratt 2003):

- Accountability
- Openness
- Probity

In the context of corporate governance, these will whittle down to

- Accountability to owners
- Honest dealing within and outside the board
- Transparency of risk-assessment and decision-taking process to the owners

Accountability to owners   The appointment of directors and the board is essentially based on the assumption that the directors will be fully accountable for their actions. As Monks and Minow (2005) say: 'Accountability is what makes delegated authority legitimate; without accountability there is nothing to prevent abuse.' While this accountability is the essential premise of the fiduciary duty of the directors, often governance failures have occurred due to the collapse of this basic premise. This lack of accountability has led to recurrent crises in the area of corporate governance. And this has prompted regulators and law makers to modify the existing laws to make those who are responsible accountable too. NYSE has made it mandatory for the CEOs and CFOs not only sign the financial statements (even quarterly) but also be personally liable for the facts therein.

Honest dealings within and outside the board   Honest behaviour within the board is based on mutual trust. Each director must have confidence in their colleagues. Any conflict of interest arising from his/her position as director shall be disclosed. Also, there shall be a clear understanding among the directors that nobody shall indulge in any activity that is targeted at personal gain arising from his membership of the board. The board should have a stringent code of conduct communicated to and understood by everybody. The code should as far as possible try to identify and eliminate all grey areas which may test a director for his behaviour.

Garratt suggests that the board should insist on

(a) Maintenance of a register of directors' interests by the company secretary, which is kept up-to-date with the onus on directors to make accurate and timely declaration or face action by the board
(b) An agreement among directors that all directors will declare on their own, and close family and friends in any item under board discussion
(c) Withdrawal from discussion by directors of any item under discussion after their declaration of interest in it
(d) Not voting on any item that affects their personal interests
(e) The register of directors' interests be open to inspection by shareholders at any time

The issue of honesty outside the board has to do with obeying all the laws and regulations of the land that are applicable and being transparent to outside stakeholders for all its actions. The board can also set its own rules. For example, Infosys Chairman N.R. Narayana Murthy has set a dictum for the company: 'When in doubt, disclose.' Of course, there is a risk committee which decides on what is to be disclosed to the outside world.

Transparency of risk-assessment and decision-taking process to owners   Many boards do not show rigour in the decision-making process. While in today's world decisions have to be made fast, it does not mean that decisions have to be made on ad-hoc basis. It should be remembered that the Board's decisions will have far reaching consequences. This was in evidence in the Satyam's board decision to acquire two companies promoted and managed by the members of the family of Mr Ramalinga Raju, the founder and chairman of Satyam. The board had to make a hasty retreat within 12 hours after taking the decision. The decision-taking by the board requires information collection, idea generation, assessment of risks, strategic thinking, critical questioning and review, and even a values test to ascertain whether the decisions will be in adherence to the value systems imbibed by the company. Even though all the stringent requirements have been adhered to, shareholders may still complain about transparency. Shareholders would like to know the process of decision-making used by the board and the consequences of those decisions. Diversity within the boardroom will help boards to have as many different viewpoints of an issue as possible enabling them to develop a new perspective and make better, informed decisions.

The duty of trust   Directors are required by law to hold their company 'in trust' for the future. This is another fundamental premise of the fiduciary duty that directors are responsible for. It must be noted that the directors have a duty to the company to hold it in trust than to the shareholders. While trying to execute this duty to the company, the directors might at times act against the narrow interests of the shareholders to protect the larger interests of the company. There have been a number of instances where certain shareholder(s) try to further or protect their interests at the expense of the company's overall interests or what is good for the company. The Satyam incident is a case in point. The board tried to protect the interests of a few shareholders (and that too those with a minority stake compared to the outside stake) at the expense of the interests of the company. Or in short, they did not hold Satyam 'in trust' for the future. But for the revolt of the outside shareholders whose total holding was much bigger than that of the promoters, the whole Satyam story would not have been made public.

The duty of upholding the primary loyalty of a director   The moment one gets elected as a director, his primary loyalty must be to the company as a legal entity rather than the shareholders who appointed them. The shareholders will always expect that the directors elected by them will act in their interests. But, the directors have to choose a view that what is good for the company over a long-term must be good for the shareholders too. Directors must concentrate on the current as well as on the future health of the company as an economic entity and refrain from doing or encouraging anything that challenges these. They have to exercise their power of judgement in times of difficulty by arriving at (sometimes) hard decisions.

The duty of care   The directors and the board as a body has to be caring for the company when they take their decisions just like a mother cares for the child. The board has a duty to protect the company from different threats, or risks, identify its weakness, make good use of its strengths to exploit the opportunities that come by in order to sustain and grow. Exercising such duty of care will require directors to observe the following:

(a) Be fully involved and committed to the company rather than cursorily attend board meetings and vote for or against resolutions.

(b) Prepare themselves for their active and full participation in the board meetings.

(c) Be properly inducted, trained to gain competence and appraised on a regular basis.

(d) Reduce the number of directorships in order to be fully committed to wherever one is a director.

(e) Continuously monitor the environment (internal and external), in order to make suitable changes in their strategies, processes, people, and even businesses.

The duty of critical review and independent thought   According to law, all directors on the board are equal. A chairman is elected from the directors to enable the board to conduct well. Hence, 'each director is expected to be sufficiently self-aware and mature to be able to make their own judgement on the best direction and prudent control systems for the health of the company' (Garratt 2003). While directors are expected to be applying independence of thought and indulging in critical review, they might be running a risk of being isolated in the short run and not getting re-elected in the long run. Many of the colleagues on the board, especially the promoters and their nominees, expect other directors to toe their line. In the conventional setting, toeing the promoter line or majority line was the expectation. But, in today's environment, while collegiality and harmony are encouraged to co-exist with diverse opinions and even dissent, many think that the dissenting director is a nuisance and forget that he/she might be expressing his/her dissent or concern for the good of the company, which is expected of him as a director. The other board members should discuss threadbare the reasons for the dissenting directors' concerns and address them before taking further decisive actions.

The duty of delivering the primary roles and tasks of the board   Garratt (2003) says that this can better be discussed by considering the four 'interlinked directoral dilemmas', namely:

- Driving the enterprise forward, while keeping it under prudent control
- Being required to be sufficiently aware of the workings of the business to be responsible for its actions, while having time to develop a longer-term more objective view of developments outside the business
- Being sensitive to short-term local demands, while balancing these against broader regional, national, and international trends
- Being focused on the commercial needs of the business, while acting responsibly to other stakeholders in your society

The board has to subdivide the broader roles into board tasks, which is explained in Chapter 4.

The duty of protecting minority owners' interests   The position of minority shareholders is precarious in most countries. While developed countries have tried to protect the interests of minority shareholders by stringent regulatory measures, in developing and underdeveloped countries this is still a major issue. The directors owe their positions to the owners or the CEO who is a nominee of the owners and hence will try to protect the interests of those who nominated them than performing and executing the duties of a 'director'. Sometimes the MOA and the AOA may specifically mention the company's intention to protect the minority interests. In countries like India, where governance conscious institutions of the California Public Employees' Retirement System (CalPERS), Teachers Insurance and Annuity Association, College Retirement Equities Fund (TIAA-CREF) or LENS type are not available, share-owners' associations take lead in protecting the interests of the minority shareholders. The directors must not forget that they represent the entire shareholding community and their allegiance is not only to the large shareholders.

The duty of corporate social responsibility   Garratt (2003) is of the opinion that it is extremely difficult for any board to take a balanced and pragmatic approach with respect to this aspect. Primarily, business enterprises are profit-driven and they must according to conventional wisdom do anything within the frontiers of law to maximize profit. This is underscored by the free market regime which is the touchstone of capitalism. On the one side, we have proponents of free markets where any action to further profit was legitimate. On the other extreme, we have anti-capitalist groups crying for an equitable distribution of wealth, protecting environments, protecting human rights, and even development of local economies rather than international development and creation of economic power blocks. In the 1970s, the free market proponents got the moral support from reputed economists like Milton Friedman, who said that 'the business of business is to make profits' and hence the social responsibility of business is to make more profits. But very early on, Peter Drucker (1970) had stated that companies had clearly set objectives in the area of public responsibility while identifying areas where management had to invariably set objectives. Drucker included it under the three intangible areas but warned that 'to neglect them is to risk not only business incompetence but… public restriction on business provoked by irresponsible business conduct.'

Recently, Charan (2005) has stated that 'money making is your (CEO's) job. You spend most of your time and energy thinking about your business. Is it positioned correctly? Is your team of leaders synchronized in the pursuit of your goals? Are the priorities right? Is the social system healthy? But the job doesn't stop there. Every business today operates in a complex and societal milieu that demands more of it than just profits… It is a foregone conclusion that business leaders have to be able to deal with market forces, and over the years they've learned to live with them. In the 21st century, business leaders will be required to deal with issues that go beyond the market' (Charan 2005). Any issue arising from a neglect of the responsible behaviour of the company towards society will lead to a backlash on the very business and its conduct. Garratt (2003) quotes the example of Shell Inc., which has developed the concept of the *triple bottom line* that enables a corporation to be concerned about the progress of not only the financial performance but also of the physical environmental performance and performance on the corporate social responsibility front. At Shell, targets and standards are set for all the three bottomlines and all the three outputs have independent, external auditors appointed who report back as part of the annual auditing process. In India, Tata Steel took leadership in implementing a social audit process. Stock markets have also woken up to the emergent need to encourage companies with concerns for society. For example *Financial Times* has constituted the *Financial Times* FTSE4 Good Index (www.ftse4good. co.uk) and Dow Jones has constituted Dow Jones Sustainability World Index, both of which have become significant in screening good corporate citizenship of companies. Companies have also come to the view that good corporate citizenship pays to bettering business. According to a survey on corporate social responsibility (CSR) trends published by the *Financial Times*, British Telecom has 'calculated that its social and environmental performance accounts for more than 25 per cent of its overall business and reputation, which in turn is the second biggest factor driving change in its customer satisfaction rates' (Hollender and Fenichell 2004). Directors and boards have to be fully aware of the realities of the expectations of performance of the company on the corporate citizenship front.

The duty of learning, developing, and communicating   According to Garratt (2003), many directors assumed that the reward of a directorship is simply the acknowledgement of the end of a long and successful executive or professional career, not the beginning of a new one. This led them to believe that there was no need for them to learn anything new and that their experience will carry them through to a cozy retirement. But today, with the corporate governance being the cynosure of attention, accepting directorship is not an easy option anymore. Directors have to look at the directorship as the start of a new and challenging career. While certain parts of managerial learning might be useful, directors' learning has to be different and broader than that of managers as their roles are different than those of the managers. To be effective and successful at directing, one must not only train but retrain in an ever changing environment. Their learning has to be more focused on the need to perform their roles, duties, and tasks. The chairman or the lead director can take initiative in getting a new director inducted and trained in the essential directorial duties. The board as a whole should also review its training needs in view of the changes in the regulatory, social, economic, technological, and competitive environments. They should invite experts in the field from industry, consulting, and academia to meet the training and learning needs. They should be on a continuous learning mode by acquiring, interpreting, and applying the knowledge available from innumerable sources.

THEORIES OF CORPORATE GOVERNANCE

Considering the structural processes of the corporate form and the fiduciary responsibilities that the directors and boards have to execute, various theories have evolved. The evolution in the theoretical approach here more or less reflects the evolution in management theories ever since management became a professional and academic discipline. These theories are drawn from a variety of disciplines: economics, finance, accounting, law, organizational behaviour, etc. It should also be noted that the process of development of corporate governance in any particular country has been unique and depended on the business and organizational culture, legislative mechanisms, ownership patterns, and other structural differences related to industry. And the stage of evolution of corporate governance in any country will depend on how the above factors have been evolving, over a period of time. For example, ownership-related control is the prevailing feature in countries like India and many other developing countries, growth of the enterprise and acquisition of size and command over markets even at the risk of diluted ownership and control could be the drivers in developed countries like the US and the others. The stage of governance might also depend on how active the shareholders are and the power enjoyed and wielded by the various institutions in the economy. For example, many Indian business enterprises and industry houses were conscious of the necessity of good governance much before the concept of corporate governance came into being. For example, the house of Tatas in India had enlightened leaders who were thoughtful of implementing a regime of good governance right from the beginning.

Tata Steel for example set a precedence of excellent, uninterrupted labour relations for decades, took responsibility for the development of Jamshedpur, where its plant is located as part of its social responsibility much before the term was constituted or became fashionable. The house of Tatas also was instrumental in establishing centres of learning excellence like the Indian Institute of Science (IISc) at Bangalore and Tata Institute of Fundamental Research (TIFR) at Mumbai, which enabled the country to produce high caliber scientists and technologists capable of taking India to the next level in scientific and technological development. The house of Lalbhais from Gujarat played a very prominent role in the establishment of the first national level management institute in India, the Indian Institute of Management, Ahmedabad, which sowed the seeds of management education in India. Over a period of about 15–20 years ever since corporate governance assumed importance and started receiving attention, a number of theories have been evolved. The major theories are agency theory, theory of transaction cost economics, stewardship theory, and stakeholder theory.

Agency Theory

According to the agency theory developed by Michael Jensen and William Meckling, in the typical corporate form, the owners are content with the ownership and control over the assets and the resources of the company are in the hands of managers who by convention need not hold any stake in the company. The tacit understanding arising out of the convention is that the managers will act as agents of the principals—the owners or the shareholders of the company. According to the theory, it is a relationship where the principal delegates work and authority to another party, the agent. But the framework is beset with pitfalls as the agent may not always act in the best interests of the principal. The agent being a human being with his/her own ambitions might try to further their selfish motives rather than safeguard the interests of the principal.

As Adam Smith (2003) says, 'The direction of such companies however being the managers rather of other people's money than of their own, it can't well be expected that they should watch over it with the same anxious vigilance.' While the managers (agents) have always been rewarded for their efficient utilization of resources which will mostly be reflected in the short term, it might not necessarily be the best thing for the company and its resources from a sustainable economic entity point of view. Thus, there can be costs in the agency framework which will have to be absorbed by the owners and the company.

For example, the management may not assess the risk of a new venture properly and thus may inflict loss of money or even reputation which can give rise to direct or indirect cost to the owners. A standard principal—agency relationship is governed by contracts (Eisenhardt 1989). Such contracts spell out the terms of performance of the contracting parties. And usually contracts are well defined in terms of timing, scope, and redress of grievances arising out of non-performance by the parties. But, when agency theory is applied to a corporation context, such a contract is missing. Demsetz and Lehn (1985) say that contracts between the shareholder and the manager are very costly to write and enforce because of the following: (1) The information asymmetry between managers and owners (shareholders) (managers usually have skills and knowledge not available to shareholders) lead to the underspecification of performance standards for the managers, (2) monitoring is difficult as shareholders are not in a position to observe everything a manager does, and (3) redress of problems even when detected is difficult because of the widely dispersed nature of shareholders and coordinating their actions is costly. According to Jensen (1993), even shareholders with significantly large shareholdings have had little success in replacing a poorly performing management through a proxy method. And Phan (2000) says that 'Even when it becomes apparent that the management is not doing its job, all a shareholder can do is to vote with his feet by selling the stock. Further, selling stock is not an effective way of changing management unless there is a run on the stock of a company, which is unlikely in most situations, because management still gets to keep its job when an individual shareholder sells out.' This inability to enforce contracts meant concentration of 'great economic power into the hands of a few professional managers who themselves were not significant owners of the companies they led. They served as 'agents' for the public shareholders who owned the company but did not manage it and the risks associated with it, had become subject to 'agency conflicts'—potential conflicts of interest between corporate managers and their owners' (Smith and Walter 2006). But according to many experts, these types of conflicts were anticipated and authorities (either at state or national level) had been implementing laws and regulations, which were intended to limit corporate freedom of actions in areas where it might come into conflict with the interest of shareholders, other stakeholders, and even general public. Even the media has been very active in bringing out such conflicts and the need for better governance.

According to Phan (2000), there are two categories of solutions to overcome the agency related problems. One is 'the board of directors represents shareholders when the ownership of capital is separated from the control of capital, as in the case of large, public corporations with dispersed ownership of shares. This is the internal mechanism of control. It relies on the expertise and goodwill of corporate watchdogs to ensure that managers abide by the principles of maximizing efficiency. The other category of solution is the external mechanisms of control. Here, the behaviour of managers is indirectly constrained by the workings of a series of competitive markets that systematically punish the company for deviating from efficiency maximization.' Thus, the internal control ends with the board's role of ratifying managerial decisions and acting as a liaison between the firm and its stockholders. Mr Kenneth E. Scott, while discussing the essence of corporate governance says: 'If the position of stockholders can't be well protected by contract, then how is it made viable? There are two mechanisms in particular that serve this function. One is the law: rules that require managers (agents) to act in the best interests of shareholders (principals). The other is governance: a set of provisions that enable stockholder by exercising voting power to compel those in operating control of the firm to respect their interests. Legal rules can but address relatively clear conflicts of interests; management competence, except in occasional cases such as Enron and Parmalat, fall in the domain of governance.

Obviously, corporate governance is not a problem for the 100 per cent-owner-manager of a business. Nor is it much of a problem for the majority stockholder (or group) which controls the board of directors and can fire managers at any time (protection of minority interests in such a form will have to come primarily from legal rights, since their voting power is generally ineffectual). So, corporate governance is an issue mainly for minority stockholders, in a firm controlled by the managers where there are no significant stockholders that can easily work together' (Wallace and Zinkin 2005).

While Scott has addressed most of the issues, one issue or context typical of most of the Indian family promoted companies doesn't get addressed: the scenario where the majority owner acts as a manager (agent) and also sits on the board of directors. This is a very intriguing situation in the area of corporate governance. While there can be lots of advantages of the owner getting actively involved in management and control, this can also become a deadly combination. The principal-agent framework can result in a number of costs for the principal as well as the agent, termed agency costs. The principal's costs may include all costs incurred in monitoring and controlling the behavior of the agent. The agent may also incur bounding costs in convincing the principal will not be harmed. In short, agency costs are the inefficiencies associated with employing a representative to carry out a task for you, rather than carrying out yourself. Any residual loss arising from a poor judgement on the part of the agent will also form part of the agency costs. The agency theory has been put to severe tests as managers are likely to have their own goals and objectives that do not directly accord with those of the owners. The theory was criticized by renowned management gurus and academics like the late Sumantra Ghoshal and Peter Moran. According to Ghoshal and Moran (2005), 'Academic theories support this justification of determinism that denies any role of moral or ethical considerations in the practice of management. The theory of principals and agents that now dominate economic analysis of the role of managers see them as having a single obligation: that of serving as agents of the shareholders who are the principals, and therefore having a single goal, viz that of maximizing the returns derived by the principals from their investments in the business.'

Whatever be the criticisms against the proponents of the agency theory or the theory itself, the theory is going to remain. One reason for its ability to sustain is that most of the governance failures can be attributed to it.

Transaction Cost Economics Theory

The transaction cost economics theory, evolved through the works of Oliver Williamson, has close relations or similarities with the agency theory but goes a little further. While agency theory states that agents (professional managers) are human beings with their own individual goals and aspirations and would like to further them while acting as agents for their principals, transaction cost economics theory assumes that individuals are self-interested and opportunistic in nature, and they will cheat the system if they can (Ghoshal & Moran 2005). The behaviour of the manager is opportunistic, i.e., an expression of 'self-interest unconstrained by morality' (Milgrom and Roberts 1992).

The theory implies that mangers should put in place control systems and legal mechanisms to guard against such opportunistic behaviour. But Ghoshal and Moran (2005) feel that such systems often encourage the very behaviour that they are trying to curb, and as a side-effect drive out such desirable attributes as initiative and co-operation. For them, transaction cost economics is 'bad for practice' because it fails to recognize the difference. According to Williamson's theory, 'organizations exist because of the superior ability to attenuate human opportunism through the exercise of hierarchical control that is not accessible to markets.' But, Ghoshal and Moran argue that 'such hierarchical controls need not necessarily curtail opportunistic behaviour. Indeed, they are more likely to cause precisely the opposite effect. The assumption of opportunism can become a self-fulfilling prophecy whereby opportunistic behaviour will increase with sanctions and incentives imposed to curtail it, thus creating the need for even stronger and more elaborate sanctions and incentives. Caught in such a vicious cycle, 'hierarchies' as organizations as described by Williamson, would, over time, lose their initial raison detre' (Ghoshal and Moran). In many of the modern organizations, where leaders insist on candor and transparency and are tolerant of dissent with thrust on collaborative excellence rather than individual excellence, the transaction cost economics theory has been finding lesser relevance.

Stewardship Theory

This is also called as shareholder theory. According to this, the boards have a stewardship role for the resources entrusted to them by the shareholders. The power over the corporation is exercised by directors who are nominated and appointed by shareholders and hence accountable to them for the stewardship over the company's resources. The theory is based on the belief that the directors can be trusted. This is also the theoretical foundation for most of the legislations and regulations in almost all the countries and the basis of most of the best practices recommended for good governance. The roles, duties, and tasks of directors are essentially based on this. This theory also underscores Garratt's contention that the distinction of managing, executive, non-executive or independent is irrelevant because according to the law, all directors are expected to fulfil the same kind of duties and behaviour. According to Peter Block (1996), 'Stewardship begins with the willingness to be accountable, for some larger body than ourselves—an organization, a community. Stewardship springs from a set of beliefs about reforming an organization that affirms our choice of service over the pursuit of self-interest. When we choose service over self-interest, we say we are willing to be deeply accountable choosing to control the world around us. It requires a level of trust that we are not used to holding.'

Stewardship is a holistic concept which promises the means of achieving a grassroot level change in the way the institutions have been governed. As Block (1996) says, 'Stewardship is to hold something in trust for another.' Block defines stewardship 'as the choice to preside over the orderly distribution of power.' This means giving people at the bottom and the boundaries of the organization choice over how to serve a customer, a citizen, a community. It is the willingness to be accountable for the well-being of the larger organization by operating in service rather than in control of those around us. Stated simply, it is 'accountability without control or compliance' (Block).

Thus, at the heart of the stewardship theory is the commitment to service. The directors on the boards acting on the principle of stewardship will hold the company in trust on behalf of the different stakeholders. While conventional agency theory attributed that agents have their own self-interest in the way they managed, led, and governed. According to Block (1996), 'Stewardship begins with the willingness to be accountable for some larger body than ourselves—an organization, a community. Stewardship springs from a set of service over the pursuit of self-interest. When we choose service over self-interest we say we are willing to be deeply accountable without choosing to control the world around us. It requires a level of trust that we are not used to holding.'

Stakeholder Theory

While corporations have been concentrating on value maximization for more than 200 years, starting with Adam Smith who thought that social wealth and welfare are likely to be greatest when corporations seek to maximize the stream of profits that can be divided among their shareholders, over a period of time the goal has got transformed to one of 'maximization of the long-run market value of the firm', where the value of the firm is mainly but not necessarily entirely defined by the company's stock price. Jensen (2005) has evolved this stakeholder theory which says that 'corporations should attempt to maximize not value of their shares (or financial claims), but distributed among all corporate 'stakeholders' include employees, customers, suppliers, local communities, and tax collectors' (Chew and Gillan 2005). This theory has been getting wide acceptance among organizations, politicians and even governance conscious organizations and governments because the theory has a perspective of long-term rather than short-term in the 'value-maximization proposition' of the earlier years. The widespread use of the tool balanced score card (BSC) which is a multidimensional performance measurement process, where not only the financial performance, which is historical in nature, but also the internal business processes, the customers, and the learning and growth aspects which will consider the sustainability of the business are also taken into consideration. Jensen describes BSC as the 'managerial equivalent' of the stakeholder theory. According to Jensen, 'Stakeholder theory is completely consistent with value-maximization or value-seeking behaviour, which implies that managers must pay attention to all constituencies that can affect the value of the firm.' But with multiple constituencies competing and with conflicting interests, the decision-making process for the boards and managers becomes difficult. Then why is it that the theory has become so popular? Jensen provides the answer: '...answer lies in their personal short-run interests. By failing to provide a definition of better, stakeholder theory effectively leaves managers and directors unaccountable for their stewardship of the firm's resources. Without criteria for performance, managers can't be evaluated in any principled way. It allows managers and directors to devote the firm's resources to their own favourite causes—the environment, art, cities, medical research—without being held accountable for the effect of such expenditure on firm value…' By expanding the power of managers in this unproductive way, stakeholder theory increases agency costs in the economic system. And since it expands the power of managers, it is not surprising that stakeholder theory receives substantial support from them.

DOES GOVERNANCE MATTER?

This question might look a little out of place in the backdrop of high profile failures like Enron, WorldCom, etc. in the US at the beginning of this century and the Satyam incident in the recent past in India. These have given rise to a lot of skepticism in the minds of the stakeholders regarding business enterprises and professional management but this is only a limited and apparent concern. At the heart of it, these governance failures put the very corporate form of business enterprise, which has been the foundation for business enterprises to become institutions that command attention, and capitalism as the economic institution that fostered unlimited opportunities for entrepreneurship to flourish to question. By and large, instances of corporate failures like Enron or Satyam are few and far between, and constitute a meager percentage of the total number of business enterprises. Very few people are concerned about governance when everything is going fine but once there is an instance of governance failure, everyone suddenly wakes up and starts identifying reasons for governance failures. This could be perhaps because people are shaken up easily by bad news and are more or less not moved by good news. People usually don't get moved by normal or good things because that only gives them a confirmation of what is expected of the corporation and their managers. For example, a well-governed company like Infosys might not get any special attention in the normal course because good governance is what is expected of boards, directors, managers, and companies. Some companies resort to the loopholes in the law to cover up governance deficiencies, which usually go unnoticed (refer Exhibit 2.1). Satyam became the cynosure of all public attention because the actions of the board of directors, managers, and the company at large resulted in violation of our expectations. Hence, even if we know that such instances might happen in future too, we show our knee-jerk reaction once they happen while still ignoring all the well-governed companies.

Corporate failure also gives rise to doubts about the efficacy of the capital markets which enable the enterprise to mobilize funds. The capital markets are expected to play a dominant role in encouraging good governance by rewarding in the form of higher stock prices, exercising control, when board and management indulges in activities which are not necessarily for the health of the company, not just by beating the prices down but also through active dialogue between companies and investors, taking a position (for or against) in a threat of takeover or acquisition by other enterprises, etc. Notwithstanding the praise for the development and growth of capital markets, these crucial governance areas have so far eluded it.

According to Garratt (2003), the process of governance was beset with its own strengths and weaknesses 'but where, remarkably, 'my word is my bond'—controlled by a strong blend of individual conscience and the fear of being banned from the self-regulating club forever—still held sway. Trust was assumed to be absolute between parties to a transaction. Personal integrity

Exhibit 2.1
Companies Take Cover of Loopholes in the Law

The Annual Report of Bajaj Auto Ltd for 2007–08 opens with the company's commitment to corporate governance: The commitment of Bajaj Group to the highest standards of good corporate governance practices predates SEBI and clause 49 of the listing agreements. Transparency, fairness, disclosure and accountability are central to the working of the Group. Bajaj Auto Limited, the newly incorporated company maintains the same tradition and commitment.

The Annual Report of 2007–08 was special in that it was the first annual report of Bajaj Auto after the much talked about demerger. While all the directors of the pre-demerger Bajaj Auto retained their seats on the board in the post-demerger Bajaj Auto, it was very interesting to see an unusual development. Mr D.S. Mehta, who was whole-time director for many years including 2006–07, suddenly got transformed into a non-executive, independent director. There is no explanation in the Annual Report as to how this change has happened. The report also did not give any (even brief) bio-data of the directors. One would have expected these to be given considering that 2007–08 was the first annual report of the company in its new avatar.

Having served the company for many years as a whole-time director, there might be no question about the value that Mr D.S. Mehta could add to the board. But, if that is so, the company should have retained him as an ordinary non-executive director.

While Bajaj Auto might be complying with all SEBI regulations in force today, was it 'right' from an ethical point of view? While conformance is a must, conformance exploiting the loopholes in laws and regulations will not be respected by any.

We all respect Mr Rahul Bajaj as an elderly statesman, fearless of airing his views on business and economy. Mr Bajaj himself chaired the committee set up by the Confederation of Indian Industry (CII) in 1996 which came out with the report—*Desirable Corporate Governance: A Code* in 1998 that also influenced the establishment of Clause 49 of the listing agreement by SEBI.

Mr Bajaj and Bajaj Auto are not alone in these kinds of happenings. In the past, even after Clause 49 came into being, such deficiencies were observed in many companies including Tata Group companies. For example, J.K. Setna, director, Tata Motors Ltd (Tata Engineering & Locomotive Company Ltd till 2002–03) since 1993 and designated as non-executive, promoter director in the company's 2002–03 Annual Report, got transformed to non-executive, independent director in the 2003–04 Annual Report (Tata Motors) without any explanation regarding the change. He was also a member on the boards of Tata Sons (the apex Tata company) and four other Tata companies at the time. He continued to be designated as non-executive independent director till his retirement in 2006.

According to pension fund CalPERS, 'independence is the cornerstone of accountability' and hence, 'a substantial majority of the board consists of directors who are independent' and that 'independence also requires a lack of conflict between the director's personal, financial or professional interests, and the interests of the shareowners.'[1] On the contrary, Ram Charan, renowned board expert and advisor, feels that 'many independent directors fall silent when facing strong CEOs; their lack of knowledge of the company and its officers works against their ability to provide oversight. The best directors are those who think independently regardless of their status. In other words, independence is a state of mind, not a resume item.'[2] The opinion of Charan is a criticism of the approach by law makers and regulators to look at structure as the foundation for better governance, the argument or opinion cannot be taken as any excuse for having somebody who does not qualify to be independent and designating him/her as independent. One is not sure about SEBI's take on this.

Questions
1. Critically comment on the two incidents at Bajaj Auto Ltd and Tata Motors Ltd explained above.
2. Do you think that regulations overemphasize director independence on corporate boards?
3. Is it necessary for SEBI to plug certain regulatory loopholes to prevent such incidents from recurring?

---

[1] http//www.calpers.ca.gov
[2] *Boards That Deliver*, 2005, Jossey-Bass.

was considered above mere corporate loyalty.' But becoming a director was still considered to be driven by the quest for power and economic benefits and was not considered part of the fiduciary responsibility to the company, shareholders, and stakeholders. It was considered more of an opportunity to lead an easy going but financially rewarding life, rather than one of offering one's expertise and contributing to the well being of the company as the directoral duty was considered to be either accepting or rejecting the proposals of management. Such a thought process was never questioned as long as the goings were good and was subjected to scrutiny only when some of the failures of corporation were squarely attributed to the neglect of the essential duties which the directors had to perform. As Garratt says, 'Being a director was more important than the art of directing.'

Post Enron-like failures, at the turn of the 20th century, led to the directors being branded as corrupt, greedy, and narrow-minded capitalists concerned only about their position of directors as one to aggrandize their personal wealth and other self-interests. According to Alan Greenspan, 1990s was an era of 'infelicitous greed', 'irrational exuberance of the markets', and 'outsized increase in opportunities for avarice', which led to most of the governance-related problems in corporations (Garratt 2003). Reaction by the public and the politics against corporate greed and corruption has led to 20-year joint sentences to offending senior executives in the US, where the average term for murder is 12 years.

When GM decided to make its governance guidelines public in the 1990s, it attracted the attention of other big corporations like IBM and American Express who also undertook initiatives in establishing governance guidelines. According to MacAvoy and Millstein (2004), in the late 1990s, a study was conducted among 300 to 500 big corporations in the US to know the functioning of corporate governance. About 30 per cent of the companies had implemented good governance practices, while 50 per cent adopted the policy of shifting the control from management to board of directors.

According to Garratt (2003), 'Privatization in the UK heralded the era of the overpaid "fat cats" and the ensuing public abreaction reinforced the country's push to the forefront of corporate governance reform. Some ridiculous, short-sighted, self-serving behaviour by the boards of these newly privatized businesses speeded the reform process. They became directors simply because they were there, and in a few cases put up some small "risk" capital to reap some very undervalued assets. To make matters worse, the new director seemed to have no intention of doing anything to audit, assess, or improve their board, or their individual competencies' while speaking on the state of affairs of corporate governance in UK in the late 1980s and 1990s. The failure of the British iconic brand Rolls-Royce and the misuse of pension funds of Mirror group led by Robert Maxwell created the much needed push for better governance in UK. The Cadbury Committee was constituted by the London Stock Exchange under the Chairmanship of Sir Adrian Cadbury to look into the financial aspects of corporate governance. In 1992, the committee produced the report titled Report of the Committee on the Financial Aspects of Corporate Governance, which was one of the first ever organized attempt, anywhere in the world, to evolve a guideline for corporate governance. Most of the countries of the developed and developing world have since formulated their codes drawing extensively from the Cadbury Committee recommendations.

According to Garratt, many of the initiatives were 'driven by two distinct purposes. First was to ensure tighter accountability of board members and individual directors to their owners for their actions. Second was to counter growing corruption in many companies (private and public) and countries, and so reinforce the movement to establish the rules of law, anti-money laundering and (later) anti-terrorism practices and thus help the liberal democratic process toward its ultimate goal of a more global "civil society".'

In India, we had a number of corporate battles and scandals in the 1980s and in the 1990s, especially after economic liberalization was initiated, which eased the process of raising finances by entrepreneurs and corporates. While the battle for the control of Shaw Wallace and Company Ltd was essentially between the incumbent management led by the chairman and managing director, S.P. Acharya, arguing for and on behalf of minority shareholders, and the institutional shareholders which were supporting the acquisition of the company by the Manu Chhabria (Jumbo Group of Dubai), ultimately the raider won the battle with the support of the institutions. Another major event which shook our capital markets was the MS Shoe Scam of 1994, when the promoter and dominant shareholder, Pawan Sachdeva, in connivance with brokers took leveraged positions on the company's stock to manipulate share prices ahead of a rights issue. This led to a brokers' default on Bombay Stock Exchange and closure of the exchange for three days. Then there was the issue related to the insider trading charges against Hindustan Lever Ltd (HLL) with regard to its merger with Brooke Bond Lipton India Ltd (BBLIL) in 1996. The controversy involved HLL's purchase of 0.8 million shares of BBLIL 2 weeks prior to the public announcement of the merger of the two companies (HLL and BBLIL). SEBI, suspecting insider trading, conducted enquiries, and after about 15 months, in August 1997, SEBI issued a show cause notice to the chairman, all executive directors and the company secretary of HLL. Later in March 1998 SEBI passed an order charging HLL with insider trading.

While these scams were serious enough to shake the beliefs of shareholders in the functioning of the capital markets and the role of institutional investors, they mostly occurred in an era before the concept of corporate governance attained importance or popularity. The Satyam incident has been one of the major governance failures in the post-liberalization Indian corporate scenario. The Satyam issue has brought to the forefront the roles of the board, the independent directors, the shareholders, the auditors, and the regulators. While this is being written, even after 15 months of investigation, no major breakthroughs have been achieved other than the new board instituted by the government deciding to let Satyam be acquired by another IT major from India, Tech Mahindra Ltd, after a bidding process. While there have not been many corporate failures like Satyam that could be attributed to poor governance, the state of governance of corporates has not been put to severe tests yet.

Boards of yester years were mostly on a compliance or conformance mode. While conformance with laws and regulations is a must, today at a growing number of companies, boards are being looked upon as a competitive weapon. According to Charan (1998), 'The board not only protects shareholder value but actually helps create it.' The increase in shareholder activism led by pension funds like CalPERS and TIAA-CREF, is forcing underperforming companies to adopt better governance practices and has been successful in getting more attention to the governance of the corporations in the US. While governance conscious institutions of the CalPERS or TIAA-CREF variety have not made their presence felt in India, shareholder activism has been on the rise of late, if some of the incidents that happened in the recent past are any indication. For example, recently at the AGM of Pfizer Ltd, the institutional shareholder Life Insurance Corporation of India objected to two proposals for increasing the remuneration of Managing Director and the Commission payable to two independent directors.[1] Earlier in 2008, Reliance Mutual Fund raised certain corporate governance related issues relating to intergroup transactions in the pharma company Novartis in which it held close to 5 per cent.[2] In another instance, a shareholder was reported to have raised the management succession issue at the CIPLA AGM.[3]

Even in the case of Satyam, the major outside shareholders like Templeton Mutual Fund, Reliance Mutual Fund, SBI Mutual Fund, etc. reacted violently and took lead in opposing the board decision to acquire two family promoted companies and the promoter and chairman of Satyam, Mr Ramalinga Raju, was forced to call off the deal within 12 hours of the decision to enter into the deal. But, by and large, with the owners themselves being on the management, the possibility of the conventional approach of shareholders appointing and removing the 'agents' for their lack of integrity or the lack of performance does not exist in India.

What are the Possible Ways to Improve Shareholder Activism in India?

A few initiatives that may help are
1. The regulator should force companies to disclose information immediately or impose heavy penalties for non-disclosures. For example, in September 2007, SEBI pulled up 20 public companies (including five public sector ones) for non-compliance to Clause 49 guidelines. But, even after 1 year, investors are in the dark regarding which those companies are as apparently none of the 20 have so far voluntarily disclosed the information. After 1 year, even if the information gets disclosed, it would be too late and irrelevant for the market to react as the erring companies had sufficient time to take corrective actions.
2. Regulator should divert its attention to prevent possible problems or failure by being proactive, by disseminating information to the public immediately on finding it or getting it and also by educating and developing investors. SEBI should have disclosed the information then and there about the 20 erring companies mentioned under point no.1 above.
3. Immediate action may be taken for reforms in the pension sector, as pension funds have longer investment horizons and substantially higher incentives than mutual funds to hold firms to high standards of governance.
4. For investors to raise questions, they have to get timely information, but either they do not get or do not know where and how to get them. Investors (small and big, especially the institutions) can come together to create agencies in the private sector for continuous surveillance of the

[1] 'LIC dissents at Pfizer AGM over MD's salary', *Business Line*, 16 April 2009.
[2] 'Reliance Mutual Fund Questions Novartis Practices', *Economic Times*, 14 August 2008.
[3] 'Succession non-issue for CIPLA, feels chairman', *Economic Times*, 30 August 2008.

corporates (on the lines of Institutional Shareholder Services, ISS, in the US) which will provide information to shareholders who then can use this information to question the acts of management.

CORPORATE GOVERNANCE MODELS

According to Coombes and Watson (2001) of McKinsey, there are basically two models, namely the Anglo-Saxon model or the market model and control model to explain the governance practices as seen in different parts of the world.

The Anglo-Saxon Model or the Market Model

This is the most popularly followed model in different parts of the world today and is based on the Anglo-Saxon shareholder capitalism. This is also called the market model as according to Coombes and Watson, it provides lots of information (even to competing firms) as it perceives very high disclosure norms, has widely dispersed ownership, very high degree of equality among shareholders, very active market for corporate control, highly active market for IPOs and private equity, and highly sophisticated institutional investors taking active interest in the affairs of companies. The market model of Coombes and Watson is shown in Fig. 2.2.

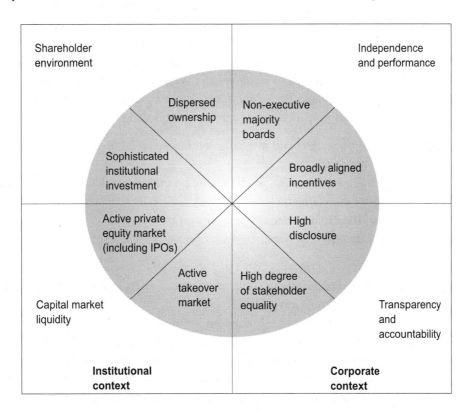

Fɪɢ. **2.2**   Market model of corporate governance prevalent in the US and UK

The model demands the directors to behave independently and take independent views even though they might feel that they have been invited by the CEO and are, hence, obliged to him for their position as directors. The model fits countries like the US and UK as the corporate governance model in these countries is market-based and market driven with the following characteristics (Wallace and Zinkin 2005):

- The shareholding is widely dispersed and led by sophisticated institutional investors, who are concerned about fundamentals and sustainability rather than reaping short-term profits and try to create an environment where shareholders have equal rights and even minority shareholders' interests are expected to be protected.
- The constitution of the board and the role assumed by it are in line with market demands. The boards are mostly constituted with majority non-executive, independent directors, whose incentives are not closely aligned with those of the dominant or controlling shareholder (if there is one) but rather aligned with the interests of the absent owners (the minority shareholders).

Control Model

According to Coombes and Watson (2001), the Asian context, where partly listed, family-owned businesses dominate, calls for a different model. According to them, the Anglo-Saxon model is not suited for these because in the Anglo-Saxon model, there is very high degree of disclosures and transparency which is not appreciated in family owned companies as these consider such disclosures and transparency will provide information to the competitors and also reduce the family's ability to run the company. Coombes and Watson are of the opinion that the governance model suitable for companies from Asia, Latin America, and Continental Europe is aimed at achieving and retaining control characterized by the following:

- Concentrated ownership and a reliance on family or bank finance which determine the shareholder context
- Boards with aligned incentives, such that the board is dependent on the same outcomes as the controlling shareholders
- Limited disclosure and inadequate minority protection
- Illiquid capital markets with restricted takeover activities and an under-developed new issues market.

The control model of corporate governance found in Asia, Latin America, and much of Continental Europe is shown in Fig. 2.3.

While the theories have evolved based on the roles, duties and responsibilities of boards and management; rights, interests and expectations of shareholders and other stakeholders; the relationships between boards, management, shareholders, and other stakeholders; issues arising out of exercise of duties, responsibilities, rights and expectations, and while they help in defining and/or addressing the issues arising therein, corporate governance as is perceived and practised in different parts of the world varies. While the governance per se varies from country to country,

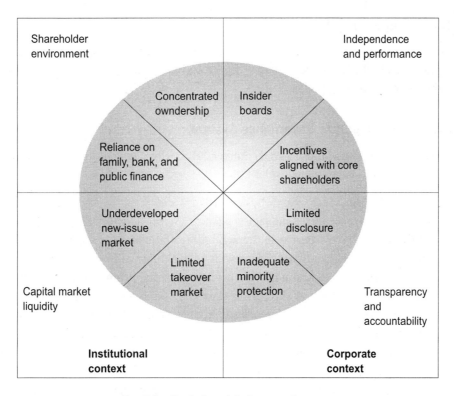

Fɪɢ. 2.3   Control model of corporate governance

most of the countries follow one of the three models, namely, the Anglo-American model, the Continental European model, and the Japanese model.

The Anglo-American Model

The model has more reliance on strong legal protection. As we have seen earlier, the first ever organized attempt to evolve a code happened in the UK, when Bank of England and LSE requested Sir Adrian Cadbury to head a committee to look into the financial aspects of corporate governance. Every country who wanted to have a good governance regime started looking at the Cadbury Report for establishing their own code and most drew very heavily from it. It is only natural that developing countries, most of which had historical links with Great Britain, started following the model as a basis. According to Som (2006), international financial institutions have also encouraged developing countries to adopt the Anglo-American model.

The Continental European Model

This model is one that seeks profits for 'pluralistic-oriented' constituencies, mostly arising out of privatization of state-owned enterprises in many countries. The influence of minority shareholders and asset managers like mutual funds are only marginal. Control mechanisms usually are shareholder agreements and discriminatory voting rights.

The Japanese Model

This model also has an objective of seeking profits for 'pluralistic-oriented' constituencies. While control is basically through the board of directors, banks, and financial institutions with majority voting shares have the ultimate control.

The Indian Corporate Governance System

India has a long history of organized commercial activity. The evolution of governance practices in India has three stages namely (Das 2008):

- *Stage I* The Managing Agency System (1850–1955)

  While the purpose of the managing agency system was to assign management of the firm to those who have expertise in managing the affairs of an enterprise including attracting investments and negotiating debt with banks, most of the time the managing agents for those enterprises promoted by Indians were the promoter families themselves. But, there were a number of enterprises started by foreign entrepreneurs or companies who needed capable managing agencies to handle their Indian operations. After a few years of establishment, it was also a practice to exit by taking a good profit on the investment, handing over the management of the company to a managing agency, either Indian or expatriate. According to Tripathi and Jumani (2007), 'There was, however, a crucial difference between the functioning of the managing agency system in the Indian-controlled concerns and expatriate firms. While in the former, the managing agencies continued to remain with the promoters' families, in the latter, the partnerships controlling the managing agencies went on changing hands as the older generations continued to return home after relinquishing their holdings. There was one more difference: no Indian managing agency firm was ever in charge of the management of companies it did not control, while the expatriate managing agencies very often assumed for a fee the responsibility to manage the affairs of sterling companies operating in India.' The managing agency system was abolished in 1972. Companies that were managed by Indian managing agents included Tata Iron & Steel, Morarjee Gokuldas Spinning and Weaving Mills, etc., and those which were managed by expatriate managing agents included Andrew Yule, Martin Burn, Binny Mills, T. Stanes, etc. While most of the managers of the companies under the Indian managing agents were family members, the Tatas under the leadership of J.R.D. Tata had taken outstanding professionals like Darbari Sheth, Sumant Moolgavkar, Russi Modi, etc. for managing their companies.

- *Stage II* The Promoter System (1956–1991)

  After the Industrial Policy Resolution was adopted in 1956, the government passed the Companies Act 1956 to prevent the abuses that were rampant in the managing agency system. The Act contained provisions about appointments and compensations, and removals of directors, AGM requirements, maintenance of records, number of maximum directorships, etc. Post the Companies Act 1956, the government promulgated the Securities Contracts

(Regulation) Act 1956 (SCRA), which enabled investors to protect their interests by enforcing stringent disclosure norms with a view to attract investors to capital markets and make it more vibrant. With the enforcement of these laws, the onus shifted from managing agencies to promoters.

• *Stage III* The Anglo-American System (1992 onwards)

Post economic liberalization and reforms that were initiated by Mr P.V. Narasimha Rao, the then prime minister, Indian economy gradually became integrated with the world economy and especially with the developed nations of the West like the US and the UK. A number of mutual funds and investment bankers from the west made a strong entry into India. It also coincided with the first ever development of a governance code in the world in the form of the Cadbury Report. The industry bodies like CII took up the mantle of initiating corporate governance reforms in India. The first-ever organized attempt in India was initiated by CII in 1998.[4] The governance failures that led to the demise of companies like Enron and WorldCom had their effects on India also. Thus followed the efforts by SEBI and the Department of Company Affairs to crystallize a code for corporates to follow, which culminated in including a clause in the listing agreements (Clause 49) between companies and the stock exchanges where their securities are listed. A number of amendments have been made to the Clause, which every listed company today has to follow. (Details of the evolution of various codes are provided in Chapter 3.)

Som (2006) provides a comparison of the these different corporate governance models and the one followed in India, based on parameters like objectives, extent of self-regulation, extent of state regulation, shareholder influence and control, as is practised today, which is presented in Table 2.1.

OWNERSHIP AND GOVERNANCE

While there are many theories that try to explain the context of corporate governance and also different models which vary from country to country, one underlying factor that is critical in influencing the corporate governance of any company is the ownership pattern. According to Som (2006), ownership is the most important factor shaping corporate governance in any country.

According to Combes and Watson (2001), the basic factor that differentiates the market model which is more prevalent in countries like the US and the UK and the control model which is mostly found in Asia, Latin America, and Continental Europe is ownership and factors related to it. While in a corporation with widely dispersed ownership, as is mostly the case in the US and UK, the most prominent conflict is the agency conflict (the conflict of interest between the shareholders—the principal and the managers—the agents, in the case of corporations where ownership is concentrated, the conflict is usually between the controlling (dominant) shareholders and the minority shareholders. The ownership structures of a company where

---

[4] Corporate Governance: A Desirable Code.

TABLE 2.1 Comparison of corporate governance models

Parameter	Model			
	Anglo-American model	Continental European model	Japanese model	Indian model
Objectives	System of Seeking Profits for individualistic shareholders	System of Seeking Profits for pluralistic constituencies	System of Seeking Profits for pluralistic constituencies	System of Seeking Profits for majority or promoters in a complex structure of group companies
Extent of self-regulation	• Single-tiered board of directors • Institutional holdings	• Cohesive group of 'insiders' with long-term stable relationships with the company, e.g., suppliers, banks, allied industrial concerns.	• System of support by main bank • Stabilization of shareholders by cross-holdings with other companies • It consists of a dual structure; the board of directors, which carries out the functions of strategic decision-making; and the board of auditors, which audits management's execution of business activities	• Single-tiered board of directors • Rule of nominee directors of FIs in the boards • Founding families and their allies usually exercise control over an extensive network of listed and non-listed companies
Extent of state regulation	None	Commercialization of corporate governance of SOEs is a twin development to privatization in many countries. The state as owner concentrates on maximizing shareholder value facilitated by floatation of SOEs.	Important sectors of economy still under state direction	Through the state owned financial institutions and banks
Shareholder Influence				
(a) Minority Shareholders	By buying and selling company shares	Marginal	Marginal	Marginal
(b) Asset Managers	Facilitating buying and selling of company shares	Marginal	Marginal	Marginal as only a minority stake is floated on the local exchanges

Contd

Table 2.1 contd

Parameter	Model			
	Anglo-American model	Continental European model	Japanese model	Indian model
(c) *Institutions*	Mutual funds, pension funds and insurance companies— operate on the principle of portfolio diversification, they have no interest in running the company and have no other relation to the company except for their financial investment	'House-banks' responsible for most financial transactions of the company	Main bank was expected to assume a leadership position within the group	Public owned FIs, banks, Mutual Funds
Other Sources of Governance	• Accountants, Credit rating institutions, Investment bankers, Financial media, Research analysts • Interlocking boards • Intercorporate investments • Market for corporate control	• Systems of inter-company holdings • Public equity markets are small. A lot of equity is financed non-publicly by families who have some degree of long-term commitment to the firm.	• Public equity markets are large, and the majority is held by shareholders that have some degree of long-term commitment to the firm. These include institutional investors, major customers, and suppliers	• Interlocking boards • Intragroup investments • Private placement of stocks • Convertibility covenant in the loan agreements of FIs. • Limited role of mergers and takeovers.
Control (a) *Proximate*	• Through voting rights shareholders select members of the board	• Parallel devices such as shareholder agreements, discriminatory voting rights	• Through the board of directors	• Minority ownership (of group companies by apex company)
(b) *Ultimate*	• By buying and selling company shares & thereby exposing the company to takeovers	• By owning an outright majority of voting shares or by owning a significant minority holding	• By owning an outright majority of voting shares by institutional investors, major customers, and suppliers.	• Majority ownership (of apex company by controlling family)

Contd

Table 2.1 contd

Parameter	Model			
	Anglo-American model	Continental European model	Japanese model	Indian model
Conformance Role	• Providing feedback to shareholders	• Questioning, judging and supervising management	• Governing, supervising, and monitoring management	• Supervising management of all group companies
Performance Role	• Developing plans for a firm's interaction with the external environment (e.g. strategic alliances, profit strategies, financing)	• Establishing rules and norms to guide a firm in achieving its strategic goals.	• Consensus management to guide a firm in achieving its strategic goals	• Formulating policies of each subsidiary by the central holding company based on cash needs of other companies in the group.
Concerns	• Conflict of interest between majority and minority shareholders • Legal reforms and their effective implementation	• Selective exchanges of information among insiders leading to lack of transparency	• Internal employees occupied positions of auditors which led to an inability to prevent improper actions • The number of directors is large which led to an inability to debate management policies of companies. Almost all directors are part of the keiretsu and are unwilling to voice opposition to decisions of the top management	• Directed credit by FIs led to credit rationing, a very low capacity to analyse credit risk and inadequate regulatory supervision of the banking and FI sector • Deficient market exit arrangements. • Insolvency legislation is rarely used as a means of reallocation of resources. • The capital structure of group-affiliated firms is usually incompatible with their asset structures • Due to group complexity, detecting opportunistic behavior by group affiliated firms is difficult.

Source: Som (2006).

ownership is concentrated not only affect how boards get constituted but also the types of funds mobilized. Consequently they affect the nature of control on the company, restrict the possibility of a market for corporate control, might influence the distribution of profits and the growth potential of the company as owners will give preferences for control over growth opportunity.

As against this, in a company with widely dispersed ownership, there is no shareholder with sufficient holding to influence the management and its decisions. In such cases the management, by and large, takes most of the decisions regarding strategy, mergers and acquisitions, distribution of profits, financing methods, growth pursuits, some even detrimental to other shareholders. The control mechanisms in the hands of shareholders are limited as many shareholders have to come together in enforcing a decision. And, management being in a dominant position not only has control over all the information but also the resources, they can pursue their plans which may not always be in the best interests of the shareholders (individuals or institutions), who will find any attempt to influence the management costly.

When the owner-managed companies decide to tap capital market to finance their growth, the issue of divergence between the objectives of the dominant shareholder and those of the newly joined shareholders usually arise. According to Wallace and Zinkin (2005), 'In these circumstances, some former owner-entrepreneurs at times continued operating as if nothing had changed. On occasion, owners undertook transactions that the other investors had no knowledge of; sometimes those transactions were simply not what the new investors had put their money into the enterprise for.' But by and large, except in case when such shareholders hold enough numbers so as to have influence on the shareholders' respective portfolios, such wide dispersal of shares tend to put the control of governance in the hands of dominant shareholders as these small shareholders will be just concerned about the return they make on their holding and mostly uninterested in other matters including governance. Take the case of the sibling rivalry at Reliance Industries. The family controlled about 34 per cent of the flagship company at the time. It is common knowledge that despite the fact that outside was holding was considerably higher than the family's, the dominant shareholder (the Ambani family) made the decision to demerge the Reliance Industries on their own and nobody raised any question regarding the roles the boards of the group companies were playing in such a crucial decision with far reaching consequences.

The Board–Owner Relationship

While the boards exist primarily due to the fact that firms are distinct legal entities, removed from the people who own (the shareholders) and those who run or operate (the managers) them. This structure is necessary to protect the owners from unlimited liability while granting freedom for the managers to act. But, despite its requirement to act on behalf of the artificial corporate entity, boards always derive its authority to act from the owners. And, with this authority comes the associated accountability to shareowners. As Carver and Carver say, '… the accountability chain is weakened when the board fails to recognize that it has the obligation, not just the authority to command. As the owners' representatives, the board has no right not to exercise those owners' rightful prerogatives. The board has no responsible alternative but to be authoritative in its role lest owners lose their voice' (Wallace and Zinkin 2005).

Ownership-related Issues in India

Family-promoted and managed companies

In India, an outstanding majority of the firms are family promoted as well as managed. Many of the families still continue to be dominant shareholders in their respective companies. Most of the families (except for the rare cases like Satyam) have significant shareholding of the order of between 25 per cent to 50 per cent. In certain cases, the family holding is as high as more than 80 per cent. For example, in Wipro, promoter Premji and family is reported to be controlling about 84 per cent holding. 'Indian business owners tend to have dominant shareholding in the companies promoted by them. The incidence of exploitation of small shareholders is very high. Financial institutions generally tend to support the existing management' says Jain (2006). Jain uses the term 'family dynamics' to explain the overlapping of the family system over business system. Figure 2.4 depicts the family dynamics.

Jain explains the characteristics of the family impact using the ten parameters discussed below.

Compensation   Family fosters equality; business needs to reward performance. In Reliance Industries, in the pre-split scenario, both Mukesh and Anil Ambani had the same salaries and other benefits.

Ownership   Family passes ownership to all, irrespective of the degree of involvement. Business needs powerful managers and therefore those who are more involved need to be given more ownership. This can lead to problems in future as has occurred in groups like Bajaj resulting in sibling rivalries.

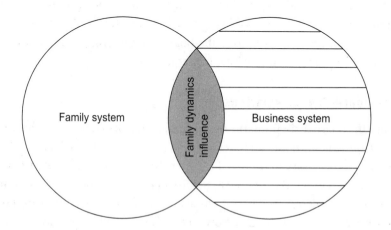

Fig. 2.4   The family and business overlap

Succession planning   Families choose the eldest as successor; business requires the most competent to succeed. With control rather than growth or other aspects on their agenda, their search for successors usually stops within the family itself.

Retirement   Family leaders continue as leader till their end; business needs leaders who are conversant with the changes and realities and capable of guiding the organization into the future.

Control   Family needs to exert control to protect their interests; business needs competent people who need freedom to flex and operate. With the thrust on control, the family may even refuse to look at opportunities for growth.

Professionalizing   Families try to provide career opportunity for all members; business needs the best for the execution of the job. Business needs professionals who can think of making the business entity grow, but family concentrating on their priorities may not be willing to let it happen.

Communication   In family, communications happen all the time: on the breakfast table, during lunch and dinner, and on many other informal occasions. Business usually demands more formal communication systems and records. Charan quotes a *Business Week* report of 2003 which found that S&P 500 companies with founding families involved in management had outperformed the remainder of the S&P 500 over the preceding decades. According to *Business Week*, 'With their intimate knowledge of the company gleaned from years of dinner time conversations, many [family directors] are as knowledgeable as the management about the [company's] inner working' (Charan 2005).

Relationships   It is very difficult for families to be unbiased and objective even in business settings. Many situations of conflicts of interests arise as a result.

Speed of action   Family reacts slowly and takes time to adopt to new situations. Business requires fast decisions and reactions. In the typical Indian context, many family groups objected to some of the liberalization policies, especially those of relaxing norms for FDI in India. This shift from a license-restricted and protected era to opening the country's markets to competition from foreign companies on the domestic turf was a little too much for many. A number of industrial houses took leadership in establishing a 'Bombay Club' demanding 'level playing' field for domestic companies. The whole issue only helped family promoted companies like Bajaj Auto to get relegated to number two position in India behind a comparatively recent entrant (Hero Honda) from a near monopolistic number one position in India and a number three scooter manufacturer in the world. Bajaj Auto has not been able to whither the storm raised by the competition. The company was forced to exit scooters on the belief that there was no market for scooters anymore, which has been proven wrong by Honda Motorcycles and Scooters India Ltd, a 100 per cent owned Honda subsidiary in India, whose Activa and Dio range of scooters redefined the market for scooters in India.

Values   Most family businesses inherit values from the founder or families. Many families expect total obedience from junior members. This may lead to a culture of lack of freshness and creativity, coupled with a lack of questioning. The family members may strictly follow certain norms when it comes to promotional methods, while the changes in the environment may demand newer approaches.

Jain (2006) puts the business orientation of the families on a continuum as shown in Fig. 2.5.

FIG. 2.5   Business orientation continuum

Family's orientation towards business   Jain (2006) uses the emphasis on words *family* and *business* to depict the family's orientation towards business. When the emphasis is more on family and less on business, the situation can be expressed as shown in Fig. 2.6(a). When the emphasis is more on business, the situation can be expressed as in Fig. 26(b).

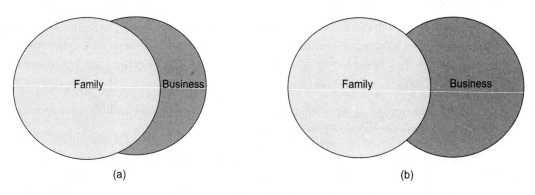

FIG. 2.6   What comes first?

Ownership motivation   Jain (2006) says that family owners have different levels of motivation during different phases of their growth. According to him, the hierarchy of motivation is very similar to Maslow's hierarchy of needs. This is depicted in Fig. 2.7.

Basic needs   At the start of a business by an entrepreneur, his prime focus is business success. His needs are basic in nature starting with survival needs.

Social needs   As his business improves, the owner moves up the ladder and seeks social recognition and looks for satisfaction of employers and customers.

Achievement needs   Having achieved financial security, and reasonable level of recognition, the entrepreneur wants to accomplish more, and looks for other opportunities for investments. He strives for leadership in his industry.

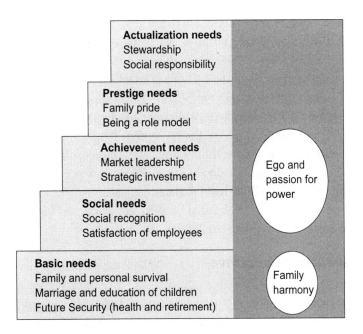

FIG. 2.7   Ownership motivation

Prestige needs   Having achieved business success, he enjoys his position. Now he takes pride in creating and building an institution and would like to be identified as a business leader and a role model.

Actualization needs   Having been acknowledged as a leader and role model, he understands that he owes much of his success to society. He knows that he will be remembered for his deeds for the benefit of the society through his business and other socially responsible activities. He gives it back to the society. Wealth is no more the most important factor for him. He needs to be remembered as an institution builder and responsible for the society's well-being.

Family-managed companies and the corporate governance conundrum

In the widely held public corporations in India, as in many other countries including developed ones, the owners/promoters have practically no role to play other than providing the financial capital and bear the risk associated with it. Examples from India could be companies like Larsen & Toubro Ltd and Infosys Technologies Ltd, etc. Of course, with Infosys, which has been promoted by a group of professionals rather than a family, the promoters are fortunate in getting a role to play in the management despite their low holding in the company. Such separation of ownership from management can lead to a divergence of interests. But regulators of corporate governance or capital markets do not distinguish between such big corporations, where shareholding is widely dispersed and ownership is separated from management, and the family managed companies, where that kind of separation does not exist. The regulators look at only whether the company has raised money from public, however small it is. While theoretically this is right, the philosophies driving the two categories (the family promoted and managed and the large public corporation, where shareholding is widely dispersed and the promoter lineage is difficult to establish) are different, they are seen as belonging to the same category. With the threat of being looked upon as another public corporation, the families might sacrifice growth for retaining control. Family promoted companies might continue to remain privately held (private limited) companies to circumvent the possibility of diluting control. The entrepreneurial instincts of the promoters/families might remain subdued. A vast majority of the companies listed 'on Indian stock exchanges continue to be low capitalized as floating external equity is often regarded by corporate managers especially family owned firms as leading to loss of control, which most managers try to avoid. Companies with low market capitalization compared to the book value of their net assets can become an easy target for acquisition and hostile takeovers' (Som 2006).

Ownership and firm performance

Is there a relationship between ownership characteristics and financial performance of a firm? Som (2006) states that 'Several empirical studies have found an inverted U-shaped relationship between the degree of ownership concentration and corporate profitability: as ownership concentration rises from a very low level, agency costs decrease due to increased shareholder monitoring and hence profitability rises; on the other hand when ownership concentration rises to a certain limit, its costs may outweigh its benefits, leading to a fall in profitability.'

The exercise of ownership depends on the extent of involvement and commitment of owners. Jain (2006) says that meaning of the term 'commitment' in this context is different from what is normally understood. Commitment in ownership means that the owner thinks in terms of value creation. A committed owner knows his limitations. He does not mind withdrawing from management if he feels that others are better suited to add more value to the business. His commitment is towards the well-being of the business and not towards satisfaction of his own ego. Similarly, an involved owner is not necessarily involved in the day-to-day management of business. He is involved in an enlightened manner through constantly keeping in touch with what is happening in the business. He is watchful, vigilant and observant.

A correlation between the degree of involvement and the degree of commitment can help the classification of owners into five different categories as shown in Fig. 2.8.

Sleeping owners   Generally aloof and indifferent towards their ownership. They might not even know about their ownership and how the company performs. Some members of the family like wives or children belong to this category. Other members of the family who are active manage holding on their behalf.

Rational owners   May not take keen interest in the activities of the company on a day-to-day basis but will be vigilant and watchful. They are emotionally indifferent to their holding and might even sell out if situation warrants it.

Concerned owners   Watchful and interested in the well-being of the firm. Actively participate in all meetings and will be careful while nominating directors to the board. Closely follow the

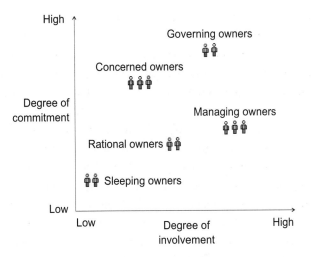

Fɪɢ. **2.8** Classification of owners (Jain 2006)

strategies adopted by the management and even question underperformance. They collaborate with other owners and see their ownership as a responsibility.

Governing owners   Act as a link between shareholders and management. Monitor the CEO's performance; will be active as members of family council, advisory board, or the board of directors. Consult and cooperate with outside directors. Implement both conformance and performance aspects of governance.

Managing owners   Get actively involved in management. Hence, usually resist governance processes. At times, they play all the three roles—ownership by holding stake, management by holding executive positions, and governance, by being member of the board. They are highly prone to conflicts of interests.

Government-promoted Companies (Public Sector Undertakings)

Another ownership-related governance issue that can arise is when the companies are promoted and fully or partly owned by the government. Such entities pose a serious challenge to the corporate governance practices in any country, especially in India where we continue to have a number of big companies in the public sector. While the leaders and planners of the country had good intentions while thinking of this structure, today they pose great challenges to the boards, regulators and even governments. The public sector was originally thought of as a means to lay a strong industrial foundation in the country, where capital was in short supply and infrastructural facilities and technology resources were poor. Even though there was no paucity of entrepreneurship in the country, building a nation in the initial years after attaining independence needed a lot of capital which the private sector was not able to mobilize considering the economic scenario on the birth of the nation. Since the capital markets were not developed enough, entrepreneurs found it difficult to mobilize capital for establishing industrial ventures.

This prompted the nation builders to think of establishing industrial undertakings under the ownership of the government.

It was the economist John Maynard Keynes who after the great depression of 1929 suggested that governments should actively intervene in economies and spend money in order to create public sector enterprises and generate employment and income. This led to the establishment of public sector enterprises even in the capitalist world of Western Europe and the US (Dewan 2006). Indian leaders perceived a mixed economy where public sector and private sector would co-exist. While in principle, the government expected the private sector to contribute to the industrialization in reasonably major ways, the lack of infrastructure, huge investment outlays needed, long gestation periods, etc. did not generate adequate interest among entrepreneurs as it necessitated sacrifices of commercial interest. Thus, the central public sector was established with its presence in areas like fertilizers, seeds, chemicals and heavy machinery in the manufacturing sector, and railways, airlines, telecom services, financial services, hospitality, etc. in the service sector. Most of the public sector units had monopoly positions in their respective industries. These units, in addition to their economic and employment generation goals, had other goals like social development, equitable income redistribution, ensuring products and services at affordable costs for the larger section of the population, etc.

But most of the governments including that of India found that while their intervention was necessary in the initial stages of industrialization of the economies, continuing with public sector was not good for the economy itself as the efficiency levels of most of the public sector companies were very poor and hence, actually leads to poor economics. The economic reforms and liberalization policies by many countries accelerated the process of encouraging private entrepreneurs through the various decontrol measures of delicensing, freeing the capital markets from the stringent controls, permitting takeovers of companies, encouraging FDIs, opening up of the capital markets for institutions from abroad (FIIs), etc. These led to a new found belief in private capitalism and skepticism about public undertakings. Many countries introduced processes of privatizing the existing public undertakings while deciding not to enter into any areas other than those of national interest like defence, internal security, or space programmes. India has been no exception. Post-liberalization, the attitude towards the public sector has changed and the government has been adopting a process of privatization or divestment of public sector undertakings; however slow the process has been.

Governance-related issues of public sector undertakings

While for all theoretical purposes, they can be considered just another company established under the Companies' Act (excluding those companies which have been established under special statutes), the governance of such companies poses many problems.

The major problems are as follow:

1. Bureacrats make most of the decisions. Even when professional managers are at the top of the companies as chairman or managing director (usually combined as CMD), most of the decisions regarding the company like board of directors (BOD), recruitment to senior positions, remunerations to managers, expansion or diversification, pricing, etc. are made

by the bureaucrats in the ministry under which the company operates. There is practically no autonomy for the managers of the company to make decisions.

2. Boards are constituted of nominees who are bureaucrats from the ministries associated with the industries in which the company falls into. For example, in a fertilizer company, nominees from the directly concerned ministry (chemicals and fertilizers) as well as from the ministry of industries will find their way to the board.

3. The pay-structure for chairman, managing director, and other directors and senior managers are not good enough to attract talent and even elicit commitment.

4. Strategies for improving economic performance take a back seat in the thrust for meeting social needs.

5. Even in the case of partly privatized companies, the government continues to make all decision regarding the company.

6. Complicated agency issues arise as the agent is not necessarily good enough to run the enterprise efficiently and the principal is not necessarily always motivated by economic performance.

While these problems raise difficulties in implementing a corporate governance system in the PSUs in general, there are delicate practice-oriented issues when it comes to implementing a corporate governance process in the PSUs.

Privatized companies or companies where government holding has been diluted partly   In all such cases, the corporate governance guidelines that are applicable to any other public limited company become applicable to them too. This puts such companies into severe difficulties to conform with all the corporate governance guidelines stipulated by SEBI as per Clause 49 of the listing agreement between the company and the stock exchange where the company's shares are listed. According to clause 49 requirements, companies with a full-time chairman must have at least 50 per cent of the directors on the board as independent. This requirement has been found to be difficult to be implemented because under bureaucratic and political pressure, the company will have to accommodate a number of people as directors. If the 50 per cent cut-off is to be maintained, the board will have a large number of members making it difficult to function. Getting good independent directors who are talented and who can contribute is difficult because independent director talents are in great demand and public sector companies with its paltry remuneration packages might find it difficult to compete with the private sector. Another problem is with respect to the dominant nature of shareholding of the government leading to neglect of minority shareholders. This problem complicates the fact that the rights of minority shareholders may get ignored as there is not enough independent component on the board, which is supposed to protect the minority shareholders' interests. While political pressures force the PSUs to follow certain paradigms, economic pressures force them to follow certain opposite paradigms. Thus, there is a paradigm conflict happening in PSUs today. With the current structure of PSUs, implementation of a full-version of corporate governance guidelines on the lines of private sector, public companies, seems to be beyond reach.

Public companies that are fully owned by government   They pose a different dilemma as far as governance is concerned. While government is theoretically the promoter of such companies and the only shareholder, governments are expected to represent the public. The capital and other funds the government invests in these companies come from the public either from funds mobilized by various agencies like RBI, postal savings schemes, and other sources or from the taxes paid by the public at large including the individuals and other companies in the private sector. Thus, while theoretically, they do not come under the purview of SEBI corporate governance guidelines as they have not made any issues to the public, they have to follow the same governance guidelines, if not it's stricter version. The utilization of public money is much more in a fully owned government company than in a private promoted public company because public would have invested only a portion in the capital of a privately promoted public company whereas it is entirely the public money that is invested in the capital of a PSU fully owned by the government. But as things stand now, the 100 per cent owned government companies are more or less closed to the public without any accessibility of information regarding their performance, management processes, and governance.

The issues related to governance of PSUs are many. Here we have only highlighted why they are different from other companies and have limited perspective of ownership patterns.

ROLES OF BOARD AND MANAGEMENT—CLARITY NEEDED

We clearly drew a distinction between managing and directing in Chapter 1. We also discussed about the questions a director should ask himself once appointed to a board. Most experts concur that the poor governance of most of the corporations is as a result of failure to distinguish between the two roles—the role of a manager and the role of a director. This was true of even Satyam. Mr Ramaliga Raju and his brother failed to perform their duties as directors while sitting on the board of directors and continued to perform their roles as managers of Satyam. They could never be considered to be incompetent, having taken Satyam from small beginnings to the third biggest IT service provider from India over a period of about 20 years. Garratt (2003) says that 'it is an open secret that the vast majority of directors are not fully competent. This is not to say that they are all therefore incompetent, but rather that most have not been able to distinguish between *managing* a business and *directing* one. They tend to be over-trained as executives and under-trained as direction givers. Their many rewards have come from being effective professional managers, not from giving strategic direction.'

Harper (2005) says that directing the company means 'focusing on providing overall leadership, judgement and enterprise and on making those decisions that are *central* to protecting and enhancing the interests of the company over time. This cannot be done if the board is bogged down with day-to-day matters that are the proper concerns of executive management. It is a prime responsibility of the chairman to maintain this focus.' But again there can be issues especially when, as in most US corporations and in a number of companies in India, the chairman is full time and hence a part of management. When the chair is full time, the chair is considered to be the de facto CEO even when the company has a CEO or an MD under the chairman.

For example, Mr Deepak Parekh as the full time chairman even with an MD under him. The case of Bajaj Auto was similar, where Rahul Bajaj was the full-time chairman while his son was designated as MD. Another issue that arises is when the chairman even though part-time is a member of the family which also has its nominee as CEO/MD. So, unless and until the individual directors understand their roles as directors with a lot of clarity, governance will be put to severe test. But, wherever the chairman is independent, he/she should encourage the directors to consider directorships as responsible professions that need meticulous attention, knowledge and a willingness to learn, courage to express truth and question when necessary, professional behaviours and attitudes, commitment and involvement. The whole-time or executive directors have to be extremely careful in exercising their role as directors on the board. Harper advises: 'Most appointments as executive director will have been made principally on the strength of success as a manager or senior specialist. Many such directors will regard their appointment to the role of director merely as a further endorsement of that success in the operational field, rather than taking a completely separate additional mantle. Their management role requires them to achieve results in the domain for which they have responsibility and to 'get things done'. In contrast, their director role requires an essentially thoughtful, reflective approach of 'thinking things through' in conjunction with their board colleagues. They must take action to create sufficient time to think and act as directors.'

According to Garratt (1996), the key task of the board of directors is to create a balance among the following four opposing forces.

Organizational effectiveness   Perception in customers' minds of all the products or services as desirable and good value for money

Organizational efficiency   The internal activities aimed at cost reduction and efficiency improvements without affecting the value perception by customers

Board performance   The board's external focus on various environments affecting the company and also about the competitive positioning and broad resource allocation in relation to the policies set by it

Board conformance   The board's internal focus of achieving business performance goals while being accountable to stakeholders

While the role of directing is different from managing, it is necessary for the board to support and bolster management (Shultz 2001). Shultz says that strategic boards 'validate good decisions. A board is there to help the CEO succeed as well as to provide policy input. It is not adversarial, as so many CEOs fear…. a board can be a CEO's best friend as a cheerleader, a helper, a counselor, advisor and listener.'

Once the necessary clarity is achieved regarding the different roles of managing and directing, many of the ownership related issues of governance can be resolved.

SUMMARY

The modern corporation as we witness today has been instrumental in the growth of business at high pace and establishing business as a formidable institution. The structure of the modern corporation works on the essential foundation of the fiduciary principles which has accountability as its base. The governance of the modern corporation works on this premise. But the same positive factors of the modern corporation have been the causes of many of their governance problems. Though impressed by the ingenuity of the concept of the corporate form, even Adam Smith was skeptical of the structure and the expectations about relationship between various constituents. Boards have fiduciary duties to the company and shareholders. While a standard principal-agent relationship can be governed by contracts that clearly specify the performance expectations of the parties, in a corporate scenario, these types of contracts are not practical considering that the shareholders are widely dispersed and their expectations are heterogeneous.

A number of theories of governance like agency theory, stewardship theory, transaction cost economics theory, stakeholder theory, etc. have been evolved in order to explain the various relationships that exist in the modern corporation. While agency theory has acquired a lot of popularity, management pundits like the late Ghoshal and Moran have criticized the theory because of the attempt there is to project managers (agents) as having only one goal, that of maximizing the returns for the principals, whereas he/she may pursue many goals on behalf of the corporation.

Most of the governance practices envisage the directors to perform their fiduciary duties. While bigger shareholders may be able to influence the boards on decisions, minority shareholders are usually protected by law. While experts have resorted to the agency theory to explain most of the relationships, it may find it difficult to explain the situation when a principal (a major shareholder) is also the agent (the manager) as is typical of most of the Indian companies.

Governance issues come to the forefront only when there has been a failure. Well-governed companies do not get much attention while bad governance attracts all eyeballs. This is because good governance is expected from all boards of directors and companies. People start with the premise of trust in a fiduciary relationship. They get shaken only when that premise of trust is broken. Governance matters because today boards are considered a competitive weapon for the corporations. Boards are expected to perform to make the firm more competitive in the marketplace than merely conform to the legal and regulatory requirements.

While in a firm there are no dominant shareholders, the typical agency conflicts occur. In a firm where there is a dominant shareholder, with the rest widely dispersed, the conflict arises between the dominant shareholder and the minority shareowners.

Different models of governance exist based on the typical relationships and practices prevalent. Typical ownership related issues prevail in India where most of the firms are family promoted as well as managed. The 'family dynamics' explains whether the family business is family oriented or business oriented. The Public Sector Undertakings (PSUs) pose another set of issues of governance in India. Public sector corporations in India, which have chosen to raise money from the public find the SEBI Clause 49 regulation a little too stringent to follow as the companies are influenced by politics and bureaucracy.

KEY TERMS

Actualization needs   A higher order of needs which defines the reasons for existence beyond the worldly ones

Agency conflicts   Conflicts arising out of entrusting the running of the company to an agent

Business prudence   Showing care and thought for the future of business

Charter   A legal framework

Concentrated ownership   A few shareholders hold majority stake

Conundrum   Puzzle

Corporate social responsibility   Responsibilities of companies towards society

Distinct legal entity   Established under definite rules and regulations

Dummies   Substitute for the real

Duty of legitimacy   Conforming to the laws or regulations

Fidelity to investors   An assurance to investors

Flagship company   The major company in an industrial group

Intangible areas   Areas which are not quantifiable and hence not measurable

Joint-stock company   An economic entity with unlimited ability to raise finances by selling shares to the public whose liabilities are limited to its shareholding

Minority owners   Shareholders who own insignificant holding

Modern corporation   The joint stock-company

Ownership motivation   The motivation to continue holding a stake in the company

Public sector undertakings   Companies set up and managed by government

Shareholder democracies   Where shareholders have a right or say

Shareholder dictatorships   Where major shareholders dictate terms

Sleeping owners   Owners who don't take active interest in the affairs of the company

Triple bottom line   Performance of the company in terms of profit, people, and protection of the planet

CONCEPT REVIEW QUESTIONS

1. Why is it said that the concept of joint-stock company has been a major reason for business growth and establishment of business as a powerful economic institution?

2. Why did Berle and Means feel that the management has to maintain the standards of conduct? What are the three rules of conduct developed according to law?

3. Distinguish between the corporate governance models observed in Asia, Latin America, and Continental Europe, and those prevalent in countries like the US and UK.

4. What are the three fundamental values on which corporate governance is built according to Bob Garratt? Explain.

5. Distinguish between agency theory and transaction cost economics theory of corporate governance.

6. Why is it that governance of Indian family promoted companies need to be looked at differently from their counterparts in the Western world?

7. What are the typical governance issues faced by PSUs in India?

CRITICAL THINKING QUESTIONS

Reliance Industries Ltd is a typical Indian family promoted and managed company. What are the typical governance issues at RIL in comparison to a professionals-promoted and managed company like Infosys Technologies Ltd?

PROJECT WORK

Analyze a typical, listed, central PSU using both primary and secondary data and prepare a report.

REFERENCES

Berle, Adolf A. and Gardiner C. Means (1932), *The Modern Corporation and Private Property*, Transaction Publishers (2009 reprint), New Jersey.

Block, Peter (1996), *Stewardship*, Berret-Koehler Publishers, San Francisco.

Brickley, James A., Clifford W. Smith, Jr., and Jerold L. Zimmerman (2005), 'Corporate Governance, Ethics, and Organizational Architecture', in *Corporate Governance at the Crossroads*, Chew, Jr., Donald H. and Stewart L. Gillan (eds), Tata McGraw-Hill, New Delhi.

Charan, Ram (1998), *Boards at Work*, Jossey-Bass, San Francisco.

Charan, Ram (2005), *Boards that Deliver*, Jossey-Bass, San Francisco.

Charan, Ram (2007), *Know-How: The 8 Skills that Separate People Who Perform and Those Who Don't*, Random House Business, London.

Chew Jr., Donald H. and Stewart L. Gillan (2005), *Corporate Governance at the Crossroads*, Tata-McGraw Hill, Delhi.

Clark, Woodrow W. and Istemi Demirag (2002), 'Enron: The Failure of Corporate Governance', *Journal of Corporate Citizenship*, 22 December 2002.

Coombes, Paul and Mark Watson (2001), 'Corporate Reforms in the Developing World', *The McKinsey Quarterly*, Number 4, Emerging Markets.

Das, Subhash Chandra (2008), *Corporate Governance in India: An Evaluation*, Prentice-Hall India, New Delhi.

Demsetz, Harold and Kenneth Lehn (1985), 'The Structure of Corporate Ownership: Theory and Consequences', *Journal of Political Economics*, No. 93.

Dewan, S.M. (2006), *Corporate Governance in Public Sector Enterprises*, Dorling Kindersley, Delhi.

Drucker, Peter F. (1970), *The Practice of Management*, Allied Publishers, Delhi.

Eisenhardt, Kathleen M. (1989), Agency Theory: An Assessment and Review, *Academy of Management Review*, 14:1, pp. 57–70.

Garratt, Bob (1996), *The Fish Rots from the Head*, Profile Books, London.

Garratt, Bob (2003), *Thin on Top*, Nicholas Brealey, London.

Ghoshal, Sumantra and Peter Moran (2005), 'Bad Practices: A Critique of the Transaction Cost Theory', *Sumantra Ghoshal on Management*, Julan Birkinshaw and Gita Piramal (ed.), Pearson Education, London.

Gopinath, C., 'Corporate Failure at Enron', *Business Line*, 4 March 2002.

Hamel, Gary S. (2000), *Leading the Revolution*, Harvard Business School Press, Boston.

Harper, John (2005), *Chairing the Board*, Kogan Page, London.

Hollender, Jeffrey and Stephen Fenichell (2004), *What Matters Most*, Random House Business Books, London.

Jain, Rajesh (2006), *Chains That Liberate: Governance of Family Firms*, Macmillan India, New Delhi.

Jensen, Michael C. (2005), Value Maximization, Stakeholder Theory, and the Corporate Objective Function, in *Corporate Governance at the Crossroads*, Chew Jr., Donald H. and Gillan, Stewart L. (ed.), Tata McGraw Hill, Delhi.

Jensen, Michel C. (1993), 'The Modern Industrial Revolution, Exit and the Failure of Internal Control Systems', *The Journal Of Finance*, 47:3, pp. 831–880.

MacAvoy, Paul W. and Ira M. Millstein (2004) *The Recurrent Crisis in Corporate Governance*, Stanford Business Books, California.

Mantle, Jonathan (2008), *Companies That Changed the World*, Quercus, London.

Milgrom, Paul R. and John Roberts (1992), *Economics, Organization and Management*, Prentice Hall, New Jersey.

Million, David (2003), 'Who "Caused" Enron Debacle', *Washington and Lee Law Review*, Winter 2003.

Monks, Robert and Nell Minow (2005), The Director's New Clothes (or the Myth of Corporate Accountability), in *Corporate Governance at the Crossroads*, Chew Jr., Donald H. and Gillan, Stewart L. (ed.), Tata McGraw Hill, New Delhi.

Phan, Philp H. (2000), *Taking Back the Boardroom*, McGraw-Hill, Singapore.

Shultz, Susan F. (2001), *The Board Book*, East-West Books, Chennai.

Smith, Adam (1761), *The Theory of Sentiments*, 2nd edn., University of Lausanne.

Smith, Adam (2003), *The Wealth of Nations*, Bantam Books, New York.

Smith, Roy C. and Ingo Walter (2006), *Governing the Modern Corporation*, Oxford University Press, New York.

Som, Lalita (2006), *Stock Market Capitalization and Corporate Governance*, Oxford University Press, New Delhi.

Tricker, Bob (2004), *Essential Director*, The Economist/Profile Books, London.

Wallace, Peter and John Zinkin (2005), *Mastering Business in Asia: Corporate Governance*, Wiley-India, New Delhi.

Weidenbaum, Murray, Mark Jensen Smith and Walter (2006).

Closing Case

Failure of Enron—The Culmination of Irrational Exuberance and Unfettered Greed

The year 2001 was a watershed year for corporate America. Enron Corporation, one of the fastest growing and highly respected corporate firm in the US went bust posing serious questions for businessmen, economics and business school academics and corporate watchers alike. In 2000, the position of Enron on the Fortune 500 list of the US's big companies was at an enviable 7, a position which the company attained in a very short period of time. It had business America in awe of disbelief. How could a highly respected and innovative company like Enron fail? As usual, the US Government and the political machinery started the damage control and debris cleaning process. Prompted by public angst and ire at the way a few powerful people control and manage public companies with contempt, the way was paved for the enactment of a law specifically aimed at improving corporate governance.

The origin

Enron was created in 1985 as a result of the merger of Houston Natural Gas and Internorth. 1989 onwards Enron began trading in commodities, buying and selling wholesale contracts in energy. The turnover grew at a fast pace, growing from $40 billion in 1999 to $101 billion in 2000, with most of the new income coming from broking of energy commodities. Everybody considered Enron a dynamic company prompted by the rapid growth it had been achieving over the years. The performance was well reflected on the price of the company's share in the stock market. In the year 2000, the market capitalization of the company was $80 billion. Senior executives reaped large rewards by exercising their share options. Company's investment bankers who received substantial fees, encouraged their analysts to persuade other investors to invest in the company.

The top management of Enron, led by CEO Jeff Skilling believed that 'old asset-based businesses would be dominated by trading enterprises such as Enron making markets for their output. Enron was credited with aggressive earnings management' (Tricker 2004). In order to indulge in the activities of growth, a large number of special purpose entities (SPEs) were created. These were partnerships with bases in tax havens, that entered into trading arrangements with Enron. Enron priced long-term energy supply contracts for future with these SPEs at market prices, while accounting for profits immediately. These SPEs made provisions for enormous fees for Enron's senior executives. They also made it appear that Enron had hedged its financial exposures with third parties whereas the third parties were actually contingent liabilities on Enron (Tricker, 2004). Immediately after the Enron debacle of 2001, the following anonymous email was in circulation in London in 2002 (Garratt 2003):

Normal Capitalism: You have two cows and buy a bull. Your herd multiplies and the economy grows. You sell the bull and retire.

Enron Capitalism: You have two cows. You sell three of them to your publicly listed corporation, using letters of credit opened by your brother-in-law at the bank. You then execute a debt/equity swap with an associate general offer so that you get all four cows back, with tax exemption for five cows. The milk rights of the six cows are transferred via an intermediary to a Cayman Islands Company, secretly owned by your chief financial officer, who then sells the rights for all seven cows back to your listed corporation. Your annual report states that your corporation owns eight cows, with an option on six more.

From the email, it is clear that SPEs and their sponsors were milking the publicly listed Enron for their private benefits. The then prevailing US accounting standards (the GAAP) did not demand such SPEs' liabilities to be consolidated with the sponsoring company's accounts 'if only 3 per cent of the equity and debt of that SPE was owned by an independent third party' (Smith & Walter 2006). And Enron had created more than 800 of them according to Smith & Walter (Smith & Walter 2006). The US laws deregulating the energy industry also favoured Enron. While deregulation was intended to benefit consumers by way of reduced energy tariff, the acute energy shortage enabled companies like Enron to push up energy prices from an average $30 per MW to over $300 per MW on an average, enabling them to make around 400 per cent to 600 per cent profits (Clark and Demirag 2002). This continued till states like California imposed consumer price caps. But, by and large, energy companies including Enron could influence White House and White House even accepted seven of the eight recommendations that Kenneth Lay, CEO of Enron, made while releasing the final report of its energy task force. 'The damage done to public by Enron, Reliant, Dynegy, among others, has been costly not only in monetary terms (in terms of billions of dollars) but also in terms of the basic belief in corporations and their operations. Aside from ethics and legal issues, the public has been dealt a blow. As one commentator put it, 'The Enron story shows just how easy it is for companies to cover their tracks, especially when the regulators are in their corner' (Clark and Demirag 2002).

It was not only the regulation that was at fault. According to Clark and Demirag, other factors like those given below also led to the fall.

Pension double standard   Executives could cash out any time while ordinary employees were locked in. Executives cashed out a billion dollars, while an employee, Janice Farmer, who retired with $700,000 in Enron told a Senate hearing that she was left with $63 monthly social security check. And Enron's retirement plan was heavily invested in its own stock according to Clark and Demirag.

Bogus accounting   Enron's method of cheating investors and regulators was by 'making its business plan so complex that neither investors nor regulators nor even its own auditors could penetrate it. While its core energy business made money (at the expense of consumers), it had speculative off-the book subsidiaries. These borrowed heavily to make risky investments and eventually took the whole company down' say Clark and Demirag.

The business press   The business press pronounced Enron as the epitome of new economy and joined the bandwagon of cheerleaders such as company insiders and stock analysts. Even management guru Gary Hamel had opined high about the company and its business processes: 'Enron is not in the business of eking the last penny out of a dying business but of continuously creating radical new business concepts with huge upside' (Hamel 2000).

Other experts highlighted other factors too. Smith and Walter questioned the auditor independence. They felt that Andersen (Enron's independent auditor) 'compromised auditor independence. Enron's SEC [Securities and Exchange Commission] filings indicated that Andersen had been paid large fees for non-audit services, in addition to its significant audit fee. Andersen also took on (outsourced internal audit work for Enron. In addition, the relationship between Enron and Andersen was seen as a revolving door, leading to several Andersen employees crossing over to Enron to work in key positions' (Smith and Walter 2006).

In 1980s, the structured finance route was used by many corporations to assist LBO transactions, and creating 'synthetic securities' through the use of swaps and other derivative contracts. These enabled the company to avail of tax advantages while being off-balance sheet. Bankers could even earn large fees if they could help corporations with such inventive and innovative transactions. They could also make money by funding such deals. Enron was no exception. They had established hundreds of SPEs, all of which needed such ingenuity. Smith and Walter mention how investment banker Merrill Lynch was involved in the structuring and financing of a particular SPE named LJM2, which was in an energy trading relationship with Enron (refer to the figure on next page). The CEO of LJM2 was simultaneously the CFO of Enron. Merrill was both a lender and investor in LJM2, as also many senior executives of Merrill and many private and institutional investors advised by them. Merrill even structured a re-purchase transaction on behalf of Enron involving a number of power-generation barges in Nigeria, with the sole purpose of off-balance sheet treatment, thereby misrepresenting Enron's financials to the market. Also, Merrill performed a range of advisory, underwriting, equity analyst coverage services, which were one of Enron's principal derivatives trading counterparts. 'Merrill's relationship with Enron provided an array of incentives for the firm to make money from the company by going along with questionable transactions or arrangements promoted by the corporation, all at the expense of investors in various Enron securities' (Smith and Walter 2006).

The US was proud of the regulation of the stockmarkets and the accounting methods and processes, as is evidenced by an ultra-Chicago economist who reportedly responded to a reporter's query on whether there was any regulating agency that he endorsed: 'the SEC, he said instantly, explaining that capitalism itself depends on honest information'. But Enron's financial deals were too complex even for the regulator to understand them (Clark and Demirag 2002).

Prof. Gopinath of Suffolk University, Boston, feels that another group that was culpable was the analysts who are part of broking houses. Gopinath says 'Even when the problems of Enron were beginning to be highlighted by newspapers, out of 17 analysts who follow Enron, 16 had 'strong buy' or 'buy' recommendations and one had 'hold'. These are the so-called experts who are knowledgeable about the firm and the industry and they failed in their duty' (Gopinath 2002). Tricker says that 'Chung Wu, a broker with UBS Paine Webber (a subsidiary of UBS, a Swiss bank), e-mailed his clients advising to sell Enron shares. He was sacked and escorted out of his office. Other UBS analysts were still recommending a strong buy on Enron. UBS Paine Webber received substantial brokerage fees from administering the Enron employee stock option programmes' (Tricker 2004).

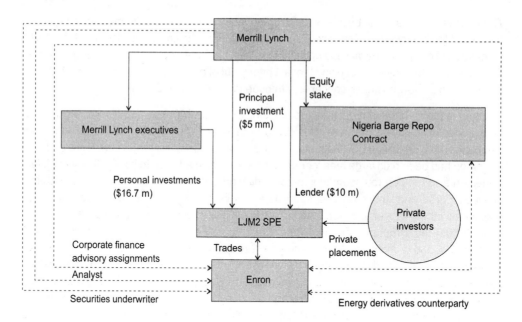

Structuring and financing of LJM2

Gopinath (2002) has also pointed to the failure of the board of directors to perform its duties. He says that the board has three roles to perform according to management theory: 'Control (overseeing the functioning of the corporation and its management, service (being a link between the corporation and its external stakeholders) and strategy (providing a direction for the enterprise into the future). Of these three roles, control is the most basic and traditional role that provides the *raison d'etre* for a board. The widely dispersed nature of ownership (shareholders) of a joint stock enterprise requires the owners to repose their authority on the board to oversee the corporation and ensure that the owners' interests are protected. This is where the board failed.' Gopinath lists five board-related issues that could have led to a lack of control:

Chairman and CEO   Best practices in corporate governance suggest separation of the roles of the chair and the CE. If the same individual occupies both the positions, 'There is too much concentration of power, and the possibility of the board supervising management gets diluted.' In Enron, after Jeff Skilling resigned as CEO in August 2001, Kenneth Lay was both chairman and CEO.

Audit committee   An audit committee oversees the work of the auditors and also must independently inquire into the workings of the organization and bring any lapses to the attention of the full board. The audit committee of Enron failed in this role. It was chaired by Robert Jadicke, formerly professor of accounting and dean of Stanford University Business School since 1985. He was there because as per regulation, audit committee must have financially literate people as its members.

Directors' independence and conflicts of interest   Good governance insists that outside directors maintain their independence and do not benefit from their board membership other than remuneration. In principle, Enron had a majority outside directors in line with the recommended best practices but they seemed to have compromised their independence. According to Gopinath, six of the IDs, suffered from serious conflicts of interest.

(a) Robert A. Beffer, Chairman, Beffer Management, bought a stake in an energy management company from an Enron partnership, thereby providing funds to start another.

(b) Ms. Wendy Gramm (wife of a Republican Senator) was formerly chairman of the Commodities Futures Trading Commission (CFTC) of the Federal Government. Enron's trading in energy derivatives was exempt from regulations by the CFTC. Shortly after the decision, she quit her position at the commission and joined Enron's board. She became Director of Regulatory Studies Programme at George Mason University, to which Enron donated $50,000.

(c) Mr John Mandelson is the President of the MD Cancer Centre at the University of Texas. Enron and related entities have donated $1.5 million to the centre since 1985.

(d) Mr William Powers (who also headed the special investigation committee constituted for damage control by Enron itself after the problems of Enron were getting public attention) was the Dean of the University of Texas Law school. Enron had given $3 million to the university after Mr Powers became Dean. The law firm that works for Enron, Vinson and Elkins, had endowed a chair at the Law School.

(e) Lord John Wakeham, a former minister for energy in UK was paid $72,000 for services as a consultant to Enron's European unit. When he was minister, he gave consent to Enron for building the country's largest power plant at Teeside. Wakeham, a CA and Chairman of British Press Complaints Council, was chairman of the nominating committee (Tricker 2004). Tricker says that in addition to annual consultancy, he was also paid a retainer fee ($ 4,600 per month).

(f) Mr Hebert Winokur was also a director of the Natco Group which is a supplier to Enron and its subsidiaries. He was also the chairman of the Board's Finance Committee.

The involvement of these directors getting other benefits compromised their independence making one wonder whether they acted in the best interests of Enron, says Gopinath.

Flow of information   For the board to perform its roles, it needs information. In Enron, the directors were pleading ignorance of the shady deals to excuse themselves of the liability. According to Gopinath (2002), if they did not have sufficient information, they should have gone seeking it. Enron was reported to have about 3500 SPEs, partnership entities that shifted debt and losses off Enron's Balance Sheet. Gopinath says that 'If the directors did not understand what was being reported to them, it was their job to educate themselves more about it by asking the right questions and getting more information.'

Too many directorships   Gopinath (2002) says that being a director of a company takes time and effort. Although the board might meet only four or five times a year, the director needs to have the time to read and reflect over all the material provided and make informed decisions. Mr Raymond Troubh, one of the directors, was a director of 11 public companies.

Other facts
Each of the directors received about $836,517 for the year 2000 by way of an annual fee of $50,000 and in stocks and stock options.

Another very interesting development at Enron which could have avoided the failure of oversight of the related party transaction by the board was the decision to suspend the company's

'Code of Ethics', which enabled an employee to set up a special partnership (SPE). While the Finance Committee under the chairmanship of Mr Winokur recommended the suspension of the Ethics Code, the chairman of the audit committee (which normally oversees the compliance of such a code) Mr Jaedicke seconded the motion. Gopinath (2002) said that 'it is the corporate equivalent of insanity defense that we see in criminal cases.'

Tricker says that 'In mid-2001, Lay was given a warning about the company's accounting techniques by Sherron Watkins, an Executive who wrote: 'I am nervous that we will implode a wave of accounting scandals'. She also advised Andersen about potential problems. By October 2001, the crisis had deepened, requiring restatement of its earlier financial statements, which revealed huge losses arising of hedging, risks taken when energy prices fell, resulting in a write-off of about $600 million in profits. SEC investigation in to the accounts revealed huge, and complex derivative positions and the transaction between Enron and the SPEs. Debts were found to be understated by $2.6 billion' (Tricker 2004).

The company filed for Chapter 11 bankruptcy in December 2001. The NYSE suspended Enron shares. John Clifford Baxter, a Vice-Chairman of Enron until his resignation in May 2001, was found shot dead. He had been one of the first to see the problems at Enron and had heated arguments about the accounting for off-balance sheet financing, which he found unacceptable (Tricker, 2004). Nearly 20,000 employees were rendered jobless. The collapse of Enron and further revelations of fraudulent and deceitful corporate behaviour in companies like WorldCom, Tyco, etc., accelerated the speed of the legislative actions and culminated in the passing of Sarbanes–Oxley Act 2002 in July 2002.

Failure of 'gatekeepers'

It was the utter failure of the various gatekeepers—the company's experts, advisors, intermediaries like banks and security analysts, auditor, independent directors, and regulators—'who seemed to disappear entirely during much of the period' according to Smith and Walter (Smith and Walter 2006). According to Gregory Van Hoey, 'Gate keepers are necessary because a corporation's assertion about itself often are inherently suspect' (Million 2003). According to Professor Coffee, 'the professional gatekeeper essentially assesses or vouches for the corporate client's transaction' (Million 2003).

According to *BusinessWeek*, 'Enron didnot just fail because of improper accounting or alleged corruption at the top. The unrelenting emphasis on earnings growth and individual initiative coupled with a shocking absence of the usual corporate checks and balances, tipped the culture from one that rewarded aggressive strategy to one that increasingly relied on unethical cornercutting. In the end, too much leeway was given to young, inexperienced managers without the necessary controls to minimize failures. This was a company that simply placed a lot of bad bets on businesses that werenot so promising to begin with.'[5]

Or, Enron's problems were firmly rooted in a flawed organizational approach or processes. According to Brickley et al, 'any concept of corporate governance, whether aimed at value maximization or some other corporate objectives, rests on the organizational underpinnings of the firm. In our view, the recent corporate scandals stem not so much from a general failure of corporate governance as from flaws in an important facet of corporate governance—the organizational design of the firm.' We use the term '*organizational architecture*' to refer to three key elements of organizational design.

---

[5] 'At Enron, the environment was right for abuse', *BusinessWeek*, 25 February 2002.

- The assignment of decision-making authority—who gets to make what decisions?
  As a general principle of corporate governance, decision management and decision control should be separated, unless decision-makers have a significant ownership stake in corporate cashflows. The most prominent example of this separation is the presence at the top of the corporation of a board of directors with fiduciary responsibility for ratifying important decisions initiated by the CEO. If the board of directors does a poor job, it can be replaced through a proxy fight or a corporate takeover specialist, financial analysts, and large blockholders (such as public pension funds) who perform the role of 'monitoring the monitor'. At Enron, the process of flattening its management structure ended up delegating too much decision-making authority deeper into the company without retaining the appropriate degree of control at higher levels.

- Performance evaluation—how is the performance of business units and employees measured?
  Any performance evaluation tries to achieve two results according to Brickley et al. One, it provides feedback on whether the company is making best use of its resources and guides new resources allocation. This also help managers to assign people to jobs that will make best use of their skills. Second, it provides a measure of the employee's or business unit's contribution to shareholder value, which in turn helps in determining rewards and penalties for compensation purposes.
  At Enron, performance was evaluated largely on the basis of near-term earnings growth, which can distort managerial decision-making.

- Compensation structure—how are employees rewarded (or penalized) for meeting (or failing) to meet performance goals?
  In earlier days, incentives used to be in the form of piece rates, commissions or cash bonus, with the employee paid on the basis of some quantifiable measure of output. But more recently, the emphasis has been on stock and stock option awards. Whatever is the form, the purpose is to increase shareholder value by motivating value adding effort. Enron offered enormous compensation to its top performers, on the basis of near-term earnings growth, which encouraged excessive risk-taking as well as business decisions geared toward propping up earnings, according to Brickley et al (2005).

Laws or codes?

Most of the laws force companies to a compliance mode, which was what happened with Enron. The letter of 'law was obeyed, but the spirit violated' according to Wallace and Zinkin (Wallace & Zinkin 2005). A code, on the other hand, emphasizes the spirit making it difficult to squarely approach governance as a box-ticking exercise.

Alignment between good governance and good financial performance is required for successful running of an enterprise, whereas in reality the reported behaviours diverged. Aligning good financial performance with good corporate governance requires the following three things that are firmly embedded within the operation of the company (Wallace and Zinkin 2005).

- A culture of making informed business decisions
  It is essential to make good, informed decisions because everything depends on them. Flawed decision-making process will not deliver the desired financial results.

Underperformance or disaster could be the likely consequences. It is the responsibility of the CEO, overseen by the board, to manage risks and maintain shareholder value as part of putting in position a practice of good corporate governance. Companies can use different parameters, tools and processes like Economic Value Added, Balanced Score-card, Six Sigma, etc. These will enable companies to take decisions that are a balance of financial as well as non-financial or intangible aspects of a business. This will make the business sustainable and the process flawless and deliver all round improvements leading to better profitability while ensuring that the business produces economic profits over and above the cost of capital.

- A culture of risk management with the appropriate processes
  '… while profit is about taking risk rather than eliminating it, the identification of risks is crucial for survival…so often, Boards only become aware of the higher risk areas when management had admitted that there is no problem, or when something has already gone wrong…' said Turnbull *Report on Internal Control: Guidance for Directors on The Combined Code* (Wallace and Zinkin 2005). An effective internal control system enables companies to manage risks while helping to achieve the objective of the company. For achieving better internal control, the company must

  - Identify the major business risks
  - Take appropriate measures to implement an effective risk management system
  - Review the company's internal control system at definite intervals
  - An attendant ability to manage a crisis should it materialize

Crisis might occur in many shapes and may take different forms and everybody will be taken by surprise. According to Wallace and Zinkin (2005), 'the damage they do the company can be mitigated if there is an understanding of the types of crisis risk the company might face, effective crisis plans are developed to address these risks and there is a good communication strategy.' A crisis can be encompassing the entire corporation or related to specific areas of product, location, employee or even initiated by a competitor. Wallace and Zinkin suggest that a crisis plan must include the following:

A vulnerabilities audit   It helps to identify the impact of a breakdown in process or procedure on the different elements of the company's value chain. It helps in answering some of the questions like what happens to production, logistics, and purchasing if there is a failure of the supply chain.

A business recovery plan   It helps to advise staff about what they are supposed to do in terms of customers and service, failing which the customers would have fled to the competitors by the time the crisis dust settles down.

A disaster recovery plan   An incident like the one that happened on 11 September 2001 could result in mass loss of data acquired over the years. Decisions like data redundancy, back up storage in different parts, off-site processing, etc. could help.

A communication plan   Even with all the above, if the company lacks in a communication plan, internally as well as externally, stakeholders will not be convinced of the action plans of the management. Communicating the actions initiated to overcome the crisis is very important and will create an apparent trust in the minds of stakeholders and shareholders.

According to Wallace and Zinkin (2005), failure to have these fundamental elements embedded in the organization will lead to spectacular collapses like those of Enron, in the US, Barings in the UK, Parmalat in Italy, or Guangdong International Trust & Investment Corporation (GITIC) in Hong Kong.

Discussion Questions

1. What major factor(s) led to the corporate governance failure at Enron?
2. Comment on the statement: The independent directors of Enron did not play their roles rightly; had they played, the failure could have been avoided.
3. Do you think that a crisis plan as suggested by Wallace and Zinkin can be of great help in preventing such crisis from occurring?

CHAPTER 3

EVOLUTION OF CORPORATE GOVERNANCE
PRACTICES AND REGULATIONS

Most of the current international debate on corporate governance has not been about improving board performance and shareholder value at all, but on such relatively arcane issues as agency theory, voting rights, and drafting of yet more regulatory legislation.

– Bob Garratt, *Thin on Top*

LEARNING OBJECTIVES

After studying this chapter, you will be able to
- Elucidate why a need was felt for better corporate governance
- Define the role played by the government in corporate governance
- Discuss the Cadbury Committee Report 1992 and its recommendations
- State the corporate governance efforts in the UK and those by UN/OECD and by ICGN and GCGF
- Explain global reporting initiatives
- Define the Sarbanes–Oxley Act 2002 and describe its salient aspects
- Enumerate the initiatives in India—the different committees, their recommendations, and Clause 49 of the Listing Agreement and subsequent amendments
- Describe the concerns regarding certain deficiencies in Clause 49 and the regulatory overlaps

Opening Case

Best Practices Are Only on Paper

According to SEBI's requirements (Clause 49 of the Listing Agreement), boards of every company must meet at least once in 3 months. Meetings for audit committees have also been made mandatory and they must meet at least once in 4 months. An analysis of the board meetings and the audit committee meetings in the latest year for which annual reports were made available (2007–08 for 19 companies and 2008–09 for 11 companies) reveals interesting data and points to the existence of a camouflaging syndrome. All companies provide details of board meetings conducted such as dates, attendance by the individual directors, etc. But six out of these companies do not provide dates of the audit committee meetings and mention only the number of meetings held. And out of the remaining 24, six companies held all the audit committee meetings on the days of board meetings. In two of the remaining companies, an overwhelming majority of the audit committee meetings (seven out of eight and six out of seven, respectively) were held on the same day as board meetings. Out of a total of 157 audit committee meetings held in these Sensitive Index (SENSEX) companies, 72 were held on the same day as that of a board meeting. As observed, most of these companies go on air (on business channels such as CNBC, NDTV Profit, or CNN-IBN) by lunch after their quarterly board meetings to announce the results. No wonder that the rigour is missing in audit and that audit happens in a very superficial manner. Most of the companies are more concerned about compliance (conformance) than performance. The details of the board meetings and audit committee meetings of these SENSEX companies are given in the table below.

Details of board and audit committee meetings

S. No.	Company	Year	No. of BMs	Dates (Y/N)	Director attendance details	No. of ACMs	Dates (Y/N)	No. of ACMs on the same date as BMs
1.	RIL	07–08	7	Y	Y	6	N	NA
2.	Infosys	08–09	6	Y	Y	4	Y	0/4
3.	L&T	07–08	8	Y	Y	6	Y	2/6
4.	ICICI Bank	08–09	8	Y	Y	6	N	NA
5.	ITC	07–08	7	Y	Y	8	Y	4/8
6.	HDFC	08–09	5	Y	Y	5	Y	5/5
7.	Bharti Airtel	07–08	4	Y	Y	4	Y	4/4
8.	HDFC Bank	08–09	10	Y	Y	7	N	NA
9.	SBI	08–09	9	Y	Y	9	Y	0/9
10.	ONGC	07–08	12	Y	Y	8	Y	8/8
11.	BHEL	07–08	8	Y	Y	5	Y	3/5
12.	HUL	08–09	8	Y	Y	7	Y	6/7
13.	TCS	08–09	7	Y	Y	8	Y	7/8
14.	Tata Steel	07–08	7	Y	Y	11	Y	3/11
15.	Tata Power	08–09	7	Y	Y	13	Y	2/13
16.	Grasim	07–08	5	Y	Y	5	N	NA
17.	NTPC	07–08	14	Y	Y	5	Y	1/5
18.	Stelite Ind.	07–08	7	Y	Y	4	Y	4/4
19.	Maruti Suzuki	07–08	6	Y	Y	4	Y	3/4
20.	Rel.Comm.	07–08	5	Y	Y	5	Y	2/5
21.	Rel.Infra.	07–08	11	Y	Y	6	Y	1/6
22.	JP Assoc.	07–08	7	Y	Y	4	Y	4/4
23.	Wipro	08–09	4	Y	Y	5	Y	1/5

Contd

Table contd

S. No.	Company	Year	No. of BMs	Dates (Y/N)	Director attendance details	No. of ACMs	Dates (Y/N)	No. of ACMs on the same date as BMs
24.	M&M	08–09	7	Y	Y	5	N	NA
25.	DLF	07–08	7	Y	Y	8	Y	3/8
26.	Hero Honda	07–08	6	Y	Y	9	Y	4/9
27.	Hindalco	07–08	5	Y	N	5	Y	NA
28.	Tata Motors	07–08	10	Y	Y	10	Y	1/10
29.	Sun Pharma	07–08	6	Y	Y	4	Y	4/4
30.	ACC	08–09	5	Y	Y	5	Y	0/5

Total ACMs: 191
Number of ACMs for which dates are not available: 34   ACM – audit committee meeting
Out of the balance 157, ACMs held on the same date as BMs: 72   BM – board meeting

Discussion Questions
1. Do you think that Indian companies are better placed compared to their Western counterparts in the context of corporate governance?
2. Most Indian companies consider corporate governance guidelines as just another box-ticking exercise. Comment.

Source: 'Corporate Governance: A Reality Check After 7 Years of Sarbanes–Oxley and nearly 4 Years of Clause 49', Paper Presented by T.N. Satheesh Kumar, at the National Conference on Corporate Governance at Hyderabad, organized by the Institute of Directors, New Delhi, and World Council of Corporate Governance, London, 21/22 August 2009.

THE NEED WAS FELT

As discussed in Chapter 2, the very concept of joint-stock companies necessitated the implementation of a governance system. This was because the number of corporate shareholders increased with the passage of time since the inception of a company and shareholding was widely dispersed. Berle and Means (1932) narrate the development of the corporate form of enterprise: '… The first important manufacturing enterprise to be so organized dates from 1813. The Boston Manufacturing Company, first of the large New England textile firms, was established at wealthier Massachusetts, during the year and was in many ways the prototype of corporations of later date. Though insignificantly small in comparison with the corporate giants of today, this company had all their essential characteristics. Within 10 years of the date of incorporation, its stock originally held by 11 stockholders, had become in a sense dispersed. By 1830, the stockholders numbered 76, no individual owned more than 8.5 per cent of the stock, it took 12 to establish majority control, and the management lay with a board of directors whose combined holdings amounted to only 22 per cent. Twenty years later there were 123 stockholders, the largest of whom still owned 8.5 per cent. Fifty-one per cent of the stock was distributed among 17 individuals while the management held only 11 per cent.' Thus, the modern corporation, as we call the joint-stock companies, is largely owned by the public while being managed by professional executives who hold minuscule stakes in them. The rewards of these professionals depend on their ability to make the company more profitable, which essentially is in the interest of the shareholders as they wait to be rewarded for the risk they assume.

But since there is no dominant shareholder, who can control the enterprise by influencing the decisions of the management, there is a situation where one leaves a large quantity of assets in the hands of a few professionals who are not necessarily interested in the long-term care of the assets and the sustainability of the business. The shareholders try to exercise their control over the affairs of the corporate through a legally constituted representative body called the board of directors. The shareholders authorize the board to act on behalf of them and the board in turn is required to exercise duty of care over the corporate as the fiduciary duty. Thus, the board has enormous responsibility on it. When the board fulfils the fiduciary duty assigned to it, protecting the interests of both the shareholders and the corporation as a distinct economic entity, we say that the corporate is well governed.

On the other hand if it fails to exercise the fiduciary duties, we say that the corporate is poorly governed. Thus, governance is the process of exercising the fiduciary duty on behalf of the shareholders and at the same time ensuring the best for the corporate as an economic entity. While these concerns existed, the joint stock company concept encouraged free enterprise, furthering the cause of capitalism through competition. As we have seen earlier, even a proponent of free markets and capitalism like Adam Smith nurtured concerns about how the concept of corporation can work in a rightful manner. Free enterprises act on the basis of the energy of competition in which the individual energies and creativity pursue their best self-interests and when individuals try to maximize their self-interests, the best interests of many get served.

According to Smith (2003), 'He generally, indeed neither intends to promote the public interest, nor knows how much he is promoting it. By preferring the support of domestic to that of foreign industry, he intends only his own security; and by directing that industry in such a manner as its produce may be of the greatest value, he intends only his own gain, and he is in this, as in many other cases, led by an invisible hand to promote an end which was no party of his intention…. By pursuing his own interest he frequently promotes that of the society more effectually than when he really intends to promote it.' When individuals try to pursue their own interest and maximize their gains, the result is competition—competition for inputs like raw materials, people, customers, capital, and profits for future investments as well as for furthering wealth. And the competitive scenario invariably leads to a 'survival of the fittest' regime, which tries to weed out the weakest competitors and enable the better fit ones to further interests (Colley et al 2003). Also, some of the better fit ones may become greedy, trying to better their interests at the expense of others and there can be conflicts of interest between the individual's intentions and society's requirements. Such things may lead to chaos and hence need some control and monitoring mechanism so that the larger interests of the different groups are protected. This mechanism that aims at peaceful coexistence of the different constituents which drive for the benefit of all the constituents is governance. Without such governance, either self-imposed or externally enforced, the system will crumble.

Competition among individuals and other economic entities cannot always be left to 'the invisible hand' as it results in the survival of the fittest. The invisible hand functions but over a long period of time. If we apply the 'invisible hand' theory to corporate failures like Enron, WorldCom, or Satyam, then it has really acted as though they have been declared unfit to compete. But then these corporates being declared unfit was a result of either their not taking actions to make themselves economically better or the action of one or two individuals in the pursuit of their own individual interests. Similarly, a governance system is required to monitor and control the use of assets of a corporate by its managers on behalf of those investors who have taken the risk of investing their savings and also for protecting the purpose for which the corporate as an economic entity has been created.

'A paradox resulting from the development of capitalism in that the collective pursuit of individual self-interest has created a prosperity that benefits all' according to Colley et al. (2003). This was actually what Smith said when he talked about the invisible hand. Individuals in their freedom to pursue their self-interests might at times act in a way that is detrimental to others' interests. While everybody approves furthering one's interests by indulging in many kinds of economic activities, certain moral standards with respect to others who might get affected must be observed. The same situations may arise with respect to corporate, which are economic entities in their own right, just like individuals. While corporate pursue their interests, they may harm the environment, exploit employees, indulge in unethical practices, exploit suppliers and customers, encourage a few who actually run the corporate, amass wealth at the expense of others, etc.

While any economically productive activity involves some kind of destruction, the issue is one of balancing the two sides—gains and damage (costs). This is what governance has to achieve in a company. Managers will try to maximize the output, which will enable them to maximize their rewards, which might result in excessive and at times wasteful use of resources, or in their anxiety to produce immediate results, they will not consider the long-term interests. To prevent such things from happening and to arrive at a balance, the corporate has to be governed. It is the duty of the board to play this balancing act role. The board will try to increase the competitiveness of the corporate while trying to protect the interests of not only the shareholders but also the stakeholders like customers, employees, suppliers, lenders, regulators, and the government. This balancing act of governance is not easy even for a corporate confined to a nation.

In a globalized context, with most of the corporations having their presence in a number of countries, process and practice of governance pose serious challenges. This is because different countries and economies follow different economic systems (capitalism, socialism, communism, or some combination of all the three as is seen in a country like China), have different cultures and moral standards, competition, behaviour of markets and customers, might be at different stages of capital market development, have different levels of economic growth, have different and varied types of regulatory framework, different judiciary practices and processes, etc.

To this Berle and Means (1932) said, 'Thus, in field after field, the corporation has entered, grown, and become wholly or partially dominant'. The date of its appearance and the degree of its dominance have in general varied with two factors, the public character of the activity in question and the amount of fixed capital necessary to carry on business… And wherever the corporate has become dominant, it has been in its quasi-public, not its private, role. It does not simply give legal clothing to the private enterprise of individuals. It adds a new quality to an enterprise—the quality of multiple ownership.'

HOW THE CORPORATE CONCEPT EVOLVED

Berle and Means describe seven dramatic changes that have happened with the introduction of the concept of the joint-stock companies and their development into big-sized corporations.

1. The position of ownership has changed from that of an active to that of a passive agent. The owner now has 'a piece of paper representing the rights and expectations with respect to the enterprise', instead of physical properties over which he had control and he could exercise direction and for which he was responsible. The owner, for all practical purposes, is powerless to affect the underlying property through any of his own efforts.

2. 'The spiritual values that formerly went with ownership have been separated from it.' This is because earlier he had attachment to the physical property which he owned and its well being could bring him direct satisfaction in addition to the satisfaction from the income. According to Berle and Means, 'this quality has been lost to the property owner much as it has been lost to the worker through industrial revolution.'

3. 'The value of an individual's wealth is coming to depend on forces entirely outside himself and his own efforts.' The value now is determined by two constituencies—one, the individual, the manager, who is in command of the resources of the enterprises, and two, the market where the securities indicating ownership get traded.

4. Not only that there is wide fluctuation in one's wealth (which could be true for most wealth) but also it gets appraised constantly. The individual owner can even verify the appraised value of his wealth or the change therein every moment.

5. The wealth of the individuals has become extremely liquid aided by the organized markets. Had the wealth been in physical assets, it would not have been so easy to convert them into cash. The individual can decide to convert his holding in one type of asset to another type practically without any notice.

6. Wealth is currently in a form which cannot be employed directly by the owner. When wealth was in the form of land or machinery, it could be used by the owner directly. The physical quality of the assets was very important for the owner. The newer form of wealth ownership does not offer its owner any chance of direct use of the wealth. He can use his new asset by resorting to a sale in the market. Or in effect, 'he becomes tied to market as never before'.

7. And finally, the owner of the corporate wealth is left with a symbol of ownership in the form of a security certificate 'while the power, the responsibility and the substance which have been an integral part of ownership in the past are being transferred to a separate group in whose hands lay control'.

The changes described above happened in the enterprises as more of them assumed the corporate form, making it amply clear as to why a governance system is necessary in the functioning of the enterprises.

The corporate, governed by law, has a legal standing independent of its owners. The corporate form has become attractive due to three reasons: its unlimited life, the limited liability of the owners, and the divisibility of ownership that allows transfer of one's ownership rights to others without disrupting the structure of the organization. And profits made by the corporate are not taxed at the ownership level but are taxed on the corporate itself. When dividends are declared from the profits made by the company and distributed among the owners (in proportion to their holdings and time period of ownership), they usually become taxable in the owners' hands in most countries. In India, however, the dividends are taxed, though different from the usual corporate tax, again at the corporate level.

This very nature of a corporate being independent of its owners is the essential reason for which there is a need for a good governance system. Colley et al. (2003) say that 'the test of effectiveness of governance is the degree to which an organization is achieving its purpose.' And the basic purpose of any business is to create and serve customers. If this purpose is executed well, it will bring in rewards for the company in terms of profits, which will result in the enhancement of shareholder value.

The evolution has a bearing on the context in which the corporate function. While initially the emphasis was on protecting the interests of owners (or shareholders), the concept has undergone a lot of changes in its meaning as the role of business as well as corporate underwent a transformation in society. In the initial stages, a governance system was felt necessary because there was an issue of loss of control from the shareholders' side to those of managers who run the corporations as agents on behalf of the owners. When it became clear that corporates live along (GE in the US established in 1890, and Bombay Dyeing and Tata Steel in India established in 1879 and 1901, respectively) and many times even have existence beyond the promoters/owners, the focus shifted from the narrow shareholders to the company itself. The company, as a unique economic entity, seemed to have an existence of its own and hence emphasis needed to be given to this corporate entity. The thinking once again underwent transformation, and for the existence and continued success of the corporation, a need was felt to take care of all those entities as well that have relations with the corporate, namely, the employees, the customers, the suppliers, the regulators, the community, society, etc., apart from shareholders, at the same time focusing on the company and its well-being. As it stands today, the concept of corporate governance has the twin objectives as discussed.

During the 1980s and 1990s, as the concept gained importance, the issues also changed over a period of time. While initially it was a neglect of shareholders and the accounting norms, 1990s saw the emphasis shifting to compensation issues. The happenings during the turn of the century in companies like Enron, Worldcom, Tyco, etc., in the US, Parmalat in Europe, GITIC in Asia, etc., took the boardrooms of corporations by storm putting a renewed thrust on the area of corporate governance. While everybody thought that the dust had more or less settled, there came a shock treatment in the form of Satyam from India. While there were no major failures in India on account of poor corporate governance, the Satyam incident shook the confidence that was bestowed upon companies from India. Indian authorities had thought that many Indian companies had a different kind of ownership and management structure compared to their Western counterparts which would ensure good governance. While majority of the governance issues were related to professional managers, their control over information, their compensation, and their decisions, in Indian companies, promoters usually held high stakes and also were actively involved in management or they were major owners and at the same time acting as agents for other smaller shareholders, which according to experts can mitigate many problems in governance. But Satyam has been a rude shock to the governance pundits. True, they were promoters but they held minority stake and still controlled the company by occupying managerial positions. They had to backtrack their decisions regarding related party transactions because of the low stake they had in the company. Had the promoters controlled high stakes in Satyam, they would still have gone ahead with the acquisitions of Maytas companies and the fraud would have taken more time to expose. While everybody believed that promoters holding high stakes and their control of management would remove the many problems that result in bad governance, the same deadly combination—owner and agent combined in one—can be very dangerous too.

An incident that happened in the case of RIL is a case in point. In June 2009, the Mumbai High Court gave a verdict in favour of the Anil Ambani-controlled Reliance Natural Resources Limited (RNRL) in their on-going tussle with the Mukesh Ambani-controlled RIL about supply of natural gas from the Krishna–Godavari basin oil block. The liability for RIL was rumoured to be around Rs 17,000 over the entire lifetime of the supply if the Supreme Court upheld the lower court verdict. Even though RIL filed for appeal in the Supreme Court, there was no information about a board meeting at RIL to discuss the issue. Why is it that the other shareholders of RIL outside the family and associates did not force the company to discuss the issue in a board meeting as they did with Satyam? The reason could be that Mukesh Ambani controls nearly 50 per cent of the RIL stock whereas Ramalinga Raju controlled only slightly above 8 per cent. (More details regarding ownership related issues will be dealt in Chapter 7.)

ROLE OF THE GOVERNMENT

While free enterprise system and the consequent capitalism gives unlimited freedom to individuals and corporations to decide, to grow, to produce, to sell, to mobilize money and other resources to acquire, and enjoy wealth, etc., certain aspects in the free enterprise system need to be monitored and at times controlled. Unfettered individual freedom can at times be detrimental to others including stakeholders. For example, a corporate in the essential goods sector becoming big and powerful and acquiring a lot, virtually converting itself into a monopoly, could be detrimental to the stakeholders like the customer. Or in their pursuit of creating wealth, they might ignore the environmental consequences, detrimentally affecting society at large. Hence, it was felt that governments should retain its right to monitor and control the enterprises and intervene wherever necessary. And, by and large, governments intervene in the free enterprise system in the following areas.

- Ensuring that the markets behave in a competitive manner through competition-related regulations like antitrust laws and fair-trade laws. The US has the Sherman Act of 1890 while in India it is the Competition Commission to create and maintain a framework. Earlier Monopolies and Restrictive Trade Practice (MRTP) Commission looked into these aspects, which has since been dismantled and replaced with Competition Commission.

- Regulation of the markets that are not competitive. By virtue of its nature, the competition in a number of areas are rather limited. For example, the oil and energy industry. Due to the large investments required and also due to the uncertainty (like in oil exploration) and long gestation periods, not many entrepreneurs enter into this area. Thus, the existing players will have a control on the market through pricing, supply, distribution, etc. Without government intervention, these companies might misuse the less competitive nature of the industry to exploit the customers.

- Endeavour to maintain a balance between capital and labour. As industries grow and technologies get upgraded, corporations try to replace labour with capital or lesser and lesser people get used in the productive operations of the corporation. This might create unrest among labour and might, at times, result in disruption of the economic activities carried out by the corporate leading to deterioration the economic output and economic strength of the country.

- Try to establish order in capital markets. While corporates by concept are characterized by diverse ownership, those investors who put their hard earned savings into the securities of the companies shall not be taken for a ride. The capital markets have to be functioning in an orderly manner so that the investors have confidence in the market system. Government has created mechanisms like Securities Exchange Commission (SEC) in the US, SEBI in India, etc., in addition to the opportunities to facilitate orderly transaction by encouraging establishment of stock exchanges.

- Protecting consumers from low quality, unsafe, and unreliable products. The government has a responsibility to see that consumers from society get the benefit of using quality, safe, and reliable products. This could be very important especially in areas like food products, pharma products, etc. Government, through its agencies like Food and Drug Administration in the US, Drug Controller's Office in India, etc., try to regulate, monitor, and control the quality of products reaching the consumers.

- The government has a duty to ensure equal opportunity and access to education, employment, shelter, and other infrastructural facilities. Corporates and other institutions in pursuit of their individual achievements could adopt a policy of serving only a limited, identified constituents for their jobs, supplies, customers, etc. This might act against the interest of the society and nation. Government usually makes a provision in the constitution itself to prevent such denial of opportunities to the deserving.

- There is a need for protecting the environment. Corporates, in pursuit of growth and profits, many a time act in such a way that it could cause harm to the environment. They may resort to methods of reducing capital investments by putting their effluents in the river water or air. They may also waste natural resources in their anxiety to make quick money. They may cut forests and establish industrial units which will affect the flora and fauna of the region. While the government does not interfere directly in the governance aspects of a company unless the situation so demands as it happened in the case of Satyam, bodies created by it like SEC in the US, SEBI in India, or the laws created for the establishment of corporate entities like Companies Act 1956 will monitor and control the governance aspects of the corporates. For example, SEC or SEBI had made it mandatory for companies to follow certain minimum broad criteria in the listing agreements between stock exchanges and companies. The acts give teeth to the regulatory bodies to enforce the laws and regulations.

WHISTLE-BLOWING MECHANISM

A whistle-blowing mechanism is considered to be highly desirable in the pursuit of better corporate governance systems. 'Prevention is better than cure' is at the core of the philosophy. It has been felt that many a corporate fraud and consequent failures causing miseries to all stakeholders could have been avoided, had the system of whistle-blowing was in place and institutionalized. Sherron Watkins in Enron tried to act as a whistle-blower once she found that whatever the CFO Andrew Fastow did was benefiting him personally at the expense of Enron by sending an anonymous mail to Kenneth Lay, the Chairman and CEO of Enron. But nothing happened as Kenneth Lay ignored the warning and failed to make any investigation on the allegations mentioned in the mail. Rest is history now and is well known.

While whistle-blowing as a policy is laudable, the intricacies involved in institutionalizing it as a process poses great challenges to corporate and the very concept of corporate governance. While most of the corporates consider the regulations for the governance themselves as a necessary pain, it is very difficult for a system of whistle-blowing mechanism to set in and get institutionalized. In fully or partly government-owned companies, this could work as they can have a system of nominating somebody at a higher level of the organizational hierarchy who will have the responsibility of the oversight of vigil and report to an outside agency rather than the top executive cadre of the company. In India, public sector organizations have a policy of appointing a chief vigilance officer in the category of general manager or above who oversees the vigilance function of the company and reports to a chief vigilance commissioner, appointed by the government. Such an arrangement will enable the process to get institutionalized. But to implement such a process in the private enterprises is a major challenge before the policy makers. While the mechanism per se can do wonders if implemented, the challenges revolve around the very implementation issue.

In India, SEBI has put the whistle-blower policy under the non-mandatory requirements under Clause 49. Companies have to present the whistle-blowing mechanism installed in their annual reports. Whistle-blowers shall be provided access to the audit committee and if necessary to the Chairperson of the audit committee. Instances of whistle-blowing have been there in India but most of them have been instigated. Mr L.C. Gupta, a former member of SEBI, hailed Mr Anil Ambani as 'an unusual whistle-blower' while writing about the issues that were raised by Anil Ambani during the sibling-rivalry days in the pre-demerged Reliance Group. Gupta (2005) wrote that 'it is a rare case of whistle-blower emerging from a company's top management cadre.' In principle there is nothing wrong about somebody from top management level blowing whistle if some frauds or unethical practices happen in the company. Although Reliance Group had been involved in many issues of violation of rules and regulations during their growth phase of 1980s and 1990s, and Anil Ambani was very much a part of it, no such issues were raised or discussed by him in public. Hence, while he might have done the right thing by pointing to various issues and refusing to sign the accounts for 2004–05, there is all the reason to believe that this was the result of the eruption of rivalry between him and his brother Mukesh Ambani with respect to the control of the Reliance Group.

But, when a company seems to be doing extremely well, or during good times, everybody has a tendency to ignore most of the issues. Most of the control mechanisms do not get enforced when the going is good. As Garratt (2003) says, 'In good times, both the cream and scum rise to the top. Very few people are willing to blow a warning whistle when every one seems to be winning in a rising market. When that market turns and the cream curdles, however the scum become only too obvious. What looked to the public like marvelously engineered marble palaces turn out to be two-dimensional lath and canvas film sets, closely held together by "creative" earnings before interest, taxes, depreciation, and amortization (EBITDA) accounting.' Such issues will get attention during tough times when everybody searches for the problems and tries to fix a culprit.

Infosys provides the details of the whistle-blowing policy under the non-mandatory requirements as: 'We have established a mechanism for employees to report concerns about unethical behaviour, actual or suspected fraud, or violation of our code of conduct or ethics policy. It also provides for adequate safeguards against victimization of employees who avail of the mechanism, and also allows direct access to the Chairperson of the audit committee in exceptional cases. We further affirm that no employee has been denied access to the audit committee' (Infosys Annual Report 2008–09). Reliance Industries Ltd, describes it under the 'Whistle-Blower Mechanism': 'The Company promotes ethical behaviour in all its business activities and has put in place mechanism of reporting illegal or unethical behaviour. Employees may report violations of laws, rules, regulations or unethical conduct to their immediate supervisor/notified person. The reports received from employees will be reviewed by the Ethics Office and the Corporate Governance and Shareholders' Interface Committee. The Directors and management personnel are obligated to maintain confidentiality of such reporting and ensure that the whistle-blowers are not subjected to any discriminatory practices'(RIL Annual Report 2007–08).

Garratt (2003) is of the opinion that 'staff with stock options or linked pension schemes do not want to rock the boat, even when they know that things are wrong, for fear of wrecking the share price.' and '…disenchanted shareholders or staff, or 'whistle-blowers' (backed increasingly by regulation)—such as IBMsucks, or SaneBP, and others too vulgarly named to mention here. Their main aim is to fight a propaganda war with the corporation to achieve their campaign ends.'

For a whistle-blowing mechanism to work, following pre-requisites are necessary:

- The corporate governance must become a culture within the entire organization rather than an annual box-ticking exercise by the board. For this, every employee should learning about its importance.

- The whistle-blowing must start from the top, the board of directors. Non-executive directors, and especially independent directors, should blow the whistle the moment they find that something is not in line.
- All employees must have access to not only the audit committee members but also to the non-executive and independent directors.
- A mechanism whereby any employee, if his concerns are not addressed by the audit committee or directors, has the freedom to convey the concern to SEBI. SEBI may open a mail-id under the control of a general manger for the purpose.
- SEBI must invite researchers on corporate governance or corporate watchers to get their inputs where there are no clear guidelines and also to get sounded of some untoward happenings in the companies.
- SEBI should encourage investors to act as whistle-blowers. A number of governance deficiencies, either due to lack of regulation or otherwise, can be brought to the notice of the audit committee, auditors and/or non-executive directors.

GOOD CORPORATE GOVERNANCE—IS IT WORTH THE WHILE?

In a study to find out whether investors put a value on corporate governance, McKinsey consultants, Felton, Hudnut, and Heeckeren (1996) said: 'We asked investors to compare two well performing companies (such as those with consistent profits and number one or two in terms of market share) and state whether they would pay more for stock of one of these companies if it were well governed. Two-thirds of the investors said they would.' As one respondent put it, 'Companies with good board governance practices have a share-holder-value focus.' According to them 'there are three major reasons why investors pay a premium for good governance.'

1. Some believe that a company with good governance will perform better over a period of time, leading to a higher stock price. This group is primarily trying to capture upside, long-term potential.
2. Some others see good governance as a means of reducing risk, as they believe it decreases the likelihood of bad things happening to a company. Also, when bad things do happen, they expect well-governed companies to bounce back more quickly.
3. And still some others regard the recent increase in attention to governance as a fad. However, they tag along because so many investors do value governance. As this group sees it, the stock of a well-governed company may be worth more, simply because governance is such a hot topic these days.

Even though this study was conducted in 1996, much before the failures of Enron, WorldCom, Tyco, or Parmalat, the apparent feeling gained through observation and analysis is that the situation has not changed much. While the percentage of those who feel reasons 1 and 2 might have increased, there is still a good percentage who considers the attention and emphasis is just another fad.

The same study by Felton et al. (1996) found that 'many investors, particularly those with lower turnover ratios, are willing to pay a premium for good governance.'

CADBURY COMMITTEE REPORT

The first-ever organized attempt at establishing a set of guidelines was in the UK. The Financial Reporting Council, the London Stock Exchange, and the British Accounting Profession sponsored to set up a committee under the chairmanship of Sir Adrian Cadbury in May 1991. This was set up essentially to address the concerns about the low level of investor confidence in fiscal reporting and in the ability of the auditors to carry out their jobs, consequent to the financial scandals and collapses like those of Coloroll, Polly Peck, etc. But as could be seen from the preface of the report, the scandals at companies like Bank of Credit and Commerce International (BCCI), Maxwell, etc., the committee looked at how governance could be improved by including independent directors, separating the roles of chairman and CEO, and establishing audit committees of the boards for all companies listed on the London Stock Exchange. The committee submitted its report in December 1992.

The Cadbury Report must be lauded as it was one of the pioneering initiatives by any country and has also been path breaking in its recommendations (see Annexure 3.1) and also has been used ever since as a reference point for many other corporate governance guidelines initiated by many other countries. The committee explains the rationale behind setting up of the committee by the sponsors as addressing the concerns which were basically 'the perceived low level of confidence, both in financial reporting and in the ability of auditors to provide the safeguards which the users of company reports sought and expected' and 'unexpected failures of major companies and by criticisms of the lack of effective board accountability for such matters as directors' pay'. And in order to address these concerns, the committee had recommended 'that the board needs to state that financial controls of the business are reviewed and in order. This has caused outrage amongst many of the top-500 companies. Curiously they have seemingly been encouraged by one of the biggest accountancy firms. Klynveld Peat Marwick Goerdeler (KPMG) is reported to have told its clients in May 1995 that 'while for accounting periods beginning on or after 1 January 1995, the directors *are* required to confirm that they have reviewed the effectiveness of the system, they are *not* [italics added] required to state their actual opinion on effectiveness—although the guideline notes that they may, wish to do so, something we advise against strongly. This must be puzzling for shareholders and other stakeholders who have assumed, reasonably, that a top-500 company would have robust financial reporting systems in place. Apparently this is not so,' says Garratt (1996), while writing about the Cadbury Committee's report.

The report begins with the structure and responsibilities of boards of directors where the committee has recommended a set of best practices and then moves on to the role of auditors and makes recommendations to the accountancy firms. Then it deals with the rights and responsibilities of the shareholders. The concluding part gives a number of appendices detailing the requirements for the concerned bodies to observe.

The report recommended that the directors make statements in the company's annual report and accounts on the effectiveness of their 'system of control' as a method of assessing and estimating risk for the stockholders. About this, Garratt (1996) says that 'it was assured that this was already high on most boards' agendas, whether listed or unlisted companies. In my experience it is not, and boards often take unnecessary risks because they do not have sufficient reporting systems, even though they are encouraged to have an audit committee of the board.' According to Gerry Acher, head of audit and accounting for KPMG, control is essential for monitoring finance and especially monitoring of expenditure, and must stretch to production, service quality, health, and safety at work, training, and monitoring systems for employees and even security of people, and physical and intellectual property. According to Garratt, corporate risk management is the ultimate responsibility of the board.

Within a very short span, the Cadbury committee made its impact in the UK. Garratt (1996) wrote that 'the pressure for change which the original Cadbury report has unleashed now looks unstoppable and it is not just the small shareholders and outraged members of the public who are squealing. The UK's National Association of Pension Funds wants to see the maximum term of directors' service contracts shortened from the present 3 years to a maximum of one, and a retirement age of 70 years for listed companies.' In about 2 years, most of the recommendations were getting implemented, despite the fact that it was voluntary in nature and there was no effort or pressure to enforce the guidelines. One of the important recommendations of the committee was to create a procedure through the use of which the independent directors could seek independent professional advice if they had lack of clarity or felt uncertain about the executives' decisions. Garratt says that 'it is one of the great innovations of Cadbury and a useful precedent that should be demanded by all executive directors, especially of subsidiary companies'. The Institute of Directors (IOD), London, provides advice for its members as a part of a wider legal advice service.

While the code was voluntary in nature, companies were expected to disclose to what extent they had followed the code, requiring explanations on gaps from the code, if any. The Cadbury Code was of a general guideline nature, offering lot of room for companies to develop their own governance practices. Being a guideline, it avoided companies from a mandatory legal and regulatory framework which is often inflexible and burdensome. Since the code was of voluntary nature and enabled corporations in the UK to better governance practices, Cadbury Code inspired many other codes including the first ever attempt by CII in India. The Cadbury Code is said to have inspired many other codes like the Bosch Report in Australia in 1995, Cardon Report in Belgium in 1998, Day Report in Canada in 1994, Vienot Report in France in 1999, King Report in South Africa in 1994, Peters Committee in Netherlands in 1997, Corporate Governance Forum of Japan in 1998, the Governance of Spanish companies in Spain in 1998, Swedish Academy Report in Sweden in 1994, German Panel Corporate Governance in Germany in 2000, and even the Sarbanes–Oxley Act 2002 in the US (Som 2006).

Highlights of Cadbury Code 1992

1. The board should include non-executive directors (NEDs) of sufficient calibre and number for their views to carry significant weight in board's decisions.
2. A procedure be established for directors to take independent professional advice if necessary, at the company's expense.
3. Non-executive directors should bring an independent judgement on issues of strategy, performance, resources including key appointment, and standards of conduct.

4. The majority of NEDs should be independent of management and free from any business or other relationship which could materially interfere with the exercise of their independent judgement, apart from their fees and shareholding.

5. The directors' total emoluments and those of the chairman and highest-paid UK director including pension benefits and stock option should be fully and clearly disclosed.

6. A remuneration committee shall be set up only of or mainly of non-executive directors who will review the performance of the executive directors.

7. The board should ensure that an objective and professional relationship is maintained with the auditors.

8. An audit committee shall be constituted only of non-executive directors and has a minimum of three members. The terms of reference shall be spelt clearly detailing authorities and responsibilities.

9. Stated very clearly about the expectations on institutional investors to try to ensure that the committee's recommendations were adopted by companies: 'we look to the institutions in particular… to use their influence as owners to ensure that the companies in which they have invested comply with the code.'

COMBINED CODE 1998

While the Cadbury Committee exceeded its brief from a purely financial aspect of governance to one of improving general governance, it was felt that certain areas needed more thrust. While compensation of directors was mentioned in passing in the Cadbury Report, the need was felt that the issue needs separate dealing as there were many cases of excessive executive remuneration that caught the attention and became a topic of debates during the 1990s. Also, there was concern about disclosure of remuneration to directors. Hence, it was felt that these issues needed to be addressed. So, a committee under the chairmanship of Sir Richard Greenbury, chairman of Marks & Spencer, was formed in response to the concerns about the size of directors' remuneration and their inconsistent and incomplete disclosure in the annual reports of companies. The committee made its recommendations in 1995. At the core of the recommendations were strengthening accountability and enhancing the performance of directors. The two aims were to be achieved by (1) the presence of a remuneration committee comprising independent, non-executive directors who would report fully to the shareholders each year about the company's executive remuneration policy, including full disclosure of the elements in the remunerations of individual directors and (2) the adoption of performance measures with which the interests of directors and shareholders were more closely aligned (Mallin 2007).

In 1995, a committee was set up under the chairmanship of Sir Ronald Hampel, Chairman, ICI Plc., to review the implementations of the Cadbury and Greenbury committee recommendations. The committee submitted its report in 1998 (see Annexure 3.2). The report endorsed the findings of the two earlier committees and their recommendations. The committee also looked into the relationships the company should consider and be concerned with various stakeholders such as employees, customers, lenders, the local community, etc., in addition to the shareholders. The report stated that 'the directors as a board are responsible for relations with stakeholders; but they are accountable to the shareholders' and 'directors can meet their legal duties to shareholders, and can pursue the objective of long-term shareholder value successfully, only by developing and sustaining these stakeholder relationships.'

The Hampel Committee, like the earlier ones, also emphasized the role of the institutional investors in improving the governance practices. It recommended that institutional investors must indulge in dialogues with companies and make discernible use of their investments in improving governance practices on the strength of their voting power.

The combined code 1998 has two parts—one aimed at companies and the other aimed at institutional investors. This also was drawn up as a voluntary code with a 'comply or explain' basis. It very clearly states its instructions about the internal controls of the business as 'the board should maintain a sound system of internal control to safeguard shareholders' investment and the company's assets' and also 'the directors should, at least annually, conduct a review of the effectiveness of the group's system of internal control and should report to shareholders that they have done so. The review should cover all controls, including financial, operational and compliance controls and risk management'.

OECD PRINCIPLES OF CORPORATE GOVERNANCE

In response to a request from the Organization for Economic Co-operation and Development (OECD) Council to develop in consultation with national governments, other relevant international organizations, and the private sector, a set of corporate governance standards and guidelines, the OECD developed a set of principles to be called OECD Principles of Corporate Governance. The OECD established an ad-hoc task force on corporate governance with a mandate to develop a set of non-binding principles that reflect the views of member committees on this issue. The task force drew from experiences of various member countries and previous work carried out by OECD like that of OECD Business Advisory Group on corporate governance. The other OECD committees that participated in the process were: the Committee on Financial Markets, the Committee on International Investment and Multinational Enterprises, the Industry Committee, and the Environment Policy Committee. In addition, they also solicited inputs from non-OECD countries, the World Bank, the International Monetary Fund, business investors, trade unions, and other interested parties.

Right from the beginning, OECD recognized that there cannot be a formula for corporate governance that can be followed by all countries or as Mallin (2007) says, 'One size does not fit all.' The principles are of such nature that they represent certain common characteristics that are fundamental to good corporate governance. The task force published its report in 1999. Subsequently, the principles were reviewed and revised in 2004. These principles approached the subject from five major aspects.

Rights of shareholders   The broad term of references included establishing the shareholder rights with reference to ownership, being informed of fundamental corporate changes, opportunity to participate effectively and vote in shareholder meetings, adequate disclosure of special rights to certain shareholders like control disproportionate to their equity ownership, ensuring transparent and efficient functioning of the market for corporate control while stating that shareholders should consider the costs and benefits of exercising their voting rights.

Equitable treatment of shareholders   There should not be any discrimination among big and small, domestic and foreign shareholders. All shareholders within the same class should be treated equally. Steps must be taken to prohibit insider trading and abusive self-dealing. Board members and managers should be required to disclose any material interests in transactions or matters affecting the corporation.

Stakeholder perspective   Care should be exercised to see that the rights of stakeholders that are protected by law are respected. In case of violation of their rights, stakeholders should have the opportunity to get redressal for their grievances. Adequate mechanisms shall be provided in the corporate governance framework to improve shareholder participation in enhancing performance. The shareholders should have access to relevant information wherever stakeholders participate in the governance process.

Disclosure and transparency   The corporate governance framework should ensure that timely and accurate disclosure is made on all matters regarding the corporation including the financial situation, performance ownership, and governance of the company. Disclosures must be available on aspects like the financial and operating results, company objectives, share ownership and voting rights, board members and other key executives and also their remunerations, foreseeable risk factors, material issues regarding employees and other stakeholders, governance structures and policies, etc. Information should be prepared, audited and disclosed in accordance with high quality standards of accounting, disclosure, and audit. Independent auditor should conduct an annual audit to provide an external and objective assurance about the preparation and presentation of financial statements. These should be fair, timely and cost efficient methods of disseminating information for access by users.

Responsibilities of the board   The governance framework should ensure the strategic guidance of the company, effective monitoring of management by the board, and the board's accountability to the company and the stakeholders. Towards achieving this, the board members should exercise due diligence and care and act in the best interests of the company and the shareholders. Board should treat all shareholders fairly especially when board decisions may affect different shareholder groups differently. Compliance with all applicable laws must be ensured while taking into account the interests of stakeholders. Board should also take necessary steps to review and guide corporate strategy, risk policy, budgets, business plans, setting of performance objectives, selection of key executives—monitor and replace them where necessary and also plan for succession. It should also monitor the implementation of corporate performance, oversee major capital expenditures, acquisitions, and divestitures, review executive remuneration, ensure a formal and transparent board nomination process, monitor and manage conflicts of interest of stakeholders like board members, executives, and shareholders, ensure integrity of the company's accounting and financial reporting systems and independent audit, constitute the board with sufficient number of non-executive board members who can exercise independent judgement, etc.

GLOBAL REPORTING INITIATIVE

In the aftermath of the Exxon Valdez oil spill in 1989, a group of socially responsible investors and environmentalists combined together to form the Coalition for Environmentally Responsible Economies (CERES), which in the beginning used 'shareholder resolutions to persuade companies to adopt a set of environmental principles and produce public standardized annual environmental reports' (Hollender and Fenichell 2004). The non-corporate members who signed for this included names from different areas such as the Calvert Group, Conservation International, Domini Social investments, AFL–CIO, Friends of the Earth, Interfaith Centre on Corporate Responsibility, National Wildlife Federation, Walden Asset Management, World Wildlife Fund (WWF), etc. It also included 60 corporate signatories such as American Airlines, Bank of America, Ben & Jerry's Homemade, GM, Ford, Nike, Timberland, Sunoco, etc. While the CERES Principles were a very important step in conditioning environmentally and socially sustainable practices, a better and sustainable impact and legacy may have been made on the disclosure and transparency aspect by what CERES developed as Global Reporting Initiative (GRI). It is an international initiative backed by a multitude of stakeholders, launched in 1997 to establish a common framework for economic, environmental, and social reporting. The thinking of the leadership of the GRI was that rather than resorting to commonly used pressure tactics like boycott of the products, or services of a corporate, or introducing shareholder resolutions towards changing the approach of corporates, filing law suits, etc., and then going public with a hot story, corporates will be induced to disclose the negative and positive impacts of their operations so that they get to know the status quo and are encouraged to improve their own performance records. According to Bob Massie, who led the CERES during the formative years, 'What the corporate world really needed, was a mutually agreed upon set of standards for environmental and social reporting. These standards would provide existing and prospective shareholders, creditors, and all those with a financial relationship with the company as well as the general public with a standardized, consistent, and independently verified window on the company's internal operations, their future risks, and the general health and viability of the enterprise' (Hollender and Fenichell). A number of companies voluntarily produced reports employing the GRI environmental and social reporting guidelines. For example, GM complied a detailed CSR report employing the GRI guidelines. According to Judith Mullins, Director of GM's Public Policy Centre at Detroit, 'GM was able to publicly identify and fix significant number of environmental problems at its manufacturing and assembly plants that might have gone undetected before committing to the analysis and review that Precedes public reporting' (Hollender and Fenichell). Judy Henderson, a member of the GRI global directorate, while speaking at a Business for Social Responsibility conference in Miami in 2002 observed that 'competitive advantage can be gained with transparency, as a question of managing risk and reputation, because discerning investors now recognize that a company managed according to interests broader than those of only shareholders is more likely to profit over the long term. Corporations with a stakeholder focus have been shown to enjoy greater sales and value growth than companies with a narrow shareholder focus' (Hollender and Fenichell). A number of companies have started producing reports on the lines of GRI. These include Intel, Dupont, Hewlett Packard, Procter & Gamble, Unilever, etc.

The GRI Guidelines are given in Exhibit 3.1.

Exhibit 3.1
GRI Guidelines—G3 Guidelines

The G3 Guidelines are the cornerstone of the GRI Sustainability Reporting Framework. In line with the GRI vision, it is recommended they be used as the basis for all of an organization's annual reporting.

The guidelines outline core content for reporting and are relevant to all organizations regardless of size, sector, or location. They are the foundation upon which all other GRI reporting guidance is based. The G3 Guidelines outline a disclosure framework that organizations can voluntarily, flexibly, and incrementally adopt. The flexibility of the G3 format allows organizations to plot a path for continual improvement of their sustainability reporting practices.

So what's in the G3?

Part 1   Reporting Principles and Guidelines
- Principles to define report content: materiality, stakeholder inclusiveness, sustainability context, and completeness
- Principles to define report quality: balance, comparability, accuracy, timeliness, reliability, and clarity
- Guidance on how to set the report boundary

Part 2   Standard Disclosures
- Strategy and Profile
- Management Approach
- Performance Indicators

How are the guidelines updated?
The guidelines are updated incrementally. This process represents a change from the previous revision cycles, in which the entire set of guidelines were subject to revision. Going forward, GRI will use a process involving incremental updates that will target specific revision goals—addressing only certain portions of the guidelines.

The Process
- On an annual basis, GRI invites stakeholders to identify their priorities in Q4 for further development of the guidelines.
- The stakeholder feedback is then reviewed and used to formulate a draft plan.
- The draft plan is posted on the GRI website for public comment.
- The board of directors will approve a final set of priorities for implementation for the next fiscal year based on feedback from the Technical Advisory Committee (TAC) and the Stakeholder Council (SC). This plan will take into account any ongoing projects from previous years that have not yet been completed.
- Based on the plan, GRI will form working groups to develop draft revisions for review by the TAC.
- Following the TAC review, the draft revisions will be forwarded to the SC for their concurrence/non-concurrence and then to the Board for a final decision.
- Updates to the guidelines will be issued when the work is completed. This means that projects may be completed and released in any given year.

In 2002, more than 200 out of an estimated 2500 companies around the world that produced some type of CSR report produced them in accordance with the GRI standards (Hollender and Fenichell 2004). The GRI guidelines enable companies to have a common framework leading to transparency through processes that are clear, unambiguous, and equivalent for all players.

The criticism against the GRI is in its utility as it is voluntary and that it lacks teeth as it cannot be enforced. Hollender and Fenichell say, 'After reviewing a collection of CSR reports that purport to follow GRI guidelines, it is clear that there is still much work to be done' and 'While no CSR report that I've read complies with all GRI's requirements, overall I regard this argument as false and misguided, since as more and more companies realize that adopting effective social and environmental policies is good for business, if not necessary for business, the pressure on them will grow to comply with a standard in place like the GRI.' Appendix A shows a typical report (abridged to include only the salient features) conforming to GRI guidelines made by Jubilant Organosys Ltd from India.

INTERNATIONAL CORPORATE GOVERNANCE NETWORK

In any corporate governance code, the attempt has been to establish certain principles that will act as guidelines for corporates. The same is true of the International Corporate Governance Network (ICGN), which has been created by investors at Frankfurt on 9 July 1999.

The ICGN principles start with praising the OECD principles referring to them as the foundation of good corporate governance. It then lists a 10-point 'Working Kit', CG Criteria (Annexure 3.3).

Assumptions made in the ICGN Approach

There are five assumptions on which the ICGN approach rests.

About shareholder rights   According to ICGN, there are five factors that need to be addressed :

1. Shareholders are entitled to be consulted before any major change is implemented to the company's strategic direction as this right affects the risk profile of the business, and shareholders have rights to have their risk profiles respected. Also, the approval of shareholders should be taken before the corporate indulges in anything that is likely to dilute the shareholder equity or erode shareholder economic interests.
2. Shareholder must be provided with adequate access to be able to exercise their right to vote and corporates must provide secure methods to enable the shareholders' voting.
3. The results of voting should be disclosed resolution-wise in a timely manner and votes cast in person or through post or proxy shall be treated alike.
4. Care should be taken to see that no shareholder enjoys power disproportionate to his/her holding or the 'one share, one vote' system be followed.
5. Institutional shareholders must exercise their vote, subject to the costs, as it is a fiduciary responsibility.

Equitable treatment of shareholders   ICGN recognizes the 'one share, one vote' principle as the best way to enable the capital markets to grow and hence agree that markets that do not recognize this principle will be disadvantaged. 'One share, one vote' prevents any differential treatment of shareholders, especially the minority and foreign shareholders.

The role of stakeholders   ICGN assumes that boards are accountable to shareholders and are responsible to interact with all stakeholders in their pursuit of creating wealth, employment and financially sustainable companies over a period of time. ICGN also assumes that there is a need to align both shareholder and stakeholder interests and is enabled to a very large extent by performance enhancing mechanisms like employee share ownership plans and profit sharing plans.

Disclosure and transparency   While disclosure of financial and operating results, risk factors, stakeholder issues, and governance structure and procedures are necessary, disclosure of information such as major shareholders, special voting rights, shareholder agreements, dominant shareholders cross-holdings if any, guarantees provided by the company, related party transactions, etc., must also be provided. Also, details of the directors, their remunerations, any material transaction with the company other than that as a board member, etc., shall be disclosed. The details of auditors and the fees paid and also, whether they have been paid fees for any non-audit related work must be disclosed.

The board responsibilities   ICGN emphasizes the fiduciary responsibilities of the board and hence expects the board as an entity and the directors as individuals being accountable to the shareholders as a whole. The board must have enough independent components with appropriate competencies and should contribute to the strategy and performance of the management, and also be responsible for constituting key committees with the right kind of skills and talents. ICGN endorses the OECD Principles fully on the independence aspect. It also suggests that relevant committees should be composed wholly or predominantly of independent, non-executive directors.

Criticism about the ICGN's approach is that it does not provide for any directives for chairpersons, CEOs, and other directors to handle their jobs effectively.

EUROPEAN UNION APPROACH TO CORPORATE GOVERNANCE

The EU guidelines for corporations was based on a study by an expert group sponsored by Global Corporate Governance Forum, which is an affiliate of International Finance Corporation (IFC). This has been done because 'promoting the private sector as an engine of growth, reducing the vulnerability of developing and transition economies to financial crises, and providing incentives for corporations to invest and perform efficiently in a socially responsible manner—these are key priorities for the World Bank Group. Strengthening corporate governance is essential in achieving these priorities because it creates the necessary climate for investment and economic development. Sound corporate governance practices inspire investor and lender confidence, spur both domestic and foreign investment and improve corporate competitiveness' says the report in its foreword. The major recommendations were about the board of directors, its constitution and structure, remuneration of directors, disclosures, shareholder rights, and guidelines for setting of EU Corporate Governance Standards. Appendix B shows the EU approach to corporate governance.

SARBANES–OXLEY ACT 2002

The high profile corporate failures that happened in the US at the beginning of the century, such as Enron, WorldCom, and Tyco, created lot of discussion, debate, and media attention. What was till then restricted to boardrooms namely, the concept of corporate governance, became a hot topic among not only business people and academics but also politicians. There was tremendous pressure on the government to control and discipline corporates so that instances of the same kind do not happen in future. Senators Paul Sarbanes and Michael Oxley sponsored a new law for regulating the governance of corporates. As is the practice in the US, the act, i.e., the Public Accounting Reform and Investor Protection Act 2002, came to be referred to as the Sarbanes–Oxley Act 2002 after its sponsors. It is also referred to as SOX, in short. According to Smith and Walter (2006), the SOX 'led to a wave of rule-tightening and enforcement actions that placed all of the US's public corporations on the defensive, with a heavy burden to adapt new and costly compliance standards and to review their own internal corporate governance practices.' 'The law has been hailed as a landmark comparable to the securities and securities exchange acts that created the Securities and Exchange Commission (SEC)' according to Waring and Pierce (2005). Smith and Walter concur: '…The 2002 Sarbanes–Oxley Act, the most extensive piece of federal securities legislation since the 1934 Securities Exchange Act. This newest of comprehensive federal laws was presumed to assure good corporate governance by the specificity and clarity of its dozen or so implementing regulations requiring actions of corporations and their boards and by insistent pressure for grater transparency.'

With a dozen sections and more than 80 subsections, the law covers extensive topics including analyst conflicts and document shredding. In addition to the coverage of various corporate governance and related aspects, the SOX have initiated steps to create a publicly funded oversight board, the Public Company Accounting Oversight Board, with a mandate to monitor auditors, strengthen auditor independence, increase CEO accountability for financial statements, make CEO and CFOs sign financial statements, ease private securities litigation, and give SEC more resources and teeth. It has also necessitated increased criminal penalties for fraudulent acts, debarring directors and officers found guilty of fraud, longer prison-term for certain categories of white-collar crimes, and even disgorgement of fraudulent gains to benefit the cheated shareholders.

One very important and notable feature of the SOX is that it has strengthened the role of the audit committee. It has resulted in increased work load for the audit committee, and the directors must devote time for audit committee work. As Carter and Lorsch (2004) say, 'Within a year of the time the law was signed by President Bush, we have heard about audit committees that have tripled the frequency of their meetings.' Commenting on the law, Senator Phil Gramm representing the Republican Party from Chicago said: 'No one sitting on a corporate board or audit committee will ever be the same' (Waring and Pierce 2005). The audit committee's new strength comes from several aspects of the new law. Sarbanes–Oxley set new standards for auditor independence, banning certain types of consulting services that auditors had been able to provide in the past, namely (Waring and Pierce):

- Book-keeping or other services related to the accounting records or financial statements of the audit client;
- Financial information system design and implementation;
- Appraisal or valuation services, fairness opinions, or contribution-in-kind reports;
- Actuarial services;
- Internal audit outsourcing services

- Management functions or human resources
- Broker or dealer, investment advisor, or investment banking services; and legal services and other expert services unrelated to audit.

Also, the audit committee must meet with the independent (external) auditors to review and discuss (Dimma 2007):

- Audit problems or difficulties and management's responses
- The responsibilities, budget, and staffing of the company's internal audit function
- Critical accounting policies and practices
- All alternative accounting treatments of financial information that have been discussed with management, the ramification of each alternative, and the auditor's preferences
- The management letter, schedule of unadjusted differences, and other material written communications between the external auditor and management.

The Act necessitates audit committees of stock exchange listed companies to disclose the presence or absence of at least one member who is 'an audit committee financial expert'. It has also defined in detail as to who is a financial expert. A 'financial expert' for the audit committee services is a person with understanding of generally accepted accounting principles and financial statements, experience in the preparation and auditing of financial statements of generally comparable issuers, and the application of such principles in connection with the accounting for estimates, accruals and reserves, experience with internal accounting controls, and an understanding of audit committee functions.

According to Smith and Walter (2006), 'The Sarbanes–Oxley Act essentially signaled that the self-regulation of the US accounting industry was over.' The Act also ushered in changes in the way executives are compensated. According to Bebchuk and Fried (2004), the major changes that happened in the area are:

- It has increased the formalization of board process thereby creating additional demands on the director's time. For example, one law firm issued to its clients a 'best practices calendar' suggesting that the compensation committee meet three days during the year, two days in February and one day in November.
- Prohibited grant of company loans to directors with a very few exceptions. Existing loans were exempted from the prohibition (Sec 402).
  Earlier firms used to grant loans to CEOs and top managers. For example, WorldCom CEO Bernie Ebbers was granted hundreds of millions of dollars in unsecured loans, approximately 20 per cent of the cash on the company's balance sheet. When Ebbers left WorldCom, he owed the firm $408 million.
- It required directors to report any trades in the company's shares the following day with grant of exemption based on determination of non-feasibility of such reporting (Sec 403). Earlier, Section 16 (a) of the SEC Act 1934 generally required executives to disclose their trades by the 10th day of the month following the trade. But when executives gave stock to the company, they had to report the transactions only within 45 days after the fiscal year in

which the transaction occurred. Thus, those insiders who had loans could hide their stock sales for up to a year. Bebchuk and Fried quote the example of Dennis Kozlowski, who continued to assert that he rarely sold his Tyco shares despite the fact that he had returned $70 million worth of stock to the company to repay the loans.

- It also made firms discontinue the practice of taking split-dollar life insurance policies for their executives with which they used to cover the executive for billions of dollars of insurance as these policies were considered as loans to the covered executive.
- It also forced the CEO and CFO to give back to the company any bonus or other incentive or equity-based compensation received during the 12 months following the filing of the misleading financial statement, or any profits realized from the sale of stock within that period in the case of a restatement of the earnings.

Refer to www.soxlaw.com for the full text of the law.

The SOX Fallouts

Tougher law means difficulty to attract good candidates. Charan (2005) says that when SOX was passed, 'a common complaint was that it would become harder to find qualified director candidates. Observers noted that individuals would likely sit on fewer boards because of the greater time demands, and some candidates would turn down the opportunity for fear of legal liability.'

The mandatory requirement that every board must have an accounting expert, 'which has led more CFOs and accounting professors to join boards. Many have strong personalities and can become a drain on the board. Unless boards explicitly consider a director candidate's ability to work within a group, they run the risk of recruiting directors who could become unwanted' (Charan 2005).

It also stipulates that the audit partners be rotated every five years and are then subject to a five-year bar. Other partners involved with the audit, but not acting as the lead partner, are subject to a seven-year rotation followed by a two-year bar. Also, for one year no member of the audit team can accept employment in a company that he/she has audited.

The Act also strengthened the already initiated moves to have a majority of the members of the boards independent in order to restrict excessive concentration of powers in management. As Smith and Walter (2006) say, 'After the cataclysmic events of the failures of Enron and WorldCom, some of these ideas were incorporated in provisions of the Sarbanes–Oxley Act and in new standards for director independence and conduct promulgated by the New York Stock Exchange and the National Association of Securities Dealers.'

There are also concerns about the role and operation of the Public Company Accounting Oversight Board (PCAOB). In fact the Free Enterprise Fund (FEF) on 7 February 2006 filed a complaint in the US district court for the district of Columbia 'challenging the formation and operation of PCAOB' (Murali 2006). The argument was that 'the Board and all the power and authority exercised by it violate the constitution. The Board's structure and operation, including its freedom from Presidential oversight and control and the method by which its members are appointed contravene the principles of the US Constitution' (Murali). Also, FEF feels that it is a very costly process to implement. Since every listed company will be subject to the SOX, smaller firms will be hit hard as companies have to bear all the costs incurred by the PCAOB. It was estimated that in the year 2003–04 alone, the SOX's regulations resulted in more than $35 billion in compliance costs imposed on the nation's businesses against the initial SEC estimates of $1.24 billion according to FEF (Murali). But SEC had formed the Small Business Advisory Committee to look at the cost of implementing Sarbanes–Oxley requirements for small businesses. According to Mike Starr, director of Global Risk Management at Grant Thornton, the fifth largest accounting firm in the US, and Chair of American Institute of Certified Public Accountants' (AICPA) special committee on Enhanced Business Reporting, 'They don't want it to be onerous' (Srivats 2005). He also said that 'the SEC and other regulators are sensitive to the perception that was gaining ground (outside the US) that the US is no longer a good place for raising capital' (Srivats).

A Survey of 450 companies conducted by Financial Executives International (FEI) in January 2004 on Section 404 costs showed that audit fees for groups with a market capitalization of around $1 billion rose by 35 per cent during the year. And a second survey whose results were published in August 2004, indicated that the cost of compliance of companies (for companies in survey with a revenue of approximately $2.5 billion) would be over $3 million and this was a 62 per cent increase over the earlier survey (D'Souza 2004).

According to Elash (2003), writer and business consultant, 'The Sarbanes–Oxley Act creates increased obligations and risks for directors personally. Directors are being asked, in effect, to underwrite their actions with their personal wealth.'

This has actually led to a rise in compensation for directors. According to D'Souza (2004), 'Compensation for directors had increased 10 per cent while insurance for these directors has in some cases more than doubled.'

There were also criticisms about how SOX 'aggravates the old and serious dilemma, the dual system of federal and state laws affecting corporations. The duties of corporations and their directors are established by the law of the state in which the corporation is incorporated. Yet all the new laws intended to restrain corporations were federal' (Smith and Walter 2006).

DESIRABLE CORPORATE GOVERNANCE—A CODE

In the years following the first-ever organized attempt to introduce a set of guidelines for governance in England in the form of Cadbury Committee Report, many countries woke up to the need for improving governance in their countries. India was no exception. There were concerns about protecting the investor interests, especially those of the minority shareholders. The Confederation of Indian Industry (CII) took the initiative in 1996 to develop and promote a code for corporate governance to be adopted and followed by Indian companies from all sectors. Apart from protecting the investor interest, the other motives were promotion of transparency within business and industry, the need to move towards international standards in terms of disclosure of information by the corporations with the ultimate aim of developing a high level of public confidence in business and industry. With India becoming integrated with the world market in a globalizing scenario, in which global investors would demand greater disclosures and transparency of decision-making it was felt necessary to have a set of governance guidelines for the Indian business and industry. With this mandate, CII set up a National Task Force, under the chairmanship of Mr Rahul Bajaj, a former president of CII and Chairman and Managing Director of Bajaj Auto Ltd, that included members from the industry, legal profession, media, and academia. The task force prepared the draft reports of guidelines in April 1997 which was then publicly debated and after incorporating the suggestions from various quarters, was published in April 1998.

The major recommendations were:

1. A single board structure as it will suffice to take care of good governance.
2. Inclusion of independent, non-executive directors. 30 per cent if the chair is non-executive and 50 per cent if the chair also holds the position of managing director.
3. Number of directorships of a person shall be restricted to 10 listed companies.
4. Non-executive directors (NEDs) to become actively involved on the board, take more responsibilities such as audit committees, and be knowledgeable on the financial aspects of the company.
5. Pay commission and offer stock options to NEDs in addition to sitting fees to attract talent, subject to certain limits.
6. Reappointment must be based on their attendance record during the previous tenure and in case of failure to attend 50 per cent or more meetings, this must be stated in the resolution that is put to vote.
7. Key information that must be placed before the board was given in detail.
8. Audit committees be constituted with at least three members, all of whom must be non-executive and the terms of reference must be clearly defined. The desirable disclosures were also detailed.
9. The annual reports shall include details in the form of additional shareholder information.
10. The consolidation of group accounts shall be optional and voluntary.
11. Major Indian stock exchanges must gradually insist on a compliance certificate signed by the CEO and the CFO stating the responsibility of the management in the integrity and fair presentation of financial statement in the annual reports.
12. About capital market related aspects such as more funding for corporate sector, not insisting on nominee directors by FIs as part of loan covenants, regarding disclosure in the offer documents of credit ratings by more than one rating agency, regarding banning companies from accepting fresh deposits or declaring dividends in the case of defaults on fixed deposit programmes. Annexure 3.4 gives the full CII report.

REPORT OF K.M. BIRLA COMMITTEE ON CORPORATE GOVERNANCE

While the CII effort was voluntary in nature from the industry side, SEBI having taken up the role of capital market regulator, tried to create and regulate a realm for corporate governance for the

Indian companies. While a number of governance guidelines were available abroad, SEBI felt that such governance guidelines have to be in consideration with the corporate environment that exists in the country and so, import of any guideline from abroad did not make sense. SEBI had already initiated a number of steps in the direction of improving governance by strengthening the disclosure norms for IPOs, reporting utilization of funds in the annual reports, quarterly results, insisting on appointment of a compliance officer, and for issues on a preferential basis, and also about takeovers and acquisitions. SEBI wanted to further strengthen the corporate governance system in the country. Hence, it appointed a committee on Corporate Governance on 7 May 1999 under the chairmanship of Shri Kumar Mangalam Birla, a member of the SEBI board to prepare a set of corporate governance guidelines for the Indian companies in the Indian context. The major recommendation of the committee, which would form the essence of the of the Clause 49 guidelines of the listing agreement between companies and the stock exchanges which forms the basis of corporate governance in India today, classified under mandatory and non-mandatory, are:

A. Mandatory

1. Not less than 50 per cent of the board shall be non-executive directors. In the case of a non-executive chairman, at least one-third of the board should comprise independent directors and in the case of an executive chairman, at least half of the board should be independent.
2. Financial institutions will appoint nominees on the boards only on selective basis and where it is essential. And such nominees, if present, will act in the same manner as any other director.
3. A qualified and independent audit committee with a minimum of three members and majority independent members with the chairman of the committee being an independent member and at least one member having financial and accounting knowledge be set up by the board, which would go a long way in enhancing the creditability of the financial disclosures and promoting transparency. The committee can get advice from executives if necessary and the company secretary will be the secretary of the committee.
4. The audit committee must meet at least thrice a year, one necessarily every six months and one for finalization of annual accounts and functions.
5. The quorum should be either two members or one-third of the audit committee, whichever is higher.
6. The committee can secure the help of outside expertise, if necessary.
7. The committee must look into the reasons for substantial defaults in the payment to depositors, debenture holders, shareholders (non-payment of declared dividends), and creditors.
8. The board should meet at least four times a year with maximum time gaps between any two meetings being 4 months.
9. A director should not be a member in more than 10 committees or act as chairman of more than five committees across all companies in which he is a director. Every director should inform the company about committee positions he occupies in other companies.

10. Management must disclose to the board all material, financial, and commercial transactions where they have personal interest or where there are potential conflicts with the interests of the company.

11. While appointing new directors or re-appointing a director, the shareholders must be provided with a brief resume of the director, details of his expertise in specific functional areas, and details of the other directorships and membership of committee of the boards.

12. A committee to redress the grievances of the shareholders be set up under the chairmanship of a non-executive director.

13. The power of share transfer should be transferred to an officer, or a committee, or to the registrar and transfer agents.

14. A separate section on corporate governance be included in the annual reports.

15. The company should obtain a certificate from the auditors of the company regarding compliance of all the mandatory recommendations.

16. The board of directors should decide the remuneration of non-executive directors.

B. Non-mandatory

1. The chairman has a distinctive role from that of the chief executive and hence even if the chairman is non-executive, he should be entitled to maintain an office at the company's expense and be reimbursed all the expenses in connection with the performance of his duties.

2. The board should set up a remuneration committee to set the company's remuneration packages for executive directors. The committee shall be constituted of at least three directors, all non-executive with the chairman being independent director. The chairman should be present at the AGM.

3. All the details of remuneration package, such as components, service contracts, notice periods, severance fees, etc., shall be provided.

4. The half-yearly declaration of financial performance including summary of the significant events in last six months should be sent to each household of shareholders.

The full committee report is available in Appendix C.

REPORT OF NARESH CHANDRA COMMITTEE ON CORPORATE AUDIT AND GOVERNANCE

In the aftermath of the corporate debacles like Enron, WorldCom, Global Crossing Qwest, etc., in the US, and also with the failure of Arthur Anderson and the enactment of Sarbanes–Oxley Act 2002, the Department of Company Affairs (DCA) under the Ministry of Finance and Company Affairs appointed a high level committee under the chairmanship of Shri Naresh Chandra, former Cabinet Secretary to the Government of India, Ambassador to the US, on 21 August 2002 to look into governance issues related to independent auditor appointment, auditor fees, rotation of audit firms or partners, and also the role of independent directors and how their independence and effectiveness can be measured. The major recommendation of the committee were:

1. Prohibition of any direct financial interest in the client by the audit firm, its partners, or members of the engagement team as well as their direct relatives and also any relative who has more than 2 per cent of the share capital of the audit client or of the share of the profit.

2. Prohibition of any loans or guarantees by the audit firm, or partners, or other members of the engagement team from the audit client.

3. Prohibition of any business relationship with the audit client by the audit firm, its partners or members of engagement, and their direct relatives.

4. Prohibition of personal relationships which would result in the exclusion of the audit firm or partners or members of engagement like with key executives or senior managers belonging to the top two managerial level of the company.

5. Prohibition of any partner or member of the engagement team from joining client before 2 years not being engaged in the audit of the client.

6. Prohibition of undue dependence on an audit client. The fee received from any one client should not exceed 25 per cent of the total revenues of the audit firm. Firms in the initial five years from the commencement of their activities and those whose total revenues are less than Rs 15 lakhs per year are exempted.

7. Prohibition of non-audit services like accounting and book keeping services, internal audit services, design and implementation of financial information systems actuarial services, services of broker, dealer, investment advisory or investment banking, other financial services which are sometimes outsourced by the client, or management services which are outsourced, recruitment services, valuation and fairness opinion services, etc.

8. Fifty percent audit partners and member of the engagement team be rotated every five years in the case of clients whose networth exceeds Rs 10 crores or whose turnover exceeds Rs 50 crores. Those who are compulsorily rotated could return after a gap of 3 years.

9. The management should provide a clear description of each material liability and its risks followed by auditor's comments on the management view.

10. Qualifications of accounts, if any, by auditors must be adequately highlighted in order to attract shareholders attention.

11. The qualification, if any, in the report shall be explained to the shareholders at the company's annual general meeting.

12. The audit firm should separately send a copy of the qualified report to the ROC, SEBI, and the principal stock exchanges with a copy of the letter marked to the management of the company.

13. The Section 225 of the Companies Act needs to be amended to require a special resolution of shareholders in case an auditor, who is otherwise eligible for reappointment, is sought to be replaced. Also, the reasons for such replacement shall be explained, about which the outgoing auditor has right to comment.

14. The audit firm should submit annually a certificate of independence to the audit committee and/or the board of directors.

15. The audit committee should review the independence of the audit firm, discuss and prepare the annual work programmes with the auditor and also recommend to the board with reasons

about the appointment/reappointment or removal of the auditors along with the annual remuneration.

16. The CEO/CFO should certify the balance sheet and profit and loss account and all the schedules and notes on accounts and cash flows in the case of companies whose net worth exceeds Rs 10 crores or whose turnover exceeds Rs 50 crores, very clearly stating any deficiencies in the design and operation of internal controls and any significant changes in the accounting policies during the year under review.

17. Three independent quality review boards (QRB) should be set up, one each for ICAI, ICSI, and ICWAI to periodically examine and review the quality of audit, secretarial and cost accounting firms, to judge and comment on the quality and sufficiency of systems, infrastructure and practices. The QRBs should review the audit quality reviews of the audit firms for the top 150 listed companies accounting to market capitalization, with the freedom for DCA to alter few samples after the period. The funding of the QRB's will be done by the respective institutes.

18. An independent prosecution directorate be created within ICAI to exclusively deal with all disciplinary cases.

19. Complaints received should be registered by the prosecution directorate and sent to the member or firm within 15 days of receipt and the prosecution directorate should ask for required documents from the complainant and the respondent within 60 days. On receipt of documents they will be placed before the disciplinary committee within 20 days of receiving the documents. The disciplinary committee shall hear the cases and decisions recorded in a report and should detail the punishment to be awarded. The ICAI council should consider the report within 45 days from the date of the report and act upon them. Appeal if any shall be placed before the appellate body headquartered in New Delhi, composed of a presiding officer and four other members. The presiding officer shall be a retired judge of the Supreme Court or a retired chief justice of a high court. Two members shall be past presidents of ICAI and the remaining two nominated by the DCA. The quorum shall be three.

20. The disciplinary committee's awards of the punishment, if any, shall be publicized through suitable media.

21. The finding of the appellate body shall be made by the central government in order to ensure independence. The expenses incurred by the disciplinary committee shall be borne by ICAI's council including the emoluments of the members, sitting fees, other allowances and expenses. All expenses of the prosecution directorate will be borne by the council of ICAI. Every complaint (other than those made by the central or state government) shall be accompanied by a fee of Rs 5000, which will be returned in case the complaint holds some ground. Fees in the case of frivolous complaints are not refunded and will go towards funding.

22. Independent disciplinary mechanisms may be designed by ICSI and ICWAI along similar lines.

23. While appointing independent directors, care must be taken to see that they have no material pecuniary relationships or transactions with the company, its promoters, senior management, or its holding company, or subsidiaries, or associate companies; are not related to promoters

or management at the board level and one level below; have not been executives of the company in the last three years; are not partners or executives of a statutory audit firm, internal audit firm or legal firm or consulting firm associated with the company for the last three years; are not significant suppliers, vendors or customers of the company; do not hold more than 2 per cent of the voting shares; and have not been directors of the company for more than three terms of three years each (maximum of nine years). However, nominee directors of a financial institution will be excluded in the determination of the number of independent directors and cross non-executive directorships of executives will not be treated as independent. The committee also recommended that the above criteria for independent directors shall be made applicable for all listed companies and also unlisted companies with a net worth of Rs 10 crores and above or a turnover of Rs 50 crores and above.

24. In the case of companies as detailed above, not less than 50 per cent of the board of directors should be independent. However, unlisted public companies with a maximum of 50 shareholders and without debt of any kind from the public, banks, or other financial institutions as long as they do not change their character and also those unlisted subsidiaries of listed companies. Nominee directors again will be excluded both from the number and the denominator.

25. Since corporate governance norms require companies to have a number of committees, the boards should have a minimum size. The minimum size should be seven with at least four independent directors in the case of all listed companies as well as unlisted public companies with a net worth of Rs 10 crores and above or turnover of Rs 50 crores and above. Again, this will not be applicable to companies with no more than 50 shareholders or those without any debt till they change their character and for unlisted subsidiaries of listed companies.

26. The minutes of meetings of the board as well as audit committees shall disclose the timing and duration of each meeting, dates of meetings, and the attendance record of members in the case of companies detailed above.

27. Those directors who find it difficult to attend the meetings physically must participate in the proceedings through tele-conference or video-conference duly minuted.

28. All information given to the press or analysts, in the case of all listed companies and unlisted companies meeting the above-mentioned criteria, should be transmitted to all board members.

29. Audit committees shall be constituted of only independent directors if the committees are indeed to be independent excepting those public companies with not more than 50 shareholders and without debt of any kind and also unlisted subsidiaries of listed companies.

30. The chairman of the audit committee must annually certify whether and to what extent each of the functions listed in the audit committee charter were discharged during the year in addition to dates and frequency of meetings. It should also provide its views on the adequacy of the internal control systems, perceptions of risks and in the event of any qualifications, why the committee accepted and recommended the financial statements with qualifications.

31. The statutory limit (of Rs 5000) on sitting fee should be revised as it is considered too small to attract talent. The present statutory limits of 1 per cent commission of net profit to independent directors and also provisions relating to the stock options are adequate and do not need any revision. The vesting of the stock options shall be staggered over at least three years.

32. The non-executive and independent directors must be granted protection from certain criminal and civil liabilities because they are not expected to be in the know of every technical infringement committed by the management.

33. DCA should encourage institutions and their proposed centres for corporate excellence to have regular training programme for independent directors. The funding could come from the Investor Education and Protection Fund (IEPF). Every independent director should undergo at least one such training course before assuming his/her responsibilities. An untrained independent director should be disqualified under Section 274(1)(g) of the Companies Act 1956, giving reasonable notice. Of course, this requirement might be introduced in a phased manner as there is paucity of the availability of such training programmes.

34. SEBI should refrain from introducing subordinate legislation in areas where specific legislations exist under Companies Act 1956. In case any additional requirements in the existing provisions are found necessary by SEBI, such requirements must be done through suitable amendments of the Companies Act 1956. DCA should respond to such requirements quickly.

35. The government should strengthen the DCA by increasing the number of DCA offices and quality and quantity of physical infrastructure. They should outsource expertise when needed. The inspection capacity needs to be strengthened and it should become a regular administrative function. It is very essential that the DCA functionaries continuously upgrade themselves through training.

36. A corporate serious fraud office (CSFO) should be set up to investigate into any instances of corporate frauds. This should be a multifunctional team which can detect frauds and also direct and supervise prosecutions. The appointments to and the functioning of this office shall be by different committees headed by the cabinet secretary.

37. The penalties in the case of offences need to be rationalized and must be related to the sums involved in the offences. The criteria for disqualification under Section 274(1)(g) of the Companies Act 1956 shall be extended beyond non-payment of debt. Independent directors must be treated differently as is done in the case of nominee directors representing financial institutions. Stricter norms should be prescribed for the companies registered as brokers with SEBI. Also, greater accountability should be provided for with respect to transfers of money. Companies Act must suitably be amended to give DCA the powers of attachment of bank accounts, etc., on the same lines as SEBI. Managers/promoters should be held personally liable when found guilty of offences. Legal fees and other charges should be recovered from the officers in default.

38. Consolidated financial statements should be made mandatory for companies having subsidiaries.

39. The workload at the offices of ROCs shall be reduced by providing for a system of 'pre-certification' by company secretaries. The system should provide strict monetary and other penalties on company secretaries who certify incorrectly even by error or oversight. The Companies Act must be amended to enable the DCA to order a compliance audit on the special audit it can enforce under section 233/8 of the Company Act.

40. The auditors should, in addition to those requirements under Manufacturing and Other Companies Auditors' Report Order (MAOCARO), to report on default in repayment of debt or interest, or failure in the redemption of debentures, or payment of interest there on, or a disqualification of directors. The committee felt that MAOCARO should be revised to include these also. The government should introduce a system of 'random scrutiny' of audited accounts, to reduce the workload in ROC officers as well as to improve auditing standards. ICAI also should reconsider the limits it has set on the number of the articles that a partner can train so that young prospective accountants get a chance to train with the best in the profession. It was also suggested that the companies established and published an internal code of ethics. DCA should sponsor and financially support research or corporate governance and allied subjects with funds from IEPF.

41. The Indian audit firms have to consolidate and grow in order to complete internationally. Towards the end, ICAI should propose that the government amend the partnership act to provide for partnerships with limited liability.

NARAYANA MURTHY COMMITTEE REPORT

While SEBI adopted most of the recommendations of the Kumar Mangalam Birla Committee, it was felt that since the governance standards have been evolving, it was necessary to evaluate the adequacy of existing governance practices and further improving them. Hence, a committee was constituted under the chairmanship of Sri N.R. Narayana Murthy, Chairman, Infosys Technologies Ltd, to recommend ways of improving governance further.

The major recommendations were:

A. Mandatory

1. Audit committees will review the following information mandatorily.
   - Financial statements and draft audit report, including quarterly/half yearly financial information
   - Management discussion and analysis (MDA) of financial condition and results of operations
   - Reports relating to compliance with laws and risk management
   - Record of related party transactions

2. All audit committee members should be 'financially literate' and at least one member should have accounting or related financial management expertise.

3. If the company has followed a treatment different from the prescribed accounting standards, management should justify why such a treatment would be more representative of the reality.

4. A statement of all transactions with related parties including their bases should be placed before the audit committee for ratification/approval. And the definition of 'related party' will be as per Accounting Standard 18 issued by ICAI.

5. The board shall be informed about the risk assessment and minimization procedures. A quarterly report on risks, mitigation plans and any limitations to the risk taking capacity of the company shall be placed before the board by the management.

6. Companies raising money through IPO should disclose the use/application of funds to the audit committee on a quarterly basis. Any diversion of funds other than those stated in the documents shall be consolidated into a statement and be certified by the auditors.

7. A code of conduct for all board members and senior management be laid down and posted on the company's website. All board members and senior management personnel shall affirm compliance with the code on annual basis. A declaration by the CEO and COO to this effect shall be provided in the annual report.

8. There shall be no nominee directors. All director appointments shall be made by shareholders.

9. Compensation to NEDs may be fixed by the board and approved by the shareholders. Companies should publish their compensation philosophy and the compensation paid to the NEDs. The details of shares held by NEDs should be disclosed on an annual basis. NEDs before joining a company should disclose their holding of the company's shares to the company.

10. Employees who observe any unethical practices should have direct access to audit committee.

11. Companies have to make an annual declaration that they have not denied any personnel access to the audit committee and that they have provided protection to 'whistle-blowers'.

12. The provisions relating to the composition of the board of directors of the holding company should be made applicable to the composition of directors of subsidiary companies. At least one independent director on the BOD of parent company shall be a director on the BOD of a subsidiary company. The audit committee of the parent company shall also review the financial statements of the subsidiary company. The board of the parent company has to declare that it has reviewed the affairs of the subsidiary company also.

13. SEBI should make compulsory the disclosures in the report issued by security analysts if the company about which they write is a client of the analyst's employer or associate of the analyst's employer and also the nature of services offered to the company, if any, and also whether the analyst, or the analyst's employer, or an associate of the analyst's employer holds or held, or intends to hold and security in the company.

B. Non-mandatory

1. Companies should be encouraged to move towards a regime of unqualified financial statements.

2. Companies should train the board members in the business model of the company as well as the risk profile of the business parameters of the company, their responsibilities as directors and the best ways to discharge them.

3. Performance evaluation of NEDs should be conducted by a peer group and shall form the basis for reappointments for further term.

The full report of the Narayana Murthy Committee is given in Appendix D.

CLAUSE 49 GUIDELINES

SEBI in January 2000 considered the recommendations of the Kumar Mangalam Birla Committee to promote and raise the standard of corporate governance of listed companies. It decided to incorporate a new clause in the listing agreement between companies and stock exchanges to include the recommendation of the committee. The following guidelines were incorporated:

I The board of directors

(a) The board shall have optimum combination of executive and non-executive directors. In case the company has an executive chairman, at least half of the board shall be independent and in the case of a non-executive chairman, at least one-third of the board shall be independent.

(b) All pecuniary relationships or transactions of the non-executive directors and the company should be disclosed in the annual report.

II Audit Committee

(a) A qualified and independent committee shall be set up. The committee shall have minimum three members, all non-executive directors, with the majority being independent, and the chairman must attend the AGM to answer shareholder queries. The committee can invite executives to be present at the meetings. The CFO/finance director, the head of internal audit, and a representative of the external auditor shall be present, if required. The company secretary will act as the secretary of the committee.

(b) The committee shall meet at least thrice a year, once before the finalization of annual accounts and others in a gap of 6 months. The quorum shall be either two members or one third of the members whichever is higher with a minimum of two independent directors.

(c) The powers of the audit committee shall include
- To investigate any activity within its terms of reference
- To seek information from any employee
- To obtain outside advice
- To secure attendance of outside experts if necessary

(d) The committee's role will include
- Oversight of the company's financial reporting with adequate disclosure
- Recommending the appointment or removal of external auditor, fixation of audit fee, and approval of fees for any other services
- Discuss with management the annual financial statements before submission to the board with focus on
  - any changes in accounting policies and practice
  - qualifications in draft audit report

- ○ significant adjustments arising out of audit
- ○ the going concern assumptions
- ○ compliance with accounting standards
- ○ compliance with requirements by stock exchanges and other legal aspects
- ○ any related party transactions that may have potential conflict with the interests of the company at large
- Review of internal control systems with management, internal, and external auditors
- Review of internal audit functions including structure, staff, leadership, reporting structure, frequency of internal audit, etc.
- Discussion with internal auditors on any significant findings and follow up there on
- Review of any internal investigations by internal auditors
- Discussion and finalization of nature and scope of audit with external auditors
- Review the company's financial risk management policies
- To look into the reasons of substantial defaults in the payments to depositors, debenture holders, shareholders (non-payment of declared dividends), and creditors

III Remuneration of Directors

- The remuneration of non-executive directors shall be decided by the board.
- All details regarding remuneration shall be disclosed in the report on corporate governance in the annual report. Details like salary, benefits, bonuses, stock options, perquisites, etc., as well as details of fixed components and performance linked incentives along with performance criteria and service contracts, notice periods, severance pays and stock option details.

IV Board Procedure

- Board should meet at least four times a year with a maximum gap of 4 months between two meetings.
- No director can be a member of more than 10 committees or act as chairman of more than five committees across all companies in which one is a director. It is mandatory for every director to declare the committee positions he occupies to the company and notify the changes as and when they take place.

V Management

- In addition to the director's report, MDA is added.

  Report is added as part of the annual report. MDA should discuss
  - ○ The industry and developments.
  - ○ Opportunities and threats
  - ○ Segment-wise or product-wise performance
  - ○ Outlook
  - ○ Risks and concerns
  - ○ Internal control systems and adequacy
  - ○ Financial performance with respect to operational performance
  - ○ Material developments in HR/industrial relations including number of people employed

○ All financial and commercial transactions made by managements, where they have a personal interest that may have a potential conflict with the interests of the company at large.

VI Shareholders

- When a new director is to be appointed, the shareholders must be provided with a brief resume of the director, nature of his expertise in specific functional areas, and names of companies where the person holds directorship and memberships of committees of the board.
- Information like quarterly results and presentation to analysts on its website be forwarded to the stock exchanges who may display them on their website.
- There must be a committee (shareholders'/investors' grievance committee) to look into the grievances of the shareholders regarding transfer of shares, non-receipt of balance sheet, non-receipt of declared dividends, etc.
- The company must expedite the process of share transfers and for this it should delegate the power to either an officer, a committee, or to the registrar and transfer agents with the delegated authority attending to the transfer formalities at least once a fortnight.

VII Report on Corporate Governance

There shall be a separate section on corporate governance in the annual reports with a detailed compliance report—compliance with any mandatory requirement and the extent to which non-mandatory requirements have been adopted shall be highlighted.

VIII Compliance

- The company shall obtain a certificate of compliance with regard to corporate governance requirements from the external auditors which shall be annexed to the corporate governance report and sent to the stock exchanges along with the annual returns.

IX Schedule of implementation:

- By all entities seeking listing for the first time, at the time of listing.
- By 31 March 2001 by all entities either in group of BSE A or in S&P Nifty Index as on 1 January 2000.
- By 31 March 2002 by all entities which are listed with paid-up capital Rs 10 crores and above or net worth of Rs 25 crores or more any time in the history of the company.
- By 31 March 2003 by all entities which are listed with paid up capital of Rs 3 crores and above.
- The non-mandatory requirements shall be implemented at the discretion of the company. Disclosures regarding adoption/non-adoption of the non-mandatory requirements shall be made in the corporate governance report.

Amendments to Clause 49

1. Institutional directors will be considered as independent directors.
2. For the purpose of the number of memberships of committees, only public limited companies (listed and unlisted) shall be included and private limited companies, foreign

companies, and companies of Section 25 of the Companies Act shall be excluded. Also, only audit committee, shareholders grievance committee and remuneration committee shall be considered for this purpose.

3. Institutional directors will be considered as independent in the case of government companies also.

4. Those companies which were required to comply with the provisions in the first phase will be required to submit a quarterly compliance report to stock exchanges within 15 days from the end of quarter.

5. The date compliance by all companies with a share capital of Rs 3 crores and above or net worth of Rs 25 crores or more at any time in the history of the company was extended to 31 March 2004. The submission of the quarterly reports also will start after 15 days from the quarter ending 31 March 2004.

6. Stock exchanges shall ensure that all provisions of corporate governance have been complied with before granting any new listing.

7. Stock exchanges shall set up a cell to monitor the compliance with the provisions of corporate governance. The cell has to submit a consolidated compliance report to SEBI within 30 days of each quarter.

8. The compliance date for companies with share capital of Rs 3 crores and above or net worth of Rs 25 crores or more will be 31 March 2005. The submission of the quarterly compliance reports also will start from 15 days from 31 March 2005.

9. Those companies which apply for listing must necessarily have audit committees and investor/shareholder grievance committee before they are granted permission for listing.

10. The definition of independent director has been detailed. An independent director shall be a non-executive director (1) who apart from receiving the director's remuneration does not have any material pecuniary relationships or transactions with the company, its promoters, its directors, its senior management or its holding company, its subsidiaries and associates which may affect the independence of the director; (2) has not been executive of the company in the immediately preceding three financial years; and (3) is not a partner or executive or was not a partner or an executive during the preceding three years of any of the following: (a) statutory audit firm or the internal audit firm that is associated with the company; (b) the legal firm(s) and consulting firm(s) that have material association with the company; (c) a material supplier, or a service provider, or a customer, or a lessor, or a lessee of the company which may affect the independence of the company; and (d) a substantial shareholder of the company owning 2 per cent or more of voting shares.

11. Minimum number of board meetings shall be four with the maximum time gap of three months between any two meetings.

12. The board shall periodically review compliance reports of all laws applicable to the company, prepared by the company as well as steps taken by the company to rectify instances of non-compliance.

13. The board shall lay down a code of conduct for all board members and senior management of the company. It shall be posted on the website of the company. All board members and

senior management personnel shall affirm compliance with the code on an annual basis. The annual report of the company shall contain a declaration to this effect signed by the CEO. The senior management shall mean personnel of the company who are members of the core management team excluding the board.

14. All members of the audit committee shall be financially literate and at least one member shall have accounting or related managerial expertise.

15. The audit committee shall meet at least four times a year with not more than four months between two meetings.

16. The audit committee shall review the functioning of the whistle-blower mechanism, in case it exists.

17. The audit committee shall mandatorily review the MDA of the financial condition and results of operations.

18. At least one independent director on the board of the holding company shall be a director on the board of a material non-listed Indian subsidiary company.

19. The audit committee shall review the financial statements in general and investments made by the unlisted subsidiary company.

20. Any change in the treatment of accounting standards shall be disclosed.

21. Procedures for risk management shall be informed to the board by the management.

22. The utilization of proceeds from public issues, right issues, preferential issues, etc., shall be disclosed to the audit committee.

23. The number of shares and convertible instruments held by non-executive directors shall be disclosed.

24. Any director candidate seeking appointment to a company shall disclose their shareholding in the company before their appointment.

25. The CEO/CFO shall certify to the board that they have reviewed the financial statements and the cash flow for the year and certify them for their verity.

26. The date for ensuring compliance with the revised clause 49 was extended to 31 December 2005.

27. The maximum time gap between two board meetings was increased from three months to four months.

28. Sitting fees paid to non-executive directors as authorized by the Companies Act 1956 would not require the previous approval of shareholders.

29. If the non-executive chairman is a promoter or is related to promoters or persons occupying management positions at the board level or at one level below the board, at least one-half of the board of the company should consist of independent directors.

30. Disclosure of relationships between directors inter-se shall be made in specified documents/filings.

31. The gap between resignation/removal of an independent director and appointment of another independent director in his place shall not exceed 180 days. However, this provision would not apply in case a company fulfils the minimum requirement of independent directors on its board (one-third or one-half as the case may be) even without filling the vacancy created by such resignation/removal.

32. The minimum age for independent directors shall be 21 years.

33. The company shall ensure that the person who is being appointed as an independent director has the requisite qualifications and experience (non-mandatory).

34. A non-executive chairman may be entitled to maintain an office at the company's expense and also allowed reimbursement of expenses incurred in the performance of his duties. Independent directors may have a tenure not exceeding, in the aggregate, a period of nine years on the board of a company (non-mandatory).

35. When the promoter is a listed entity, its directors other than the independent directors, its employees, or its nominees shall be deemed to be related to it. If the promoter is an unlisted entity, its directors, its employees, or its nominees shall be deemed to be related to it.

36. The board may set up a remuneration committee to determine, on their behalf and on behalf of shareholders with agreed terms of reference, the company's remuneration policies. It would be set up with minimum three directors, all non-executive, with the chairman being an independent director (non-mandatory).

37. The chairman of the remuneration committee shall be present at the AGM to answer the queries of the shareholders (non-mandatory).

38. Company should train directors on the business model of the company, their responsibilities as director and the best ways to discharge them (non-mandatory).

39. Every individual director should be evaluated by all other member of the board (non-mandatory).

40. The company should establish a mechanism for employees to report to the management concerns about unethical behaviour, actual or suspected fraud, or violation of the code of conduct (non-mandatory).

Clause 49—A Panacea for Corporate Governance?

Despite the rigour of exercise and claims that clause 49 is comparable to the Sarbanes–Oxley Act of US, a number of issues are yet to be resolved. There are many examples. For instance, the prescription of a maximum of nine years as tenure for an independent director on the board of a company. There has been no mention of what shall be the threshold year of reference. Or SEBI might have been under the assumption that it applies to all those who had been serving nine years or more as independent directors. By and large, companies have also given it a go by. Even the supposed to be well-governed companies like Infosys state in their annual report that 'none of the independent directors on our board have served for a tenure exceeding nine years from the date when the new Clause became effective.' What date is the company referring to? For a company like Infosys, the Clause 49 regulations and subsequent amendments became effective from 31 March 2001 eventhough the guideline regarding the tenure was introduced as an amendment. The non-mandatory provision tells about 'a tenure not exceeding, in the aggregate, a period of nine years'.

Another issue that is yet to be addressed by corporates is the strict adherence to the independent director qualification criteria. The clause provides for excluding people who are/were partners of auditors, legal firms, and consulting firms from becoming independent directors, but a number of directors continue their associations and even big companies have not implemented some of these requirements. Another major question regarding the independence of directors is whether they can be considered independent on many boards belonging to the same group. There is a lack of clarity on this count.

Another issue is related to partners of audit firms of a company holding independent directorship at another company belonging to the same group. Also, it has been found that even a large number of big companies do not report the dates of audit committee meetings or conduct audit committee meetings on the same day as board meetings. Most of the companies hold board meetings to consider the quarterly results and most of the big ones complete the processes before noon and go on air with their quarterly results, raising concerns about the rigour of the audit committee processes. While some feel that 'Clause 49 is on par with global best' (Cohen 2005), lots of issues as mentioned above need to be addressed if the regulation is to be made more meaningful and purposeful.

REGULATORY OVERLAPS

Corporate governance being an area that has implications with regard to the establishment of companies, constitution of its boards, and the powers assigned to the board to act on behalf of the company and issuing securities to public and the associated paraphernalia in respect of transparency, disclosures, compliances with investor grievance redress, etc., has to take care of both company laws and capital market regulation. In many countries, including India, these two aspects are being handled by two different agencies. In India, the Department of Company Affairs (DCA) is involved in the matters relating to the incorporation while SEBI is the agency that takes care of the regulatory aspects of the capital market related issues. In the US, incorporation is a state subject while the securities laws are federal in nature. This gives rise to some kind of an overlap when it comes to corporate governance aspects. For example, in India, while clause 49 recommended one-third or one-half of the board to be independent depending on whether the chairman is part-time, non-promoter (or their relatives) or executive or promoter (or their relatives), where as Irani Committee which was entrusted with the job of reviewing the Companies Act 1956 recommended that it needs to be only one-third in all companies. While SEBI has a bigger role to play in the practices and processes of governance, the structure for governance shall be vested with DCA. Since SEBI has actually nothing to do with structure, formation, or composition of the board such aspects shall vest with DCA since all incorporation regulations are monitored and controlled by DCA. Hence, any recommendation or guideline regarding the structure part such as formation of board, independent component, committees, etc., shall come under the purview of DCA and not SEBI (Kumar 2005). This scenario of creating confusion in the minds of companies must change and regulatory bodies should work in sync to avoid such confusion.

SUMMARY

The concept of corporate governance originated as a result of gradual dispersion of ownership of corporations. The dispersion of ownership was the outcome of the very concept of joint-stock companies. As capital requirements for corporations increased, corporations increased their reliance on outside shares, resulting in substantially reduced ownership on the part of the original owners or promoters. At the beginning, the promoter had control over the physical assets even though the assets were being managed by outside professional managers. But the gradual dispersion of ownership resulted in loss of this control and a mechanism had to be evolved for the control of the assets of the corporation and the corporation itself on behalf of the now dispersed owners. Thus originated the concept of the fiduciary duty of boards to act in the best interests of the shareholders. But the whole question was whether these boards will act as fiduciaries for the owners.

Even hard-core proponents of capitalism like Adam Smith, while strongly supporting the cause of free enterprises, believed that this pursuit of individual economic goals will promote the interests of society even without any specific interest in doing it and raised concerns about how this concept of joint-stock companies will work eventhough he was highly appreciative of the innovative concept of joint-stock corporations.

The question was one of how to get the individuals who constitute the board and the board as a body act on behalf of the interests of the shareholders. While the question was very much there ever since Berle and Means wrote their seminal book *The Modern Corporation and Private Property* in 1932, it assumed more importance when there were issues of managerial excesses in 1980s and 1990s. This forced the industry, accounting and audit profession, stock exchanges, etc., to evolve certain norms and guidelines for better governance of companies.

The first of such efforts started in the UK in the form of the Cadbury Committee, which was assigned the duty of recommending guidelines regarding the financial aspects of corporate governance but exceeded its brief by looking at other aspects of corporate governance, consequent to the emergence of governance issues in the UK during the tenure of the committee. The pioneering effort in the UK by the Cadbury Committee set a trend across the globe with almost all the major countries evolving best practice codes or guidelines of some kind for better governance of corporate in their respective countries including India. While majority of the codes have been in the form of voluntary guidelines by inserting governance-related prescriptions in the listing agreements between company and the stock exchanges, where the company's shares and other securities are listed, US went ahead with the creation of a new Act by the Congress, thanks to the high-profile failures of companies like Enron, WorldCom, Tyco, etc.

Almost every country today has a code of corporate governance. Apart from the efforts of individual countries to evolve guidelines, International Finance Corporation (IFC), World bank, United Nations (UN), etc., also have taken interest in the promotion of corporate governance guidelines for the member countries to follow. By and large, regulations have been in the form of mandatory and non-mandatory requirements for the companies to follow. Most of the regulations and guidelines try to improve the governance by tampering with the structure of the board and other governance-related aspects. In India, SEBI has implemented Clause 49 as part of the listing agreement to regulate corporate governance. Even though most of the regulations are stringent, the failure of corporate as a result of poor governance continues to happen. The recent failure of Satyam Computers in India is a case in point. The company was not only covered by Clause 49 regulations in India but also the Sarbanes–Oxley Act 2002 of the US, consequent to their raising funds from the US and getting listed on NYSE. This has raised serious questions about the efficacy of the external regulations to further the cause of governance of corporates. Many experts have felt that it is not the lack of regulation that has resulted in the continuation of governance issues but rather the enforcement of them.

KEY TERMS

Anti-trust tendencies to display monopolistic practices

Bestowed given as an honour

Cataclysm violent event that causes change

Contravene go against

Diligence concentrated and steady effort

Disclosure stating the relevant details for the understanding of interested parties

Dispersed distributed

Dominant shareholder a shareholder who has significant stake compared to others

Economic system the fundamental premise or ideology on which the various aspects of the economy are developed

Equitable fair and just

Fall-out after effect

Flora and fauna plants and animals in an area

Insider trading trading in a company's shares by executives and employees who have access to key inside information

Listing agreement agreement between a company and the stock exchange where the company's shares/other securities are listed

Mandatory compulsorily to be observed

Non-mandatory desirable but not compulsory

OECD Organization for Economic Co-operation and Development

Onerous burdensome

Pre-certification certification by qualified experts before the reports are submitted

Public character how distributed is the capital among public

Qualification of accounts remarks made by auditors for certain violation of accounting standards or norms

Ramifications sub-division of something complex

Shredding destroying

Split dollar insurance policy premiums are split between two parties (usually employee and employer)

Squeal shrill cry or sound

Sustainability ability to endure for long-term into future

Transparency throw light in such a way that there can be no doubt

Unfettered without any hinder or control

Unsecured loans loans given without any collateral

Voluntary out of one's own initiative and interest

Vulnerability not protected against attack or damage

CONCEPT REVIEW QUESTIONS

1. What are the pre-requisites for a whistle-blowing mechanism to work effectively?
2. What is the rationale for investors to pay a premium for good governance?
3. While the US has gone for a specific law to regulate corporate governance, many other countries including India have established most guidelines, some of which are mandatory while others are not. Which route do you think is better?
4. What is the difference between conventional corporate reporting and GRI?
5. How do you compare Clause 49 with the Sarbanes–Oxley Act 2002?
6. How would you rate corporate governance in India after about four years of full implementation of Clause 49?
7. Do you think that the laws of incorporation and capital market regulations need better alignment for companies to have clarity about good governance?

CRITICAL THINKING QUESTIONS

1. Bill George, former chairman and CEO of Medtronic and currently director at Goldman Sachs, Novartis, etc. and professor at Harvard, wrote in his book *Authentic Leadership*: 'It is impossible to legislate integrity, stewardship, and sound governance.' Critically evaluate and comment on this statement.

PROJECT WORK

Study the extent to which Indian companies go the extra mile beyond regulation in corporate governance with NSE 50 (Nifty) companies as a sample.

REFERENCES

Bebchuk, Lucian and Jesse Fried (2004), *Pay without Performance*: *The Unfulfilled Promise of Executive Compensation*, HBS Press, Boston.

Berle, Adolf A. and Gardiner C. Means (1932), *The Modern Corporation and Private Property*, Transaction Publishers, New Jersey.

Carter, Colin B. and Jay W. Lorsch (2004), *Back to the Drawing Board*, Harvard Business School Press, Boston.

Charan, Ram (2005), *Boards that Deliver*, Jossey-Bass, San Francisco.

Cohen, Alexander F., Interactive, *Economic Times*, 3 December 2005.

Colley Jr., John L., Jaqueline L. Doyle, George W. Logan, and Wallace Stettinius (2003), *Corporate Governance*, Tata McGraw Hill, Delhi.

Dimma, William A. (2007), *Tougher Boards for Tougher Times: Corporate Governance in the Post-Enron Era*, Wiley-India, New Delhi.

D'Souza, Dolphy, 'Better Fix It or Else....', *Economic Times*, 11 November 2004.

Elash, Daniel D., 'Developing Outstanding Performance in Boards of Directors', *Effective Executive*, October 2003.

Felton, Robert F., Alec Hudnut, and Jennifer van Heeckeren (1996), 'Putting Value On Board Governance', *McKinsey Quarterly*, Number 4.

Garratt, Bob (1996), *The Fish Rots from the Head*, Profile Books, London.

Garratt, Bob (2003), *Thin on Top*, Nicholas Brealey, London.

Gupta, L.C., 'An unusual whistle-blower', *Economic Times*, 5 May 2005.

Hollender, Jeffrey and Stephen Fenichell (2004), *What Matters Most: Business, Social Responsibility and the End of the Era of Greed*, Random House Business, London.

Kumar, T.N. Satheesh, 'How Independent Are Independent Directors?' *Indian Management*, May 2005.

Mallin, Chris (2007), *Corporate Governance*, Oxford University Press, New Delhi.

Murali, D., 'From Monica Lewinsky to Sarbanes–Oxley', *Business Line*, 9 February 2006.

Smith, Adam (2003), *The Wealth of Nations*, Bantam Books, New York.

Smith, Roy C. and Ingo Walter (2006), *Governing the Modern Corporation*, Oxford University Press, New York.

Som, Lalita (2000), *Stock Market Capitalization and Corporate Governance*, Oxford University Press, New Delhi.

Srivats, K.R., 'Sarbanes-Oxley legislation: US panel looking at easing cost of compliance', *Business Line*, 8 May, 2005.

Waring, Kerrie and Chris Pierce (eds) (2005), *The Handbook of International Corporate Governance: A Definitive Guide*, Kogan Page, London.

www.soxlaw.com.

Closing Case

Independence Only on Paper

Independent directors are supposed to be the cornerstone of corporate governance. Clause 49 of SEBI insists on a major component of independent directors on boards and has also been amended to make it more stringent. Let us look at some of the issues related to the real independence of directors in the Indian scenario. The regulatory framework in force is encouraging practices which raises questions about real independence of the directors categorized as independent.

The Issue of Independence

A lot have been written about independent directors, their roles, their effectiveness and even prescriptions for their better functioning after the Satyam episode. While every expert has suggested that directors designated as independent act really independently, the very appointment of them by companies at times is disturbing.

Whole-time/Promoter Directors Getting Transformed into Independent Directors

The Annual Report of 2007–08 was the first annual report of Bajaj Auto after the much talked about demerger. The merger scheme was with the approval of the Mumbai High Court. While all the directors of the pre-demerger Bajaj Auto retained their seats on the board in the post-demerger Bajaj Auto, it was very amusing to see an interesting development. Mr D.S. Mehta, who was whole-time director for many years including 2006–07, suddenly got transformed into a non-executive, independent director. The report did not give any (even brief) bio-data of the directors. One would have expected these to be given considering that 2007–08 was the first annual report of the company in its new avatar. So only discernible investors or corporate watchers would have taken note of this change.

According to Clause 49 of the listing agreement, which deals with the corporate governance regulations for companies, an independent director 'has not been an executive of the company in the immediately preceding three financial years' along with other criteria for independence. It is true that SEBI (Clause 49) does not mention such possible corporate transformations and the consequent changes in the board structures.

Having served the company for many years as a whole-time director there might be no question about the value that Mr D.S. Mehta could add to the board. But, if that is so, the company should have retained him as an ordinary non-executive director.

While Bajaj Auto might have emerged as a newly incorporated entity post de-merger subject to the approval of the High Court and also be complying with all SEBI regulations in force today, was it 'right' from an ethical point of view? While conformance is a must, conformance exploiting the loopholes in laws and regulations will not be respected by any.

Mr Bajaj and Bajaj Auto are not alone in these kinds of happenings. Such deficiencies were observed in other companies, including the Tata Group companies. J.K. Setna, Director at Tata Motors (TELCO till 2002–03) since 1993, was designated non-executive, promoter director in the company's 2002–03 Annual Report, was designated as non-executive, independent director in the 2003–04 Annual Report (Tata Motors). He was also a member on the board of

Tata Sons (the apex Tata Company) and four other Tata companies at that time. He continued to be designated as non-executive independent director till his retirement in 2006.

Whole-time Directors of Subsidiary Company Sitting on the Board of the Parent Company Getting Transformed into Independent Directors

Deepak Satwalekar was a Director on the board of HDFC Ltd as ED and MD and left to assume the position of MD at the subsidiary HDFC Standard Life Insurance Co. Ltd in the year 2000. He continued to be a director on the board of HDFC as a non-executive director. He retired from HDFC Ltd Life on 14 November 2008, and suddenly his designation at HDFC changed to independent director. How can such sudden transformations happen? Can he be considered independent in the real sense?

Independent Director on Many Group Companies

SEBI modified Clause 49 in April 2008 to make qualification criteria for independent directors more stringent. While SEBI's action removed certain anomalies, a lot more needs to be addressed to make the role of independent directors (IDs) more meaningful. The issue of independence gets complicated by the fact that a large number of major companies are owned by the same industrial houses like Tatas, Birlas (AVB Group), Reliance, etc. Most of the issues arise on the question of 'real' independence of the directors designated as independent by many of these companies. The basic tenet of good corporate governance is that independent, non-executive directors are appointed to provide a check-and-balance mechanism on the executive and other promoter, non-executive directors. But, if independence itself is in question, the very purpose of having IDs is defeated. An analysis of the practices of some of the highly rated and high profile companies (some of which are even recipients of awards for excellence in corporate governance) will reveal that the current practices leave much to be desired, forcing us to conclude that the scenario in other companies could be even worse. For example, Mr Nusli Wadia has been indicated as an Independent, non-executive director on the boards of Tata Steel, Tata Motors, and Tata Chemicals. While many may argue that he was nominated by the promoter group (readers may remember the reports that appeared in the business press about his closeness to JRD and the role he played on a few occasions of crises within the group), the question facing us actually is how could he be an independent director on the boards of three companies belonging to the same group. The moment he becomes director of one company of the group, his independence in the *real* sense is lost and cannot be considered for positions as independent director within the group. Similar is the case of Mr S.M. Palia who sits on the boards of Tata Steel and Tata Motors. That Mr Tata (and Mr S.M. Palia) sit on the board of Bombay Dyeing, a Wadia Group Company, of which Mr Wadia is the chairman, makes it an even interlocking directorship situation.

Independent Directors with Conflicts of Interest

Prof. Krishna Palepu was a director of Satyam Computers. For his services as a non-executive director (please note that he was not an independent director according to 2007–08 Annual Report) he was drawing a remuneration of Rs 0.124 million. He was also drawing a remuneration of about Rs 7.951 million for offering professional services to the company. This was very much disclosed in the annual report of Satyam. But everybody who mattered in corporate governance criticized it as conflicts of interest. But while they were eloquent on Mr Krishna Palepu, they seem to be silent on many other issues of conflicts of interest that exist in some of the big companies in India. Reliance Industries has Mr M. L. Bhakta classified as independent, non-executive director on the RIL board. Mr Bhakta has been a director of Reliance Industries since 1977 (the year in which the company went public and hence might have, in all probability, joined the board as a promoter nominee). He is a senior partner of the firm M/s. Kanga & Company, which functions as the Solicitors and Advocates for the company. His firm was paid professional fees (Rs 86.09 lakhs in 2007–08) for the services rendered to the company. How can he, whose firm offers legal advisory services for a fee to the company be considered *really* independent? Mr R.K. Kulkarni, non-executive, independent director at Mahindra & Mahindra Ltd is a partner of Khaitan & Co, Advocates and Solicitors for the company. (Khaitan & Co received Rs 85.63 lakhs from the company in 2007–08.) Similarly, Shailesh Haribhakti, Partner of Haribhakti & Company, used to sit on the board of IPCL while his firm was an auditor for Reliance Energy (before the brothers Mukesh and Anil split). Another instance was that of Y. H. Malegam, who while being a partner of S.B. Billimoria & Co, was also an auditor for a number of companies in the Tata Group. He also used to sit on the board of Tata Tea with which his firm was not associated as an auditor. Mr Malegam, being auditor of a number of companies in the Tata Group, was having an association with the group enjoying financial compensation for the services rendered by the firm in which he was a partner. Could he claim to be independent in the real sense?

Long Tenures of Independent Directors

Another area of concern is the tenure served by independent directors. A very large number of directors have been with the companies for long periods. Mr Wadia has been on the boards of Tata Steel, Tata Motors, and Tata Chemicals for 29, 10, and 27 years, respectively. Mr Bhakta has been on the Reliance Industries board for more than 31 years. Narayana Murthy committee recommended a maximum of nine years. But Mr Murthy has not implemented his committee's recommendation (of course, non-mandatory by SEBI) in his own company (Deepak Satwalekar and Marti Subrahmanyam have been on Infosys board since October 1997 and April 1998, respectively—an example of conformance rather than performance). The annual report of Infosys states: 'Independent director may have a tenure not exceeding, in aggregate, a period of nine years on our board. None of the independent directors on our board have served a tenure exceeding 9 years from the date when the new Clause 49 became effective' (Infosys Annual Report 2008–09). Omkar Goswami recently wrote with passion about making this recommendation mandatory but is seeking re-election at Dr Reddy's which he joined in October 2000 (of course, he says the year count should start from 2004!)

Would not such long tenures give rise to a situation where the independent directors act more like insiders? As Colin Carter and Jay Lorsch (2004) say in their book *Back to the Drawing Board*, 'Long service helps a director to understand the company better, but emotional attachment means she cannot be truly independent.' It might lead to self-defeating harmony in the boardroom than encouraging a questioning culture and facing the truth and reality.

Source: 'Corporate Governance: A Reality Check after 7 Years of Sarbanes–Oxley and nearly 4 Years of Clause 49', Paper Presented by T.N. Satheesh Kumar at the National Conference on Corporate Governance at Hyderabad, organized by Institute of Directors, New Delhi and World Council of Corporate Governance, London, 21/22 August 2009.

Discussion Questions

1. Apparently every company targets conformance than performance when it comes to corporate governance. Critically examine this in the context of the case.
2. Conflicts of interest are very difficult to remove altogether. Can you suggest some processes and procedures to overcome this problem?
3. Judiciary seems not to consider the issues related to corporate governance when it gives assent to the restructuring of corporate. Comment.

ANNEXURE 3.1   THE CADBURY REPORT

Summary of Recommendations

Compliance with the code of best practice

1. The boards of all listed companies registered in the UK should comply with the Code of Best Practice set out on pages 58 to 60. As many other companies as possible should aim at meeting its requirements (paragraph 3.1).
2. Listed companies reporting in respect of years ending after 30 June 1993 should make a statement about their compliance with the Code in the report and accounts and give reasons for any areas of non-compliance (paragraph 3.7) .
3. Companies' statements of compliance should be reviewed by the auditors before publication. The review should cover only those parts of the compliance statement which relate to provisions of the Code where compliance can be objectively verified. The Auditing Practices Board should consider guidance for auditors accordingly (paragraph 3.9).
4. All parties concerned with corporate governance should use their influence to encourage compliance with the Code (paragraph 3.14). Institutional shareholders in particular, with the backing of the Institutional Shareholders' Committee, should use their influence as owners to ensure that the companies in which they have invested comply with the Code (paragraph 6.16).

Keeping the code up to date

5. The Committee's sponsors, convened by the Financial Reporting Council, should appoint a new Committee by the end of June 1995 to examine how far compliance with the Code has progressed, how far our other recommendations have been implemented, and whether the Code needs updating. Our sponsors should also determine whether the sponsorship of the new Committee should be broadened and whether wider matters of corporate governance should be included in its brief. In the mean time the present Committee will remain responsible for reviewing the implementation of its proposals (paragraph 3.12).

Directors' service contracts

6. The Companies Act should be amended to come in line with the requirement of the Code that directors' service contracts should not exceed three years without shareholders' approval (paragraph 4.41).

Interim reporting

7. Companies should expand their interim reports to include balance sheet information. The London Stock Exchange should consider amending the continuing obligations accordingly. There should not be a requirement for a full audit, but interim reports should be reviewed by the auditors and the Auditing Practices Board should develop appropriate guidance. The Accounting Standards Board in conjunction with the London Stock Exchange should clarify the accounting rules which companies should follow in preparing interim reports. The inclusion of cash flow information should be considered by the Committee's successor body (paragraph 4.56).

Enhancing the perceived objectivity of the audit

8. Fees paid to audit firms for non-audit work should be fully disclosed. The essential principle is that disclosure should enable the relative significance of the company's audit and non-audit fees to the audit firm to be assessed, both in a UK context and, where appropriate, a worldwide context. The 1991 Regulations under the Companies Act should be reviewed and amended as necessary (paragraph 5.1 I).
9. The accountancy profession should draw up guidelines on the rotation of audit partners (paragraph 5.12).

Enhancing the effectiveness of the audit

10. Directors should report on the effectiveness of their system of internal control, and the auditors should report on their statement. The accountancy profession together with representatives of preparers of accounts should draw up criteria for assessing effective systems of internal control and guidance for companies and auditors (paragraphs 4.32 and 5.16).
11. Directors should state in the report and accounts that the business is a going concern, with supporting assumptions or qualifications as necessary, and the auditors should report on this statement. The accountancy profession together with representatives of preparers of accounts should develop guidance for companies and auditors (paragraph 5.22).
12. The question of legislation to back the recommendations on additional reports on internal control systems and going concern should be decided in the light of experience (paragraphs 5. I7 and 5.22).
13. The government should consider introducing legislation to extend to the auditors of all companies the statutory protection already available to auditors in the regulated sector (banks, building societies, insurance, and investment business) so that they can report reasonable suspicion of fraud freely to the appropriate investigatory authorities (paragraph 5.28).
14. The accountancy profession together with the legal profession and representatives of preparers of accounts should consider further the question of illegal acts other than fraud (paragraph 5.30).
15. The accounting profession should continue its efforts to improve its standards and procedures so as to strengthen the standing and independence of auditors (paragraph 5.36).

Voting by institutional investors

16. Institutional investors should disclose their policies on the use of their voting rights (paragraph 6.12).

Endorsement of work by others

17. The Committee gives its full support to the objectives of the Financial Reporting Council and the Accounting Standards Board. It welcomes the action by the Financial Reporting Review Panel over companies whose accounts fall below accepted reporting standards (paragraphs 4.52 and 5.8).

18. The Committee supports the initiative of the Auditing Practices Board on the development of an expanded audit report. It also gives its full support to the lead which it is taking on the development of auditing practice generally (paragraphs 5.14 and 5.15).

19. The Committee welcomes the statement by the Institutional Shareholders' Committee on the Responsibilities of Institutional Shareholders in the UK (paragraph 6.1 I).

Issues for the Committee's successor body

20. Issues which the Committee has identified that its successor body may wish to review or consider in greater depth include: the application of the Code to smaller listed companies (paragraph 3. IS); directors' training (paragraph 4.20); the rules for disclosure of directors' remuneration, and the role which shareholders could play (paragraph 4.46); a requirement for inclusion of cash flow information in interim reports (paragraph 4.56); and the procedures for putting forward resolutions at general meetings (paragraph 6.4). The Committee and its successor will also keep watch on developments regarding the nature and extent of auditors' liability (paragraph 5.35).

ANNEXURE 3.2   THE COMBINED CODE

PRINCIPLES OF GOOD GOVERNANCE AND CODE OF BEST PRACTICE

Derived by the Committee on Corporate Governance from the Committee's Final Report and from the Cadbury and Greenbury Reports

Preamble

1. In the Committee's final report we said that in response to many requests, we intended to produce a set of principles and code which embraced Cadbury, Greenbury and the committee's own work. This Combined Code fulfils that undertaking.

2. The Combined Code is now issued in final form, and includes a number of changes made by the London Stock Exchange, with the Committee's agreement, following the consultation undertaken by the London Stock Exchange on the committee's original draft.

3. The Combined Code contains both principles and detailed Code provisions. We understand that it is the intention of the London Stock Exchange to introduce a requirement on listed companies to make a disclosure statement in two parts.

4. In the first part of the statement, the company will be required to report on how it applies the principles in the Combined Code. We make clear in our report that we do not prescribe the form or content of this part of the statement, the intention being that companies should have a free hand to explain their governance policies in the light of the principles, including any special circumstances applying to them which have led to a particular approach. It must be for shareholders and others to evaluate this part of the company's statement.

5. In the second part of the statement the company will be required either to confirm that it complies with the Code provisions or—where it does not—provide an explanation. Again, it must be for shareholders and others to evaluate such explanations.

6. In our report we make clear that companies should be ready to explain their governance policies, including any circumstances justifying departure from best practice; and that those concerned with the evaluation of governance should do so with common sense, and with due regard to companies' individual circumstances.

7. We also make clear in our report that it is still too soon to assess definitively the results of the Cadbury and more especially the Greenbury codes. We see this Combined Code as a consolidation of the work of the three committees, not as a new departure. We have therefore retained the substance of the two earlier codes except in those few cases where we take a different view from our predecessors. We should in particular like to make clear, in relation to the detailed provisions in the Listing Rules on directors' remuneration, that we envisage no change except where we take a different view from the Greenbury committee. With two exceptions, relating to the status of the remuneration committee, and the compensation payable to an executive director on loss of office, these changes are minor.

8. Section 1 of the Combined Code contains the corporate governance principles and code provisions applicable to all listed companies incorporated in the United Kingdom. These would be covered by the statement referred to in paragraphs 3–5 above, which will be required by the Listing Rules. Section 2 contains principles and code provisions applicable to institutional shareholders with regard to their voting, dialogue with companies and evaluation of a company's governance arrangements. These are not matters which are appropriate for the Listing Rules to include within the disclosure requirement. Nevertheless we regard Section 2 of this Combined Code as an integral part of our recommendations; we commend it to the organizations representing institutional shareholders and we hope that at least the major institutions will voluntarily disclose to their clients and the public the extent to which they are able to give effect to these provisions.

9. We have not included in the Combined Code principle D.IV in Chapter 2 of our final report, which reads as follows:

'External Auditors. The external auditors should independently report to shareholders in accordance with statutory and professional requirements and independently assure the board on the discharge of its responsibilities under D.I and D.II above in accordance with professional guidance.' We say in paragraph 6.7 of the report that we recommend neither any additional prescribed requirements nor the removal of any existing requirements for auditors in relation to governance or publicly reported information, some of which derive from the Listing Rules. This recommendation is accepted by the London Stock Exchange. But the existing requirements for auditors will be kept under review, as a matter of course, by the responsible organizations. Committee on Corporate Governance June 1998.

PRINCIPLES OF GOOD GOVERNANCE

Section 1   Companies

A. Directors

The Board

1. Every listed company should be headed by an effective board which should lead and control the company.

Chairman and CEO

2. There are two key tasks at the top of every public company—the running of the board and the executive responsibility for the running of the company's business. There should be a clear division of responsibilities at the head of the company which will ensure a balance of power and authority, such that no one individual has unfettered powers of decision.

Board Balance

3. The board should include a balance of executive and non-executive directors (including independent non-executives) such that no individual or small group of individuals can dominate the board's decision taking.

Supply of Information

4. The board should be supplied in a timely manner with information in a form and of a quality appropriate to enable it to discharge its duties.

Appointments to the Board

5. There should be a formal and transparent procedure for the appointment of new directors to the board.

Re-election

6. All directors should be required to submit themselves for re-election at regular intervals and at least every three years.

B. Directors' Remuneration

The Level and Make-up of Remuneration

1. Levels of remuneration should be sufficient to attract and retain the directors needed to run the company successfully, but companies should avoid paying more than what is necessary for this purpose. A proportion of executive directors' remuneration should be structured so as to link rewards to corporate and individual performance.

Procedure

2. Companies should establish a formal and transparent procedure for developing policy on executive remuneration and for fixing the remuneration packages of individual directors. No director should be involved in deciding his or her own remuneration.

Disclosure

3. The company's annual report should contain a statement of remuneration policy and details of the remuneration of each director.

C. Relations with Shareholders

Dialogue with Institutional Shareholders

1. Companies should be ready, where practicable, to enter into a dialogue with institutional shareholders based on the mutual understanding of objectives.

Constructive Use of the AGM

2. Boards should use the Annual General Meeting (AGM) to communicate with private investors and encourage their participation.

D. Accountability and Audit

Financial Reporting

1. The board should present a balanced and understandable assessment of the company's position and prospects.

Internal Control

2. The board should maintain a sound system of internal control to safeguard shareholders' investment and the company's assets.

Audit Committee and Auditors

3. The board should establish formal and transparent arrangements for considering how they should apply the financial reporting and internal control principles and for maintaining an appropriate relationship with the company's auditors.

Section 2   Institutional Shareholders

E. Institutional Investors

Shareholder Voting

1. Institutional shareholders have a responsibility to make considered use of their votes.

Dialogue with Companies

2. Institutional shareholders should be ready, where practicable, to enter into a dialogue with companies based on the mutual understanding of objectives.

Evaluation of Governance Disclosures

3. When evaluating companies' governance arrangements, particularly those relating to board structure and composition, institutional investors should give due weight to all relevant factors drawn to their attention.

CODE OF BEST PRACTICE

Section 1   Companies

A. Directors

A.1 The Board

Principle   Every listed company should be headed by an effective board which should lead and control the company.

Code Provisions

A.1.1   The board should meet regularly.

A.1.2   The board should have a formal schedule of matters specifically reserved to it for decision.

A.1.3   There should be a procedure agreed by the board for directors in the furtherance of their duties to take independent professional advice if necessary, at the company's expense.

A.1.4   All directors should have access to the advice and services of the company secretary, who is responsible to the board for ensuring that board procedures are followed and that applicable rules and regulations are complied with. Any question of the removal of the company secretary should be a matter for the board as a whole.

A.1.5   All directors should bring an independent judgement to bear on issues of strategy, performance, resources, including key appointments, and standards of conduct.

A.1.6   Every director should receive appropriate training on the first occasion that he or she is appointed to the board of a listed company, and subsequently as necessary.

A.2 Chairman and CEO

Principle   There are two key tasks at the top of every public company—the running of the board and the executive responsibility for the running of the company's business.

There should be a clear division of responsibilities at the head of the company which will ensure a balance of power and authority, such that no one individual has unfettered powers of decision.

Code Provision

A.2.1   A decision to combine the posts of chairman and chief executive officer in one person should be publicly justified. Whether the posts are held by different people or by the same person, there should be a strong and independent non-executive element on the board, with a recognized senior member other than the chairman to whom concerns can be conveyed. The chairman, chief executive and senior independent director should be identified in the annual report.

A.3 Board Balance

Principle   The board should include a balance of executive and non-executive directors (including independent non-executives) such that no individual or small group of individuals can dominate the board's decision taking.

Code Provisions

A.3.1   The board should include non-executive directors of sufficient calibre and number for their views to carry significant weight in the board's decisions. Non-executive directors should comprise not less than one-third of the board.

A.3.2   The majority of non-executive directors should be independent of management and free from any business or other relationship which could materially interfere with the exercise of their independent judgement. Non-executive directors considered by the board to be independent in this sense should be identified in the annual report.

A.4 Supply of Information

Principle   The board should be supplied in a timely manner with information in a form and of a quality appropriate to enable it to discharge its duties.

Code Provision

A.4.1   Management has an obligation to provide the board with appropriate and timely information, but information volunteered by management is unlikely to be enough in all circumstances and directors should make further enquiries where necessary. The chairman should ensure that all directors are properly briefed on issues arising at board meetings.

A.5 Appointments to the Board

Principle   There should be a formal and transparent procedure for the appointment of new directors to the board.

Code Provision

A.5.1   Unless the board is small, a nomination committee should be established to make recommendations to the board on all new board appointments. A majority of the members of this committee should be non-executive directors, and the chairman should be either the chairman of the board or a non-executive director. The chairman and members of the nomination committee should be identified in the annual report.

A.6 Re-election

Principle   All directors should be required to submit themselves for re-election at regular intervals and at least every three years.

Code Provisions

A.6.1   Non-executive directors should be appointed for specified terms subject to re-election and to Companies Act provisions relating to the removal of a director, and reappointment should not be automatic.

A.6.2   All directors should be subject to election by shareholders at the first opportunity after their appointment, and to re-election thereafter at intervals of no more than 3 years. The names of directors submitted for election or re-election should be accompanied by sufficient biographical details to enable shareholders to take an informed decision on their election.

B. Directors' Remuneration

B.1 The Level and Make-up of Remuneration

Principle   Levels of remuneration should be sufficient to attract and retain the directors needed to run the company successfully, but companies should avoid paying more than what is necessary for this purpose. A proportion of executive directors' remuneration should be structured so as to link rewards to corporate and individual performance.

Code Provisions
Remuneration policy

B.1.1   The remuneration committee should provide the packages needed to attract, retain and motivate executive directors of the quality required but should avoid paying more than what is necessary for this purpose.

B.1.2   Remuneration committees should judge where to position their company relative to other companies. They should be aware what comparable companies are paying and should take account of relative performance. But they should use such comparisons with caution, in view of the risk that they can result in an upward ratchet of remuneration levels with no corresponding improvement in performance.

B.1.3   Remuneration committees should be sensitive to the wider scene, including pay and employment conditions elsewhere in the group, especially when determining annual salary increases.

B.1.4   The performance-related elements of remuneration should form a significant proportion of the total remuneration package of executive directors and should be designed to align their interests with those of shareholders and to give these directors keen incentives to perform at the highest levels.

B.1.5   Executive share options should not be offered at a discount save as permitted by paragraphs 13.30 and 13.31 of the Listing Rules.

B.1.6   In designing schemes of performance related remuneration, remuneration committees should follow the provisions in Schedule A to this code.

Service Contracts and Compensation

B.1.7   There is a strong case for setting notice or contract periods at, or reducing them to, one year or less. Boards should set this as an objective; but they should recognize that it may not be possible to achieve it immediately.

B.1.8   If it is necessary to offer longer notice or contract periods to new directors recruited from outside, such periods should reduce after the initial period.

B.1.9   Remuneration committees should consider what compensation commitments (including pension contributions) their directors' contracts of service, if any, would entail in the event of early termination. They should in particular consider the advantages of providing explicitly in the initial contract for such compensation commitments except in the case of removal for misconduct.

B.1.10 Where the initial contract does not explicitly provide for compensation commitments, remuneration committees should, within legal constraints, tailor their approach in individual early termination cases to the wide variety of circumstances. The broad aim should be to avoid rewarding poor performance while dealing fairly with cases where departure is not due to poor performance and to take a robust line on reducing compensation to reflect departing directors' obligations to mitigate loss.

B.2 Procedure

Principle   Companies should establish a formal and transparent procedure for developing policy on executive remuneration and for fixing the remuneration packages of individual directors. No director should be involved in deciding his or her own remuneration.

Code Provisions

B.2.1   To avoid potential conflicts of interest, boards of directors should set up remuneration committees of independent non-executive directors to make recommendations to the board, within agreed terms of reference, on the company's framework of executive remuneration and its cost; and to determine on their behalf specific remuneration packages for each of the executive directors, including pension rights and any compensation payments.

B.2.2   Remuneration committees should consist exclusively of non-executive directors who are independent of management and free from any business or other relationship which could materially interfere with the exercise of their independent judgement.

B.2.3   The members of the remuneration committee should be listed each year in the board's remuneration report to shareholders (B.3.1 below).

B.2.4   The board itself or, where required by the Articles of Association, the shareholders should determine the remuneration of the non-executive directors, including members of the remuneration committee, within the limits set in the Articles of Association. Where permitted by the Articles, the board may however delegate this responsibility to a small sub-committee, which might include the chief executive officer.

B.2.5   Remuneration committees should consult the chairman and/or chief executive officer about their proposals relating to the remuneration of other executive directors and have access to professional advice inside and outside the company.

B.2.6   The chairman of the board should ensure that the company maintains contact as required with its principal shareholders about remuneration in the same way as for other matters.

B.3 Disclosure

Principle   The company's annual report should contain a statement of remuneration policy and details of the remuneration of each director.

Code Provisions

B.3.1   The board should report to the shareholders each year on remuneration. The report should form part of, or be annexed to, the company's annual report and accounts. It should be the main vehicle through which the company reports to shareholders on directors' remuneration.

B.3.2   The report should set out the company's policy on executive directors' remuneration. It should draw attention to factors specific to the company.

B.3.3   In preparing the remuneration report, the board should follow the provisions in Schedule B to this code.

B.3.4   Shareholders should be invited specifically to approve all new long-term incentive schemes (as defined in the Listing Rules) save in the circumstances permitted by paragraph 13.13A of the Listing Rules.

B.3.5   The board's annual remuneration report to shareholders need not be a standard item of agenda for AGMs. But the board should consider each year whether the circumstances are such that the AGM should be invited to approve the policy set out in the report and should minute their conclusions.

C. Relations with Shareholders

C.1 Dialogue with Institutional Shareholders

Principle   Companies should be ready, where practicable, to enter into a dialogue with institutional shareholders based on the mutual understanding of objectives.

C.2 Constructive Use of the AGM

Principle   Boards should use the AGM to communicate with private investors and encourage their participation.

Code Provisions

C.2.1   Companies should count all proxy votes and, except where a poll is called, should indicate the level of proxies lodged on each resolution, and the balance for and against the resolution, after it has been dealt with on a show of hands.

C.2.2   Companies should propose a separate resolution at the AGM on each substantially separate issue, and should in particular propose a resolution at the AGM relating to the report and accounts.

C.2.3   The chairman of the board should arrange for the chairmen of the audit, remuneration, and nomination committees to be available to answer questions at the AGM.

C.2.4   Companies should arrange for the Notice of the AGM and related papers to be sent to shareholders at least 20 working days before the meeting.

D. Accountability and Audit

D.1 Financial Reporting

Principle   The board should present a balanced and understandable assessment of the company's position and prospects.

Code Provisions

D.1.1   The directors should explain their responsibility for preparing the accounts, and there should be a statement by the auditors about their reporting responsibilities.

D.1.2   The board's responsibility to present a balanced and understandable assessment extends to interim and other price-sensitive public reports and reports to regulators as well as to information required to be presented by statutory requirements.

D.1.3   The directors should report that the business is a going concern, with supporting assumptions or qualifications as necessary.

D.2 Internal Control

Principle   The board should maintain a sound system of internal control to safeguard shareholders' investment and the company's assets.

Code Provisions

D.2.1   The directors should, at least annually, conduct a review of the effectiveness of the group's system of internal control and should report to shareholders that they have done so. The review should cover all controls, including financial, operational and compliance controls, and risk management.

D.2.2   Companies which do not have an internal audit function should from time to time review the need for one.

D.3 Audit Committee and Auditors

Principle   The board should establish formal and transparent arrangements for considering how they should apply the financial reporting and internal control principles and for maintaining an appropriate relationship with the company's auditors.

Code Provisions

D.3.1   The board should establish an audit committee of at least three directors, all non-executive, with written terms of reference which deal clearly with its authority and duties. The members of the committee, a majority of whom should be independent non-executive directors, should be named in the report and accounts.

D.3.2   The duties of the audit committee should include keeping under review the scope and results of the audit and its cost effectiveness and the independence and objectivity of the auditors. Where the auditors also supply a substantial volume of non-audit services to the company, the committee should keep the nature and extent of such services under review, seeking to balance the maintenance of objectivity and value for money.

Section 2   Institutional Shareholders

E. Institutional Investors

E.1 Shareholder Voting

Principle   Institutional shareholders have a responsibility to make considered use of their votes.

Code Provisions

E.1.1   Institutional shareholders should endeavour to eliminate unnecessary variations in the criteria each of which applies to the corporate governance arrangements and performance of the companies in which they invest.

E.1.2   Institutional shareholders should, on request, make available to their clients information on the proportion of resolutions on which votes were cast and non-discretionary proxies lodged.

E.1.3   Institutional shareholders should take steps to ensure that their voting intentions are being translated into practice.

E.2 Dialogue with Companies

Principle   Institutional shareholders should be ready, where practicable, to enter into a dialogue with companies based on the mutual understanding of objectives.

E.3 Evaluation of Governance Disclosures

Principle   When evaluating companies' governance arrangements, particularly those relating to board structure and composition, institutional investors should give due weight to all relevant factors drawn to their attention.

Schedule A: Provisions on the Design of Performance Related Remuneration

1. Remuneration committees should consider whether the directors should be eligible for annual bonuses. If so, performance conditions should be relevant, stretching and designed to enhance the business. Upper limits should always be considered. There may be a case for part payment in shares to be held for a significant period.

2. Remuneration committees should consider whether the directors should be eligible for benefits under long-term incentive schemes. Traditional share option schemes should be weighed against other kinds of long-term incentive scheme. In normal circumstances, shares granted or other forms of deferred remuneration should not vest, and options should not be exercisable, in under 3 years. Directors should be encouraged to hold their shares for a further period after vesting or exercise, subject to the need to finance any costs of acquisition and associated tax liability.

3. Any new long-term incentive schemes which are proposed should be approved by shareholders and should preferably replace existing schemes or at least form part of a well considered overall plan, incorporating existing schemes. The total rewards potentially available should not be excessive.

4. Payouts or grants under all incentive schemes, including new grants under existing share option schemes, should be subject to challenging performance criteria reflecting the company's objectives. Consideration should be given to criteria which reflect the company's performance relative to a group of comparator companies in some key variables such as total shareholder return.

5. Grants under executive share option and other long-term incentive schemes should normally be phased rather than awarded in one large block.

6. Remuneration committees should consider the pension consequences and associated costs to the company of basic salary increases and other changes in remuneration, especially for directors close to retirement.

7. In general, neither annual bonuses nor benefits in kind should be pensionable.

Schedule B: Provisions on what should be Included in the Remuneration Report

1. The report should include full details of all elements in the remuneration package of each individual director by name, such as basic salary, benefits in kind, annual bonuses and long term incentive schemes including share options.

2. Information on share options, including Save As You Earn (SAYE) options, should be given for each director in accordance with the recommendations of the Accounting Standards Board's Urgent Issues Task Force Abstract 10 and its successors.

3. If grants under executive share option or other long-term incentive schemes are awarded in one large block rather than phased, the report should explain and justify.

4. Also included in the report should be pension entitlements earned by each individual director during the year, disclosed on one of the alternative bases recommended by the Faculty of Actuaries and the Institute of Actuaries and included in the UK Listing Authority's Listing Rules. Companies may wish to make clear that the transfer value represents a liability of the company, not a sum paid or due to the individual.

5. If annual bonuses or benefits in kind are pensionable the report should explain and justify.

6. The amounts received by, and commitments made to, each director under 1, 2, and 4 above should be subject to audit.

7. Any service contracts which provide for, or imply, notice periods in excess of one year (or any provisions for predetermined compensation on termination which exceed one year's salary and benefits) should be disclosed and the reasons for the longer notice periods explained.

Bibliography

1. Copies of the following Reports can be obtained from Gee Publishing, 0345-573 113.
   • Report of the Committee on the Financial Aspects of Corporate Governance: The Code of Best Practice (Cadbury Code)—1 December 1992
   • Report of the Committee on the Financial Aspects of Corporate Governance: Compliance with the Code of Best Practice—24 May 1995
   • Directors' Remuneration: Report of a Study Group chaired by Sir Richard Greenbury (Greenbury Committee report)—17 July 1995
   • Committee on Corporate Governance: Final Report (Hampel Committee report)—28 January 1998

2. Copies of the following Guidance documents can be obtained from the Institute of Chartered Accountants in England and Wales, tel: 020 7920 8100 extn 8487.
   • Going Concern and Financial Reporting: Guidance for Directors of Listed Companies registered in the UK—November 1994
   • Internal Control and Financial Reporting: Guidance for Directors of Listed Companies registered in the UK—December 1994

3. Copies of the following Guidance Note can be obtained from the Institute of Actuaries, tel: 020 7632 2100.
   • Faculty and Institute of Actuaries Guidance Note GN11: Retirement Benefit Schemes, Transfer Values—updated March 1998

4. Copies of the following bulletins can be obtained from Accountancy Books, tel: 01908-248 000
   • APB bulletins (1995/1 and 1996/3): Disclosures Relating to Corporate Governance

5. Copies of the following document can be obtained from the DTI, tel: 020 7215 1994
   • Developing a Winning Partnership: How companies and institutional investors are working together (the Myners recommendations) —updated September 1996

6. Copies of the following Statements can be obtained from the ABI, tel: 020 7600 3333
   • Institutional Shareholders' Committee: The Role and Duties of Directors—A Statement of Best Practice
   • Institutional Shareholders' Committee: The Responsibilities of Institutional Investors—A Statement of Best Practice

7. Association of British Insurers: produce a range of corporate governance related publications, tel: 020 7600 3333

8. National Association of Pension Funds: produce a range of corporate governance related publications, tel: 020 7730 0585

9. The Listing Rules—copies of these rules can be obtained from the Financial Services Authority (Sales and Distribution), tel: 020 7676 3298, fax: 020 7676 9728.

Source: www.fsa.gov.uk/Pubs/ukla/lr_comcode.pdf.

ANNEXURE 3.3   ICGN STATEMENT OF PRINCIPLES

INTERNATIONAL CORPORATE GOVERNANCE NETWORK

Statement on Global Corporate Governance Principles

Adopted on 9 July, 1999 at the Annual Conference in Frankfurt

The International Corporate Governance Network (ICGN), founded in 1995 at the instigation of major institutional investors, represents investors, companies, financial intermediaries, academics, and other parties interested in the development of global corporate governance practices. Its objective is to facilitate international dialogue on the issues concerned. Through this process, the ICGN holds, companies can compete more effectively and economies can best prosper. The organization's charter empowers it to adopt guidelines when it feels they can contribute to achieving this objective.

Statement on the OECD Principles

In May 1999 ministers representing the 29 governments which comprise the OECD voted unanimously to endorse the *OECD Principles of Corporate Governance*. These principles were negotiated over the course of a year in consultation with key players in the market, including the ICGN. They constitute the chief response by governments to the G-7 Summit Leaders' recognition of corporate governance as an important pillar in the architecture of the twenty-first century global economy. The Principles were welcomed by the G7 leaders at the Cologne summit in June 1999 and are likely to act as signposts for activity in this area by the International Monetary Fund, the World Bank, the United Nations, and other international organizations.

The ICGN applauds the OECD Principles as a declaration of minimum acceptable standards for companies and investors around the world. Much of the document reflects perspectives promoted by ICGN representatives serving on the OECD's Ad-Hoc Task Force on Corporate Governance, relying on the draft principles under discussion at the ICGN. The ICGN welcomes the OECD Principles as a remarkable convergence on corporate governance common ground among diverse interests, practices, and cultures.

The ICGN affirms—with the OECD Principles—that along with traditional financial criteria, the governance profile of a corporation is now an essential factor that investors take into consideration when deciding how to allocate their investment capital. The Principles highlight elements that ICGN investing members already take into account when making asset allocation and investment decisions.

While the ICGN considers the OECD Principles the necessary bedrock of good corporate governance, it holds that amplifications are required to give them sufficient force. In particular, the ICGN believes that companies around the world deserve clear and concrete guidance on how the OECD Principles can best be implemented. Practical guidance can help boards meet real-world expectations so that they may operate most efficiently and, in particular, compete for scarce investment capital effectively. The ICGN contends that if investors and managers succeed in establishing productive communication on issues, they will have enhanced prospects for economic prosperity, fuller employment, better wages, and greater shareholder wealth.

The ICGN therefore advocates that companies adopt the OECD Principles as amplified in the attached statements. First, to offer more concise guidance, the ICGN distills the most significant points in its statement on the OECD Principles into a short-form roster of corporate governance tenets—a 'Working Kit'—that reflects the viewpoints of ICGN members. Then the ICGN statement amplifying the OECD Principles tracks that document's format, underscoring or interpreting as appropriate.

It is the ICGN's view that it is in companies' best interests to adhere to these recommendations even in the absence of any domestic legal requirements for their implementation.

THE INTERNATIONAL CORPORATE GOVERNANCE NETWORK

ICGN Approach to the OECD Principles:

A 'Working Kit' Statement of Corporate Governance Criteria

1. Corporate Objective

The overriding objective of the corporation should be to optimize over time the returns to its shareholders. Where other considerations affect this objective, they should be clearly stated and disclosed. To achieve this objective, the corporation should endeavor to ensure the long-term viability of its business, and to manage effectively its relationships with stakeholders.

2. Communications and Reporting

Corporations should disclose accurate, adequate, and timely information, in particular meeting market guidelines where they exist, so as to allow investors to make informed decisions about the acquisition, ownership obligations and rights, and sale of shares.

3. Voting Rights

Corporations' ordinary shares should feature one vote for each share. Corporations should act to ensure the owners' rights to vote. Fiduciary investors have a responsibility to vote. Regulators and law should facilitate voting rights and timely disclosure of the levels of voting.

4. Corporate Boards

The board of directors, or supervisory board, as an entity, and each of its members, as an individual, is a fiduciary for all shareholders, and should be accountable to the shareholder body as a whole. Each member should stand for election on a regular basis.

Corporates should disclose upon appointment to the board and thereafter in each annual report or proxy statement information on the identities, core competencies, professional or other backgrounds, factors affecting independence, and overall qualifications of board members and nominees so as to enable investors to weigh the value they add to the company. Information on the appointment procedure should also be disclosed annually.

Boards should include a sufficient number of independent non-executive members with appropriate competencies. Responsibilities should include monitoring and contributing effectively to the strategy and performance of management, staffing key committees of the board, and influencing the conduct of the board as a whole. Accordingly, independent non-executives should comprise no fewer than three members and as much as a substantial majority. Audit, remuneration and nomination board committees should be composed wholly or predominantly of independent non-executives.

5. Corporate Remuneration Policies

Remuneration of corporate directors or supervisory board members and key executives should be aligned with the interests of shareholders. Corporations should disclose in each annual report or proxy statement the board's policies on remuneration—and, preferably, the remuneration break up of individual board members and top executives—so that investors can judge whether corporate pay policies and practices meet that standard. Broad-based employee share ownership plans or other profit-sharing programs are effective market mechanisms that promote employee participation.

6. Strategic Focus

Major strategic modifications to the core business(es) of a corporation should not be made without prior shareholder approval of the proposed modification. Equally, major corporate changes which in substance or effect materially dilute the equity or erode the economic interests or share ownership rights of existing shareholders should not be made without prior shareholder approval of the proposed change. Shareholders should be given sufficient information about any such proposal, sufficiently early, to allow them to make an informed judgement and exercise their voting rights.

7. Operating Performance

Corporate governance practices should focus board attention on optimizing over time the company's operating performance. In particular, the company should strive to excel in specific sector peer group comparisons.

8. Shareholder Returns

Corporate governance practices should also focus board attention on optimizing over time the returns to shareholders. In particular, the company should strive to excel in comparison with the specific equity sector peer group benchmark.

9. Corporate Citizenship

Corporations should adhere to all applicable laws of the jurisdictions in which they operate. Boards that strive for active cooperation between corporations and stakeholders will be most likely to create wealth, employment, and sustainable economies. They should disclose their policies on issues involving stakeholders, for example workplace and environmental matters.

10. Corporate Governance Implementation

Where codes of best corporate governance practice exist, they should be applied pragmatically. Where they do not yet exist, investors and others should endeavor to develop them. Corporate governance issues between shareholders, the board and management should be pursued by dialogue and, where appropriate, with government and regulatory representatives as well as other concerned bodies, so as to resolve disputes, if possible, through negotiation, mediation, or arbitration. Where those means fail, more forceful actions should be possible. For instance, investors should have the right to sponsor resolutions or convene extraordinary meetings.

THE INTERNATIONAL CORPORATE GOVERNANCE NETWORK
OECD Principles as Amplified

Preamble

The ICGN affirms that to be effective, corporate governance practices should focus board attention on optimizing over time the returns to shareholders with a view to excel in comparison with the company's equity sector peer group. To achieve this objective, the board is expected to manage successfully its relationships with other stakeholders, i.e. those with a legitimate interest in the operation of the business, such as employees, customers, suppliers, creditors, and the communities in which the company operates.

I The Rights of Shareholders

Overall strategy   Major strategic modifications to the core business(es) of a corporation should not be made without prior shareholder approval of the proposed modification. Equally, major corporate changes which in substance or effect materially dilute the equity or erode the economic interests or share ownership rights of existing shareholders should not be made without prior shareholder approval of the proposed change. Shareholders should be given sufficient information about any such proposal, sufficiently early, to allow them to make an informed judgement and exercise their voting rights.

Access to the vote   The right and opportunity to vote at shareholder meetings hinges in part on the adequacy of the voting system. The ICGN believes that markets and companies can facilitate access to the ballot by following the ICGN's *Global Share Voting Principles*, adopted at the 10 July, 1998 annual meeting in San Francisco. In particular, the ICGN supports initiatives to expand voting options to include the secure use of telecommunication and other electronic channels.

Disclosing results   The ICGN underlines both the OECD assertion that 'equal effect should be given to votes whether cast in person or in absentia' and the Annotation's statement that 'as a matter of transparency, meeting procedures should ensure that votes are properly counted and recorded, and that a timely announcement of the outcome be made.' To implement this recommendation, the ICGN believes that corporations should disclose voting levels for each resolution in a timely manner.

Unequal voting   The ICGN affirms that divergence from a 'one-share, one-vote' standard which gives certain shareholders power disproportionate to their equity ownership is undesirable. Any such divergence should be both disclosed and justified.

Duty to vote   The ICGN believes that institutional investors have a fiduciary obligation to vote their shares, subject to considerations of excessive cost and obstacles.

II The Equitable Treatment of Shareholders

One-share, one-vote   The ICGN affirms the OECD's recognition that 'many institutional investors and shareholder associations support…the concept of 'one-share, one-vote.' The ICGN holds that national capital markets can grow best over the long-term if they move toward the 'one-share, one-vote' principle. Conversely, capital markets that retain inequities are likely to be disadvantaged compared with markets that embrace fair voting procedures.

Protections   As the OECD declares, boards should treat all the corporation's shareholders equitably and should ensure that the rights of all investors, 'including minority and foreign shareholders,' are protected.

III The Role of Stakeholders in Corporate Governance

Board member duties   The ICGN is of the view that the board should be accountable to shareholders and responsible for managing successful and productive relationships with the corporation's stakeholders. The ICGN concurs with the OECD Principle that 'active cooperation between corporations and stakeholders' is essential in creating wealth, employment, and financially-sound enterprises over a period of time.

Stakeholder participation   The ICGN affirms that performance-enhancing mechanisms promote employee participation and align shareholder and stakeholder interests. These include broad-based employee share ownership plans or other profit-sharing programmes.

IV Disclosure and Transparency

Objective   The ICGN holds that corporations should disclose accurate, adequate and timely information, in particular meeting market guidelines where they exist, so as to allow investors to make informed decisions about the acquisition, ownership obligations and rights, and sale of shares.

Ownership and voting rights   In addition to financial and operating results, company objectives, risk factors, stakeholder issues and governance structures, the information enumerated in the OECD Annotations is needed. These are 'data on major shareholders and others that control or may control the company, including information on special voting rights, shareholder agreements, the beneficial ownership of controlling or large blocks of shares, significant cross-shareholding relationships and cross-guarantees' as well as information on differential voting rights and related party transactions.

Board member information   The ICGN further asserts that corporations should disclose upon appointment to the board and thereafter in each annual report or proxy statement sufficient information on the identities, core competencies, professional backgrounds, other board memberships, factors affecting independence, and overall qualifications of board members and nominees so as to enable the assessment of the value they add to the company. Information on the appointment procedure should also be disclosed annually.

Remuneration   Remuneration of corporate directors or supervisory board members and key executives should be aligned with the interests of shareholders. Corporations should disclose in each annual report or proxy statement the board's policies on remuneration—and, preferably, the remuneration break up of individual directors and top executives—so that it can be can judged whether corporate pay policies and practices meet that standard.

Audit   The ICGN advocates annual audits of corporations by independent, outside auditors, together with measures that enhance confidence in the quality and independence of the audit. The ICGN itself has voted support for the development of the highest-quality international accounting standards, and would encourage corporations to apply those or other standards of comparable quality. The ICGN also backs active, independent board audit committees and, to limit the risks of possible conflicts of interest, disclosure of the fees paid to auditors for non-audit services.

V The Responsibilities of the Board

The ICGN agrees with the OECD's enumeration of board duties and responsibilities.

Independent board members   It endorses the assertion that 'the board should be able to exercise objective judgement on corporate affairs independent, in particular, from management.' To meet this challenge, the ICGN holds that each company should take the following steps. First, it should acknowledge that the board of directors, or supervisory board, as an entity, and each of its members, as an individual, is a fiduciary for all shareholders, and should be accountable to the shareholder body as a whole. Each elected member should stand for election on a regular basis. Second, each board should include sufficient independent non-executive members with appropriate competencies.

Responsibilities should include monitoring and contributing effectively to the strategy and performance of management, staffing key committees of the board, and influencing the conduct of the board as a whole. Accordingly, independent non-executives should comprise no fewer than three members and as much as a substantial majority.

Independent Committees   To further strengthen the professionalism of boards, the ICGN endorses earlier language considered by the OECD. 'Certain key responsibilities of the board such as audit, nomination and executive remuneration, require the attention of independent, non-executive members of the board. Boards should consider establishing committees containing a sufficient number of independent non-executive board members in these areas where there is a potential for conflict of interest or where independent business judgement is advisable.' The ICGN considers that to meet this challenge audit, remuneration and nomination board committees should be composed wholly or predominantly of independent non-executives.

ANNEXURE 3.4   DESIRABLE CORPORATE GOVERNANCE—A CODE

Foreword

In 1996, CII took a special initiative on corporate governance—the first institutional initiative in Indian industry. The objective was to develop and promote a code for corporate governance to be adopted and followed by Indian companies, be these in the private sector, the public sector, banks or financial institutions, all of which are corporate entities. This initiative by CII followed from public concerns regarding the protection of investor interest, especially the small investor; the promotion of transparency within business and industry; the need to move towards international standards in terms of disclosure of information by the corporate sector and, through all of this, to develop a high level of public confidence in business and industry. A national task force set up with Mr Rahul Bajaj, past president, CII and chairman and managing director, Bajaj Auto Limited, as the chairman included membership from industry, the legal profession, media, and academia.

This task force presented the draft guidelines and the code of corporate governance in April 1997 at the National Conference and Annual Session of CII. This draft was then publicly debated in workshops and Seminars and a number of suggestions were received for the consideration of the task force. Reviewing, these suggestions, and the development, which have taken place in India and abroad over the past year, the task force has finalized the Desirable Corporate Governance Code. CII has the pleasure in presenting this Code in this document for information, for understanding, and for implementation of Indian business and industry.

CII would like to acknowledge, with deep gratitude, the role and leadership provided by the task force chairman, Mr Rahul Bajaj, and the economist in the group, Dr Omkar Goswami, who undertook a great deal of research and too special responsibility for drafting the Code.

Since 1974, CII has tried to chart new path in terms of the role of an industry association such as itself. It has gone beyond dealing with the traditional work of interacting with government of policies and procedures, which impact on industry. CII has taken initiatives in quality, environment, energy, trade fairs, social development, international partnership building, etc. as part of its process of development and expanding contribution to issues of relevance and concern to industry. This Code of Corporate Governance continues this process and takes it one step further. Fortunately there is very little difference between the draft Code released in April 1997 and the final Code, which is now published. It reflects the comprehensiveness of the task force's work and the thought, which has gone into preparing this Code. It is pioneering work, it is path-breaking initiative and we are delighted to release the Code in the hope that the corporate sector will implement it seriously and sincerely.

N. Kumar
President, CII
April 1998

Although 'corporate governance' still remains an ambiguous and misunderstood phrase, three aspects are becoming evident.

- First, there is no unique structure of 'corporate governance' in the developed world; nor is one particular type unambiguously better than others. Thus, one cannot design a code of corporate governance for Indian companies by mechanically importing one form or another.
- Second, Indian companies, banks and financial institutions (FIs) can no longer afford to ignore better corporate practices. As India gets integrated in the world market, Indian as well as international investors will demand greater disclosure, more transparent explanation for major decisions, and better shareholder value.
- Third, corporate governance goes far beyond company law. The quantity, quality, and frequency of financial and managerial disclosure, the extent to which the board of directors exercise their fiduciary responsibilities towards shareholders, the quality of information that management share with their boards, and the commitment to run transparent companies that maximize long term shareholder value cannot be legislated at any level of detail. Instead, these evolve due to the catalytic role played by the more progressive elements within the corporate sector and, thus, enhance corporate transparency and responsibility.

A Minimal Definition

Corporate governance deals with laws, procedures, practices, and implicit rules that determine a company's ability to take managerial decisions vis-à-vis its claimants—in particular, its shareholders, creditors, customers, the State, and employees. There is a global consensus about the objective of 'good' corporate governance: maximising long term shareholder value. Since shareholders are residual claimants, this objective follows from a premise that in well performing capital and financial markets, whatever maximizes shareholder value must necessarily maximize corporate prosperity, and best satisfy the claims of creditors, employees, shareholders, and the State.

For a corporate governance code to have real meaning, it must first focus on listed companies. These are financed largely by public money (be it equity or debt) and, hence, need to follow codes and policies that make them more accountable and value oriented to their investing public. There is a diversity of opinion regarding beneficiaries of corporate governance. The Anglo-American system tends to focus on shareholders and various classes of creditors.

Continental Europe, Japan, and South Korea believe that companies should also discharge their obligations towards employees, local communities, suppliers, ancillary units, and so on. In the first instance, it is useful to limit the claimants to shareholders and various types of creditors. There are two reasons for this preference.

1. The corpus of Indian labour laws are strong enough to protect the interest of workers in the organized sector, and employees as well as trade unions are well aware of their legal rights. In contrast, there is

very little in terms of the implementation of law and of corporate practices that protects the rights of creditors and shareholders.

2. There is much to recommend in law, procedures and practices to make companies more attuned to the needs of properly servicing debt and equity.

If most companies in India appreciate the importance of creditors and shareholders, then we will have come a long way. Irrespective of differences between various forms of corporate governance, all recognize that good corporate practices must—at the very least—satisfy two sets of claimants: creditors and shareholders. In the developed world, company managers must perform to satisfy creditors' dues because of the disciplining device of debt, which carries with it the credible threat of management change via bankruptcy. Analogously, managers have to look after the right of shareholders to dividends and capital gains because if they do not do so over time, they face the real *risk of take-over*. An economic and legal environment that puts a brake on the threat of bankruptcy and prevents take-overs is a recipe for systematic corporate mis-governance.

Board of Directors

The key to good corporate governance is a well functioning, informed board of directors. The board should have a core group of excellent, professionally acclaimed non-executive directors who understand their dual role: of appreciating the issues put forward by management, and of honestly discharging their fiduciary responsibilities towards the company's shareholders as well as creditors.

Recommendation 1

There is no need to adopt the German system of two-tier boards to ensure desirable corporate governance. A single board, if it performs well, can maximise long term shareholder value just as well as a two- or multi-tiered board. Equally, there is nothing to suggest that a two-tier board, per se, is the panacea to all corporate problems. However, the full board should meet a minimum of six times a year, preferably at an interval of two months, and each meeting should have agenda items that require at least half a day's discussion. It has been proved time and again in the US, Great Britain, Germany, and many other OECD countries that the quality of the board—and, hence, corporate governance—improves with the induction of outside professionals as non-executive directors. As a recent article puts it: Obviously not all well governed companies do well in the market place. Nor do the badly governed ones always sink. But even the best performers risk stumbling some day if they lack strong and independent boards of directors (*Business Week*, 25 November 1996, p. 84).

Securing the services of good, professionally competent, independent non-executive directors does not necessarily require the institutionalising of nomination committees or search committees. However, it does require a code that specifies a minimal thumb rule. This leads to the second recommendation.

Recommendation 2

Any listed companies with a turnover of Rs 100 crores and above should have professionally competent, independent, non-executive directors, who should constitute

- at least 30 per cent of the board if the chairman of the company is a non-executive director, or
- at least 50 per cent of the board if the chairman and managing director is the same person.

Getting the right type of professionals on the board is only one way of ensuring diligence. It has to be buttressed by the concept of limitation: one cannot hold non-executive directorships in a plethora of companies, and yet be expected to discharge one's obligations and duties. This yields the third recommendation.

Recommendation 3

No single person should hold directorships in more than 10 listed companies.

As of now, section 275 of the Companies Act allows a person to hold up to 20 directorships. The Report of the Working Group on the Companies Act (February 1997) has kept the number unchanged. It is felt that with 20 directorships it would be extremely difficult for an individual to make an effective contribution and ensure good governance, and yet discharge his fiduciary responsibilities towards all. In this context, it is useful to give the trend in the US. According to a recent survey of over 1,000 directors and chairmen of US corporations, the directors themselves felt that no one should serve on an average more than 2.6 boards. On 12 November 1996, a special panel of 30 corporate governance experts co-opted by the National Association of Corporate Directors of the US recommended that senior executives should sit on no more than three boards, including their own. Retired executives and professional non-executive directors should serve on no more than six.

Recommendation 4

For non-executive directors to play a material role in corporate decision-making and maximising long-term shareholder value, they need to

- become active participants in boards, not passive advisors;
- have clearly defined responsibilities within the board such as the audit committee; and
- know how to read a balance sheet, profit and loss account, cash flow statements and financial ratios, and have some knowledge of various company laws. This, of course, excludes those who are invited to join boards as experts in other fields such as science and technology.

This brings one to remuneration of non-executive directors. At present, most non-executive directors receive a sitting fee which cannot exceed Rs 2,000 per meeting. The working group on the Companies Act has recommended that this limit should be raised to Rs 5,000. Although this is better than Rs 2,000, it is hardly sufficient to induce serious effort by the non-executive directors.

Recommendation 5

To secure better effort from non-executive directors, companies should:

- Pay a commission over and above the sitting fees for the use of the professional inputs. The present commission of 1 per cent of net profits (if the company has a managing director), or 3 per cent (if there is no managing director) is sufficient.
- Consider offering stock options, so as to relate rewards to performance. Commissions are rewards on current profits. Stock options are rewards contingent upon future appreciation of corporate value. An appropriate mix of the two can align a non-executive director towards keeping an eye on short-term profits as well as longer term shareholder value.

The above recommendation can be easily achieved without the necessity of any formalized remuneration committee of the board. To ensure that non-executive directors properly discharge their fiduciary obligations, it is, however, necessary to give a record of their attendance to the shareholders.

Recommendation 6

While re-appointing members of the board, companies should give the attendance record of the concerned directors. If a director has not been present (absent with or without leave) for 50 per cent or more meetings, then this should be explicitly stated in the resolution that is put to vote. As a general practice, one should not reappoint any director who has not had the time attend even one-half of the meetings.

It is important to recognize that under usual circumstances, non-executive directors in India suffer from lack of quality information. Simply put, the extent to which non-executive directors can play their role is determined by the quality of disclosures that are made by the management to the board. In the interest of good governance, certain key information must be placed before the board, and must form part of the agenda papers.

Recommendation 7

Key information that must be reported to, and placed before, the board must contain:

- Annual operating plans and budgets, together with updated long-term plans.
- Capital budgets, manpower and overhead budgets.
- Quarterly results for the company as a whole and its operating divisions or business segments.
- Internal audit reports, including cases of theft and dishonesty of a material nature.
- Show cause, demand and prosecution notices received from revenue authorities which are considered to be materially important. (Material nature is any exposure that exceeds 1 per cent of the company's net worth.)
- Fatal or serious accidents, dangerous occurrences, and any effluent or pollution problems.
- Default in payment of interest or non-payment of the principal on any public deposit, and/or to any secured creditor or financial institution.
- Defaults such as non-payment of inter-corporate deposits by or to the company, or materially substantial non-payment for goods sold by the company.
- Any issue which involves possible public or product liability claims of a substantial nature, including any judgement or order which may have either passed strictures on the conduct of the company, or taken an adverse view regarding another enterprise that can have negative implications for the company.
- Details of any joint venture or collaboration agreement.
- Transactions that involve substantial payment towards goodwill, brand equity, or intellectual property.
- Recruitment and remuneration of senior officers just below the board level, including appointment or removal of the chief financial officer and the company secretary.
- Labour problems and their proposed solutions.
- Quarterly details of foreign exchange exposure and the steps taken by management to limit the risks of adverse exchange rate movement, if material.

The Report of the Working Group on the Companies Act was in favour of audit committees, but recommended that these be set up voluntarily 'with the industry associations playing a catalytic role' [p. 23]. The group felt that legislating in favour of audit committees would be counter-productive, and could lead to a situation where such committees would be often constituted to meet the letter—and not the spirit—of the law. Nevertheless, there is a clear need for audit committees, which yields the next recommendation.

Recommendation 8

1. Listed companies with either a turnover of over Rs 100 crores or a paid-up capital of Rs 20 crores should set up audit committees within two years of inception.
2. Audit committees should consist of at least three members, all drawn from a company's non-executive directors, who should have adequate knowledge of finance, accounts, and basic elements of company law.
3. To be effective, the audit committees should have clearly defined terms of reference and its members must be willing to spend more time on the company's work vis-à-vis other non-executive directors.
4. Audit committees should assist the board in fulfilling its functions relating to corporate accounting and reporting practices, financial and accounting controls, and financial statements and proposals that accompany the public issue of any security—and thus provide effective supervision of the financial reporting process.
5. Audit committees should periodically interact with the statutory auditors and the internal auditors to ascertain the quality and veracity of the company's accounts as well as the capability of the auditors themselves.
6. For audit committees to discharge their fiduciary responsibilities with due diligence, it must be incumbent upon management to ensure that members of the committee have full access to financial data of the company, its subsidiary and associated companies, including data on contingent liabilities, debt exposure, current liabilities, loans, and investments.
7. By the fiscal year 1998–99, listed companies satisfying criterion (1) should have in place a strong internal audit department, or an external auditor to do internal audits; without this, any audit committee will be toothless.

Why should the management of most Indian companies bother about giving such information to their audit committees? The answer is straightforward. Over a period of time, they will have to, for there will be a clear-cut signalling effect. Better companies will choose professional non-executive directors and form independent audit committees. Others will either have to follow suit, or get branded as the corporate laggards. Moreover, once there is an established correlation between audit committees on the one hand, and the quality of financial disclosure on the other, investors will vote with their feet. The last two years have seen domestic investors escape from equity in favour of debt, particularly bonds issued by public financial institutions. If the corporate sector wants to create a comeback for equity, it can only do so through greater transparency. Audit committees ensure long-term goodwill through such transparency.

Desirable Disclosure

Our corporate disclosure norms are inadequate. With the growth of the financial press and equity researchers, the days of having opaque accounting standards and disclosures are rapidly coming to an end. As a country which wishes to be a global player, we cannot hope to tap the GDR market with inadequate financial disclosures; it will not be credible to present one set of accounts to investors in New York and Washington DC, and a completely different one to the shareholders in Mumbai and Chennai. So, what is the minimum level of disclosure that Indian companies ought to be aiming for? The Working Group on the Companies Act have recommended many financial as well as non-financial disclosures. It is worth recapitulating the more important ones.

Non-financial disclosures recommended by the Working Group on the Companies Act

1. Comprehensive report on the relatives of directors—either as employees or board members—to be an integral part of the directors' report of all listed companies.

2. Companies have to maintain a register which discloses interests of directors in any contract or arrangement of the company. The existence of such a register and the fact that it is open for inspection by any shareholder of the company should be explicitly stated in the notice of the AGM of all listed companies.

3. Similarly, the existence of the directors' shareholding register and the fact that it can be inspected by members in any AGM should be explicitly stated in the notice of the AGM of all listed companies.

4. Details of loans to directors should be disclosed as an annex to the directors' report in addition to being a part of the schedules of the financial statements. Such loans should be limited to only three categories—housing, medical assistance, and education for family members—and be available only to fulltime directors. The detailed terms of loan would need shareholders approval in a general meeting.

5. Appointment of sole selling agents for India will require prior approval of a special resolution in a general meeting of shareholders. The board may approve the appointment of sole selling agents in foreign markets, but the information must be divulged to shareholders as a part of the directors' report accompanying the annual audited accounts. In either case, if the sole selling agent is related to any director or director having interest, this fact has to not only be stated in the special resolution but also divulged as a separate item in the directors' report.

6. Subject to certain exceptions, there should be a secretarial compliance certificate forming a part of the annual returns that is filed with the Registrar of Companies which would certify, in prescribed format that the secretarial requirements under the Companies Act have been adhered to.

Financial disclosures recommended by the Working Group on the Companies Act

1. A tabular form containing details of each director's remuneration and commission should form a part of the directors' report, in addition to the usual practice of having it as a note to the profit and loss account.

2. Costs incurred, if any, in using the services of a group resource company must be clearly and separately disclosed in the financial statement of the user company.

3. A listed company must give certain key information on its divisions or business segments as a part of the directors' report in the annual report. This should encompass (i) the share in total turnover, (ii) review of operations during the year in question, (iii) market conditions, and (iv) future prospects. For the present, the cut-off may be 10 per cent of total turnover.

4. Where a company has raised funds from the public by issuing shares, debentures or other securities, it would have to give a separate statement showing the end-use of such funds, namely: how much was raised versus the stated and actual project cost; how much has been utilized in the project up to the end of the financial year; and where are the residual funds, if any, invested and in what form. This disclosure would be in the balance sheet of the company as a separate note forming a part of accounts 5. The disclosure on debt exposure of the company should be strengthened.

6. In addition to the present level of disclosure on foreign exchange earnings and outflow, there should also be a note containing separate data on of foreign currency transactions that are germane in today's context: (i) foreign holding in the share capital of the company, and (ii) loans, debentures, or other securities raised by the company in foreign exchange.

7. The difference between financial statements pertaining to fixed assets and long-term liabilities (including share capital and liabilities which are not to be liquidated within a year) as at the end of the financial year and the date on which the board approves the balance sheet and profit and loss account should be disclosed.

8. If any fixed asset acquired through or given out on lease is not reported under appropriate subheads, then full disclosure would need to be made as a note to the balance sheet. This should give details of the type of asset, its total value, and the future obligations of the company under the lease agreement.

9. Any inappropriate treatment of an item in the balance sheet or profit and loss account should not be allowed to be explained away either through disclosure of accounting policies or via notes forming a part of accounts but should be dealt with in the Directors' Report.

While the disclosures recommended by the Working Group in its report as well as in the modified Schedule VI that would accompany the Draft Bill go far beyond existing levels, much more needs to be done outside the framework of law, particularly (i) a model of voluntary disclosure in the current context, and (ii) consolidation of accounts.

All other things being equal, greater the quality of disclosure, the more loyal are a company's shareholders.

Besides, there is something very inequitable about the present disclosure standards: we have one norm for the foreigners when we go in for GDRs or private placement with foreign portfolio investors, and a very different one for our more loyal Indian shareholders. This should not continue. The suggestions given below partly rectify this imbalance.

Recommendation 9

Under 'Additional Shareholder's Information', listed companies should give data on:

1. High and low monthly averages of share prices in a major Stock Exchange where the company is listed for the reporting year.

2. Greater detail on business segments up to 10 per cent of turnover, giving share in sales revenue, review of operations, analysis—The Working Group on the Companies *Act* has recommended that consolidation should be optional, not mandatory. There were two reasons: (i) first, that the Income Tax Department does not accept the concept of group accounts for tax purposes—and the Report of the Working Group on the Income Tax Act does not suggest any difference, and (ii) the public sector term lending institutions do not allow leveraging on the basis of group assets. Thus:

Recommendation 10

1. Consolidation of Group Accounts should be optional and subject to
   o the FIs allowing companies to leverage on the basis of the group's assets, and
   o the Income Tax Department using the group concept in assessing corporate income tax.

2. If a company chooses to voluntarily consolidate, it should not be necessary to annex the accounts of its subsidiary companies under section 212 of the Companies Act 1956.

3. However, if a company consolidates, then the definition of 'group' should include the parent company and its subsidiaries (where the reporting company owns over 50 per cent of the voting stake).

One of the most appealing features of the Cadbury Committee Report (Committee on the Financial Aspects of Corporate Governance) is the compliance certificate that has to accompany the annual reports of all companies listed in the London Stock Exchange. This alone has created a far more healthy milieu for corporate governance despite the cosy, club-like atmosphere of British boardrooms. It is essential that a variant of this be adopted in India.

Recommendation 11

Major Indian stock exchanges should gradually insist upon a compliance certificate, signed by the CEO and the CFO, which clearly states that:

- The management is responsible for the preparation, integrity, and fair presentation of the financial statements and other information in the annual report, and which also suggest that the company will continue in business in the course of the following year.
- The accounting policies and principles conform to standard practice, and where they do not, full disclosure has been made of any material departures.
- The board has overseen the company's system of internal accounting and administrative controls systems either director or through its audit committee (for companies with a turnover of Rs 100 crores or paid-up capital of Rs 20 crores).

As mentioned earlier, there is something inequitable about disclosure by a company substantially more for its GDR issue as compared to its domestic issue. This treats Indian shareholders as if they are children of a lesser God.

Recommendation 12

For all companies with paid-up capital of Rs 20 crores or more, the quality and quantity of disclosure that accompanies a GDR issue should be the norm for any domestic issue.

Capital Market Issues

Since 'take-over' is immediately associated with 'raider', it is considered an unethical act of corporate hostility. The bulk of historical evidence shows otherwise. Growth of industry and business in most developed economies have been aided and accompanied by take-overs, mergers, and strategic acquisitions. International data shows that take-overs usually serve three purposes: (i) creates economies of scale and scope, (ii) imposes a credible threat on management to perform for the shareholders, and (iii) enhances shareholder value in the short- and in the medium-term. Because the targets are typically under-performing companies, take-over typically enhance short as well as longer term shareholder value.

The short-term value rises because the bidder has to offer shareholders a price that is significantly higher than the market. Longer term gains tend to occur because the buyer has not only bet on generating higher value through cost cutting, eliminating unproductive lines and strengthening productive ones but also put in his money to own the controlling block of equity. The new Take-over Code has been introduced in India. Although the code has its problems—especially after a 50 per cent acquisition—it is a step in the right direction. However, the code is, at best, necessary for facilitating take-overs; it is hardly sufficient.

There lies a basic problem with take-overs in India. One cannot have a dynamic market and a level playing field for take-overs when there are multiple restrictions on financing such acquisitions.

- Banks do not lend for such activities. Until the slack season credit policy announced on 15 April 1997, banks had imposed a credit limit of Rs 10 lakhs against share collateral—hardly the kind of money that can fund domestically financed take-overs.

- There is no securitization. This prevents the value of underlying assets to be used in refinancing—something which could not only reduce cost of funds but also facilitate take-overs by dynamic but not necessarily cash rich entrepreneurs.
- FIs do not finance take-overs.
- There are not enough corporate debt instruments which a company could use to finance a takeover—and even these attract very high rates of Stamp Duty.

In such an environment, it is not surprising that one ends up with a severely limited take-over code where an acquirer can go into take-over mode and, yet need not increase its equity exposure to more than 30 per cent. Moreover, it queers the pitch in favour of those who have access to off-shore funds, which do not operate under these artificial constraints. As things stand, there will be only two types of raiders: (i) entrepreneurs from cash rich industries, and (ii) foreign investors who can garner substantial cheap funds from abroad. From a perspective of industrial growth—where take-overs become vehicles for synergy, scale, new technological and managerial inputs, corporate dynamism, and long term enhancement of shareholder value—it is essential that dynamic Indian firms and entrepreneurial groups attempting take-overs be treated the same way by Indian banks and FIs as their buyout counterparts are in the west. This leads to an important recommendation.

Recommendation 13

Government must allow far greater funding to the corporate sector against the security of shares and other paper.

When this is in place, the take-over code should be modified to reflect international norms. Once takeover finance is easily available to Indian entrepreneurs, the trigger should increase to 20 per cent, and the minimum bid should reflect at least a 51 per cent take-over.

Creditors' Rights

It is a universal axiom that creditors have a prior and pre-committed claim on the income of the company, and that this claim has to be satisfied irrespective of the state of affairs of the company. Important creditors can, and do, demand periodic operational information to monitor the state of health of their debtor firms; but, so long as their dues are being repaid (and expected to be repaid) on schedule, pure creditors have no legal say in the running of a company. Therefore, insofar as creditors are not shareholders, and so long as their dues are being paid in time, they should desist from demanding a seat on the board of directors.

This is an important point in the Indian context. Almost all term loans from FIs carry a covenant that it will represented on the board of the debtor company via a nominee director. This yields the next recommendation.

Recommendation 14

It would be desirable for FIs as pure creditors to re-write their covenants to eliminate having nominee directors except:

(a)   in the event of serious and systematic debt default; and
(b)   in case of the debtor company not providing six-monthly or quarterly operational data to the concerned FI(s).

Today, credit-rating is compulsory for any corporate debt issue. But, as in the case of primary equity issues, the quality of information given to the Indian investing public is still well below what is disclosed in many other developed countries. Given below are some suggestions.

Recommendation 15

1. If any company goes to more than one credit rating agency, then it must divulge in the prospectus and issue document the rating of all the agencies that did such an exercise.
2. It is not enough to state the ratings. These must be given in a tabular format that shows where the company stands relative to higher and lower ranking. It makes considerable difference to an investor to know whether the rating agency or agencies placed the company in the top slots, or in the middle, or in the bottom.
3. It is essential that we look at the quantity and quality of disclosures that accompany the issue of company bonds, debentures, and fixed deposits in the US and Britain—if only to learn what more can be done to inspire confidence and create an environment of transparency.
4. Finally, companies which are making foreign debt issues cannot have two sets of disclosure norms: an exhaustive one for the foreigners, and a relatively minuscule one for Indian investors.

There is another area of concern regarding creditors' rights. This has to do with holders of company deposits. In the last three years, there have been too many instances where manufacturing as well as investment and finance companies have reneged on payment of interest on company deposits or repayment of the principal. Since these deposits are generally unsecured loans, the deposit holders are prime targets of default.

Recommendation 16

Companies that default on fixed deposits should not be permitted to
- accept further deposits and make inter-corporate loans or investments until the default is made good; and
- declare dividends until the default is made good. Both have been suggested by the Working Group on the Companies Act, and are endorsed by CII.

On FIs and Nominee Directors

Consider two facts: (i) the largest debt-holders of private sector corporate India are public sector term lending institutions such as IDBI, IFCI, and ICICI; and (ii) these institutions are also substantial shareholders and, like in Germany, Japan, and Korea, sit on the boards as nominee directors. So, in effect they have combined inside debt-cum-equity positions so common to German, Japanese, and Korean forms of corporate governance. But informed insiders in India do not seem to behave like their German counterparts; corporate governance and careful monitoring do not happen as they are supposed to when a stake-holder is both creditor and owner of equity, as in Germany. The apparent failure of government controlled FIs to monitor companies in their dual capacity as major creditors and shareholders has much to do with a pervasive anti-incentive structure. There are several dimensions of this structure. First, major decisions by public sector financial institutions are eventually decided by the Ministry of Finance, and not by their board of directors. De jure, this cannot be cause for complaint—after all the Government of India is the major shareholder and, hence, has the right to call the shots. However, at issue is the manner in which the government calls the shots, and whether its decisions enhance shareholder value for the FIs. Second, nominee directors of FIs have no personal incentive to monitor their companies. They are neither rewarded for good monitoring nor punished for non-performance. Third, there is a tradition of FIs to supporting existing management except in the direst of circumstances. Stability of existing management is not necessarily a virtue by itself, unless it translates to greater transparency and higher shareholder value. Fourth, compared to the number of companies where they are represented on the board, the FIs simply do not have enough senior-level personnel who can properly discharge their obligations as good corporate governors. In a nutshell, therefore, while nominee directors of FIs ought to be far more powerful than the disinterested non-executive directors, they are in fact at par. Consequently, the institutions which could have played the most proactive role in corporate governance—India's largest concentrated shareholders-cum-debtholders—have not done so. The long term solution requires questioning the very basis of majority government ownership of the FIs, and whether it augurs for better governance and higher shareholder value for India's companies as well as the FIs themselves. As a rule, government institutions are not sufficiently concerned about adverse income and wealth consequences arising out of wrong decisions and inaction; their incentive structures do not reward performance and punish non-performance; and, most of all, they remain highly susceptible to pulls and pressures from various ministries which have little to do with commercial accountability, and which often destroy the bottomline. Therefore, it is necessary to debate whether the government should gradually become a minority shareholder in all its financial sector institutions. This debate needs to be thrown open to taxpayers and the investing public. But, for the present, there is a short term solution that must be considered as quickly as possible.

Recommendation 17

Reduction in the number of companies where there are nominee directors. It has been argued by FIs that there are too many companies where they are on the board, and too few competent officers to do the task properly. So, in the first instance, FIs should take a policy decision to withdraw from boards of companies where their individual shareholding is 5 per cent or less, or total FI holding is under 10 per cent.

Concluding Remarks

A code of corporate governance cannot be static. It must be reviewed. Therefore, CII must review this report after some time, preferably within the next five years. Having said this, the report focuses on two more issues: (i) What does one mean by a 'code' of corporate governance? (ii) A vision of things to come in the next few years, and its implications for corporate governance. Simply put, corporate governance refers to *an* economic, legal, and institutional environment that allows companies diversify, grow, restructure and exist, and do everything necessary to maximize long term shareholder value. Thus, non-executive directors and disclosures are parts, and not the whole, of corporate governance. To most international experts on the subject, corporate governance is an interplay between companies, shareholders, creditors, capital markets, financial sector institutions, and company law. Hence, a code of corporate governance must attempt to address all these issues. This report, therefore, does constitute a code of corporate governance; and it consciously goes beyond the duty of boards and non-executive directors. Moreover, this code of corporate governance—despite its possible lacunae—will not become a reality with the stroke of a magic wand. It is a fairly substantive and radical code; it will therefore have its detractors; and putting it into effect will be a long haul. Nevertheless, it is vital for the corporate well being of India. To appreciate this, it is useful to take a peep at the vision of the near future. It is a vision that will almost certainly come to bear, and shall, willy-nilly, shape tomorrow's corporate governance.

1. First, a larger number of foreign portfolio investors will constantly raise their demand for better corporate governance, more transparency, and greater disclosure. This is precisely what happened in the US from the early 1980s and in Britain since the early 1990s.

2. Second, in a year or at most two there will be the entry of foreign pension funds. Since these funds tend to hold on to their stocks longer than mutual funds, their fund managers will be even more active in insisting upon better corporate governance.

3. Third, in the foreseeable future, there could conceivably be, at least half a dozen private equity or leveraged buy-out funds, each with an investment base of US $50 million or more. These funds will take a 2-3-year view on under-performing but asset rich Indian companies, take them over, de-list for a couple of years, and then return to the market to exit from their portfolio after successful turnaround. Thus, Indian companies will become targets for take-over. The target becomes all the more attractive if management has not given long term shareholder value.

4. Fourth, Indian FIs will not continue to support management irrespective of performance. Therefore, one will see FIs converting their outstanding debt to equity, and setting up mergers and acquisition subsidiaries to sell their shares in underperforming companies to more dynamic entrepreneurs and managerial groups.

5. Fifth, even if FIs do not have M&A wings, they will still unintentionally queer the pitch for equity. So long as IDBI, ICICI, and IFCI have maturity mismatch between their assets and liabilities, they will in all probability, periodically come to the market for raising resources with high yield instruments like 15 per cent to 16 per cent bonds. Such a high yield on what is effectively a risk-free instrument will put an upper bound to the demand for relatively more risky equity. This is expected to continue for a few years. It implies that Indian companies will have to rely much more on GDRs, other ECBs and private placement—all of which will necessarily require more transparency and disclosure and better governance.

6. Sixth, the financial press will get stronger than ever before. In the last five years, the press and financial analysts have induced a level of disclosure that was inconceivable a decade ago. This will increase and force companies to become more transparent—not just in their financial statements but also in matters relating to internal governance.

7. Finally, when India has full capital account convertibility, an Indian investor who has money to invest would have the option of investing either in an Indian or a foreign company. The investor would be inclined to invest in the Indian company if it follows some standards of transparency, disclosure, and corporate governance. What does all this mean for better corporate governance? It means everything. The loyalty of a typical Indian investor is far greater than his counterparts in the US or Britain. But, our companies must not make the mistake of taking such loyalty as a given. To nurture and strengthen this loyalty, our companies need to give a clear-cut signal that the words 'your company' has real meaning. That requires well functioning boards, greater disclosure, better management practices, and a more open, interactive and dynamic corporate governance environment. Quite simply, shareholders' and creditors' support are vital for the survival, growth and competitiveness of India's companies. Such support requires us to tone up our act today.

PART II

BOARDS AND GOVERNANCE

- Structure of the Board—Directors, Types of Boards, and Committees
- The Board Development Process— Selection, Development, Compensation, and Performance Review
- Boards and Leadership

CHAPTER 4

STRUCTURE OF THE BOARD

DIRECTORS, TYPES OF BOARDS, AND COMMITTEES

The concept of independent directors is a myth, offering a false sense of security to small shareholders.

— Prithvi Haldea, Founder-Managing Director, Prime Database

LEARNING OBJECTIVES

After studying this chapter, you will be able to

- Describe the constitution and purpose of the board
- Enumerate the board types usually observed
- Define the roles of the board and describe the evolution of boards based on roles and responsibilities
- List the different categories of directors
- Discuss the need for independent directors and the various concerns about real independence
- State director compensation-related issues
- Explain the committee structure for better governance and enumerate the different types of committees and their roles

Opening Case

Should Directors' Age Be Investors' Concern?

A large number of directors (including independent directors) have been in service for long periods. While both companies and directors will refute any allegation of their losing independence due to such long association, would not a company with long-serving directors at least lose a chance of getting independent views of the managers of a later generation? Businesses outgrow their boards over a period of time. A successful board of the past is no guarantee of success in the future. As the environment of business changes, new thinking and sometimes new faces are required. Most companies do not talk about a retirement policy for directors. Even Tatas do not mention a retirement policy for their directors in their annual reports, except in the case of Tata Power, which mentions only about executive chairmen and executive directors, non-executive chairmen and non-executive deputy/vice-chairmen and not ordinary directors. Indian Hotels Company Ltd had a 93-year-old director, according to its 2006–07 annual report, who expired in 2007 after serving the board for more than 43 years. Companies' Bill 1997 proposed a limit of 75 years for all directors, except for those who were appointed earlier for a specific period but where yet to complete their tenures. Of course, there is a difficulty in knowing the age or the association of a particular director with a company since such details appear in the annual report only when the directors retire by rotation and seek re-election or when new directors are inducted into the board. In August 2004, three directors of Nike aged 77, 84, and 85 years reportedly resigned citing increased scrutiny of age as the reason for their quitting the board. One of them, John Jaqua, 84 years, who had been director since the founding of Nike in 1968, is reported to have said, 'People who buy stock look at the age of the directors.' In India too, the time may not be far away when investors start looking at the age of directors. Only very limited number of companies provide details of all the current directors (except their ages) in their annual report. Many companies do not give the ages of the directors even when they seek re-appointment.

Discussion Questions
1. Do tenure and age of directors on the boards matter in governance?
2. Does it help investors if companies disclose age details of directors in every annual report?

Source: Annual reports of Tata Group companies like Tata Steel, Tata Power, Tata Chemicals, and Indian Hotels Company Ltd for years 2002–03 to 2007–08; *The Economic Times*, 'Nike's three oldest members step down', 3 August 2004, p. 10.

BOARDS AND GOVERNANCE

We drew a clear distinction between governance and management of corporates. Also, we saw that while differences in the structure of the boards exist, the board of directors (BOD) is the ultimate responsible body for the governance of a firm. The fiduciary responsibility to act on behalf and in the interests of the shareholders rests with the BOD. Laws relating to the establishment of firms are proposed by the state/federal government. In the US, most corporations are incorporated under state laws and there are practically no federally incorporated corporations. States were in fact competing against each other for attracting corporations to be established. The state of Delaware was seen as being more 'company friendly' and the majority of US companies listed on New York Stock Exchange (NYSE) registered in the state, taking advantage of the easier and flexible incorporation norms. According to Smith and Walter (2006), Delaware has continued to be the preferred state for incorporation of large businesses since 1916. Of course, federal laws and regulations like Securities Act 1933 and Securities Exchange Act 1954 are applicable to all companies irrespective of their state of incorporation.

In India, all companies are incorporated under the Companies Act 1956, which is applicable to all the states. A company has a characteristic of 'perpetual succession'. It is a stable form of organization and does not have any fixed span of life. It continues its existence despite the mental or physical incapacity, insolvency, or death of its members. Since it has been created by law, it can only be dissolved by an act of law. Notwithstanding the changes in the composition of its members, the company goes on forever. Thus, it is also created as an artificial person by law, different from its members. Since it is an artificial person, a company operates through a body constituted of individuals, called the BOD, which acts on behalf of and in the interest of the company and the members who own it. The company can and does act only through the BOD. Also a company has been considered to be a separate legal entity distinct from its members. This enables the company to own properties which are expected to be for the benefit of the company as a whole and not for the personal benefit of the owners. A company being a legal person can enforce its rights legally and it can also be sued for breach of its statutory requirements. The limited liability and the transferability features enable a company to mobilize funds from many investors. Thus, the corporate form has a lot of advantages in order to establish and grow business ventures. On the advantages of the corporation and the role of the BOD in a large corporation, Drucker (1946) opined that 'whoever works in a big organization especially at or near the top, will inevitably be bounded by it wherever he comes from. Hence the question is how can the corporation give its management the imagination, the understanding of the outside point of view, of the public's (consumers, workers, voters, and government) imagination and of the limits thereof.' Drucker continues: 'In the large corporation, the automatic contact with the outside world is lacking almost entirely and by necessity. The BOD can't function as it does in a small business. The control of a large corporation is such complex job and requires such constant attention that the outside board member, who has his own affairs to look after, can know very little about the business—too little on the whole to be useful as an outsider.'

Conventionally, political governments of states used to enjoy unlimited source of power but the twentieth and twenty-first centuries have been witnessing a dramatic change in the power resources. The power resources have shifted from government (politics) to economic forces like corporations which act as creators of wealth. And such corporations have been going multinational and are in effect becoming the drivers of the future. With this power shift, the government's ability to regulate is getting eroded, thereby making corporations even more powerful and making governance more corporation-centric (or board-centric). Thus, the corporate form as the posterboy of capitalism has enormous advantages because of the shift in power explained above. The onus is now on the corporations and their boards to see that they are well governed.

BOARD ORGANIZATION
Purpose of the Board

According to the Institute of Directors (IOD), the purpose of the board is 'to ensure the company's prosperity by collectively directing the company's affairs, whilst meeting the appropriate interests of its shareholders and relevant stakeholders.' But there exists a lot of confusion about what are the really important issues that come under the purview of the board and what are to be left to others (management). Whole-time or executive directors are very often not sure of what is expected of them in their role as members of the board. Management issues usually get entangled with matters that the board has to deal with. Directors have to act in a fiduciary capacity and hence have to act as stewards of the company on behalf of the shareholders. The investors of the company leave the company in the hands of the directors as a body (the board), acting as fiduciary and thus lending a lot of power to them. Fiduciary responsibility requires the board to act in good faith in the best interests of the company, not to misuse the powers, and also not to indulge in acts that give rise to conflicts between their duties to the company and their personal interests or duties to third parties. While on board, executives, managers, or shareholders have to remember that their responsibilities as directors are different from those they have as managers or shareholders. This is because, the primary purpose of the board is to shape the destiny of the company, ensure that its financial performance is adequate to meet the expectations of shareholders, encourage stakeholders to continue their association with the company, manage its risks in a prudent manner, and take all safeguard measures to protect its reputation. In short, one can say that the purpose of the board is to ensure the company's continuing prosperity.

Whatever be the information that the board considers, the questions they pose, and the discussions that take place at board meetings, they have only two fundamental outcomes: *to make decisions*, the most fundamental one, and *to learn*, the other (Harper 2005). Confusion regarding roles often arises when some of the directors are also significant shareholders in the company. This may at times lead to diversion of attention from the objectives of the board. This is where the leadership of the board (the chairman) has to remind the board that the directors have a collective legal responsibility to act in the best interests of the company at all times rather than just the interests of the shareholder(s). The issue gets even more complicated when the chairman happens to be a shareholder and sometimes the largest shareholder, which is the situation in most of the family promoted and managed companies in India. In such a case, the board has to see that the independent component is strong and that a lead independent director (LID) is appointed who reminds the board of its legal responsibilities.

Harper suggests that the executive directors be asked a few questions to ascertain how well they understand what is required of them as directors. It is felt that the same questions are not necessarily customized for executive directors and are applicable to all directors (except for the last question):

- Are they quite clear about the responsibilities and purpose of the BOD?
- Do they have a clear understanding of how they should behave as directors and what duties they have under the law?
- Have they seen the memorandum and articles of association of the company they are directors of and do they know what those documents are for?
- Are they familiar with the various tasks that a board should be competent in addressing and how they can add to that competence?
- Can they effectively separate their roles as director from their executive management roles?

If the answer to all the four (all the five in case of an ED) or any of the first four (for NEDs) of the above questions is 'no' or 'not adequately' there is a cause for concern. The board members need to be made aware of their responsibilities and duties as directors. A number of programmes are being organized by different industry bodies, business schools, and the IOD to equip the existing directors as well as potential director candidates with the essential requirements to assume the responsibilities of directorship. IOD, London, for example, conducts a course and examinations to enable people acquire a chartered director certification. IOD, India, has been organizing programmes for directors and those who aspire to become one under the title Masterclass for Directors (MFDs).

IOD, London, has laid down a code of professional conduct for directors. The code (see Exhibit 4.1) contains a comprehensive list of twelve articles.

Exhibit 4.1
The Code of Professional Conduct

All references to the masculine gender include the feminine.

A Chartered Director ('director') shall

Article 1
Exercise leadership, enterprise, and judgement in directing the company so as to achieve its continuing prosperity and act in the best interests of the company as a whole.

Article 2
Learn the standards of good practice set out in the Institute's publications, *The Director's Handbook* (2007) and *The Effective Director* (2007) and act accordingly diligently.

Article 3
Serve the legitimate interests of the company's shareholders.

Article 4
Exercise responsibilities to employees, customers, suppliers, and other relevant shareholders, including the wider community.

Article 5
Comply with relevant laws, regulations and codes of practice, refrain from anticompetitive practices, and honour obligations and commitments.

Article 6
At all times have a duty to respect the truth and act honestly in his business dealings and in the exercise of all his responsibilities as a director.

Article 7
Avoid conflicts between his personal interests, or the interests of any associated company or person, and his duties to the company.

Article 8
Not make improper use of information acquired as a director or disclose, or allow to be disclosed, information confidential to the company.

Article 9
Not recklessly or maliciously injure the professional reputation of another member of the IOD and not engage in any practices detrimental to the reputation and interests of the institute or the profession of director.

Article 10
Keep abreast of current good practice.

Article 11
Set high personal standards by keeping aware and adhering to this Code, both in the spirit and in the letter, and promoting it to other directors.

Article 12
Apply the principles of this Code appropriately when acting as a director of a non-commercial organization.

Source: http://www.iod.com/intershoproot/eCS/Store/en/pdfs/training_Code_of_Professional_Conduct.pdf

Delineating the Board's Role from that of the Management

Since it is very difficult to clearly draw a fine line dividing the board from the management (especially for the executives of the company who sit on the board), it is very essential that the board discusses and agrees on those areas which will be considered in its domain. Experts like Harper (2005) say that such domains are referred to as the board's reserved powers and should be listed. According to him, matters 'that will shape and determine the destiny of the organization, its ethos, achievements, structure, reputation, wellbeing, and posture within the law' will form part of the reserved powers.

Board Organizations Usually Found

As we have seen, a BOD is a statutory requirement of a corporate. The duty of this statutory body is to represent and protect primarily the interests of the shareholders who have taken the risk of investing their hard-earned savings in the shares of the corporate and also the interests of other stakeholders. The board thus has the primary role of exercising accountability to shareholders. A board's responsibilities are derived from laws, customs, traditions, and contemporary practices. While it is not expected to 'run' the company, it has to exercise an 'oversight' on what the management does while running the company to ensure that the mission of the corporate is implemented.

Boards can be organized either as

(a) All-executive
(b) Majority-executive
(c) Majority non-executive, or
(d) Two-tier (where there will be two boards instead of one)

We will use the common framework as given in Fig. 4.1 to differentiate between governance and management, and also describe the various types of boards:

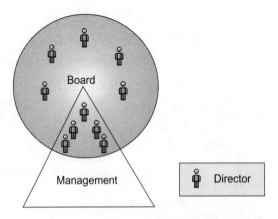

Fig. 4.1   The board–management differentiation

An *all-executive board* is made up entirely of executive (full-time) directors (see Fig. 4.2).

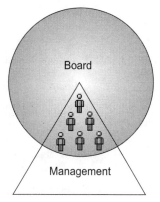

Source: Tricker, Bob, (2001), *Pocket Director*, London, Profile Books/Economist.

Fɪɢ. **4.2**   The all-executive board

In such boards, every director is also a full-time employee of the company and is paid for his full-time services for the company. The potential issue that can arise is that the board is monitoring and supervising its own performance. In effect, the board members are evaluating their own answer sheets written by them as managers. While this can have advantages of less or no communication gap and information blocks, it can give rise to conflicts of interest.

A *majority executive board* will have its membership dominated by whole-time directors (WTDs). While there may be a few non-executive directors (NEDs), members of the executive clan will far outnumber the NEDs (see Fig. 4.3).

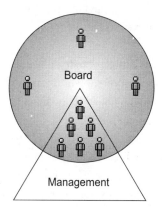

Source: Tricker, Bob, (2001), *Pocket Director*, London, Profile Books/Economist.

Fɪɢ. **4.3**   The majority-executive board

The NEDs get appointed because there is a need—a need for certain expertise which is not available within the company. Or they may come in as nominees of a few major investors to protect their interests or may be appointed to take care of strategic suppliers, customers, or government bodies.

The *majority non-executive (outside) board* will have more outside directors than executive directors (see Fig. 4.4).

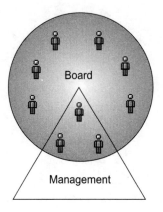

Source: Tricker, Bob, (2001), *Pocket Director*, London, Profile Books/Economist.

FIG. 4.4   The majority-non-executive board

The members of unitary boards, whether executive or non-executive, have to be elected by the shareholders at a general meeting. While theoretically the law requires that the members have to be elected by the shareholders, shareholders usually end up ratifying the nominations made by the board or the nomination committee of the board.

The types of board structures mentioned above fall under the unitary board category. There is only one board for the company and hence unitary. Whereas most of the developed and developing countries follow the Anglo-American system of a unitary board structure, European countries like Germany, Austria, and Scandinavian countries like Denmark and Netherlands require a two-tier board or dual-board system consisting of a supervisory board and a management board (see Fig. 4.5).

The management board is responsible for managing the enterprise, with its members jointly accountable for the management of the enterprise. All of a company's major functions shall be represented on the management board. It is the chairman of the management board who co-ordinates the work of the management board. The supervisory board appoints, supervises, and advises the management board, and is responsible for decisions of fundamental importance to the enterprise. The supervisory board will have a chairman appointed to co-ordinate the work of the supervisory board. The supervisory board consists of representatives of the shareholders and employees. The members of the supervisory board are appointed by shareholders (shareholder representatives) at a general meeting and employee representatives are nominated by the employees of the enterprise. Employee representation is compulsory on the supervisory board. The supervisory board appoints, supervises, advises, and, if necessary, dismisses members of the management board. It is responsible for taking decisions of fundamental importance to the enterprise. Representatives elected by shareholders as well as employees are equally obligated to act in the company's interests. It also approves the distributions of profit proposed by the management board. It has to ensure the integrity of the company's accounting, audit, and financial

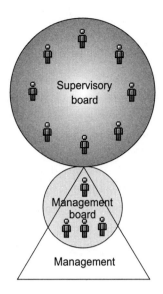

Source: Tricker, Bob, *Pocket Director*, Profile Books/Economist, 2001.

Fɪɢ. **4.5**   The two-tier board

reporting systems. The supervisory board can never have more than two former members of the management board so as to maintain its independence from the management board. The differences between supervisory and management boards are given in Table 4.1.

Tᴀʙʟᴇ **4.1**   Differences between supervisory and management boards in two-tier boards

Supervisory board	Management board
1. Members who are shareholder representatives are elected by shareholders in general meeting and members who are employee representatives are nominated by employees	Members are appointed by the supervisory board
2. Controls the direction of the business enterprise	Manages the business
3. Oversees the establishment of the operating systems and information systems by the management board	Provides the various financial information and other reports to supervisory board and implements appropriate systems for better management of business

Role, Duties, and Responsibilities of the Unitary Board

Even though company laws of most countries talk only about the requirements of directors (the term board is conspicuously missing in most), since they specify certain minimum numbers of directors for different types of companies, a board becomes mandatory as a board is an association of directors. According to Companies Act 1956 (Section 252), every public limited company must have at least three directors and every private limited company must have a minimum of two directors. The AOA of the company will usually specify the minimum and maximum number of directors. Within the limits prescribed by the articles, the company may increase or decrease the number of directors by ordinary resolution at the general meeting. Whenever a public limited company wants to increase the number of directors beyond the maximum specified by the AOA, approval from the central government must be obtained except in case where the expanded number of directors is less than twelve.

It is the board (association of directors) which takes care of governance matters in a company. Theoretically, executive powers are vested in the board as a whole. But in practice, the board delegates executive powers to the executive directors, especially the managing director, who acts as the chief executive officer (CEO) and heads the management of the business. But this arrangement does not absolve the board's ultimate responsibility and it is accountable for the company's affairs. The board has to monitor what the management does and must provide a system of checks and balances and will have the ultimate authority to appoint, change, and remove the management/ managing director (CEO) whenever necessary.

Role depends on need and context

There is a widely held myth that all boards do the same thing and every director has the same job irrespective of the board or boards associated with. This is not true. The role of the board and hence that of any director depends on the specific needs of the company and also the context in which the company and the board is expected to function.

In some companies, the board plays a very 'active' role, though not in the day-to-day running of the business, in the formation of strategy; in according assent to long-term, medium-term, and short-term objectives and plans set by management; in allocation of resources; in monitoring the progress and results; in appointment, evaluation, and fixing compensation of CEO and other senior management personnel; in risk management; in ensuring compliance with regulatory requirements; and in establishing ethical standards, meeting societal expectations, and taking control actions on performance.

As against this, in some companies, directors have been found to be playing very 'passive' roles. These boards more or less performed a compliance role: the board is a statutory requirement and the company had a board to comply with the statutory requirement and all matters relating to the company were handled by the promoter CEOs or other CEOs. Charan (2005) calls such boards *ceremonial boards* and this was the practice in many countries and even in the US before the Sarbanes–Oxley Act was introduced in 2002. Meetings were more of a ritual, driven by a tight agenda with very little communication from the CEO, practically no discussions, or questioning, or dissent. Directors used to be on boards for the prestige and/or money and did not communicate with each other.

The role of the board is largely determined by the context in which the company operates. The economic scenario of the country and across the globe, the nature of the industry, competition in the marketplace, the globalization pressures, the outsourcing pressures and opportunities, culture within the firm, the social set-up of the country, etc., would exert their influence in determining the role of a board and its functions.

For example, in a country where the economic and industrial development and growth were guided, by and large, by the government (as it was in India in the pre-liberalization era), the board's role was very limited to one of maintaining status-quo. Entrepreneurial urge to enter into new businesses by adopting new strategies was not encouraged and hence the role of the board was one of survival and continuation rather than growth and leadership. The competitive scenario in such countries was limited to a few players operating in a closed, seller's market. Hence, the board and directors did not have to worry about multitude of options, opportunities, and strategies available for the company. Most of such economies were dominated by conventional industries such as textiles, utility, essential food and other items, etc. These industries were not dramatically affected by normal economic changes. The culture within the firm is the one which determines the style of operations and hence the role played by the BOD. In companies where a patriarchic kind of culture prevails, the board and the directors are likely to be passive witnesses to the dominating role played by the patriarch founder or his family descendents. Again, the social set up of a country affects the role played by the board. In a country like India, we lay more emphasis on family ties rather than on business or entrepreneurial mindset. Harmony most of the time wins over truth.

To cite practical examples, the role of the board of a petroleum refining and marketing company like Exxon-Mobil or Reliance Petroleum will be different from that of IBM or Infosys. The essential role of the BOD in Exxon-Mobil may be to meet the societal pressures on environment protection, whereas that of IBM BOD could be outsourcing or making strategic acquisitions, and that of Infosys could be related to global reach.

These factors give rise to different board styles. Tricker (2001) describes four different board styles based on the extent of directors' concern for interpersonal relationships at the board level, and the tough-minded concern for tasks of the board. They are rubber stamp, country club, representative, and professional. See Fig. 4.6.

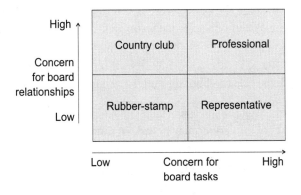

Source: Tricker, Bob, *Pocket Director*, Profile Books/Economist, 2001.

Fig. 4.6 Different board styles

Rubber-stamp board   The directors have little concern for either the tasks of the board or the relationships among directors. The meetings of the board are usually a formality. They even get minuted without the meetings actually taking place. Even if the board meets, the promoter CEOs or the dominant CEOs take decisions and other directors usually give their unconditional assent.

Country-club board   Since boards are more concerned about their interpersonal relationships between board members, the major tasks related to the business gets relegated to low priority. Harmony in the boardroom becomes the primary focus and business related issues are usually given a go-by.

Representative boards   Here the emphasis is on business-related tasks at hand with the directors representing different shareholders or stakeholders trying to drive for the accomplishment of tasks which might affect the shareholder/stakeholder they represent. Since selfish interests are at the forefront, discussion can turn out to be adversarial. It functions like a parliament with representatives from different parties each trying to push for their interests.

Professional boards   Professional boards show concern for both tasks and interpersonal relationships between directors. The board chairman generally shows enormous depth of leadership. The members indulge in heated discussions and debates with the interests of the company at the top of their minds. They even dissent while showing mutual understanding and respect for each other.

Evolution of boards

Ram Charan, an accomplished board and governance expert, describes the roles of the boards based on the evolution they have undergone. According to him, the landmark event in the corporate governance scenario is the Sarbanes–Oxley Act of 2002 in the US, popularly referred to as SOX, introduced in the aftermath of high profile financial scandals and corporate failures and the consequent political and public ire in the early 2000s. According to him, the SOX has been instrumental in making the boards and directors more responsible ushering in new ways of board functioning, hitherto unheard of. According to him, even though the changes are far from necessary and satisfactory, the encouraging news is that changes are happening and that too in the right direction. Charan (2005) identifies three stages in the board evolution, namely, the ceremonial board, the liberated board, and the progressive board, and the role of the board varies, depending on where the board is in the cycle of evolution.

Ceremonial board   The ceremonial board, by and large, performed a compliance role. Directors fulfilled their obligations, such as attending the minimum required board meetings and giving assent to board resolutions proposed by the management. The criteria for a director to choose membership of a board were prestige and money associated with it, eventhough public in general never knew them or their contribution. Many boards of the past, including those of the failed high profile companies, typically represented the ceremonial category.

Liberated board   Charan feels that most boards left their ceremonial style behind after SOX. This is because the CEO now expects boards to contribute. The prospective directors also expect and want to actively participate in the proceedings of the board as a pre-requisite for accepting directorships. A few companies have already embarked on such changes even before

SOX. The General Motors board, to cite an example, had as early as in 1994 come out with 'Guidelines for Corporate Governance' which resulted in the Chairman and CEO Mr Robert Stempel's stepping down following his losing confidence of the NEDs of the company. The said guidelines were prepared with the advice of Ira Milstein, the company's counsel (Ward 1997). The shareholder activism, given momentum by pension fund CalPERS, also took its roots in early 1990s when CalPERS announced a formal strategy of meeting directly with the board members of underperforming companies. CalPERS, in the year 2000, holding 10.2 million Disney shares, withheld its votes for the re-election of directors Senator George J. Mitchell and Robert A.M. Stern citing conflict of interest as they were drawing consulting fees from the company. Such actions on the part of companies and investors made companies to shed their ceremonial style and embark on a more liberated style. Directors felt that there needs changes in the way the companies are governed. Charan says that though a number of corporate activists and watchers were pressing for governance reform, many companies were still reluctant to make radical changes in their governance practices. However, the new liberated thinking has enabled many companies to adopt changes eventhough the pace of changes has been slow.

Progressive board   This style is the one that shows how the board shall function so as to be reckoned as a competitive advantage for the company. The directors of a progressive board 'gels into a coherent and effective group' encouraging discussion, debate and dissent 'without breaking the harmony of the group'. Directors find such meetings 'energizing'. Such boards conform to the definition of learning boards by Garratt (1996). Meticulously complying with rules and regulations, accountability aspects and the supervision of management (the conformance aspect of governance), they also get involved in the overall policy formulation and strategic thinking in order to drive home competitive advantage to the company (the performance part of governance). Garratt feels that directors need a 'brain-on' attitude rather than a 'hands-on' attitude, which suits the managers. The Learning Board Model of Garratt is given in Fig. 4.7.

While in general the roles of most of the boards and directors look similar, they may vary widely in real practice because such general lists are drawn from the best practices for any board to follow. Usually boards act in such a manner as to handle the issues at hand and they will mostly be pressed into action when there is a fire. Otherwise, they usually lie low.

Duties and Responsibilities in the Two-tier Board Composition

The supervisory board has the responsibility for:

- Appointing, remunerating, and dismissing the management board.
- Approving distributions of profit proposed by the management board.
- Ensuring integrity of the company's accounting, audit, and financial reporting systems. Of course, the supervisory board participates in the preparation of the annual financial statements and oversees the audit.
- Managing the business with care, diligence, and prudence.

The management board has the responsibility for:

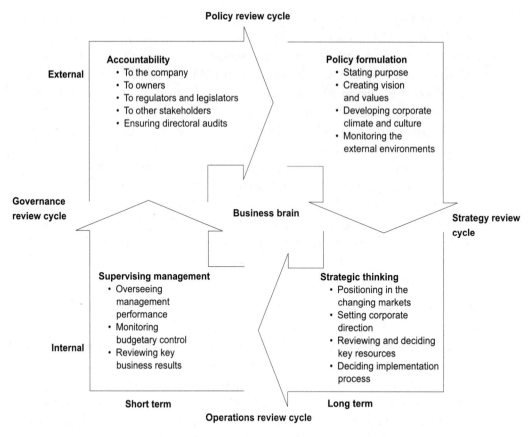

Source: Garratt, Bob (1996), *The Fish Rots from the Head*, London, Profile Books.

Fɪɢ. **4.7**   The learning board model

- Preparing business policy and strategy for future direction of the company and reporting the same to the supervisory board
- Running the company profitably
- Reporting to the supervisory board the state of business and the condition of the company
- Internal risk management
- Reporting to the supervisory board on finance, investment, and personnel planning and putting in place adequate internal monitoring and control structures

The Board's Complex Role—Many a Conflicting Roles

As per Standards for the Board (IOD 1999).
- Be entrepreneurial to drive the business while having prudent control.
- Be knowledgeable about the working of the company to be answerable for all its actions, yet be able to stand back from the routines of management and retain an objective and holistic view (helicopter view).

- Be sensitive to the pressures of short-term issues while retaining the broader, long-term perspective.
- Be knowledgeable about local issues but be aware of global competitive and other influences.
- Be focused on commercial needs of the business while concerned with social responsibility towards employees, partners, community, and society.

Tasks of the board

The tasks of the board have to be in line with the overriding purpose of the board—ensuring sustained prosperity of the company. Harper divides the tasks into two major categories: *conditioning* tasks and *enterprise* tasks. The conditioning tasks have mostly to do with the company's aspirations, values, and its interface with other parties. The enterprise task is concerned with the specific direction which the company wants to take. In effect, we can say that *enterprise* tasks talk about 'what' the company wants to do and achieve, whereas the *conditioning* tasks deal with the 'how' the company wants to realize its achievement.

Broadly speaking the board can be said to be performing the following tasks (IOD Standards for the Board):

- Establish vision, mission, and values
- Set strategy and structure
- Delegate to management
- Exercise accountability to shareholders and be responsible to relevant stakeholders

Establishing vision, mission, values, and exercising accountability to shareholders and being responsible to relevant stakeholders form part of the conditioning tasks, whereas setting strategy and structure and delegating to management form part of the enterprise tasks.

The board has to set a clear direction to the organization in terms of its vision, mission, and also the set of values which it will adhere to while driving for achievement of its mission and vision.

The broad strategy framework and the organizational and operational execution of strategy also have to be set by the board. The board also has a duty to delegate responsibility and necessary authority to execute those responsibilities to the management, so as to achieve the mission and vision set by the organization.

According to Gupta (1997), the board has two-way responsibility: one towards enterprise and the other towards society. It is depicted in Fig. 4.8.

Based on this two-way responsibility of the board, the board has two fundamental tasks: those relating to the organizational needs and those relating to the societal needs. The tasks relating to the organizational needs are as follows.

Overseeing and evaluating executive management   The board serves as a mechanism for ensuring that the management is doing its job. Executive power without a system of accountability is dangerous, whether in politics or in business.

Setting long-term strategies   Day-to-day problems pre-empt the executive management's time and attention. Hence, long-term tasks such as broad policy and strategy formulation tend to be neglected by operating executives.

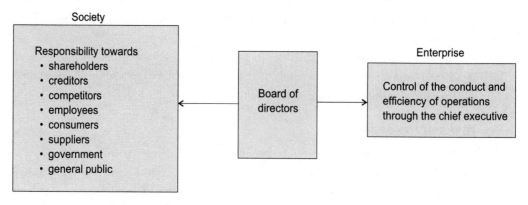

Source: Gupta, L.C. (1997), *Corporate Boards and Nominee Directors*, New Delhi, Oxford University Press.

FIG. 4.8   Board's two-way responsibility

Removing non-performing top management   This need arises when the top management fails to perform. Undoubtedly, it is the most difficult and delicate of the board's responsibilities. A board which is incapable of removing non-performing top management will itself be regarded as an ineffective and non-performing board.

Serving as a 'sounding board'   A company's top management needs a multi-talented group of independent, experienced people whom it can use as a 'sounding board' for its plans and whom it can consult in confidence. The executive management cannot itself perform this advisory task impartially and objectively.

The other part of the board's responsibility according to Gupta is its duty to society. A large corporate enterprise of today affects the lives of a large number of citizens in many ways. Hence, it is the board's moral duty, as part of its function of trusteeship, to ensure that the company acts responsibly towards society. The concept is sometimes summed up by terms 'corporate morality' or 'corporate conscience'. The tasks relating to the societal needs are:

*   Cost-efficient operation
*   Balancing the interests of all shareholders with those of creditors, employees, customers, suppliers, government, and the community in general
*   Compliance with all laws
*   Ethical behaviour on the part of the executive management

Ultimately, the board should be accountable to shareholders who have assumed the risk of investing in the company and also to act in a highly responsible manner with all the other relevant stakeholders.

Board—A Decision-making Body

The BOD is fundamentally a decision-making body. It does not have the time or resources to do other things. Hence, the board's duty will be to make the best possible decision at a given situation.

This puts the director and board in a position where they have to ensure that they collect and skim through the information the management provides, consider a number of alternatives and estimate the possible outcomes of each of them, and then arrive at decisions. Decision-making involves a lot of complexity and at times will have to be made amidst ambiguity. This is where the board should draw on its collective experience and judgements of its individual members. As Garratt (1996) says, directors are 'brain-on' which essentially makes their major job that of thinking and that is what they are paid for.

TYPES OF DIRECTORS

A unitary board, which is mostly observed to exist will consist of basically two types of directors: executive and non-executive directors. *Executive directors* (EDs) are in full-time employment of the corporate and are expected to devote their energy and efforts to the corporation full-time. Managing directors and other full-time (whole-time) directors belong to this category. They are on regular roles of the company and hence draw remuneration by way of salaries and other perks which get fixed at intervals during their tenures. Even though they are in full-time employment, they may also be retiring after a specific tenure, depending on the AOA of the company. Some of these directors may be the promoters or members belonging to the promoter families.

Non-executive directors (NEDs) on the other hand are not in full-time employment with the company. They devote only part of their time for the company. Of course, being on the board of the company only part-time does not exonerate them from any of the directoral duties. Since they are not in full-time employment of the company, they do not draw any remuneration by way of salaries and perquisites which the EDs are paid but get remunerated by way of sitting fees for attending the board meetings/board committee meetings and also by way of commission which is usually fixed as subject to a maximum percentage of net profit and payable to all the non-executive directors together. Of course, incidental expenses in connection with attending board meetings and/or audit committee meetings like travel, accommodation, conveyance, etc., will also be reimbursed. Some companies choose to pay only commission without any sitting fees, some others pay only sitting fees, and many pay both. Of course sitting fees for attending committee meetings is usually lower compared to those for attending board meetings.

There are different classifications for the NEDs.

Promoter nominee directors They usually belong to the promoter families or their associates. They might hold shares or not. In the company they are expected to strengthen the hands of the promoter group in the boardroom.

Institutional nominees Many institutions invest in the company by lending to the company or investing in the equity capital of the company. Such institutions would like to protect their interests in the company. Hence, they will nominate directors on to the board. Development financial institutions (DFIs), mutual funds, venture capital companies, investment banks all invest in companies. Normally those institutions who have a major stake in the company by way of equity or debt would like to nominate their representatives to the board.

In India, in the early days of industrial development post independence, when DFI financing was the major source of long-term finance for corporates, DFIs used to insist on nomination of directors to the boards of the borrower companies as a part of the protective covenants. The practice was given more thrust as a result of the report of the Dutt Committee of 1969, when the government decided as a matter of policy that the public financial institutions should appoint nominee directors on the boards of all assisted companies. The committee's recommendations were essentially based on two considerations: one, preventing concentration of economic power and two, need for ensuring that 'public interest and not merely private profit would guide the operations of the large industrial undertaking in the private sector'. According to L. C. Gupta, 'Nominee directors are expected to change the board's atmosphere by their presence. They can contribute by improving the board process of decision-making' (Gupta 1997).

Independent directors   A third category of NEDs is the independent director. These directors are nominated to the board for their expertise and they are expected to have an independent view and judgement of the company and the business (Exhibit 4.2 depicts the Indian scenario). Most of the countries have made regulations regarding the inclusion of independent directors on corporate boards up to a certain percentage of the total board strength.

Lead independent director (LID)   Companies may also decide to have an LID who will chair all the meetings of the independent directors. Most companies with forward-looking boards today encourage separate meetings of independent directors without the other members present. The independent directors will appoint a lead director to chair such meetings of IDs. The decisions or concerns arising from such meetings will be conveyed to the full board by the lead director. The LID will also usually chair the board meetings in the absence of the regular chairman.

Most of the regulations on corporate governance stipulate an upper limit of shareholding that an independent director can have in the company. In India, according to Clause 49 of the Listing Agreement, this limit is set at 2 per cent. Institutional nominees are usually considered as IDs irrespective of their holdings under many regulations.

While these types of classifications are in common use, there are people like Bob Garratt who feel that 'directors are designed to be a group of equals who meet collegially around the boardroom table under the natural guidance of the chairman, elected by them as *primus inter pares* to agree the future directions of the business and ensure its prudent control. In this strict sense, directors are never executives. The term "executive director" is a legal nonsense, as is "non-executive" or "independent director". A director is a director' (Garratt 2003).

NEED FOR INDEPENDENCE

While the class of independent directors is a new addition, the concept of independence and independent judgement of directors was in existence even in earlier days. The Cadbury Committee Report 1992, considered to be the first-ever organized attempt to provide a set of guidelines for corporate governance while describing the best practices for boards, explained that 'where the chairman is also the chief executive, it is essential that there should be a strong independent element

Exhibit 4.2
An Independent Director's Track Record in a Typical Indian Company

Mr K.M. Birla's record of attendance at board meetings and committee meetings of Maruti Suzuki India Ltd

Date of Appointment: 7 July 2003
Committee membership: Shareholders'/investors' grievance

Year 2003–04 (for part of the year)
Number of board meetings during his presence: 5
Number of board meetings attended: None
Previous Annual General Meeting: Not Applicable (joined after AGM)
Number of Committee (Investor Grievance) meetings held during his presence: 2
Number of committee meetings attended: None
Remuneration shown paid/payable in the annual report: Rs1,00,000

Year 2004–05 (for full year)
Number of board meetings during the year: 6
Number of board meetings attended: None
Attendance at previous AGM: Nil
Number of committee (Investors' Grievance) meetings held: 1
Number of committee meetings attended): None
Remuneration shown paid/payable in the annual report: Rs 1,00,000

Year 2005–06 (for full year)
Number of board meetings held during the year: 8
Number of board meetings attended: None
Attendance at previous AGM: Nil
Number of committee (Investors' Grievance) meetings held: 2
Number of committee meetings attended: none

Remuneration shown paid/payable in the annual report: Rs1,00,000

Year 2006–07 (for part of the year)
Number of Board meetings held during his presence: 4
Number of board meetings attended: None
Attendance at the previous AGM: Nil
Number of committee (Investors' Grievance) meetings held during his presence: None
Number of committee meetings attended: None
Remuneration shown paid/payable in the annual report: Nil

Common to all annual reports
While discussing about the Shareholders'/investors' Grievance Committee, the report states that 'the committee consists of two executive directors and three NEDs, one of whom is independent'. Mr Birla was the only independent director on the committee in the years 2003–04, 2004–05, and 2005–06.

Date of Resignation: 27 July 2006

Discussion Questions
1. Comment on the concept and practice of director independence in India.
2. Evaluate the leadership role of Shri K.M. Birla as a captain of Indian industry and the architect of CG guidelines (Clause 49) in India.
3. What action should be taken by the company in such situations?

Source: Annual reports of Maruti Udyog Ltd (presently Maruti Suzuki India Ltd) for the years 2003–04, 2004–05, 2005–06, and 2006–07

on the board with a recognized senior member other than chairman to whom the concerns can be conveyed'. And while discussing about NEDs the report said: 'NEDs should bring an independent judgement to bear on issues of strategy, performance, resources including key-appointments, and standards of conduct' and 'The majority (of NEDs) should be independent of management and free from any business or other relationships which could materially interfere with the exercise of their independent judgement, apart from their fees and shareholding' (Cadbury 1992).

So, the concept and requirement of independence were well thought of. The basic reason behind the concept is to have an independent judgement of the various aspects relating to business and the organization. Such an independent judgement will enable the company to have checks and balances in the governance process, in addition to the possibility of bringing their expertise to the company. While the concept and the suggestion are meritorious, most of the companies bring in independent directors who just meet the qualification criteria (the hardware requirements) rather than the requisite independent mindset (the software requirements).

For example, Clause 49 of the listing agreement between the company and the stock exchange where the company's shares are listed stipulates that no shareholder with more than two per cent stake in the company becomes eligible; and no partners of current legal, audit, and consulting firms, as well as partners of such firms that had worked with the company in the preceding three years become eligible as also a relative of a promoter, an executive director, or a senior executive one level below an ED to be appointed as an ID of the company. While the company appoints a person who meets all these qualification criteria (the so-called material relationships) sans an independent mindset (the non-material requisite), it again is meaningless. Most consider the requirement of IDs as a structural one rather than a process one. The ID's independent mindset must be contributing to the process of achieving better governance. IDs for namesake will only help in achieving the structural requirements.

Till very recently IDs used to be getting nominated because the CEO and the person thus nominated used to be members of the same local club or they worked together on the boards of another company or a non-profit organization. The spirit behind the requirement of IDs is very clear: it is to have an independent mindset. Most boards and companies appoint IDs to meet the regulatory requirements as a box-ticking necessity rather than to gain from their independent judgement. Even when they have an independent mindset, very often they will be constrained by the threat of losing their positions on the board. As Smith and Walter (2006) say that 'the theoretical benefits of independence are fully offset by their practical limitations', suggesting the limitations of the possibility of independent directors criticizing the CEO as such directors will find their re-election to the board in jeopardy.

Concerns about Independence

While every company talks about 'substance' over 'form' in their reports on corporate governance, many of them would fail if we administered a test for 'real' independence of the designated IDs. If the independence itself becomes questionable, the very purpose of having IDs on the boards gets defeated. The following are some of the concerns that have been raised in India. Some of these concerns may not be against the regulator's (SEBI) guidelines, but nonetheless they remain as concerns.

Same persons sitting on the boards of many companies belonging to the same group but considered to be independent in each of the companies   For example, Nusli Wadia sits on the boards of TISCO, Tata Motors, and Tata Chemicals and designated independent in all the three companies. How could he be an independent director on the boards of three companies belonging to the same group? The moment he becomes director of one company of the group, his independence in the real sense is lost. Please note that these companies have a number of common directors from the promoter group. Similar is the case of Mr S.M. Palia who sit on the boards of Tisco and Tata Motors. That Mr Tata (and Mr S.M. Palia) sits on the board of Bombay Dyeing, a Wadia Group Company, of which Mr Wadia is the chairman, makes it an even interlocking directorship situation. Another very interesting example was that of Mr N.S. Sekhsaria and Mr A.L. Kapur, being classified as independent directors on the board of ACC. How could Mr Sekhsaria and Mr Kapur, managing director and WTD, respectively of GACL, which held about 14 per cent of ACC through its subsidiary Ambuja Cement India Ltd (then a 60 per cent subsidiary of GACL), be classified as independent directors on the board of ACC in 2003–04? They had to be nominees of a major (non-institutional) shareholder. Surprisingly, in the subsequent annual report, it was stated that they ceased to be independent directors pursuant to the acquisition of shares of ACC by Holdcem Cements Pvt. Ltd, with Ambuja Cement India Ltd and GACL acting in concert, and thus Ambuja Cement India Ltd, effectively holding 34.69 per cent of ACC.

Partner of an auditing firm which does audits of many companies belonging to a group but designated as independent in another firm belonging to the same group with which he is not associated as an auditor   Yezdi H. Malegam was a partner of S.B. Billimoria & Company and was an auditor for many companies belonging to the Tata Group (Tata Motors, Tata Steel, TCS, etc.). He was on the board of Tata Tea as an independent director, another company belonging to the group with which his firm was not associated as an auditor. Similarly, Shailesh Haribhakti, partner of Haribhakti & Company, was on the board of IPCL whereas his firm is an auditor for Reliance Energy while both the companies were part of the same group. Today, the companies belong to two different groups, thanks to the split between the Ambani brothers.

Independent directors not attending the board meetings or AGMs for years but still mentioned as independent directors (and at times enabling the company to meet the requisite percentages of independent directors according to SEBI guidelines)   Tata Steel used to have Mr Kumar Mangalam Birla on the board as an ID (whether he was independent was another puzzle as his investment company Pilani Investments used to own more than 2 per cent of Tata Steel). Mr Birla attended only one board meeting and two AGMs out of 47 board meetings and six AGMs held from 2000–01 to 2006–07.

Changing the designation of other types of directors to IDs from one year to subsequent years   Mr J.K. Setna was a director of Tata Motors since 1993 and was mentioned as non-executive promoter director in the 2002–03 annual report, but was shown as non-executive, independent director in the 2003–04 annual report with no mention of how this change happened. Till his retirement in 2006, he continued to be designated as independent. At the time he was also a member on the boards of Tata Sons and other four Tata companies, confirming his promoter director status. An executive director can become independent after a period of 3 years of non-association according to the SEBI guidelines. But how could a promoter nominee become independent?

Partners of firms offering services to the company sitting on the board of the company as IDs   Reliance Industries has Mr Mansingh L. Bhakta, a director since 1977, classified as independent director (and LID too). Mr Bhakta is a senior partner of the law firm, Kanga & Company, which functions as the solicitors and advocates for the company, according to the annual report of 2007–08, despite the revised Clause 49 stipulation that 'partners of current legal, audit, and consulting firms as well as partners of such firms that had worked in the company in the preceding three years, too, cannot be independent directors.' How can he whose firm offers legal advisory services for a fee to the company, be considered really independent?

IDs offering consulting or other services to the company   Many companies have IDs offering different services to the company like consulting, training, legal, etc. Even the most stringent of the corporate governance regulations (SOX) only says that a director is 'not considered independent if he/she accepts any compensation from the company or any of its affiliates in excess of $60,000 during the fiscal year other than compensation for board service' (Kumar 2005). If the purpose and intention of the regulation is to prevent conflicts of interest, putting any limit in value for the services is absurd. It is not the monetary value that matters; it is the spirit that matters. A conflict of interest remains a conflict of interest even if the value ascribed to the contributing issue is limited.

The erstwhile full-time chair steps down to become part-time chair with a possibility to change board composition Clause 49 stipulates that a minimum of 50 per cent of the board must be IDs in case the chairman is full-time and one-third of the board must be independent if the chairman is part-time. Mr Ratan Tata was full-time chairman of Telco (now Tata Motors). Suddenly he relinquished his post of executive chairman and decided to become non-executive chairman, in conformance with the then famous Tata Retirement Policy for Directors. Please note that there was no CEO or MD for the company at the time of his relinquishment from the chairman's post. And for quite a number of years after he relinquished the executive post, there was no MD/CEO for the company till it was later conferred on Mr Ravi Kant. For all practical purposes, the power equations in the company remained the same whereas the company had an opportunity to change the composition of the board and bring in more executive directors (at fat salaries) or promoter directors which might not have been in the interest of all the stakeholders. Theoretically, the company could reduce the number of independent directors.

Long tenures of independent directors making them behave more like insiders   A very large number of independent directors have been with the companies for long periods. Would not such long tenures give rise to a situation where the independent directors act more like insiders? While experience and learning result in better expertise, the concern is whether it can result in only congeniality and no dissent even when necessary. As Colin Carter and Jay Lorsch (2004) say, 'Long service helps a director to understand the company better, but emotional attachment means she cannot be truly independent'. It might lead to a situation causing self-defeating harmony in the boardroom than encouraging a questioning culture and facing truth and reality. Mr Wadia has been on the boards of Tata Steel, Tata Motors, and Tata Chemicals for 31, 12, and 29 years, respectively. While Narayana Murthy committee on Corporate Governance constituted by SEBI recommended a maximum tenure of 9 years for IDs, many companies have given it a cursory pass by as this is only a non-mandatory guideline. With the directors who get their first appointment to directorship in the upper age group, this period of 9 years looks a little too long a tenure. While writing on the Satyam issue, Goswami (2009), founder and chairman of CERG Advisory Pvt. Ltd (former

Chief Economist, CII) and director on many boards including Infosys, Dr Reddy's Laboratories, IDFC, etc., commented that 'We need a re-think. I believe it makes sense, because very long association with any board can potentially diminish the objectivity and watchdog-like behaviour that shareholders have the right to expect from their independent directors. My preference is to start with 2004, when the new Clause 49 came into being; and count off 9 years from then. So, anyone who was an outside director on the board of a company in 2004 ought to demit office not later than 2013.'

Number of independent directorships   It has been found that most of the directors have large number of directorships. For example, Deepak Parekh, who recently was appointed by the government on the reconstituted Satyam board, sits on at least 13 other boards of listed public companies in India in addition to being full-time chairman of HDFC. While one cannot specify a number as the most appropriate, more numbers can be a serious issue when it comes to commitment and contribution. Research shows that if a company's directors are on multiple boards, the company is significantly more likely to become defendant in a securities fraud lawsuit, a result suggesting that directors with less available time tend to be less vigilant (Finkelstein 2003). SEBI stipulates that no director can be a member of more than 10 committees of the board or be a chairman of more than five such committees, indirectly saying that an independent director cannot be on more than 10 boards based on the assumption that an ID has to be at least on one committee of the board. If we assume that on an average an independent director/NED has to put in about 100–150 hours per company per year, depending on whether he is or not a member or a member of committees, if one is on the board of say, 10 companies, he has to put in 1000–1500 hours in total or approximately 85–125 working days a year, considering a 12-hour working day. Can anybody working full time with one company devote this kind of time to other companies? It would be impossible. If one is retired but still very active as a consultant, he may again find it difficult. For retired people beyond a certain age, say 65 years, it may not be very easy to be on the board of many companies if it involves a lot of traveling. Thus, while the number of directorships one can take depend on one's pre-occupation, the role of the board where he/she is a member, health, energy levels, etc., and theoretically, we cannot set an upper limit. But, this study points to the fact that if the majority of directors are either CEOs or chairmen of their own companies, the time they can allot to other directorships must be severely limited. This explains why Mr Birla did not attend many board meetings or AGMs at Tata Steel or any board meeting or AGM at Maruti Udyog (now Maruti Suzuki India).

In a study conducted by the author on the corporate governance of Indian family managed companies, based on Sensex companies as a sample, it was found that more than 60 per cent of the sample companies had even independent directors who were members on 11 or more boards (Kumar 2008). There is another argument suggested by the industry that since independent directors are a recent regulatory requirement, there is a problem of getting the right candidates to sit on the boards. Who should be blamed for this? The industry itself is to be blamed. If you have a person like Nusli Wadia sitting on three major Tata companies for continuous stretches of nearly 30 years, how do we expect well-trained and groomed director material to be available for India Inc. to grab? Hitherto companies had a tendency to overload good director material with too many directorships. This should change. Companies should look at below board level like vice-presidents, general managers, etc. for board positions. The point must be to select the right and functional rather than the best and the famous.

The compensation of independent directors   The compensation issue of IDs has only been emerging in India. Earlier, professionals used to assume directorships primarily for the prestige associated with the directorship. They used to get meager compensation for their directoral roles. The sitting fee used to vary from as low as Rs 250 to Rs 5,000 till recently. Today, most of the companies have set and also pay an upper limit of Rs 20,000 per board meeting with additional payments for attending committee meetings if they happen to sit on committees too. Many companies have also started compensating the IDs (and other NEDs) by way of commission by allocating a maximum percentage (subject to rules which limit it to one per cent) of net profit payable to them. Ever since SEBI has made the presence of IDs mandatory on boards, we have been witnessing a competition among companies to attract talented professionals to their boards. As a consequence, the compensation levels have been increasing and in some cases the ratio of compensation between WTDs and IDs (NEDs) is as low as 1.5:1. Of course, this is rather an exception than the rule. This ratio for India Inc. varies from about 1.5:1 as is the case with Infosys to about 494:1 in the case of Hero Honda (2007–08 figures). While on the positive side the hikes in compensation for IDs is welcome, but there could be not-so-positive sides to the whole issue. One of them may emerge if one looks at the issue from the Infosys WTDs' point of view.

Any independent director along with other NEDs will have to only attend the board meetings and the committee meetings.

Estimates by experts like Carter and Lorsch (2004) put the time to be devoted by any NED for a company from about 80 hours (for a stable and satisfactory company situation and industry complexity and where the board plays a watchdog role) to 320 hours (for a challenging company situation and industry complexity where the board plays the role of a pilot).

Even if we assume that at Infosys the board's role may be that of a pilot, it may not be anything beyond 320 hours. And one can be sure that none of the IDs on the board of Infosys will be able to devote anything beyond this considering their full time engagements, directorships on other companies, etc.

So, what is the incentive for Mr Nilekani, Mr Gopalakrishnan, and other WTDs to toil 24×7×52 for the company? And, according to the Infosys code of conduct for WTDs, the WTDs can become director of only one outside company.

On the other hand, many of the IDs on the Infosys board are members of boards of many other reputed companies, where there are opportunities for broadening one's experience and learning besides being well compensated. On the whole, these IDs may end up earning much more than what a WTD at Infosys earns (of course other than dividends which the WTDs can continue to get if they continue to hold on to their stakes even after they quit), coupled with the freedom to join many more if they can meet the demands of directoral duties and time.

On another side, would not such high salaries tempt independent directors to behave like internal directors leading to a mockery of the very concept of having IDs? Whether they would continue to behave like true IDs or become rubber stamps of the management, since this kind of pay might create a situation where they become obliged to the company board and management, is the moot question.

By being on the board of a company if one can get rewarded to the tune of Rs 1.65 crore during a 3-year tenure by devoting a maximum of 960 hours, and that too in a country like India, it could be very enticing even for the best-of-the-lot IDs and might lead to a situation leading to more self-defeating harmony in the boardroom than facing the truth and reality. While IDs need to be rewarded well for their contribution to the company, it has to be in line with the effort they are required to make. Too less will not motivate them to be committed and too much may make them too committed to act like insiders, making a mockery of the independence. A suggestion can be to pay them on the basis of days (or hours) expected to be devoted to the company at the same daily (hourly) rate the CEO is paid as the IDs are expected to advise the CEOs.

Independent directors holding shares in the companies   (either in the form of stocks or options issued as part of the compensation package). The general assumption about corporate governance is that directors holding stake in the company will have greater commitment towards the performance of the company. The fundamental premise for director stakeholding is: If we want directors to think like shareholders, they should be shareholders (Carter and Lorsch 2004). It was also assumed that directors who held substantial chunks of equity in a company are much more likely to ask discerning questions of management than an outside director who does not own any stock (Carter and Lorsch). But Mr A.W. Smith Jr in an article in 1988 raised the concern that share ownership by directors especially through options would tempt directors toward short-term decision-making to boost stock prices (Smith 1988). Lorsch (1989) while favouring part payment to director through options, had admitted that his research found that stock ownership was not a prime motivator for board service. According to Carter and Lorsch, 'The more shares a director owns, the more he has a personal interest to worry about—in effect, the more in danger he is of losing some aspects of his independence.' Here, the author takes a view that if independent directors own any stock, their independence will be lost. Instead of being independent, they would align themselves with other shareholders like promoters or other institutions. And, this may also give rise to opportunities for insider trading because he/she has all strategic information. Robert Gumbiner, former chairman of FHP International, feels that 'ownership of stock options by members of the board has a strong tendency to compel them to act in a short-term, deleterious manner' (Ward 1997). Another problem with pay through stock options is that the exercise of options will have bearing only on the stock price (or the market) and may not have much relevance to the actual performance of the company. While some may suggest that safeguards can be built in to assure that directors become long-term shareholders, this gives rise to another question: Should directors be serving the boards long-term? If your interest is to create a strategic board, you would like to shuffle the board to meet the requirements of the current, changed scenario. In a study on the governance of 30 BSE Sensex companies, in 19 companies out of 25 for which shareholding details have been made available, independent directors either hold stock already or have been issued stock options.

IMPROVING ADMINISTRATION OF GOVERNANCE THROUGH COMMITTEES

While board as a whole has the responsibility for the governance of the corporation, it may not be easy and advisable for the full board to be available for carrying out various governance activities. According to Carter and Lorsch (2004), 'The rationale for establishing board committees is to divide up the work among board members so that they can accomplish more in their limited time and the risk of the "whole board approach" on complex matters is that in theory every director is involved, but in practice no one takes responsibility; it is simply too difficult for all the directors to understand the technical details.'

Some of the areas like auditing of the financial position of the company require specific expertise which every director may not have. Getting the full board for the process of appointing the auditors or vetting the audit statements is unwarranted and may even delay the processes and requirements. Hence, boards have developed a practice of forming committees intended for specific purposes. The number of committees varies from company to company. And some committees are permanent in nature while some are constituted to meet temporary needs. A number of committees may be mandatory in a country depending on the regulation prevailing there.

The most commonly observed committees are:

1. Audit
2. Remuneration/compensation
3. Nomination/corporate governance
4. Investor/shareholder grievance
5. Special committees–managing committee, risk management committee, committee of directors, etc.

While audit and investor grievance committees are mandatory under most regulatory frameworks, some countries have made certain other committees also mandatory. For example, the SOX in the US makes the compensation and nomination committees also mandatory. Banking companies usually have a risk management committee to oversee the management of risky exposures of banks. All the committees have to be constituted of only directors. Management job is restricted to providing information to the committees. Each of these committees will have a chairman. The tasks and requirements of the different committees are detailed below.

Audit Committee

It is mandatory under almost all regulatory frameworks. While SEC insists that the committee be constituted only from IDs, Clause 49 of the SEBI guidelines for listing agreement stipulates that minimum number shall be three and majority shall be independent directors. SOX insists that at least one of the members shall be a 'financial expert'. Clause 49 in India requires that at least one member has financial and accounting knowledge. Clause 49 necessitates that every listed company adopt an appropriate audit committee charter. SEC also recommends that every listed company adopt an audit committee charter. A charter, if available, will clearly state the objective, the responsibilities, the composition, relationship with independent and internal auditors, disclosure requirements, delegation of authority, etc. The committee usually has the authority to select, evaluate, and replace the independent director.

The basic functions of a typical audit committee might include:

- Advising and appraising the board on various systems of internal controls and matters of internal audit
- Liaising with independent auditors and reporting to the board on the audit process and on specific audit issues
- Reviewing the financial information to be provided to shareholders and others
- Advising the board on matters of broad accountability.

While, by and large, most of the companies have only IDs on the audit committees, companies like Tata Steel seem to be an exception. They have non-independent directors on the audit committee even in the year 2007–08.

Audit committee is expected to meet at least once in 3 months according to revised Clause 49 guidelines. With every board meeting having something to discuss about audit function, it is only likely that the number of audit committee meetings exceed the number of board meetings under normal circumstances.

Remuneration/Compensation Committee

The purpose of this committee is to decide on the remuneration to be paid to the CEO/ MD, other executive/whole-time directors, and the NEDs. It decides on the composition of the remuneration package including bonuses and incentives. Its responsibility is to establish a compensation criterion that is sufficient to attract and retain talent and expertise within the company. It makes the recommendations to the board and the board seeks the approval of the shareholders in a general meeting.

In certain companies, it even deals with the remuneration packages of senior executives below the board level. Remuneration committee is mandatory according to SOX; whereas in India, according to Clause 49, it is non-mandatory. The US laws stipulate that it be constituted of only IDs, those Indian companies which are listed only in India and which have these committees have a combination of IDs, other NEDs including promoter nominees, and even WTDs. Ideally it should be composed only of IDs. On the compensation committee continuum, we can see very big and highly respected companies without them and small and not necessarily reputed ones with them and constituted only of IDs. Since this is non-mandatory, there is no specified number of meetings. The number of meetings will depend on the necessity to fix the remuneration package for directors and other senior managers.

To cite examples from India, big companies like Grasim or Hindalco belonging to the AV Birla Group of companies do not have remuneration committees, whereas much smaller companies like Carborundum Universal or Pricol have the remuneration committees that are, constituted only of independent directors. Tata companies like Tata Steel, Tata Motors, or TCS have remuneration committees but all have a promoter nominee (R.N. Tata) as member. While, in general, the purpose of committees is to relieve the full board from involving in every detail, a certain committee that is expected to be composed of independent directors only shall not be considered to be just another committee but as independent committee because the very nature of the work and the responsibility they are expected to handle, even when they belong to non-mandatory requirements. If the remuneration committee includes promoter nominees (even when they are NEDs) in a family promoted and managed company, it is like one family member evaluating the answer sheets of another family member. Another issue relates to the leadership shown by some of these companies and promoters. Both Grasim and Hidalco are chaired by Kumar Mangalam Birla, who can be said to be a major architect of corporate governance guidelines in India. Major companies in his group have been doing just enough on the corporate governance front to meet the mandatory requirements. They do not seem to be providing any kind of leadership for others to be inspired on the corporate governance front.

Nomination/Corporate Governance Committee

The primary purpose of a nomination committee is to identify new directors on to the board whenever an existing member retires after his tenure and do not offer himself for re-election, or when the board wants to expand. It oversees the nomination process to identify, screen, and review potential director material to serve as EDs, NEDs, and IDs and recommend them to the board for the final decision on appointment. The committee also may play a role of evaluation of individual directors and the board as a whole. They may also review the company's corporate governance guidelines (like governance charters) periodically and recommend amendments to the board as may deem necessary, where it fulfills the role of a corporate governance committee too. The committee may use outside consultants' help in its execution of duties.

The nomination committee again is not mandatory in India but many companies have chosen to have them. While companies like Infosys (Nasdaq listed) have all IDs as members of the committee, companies like Tata Steel, Tata Motors, and TCS have promoter nominee (R.N. Tata) on them. Major companies in AV Birla Group again do not have nomination committees. Since this is also non-mandatory, the number of meetings will depend on the necessity for the committee to meet as and when directors are to be nominated.

Investor Grievance Committee

This committee looks into the grievances and complaints of the investors with respect to their shareholding like non-receipt of shares/debentures/dividends/interest warrants/financial reports and other communications on time, loss of shares/debentures, issue of duplicate certificates, delays in transfers, other queries regarding their holdings, etc. The committee might also monitor the implementation and compliance of the company's code of conduct relating to insider trading. This committee was already in vogue and mandatory before the Clause 49 came into being. This continues to be mandatory even today. Usually constituted from executive as well as non-executive/independent directors, companies like Infosys have only IDs as members with the company's compliance officer functioning as secretary to the committee.

Risk Management Committee

This again is not mandatory according to SEBI but banking regulator RBI insists that banks and other financial institutions which have exposed themselves to risks must have risk management committees. But apart from banks, many other companies have also constituted risk management committees. Infosys, for example, have constituted a risk management committee, exclusively of IDs with the assigned role of identification, evaluation, and mitigation of operational, strategic, and external environment risks 'with the responsibility of monitoring and approving the risk policies and associated practices of the company' (Infosys Annual Report 2007–08). It is also responsible for 'reviewing and approving risk disclosure statements in many public documents or disclosures'. It is very interesting to note that even some of the bigger companies like RIL (which apparently is subject to many risks), Tata Steel, Wipro, or TCS, which are by no means lesser exposed to risk, have not constituted risk management committees yet.

Special Committees

Many companies will constitute special 'functional' committees for specific purposes. For example, they may constitute Investment Committees, Project Committees, Disaster Management Committees, Merger & Integration Committees, etc., depending on the requirements at specific periods of time. The terms of references for such committees will be detailed once they are constituted.

DIRECTOR INDEPENDENCE—NEED IS FOR INDEPENDENT MINDSET

While the law and regulator demand that half or one-third of the directors shall be independent, the very presence of IDs meeting all the qualification criteria for IDs will not serve the purpose. Enron failed despite having majority independent directors. Satyam in India is another case in point. It had IDs who were eminent personalities and experts in their respective fields. These examples show clearly that it is just not the presence of IDs that matters; instead, it is how they behave and act. They should have the capability as well as courage to question the actions and decisions of the WTDs, promoters, and the management in times of doubt and need. Company's interests must be at the top of their minds. It is not very easy to achieve these desired states without the board encouraging and being comfortable with a questioning culture.

While it may not be very easy to raise questions against a group of WTDs or NEDs representing the promoters, many a time with the largest shareholder, if not holding majority stake in the company, it is possible to succeed in impressing that they keep the company and its well-being as the highest beneficiary of their efforts. The first effort is to make the board comfortable with a questioning culture, without forgetting that the board members have to act as a cohesive team. It is not necessary to have directors strictly meeting the requisite criteria for IDs to have an independent mindset. The problem here is that the boards have to make the investors and the public in general believe that they will act independently and with an independent mindset, and a family member of the board, even with a highly independent mindset, will find it extremely difficult to convince them. Whatever it is, at the end of the day, independent directors will add value to the boards only if they have an independent mindset and act accordingly.

SUMMARY

While differences in their constituents and structures exist, boards are the ultimate responsible bodies for the governance of a firm. Different countries follow different types of incorporation laws. In the US, laws are generally framed by states and there are very few federal company laws. In India, all the states follow the same federal act, the Companies Act 1956. A board of directors is a legal requirement in almost every country. Board's responsibilities are derived from laws, customs, traditions, and current practices. While boards can be organized in different ways, the purpose of the board is same everywhere: to ensure the company's prosperity by collectively directing the company's affairs. While most countries follow a unitary board system, European countries like Germany and Austria and Scandinavian countries like Denmark and the Netherlands follow a two-tier or dual-board structure.

The role of the board may vary from company to company and will depend on need and context. Boards can also operate in different styles. Boards have been evolving over a period. Of late, because of stringent regulations as well as pressure from stakeholders, boards as well as directors have become more demanding. Boards have to play roles which many a time look conflicting.

Boards usually will have executive and non-executive members with some of the non-executive members being independent. While there is a consensus today that boards should have a good independent element, practices give rise to many concerns.

Committees are an usual phenomena in order to relieve the entire board from getting in the way of decision-making. Regulation in many countries has made constitution of certain committees mandatory.

The question of director independence is a ticklish issue. While regulations demand that IDs meet certain qualification criteria, it is the independent mindset that matters. Sans independent mindset, independent directors are not going to make any difference to governance.

KEY TERMS

Board committees Committees formed with directors to handle specific responsibilities without the need for the entire board to get involved

Board styles Different styles of functioning of boards

Box-ticking Indicating whether the process complies with the requirements

CalPERS California Public Employees Retirement System, a US-based pension fund

Country-club board Board where directors get selected due to their informal association outside the company

Fiduciary capacity Assigned position to act responsibly on behalf of somebody

Holistic view An overall perspective

Lead independent director Director who will co-ordinate the activities of independent directors including chairing the meetings of independent directors without management representatives

Nominee directors Directors nominated by financial institutions

Power shift Shift of ability to exercise power (from one agency to another)

Prudent control Careful control of the corporation and its resources

Rubber-stamp board Board which simply agrees with the decisions taken by the CEO or promoters without verification

Sarbanes–Oxley US law specifically meant for corporate governance

CONCEPT REVIEW QUESTIONS

1. Business has surpassed politics and governments as a source of power. Do you agree? Explain the rationale behind your stand.

2. What is the purpose of a corporate board?

3. The role of the board depends on context. Critically comment on the statement.

4. Do you feel that boards have undergone an evolution?

5. The different roles of the board are conflicting within themselves. Do you think that this puts a serious limitation to its effectiveness?

6. Do you feel that the number of directorships shall be limited by regulation?

7. Independent directors shall not hold a stake in the company. Comment.

CRITICAL THINKING QUESTIONS

If independence is a mindset, is it necessary for the regulator to insist on having a separate category of directors known as independent directors? Explain giving rationale with examples.

PROJECT WORK

Analyse the effectiveness of committees in governance based on publicly available information for the 30 companies constituting the Bombay Stock Exchange Sensitive Index (SENSEX).

REFERENCES

Cadbury, Sir Adrian (1992), The Report of the Committee on the Financial Aspects of Corporate Governance, Gee and Co, London.

Carter, Colin B. and Jay W. Lorsch (2004), *Back to the Drawing Board*, Harvard Business School Press, Boston.

Charan, Ram (2005), *Boards that Deliver*, Jossey-Bass, San Francisco.

Clause 49 of the Listing Agreement between Company and Stock Exchanges, www.sebi.gov.in.

Drucker, Peter (1946), *The Concept of the Corporation*, Transaction Publishers, New Jersey.

Finklestein, Sydney (2003), *Why Smart Executives Fail*, Penguin Portfolio, New York.

Garratt, Bob (1996), *The Fish Rots from the Head*, Profile Books, London.

Garratt, Bob (2003), *Thin on Top*, Nicolas Brealey, London.

Goswami, Omkar S. (2009), Aftermath of Satyam, *Businessworld*, 2 February, pp. 20.

Gupta, L.C. (1997), *Corporate Boards and Nominee Directors*, Oxford University Press, New Delhi.

Harper, John (2005), *Chairing the Board*, Kogan Page, London.

Kumar, T.N. Satheesh (2005), 'How Independent Are Independent Directors?' *Indian Management*, May 2005.

Kumar, T.N. Satheesh (2008), 'Strategic Corporate Governance: Looking Beyond Regulations,' *ICFAI Journal of Corporate Governance*, April, pp. 42–57.

Lorsch, Jay W. and Elizabeth MacIver (1989), *Pawns & Potentates*, HBS Press, Boston.

Mace, Myles (1971), *Directors: Myth & Reality*, HBS Press, Boston.

Public Accounting Reform and Investor Protection Act (Sarbanes–Oxley Act) 2002, US.

Smith Jr., A.W. (1988), 'Stock Options for Directors?', *Corporate Board*, March/April 1988, pp. 14.

Smith, Roy C. and Ingo Walter (2006), *Governing the Modern Corporation*, Oxford University Press, New York.

Tricker, Bob (2001), *Pocket Director*, Economist/Profile Books, London.

Ward, Ralph D. (1997), *21st Century Corporate Board*, John Wiley & Sons, New York.

Closing Case

Board Structure—Professional vs Family Firms

Excerpts from the corporate governance reports of two major companies from India, namely, Infosys Technologies Ltd and Reliance Industries Ltd, for the year 2007–08 are given below. Analyse the practices of the two companies and answer the questions that follow. You may use other published information in support of your answers.

Infosys Technologies Ltd

In the last decade, two events significantly contributed to making corporate governance nearly a household term. The first was the wave of financial crises in Russia, Asia, and Brazil in 1998, when the activities of the corporate sector influenced entire economies and the global financial system. Three years later, the corporate scandals in the US had highlighted the macroeconomic consequences of weak corporate governance systems. In the aftermath, economists, the corporate world, and policy-makers everywhere began to recognize the importance of corporate governance. The traditional analysis of corporate governance focused on the allocation of power and duty among the BOD, management, and shareholders. As the sole residual claimants on company assets, shareholders were presumed to have the most incentive to maximize company value. According to that perspective, the BOD acted as the shareholders' agent and management was responsible for daily operations. In today's scenario, the board and the management play the role of trustees. Effective corporate governance requires a clear understanding of the respective roles of the board and the senior management, and their relationships with others in the corporate structure. The relationship of the board and the management with stockholders should be characterized by candour; their relationship with employees should be characterized by fairness; their relationship with the communities in which they operate should be characterized by good citizenship; and their relationship with the government should be characterized by a commitment to compliance. We believe that sound corporate governance is critical to enhance and retain stakeholders' trust. Accordingly, we always seek to ensure that we attain our performance rules with integrity. Our board exercises its fiduciary responsibilities in the widest sense of the term. Our disclosures always seek to attain best practices in international corporate governance. We also endeavour to enhance long-term shareholder value and respect minority rights in all our business decisions. Our corporate governance philosophy is based on the following principles:

- Satisfy the spirit of the law and not just the letter of the law. Corporate governance standards should go beyond the law.
- Be transparent and maintain a high degree of disclosure levels. When in doubt, disclose.
- Make a clear distinction between personal conveniences and corporate resources.
- Communicate externally, in a truthful manner, about how the company is run internally.
- Comply with the laws in all the countries in which we operate.
- Have a simple and transparent corporate structure driven solely by business needs.
- Management is the trustee of the shareholders' capital and not the owner.

The BOD is at the core of our corporate governance practice and oversees as to how the management serves and protects the long-term interests of all our stakeholders. We believe that an active, well-informed and independent board is necessary to ensure highest standards of corporate governance. The majority of our board, 8 out of 15, are independent members. Further, we have audit, compensation, investor grievance, nominations, and risk management committees, which comprise only independent directors.

As a part of our commitment to follow global best practices, we comply with the Euro-shareholders Corporate Governance Guidelines 2000, and the recommendations of the Conference Board Commission on Public Trusts and Private Enterprises in the US. We also adhere to the UN Global Compact Programme. Further, a note on our compliance with the corporate governance guidelines of six countries—in their national languages—is presented elsewhere in the Annual Report.

Corporate governance guidelines

Over the years, the board has developed corporate governance guidelines to help fulfill our corporate responsibility to various stakeholders. These guidelines ensure that the board will have the necessary authority and practices in place, to review and evaluate our operations when required. Further, these guidelines allow the board to make decisions that are independent of the management. The board may change these guidelines from time to time to effectively achieve our stated objectives.

Board Composition
Size and composition of the board

The current policy is to have an appropriate mix of executive and independent directors to maintain the independence of the board, and to separate the board functions of governance and management. The board consists of 15 members, six of who are executive or full-time directors, one is non-executive and 8 are independent directors. Four of the executive directors are our founders. The board believes that the current size is appropriate, based on our present circumstances. The board periodically evaluates the need for change in composition of its size.

Responsibilities of the chairman, co-chairman, CEO, and the COO

Our current policy is to have a non-executive chairman and chief mentor—N.R. Narayana Murthy; a co-chairman—Nandan M. Nilekani, a chief executive officer (CEO) and managing director—S. Gopalakrishnan; and chief operating officer (COO)—S. D.Shibulal. There are clear demarcations of responsibility and authority among these officials.

- The chairman and chief mentor is responsible for mentoring our core management team in transforming us into a world-class, next-generation organization that provides state-of-the-art, technology-leveraged business solutions to corporations across the world. He also interacts with global thought leaders to enhance our leadership position. In addition, he continues to interact with various institutions to highlight and help bring about the benefits of IT to every section of society. As chairman of the board, he is also responsible for all board matters.
- The co-chairman of the board focuses on key client relationships, deals with broader industry issues, provides global thought leadership, leads transformation initiatives, contributes to strategy, and is a brand ambassador.

- The CEO and MD is responsible for corporate strategy, brand equity, planning, external contacts and other management matters. He is also responsible for achieving the annual business plan and acquisitions.
- The COO is responsible for all customer service operations. He is also responsible for technology, new initiatives, and investments. The co-chairman, CEO, COO, the other executive directors and the senior management make periodic presentations to the board on their responsibilities, performance, and targets.

Board definition of independent directors

According to Clause 49 of the listing agreement with Indian stock exchanges, an independent director means a person other than an officer or employee of the company or its subsidiaries or any other individual having a material pecuniary relationship or transactions with the company which, in the opinion of our BOD, would interfere with the exercise of independent judgement in carrying out the responsibilities of a director. We adopted a much stricter definition of independence than required by the NASDAQ listing rules and the Sarbanes–Oxley Act 2002 of US. The same is provided in the *Audit committee charter* section of this Annual Report.

Lead independent director

Deepak M. Satwalekar is the LID. He represents and acts as spokesperson for the independent directors as a group, and is responsible for the following activities:

- Presiding over all executive sessions of the board's independent directors
- Working closely with the chairman, co-chairman, and the CEO to finalize the information flow, meeting agendas and meeting schedules
- Liaising between the chairman, co-chairman, CEO, and the independent directors on the board, and
- Along with the chairman and co-chairman, taking a lead role in the board evaluation process

Board membership criteria

The nominations committee works with the entire board to determine the appropriate characteristics, skills and experience required for the board as a whole as well as its individual members. Board members are expected to possess the expertise, skills, and experience required to manage and guide a high-growth, high-tech software company, deriving revenue primarily from G-7 countries. Expertise in strategy, technology, finance, quality, and human resources is essential. Generally, the members will be between 40 and 60 years of age, and will not be related to any executive directors or independent directors. They are generally not expected to serve in any executive or independent position in any company that is in direct competition with us. Board members are expected to rigorously prepare for, attend, and participate in all Board and applicable committee meetings. Each member is expected to ensure that their other current and planned future commitments do not materially interfere with their responsibility as our director.

Selection of new directors

The board is responsible for the selection of new directors. The board delegates the screening and selection process involved in selecting new directors to the nominations committee, which consists exclusively of independent directors. The nominations committee in turn makes recommendations to the Board on the induction of any new directors.

Membership term

The board constantly evaluates the contribution of the members and periodically makes recommendations to the shareholders about re-appointments as per statute. The current law in India mandates the retirement of one-third of the board members (who are liable to retire by rotation) every year, and qualifies the retiring members for re-appointment. Executive directors are appointed by the shareholders for a maximum period of 5 years at a time, but are eligible for re-appointment upon completion of their term. Non-executive/independent directors do not have a specified term, but retire by rotation as per law. The nominations committee of the board recommends such appointments and re-appointments. However, the membership term is limited by the retirement age for members.

Retirement policy

Under this policy, the maximum age of retirement for executive directors is 60 years, which is the age of superannuation for our employees. Their continuation as members of the Board upon superannuation/retirement is determined by the nominations committee. The age limit for serving on the board is 65 years.

Succession planning

The nominations committee constantly works with the board to evolve succession planning for the positions of the chairman, CEO, COO, and CFO and also develops plans for interim succession for any of them, in case of an unexpected occurrence. The board, if required, may review the succession plan more frequently.

Board compensation policy

The compensation committee determines and recommends to the board, the compensation payable to the directors. All board-level compensation is approved by the shareholders, and separately disclosed in the financial statements. Remuneration of the executive directors consists of a fixed component and a performance incentive. The compensation committee makes a quarterly appraisal of the performance of the executive directors based on a detailed performance-related matrix. The annual compensation of the executive directors is approved by the compensation committee, within the parameters set by the shareholders at the shareholders' meetings. The compensation payable to independent directors is limited to a fixed amount per year as determined and approved by the Board, the sum of which is within the limit of 1 per cent of our net profits for the year, calculated as per the provisions of the Companies Act 1956. The performance of independent directors is reviewed by the full Board on an annual basis. The compensation paid to independent directors and the method of calculation is disclosed separately in the financial statements.

Non-executive/Independent Directors' remuneration

Section 309 of the Companies Act 1956 provides that a director who is neither in the whole-time employment of the company nor a managing director may be paid remuneration by way of commission, if the company, by special resolution, authorizes such payment. Members of the company at the annual general meeting held on 12 June 2004, approved payment of remuneration by way of commission to NEDs, at a sum not exceeding 0.5 per cent per annum of our net profits. We have paid Rs 4.19 crore (US $10,47,500) as commission to our NEDs. The aggregate amount was arrived at as per the criteria in the following tables.

Cash compensation paid to directors in fiscal 2008 (in Rs crores)

Name of the director	Fixed Salary				Bonus/ incentives	Commission	Total
	Basic salary	Perquisites/ allowances	Retiral benefits	Total fixed salary			
Founder and Non-executive Director							
N. R. Narayana Murthy	–	–	–	–	–	0.50	0.50
Founder and Whole-time Directors							
Nandan M. Niekani	0.21	0.06	0.05	0.32	0.49	–	0.81
S. Gopalakrishnan	0.21	0.06	0.05	0.32	0.49	–	0.81
S. D. Shibulal	0.20	0.06	0.05	0.31	0.47	–	0.78
K. Dinesh	0.21	0.07	0.05	0.33	0.49	–	0.82
Whole-time Directors							
T. V. Mohandas Pai	0.33	0.13	0.08	0.54	1.24	–	1.78
Srinath Batni	0.30	0.11	0.08	0.49	0.77	–	1.26
Independent Directors							
Deepak M. Satwalekar	–	–	–	–	–	0.56	0.56
Prof. Marti G. Subrahmanyam	–	–	–	–	–	0.47	0.47
Dr Omkar Goswami	–	–	–	–	–	0.44	0.44
Rama Bijapurkar	–	–	–	–	–	0.44	0.44
Claude Smadja	–	–	–	–	–	0.42	0.42
Sridar A. Iyengar	–	–	–	–	–	0.46	0.46
David L. Boyles	–	–	–	–	–	0.47	0.47
Prof. Jeffrey S. Lehman	–	–	–	–	–	0.43	0.43

Note: None of the above directors are eligible for any severance pay.

	in Rs crore	US $
Fixed pay	0.30	75,000
Variable pay*	0.10	25,000
Chairperson of the board	0.10	25,000
Lead independent director	0.06	15,000
Chairperson of audit committee	0.08	20,000
Members of the audit committee	0.04	10,000
Chairperson of other committees	0.02	5,000
Members of other committees	0.01	2,500

Based on the attendance at board meetings; US $1 = Rs 40.02

At the meeting held on 15 April 2008, the board further decided that effective 1 April 2008, independent directors based overseas and travelling to India to attend board meetings will be eligible to receive an additional US $5,000 per meeting. The decision considers the fact that these independent directors have to spend at least two additional days in travel while attending board meetings in India. The board believes that the above commission structure is commensurate with global best practices in terms of remunerating NEDs of a company of similar size and adequately compensates for the time and contribution made by the NEDs.

Memberships in other Boards

Executive directors may, with the prior consent of the chairperson of the BOD, serve on the board of one other business entity, provided that such a business entity is not in direct competition with our business operations. Executive directors are also allowed to serve on the Board of corporate or government bodies whose interests are germane to the future of the software business, or are key economic institutions of the nation, or whose prime objective is benefiting society. Independent directors are not expected to serve on the boards of competing companies. Other than this, there are no limitations on them, save those imposed by law and good corporate governance practices.

Reliance Industries Ltd

Corporate governance is based on the principles of integrity, fairness, equity, transparency, accountability, and commitment to values. Good governance practices stem from the culture and mindset of the organization. As stakeholders across the globe evince keen interest in the practices and performance of companies, corporate governance has emerged on the centre stage. Over the years, governance processes and systems have been strengthened at Reliance. In addition to complying with the statutory requirements, effective governance systems and practices towards improving transparency, disclosures, internal controls, and promotion of ethics at work-place have been institutionalized. Reliance recognizes that good corporate governance is a continuing exercise and reiterates its commitment to pursue highest standards of corporate governance in the overall interest of all the stakeholders. For implementing the corporate governance practices, Reliance has a well defined policy framework consisting of the following:

- Reliance's values and commitments policy
- Reliance's code of ethics
- Reliance's business policies
- Reliance's policy for prohibition of insider trading
- A detailed programme of ethics management

These policies and their effective implementation underpin the commitment of the Company to uphold the highest principles of corporate governance consistent with the company's goal to enhance shareholder value.

Corporate Governance Monitoring and Review Process at Reliance
Reliance continuously reviews its policies and practices of corporate governance with a clear goal not merely to comply with statutory requirements in letter and spirit but also constantly endeavours to implement the best international practices of corporate governance, in the overall interest of all stakeholders. Some of the major initiatives taken by the company towards strengthening its corporate governance systems and practices include the following:

(a) Corporate Governance and Stakeholders' Interface Committee
The Corporate Governance and Stakeholders' Interface Committee consisting of independent directors examines various corporate governance practices from time to time and recommends to the board for adoption. Establishment of a dedicated independent board committee demonstrates the level of management's commitment in putting in place a pervasive governance framework flowing from the top. The scope of the Corporate Governance and Stakeholders' Interface Committee was enhanced to act as Nomination Committee as well. Accordingly, the committee evaluates and recommends to the board the appointment of directors on the board. This move of the management aims at ensuring increased level of transparency, objective evaluation of the board strength, and impartial selection of new directors on the board.

(b) Corporate Governance Manual
The Corporate Governance Manual ('the Manual') of the company sets out amongst others the procedures for effective functioning of the board and its committees. The manual also incorporates the code of business conduct and ethics for directors and management personnel, code of ethics for employees, code of conduct for prohibition of insider trading, and key accounting policies. These policies are constantly monitored and reviewed by the Corporate Governance and Stakeholders' Interface Committee, from time to time.

(c) Secretarial Audit
The company has appointed an independent practising company secretary to conduct secretarial audit. The quarterly audit reports are placed before the board and the annual audit report placed before the board is included in the Annual Report. This audit has been introduced to report to the management as well as the shareholders of the status of compliance with various applicable corporate and securities laws.

(d) Guidelines for the Board/Committee Meetings
The company has defined guidelines for meetings of the board and board committees. These guidelines seek to systematize the decision-making process at the meetings of the board and board committees in an informed and efficient manner. The salient features of the guidelines have been dealt with in detail elsewhere in this report.

(e) Best Governance Practices

It is the company's constant endeavour to adopt the best governance practices as laid down in international codes of corporate governance and as practised by well known global companies.

Some of the best global governance norms put into practice at Reliance include the following:

(i)   The company has a designated LID with a defined role.

(ii) All securities related filings with stock exchanges and SEBI are reviewed on a quarterly basis by the Shareholders'/Investors' Grievance Committee.

(iii) The Company has established policies and procedures for corporate communication and disclosures.

In accordance with Clause 49 of the listing agreement with the stock exchanges in India (Clause 49) and some of the best practices followed internationally on corporate governance, the report containing the details of governance systems and processes at Reliance Industries Limited is as under:

1. Company's Philosophy on Code of Governance

Reliance's philosophy on corporate governance envisages attainment of the highest levels of transparency, accountability, and equity in all facets of its operations, and in all its interactions with its stakeholders, including shareholders, employees, lenders, government, and the society at large. Reliance is committed to achieve and maintain the highest standards of corporate governance. Reliance believes that all its actions must serve the underlying goal of enhancing overall shareholder value on a sustained basis. Reliance is committed to the best governance practices that create long term sustainable shareholder value. Keeping in view the company's size, complexity, global operations, and corporate traditions, the Reliance governance framework is based on the following main principles:

- Constitution of a BOD of appropriate composition, size, varied expertise, and commitment to discharge its responsibilities and duties.
- Ensuring timely flow of information to the board and its committees to enable them to discharge their functions effectively.
- Independent verification and safeguarding integrity of the company's financial reporting.
- A sound system of risk management and internal control.
- Timely and balanced disclosure of all material information concerning the Company to all stakeholders.
- Transparency and accountability.
- Compliance with all the applicable rules and regulations.
- Fair and equitable treatment of all its stakeholders including employees, customers, shareholders, and investors.

2. Board Composition and Particulars of Directors

Board Composition

The company's policy is to maintain optimum combination of executive and non-executive directors. The board consists of 13 directors, out of which 8 are independent directors. Composition of the board and category of directors are as follows:

Category	Name of Directors
Promoter director	Mukesh D. Ambani *Chairman and Managing Director*
Executive directors	Nikhil R. Meswani Hital R. Meswani Hardev Singh Kohli
Non-executive, Non-independent director	Ramniklal H. Ambani
Independent directors	Mansingh L. Bhakta Yogendra P. Trivedi Dr Dharam Vir Kapur Mahesh P. Modi S. Venkitaramanan Prof. Ashok Misra Prof. Dipak C. Jain Dr Raghunath A. Mashelkar

All the independent directors of the company furnish a declaration at the time of their appointment as also annually that they qualify the conditions of their being independent as laid down under Clause 49. All such declarations are placed before the board.

No director is related to any other director on the board in terms of the definition of 'relative' given under the Companies Act 1956, except Shri Nikhil R. Meswani and Shri Hital R. Meswani, who are brothers.

What constitutes independence of directors

For a director to be considered independent, the board determines that the director does not have any direct or indirect material pecuniary relationship with the company. The board has adopted guidelines to determine independence, which are in line with the applicable legal requirements.

Lead independent director

The BOD of the company has designated Shri Mansingh L. Bhakta as the LID. The role of LID is as follows:

- To preside over all meetings of independent directors.
- To ensure that there is adequate and timely flow of information to independent directors.
- To liaise between the chairman and managing director, the management and the independent directors.
- To advise on the necessity of retention or otherwise of consultants who report directly to the Board or the independent directors.
- To preside over meetings of the board and shareholders when the chairman and managing director is not present or where he is an interested party.
- To perform such other duties as may be delegated to the LID by the board/independent directors.

Remuneration paid to the chairman and managing director and the whole-time directors, including the number of stock options granted during 2007–08

Name of the director	Salary	Perquisites and allowances	Retiral benefits	Commission payable	Total	Stock options granted
		Rs in lakhs				Nos
Mukesh D. Ambani	60.00	48.00	18.75	4275.44	4,402.19	Nil
Nikhil R. Meswani	15.00	24.00	4.54	1068.86	1,112.40	7,00,000
Hital R. Meswani	15.00	24.00	4.51	1068.86	1,112.37	7,00,000
Hardev Singh Kohli	41.67	67.09	17.34	Nil	126.10	50,000

The NEDs are paid a sitting fee of Rs 20,000 for attending each meeting of the board and/or committee thereof. Each of the NED is also paid a commission amounting to Rs 21,00,000 on an annual basis, provided that the total commission payable to such directors shall not exceed one per cent of the net profits of the company.

Sitting fee and commission to the NEDs for 2007–08 are as detailed below (Rs in lakhs)

Name of the non-executive director	Sitting fee	Commission	Total
Ramniklal H. Ambani	1.40	21.00	22.40
Mansingh L. Bhakta	2.60	21.00	23.60
Yogendra P. Trivedi	5.00	21.00	26.00
Dr Dharam Vir Kapur	3.00	21.00	24.00
Mahesh P Modi	3.80	21.00	24.80
S. Venkitaramanan	2.60	21.00	23.60
Prof. Ashok Misra	1.40	21.00	22.40
Prof. Dipak C. Jain	1.80	21.00	22.80
Dr Raghunath A. Mashelkar	0.80	17.50	18.30
Total	22.40	185.50	207.90

During the year (2007–08), the company has paid Rs 86.09 lakhs as professional fees to M/s. Kanga & Co., a firm in which Shri M. L. Bhakta, Director of the company, is a partner. There were no other pecuniary relationships or transactions of the NEDs vis-à-vis the company. The company has not granted any stock option to any of its NEDs.

Discussion Questions
1. Do you think that ownership pattern has any influence on the governance practices of these companies? Justify your view with substantiating arguments.
2. Comment on the composition of the boards of the two companies.
3. Compare and comment on the director nomination and compensation policies of the two companies.

CHAPTER 5

THE BOARD DEVELOPMENT PROCESS
SELECTION, DEVELOPMENT, COMPENSATION, AND PERFORMANCE REVIEW

There is a need for the promoter CEOs to have a voluntary restraint on their salaries/ emoluments. Promoters, by definition, have other income and in any case will not leave their company to join another one. Hence, they must set an example.

– Rahul Bajaj, Chairman, Bajaj Auto Ltd, quoted in *Business Today*, 15 November 2009

LEARNING OBJECTIVES

After studying this chapter, you will be able to
- Explain how to make boards more effective and a force to reckon with
- Discuss the recruitment of the right candidates to the board
- Explain where to locate director candidates and what to look for in them
- Enumerate the desirable personal qualities and characteristics of directoral candidates
- Elucidate performance evaluation of individual directors and the board as a whole
- Explain the importance and relevance development of individual directors and the board as a whole
- Describe succession planning at CEO and other director levels
- Understand the CEO and other executive director compensation and related issues and define the board's role
- Elucidate the non-executive director compensation
- Distinguish between the Indian scenario of CEO and other director compensation
- List the components of CEO and director compensation

Opening Case

Determinants of Executive Pay

Prime Minister Manmohan Singh, while sharing his thoughts on 'Inclusive Growth—Challenges for Corporate India' organized by CII at Delhi on 24 May 2007, advised the corporate captains to 'resist excessive remuneration to promoters and senior executives, and discourage conspicuous consumption. In a country with extreme poverty, industry needs to be moderate in the emolument levels it adopts. Rising income and wealth inequalities, if not matched by a corresponding rise (in) income across the nation, can lead to social unrest.' In reaction to the PM's comments, it was suggested from many quarters that deciding chief executive officer (CEO) compensations is not the business of legislations or regulations, but rather that of market forces and shareholders. Speaking on the issue, Mr Rahul Bajaj reportedly commented: 'I think the Prime Minister was referring to the emoluments of the promoters, and I share his view that promoters should voluntarily exercise self-restraint.' As a response to the issue, Kumar wrote 'it is not just the market mechanism of supply and demand for talent that determines CEO salaries. What role does the market play when a relatively smaller company like Cipla pays its founder-promoter CEO Rs 7.88 crores, while the salary of the professional, outsider CEO of a much bigger and profitable company like Maruti Udyog is only Rs 1.47 crore? It is true that markets, by and large, have shown tremendous

Performance of Bajaj Auto Ltd

	2006–07	2007–08	2008–09
Total vehicles sold (numbers in millions)	2.72	2.43	2.19
Motor cycle sales (numbers in millions)	2.38	2.14	1.91
Market share (per cent)	33.75	32.7	28.0
Exports (numbers in millions)	0.44	0.62	0.77
Gross sales (Rs millions)	106000	96900	90500
PBT (Rs millions)	17280	10120	9580
PAT (Rs millions)	12380	7559	6570
EPS (Rs)	122	54.2	45.2
DPS (Rs)	40	20	22
Share price (Rs) (Closing price on 31 March)		945[a]	618.45
Shareholding of promoter + friends, associates	46.59	61.65	61.65
Executive compensation details (Rs millions)			
Rahul Bajaj, Executive Chairman	39.55	38.06	62.69
Madhur Bajaj, Executive Vice-chairman	27.55	25.31	41.40
Rajiv Bajaj, Managing Director and CEO	20.15	20.23	33.12
Sanjiv Bajaj, Executive Director	14.79	14.83	8.92
Total managerial remuneration	102.04	98.43	146.13
Increase (Decrease) (%)		(3.54)	48

[a] Opening price after the demerger on BSE on 26 May 2008, the date of listing.

resilience by more or less correctly valuing shares of companies. And, the market mechanism may work well up to senior/top management positions below the board level. But CEO salaries in India are a different game altogether and are not entirely determined by the demand-supply scenario in the CEO job market.' And 'the CEOs of most Indian companies are family members who have not been competing with others for the top job. Salaries and compensation packages of CEOs/whole time directors (WTDs) are fixed through resolutions, passed or rejected through a voting system. The voting system is considered to be a democratic process and goes well with any free market system. But the problem arises because the promoters or other interested parties may hold or control a very large percentage of shareholding and can thus ensure that resolutions are either passed or defeated to suit their needs.'

The performance of Bajaj Auto Ltd for the years 2006–07, 2007–08, and 2008–09 are shown above.

Additional Information

1. The company underwent a demerger to bifurcate the various businesses into automobiles, financial services, and a holding company.
2. The year 2008–09 was bad for the economy consequent to the economic meltdown in the developed world.

Discussion Questions

1. Do you believe that executive compensation is market driven? Substantiate with arguments and examples.
2. Comment on the compensation policy of Bajaj Auto Ltd. Does it fall under the pay-for-performance regime?

Sources: 'Are Indian CEOs Overpaid, *Business Today*, 1 July 2009; Satheesh Kumar, 'Can market decide salaries of CEOs?' *Economic Times*, 8 June 2007; Annual Reports, Bajaj Auto Ltd for years 2006–07, 2007–08, and 2008–09.

MAKING BOARDS A FORMIDABLE FORCE

As we have seen in earlier chapters, the board today is considered to be a competitive weapon for a company. Any competitive weapon must have competence, and board competence depends on the competencies of the individual directors and how they come together to become a formidable force. The composition of the board is very important in this pursuit. According to Charan (1998), 'Without the right composition, the dialogue may never take off, the board's competitive power may never get released.' The board should be able to attract the best talent suitable for the job, and best governance means best people. While companies spend a lot of time, energy, and effort in getting the right people below the board, the same rigour is not usually seen in the recruitment of directors. Despite the requirement of large numbers (rough estimates range from 18,000 to 50,000) of independent directors (IDs) in Indian companies, we are yet to see any advertisement from a company for the recruitment of independent directors. The Satyam fall-out and the allegation that the IDs did not play their roles well, and the possible liabilities of those independent directors in the event they are held responsible, will definitely force potential director candidates to think twice before they accept an invitation. Also, with the expectation of the time to be devoted by an ID in a company, directors from now on would choose fewer board seats. The rigour down the line is seen not only in the recruitment but also in training, development, appraisal, etc. But very rarely do these things happen at the board level.

There have been positive changes in developed economies like the US, thanks to the high profile failures like Enron, WorldCom, etc., and the subsequent enactment of the Sarbanes–Oxley Act of 2002, which is highly stringent and necessitates that nomination committees be constituted and that they be constituted only of independent directors. This has definitely resulted in a shift from the conventional method of recruiting celebrities or recruiting people who are members of the same club where the chairman or the CEO of the company frequents, or who play golf with the chairman or the CEO or who happen to be colleagues of the CEO or chairman on the board of another company. When a nomination committee, which is responsible for recruitment is constituted only of IDs, objectivity is expected. While recruiting, the committee also has to give importance to diversity. Without diversity, one cannot achieve diversity of thinking, which is essential in today's business conduct. Diversity brings in diverse points of view, which will lead to different perspectives on a subject.

While diversity must be encouraged, the director-to-be must have fundamental business acumen and Charan says that 'boards need, first and foremost, people who are keen business people who can cut through complexity.' They need to be fully involved and actively engaged in the directoral profession. Many attributes which are taken as 'givens' like integrity, openness, courage, collegiality, walking the talk, etc., are expected to be met by every director candidate. If the board is filled with the right and competent directors, it will demonstrate its competitive advantage. After the right candidates are chosen, they should be properly inducted onto the board and into the company, their development needs be identified to meet the specific needs of the company or the changes in the environment, and be motivated to contribute their best to the company. Talents are always in short supply. So, they must be encouraged to stay on for a reasonable period of time. They should be appraised at frequent intervals to ascertain their contribution. And their exits should be planned if they fall short of expectations or the changing environment demands fresh talent.

How to Get the Right People

Carter and Lorsch (2004) has suggested the following five-step process in order for boards to get good people in the right mix.

Widen the talent   Think broader than just about current and former CEOs. Widen the age and experience criteria to add younger but experienced executives as board members.

Think strategically about the skill mix   Particularly in light of the challenges facing the business and the board's agreement about its role, the skills and experience that the board specifically needs to oversee its company need to be well thought out.

Raise the performance bar   Develop a performance culture in the boardroom. The corporate governance or nominating committee should review the performance of each director who is being considered for re-nomination to be certain that they meet the board's criteria for performance. This will make re-nomination more than a formality and provide a realistic way to remove underperforming directors.

Insist on education process for new directors   Regularly refresh the existing directors. Help them to keep up with rapid change by educating them about the company's changing environment. Help them to learn and stay excited about the business.

Be realistic about compensation   Cultivate professionalism rather than greed while making it worthwhile for board members to put in the required effort.

Director Selection Process

Excellence in governance requires excellent boards. Excellent boards need excellent people. As Charan (1998) says, 'The power of board as a competitive weapon depends on the quality and diversity of directors.' Shultz (2001) concurs: 'If you get the people right, little else matters. Because good governance will follow. A board's power is a function of its directors and how they are chosen.' Most the companies do not give much importance to this crucial aspect. Regulations and guidelines in most countries require that a good majority of directors be independent. For example, the Sarbanes–Oxley Act 2002 demands that a majority of the directors must be independent and the audit, nomination, and remuneration committees shall be constituted only of independent directors. Once the structural requirements are met, companies will 'conform' to the requirements. But what is the guarantee that these directors will perform? Having the requisite number or percentage of independent directors is a box-ticking exercise for many. While conformance is essential, companies and boards have to worry about performance too. As Carter and Lorsch (2004) say, 'Good people—and people who are suited to the job at hand—will perform even if the structure is less than ideal, but the opposite is certainly not true.' A company like Infosys Technologies Ltd is reputed for its governance practices not just because it has the requisite structure but because it has packed its board with excellent talent.

Where to look for

While recruiting new directors, the board has to keep in mind the right mix that is appropriate not only now but also in future. The board also has to 'examine the variety and complexity of the issues that your board needs to address' (Harper 2005). Till recently, whenever there was a vacancy on the board, the company and board would immediately approach CEOs of other major companies or retired CEOs from other companies. Or, in short, the search used to stop at the CEO level. But, in today's context, a director has to devote considerable time to a company.

Take the case of an Indian company. The regulators demand that at least four board meetings apart from AGM have to be held. Assuming that each meeting lasts at least 4 hours, time required for meetings alone is 16 hours. At least an equal amount of time must have been spent on preparation. So, another 16 hours. If the director happens to be on at least one committee which meets at least twice a year (if audit committee, the number of meetings may be more) and lasts for 4 hours each, with a preparation time of 4 hours/meeting, he/she must spend another 8 to 16 hours. Thus, only for the attendance of the meeting, a director has to devote 40 to 48 hours a year or five to six 8-hour working days. Again, one has to add travel time. At least an equal amount of time might have been planned for travel. That means another 40 to

48 hours (this could be in fact much more). Can a full-time CEO, committed to his company, devote this kind of time in the service of another company to execute his responsibilities as a director? It is extremely difficult. If at all they have the energy, skills, and health, there are at least seven boards in India for each, CEO considering the number of companies listed on Indian stock exchanges and the demand for independent directors. So, companies have to look for alternatives.

Charan (1998) suggests that boards should look at 'other number ones and number twos', meaning that they should look at people below the board level like direct reports of the CEOs, who head divisions which are big businesses inside a corporation. For example, GE has a number of businesses which are bigger (between $5 billion and $10 billion) compared to the revenues of many other companies. In India, for example, Reliance Industries has divisions which have very high turnovers. These division heads are not CEOs in the strict sense of the term but manage reasonably big businesses with profit-centre responsibilities. The most important criterion is whether the candidate has business acumen. Director experience is also a must. Charan (2005) says that 'by broadening their searches to include direct reports of CEOs for example move aggressively seeking gender, ethnic, and geographic diversity, boards have discovered that the pool of qualified directors is much larger than they first thought.' Such people will be keen and more likely to be motivated to contribute to the company. They would be showing more learnability than CEOs, many of whom may have an air of 'all-knowing' around them.

What to look for

Having widened the net for talent, by looking at one or two levels below the CEO level, the board should concur on the competencies and qualities that every director should possess. Carter and Lorsch (2004) have suggested that boards should look at six attributes in the director to be:

Intellectual capacity   The work of a board in a highly cerebral—intellectual capacity is a must. Can the candidate understand a business in which he/she has no experience? The candidate must have business acumen and should understand what drives performance in the business.

Interpersonal skills   Can the candidate work as part of a group? Can he/she gel well with other members? Can he/she be both challenging and supportive of management? Are they open to being dissented? Do they show courage to express their concerns while driving for collegiality and harmony in the boardroom?

Instinct   Does the prospective director have good business instincts and judgement? It is different from intelligence; it deals with business acumen.

Interest   Is the director genuinely interested in the job, the company, the business, and its people? Is he/she committed and willing to go the extra mile when necessary? Does he/she appreciate that it is a position of responsibility and not just one of making money and providing prestige?

Commitment to contribute   Can he/she find time to be committed to the company in his/her busy schedule? Regulations or guidelines may suggest certain limits. But can he/she stretch enough to many directorships while keeping his/her commitment to each intact?

Integrity   Director candidates must be truthful and honest. Will he/she be accountable to the shareholders on whose behalf he/she is expected to act? Will he/she declare conflicts of interest, if any, upfront? Will he/she keep the interests and reputation of the company at the top of his/her mind beyond his/her personal interests and reputation?

Nomination committees must fix certain criteria/qualifications/qualities which the director candidates have to meet.

While some or all of the things that Carter and Lorsch prescribe can be adopted in a basic and general framework, nomination committees must look for specific requirements their specific boards need. Charan (1998) says that 'the board should articulate its needs and expectations for new members and then list the criteria.' Charan has suggested that every board should raise a number of questions, which are categorized under three heads: Perspective, Board Dynamics, and Leadership (Exhibit 5.1):

Exhibit 5.1
Should This Person Be on Our Board?

1. Perspective: How will this individual add to this composite perspective of the group of outside directors?

Does this individual	Yes	No
• have a track record of success (in the top quartile of his or her profession)?	—	—
• have an affinity for and expertise in some aspect of the external environment?	—	—
• have the ability to see the business as a whole?	—	—
• focus on the big picture rather than operational details?	—	—
• exercise that perspective in his/her full-time work?	—	—
• have the ability to cut through complex issues and ask incisive questions?	—	—
• have the courage to remain independent while possessing the compassion to help management by counselling, coaching, and giving feedback?	—	—
• help create balance between directors who are creative and probing and those who are focused and pragmatic?	—	—
• have a set of experiences that is additive to those of other directors?	—	—

2. Board dynamics: Will this individual enhance the dynamics of interaction among directors in committees and/or board meetings by constructively challenging management and other directors, stimulating creative thought, contributing incisiveness to discussions, and helping bring closure to debate?

Is this individual	Yes	No
• a good collaborator, not someone who prefers to fly solo?	—	—
• able to exercise independent judgement while being collegial?	—	—
• aware of the importance of group dynamics?	—	—
• a strong presence?	—	—
• someone who is willing to participate and challenge fellow directors?	—	—
• someone who will make this board more effective?	—	—

3. Leadership: Does this person have a record of leadership in his/her area of activity and have the gut instinct of a CEO?

	Yes	No
• Will this individual be willing to serve as a Sounding board for the CEO when necessary?	—	—
• Will this person support the CEO's and/or the board's efforts to ensure an orderly and well-executed succession planning?	—	—

- Is this person truly interested in learning the industry and the business? — —
- Is this person articulate and cogent? — —
- Is this person free of conflicts of interest? — —

- Will this person devote enough time and be accessible? — —
- Is this person of high integrity and ethical standards? — —

While general criteria like integrity, time (demanding limits on the number of directorships), independence, etc. are important, Charan (1998) warns that 'not all criteria should be generic. The criteria should help define people who can help with the company's current challenges' and that 'boards can and should go hard on the issue of racial, gender, ethnic, and global diversity but not at the expense of other criteria.'

Harper (2005) has listed 35 personal attributes for directors under six categories (Exhibit 5.2):

Exhibit 5.2
Director's Personal Characteristics

1. Decision-making

Critical faculty Probes the facts, challenges assumptions, identifies the (dis)advantages of proposals, provides counter arguments, ensures discussions are penetrating

Decisiveness Shows a readiness to take decisions and take action. Is able to make up his or her mind.

Judgement Makes sensible decisions or recommendations by weighing evidence. Considers reasonable assumptions, the ethical dimension, and factual information.

2. Communication

Listening skills Listens dispassionately, intently, and carefully so that key points are recalled and taken into account, questioning when necessary to ensure understanding.

Openness Is frank and open when communicating. Willing to admit errors and shortcomings.

Presentation skills Conveys ideas, images, and words in a way that shows empathy with the audience.

Responsiveness Is able to invite and accept feedback.

Verbal fluency Speaks clearly, audibly and has a good diction. Is concise, avoids jargon and tailors content to the audience's needs.

Written communication skills Written matter is readily intelligible; ideas, information, and opinions are conveyed accurately, clearly, and concisely.

3. Interaction with others

Confidence Is aware of own strengths and weaknesses. Is assured when dealing with others. Is able to take charge of a situation when appropriate.

Coordination skills Adopts appropriate interpersonal styles and methods in guiding the board towards task accomplishment. Fosters cooperation and effective teamwork.

Flexibility Adopts a flexible (but not compliant) style when interacting with others. Takes their view into account and changes position when appropriate.

Integrity Is truthful and trustworthy and can be relied upon to keep his or her word. Does not have double standards and does not compromise on ethical and legal matters.

Learning ability Seeks and acquires new knowledge and skills from multiple sources, including board experience.

Motivation Inspires others to achieve goals by ensuring a clear understanding of what needs to be achieved and by showing commitment, enthusiasm, encouragement, and support.

Persuasiveness   Persuades others to give their agreements and commitment; in face of conflict uses personal influence to achieve consensus and/or agreement.

Presence   Makes a strong positive impression on first meeting. Has authority and credibility, establishes rapport quickly.

Sensitivity   Shows an understanding of the feelings to provide personal support or to take other actions as appropriate.

4. Analysis and use of information

Consciousness of detail   Insists that sufficiently detailed and reliable information be taken account of and reported as necessary.

Eclecticism   Systematically seeks all possible relevant information from a variety of sources.

Numeracy   Assimilates numerical and statistical information accurately, understands its derivation and makes sensible, sound interpretations.

Problem recognition   identifies problems and identifies possible or actual causes.

5. Strategic perception

Change-orientation   Alert and responsive to the need for change. Encourages new initiatives and the implementation of new policies, structures, and practices.

Creativity   Generates and recognizes imaginative solutions and innovations.

Foresight   Is able to imagine possible future states and characteristics of the company in a future environment.

Organizational awareness   Is aware of the company's strengths and weaknesses and of the likely impact of the board's decisions upon them.

Perspective   Rises above the immediate problem or situation and sees the wider issues and implications. Is able to relate disparate facts and see all relevant relationships.

Strategic awareness   Is aware of the various factors that determine the company's opportunities and threats (for example, shareholder, stakeholder, market, technological, environmental, and regulatory factors).

6. Achievement of results (business competence)

Business acumen   Has the ability to identify opportunities to increase the company's business advantage.

Delegation skills   Distinguishes between what should be done by others or by him or her. Allocates decision-making or other tasks to appropriate colleagues and subordinates.

Drive   Shows energy, vitality, and commitment.

Exemplar   Sets challenging but achievable goals and standards of performance for self and others.

Resilience   Maintains composure and effectiveness in the face of adversity, setbacks, opposition, or unfairness.

Risk acceptance   Is prepared to take action that involves calculated risk in order to get a desired benefit or advantage.

Tenacity   Stays with a position or plan of action until the desired objectives are achieved or require adaptation.

Strategic recruiting

One of the first mistakes that a board commits is its failure to recruit strategically. According to Shultz (2001), good governance is the result of good people on the board. Any other step towards better governance has its foundation on getting the right people.

Shultz has listed the following nine steps for strategic recruiting.

Create a board charter   The board charter (governance guidelines) defines the role and mission of the board. This is important because it specifies the purpose of the board, the directors, and the management. The critical focus must be the role of the board. This will make clear for the board to decide on what to look for in a new recruit and for the director candidate to know what is expected of him.

Create a needs matrix   After drafting a charter, the next step is to create a matrix that defines the critical governance needs. Shultz suggests a two-step process for creating the matrix.

List your critical needs   The criteria shall be detailed by thinking through the company's strategic plan, what it will be in future in terms of size, complexity, geographical reach, technology, organic or inorganic growth, etc. Prioritize your critical needs. Then list out the competencies that will be needed to meet the future needs in terms of knowledge, skills, operating experience, interpersonal and team relationships, successes and failures, leadership attributes, experience at board level, expertise in corporate governance matters, etc.

Map the current board members in the context of the need matrix.   List the qualities and experiences of the existing board members. Find out whether there are gaps. Are there any weak spots in the existing set up in the context of future needs? How many will be required to move out and how many shall be brought in? The needs matrix has to be revisited at regular intervals, at least once a year in this dramatically changing business environment. Thomas Horton, Chairman of National Association of Corporate Directors and CEO of American Management Association says, 'Begin with criteria, not names' (Shultz 2001). Refer to Exhibit 5.3.

Define board size   Smaller board means greater director involvement. Larger the number, it might be more difficult for the board to hear everybody. Shultz says that 'deliberations and decision-making tends to get pushed down to the committee level, with the result that the full board evolves into an increasingly passive forum'. 'Although the precise number of directors may vary, the rationale for having a relatively small board is consistent' (Charan 1998). Bill Adams, former chairman of Armstrong, is of the opinion that boards can function very effectively with just six outside directors and one inside director. Beyond that you are not adding any new perspectives, and the larger number diminishes the board's ability to have long, intensive discussions either across the top or drilling down into the issues. 'If you take a board of say, 12 directors, you usually have about six who are pulling the weight anyway' (Charan, 1998). 'Boards should be as small as feasible. A smaller group of directors will find it easier to interact and reach decisions subject to the need for enough director to do the work of the board and its committees' while speaking about today's best practices (Carter and Lorsch, 2004).

Develop a profile for each open board position   All good companies invariably create a profile for key management positions. Do the same for director positions. 'Develop position specifications around your key needs—a statement of director qualifications—and recruit to those specifications' says Shultz (2001). After creating a profile, one has to decide on what shall be the composition of the board to include serving CEOs, retired CEOs, consultants, academics, lawyers, etc. Depending on the specific policies and requirements, the percentage of women, international representation, etc., shall also be looked into.

Recruit proactively   Now, one has to identify people who have successfully dealt with the critical issue you have identified. Get inputs from other directors and even the management

Exhibit 5.3
Board Needs Matrix

Rank in each area from 1 to 5 with 1 minimal and 5 outstanding

	Directors	Prospects	Total
Expertise	1 2 3 4 5	1 2 3 4 5	–
Operations leadership	– – – – –	– – – – –	–
Strategic planning	– – – – –	– – – – –	–
Organizational development	– – – – –	– – – – –	–
Human resources	– – – – –	– – – – –	–
Finance	– – – – –	– – – – –	–
Mergers and acquisitions	– – – – –	– – – – –	–
Corporate governance			
Expertise	– – – – –	– – – – –	–
Technology	– – – – –	– – – – –	–
E-commerce	– – – – –	– – – – –	–
International	– – – – –	– – – – –	–
Legal	– – – – –	– – – – –	–
Marketing	– – – – –	– – – – –	–
Federal Government	– – – – –	– – – – –	–
Healthcare	– – – – –	– – – – –	–
Qualities			
Team player	– – – – –	– – – – –	–
Leadership	– – – – –	– – – – –	–
Visionary	– – – – –	– – – – –	–

Length of board service	—
Committees/board officer positions	—
Number of for-profit boards	—
Number of non-profit boards	—
Date of end of term, if applicable	—
Attendance percentage	—
Geographic location	—

Total Number of

Age: —— Under 35
        —— 36–50
        —— 51–65
        —— Over 65

Ethnic —— Asian
       —— African-American
       —— Caucasian
       —— Hispanic
       —— Other

Gender —— Female
       —— Male

* Support this matrix with resumes of individuals together with a key sheet with names and numbers. This document can be circulated to the board and managers while preserving confidentiality.

and other constituencies like CEOs of other companies who had a chance to interact with the potential candidates, customers who had dealt with them, creditor, investors, etc. Shultz is of the opinion that one has to talk to at least three qualified candidates for each director position. Since a company evolves through different stages of growth, so do its needs and challenges. Hence, 'recruit one or two directors who are there ahead of you, who have had success managing through those growth stages, and who know the issues'. Since directorship is a huge responsibility today, those who are otherwise qualified but look for leading a cozy life shall be discouraged. Today, no director can be there for the glory of it. Also, do not recruit celebrities for the glamour they bring. While deciding on the people, see whether there is a need for supplementing management in certain areas like finance, technology, mergers and acquisitions, etc. While specific expertise must be encouraged, care should also be taken to see that they have broader views about business. Thomas Horton, chairman of National Association of Corporate Directors (NACD), suggests that the board should look for directors who are 'a few notches better' than those already on the board so as to elevate the caliber of the entire board (Shultz 2001). Shultz is of the opinion that boards have to 'cross fertilize'. Doug Foshee, CEO of Neuvo Energy, says: 'I see some companies too focused on attracting only board members with similar experience in the same industry as that company. This approach can lead to corporate myopia and an inability to respond to the pace of change in industry in general' (Shultz).

Shultz suggests that intangibles like the following must be ensured to make the board more effective:

Integrity   Indicates the strength of character

Business sense   The director should have business acumen which has already been discussed earlier.

Thinking strategically   The approach to problem solving, original thinking qualities, ability to substantiate points, willingness to change opinion, etc.

Good nature   Looking at issues in an objective manner than a personal manner

Focus   Ability to get the issue quickly

Sound judgement   Applies good common sense

Scope   Ability to see the big picture and contribute

Curiosity   Enthusiasm for learning new things

Listening   Is he/she a good listener or loudmouthed?

'For the board to be a competitive advantage, its composition must be relevant to the time and needs of the company. The governance committee should periodically debate the criteria to make sure the current composition is appropriate, not only when there is turnover on the board but also when a change in strategies or in the external context might argue for new skills.' (Charan, 2005). Charan is of the opinion that every board should include at least two directors who are sitting or recently retired CEOs. Charan (2005) says that they 'not only bring a great deal of relevant experience to the board but also have great instincts about changes in the external environment, strategy, people, and operational effectiveness.'

But Shultz (2001) warns: 'Just because someone has been successful in driving a company does not mean that she is effective in the boardroom. It is not easy for a decision, action-oriented CEO or entrepreneur to metamorphose into a collaborative team member, to sit quietly, to be a good listener, a good advisor and a consensus builder, CEOs are mired in the business of a single company, so their perspective is limited in that sense.' Robert Monks, Chairman of LENS, says: 'It is a question of time, of commitment, of balance.' Shultz is of the opinion that it is better to include some directors with prior board experience 'because of their ability to mentor new board members and the governance knowledge they bring.'

Charan has suggested that a detailed background of the NEDs be compiled to establish how the director-mix and the domain knowledge fit together. The major strengths required by the board are entered on the left hand side in rows and the directors are plotted across in columns. This exercise helps in codifying the most prominent experiences of the individual directors and in finding out how they match with the requirements of the company. Exhibit 5.4 gives typical board candidate criteria for a typical board (Charan 2005).

Exhibit 5.4
Board Candidate Criteria for a Typical Board

General Criteria
Having high ethical standards and integrity. Willing to act on and be accountable for board decisions. An ability to provide wise and thoughtful counsel on a range of issues. Have a history of achievements that reflect high standards for themselves and others. Be loyal and committed to driving the success of the company. Able to take tough positions while being a team player.

Specific Criteria

Major strength	Williams	Jeter	Rodriguez	Giambi	Sheffield	Posada	Matsui	Clark	Wilson
1. Business management (CEO or president) operations	x	x	x	x	–	x	–	–	x
2. Financial literacy	x	x	x	–	–	–	x	–	x
3. Financial expertise	x	x	x	x	x	x	–	x	x
4. Marketing	–	–	–	–	x	x	–	x	x
5. Global experience	x	–	–	x	–	–	–	–	–
6. Other (R&D, PR, public accounting, government....)	x	–	–	–	–	–	x	x	–
7. Human resources	–	–	–	–	–	–	x	–	–
8. Business development/ M&A expertise									
9. Change management									

Source: Boards that Deliver, Ram Charan, Jossey-Bass, 2005

Using outside agencies for recruiting   More boards use head hunters for recruiting directors these days. This helps in making the search process more objective, without any reluctance to pose hard questions. While headhunters can be of great help, the board has to be fully involved in the interview process, the reference checks, etc. They also must ascertain the chemistry—after all the candidate has to gel into the existing/new team.

Induction and orientation   Having recruited the new directors, they shall be properly inducted onto the board. An induction programme will ensure that the new recruits are fully informed about the company, its business, and financials. Directors will vary widely in their knowledge about the company and its business. Hence, Tricker (2004) has suggested that a checklist be prepared for the induction purpose. According to him, the checklist can be used by chairmen and CEOs planning an induction programme for their board members as well as by newly appointed directors wanting to brief themselves.

Knowledge about the company   The prime focus of the induction programme must be on the company and its governance. The chairman, directors who have been serving the company for long, lead independent director, and even the company secretary can be very helpful in this aspect. The director must basically know about the following things, namely:

- Ownership power—In a joint-stock limited company, ownership is the ultimate basis of governance power. What is the pattern of ownership? Are there a few dominant shareholders with the balance widely distributed? Or, is there no shareholder who can be said to be influential with the kind of shareholding? How were ownership-related issues resolved in the past? Is it a family promoted and managed company where succession lines are clear? Is the company under a threat of takeover due to its shareholding pattern? Is the relationship among owners, board, and management healthy, progressive, and meaningful? How could all these change in future?
- Rules, regulations, and company law—The board/ chairman should educate the new director recruit about the various rules, regulations, and the company law provisions. The director must become conversant with the articles of association, memorandum of association, and the company rule book (like the code of ethics, and code of conduct for all employees and directors particularly), the company's governance charter, listing rules and agreements with stock exchanges, and the governance guidelines in the listing agreement (like Clause 49 in India). In countries like the US, where company laws are made by states rather than at federal level, one must be familiar with specific state laws applicable. The new director must also be thorough with the specific provisions regarding audit requirements.
- Board structure, membership, and processes—How is the board constituted? What is the regulation regarding the composition? Is the board meeting regulations or guidelines as far as structure is concerned? Is it balanced in such a way as to get an outside perspective and at the same time get the board decisions delegated and executed well? Are the independent directors really acting independently or are they there just to meet the governance regulations? Is the insider-outsider ratio acceptable? Is the chairmanship separated from the CEO position? Is the chairman non-executive? What are the backgrounds of the other directors

on the board? Is there a succession plan for every position in management? How often does the board meet? Which are the committees that have been constituted? What is the kind of discussion that takes place? Have there been debates and dialogues before decisions are made? What is the information architecture for the board to get the necessary information? Is there a lead (independent) director? Do independent directors discuss issues without the other members present? Are there charters for different committees? Are committees like audit, nomination, and remuneration constituted of only independent directors? The new director should have answers to all these questions.

Knowledge about the business   The next focus area of the induction checklist is the business itself. Is the new recruit familiar with the business/es? Does he have the business acumen to understand how the business makes money? Does he have a broad picture of the competitive scenario in which the company's business operates?

- The basic business process—Are you familiar with the value chain of the company? Are you familiar with the major sources of the business inputs, where they come from, and who makes them available to the company? Which factors in the business processes are critical, which provide competitive advantages, and which drive costs? What are the core competencies of the business? What is the range of products/services offered by the business? Who are the customers? What need of the customers does the business meet? What needs of the end customers does the business meet? Who are your major customers? Who contribute mostly to your business?
- Corporate strategies—What are the firm's vision, mission, and values? Is the vision shared, clearly articulated in strategies, plans, and projects? The new recruit can get copies of them and discuss with chairman, CEO, or any other senior director. What is the current strategy for growth? Is the growth organic or inorganic? Who are the principal competitors? What strategies do they pursue? What competitive advantages and disadvantages do they have? Are the entry barriers strong? Are their potential entrants into the business? What is the level of technology in the industry? Is the company ahead of the rest in terms of technology? Does the company invest in R&D? Is the business of the organization complex or simple? How are strategies made? Is there involvement of people from different levels in the making of strategy? What is the role of the board in the strategy making? The director should read the annual reports of the company for the past few years with special emphasis on management discussion and analysis.

Organization, management, and people   What is the formal organizational structure? How does it work? This may be discussed with the chairman, CEO, or other senior executives. Is the structure suited to strategy? Develop an insight into the culture of the organization. How does communication take place? What are the management control systems in place like budgetary planning and control, profit centre accountability, etc.? How is management performance measured? How is management compensated? Are there stock-option schemes for directors and management?

What is the strength of employees in the total organization? Have there been disruptions in work due to poor industrial relations? Does the company have adequate skill sets at the employee levels? Are there regular training and development programmes for managers and other employees?

Knowledge of financials   The director should study the annual financial statements and other details like directors' report, management discussion and analysis (MDA), etc., from the annual reports. He/she should also study trends in key financial ratios like return on equity (ROE), return on capital employed (ROCE), current ratio, inventory turnover ratio, asset turnover ratio, interest coverage ratio, etc., and give emphasis to trends rather than to absolute ratios. What the future holds? How is business financed? What is the financial structure? How does the debt/equity (D/E) ratio compare with competitors' and industries? Will changes in interest rates affect the company's investment plans? What is the auditing process? How often the audit committee reviews the accounts? Have there been any qualification remarks from the auditors in the past? How did the board deal with such issues to straighten them?

Expectations on appointment   All directors should discuss with the chairman what is expected of their directorship before accepting their nomination. The induction briefing should review the expectations of the chairman, CEO, and other directors. Is there a specific role identified for you? Was there any specific reason why you were nominated to the board? Are there any other expectations? Is the director capable of fulfilling these expectations? How much time are you expected to devote to the board work? What is the channel for getting the information necessary for your functioning as a director? What are the arrangements for sharing of information among directors when they are not meeting?

- Courage—Does he/she have the moral fortitude to speak up, question, express a thinking which is different from others? Garry Tooker, former CEO of Motorola says: 'Best are board members who are independent and vocal, but collegial. They used to be able to disagree without being disagreeable' (Shultz 2001).
- Ability to evaluate people—Directors are not hands-on people. So, focusing on skill sets and their ability to get things done may not help. Instead, focus should be on their ability to ensure that the best people are managing the affairs of the company and thus the interests of the shareholders.
- Commitment to the company and management—The director must show commitment to make a contribution to the company and be supportive of the efforts of the management led by the CEO.
- Being not too hungry—Be it ego, be it position, be it power, or be it money.
- Avoid the 'good-old-boy' syndrome—Conventionally, directors got recruited because they were known to the CEO either because they went to the same club, or played golf together; or they were bankers, consultants, attorneys, or venture capitalists to the company. This has to be discontinued with. Since the company has created a needs matrix, it knows what is needed and so it is better to venture out and find someone who can meet the needs of the company.

Interview and reference check   Even experienced directors should be interviewed thoroughly in the context of the company's board and its requirements. Candidates must be met both formally and informally to know how they behave in different situations and places like office, home, club, etc. Such interactions will help the recruiter to see the culture in which they operate.

Shultz (2001) suggests a list of questions to be asked to a prospective board member:

1. Why do you want to serve?
2. What is your opinion about the company?
3. How will you contribute? Elaborate with examples.
4. What are your specific areas of expertise? How will you add value to the board?
5. What is your level of financial acumen?
6. How many other boards do you sit on? What role do you play on those boards?
7. What is your view of the role of a board and corporate governance?
8. Do boards add value? How?
9. What are the downsides of being a member of a board?
10. How do you use your board? (If applicable)
11. What is your most rewarding experience on a board?
12. How specifically have you added value? Provide examples
13. What has been your most difficult experience as a director?
14. Are you willing to commit to the level of participation and support that we need?
15. What committees would you like to sit on? Why?
16. Do you prefer to be compensated in stock or cash?
17. Are your goals and values compatible with those of our company? Explain.
18. What are your strengths and weaknesses?
19. Would you like to make comments on our financial statements?
20. What are your concerns?

After the interview, reference checks shall be conducted. Find out how the candidate has performed on other boards, both profit and non-profit. This is one area which usually gets neglected or not enough importance is given. Most of the people find it difficult to ask hard questions but this step is crucial in the recruitment process. It is the only way to know the experience-related aspects of the directoral candidate.

Questions like the one given below can help while asking for references (Shultz 2001).

- Does he attend meetings?
- Does he contribute? How?
- Does he enhance the dynamics? Does he care?
- How does he move his thoughts into action?
- What differentiates him in the boardroom?
- What style does he use to express himself?
- Is he fair?
- Doe he focus on issues? Or does he just want air time?
- Does he do his homework?

- How does he resolve problems and disputes?
- Why is he interested?
- What about his attitude? Does he always want to win his point?
- What are his strengths?
- What is he weak at?
- Is there any other information which is important?

Recruit in a continuum   Boards have to continually monitor their needs matrix and competencies needed. They have to continuously scout around for good candidates to replace those who retire or to fill emerging needs.

DIRECTOR DEVELOPMENT AND SUCCESSION PLANNING
Director Development

Getting recruited and inducted on to the board is not an end in the director's journey; the journey has only begun. The director himself and the board under the leadership of the chairman should see that the director is on a continuous learning mode. The environment in which the corporation is functioning undergoes dramatic changes over a period of time. Some of the changes could be slow and steady which the director and board may be able to foresee, but some of the changes could be sudden and disruptive and the directors and boards will have to get themselves conditioned to such changes in order to guide the organization to survive such challenges. The board under the leadership of the chairman should identify the needs of development for individual directors and the board as a whole. This type of continuing education is essential for boards in their pursuit of directoral duties. Changes may happen in the economic situation of the country and the entire globe, in the marketplace, in the competitive environment, in technology, in the consumers, in the value chain components, in the legal and the regulatory environment, in the strategic approaches to business, in the way people need to be managed and led, and in the public perception about business and business organizations. All these may necessitate a board to move from the conventional approach to governance to some new approach in line with the changes. This will necessitate individual directors and board as a whole to educate themselves so as to be prepared for the changes in the environment. Thus, continuing education and development of directors and board as a whole becomes important and relevant.

The purpose

The purpose of development processes is to increase the effectiveness of the individual directors and the board. As Harper (2005) warns, 'If the board is not as effective as it needs to be in today's fast changing and demanding environment, the company could well lose its way. In such circumstances, the company may be acquired or bought out, involving changes to the board in either case. Alternatively, the shareholders may insist on board changes being made. The ultimate catastrophe would be the company to founder completely.'

Who is responsible for director development?

According to Phan, the director and board development responsibility is one of the three responsibilities of the chairman, the other two being the liaison responsibility (i.e. liaising with the stakeholders) and the responsibility for the agenda (i.e. setting the agenda for and managing the board meetings) (Phan 2000). The chair together with the nomination/governance committee has to decide on the competencies required in the directors at intervals and has to map the existing competencies and experiences in the directors and the board as a whole. The chairman, usually, will have to play a mentor's role to the CEO. And the current thinking that the positions of chair and CEO be separate must have its roots in this mandate. In such situations where the chair is usually non-executive, the chair can also act as a mentor for other NEDs and/or IDs. When there is a lead independent director on the board, he can take the lead in mentoring the other IDs.

Assessing development needs

Appraisal phase: assessing performance of the board and directors

Any approach to improving the board effectiveness and performance must start with the basic review of the board itself, what it adopts as its roles, duties and responsibilities, and how it executes them. This must be done in view of the changes in the environment and the emerging needs of the company. Harper (2005) says that a comprehensive review of the board will explore.

The composition of the board   Personal characteristics needed; achieving balance in intellectual capacity, special knowledge and experience; board size and structure.

The matter it addresses   Directing not managing, deciding major issues, and delegating the rest.

Its style and response   Planning and managing board meetings, boardroom behaviour, using board committees, credibility, personalities, and power and politics using the NEDs.

Its focus   Focusing on strategic issues; anticipating the future; corporate culture and values; thinking and acting strategically; and considering risk, compliance, and ethics.

The outcomes of this review must be evaluated by the board and various ideas and options for improvements and change identified shall be considered. The course of action arising out of such ideas and options shall be implemented under the chairman's leadership. During and after the implementation, a review must be carried out. Harper (2005) suggests a number of questions for conducting an active review.

How effective are our board meetings?

- Are our objectives being achieved?
- Are we a well-informed board?
- Is the quality and depth of discussion good enough?
- Were our important decisions good?
- Do we seek the best advice when we need it?
- Are all the board's tasks being tackled effectively?
- Are only proper board issues being addressed?
- Are we an effective working group?

- Is everyone contributing and behaving effectively?
- Is the company's future prosperity being assured?

How well is our board doing in each of the following areas?

- Determining the company's values and aspirations
- Setting corporate vision/aims/mission/objectives
- Contributing to strategic thinking and agreeing strategic plans
- Ensuring availability of required resources
- Ensuring reputation and achievements are protected
- Determining and reviewing policies
- Monitoring performance against plans, budgets, and agreements
- Monitoring adherence to laws, regulations, and policies
- Exercising responsibility to shareholders and other parties

Board evaluation   'Progressive boards have known all along that self-evaluation is a vital process—one that ensures continuous improvement and renewal. The external environment is ever changing and the board must be prepared to change with it. There is always room to improve, says Charan (1998) while emphasizing on the need for evaluation. Lois Juliber, former Vice-Chairman of Colgate-Palmolive and Director of Du Pont says: 'The height of a good board is its willingness to evaluate itself' (Charan). Charan suggests the use of a corporate board self-evaluation instrument, designed to help the board identify specific areas for improvement (Exhibit 5.5).

Exhibit 5.5
Corporate Board Self-evaluation Instrument

The instrument is designed to help the board identify specific areas for improvement. It is similar to instruments used at several companies. It can of course be abbreviated to include only a few questions in each section.

This instrument can be used in several ways. One option is to use it as a discussion guide only. Another is to ask each director to complete the instrument and have the results compiled by a third party. The board chairman or the corporate governance committee can then lead discussion of the results. Alternatively, the chairman of the corporate governance committee can compile the results. Confidentiality will encourage candor.

The instrument should be used in the spirit of constructive criticism.

Directors should avoid choosing 4. The instrument is more useful when directors take a position.

	Deteriorating				Improving		
Section 1. The Company as a Whole							
1. Is the company's health improving or declining							
(a) compared to the last 2 years?	1	2	3	4	5	6	7
(b) compared to the competition?	1	2	3	4	5	6	7
(c) compared to the external environment?	1	2	3	4	5	6	7

	Definitely not					Definitely yes	
2. Is the company fully capturing potential opportunities?	1	2	3	4	5	6	7
3. In your assessment, does the board as a whole expect the company to perform well							
(a) This year?	1	2	3	4	5	6	7
(b) Over the next 3 years?	1	2	3	4	5	6	7
4. Do you yourself expect the company to perform well							
(a) This year?	1	2	3	4	5	6	7
(b) Over the next 3 years?	1	2	3	4	5	6	7
5. In your assessment, does the board as a whole concur with the company strategy?	1	2	3	4	5	6	7
6. Do you yourself concur with the company strategy?	1	2	3	4	5	6	7
7. In your assessment, does the board as a whole believe that the company has the right balance between short-term and long-term goals?	1	2	3	4	5	6	7
8. Do you yourself believe that the company has the right balance between short-term and long-term goals?	1	2	3	4	5	6	7
9. In your assessment, does the board as a whole feel that the company has the right CEO?	1	2	3	4	5	6	7
10. Do you yourself feel that the company has the right CEO?	1	2	3	4	5	6	7
11. Does the board as a whole believe the company is confronting the fundamental realities that, if not dealt with, are likely to cause a decline in long-term health and performance?	1	2	3	4	5	6	7
12. Do you yourself believe the company is confronting the fundamental realities that, if not dealt with, are likely to cause a decline in long-term health and performance?	1	2	3	4	5	6	7
13. Does the board as a whole believe that the company has the right compensation strategy?	1	2	3	4	5	6	7

14. Do you believe that the company has the right compensation strategy?	1	2	3	4	5	6	7
15. Does the board as a whole think the top management succession process is effective?	1	2	3	4	5	6	7
16. Do you think the top management succession process is effective?	1	2	3	4	5	6	7

Section II. The Board as a Whole

17. Does the board as a whole seem to have a clear understanding of its roles and responsibilities?	1	2	3	4	5	6	7
18. Does the board have a sufficient understanding of the company's philosophy and strategy?	1	2	3	4	5	6	7
19. Does the board confront the real issues?	1	2	3	4	5	6	7
20. Does the board have a full-year agenda?	1	2	3	4	5	6	7
21. Is the leadership of the board effective?	1	2	3	4	5	6	7
22. Do board meetings allow enough time for the exchange of ideas?	1	2	3	4	5	6	7
23. Is the information the board receives for board meetings							
(a) useful?	1	2	3	4	5	6	7
(b) adequate?	1	2	3	4	5	6	7
(c) in an efficient format?	1	2	3	4	5	6	7
(d) sufficiently related to the external environment?	1	2	3	4	5	6	7
24. Do board members come to board and committee meetings fully prepared?	1	2	3	4	5	6	7
25. Are presentations to the board.....							
(a) focused on the right issues?	1	2	3	4	5	6	7
(b) clear and succinct?	1	2	3	4	5	6	7
(c) helpful?	1	2	3	4	5	6	7
26. Is the board functioning to its full potential?	1	2	3	4	5	6	7

Why or why not?   _____

_____

_____

Section III. The Board's Group Dynamics

27. Is the board's dialogue of high quality?	1	2	3	4	5	6	7
28. Does the board have sufficient dialogue?	1	2	3	4	5	6	7
29. Is participation in the dialogue sufficiently broad?	1	2	3	4	5	6	7
30. Is the dialogue exciting and insight generating?	1	2	3	4	5	6	7
31. Is the dialogue focused?	1	2	3	4	5	6	7
32. Does dialogue take place among directors?	1	2	3	4	5	6	7
33. Do board members take a reasoned, independent positions?	1	2	3	4	5	6	7
34. Do board members share their knowledge and experience to help the CEO and the company?	1	2	3	4	5	6	7
35. Are board discussions open and candid?	1	2	3	4	5	6	7
36. Do members listen to and consider each other's comments?	1	2	3	4	5	6	7
37. Does the atmosphere of the boardroom encourage critical thinking?	1	2	3	4	5	6	7
38. Do board discussions reach closure?	1	2	3	4	5	6	7

Section IV: Committee Performance

Board members should complete this section for each committee they are on.

Committee: _____

	Definitely not				Definitely yes		
1. Is this committee effective?	1	2	3	4	5	6	7
2. Is the output of the committee supporting the full board?	1	2	3	4	5	6	7
3. Does the committee confront the real issues?	1	2	3	4	5	6	7
4. Does the committee give the CEO candid, decisive feedback?	1	2	3	4	5	6	7
5. Does the committee's feedback accurately reflect the views of all committee members?	1	2	3	4	5	6	7
6. Is the committee able to make collective judgements about important matters?	1	2	3	4	5	6	7

7. Has the committee laid out a full-year agenda?	1	2	3	4	5	6	7
8. Is the committee's composition appropriate?	1	2	3	4	5	6	7
9. Is the leadership of the committee effective?	1	2	3	4	5	6	7
10. Does the committee chairperson elicit contributions from all members?	1	2	3	4	5	6	7
		Not enough		**Just right**		**Too much**	
11. Does the committee allocate the right amount of time for its work?	1	2	3	4	5	6	7

Administration of the instrument   Charan suggests that it can either be used as a discussion guide within the boardroom with every director present or by asking each director to complete the instrument and have the results compiled by the chairman or a third party. In the second case, confidentiality will encourage candid expression of their opinions.

Director evaluation   Charan (1998) suggests a board member peer review instrument which identifies the specific areas for individual directors to improve (Exhibit 5.6).

Exhibit 5.6
Board Member Peer Review Instrument

This instrument identifies specific areas for individual directors to improve. It is similar to an instrument in actual use. If the board chooses to use an abbreviated version of this instrument, be sure it covers a range of contributions. Directors add value in a variety of ways.

Note: Peer review is best suited for use by boards that are functioning well and have a high level of trust. If serious tensions exist among board members or between the CEO and certain directors, peer review is likely to exacerbate those tensions. Under no circumstances should it be used to remove targeted individuals. If the board indicates resistance to the process, it is best to find other means of improving board performance. Misuse, whether intentional or inadvertent, will breed distrust.

When board dynamics are healthy, peer review can strengthen individual performance. It can be exercised in several ways. One option is for each board member to complete a review instrument of each of his or her colleagues and have the results compiled by a third party. The board chairman or the chairman of the corporate governance committee can discuss the composite results with individual directors one-on-one. Alternatively, the corporate governance committee can use the instrument as a guide for discussing the performance of individual directors as they come up for nomination. The fact that the process exists will begin to influence behaviour. Confidentiality is crucial.

Director's Name: _____

A. Preparation and Participation

		Definitely not					Definitely yes		
1. Does this person come to board and committee meetings fully prepared?		1	2	3	4		5	6	7
2. Does this person seem to understand the company's philosophy and strategy?		1	2	3	4		5	6	7

B. Behaviour

3. Does this person enhance group discussions in the following ways								
(a) pushes the discussion forward	1	2	3	4		5	6	7
(b) integrates various viewpoints	1	2	3	4		5	6	7
(c) helps discussion reach closure	1	2	3	4		5	6	7
(d) encourages openness and candour	1	2	3	4		5	6	7
(e) pushes the group to confront reality	1	2	3	4		5	6	7
(f) brings new thinking	1	2	3	4		5	6	7
(g) challenges other directors who sidetrack discussions or dwell in minutiae	1	2	3	4		5	6	7
(h) helps draw out contributions from others	1	2	3	4		5	6	7
4. Is this person a 'good' board member in the following ways:								
(a) is a team player	1	2	3	4		5	6	7
(b) listens to and considers others' comments	1	2	3	4		5	6	7
(c) is willing to change his or her viewpoint	1	2	3	4		5	6	7
(d) accepts challenge from others without becoming defensive	1	2	3	4		5	6	7
(e) has the courage to say what is on his or her mind	1	2	3	4		5	6	7
(f) is free of conflicts of interest	1	2	3	4		5	6	7
(g) exercises independent judgement	1	2	3	4		5	6	7
5. Does this person's behaviour reflect an understanding of the difference between managing and governing a corporation?	1	2	3	4		5	6	7

C. Quality of Value Added

6. Does this person understand and focus on issues that are key to the business?	1	2	3	4		5	6	7

7. Does this person helps colleagues understand and focus on issues that are key to the business?	1	2	3	4	5	6	7
8. Does this person cut through complex issues?	1	2	3	4	5	6	7
9. Does this person help colleagues cut through complex issues?	1	2	3	4	5	6	7
10. Do you consider this person's questions or comments to be:						
(a) incisive and penetrating?	1	2	3	4	5	6	7
(b) appropriately timed?	1	2	3	4	5	6	7
(c) value-adding?	1	2	3	4	5	6	7
11. Does this person keep discussions on track by avoiding talking too much, reminiscing, or engaging in philosophical arguments?	1	2	3	4	5	6	7
12. Are this person's judgements genuinely independent of management?	1	2	3	4	5	6	7
13. Does this person apply his or her experience and business wisdom to matters that come before the board	1	2	3	4	5	6	7
14. Does this person take into account the viewpoints of all stakeholders?	1	2	3	4	5	6	7
15. Does this person contribute to the CEO's perspective and wisdom in running the company by sharing his or her knowledge and experience:						
(a) privately (in person or by phone)	1	2	3	4	5	6	7
(b) in board or committee meetings	1	2	3	4	5	6	7
16. Does this person open doors to his or her network to help the CEO and the company?	1	2	3	4	5	6	7

Development of directors and the board

The appraisal and reviews of performance conducted on board as a whole and the individual directors will reveal the development needs for the total board and at individual director levels, for the directors and board to be more effective. Boards can seek the help of outside experts on board functioning. There are many good coaches and mentors who help boards as a whole and directors at individual levels to improve their effectiveness and performances. Board experts like Ram Charan and Marshall Goldsmith are in great demand today. An experienced chairman can also identify the needs at the board level and also at individual director level and make arrangements for meeting the development needs. Individual directors should try to develop themselves and update their knowledge on a continuous manner, so that they become more competent in an ever changing demanding environment. Some of the learning methods and sources available are:

- Seminars, courses, and workshops on corporate governance organized by universities/ consultants
- Conferences organized by bodies like Institute of Directors (IOD), National Association of Corporate Directors (NACD), etc., in the UK and US and industrial bodies like Federation of Indian Chambers of Commerce and Industry (FICCI), Confederation of Indian Industry (CII) or Assocham, and IOD local arm in India
- Seminars/sessions organized by regulators like SEC/SEBI, etc., and by stock exchanges.
- Individual and group coaching and mentoring by board experts
- Books and other publications like journals, newspapers, and business magazines
- Board retreats where experts will engage directors in discussion on various corporate governance matters.

What to get educated in   Charan says that while most boards have already been aware of the need to broaden their understanding of accounting and finance to improve their oversight of financial health along with top management succession, boards have also been alerted to changes in securities laws, policies, and other compliance roles in their home country as well as around the world. Charan (2008) says that there are other areas too which a board must be conversant with, some of which need to be custom designed for a particular board.

Strategy   Changes in environment make strategies obsolete and business models invalid. Directors may need focused education on specific industries, global regulatory environment, and external trends. They can learn how what is happening in the world affects their industry from diverse sources and points of view.

Performance measurements   New conventions in measuring and reporting performance are emerging and directors need to learn how performance reporting can be done in a given company and industry.

How financial markets function   The board and the audit committee should have an up-to-date review of the role financial reporting and disclosure plays, and of how financial markets function. How do different types of investors influence the capital markets? How do professional investors make decisions and how should boards influence those decisions?

Risk management   Boards are taking on great responsibility in understanding risk. What contributes to financial, business, and geopolitical risk? How will these risks change? What are the ways to eliminate, mitigate, transfer, or otherwise live with these risks?

Changing legal responsibilities of directors   Directors need to keep themselves abreast with fundamentals: How are laws being interpreted? What laws will be created? What are the grey areas? Lawyers have observed that some courts are taking more active stances on hearing cases regarding director liabilities.

Top executive compensation   CEO compensation is a classic area for board education, but it is a top-of-mind issue. But practices in compensation are ever-changing. Boards need to know what the new issues are and what the best practices are to attract, motivate, and retain their leaders.

Technologies   Directors should be educated on key technical issues affecting the industry and the management processes. Since technologies evolve at rapid rates, they can affect a company at many fundamental levels.

Succession planning   The moment we talk about succession planning, what comes to our mind is the CEO succession. While CEO succession is one of the most important succession planning, the board has also to be concerned about succession issues of other executive directors and other NEDs on the board, and at senior management level. But the most important of all these is CEO succession. Charan (1998) says, 'Make no mistake about it: that the responsibility for a smooth leadership transition rests squarely with the board. Boards at work can act confidently and fast, even when the CEO's exit is not planned.' Such crises are not uncommon. Many events like the sudden resignation (or sudden demise) of a CEO, an accounting irregularity leading to overstatement of revenues and/or profits in the financial statements, or a confession like the one Mr Ramalinga Raju made at Satyam—can all be reasons for such crises. The board has to deal with these at break-neck speed. Charan quotes the McDonald's board which was able to act with speed after CEO Jim Cantalupo's untimely demise in 2004. The board met immediately after and was able to name President and COO Charlie Bell as CEO within hours. In contrast, when the CEO of TRW resigned suddenly in 2002, the board was caught unaware and unprepared. There was no internal candidate who could take over. Within 3 days, the board received a take-over bid from Northrop Grumman, which had been lying in wait. Without a succession plan that could put a credible CEO in place quickly, the board had to accede to the takeover (Charan 2005). It would be interesting to note that Charan himself had hailed TRW along with Conrail, GE, and Coca-Cola among large companies having good succession planning process (Charan 1998). But, the continuity of the process seemed to have broken resulting in a void of leadership leading to the takeover by Northrop Grumman.

Boards must understand that the decision of the sort at McDonald's could be taken only with a systematic planned approach to succession issue. McDonald's could do it because the board had considered succession planning as an important part of its role and job. The process of identifying successors to any positions, especially those of CEOs or other key senior management positions must start early. No board can identify a successor suddenly if it has not planned for it. GE is often cited as the best example where board considers succession planning as one of its most important jobs. The process has been in place for the last many decades. It is often said that there are at least five to six candidates who could jump into the shoes of the CEO if he suddenly exits. Charan (1998) says that 'succession planning works best when the roles of the board, the CEO, the human resources executive, and the organization and personnel committee are clear. The board must choose the CEO, but not in isolation. Rather, that decision is part of an organization-wide effort to identify and develop talent. The CEO, the top human resources executive, and the board's organization and personnel committee play important roles in that effort.'

The board must see that the corporation has a process in place for identifying talent for today as well as for future. According to Charan (1998), it must continually challenge the criteria for promotion and recognition. It must give management its collective judgement on key insiders and take ownership of the final decision. The board must force the CEO and the HR head to take initiative and lead in establishing a process to continually evaluate people inside the company and board must insist on them to supply information about people at least 3–4 levels below the CEO. This will enable the board to create a leadership inventory with desirable criteria. While identifying potential CEO candidates, the board has to look not only at successes but also the failures the person has had. This is because failures often give a lot of opportunities for learning. In business, as in many other areas, failures are likely. So, somebody who has faced only successes, may find failures very difficult to absorb. Failures will be shocking to him/her and such people will not be able to look at failure with a controlled mind. Experience of only successes in the past will make one complacent.

CEO's role in succession planning   The board has to take CEO into confidence to actively initiate a process of identifying a leadership pipeline. But, many CEOs do not get actively involved in the process of identifying talent and developing them to take the mantle of leadership from him/her, because either he/she is too busy to devote time or he/she feels threatened. Charan (1998) suggests including succession planning as a criterion in the CEO's performance evaluation. The board can also make it a practice to meet and interact with managers below the CEO level to identify talents among them. Potential people may be invited to be present at board meetings as observers or to assist their respective executive directors or CEO, which will give the board members opportunities to interact with them. The CEO should take keen interest in developing the potential leaders by providing them with challenging assignments. Their performance should be closely monitored and evaluated. He should work with the HR head to establish a leadership development process within the company. The CEO should take all formal and informal opportunities to evaluate the potential leaders.

HR head's role   The HR head can evolve a process with inbuilt design to hire, promote, transfer, evaluate, and reward the future leaders. He/she can provide wonderful judgements about people. The HR person should know what type of leaders will be required for handling the business in this changing environment. HR people should become business oriented to understand the qualities required for the business to succeed. The board should encourage the HR people to get in interactive mode with the board, to get information about the talents that exist in the company.

Role of the nomination committee   While the CEO and HR people are actively involved in the process of developing leadership pipeline within the company, it is the responsibility of the nomination committee to scout around for talent to fill other board vacancies (NEDs and IDs). They should plan for succession of directors whenever somebody retires or resigns. While retirement can be better planned, resignations are not that easy to handle. They must be constantly scouting around for talented candidates to fill vacancies that may arise in future. The talent search must be aligned with the company's business plan for the future too. The committee must identify candidates to meet the profiles created for meeting the varying needs and meeting other general and specific functional criteria. After having identified and short-listed a number of candidates, the committee should conduct due diligence, meaning really getting to know the individual candidates and their reputations (Colley et al. 2003). The committee also needs to know whether there would be good chemistry between the candidate, other members of the board, and the CEO (Charan 1998; Colley et al.).

CEO COMPENSATION

One of the most important tasks of a board is to decide on the compensation package for CEO and other executive directors. At times, they may also be required to take decisions on the remuneration to be paid to senior executives below the board level. But, of all these, fixing of compensation for the CEO tops the list. This is because 'the most inflammatory governance issue is the massive surge in CEO pay, which many say is enabled by indifferent boards, at best, and conflicted boards, at worst' (Shultz 2001). There were many reasons for the shareholder and public reaction to the CEO compensation. Citigroup CEO Sanford Weil took home more than $52 million in compensation and exercised $156 million in 'reloading' options in 1998. The return to the shareholders in 1998 was a minus 93 per cent. In the same year, Rental Service Corp Chairman Martin Reid's pay soured by 592 per cent to about $4.5 million when the company's stock nosedived by over 36 per cent.

CEO compensation has been attracting more attention than ever before. As Charan (2005) says, 'the compensation committee everywhere are feeling the heat of intense public scrutiny. Nothing tarnishes a board (or attracts regulators) like a CEO walking away with a huge pay package while being forced out for non-performance or when a bull market makes the dollar amount of compensation obscenely large. Michael Ovitz's $140 million severance package, Jean-Marie Messier's €21 million severance, and Richard Grasso's $187.5 million pay package may be exceptional, but they made headlines and put all boards under fire.' The publicity the subject has received in recent years is enormous. The media actively publicizes CEO salaries. For example, every year, business magazines like *Business India*, *Business Today*, etc., publish the list of 500 or 1000 CEOs and other top executives drawing the highest compensation packages in India. Such lists were not prepared or published about 15 years back. Such exposure of executive compensations draws even the attention of politicians. Colley et al. say that 'reporting the total compensation of CEO makes for sensational journalism, usually at the expense of informed debate. The predictable result has been that politicians have attempted to regulate CEO salaries.'

Most of these problems arise because of the lethargic or lacklustre performance of the board in this area. The board usually entrusts the responsibility of evaluating managerial performance and set appropriate reward and incentive criteria to the compensation committee. According to Phan (2000), 'The work of this committee has become strategic because the right compensation structure ensures that the management is focused on the appropriate performance targets and therefore strongly influences the strategic plans that they formulate for the firm.'

Charan (2005) says that 'the challenge to compensation committee is clear: ensure that compensation plans pass the test of common sense and reward top management for building the intrinsic value of the business. Compensation is the sharpest tool for ensuring that the CEO acts in the best interest of the company and its investors, and boards have to use it effectively.'

The problem most boards face is how to arrive at a performance criterion. Pay for performance is wonderful in rhetoric but difficult in practice. While a number of performance outcomes are tangible and can be measured, many are not and cannot be measured. Hence, as Charan (1998) says, 'Goals should not be strictly formulaic or quantitative. They should establish what the CEO has to do in terms of management development, customer satisfaction, changing the organization's culture or "genetic code", or building competence for the future.' Colley et al. (2003) say that 'the goal of the executive compensation is to find an equilibrium level that provides shareholders with the greatest return consistent with their risk tolerance, net of the cost of the compensation. The challenge facing the board is how to find and make the best deal for shareholders.'

Colley et al. feel that the board must resolve a number of basic philosophical issues in forming the foundation for its compensation strategies like:

What constitutes good performance?   Colley et al. feel that the performance has to be looked at from current circumstances, its goals, and the execution of its strategies. The time dimension must be kept in mind. Goals should be both short-term and long-term, necessitating compensation plans to include both short-term and long-term components. There must be a good balance between these and boards should not be blinded by good current performance while long-term outlook is deteriorating or vice-versa. But boards have to be cautious about sacrificing the sustainability of long-term performance for short-term gains.

The short-term performance may be measured more objectively with the financial performances. At the same time, the board should see that the strategic goals are essentially aimed at long-term sustainability of financial health and more wealth for shareholders. The performance also has to be consistent with the age of the company. A start-up may not be performing well financially, so other criteria like current execution of strategy to make the long-term financial viability good has to be looked at. Another thing that has to be kept in mind is the compensation level in the industry of which the company is a part of. Also, the nature of the industry must be understood. Some industries are cyclical and hence the compensation has to be looked at from a different perspective.

Does management make a difference in performance?   The answer to this question generally is very easy. The management is capable of making a difference in the firm performance. Management is one of the major reasons why some companies perform better than others belonging to the same industry. Management contributes by way of ideas, commitment, innovative practices, attracting, developing, and enabling people and talent, creating brand equity for products and company, integrity, candour, creating a culture of questioning and learning, encouraging team performance, etc., and can make a genuine difference in the way the company operates and achieves its targets. Companies like GE, Johnson & Johnson, Medtronic, etc., in the US and companies like HUL, Infosys, ITC, Hero Honda, etc., in India have been examples of where the management has been consciously making efforts to improve the performance of the company and succeeding in its efforts.

Does compensation make a difference in getting good management?   While pay is only one of the factors in attracting and retaining talent, there is a competitive market-place for talent in the current scenario, which makes compensation an important factor. By pricing the talent right, companies will be able to attract and retain the talent better. In modern progressive organizations, where management puts in place many of the soft requirements of managers, pricing can once again become the important criterion.

How much, if any, of management's compensation should be 'at risk'?   The question looks at the answer of how much of the compensation is directly and closely linked to performance only and how much will be guaranteed. Or, how much of the compensation will be fixed (as monthly salary and allowances irrespective of performance) and how much will be variable (related to performance like incentives, bonuses, stock options, which will be paid only on the achievement of certain minimum parameters). The tendency today is towards more percentages (sometimes as high as 70 per cent) by way of variable component.

Charan (2005) says that 'performance is measured by more than nominal stock price or any one other variable. Instead, compensation plans should be clear, straightforward and built around a combination of objectives that reflect the board's careful judgements about what is truly important for the company. Some of the objectives will be qualitative and therefore harder to measure, but this is where boards can shine by consistently exercising keen judgements and business savvy.'

Charan divides the entire CEO compensation decision-making by boards into different tasks.

Define a compensation philosophy that captures the board's intentions for the company   Sometimes it may happen that the CEO meets the agreed targets, there might have been a few sacrifices which were important to business, like a cut in the marketing expenses too steeply diluting the brand equity of the products, a loss of critical talent during the year, reduction of R&D expenses to such levels that the technology edge of the company will be put to question, etc. CEO must be rewarded only when the company is really better off. Working with a compensation philosophy will prevent the occurrence of problems of the above-mentioned sort. According to Charan, the philosophy has to capture the essence of what the board has in mind for the business. The philosophies must aim for a balance of factors that are attractive for short-term investors and factors that build the corporation for the future. Also, the philosophy must indicate what level of risk the board is willing to accept. Factors like nature of business, risk (which again may depend on nature), particular situation (fast growth, turn-around, acquisitions, or getting ready to be acquired, etc.) of the company, industry dynamics and compensation, etc.

Charan suggests that while the philosophy is on the periphery, one must dig deep into four areas to make sure that the right behaviours are rewarded.

Strategy   Whether the firm's strategy provides clear outcome.

Resource allocation   How the CEO allocates resources, lion's share for the short-term or in a balanced manner, so that market development, product development, brand development, and people development are given adequate care.

Borrowing   Is the company carrying debt at an appropriate level? Is the CEO taking on more debt to push the company into the risky category?

Critical people   Does the CEO take care of the critical needs on the people aspect which could make or break the business?

Define multiple objectives that reflect the compensation philosophy   Charan says that many pay-for-performance schemes fall short of expectations because the objectives are too narrow or too far removed from what the board wants the CEO to do. Many boards make the mistake of putting their trust for a single objective, like increasing shareholder return or EPS, as a proxy for a CEO's performance. But, such a single objective rarely captures the range of behaviours a board wants to encourage in the CEO. Many companies were grounded because of the reckless acquisition spree of the CEO using heavy debt in pursuit of EPS or stock price appreciation. Charan cautions against the use of stock market value as the intrinsic value of the company. This is because stock prices are subject to psychological whims of investors as well as to cyclical swings as valuation methodologies go out of fashion and are reinvented. Charan quotes Dennis Donovan, head of HR at Home Depot: 'Relying on stock-market values for incentives when the market under-recognizes the company's intrinsic value can be very de-motivating to key employees'. So, Charan feels that to keep behaviours in balance, the CEO needs multiple objectives. But these cannot be too many. They must be fewer but enough to capture the performance essentials. The set of objectives may vary from company to company.

Match objectives with cash and equity rewards   The compensation plans have to be matched with the time horizons of the objectives. Cash awards are best for rewarding annual performance objectives while equity awards with long vesting periods will encourage the CEO to be very much concerned about the long-term. While a starting proportion could be 50:50, it may vary from industry to industry. In mature industries, where growth opportunities are less, the compensation should be weighted towards cash, whereas in the case of emerging high-tech industries like biotech or IT, compensation weighted towards equity would augur better. Boards should not pay bonuses as a right of the CEO. Bonus is to be paid based on the board's judgement of performance of the CEO vis-à-vis objectives. Some boards also insist that bonus will be paid only on the accurate portrayal of financial performance.

Create a compensation framework that shows total picture of compensation as well as how objectives and rewards are matched   Charan suggests that a grid be built with categories of objectives in the left hand column and the components of compensation (cash bonus, deferred compensation, stock options or restricted stocks, etc.) across the top.

- The categories of objectives can be something like
- Financial and operating accomplishments for the year
- Upgrading the human resource of the company
- Progress on multi-layer strategic building blocks

The multitude of objectives can be grouped under different categories given above.

The components of compensation can be base salary, annual cash incentives, and equity incentive as shown in the Exhibit 5.7.

Exhibit 5.7
Sample CEO Compensation Framework

(Provide the scenario applicable to the company. Eg: Discount retailer with low debt.)

Philosophy: To make incremental improvements to financial condition, while improving the company's positioning versus major competitors within three years and avoiding the issuance of long-term debt.

Short-term objectives:
1. Improve operating cash flow by x per cent over one year.
2. Meet specific margin and company sales goals.
3. Meet total revenue goals.
4. Do not let debt increase beyond y level.
5. Open z new stores in the coming year.

Long-term objectives, for which this year's tasks and milestones must be defined.
1. Differentiate the brand against Wal-Mart.
2. Execute relevant systems and logistics actions that will match or exceed Wal-Mart's inventory turns and out-of-stock levels.
3. Improve pool of store managers, regional managers, and merchandise managers.
4. Initiate processes for increasing imports from low-cost producers in China.

Base salary was set at the 50th percentile against 10 comparable firms.

	Base salary (25 per cent of potential component)	**Annual cash incentive** (25 per cent of potential component)	**Equity incentive** (50 per cent of potential component)
Financial and operating accomplishment	N/A	• Improve operating cash flow by x% • Meet specific margin and company sales goals • Meet total revenue goals • Do not let debt increase beyond y level • Open z new stores	N/A
Upgrading the human resources of the company	N/A	N/A	• Specific 1-year tasks to improve the pool of: ◦ store managers ◦ regional managers ◦ merchandise managers
Multi-year strategic	N/A	N/A	• Specific one-year tasks building blocks to differentiate the brand against Wal-Mart • Specific one-year tasks to match or exceed Wal-Mart's inventory turns and out of stock levels. • Specific one-year tasks to increase imports from China.

The board has to decide what portion of equity is to be vested after retirement

Source: Boards that Deliver, Ram Charan, Jossey-Bass, 2005

Perform meaningful quantitative and qualitative evaluation of CEO performance
Having established a philosophy for compensation, identified the multitude of objectives, decided on the different types of components, and established a framework, now the performance of the CEO has to be evaluated. When the board has decided to move beyond a mechanical formula, the board has to be meticulous in assessing the relative as well as qualitative performance measures. The board has to exercise care and rigour in this process and also in the collection of data. Every factor has to be compared with those of competitors and whether there were one-time influences on them. Comparing with competitors is not always easy as some of the bigger competition may be part of multi-business corporations. Competition may even use different accounting methods. Whenever there were contingent situations, board should consider those factors too while evaluating performance. 'Successfully navigating a crisis, for instance usually merits reward' says Charan. Charan suggests that boards should make transparent not only the compensation packages but also the criteria used to assess the CEO performance.

Address real-world issues like severance pay and getting advice from HR and compensation consultants   When companies recruit CEOs from outside on an urgent basis, the candidates may at times have to forgo the part of compensation which will become due to him in the future. The candidate may insist on being compensated for such opportunity losses. The payment could take the form of signing bonuses, part of which is deferred, or accumulated unvested stock options, or even a golden handshake mentioned in the event of premature forced exit by the board. The compensation committee and the board have to keep in mind the implications of these when they formulate a compensation policy. With the kind of complexity involved in the design of a compensation package, boards and compensation committees may need help from HR group within or outside HR and compensation consultants. The HR people or consultants should clearly imbibe the performance objectives and the evaluation criteria for being of any assistance.

According to Smith and Walter (2006), 'it was a sellers' market for CEOs in the 1980s and 1990s, and CEOs could largely write their own tickets. Often it was "golden hellos" when CEOs arrived, "golden handcuffs" while they served, and "golden goodbyes" when they resigned or were terminated. This was a far cry from the dedicated, professional managers of the establishment corporation of the past' while talking about how there has been a shift in the way CEOs were compensated. While the US has been a cradle for compensation notoriety (remember Richard Grasso at NYSE, Robert Nardelli at Home Depot, or Jill Barad at Mattel who were all paid tens and hundreds of millions in the form of severance pay), such compensations have also started making their entry in India of late. Recently, it was reported that Mr Malvinder Singh, quit as CEO of Ranbaxy (in the year 2008 the Japanese drug company Daiichi Sankyo acquired controlling stake in Ranbaxy from the promoters but let Malvinder continue as CEO as per the terms of acquisition) would receive Rs 450 million for leaving before the expiry of his five-year term.

CEO Compensation Reach for the Stratosphere

Over 1980s and 1990s, CEO compensation methods and processes took a different turn. The valuation processes of the contribution of the executives underwent dramatic change. As Ward (1997) says, 'Corporate executives of earlier decades were valued by the growth and the size of their results and empires. Although such yardsticks remained, especially for the exploding high-tech industries, most CEOs were now being judged by how much they cut-cut expenses, cut facilities, cut fat, and of course, cut employees.' With the establishment of stock market as the most powerful institution and stock prices as the primary yardstick of performance of a CEO, the emphasis was on short-term growth rather than long-term sustainability. This was also overwhelmingly aided by the recommendations by governance and compensation experts that in order for the CEO and top management to better align with the interests of the shareholders, a good part of their compensation shall be stock-related, either as stock options, restricted stock issues, etc. Hence, the management with the thrust on short-term stock-market performance, resorted to what Hamel and Prahalad describe as denominator management (discussed in Chapter 6 in detail) (Hamel and Prahalad 1994). While there has been political, public, and stockholders' ire as a result of the high-profile corporate failures in the early 2000s, nothing much seems to have changed. While 'pay for performance' has been the motto, it has mostly been 'pay without performance'. Stories of increased CEO remuneration even when there is deterioration in the company's performance have been commonplace, but investors, the public, and even the so called 'gate keepers' usually are in a slumber and wake up only when there is a crisis.

Compensation—The Ratio between CEO and the Lowest-paid Employee

Drucker had very early on suggested that this ratio shall never be greater than 50. But in 2000, the multiple for S&P 500 companies in the US was about 450 and for the largest 100 US companies, it was about 1000 (Dimma 2006). Dimma says that in Canada, the multiples are dependent on the company size and the multiples for various sized are as shown in Table 5.1.

TABLE 5.1   Multiples and the company sizes

Company size	Total cash compensation multiple
Small-cap (< $1 billion)	Up to 40
Mid-cap ($1–$3 billion)	Up to 60
Large-cap (>$3 billion)	Up to 100

When the CEO or the top management gets increased pay while the shareholders get lesser returns as a result of poor performance of the company, there is a wealth transfer from shareholders to management. 'Warren Buffet called it, famously, the largest peacetime transfer of wealth in US history. And shareholders have noticed' (Dimma, 2006). In 2001, for example, Larry Ellison, CEO of Oracle, took home $706 million a year when Oracle's shareholders got the least return' (Prasuna 2002). Prasuna points out that 'CEO compensation in the US has been high. There are historical reasons for the phenomenon. Most of the American businesses have long past their founding fathers and come into the hands of "professional managers", who are rarely from the founding family. Which means that they do not necessarily bring the ownership, belongingness, and involvement with the fortunes of the company. Their goal would be limited to accomplishing tasks rather than achieving new heights that successful companies need to go. To create surrogate entrepreneurs who would aim beyond survival, it becomes necessary to provide higher compensation packages.' While there have been instances like Glaxo Smithkline in the UK where shareholders voted against the pay policies for senior management including a 'golden parachute' for the CEO Jean Pierre Garnier (Ratna 2003), such instances are few and far between.

While higher compensation packages in the US could have arisen out of a necessity to create surrogate entrepreneurship because businesses and enterprises had outgrown their familial ownerships (Prasuna 2002) or due to the fact that the founding fathers and their next generations had the wisdom that enterprises would be better managed by professionals, the Indian compensation scenario provides a different picture. The Owner Executive Chairman and/or CEO of family promoted and managed companies beat the professional CEOs hands down. A comparison of the top 10 compensation for owners as well as professional executives for the years 2003–04 and 2007–08 is as shown in Tables 5.2 and 5.3.

TABLE 5.2   Owner CEOs and professional CEOs

Company owners remuneration			Company professional executives remuneration		
	Name	(Rs million)		Name	(Rs million)
Hero Honda	B.L. Munjal	117.12	Wipro	Vivek Paul	57.02
Reliance Ind.	M.D. Ambani	116.20	Ranbaxy	D.S. Brar	40.52
Reliance Ind.	A.D. Ambani	116.20	I-flex Sol.	Rajesh Hukku	31.13
Hero Honda	Pawan Munjal	115.35	Ranbaxy	Brian Tempest	36.49
Cadila Hlth	P.R. Patel	84.00	Ranbaxy	V.K. Kaul	28.79
Wockhardt	H.F. Khorakiwala	68.18	Nestle	Carlo Donati	27.49
Apollo Tyres	O.S.Kanwar	56.10	I-flex Sol.	R. Ravisankar	26.40
HCC	Ajit Gulabhchand	37.92	HLL	M.S. Banga	24.66
Divi's Lab.	Murali K. Divi	37.36	Ranbaxy	B. Rashmi	22.37
Dr Reddy's	K. Anji Reddy	33.34	ITC	Y.C. Deveshwar	18.68

Source: Business India, 2–15 April 2004.

TABLE 5.3   Remuneration comparison for the year 2007–08

Remuneration			Professional remuneration		
Company	Owner name	(Rs million)	Company	Executives name	(Rs million)
Reliance Ind.	M.D. Ambani	440.22	Cipla	Amar Lulla	123.25
Sun TV	Kalanithi Maran	324.10	L & T	A.M. Naik	83.92
Sun TV	Kavery Kalanithi	324.10	Hindalco	D. Bhattacharya	82.37

Contd

Table 5.3 contd

	Remuneration			Professional remuneration	
Company	Owner name	(Rs million)	Company	Executives name	(Rs million)
Madras Cem.	P.R.R. Rajha	324.05	Cairn Ind	Rahul Dhir	68.31
Reliance Com.	A.D. Ambani	300.30	Ranbaxy	Brian Tempest	66.99
Ranbaxy	Malvinder Singh	195.86	Ambuja Cem.	Anil Singhvi	66.68
Bharti Airtel	Sunil Mittal	195.51	East Ind. Hot.	S.S. Mukherji	65.26
Jindal St&Pow.	Naveen Jindal	169.30	Shobha Dev.	J.C. Sharma	58.40
JSW Steel	Sajjan Jindal	167.30	Zee Ent.	Pradeep Guha	53.31
Hero Honda	B.L. Munjal	157.62	Nestle	M.G. Rolland	53.11

Source: *Business India*, 30 November, 2008.

Rising Concerns about CEO Compensation

While CEO and senior executive compensation has been a hotly debated topic, it gained in intensity in the post-Enron era. While there have been many critics of the skyrocketing compensation packages of executives, there have also been powerful defenders in whose view, 'despite some lapses, imperfection, and cases of abuse, executive pay arrangements have largely been shaped by market forces and boards loyal to shareholders' (Bebchuk and Fried 2004). Whatever be the case, the board's task and ability in developing an executive compensation plan has received much public attention these days. Since it caught so much public attention, politicians have taken serious steps to influence regulators to regulate CEO salaries. Everybody agrees that the compensation package be right enough to cultivate an entrepreneurial mindset, most are concerned about the diverging trend between performance and compensation. As Ward (1997) says, 'By 1991, the United States was enduring both a recession and major economy-wide corporate restructuring, both of which brought falling corporate profits and major layoffs. At the same moment, the pay of those famous CEOs was headed violently upward.' According to Charan, a progressive board has to arrive at a framework to view the total compensation package.

According to him, 'Get the compensation right and the CEO adds significant long-term value. Get it wrong, and a CEO could go on a debt-fuelled acquisition spree that at the extreme lands the company in bankruptcy' (Charan 2005). According to Bebchuk and Fried (2004), 'During the extended bull market of the 1990s, executive compensation at public companies—companies whose stocks are traded on stock exchanges—soared to unprecedented levels. Between 1992 and 2000, the average real (inflation-adjusted) pay of CEOs of S&P 500 firms more than quadrupled, climbing from \$3.5 million to \$14.7 million... The growth of executive compensation far outstripped that of compensation for other employees. In 1991, the average large company CEO received approximately 140 times the pay of an average worker; in 2003, the ratio was about 500:1.' Even pro-business and pro-executive magazines like *Business Week* and *Forbes* dealt with cover stories on CEO pay excesses. According to Ward, 'Even such a normally doughty defender of free enterprise as George Will in September 1991 wrote of executives of "ripping of capitalism" with CEO compensation that was "generally disproportionate and often ludicrous".'

The executive compensation excesses caught such public glare that it forced political intervention. According to Ward, 'In May 1991, a sub-committee of the US Senate held hearings on executive compensation and tax policy and drew some damning testimony. Nell Minow, who was then president of Institutional Shareholder Services, paraphrased Churchill to note that "never have so few done so little to get so much money".'

Post Senate hearings in 1991, a number of legislative bills were moved in the Senate with Sen. Carl Levin sponsoring the Corporate Pay Responsibility Act followed by another by Repr. Martin Sabo to disallow tax deductions for top manager pay exceeding 25 times that of the company's lowest paid workers. The first one would have permitted shareholders to vote on top executive pay policies, forcing a simplified and uniform disclosure of executive and director pay and demanded calculation of the value of executive stock options. Also, 'the tax laws were modified in 1993 to make the portion of salaries in excess of $1 million per year in the public companies a non-taxable expense' (Colley et al 2003).

According to Bebchuk and Fried (2004), 'The dominant paradigm for financial economists' study of executive compensation has assumed that pay arrangements are the product of arm's-length bargaining—bargaining between executives attempting to get the best possible deal for themselves and boards seeking to get the best possible deal for shareholders. This assumption has also been the basis for the corporate law rules governing the subject.'

Most boards have been worried about losing their CEOs and other senior executives in an era when talent is at a premium. Thus, on the strength of the reason that they want to retain their CEOs who they think are the best and thus yield to the arm-twisting by the CEO and other top managers. The whole process of raising the compensation levels were aided largely by the so-called professional compensation consultants. According to Smith and Walter, 'To be sure that they were meeting market standards, they retained compensation consultants, who conducted surveys of the compensation arrangements at comparable companies and reported back to the board. They might show that the median compensation for a CEO was $4 million, the upper quartile was $6 million, but their own CEO was receiving $3.8 million, less than the median and much less than the upper quartile, where board thought their CEO should really be ranked. So they got a raise to adjust his or her compensation to where the board thought it should be, on the basis of the consultant's analysis. The adjustments raised the median for the group to, say $4.2 million and the consultants reported the information to other companies, and the level of compensation required to keep one's own CEO in line continued to rise—all by itself and without any direct contribution by the CEO.'

The media and the business press usually emphasize the focus on the level of pay, rather than how the CEOs are paid. Michael Jensen and Kevin Murphy argue that 'the relentless focus on how much CEOs are paid diverts public attention from the real problem—how CEOs are paid' (Chew and Gillan 2005). The challenge before companies grew whenever there was a need for replacing the incumbent CEO, especially when the company was passing through a rough patch and the intention for replacing was a vice-like tough turn-around assignment. The leeway available for the company for negotiation was, most of the time, narrow. A lot of incentives like a big sign-in bonus, a number of perquisites of which some could be outlandish (a posh accommodation in an up-market area, luxury cars for private use, private jets, exquisite holiday location listed, a number of care-takers at the apartment, etc.), fancy titles, stock-options or restricted stock issues, huge retirement benefits, and even a huge severance pay in case the candidate was terminated before the term. Since the board's primary responsibility at times was to find the best candidate for the job to tide over the crisis (which many companies like even IBM succumbed to), they yielded to any demands that would ensure the candidate would come on board. Senior executives even used to negotiate contracts with the boards of companies to pay them exorbitantly in the event of the company's takeover by other companies, sometimes irrespective of whether they were removed or asked to stay on. While conventionally it is called 'golden parachute', 'the *Wall Street Journal* once referred rather indelicately to the practice as "the golden condom" because it protects senior management while screwing shareholders' (Dimma 2006). Supporters and defenders of the at-times-outrageous compensation practices often cite the war for talent in the so-called efficient market. Bebchuk and Fried (2004) quote Ira Kay, a noted compensation consultant, who argued that 'the CEO labour market meets all the criteria of any market', while testifying before US Senate Committee. And Bebchuk and Fried say that 'in this view, compensation arrangements are the outcome of market interactions, a product of the combined forces of the supply and demand for managerial talent.'

Board's Role in Compensation

Jensen and Murphy are of the opinion that 'one of the most critical roles of the board of directors is to create incentives that make it in the CEO's best interest to do what is in the shareholders' best interest' (Chew and Gillan 2005). According to them, some combination of three basic policies will create the right monetary incentives for CEOs to maximize the value of their companies:

Boards can require that CEOs become substantial owners of company stock   The most powerful link between shareholders' wealth and executive wealth is direct ownership of shares by the CEO. The larger the share of company stock controlled by the CEO and senior management, the more substantial is the link between shareholders' wealth and executive wealth. Jensen and Murphy cite the example of Warren Buffet who controls directly and indirectly about 45 per cent of Berkshire Hathaway's equity. The stock-related feedback effect of a $10 million decline in market value is nearly $4.5 million, a powerful incentive to resist wasteful spending. While it is unreasonable to expect all public-company CEOs to own as large a percentage of their company's equity as Warren Buffet's share of Berkshire Hathaway, the lesson is still valid. The larger the share of the company stock controlled by the CEO and the senior management, the more substantial the linkage between shareholder wealth and executive wealth. In most of the Indian companies today, the CEOs hold substantial stakes. For example, in RIL, promoter CEO Mukesh Ambani controls about 51.37 per cent while promoter Azim Premji controls about 80 per cent of the outstanding stock of Wipro.

Cash compensation should be structured to provide big rewards for outstanding performance and meaningful penalties for poor performance   Creating better incentives for CEOs almost necessarily means increasing the financial risks CEOs face. This way, cash compensation has certain advantages over stock and stock options. Stock-based incentives subject a CEO to the vagaries of the stock market that are clearly beyond their control. Compensation contracts based on company performance relative to comparable companies could provide sound incentives while insulating the CEO from factors such as stock-market crash of 1987. Jensen and Murphy say that if CEOs owed a large percentage of corporate equity, the usually observed weak link between cash compensation and corporate performance would be less troubling. According to them, it would make sense for CEOs with big chunks of equity to have their cash compensation less sensitive to performance than CEOs with small stockholdings.

Make real the threat of dismissal   The threat of being fired as a result of poor performance can provide powerful monetary and non-monetary incentives for CEOs to maximize company value. This is because much of an executive's 'human capital' (and thus his or her value in the job market) is specific to the company; CEOs who are fired from their present jobs are unlikely to find new jobs that pay as well. A high-visibility dismissal is a public humiliation and this should make managers weigh carefully the consequences of taking action that increase the probability of being dismissed. But Jensen and Murphy say that while the prospect of dismissal can be a monetary and non-monetary incentive, the evidence is not all that clear. The CEO's position is not a risky job as very few of a large number get dismissed even after years of underperformance. The reasons are not hard to find: (a) The CEOs have organization specific capital; it is difficult for an outsider to come in and run a giant company. (b) There can be a lag between input and output. The CEO's efforts taken now may not be reflected this year or next year but might add long-term competitiveness and firm value.

Arm's-length Bargaining and Contracting

According to Bebchuk and Fried, the generally accepted principle (or 'the official view') is that pay considerations are the result of arm's-length bargaining—bargaining between the executives attempting to get the best possible deal for themselves and the boards, seeking to get the best deal for shareholders. According to them this assumption has been at the foundation of corporation-related laws and regulations governing the subject. The underline theory is the agency theory, which assumes that executives acting as agents are selfish and would try to elicit maximum monetary rewards from the boards while boards acting in a fiduciary capacity on behalf of the shareholders will try to maximize the shareholders' value. While apparently these may look like forces acting in opposite directions, boards can always achieve a balance by linking the executives' financial gains to the creation of wealth for the share holders. Considering that shareholders' value creation has always been measured on the basis of the company's performance in the stock markets, there can be aberration in the executive and company's performance vis-à-vis stock market performance. Financial experts have devised other parameters like return on investment (ROI), ROE, ROCE and Economic Value Added (EVA), all of which can act as effective tools to measure the firm's performance, if used prudently. Whatever be the method of assessing the performance of the executive, 'arm's-length model implicitly assumes that unlike corporate executives, corporate directors can be relied on to serve shareholders' according to Bebchuk and Fried (2004). But they also caution: 'Given that executives do not instinctively seek to maximize shareholder value, however there is no reason to expect a priori that directors will act in this way. Directors' on incentives and preferences do matter. Directors have financial and non-financial incentives to favour, or at least to get along with executives.'

According to Gillan (2005), 'Compensation issues have become an increasingly important component of corporate governance for a number of reasons.' Gillan lists four reasons.

1. A well-crafted compensation plan should result in the alignment of the interests of executives and employees with those of shareholders. The policy should be effective enough to attract, motivate, and retain employees. But, many a time, the costs and benefits of large pay packages and option grants to executives in particular are not always obvious.
2. Most companies, especially knowledge-based companies consider the role of employees or 'human capital' critical in the generation of returns to shareholders. Employees are well-aware of this, and hence desire (and demand) a 'piece of action', i.e.—to be compensated by way of equity for their contribution to value creation.
3. Concerns about how costly are the stock options for shareholders, considering that the use of options as a component of compensation has exploded.
4. The fundamental disconnect between pay and performance arising out of a misuse of the stock-based compensation, especially in the context of a booming economy and rising stock market.

However, while a compensation programme needs to be monitored and should incorporate the latest developments in the field, most of the ills are related not to the design of the components but the administration of it. Almost all governance and compensation experts concur that there is a need to align the compensation with the shareholders' rewards. By making stock options a major component of the total compensation package, the board and the company is trying to implement and achieve this paradigm. As Pearl Meyer, Founder and CEO of Pearl Mayer and Partners, says: 'The most significant change in executive compensation has been the shift to pay-for-performance programmes that are focused on stock based incentives, to motivate and reward the creation of the shareholder value... These trends and the historic rise in the stock prices over the past decade have resulted in a sharp increase in compensation and extraordinary levels of executive wealth. For 2000 and 2001, 91 per cent of the CEO's pay at the top 200 US industrial and service companies was variable, with as much as 70 per cent based on the price of the stock, and only 20 per cent based on business and financial performance' (Ashby and Miles 2002).

However, suddenly the stock option programme comes under attack when in a particular year the stock markets skyrocketed and the executives who suddenly got paid in large numbers of millions got all the attention and flack. Comparisons made with previous years, with other companies in the same country, even with the company's financial performance (which need not have any relationship with the stock market movements), and with companies abroad and led to making all funny and sometimes nasty comments attributing the large package to greed of the executive clan. But Dimma does not find much fault with greed. He is of the opinion that 'greed is inherent in the human condition, though it is more evident in some sets of gene than in others. Greed is not without redeeming qualities (energy, achievement, wealth creation), but for society's sake, it must be channeled and held within bounds' and 'Greed will, of course, always be with us. Properly controlled and kept in check, it is an important incentive to accomplishment. But the key word is "controlled" and I fear that incrementalism does not get at the heart of the problem' (Dimma 2006).

Despite the occurrence of financial scandals and the consequent failure of corporates, and the fact that the CEO's pay continued to be under limelight putting the whole approach and its validity under question, 'financial economists have continued to use arm's-length contracting as the main lens through which to view compensation arrangements' say Bebchuk and Fried (2004). But they say that 'directors have neither the time nor the information necessary to monitor all managerial actions to ensure that they benefit the shareholders. Given the considerable discretion inherent in a CEO's position, inducing the CEO to focus on shareholder interest and avoid self-serving choice is therefore important. The board can influence the CEO to behave in this manner by designing compensation arrangement that provides the CEO with an incentive to increase shareholder value. Thus, it is argued, a well designed compensation scheme can make up for the fact that the directors cannot directly monitor or evaluate many of the top executives' decisions' (Bebchuk and Fried).

A CEO and Executive Compensation 2009 Survey co-sponsored by Farient Advisors LLC and *directors and boards* reveals that 'corporate directors, executives, and shareholders believe that excessive executive compensation is a significant issue.'[1]

Compensation for CEOs in India

While all listed companies mandatorily disclose the total compensation paid to the CEOs and other EDs as well as NEDs, very few disclose the various components and the performance criteria. Infosys provides the director compensation policy in greater detail in their annual report. Their broad board compensation policy states that 'the compensation committee determines and recommends to the board, the compensation payable to all directors. All board-level compensation are approved by the shareholders and separately disclosed in the financial statements. Remuneration of the executive directors consists of a fixed component and a performance incentive. The compensation committee makes a quarterly appraisal of the performance of the executive directors based on a detailed performance-related matrix. The annual compensation of the executive directors is approved by the compensation committee, within the parameters set by the shareholders at the shareholders' meetings'.[2] As a note to the details of compensation paid to the board members, the company states that 'none of the directors are eligible for any severance pay.'[3] The specific charter of the compensation committee describes its responsibilities and authorities as 'the compensation committee shall annually review and approve for the CEO, the executive directors, and senior management (a) the annual base salary, (b) the annual incentive bonus, including the specific goals and amount, (c) equity compensation,

---

[1] *Directors and Boards*, Spring 2009.

[2] Infosys Annual Report 2008–09.

[3] Infosys Annual Report 2008–09.

(d) employment agreements, severance arrangements, and change in control agreements/ provisions, and (e) any other benefits, compensation or arrangements'.

Another major company in India, Reliance Industries Ltd, provides only minimum (and even vague about the criteria) details regarding the Remuneration Committee's functioning. It details the process as Terms of Reference, which says: 'The Remuneration Committee has been constituted to recommend/review remuneration of the managing director and whole-time directors, based on their performance and defined assessment criteria'.[4] The remunerations paid to CMD and whole-time directors include a basic salary, perquisites and allowances, retiral benefits, commission, and a grant of stock options (except for Mr Mukesh Ambani, being promoter). One of the four full-time directors (non-family member) is not paid any commission. The report also states that 'there is no separate provision for payment of severance fees.' There is another committee, Employees Stock Compensation Committee, which does not say anything about whether option grants for directors are covered by this committee or not.

A Better Way Forward in Executive Compensation

While compensation has been a controversial issue becoming the cynosure of all corporate watchers, a good percentage of them feel that the CEO pay levels are more or less correct. For example, while 55 per cent of the respondents of the Executive Compensation and Governance Survey 2009, mentioned above, felt that executive compensation is a significant issue, about 76 per cent of the respondents indicated that the CEO pay levels in their organization were 'about right'. Whereas 34 per cent of the respondents strongly turned down the idea of establishing more rules, 40 per cent felt that more rules be established only for organizations receiving governmental assistance. Only 26 per cent felt that more rules be established for all organizations. About 69 per cent of the respondents strongly advocated the necessity of steps to improve the degree of alignment between performance and pay. Charan (2005) suggests that 'boards must get a handle on CEO compensation once for all. Pay for performance has long been the goal, but even well-intentioned boards have had trouble in practice. Something goes wrong in defining performance, measuring it, and matching rewards to it, whether it is over relying on a single measure of performance or creating complex systems that obscure the total package.'

COMPONENTS OF CEO COMPENSATION

Since the total compensation paid to CEOs catch attention of not only the pay or governance watchers, those analysts or experts who track a company, but also those of members of public, it would be appropriate at this stage to understand what constitutes the CEO pay. The components of CEO pay can be divided into what constitutes the current compensation, what constitutes the long-term, and also the contingent component which is to be paid in the case of unexpected events, usually a part of the contract these days (see Table 5.4).

---

[4] RIL Annual Report 2007–08.

TABLE **5.4**   Components of CEO compensation

Current	Long-term	Contingent
Base salary	Cash bonuses	Severance pay
Perquisites	Stock options	
Fringe benefits	Stock grants	
Cash bonuses	Stock ownership plan	
Commission		

Current Compensation

Base salary

This is the monthly compensation which will depend on the pay structure within the company, competitive forces acting on the pay, and is usually the basis for calculation of the other components like perquisites or fringe benefits. It usually forms a very small percentage of the total package to enable an executive to sustain even in the absence of superior performance. While this is usually not related to performance, performance enables one to bargain for a fixation of basic pay at higher levels on entry, bargain for increments as years pass by, etc. The basic pay is not intended at the creation of any wealth for the CEO. For example, the basic salary of the highest-paid CEO in India, Mr Mukesh Ambani, CMD of Reliance Industries Ltd in the year 2007–08 was only Rs 6 million while his total compensation package was Rs 440.22 million. The basic salary of Mr Gopalakrishnan, CEO of Infosys, was Rs 3 million whereas his counterpart at TCS (Mr Ramadorai) was paid Rs 7.62 million in 2008–09. Since most companies offer higher at-risk-component as an incentive for higher performance, the basic salaries in most cases are very reasonable-looking.

Perquisites

Perquisites can at times prove very costly to the company. These include club memberships, business expense reimbursements for entertaining customers, chauffeur-driven luxury cars, private jets, luxurious residential apartments in up-market locations, servants for home at company expenses, private security arrangements, reservation in major games/sports, events/theatre, subscriptions to important management journals and business publications, book allowances, advice for financial planning, etc. Mukesh Ambani enjoyed perquisites worth Rs 4.8 million in 2007–08. S. Gopalakrishnan of Infosys was paid Rs 1.1 million while S. Ramadorai was paid Rs 8.335 million (which includes benefits, perquisites, and allowances).

The term perquisites in India include contribution to provident fund, superannuation fund, gratuity, and encashment of leave according to Companies Act 1956. The global scenario is not very different.

Cash-bonus for short-term performance

This is paid on the achievement of short-term goals and objectives. These may include new product launches within specified times; completing a planned acquisition; reducing flab, especially units that are unviable; progress on identifying and developing potential leaders including those for COO and CEO positions; and awards won by the company during the year, which will improve its competitive advantage as well as social standing, in addition to routine financial measures. No cash bonus component has been shown in the case of Mukesh Ambani in 2007–08 and S. Ramadorai in 2008–09, while Gopalakrishnan at Infosys was paid Rs 4.4 million during the year 2008–09.

Fringe benefits

Firms usually include insurance premium for both medical and life coverage, costs of holidaying and vacationing (Leave Travel Concessions–LTC or Leave Fare Concessions—LFC, in India), retiral benefits (a few of the perquisites which the CEO used to enjoy during his employment may be negotiated to continue even after retirement) like pension, gratuity, and other benefits. Not every company provides details of fringe benefits enjoyed by the executives and might be covered together with perquisites. As Colley et al. (2003) say: 'In fact, fringe benefits can be an area of major abuse by boards and CEOs, especially with regard to retirement packages.' The retiral benefits of Jack Welch came under lens after a divorce suit made the package public. Welch was to enjoy the use of private jets, hotel suites, apartments, daily flowers, and even theatre tickets (Dimma). Payments towards pension have also been catching attention as sometimes they are exorbitantly high. *New York Times* in April 2005 listed the largest pension entitlements of retired US senior executives, primarily CEOs. The annual pensions ranged from $3 million to $6 million per annum (Dimma 2006). Some companies even indulge in such actions as crediting two or more years of service for every year of actual service or add anywhere from five years to sometimes 20 years of service arbitrarily when faced with instances of luring executives from other companies whose pensions in those companies are not transferable (Dimma).

Commission

Globally, commission is not a component of CEO compensation, but most of the Indian companies have adopted a system of paying commission to their CEOs, other working directors, and NEDs. The Company Law in India (Part II of Schedule XIII) provides guidelines for managerial remuneration which states that 'remuneration may be by way of salary, dearness allowance, perquisites, commission, and other allowances.'[5] Pre-liberalization regulation in India was very stringent on managerial remuneration. But post-liberalization, the regulations have been relaxed and a company making profits can pay up to 5 per cent of net profits, calculated according to the provisions under Section 148 and 309 of the Companies Act, to the managing director. If there are more than one 'managerial person' (more than one director with executive responsibilities), total managerial remuneration shall not exceed 10 per cent of the net profits calculated as mentioned above. Thus, in the post-liberalized scenario, remuneration levels of companies increased considerably and the major part of remuneration has been started to be paid in the form of commissions. For example, out of Mukesh Ambani's total remuneration package of Rs 440.22 million, Rs 427.54 million was in the form of commission. While TCS

[5] Taxman's Company Law Ready Reckoner 2009.

paid a commission of Rs 25 million to CEO Ramadorai, Infosys does not pay any remuneration in the form of commission to executive directors.

Compensation Components for Long-Term

Since a CEO is very actively involved in the strategy-making, the results of which will be reflected only in the future, a certain (according to experts, a majority) part of the compensation shall be designed for the long-term and such components will fall due as and when the long-term targets are achieved. Care must be taken to see that it is simply not the achievement of a specific target, but that achievement is within a time-frame and also within the target resource budget.

Cash-bonus for long-term achievement of long-term objectives

The performance criteria fixed could be the timely development and launch of a radically new product currently under R&D, or implementation of a long-gestation project within time, or achievement of the company's stated objectives like revenues, which must constitute of say 60 per cent from products which were introduced not more than 5 years ago, or attainment of a stated market share after a specified time period, or creation of a leadership cadre through the conscious efforts of the CEO making the company strong on succession issues, or establishing better relations with unions which will result in improved productivity, etc. Out of the total cash-bonus components, a large part shall be based on the CEO's performance for the long-haul.

Stock options

Compensation by way of stock options has been in vogue for quite some time now. Usually paid as incentives for performance, they give the CEO/executives the right to purchase a specified number of shares of the firms' stock at a stipulated price sometime in future. The award is staggered over a period of time, usually year-by-year. The technical term for the point in time at which the stock options actually become the property of the holder is known as 'vesting'. For example, a CEO may be awarded options to purchase say one million shares at say Rs 100 per share. This price is known as the strike price. The options however may be distributed or vested over a period of say 10 years entitling the CEO to buy the shares from the company at Rs 100 a share of 100,000 shares a year for 10 years. Since the award is spread over a period of 10 years, there is a strong incentive for the CEO to see that the performance of the company over the term is good, and that the company's shares in the stock market sell at a premium beyond Rs 100 as such a price only will provide him any incentive as the price of Rs 100 has to be paid by the CEO. It also encourages the CEO to stick with the company for long-term as his incentives are spread over the long-term. The difference in the exercise price and the market price on the date of exercise was subject to fringe benefit tax (FBT) in India after it was introduced but has been changed to perquisite tax according to the 2009–10 budget presented at the parliament in July 2009.

The CEO can sell the shares in the market and make gains or hold them. Options in India are *qualifying* in the sense that any profits arising out of exercising the option will be subjected to capital gains tax. In the US, there are *non-qualifying* options also which are not taxed for capital gains but are taxed as ordinary income.

Underwater and in-the-money options

Underwater options are those for which strike price is higher than the market price, making the options valueless.

In-the-money options are those where the current market price of shares is greater than the options price. Stock options that are vested and in the money can be exercised (encashed) at any time up to their expiration date.

Usually, companies do not reset the price of *underwater* options (as repricing downward will in effect reward executives for failure or for not meeting objectives) unless some contingency arises. But, at times boards may, with shareholder approval, reset the exercise price to act as an incentive for executives to continue or attract new executives on to the board.

Implications of CEO's actions in options   Shareholders expect the CEO to hold on to the options acquired by him/her if he/she has confidence in the company's future. If a CEO sells the shares vested, that would be sending a negative signal to the shareholders, investment analysts, and even public at large about the future of the company. Recently, when Manoj Kohli, CEO, Bharti Airtel, sold the shares he had acquired, the share price of Bharti Airtel tumbled by 6.4 per cent on the Bombay Stock Exchange (BSE) on that day.

According to Dimma (2006), options are a good method of compensating executives if a few important conditions are established and met:

- Performance options should be used much more than they are. They should in fact, become the norm. Of course, in a strong bull market, these compensations touch very high levels as P/E ratios reach for the stratosphere. According to Dimma, performance options pay-off generously only when there is superior performance, that is when pre-determined stretch targets are met or exceeded.
- Insistence that shares acquired through options be held for not less than one year, and preferably two years. Dimma says that executives may be permitted based on their request to sell enough shares to cover the cost of acquisition and the related tax incidence.
- All senior executives should hold, as long as they are employed, the company shares to the tune of an amount of not less than three to seven times their annual salary. Dimma advises that the more senior the position, the greater shall be the multiple.
- Full vesting shall not be made at the time of grant of options. Dimma suggests that vesting at 20 per cent per year over five years as the best practice.
- Options must be expensed. This will have a moderating effect on some of the more outrageous levels of options granted in recent years according to Dimma. In the US all options have been expensed from 2005. In Canada also companies expense options.

Stock grants

Some companies opt for stock grants in place of stock options. Grants are taxable when granted and are more expensive per share to the company than options. For tax purpose, stock grants are on par with cash compensation.

Stock purchase plans

Here the company provides loans to the executives to enable them to purchase the stipulated number of shares. The loans are then set off against bonuses earned for meeting or exceeding objectives set.

Stock options vs outright share issues

Experts are divided on whether issue of stock options or outright issue of shares to the executives is better. There are people like Warren Buffet who feel against options as they provide no downward risk to the management. Hence, he prefers stock grants or stock purchase plans to options (Colley et al. 2003). Bill Miller of Legg Mason is another who has advocated that options be abolished. According to him, outright ownership is the best way of aligning management with shareholder interests (Dimma 2006). But Dimma feels that the problems with options lie not in the principle but in the practice. He feels that abolishing options for the ills in practice is like throwing the baby with the bathwater (Dimma).

Dimma suggests four remedial measures in order to make options more palatable to those who are concerned:

The value of options granted need to be limited and controlled by compensation committees constituted only of independent directors. If necessary, they may take advice from an external compensation consultant, hiring of which is done by the committee and not management. Dimma suggests that the net present value of an option grant, when calculated for each year of its term, should not exceed the salary of the executive. The use of the Black Scholes formula to price the options has an inherent undervaluing flaw as the model looks at only short-term options.

Options shall be issued only when performance is demonstrably superior, measured in absolute as well as relative terms.

The cost of options granted should be expensed. This will act as a disincentive for the company and thus prevent excesses. Dimma (2006) says that 'a hit to the bottomline always sobers the mind.'

The rules about the length of time for which the shares acquired through the options need to be tough. Dimma favours that the guidelines be framed by the boards rather than regulated by the government. The executives should be encouraged to hold on to the shares for the long term. Dimma suggests that government regulation must be in the form of tax incentives on shares arising out of options. Shares held for short term should be taxed high and those held for longer periods should be taxed low.

Severance Pay and Other Gratuitous Payments

Severance pays are common in countries like the US whereas they have not become very popular in India. Severance pays usually form a part of the contract between a new CEO and the company which may be paid in the event of the company getting acquired and the CEO deciding to move on or the CEO being removed from the position as a result of underperformance before the expiry of the term. These types of packages made a strong entry in the 1990s and is still continuing. These packages have been catching attention as in some cases they have turned out to be at obscene levels. For example, Bob Nardelli, CEO of Home Depot was reported to be paid $210 million severance package (in addition to the $225 million he was paid during the six-year period from 2001 to 2006) when he was asked to go by the board after the company's shares dropped 7.9 per cent and the company lost market share to Lowe's companies ('Nardelli Exit Package Called "Outrage" Heighten Pay Debate'[6]).

Exotic names like golden or platinum parachutes have been given to such packages to reflect how valuable they are and how they permit the exiting CEOs a safe landing. Colley et al. (2003) narrate examples: 'CEOs whose unsatisfactory performance called for their dismissal have been perversely rewarded with payments of $1 million or $2 million per year for life, with provision that if their spouses outlive them, the spouse will get half the amount for the rest of their lives… In one instance, the terms of the merger between two companies called for the CEOs who was leaving to receive $5 million per year for life, alongwith the generous extension of the benefit to his wife. In some cases involving the merger of two firms, the package is so rich that both CEOs prefer to leave rather than stay and work.' Bebchuk and Fried explain the case of Mattel CEO Jill Barad. When she was forced out by the board, 'she had $4.2 million loan forgiven, and received an additional $3.3 million in cash to cover the tax liability arising from the forgiveness of another loan. In addition, her unvested options were allowed to vest automatically and to remain exercisable until the end of their original terms. These gratuitous benefits accompanied the severance package already granted under her contract which included a termination payment of $26.4 million, annual retirement benefits of more than $700,000 and other benefits' (Bebchuk and Fried 2004). Charan (2009) highlights the case of Stanley O'Neal 'who left Merrill Lynch after announcing a $2.24 billion quarterly loss in 2007 yet received $161.5 million in equity awards and retirement benefits.' The problem gets even more complicated when the board is forced to recruit a CEO from outside to suddenly replace the CEO who is forced out. Charan again quotes the example of Merrill Lynch: 'To hire John Thain from NYSE Euronext as a replacement for O'Neal, Merrill had to offer him substantial compensation for giving up awards from NYSE.'

The fringe benefits for Mukesh Ambani in 2007–08 were in the form of retiral benefits at Rs 1.75 million. For Gopalakrishnan of Infosys, these were Rs 0.7 million and this component is not shown separately in the case of Ramadorai of TCS.

Supplemental Executive Retirement Plans

In the US, the qualified retirement plans for those which get a favourable tax treatment for the firm have certain limitations as far as pension amounts are concerned. Suppose an executive was earning say $1 million per annum at the time of retirement and the company plan promises to pay 50 per cent of the compensation earned during the last year of service, it cannot pay $500,000 annually as there is a stipulation to limit the same to $100,000 annually. Thus, firms do not have the ability to provide executives with pensions that are similar in size to their annual compensation while in service. To circumvent this, firms usually provide executives with non-qualified 'supplemental' executive retirement plans (SERPs). According to Bebchuk and Fried,

[6] Bloomberg.com, 3 January 2007.

'SERPs differ from typical qualified pension plans in two critical ways. First, they do not receive the favourable tax treatment enjoyed by qualified plans; no investment income goes untaxed under a SERP. The company pays taxes on investment income it must generate in order to pay the executive in retirement. If the money had been distributed as salary, on the other hand, the executive who invested the money for retirement would have had to pay taxes on any income generated. The effect of SERP, therefore, is to shift some of the executive's tax burden to the firm' (Bebchuk and Fried 2004). One very unfortunate aspect of this compensation component is that it is only related to the executive's salary at the time of retirement and has no link to performance. The longer the service of the employee and the higher the pay at the time of retirement, the higher the SERP payout. Bebchuk and Fried note that 'many firms have also credited executives with years that they did not actually serve, ratcheting up the final payout under the plan's formula' (Bebchuk and Fried 2004). While the normal pension plans would be invariably reported in the regular compensation tables, plans under SERP are largely not disclosed and thus hidden from view. This is because firms are mandatorily required to disclose only those paid to the current executives. Since the payments under SERPs happen after the executives leave the company, they are rarely shown in the compensation tables.

Getting the CEO Compensation Right

The well-publicized stories on CEO compensation in the past clearly led to the belief that there were serious problems. Higher pay for lesser performance was being accorded. The outrageous pay packages caught the attention of everybody who was interested. The need for reform was seriously felt. Companies and boards are making a move (though very slowly) to a pay-for-performance regime. Whenever CEO (and other executive) compensation is looked into by the board, it should be done in such a way that it provides executives enough incentives to generate value for shareholders. Bebchuk and Fried (2004) suggest a framework for investors to pursue while according their assent to compensation plans.

Reduce windfalls in equity-based plans   Investors should encourage equity-based plans that filter out at least some of the gains in the stock price that are due to general market or industry movements. With such filtering, same amount of incentives can be provided at a lower cost or more incentives can be provided at the same cost. Investors must refrain from rewarding the executives with restricted stock grants, as they might provide even higher windfall than options, which again is detrimental to the interests of the shareholders (remember Buffet is of the opinion that stock grants are better, which clearly indicates that opinions are divided).

Improving the link between bonus plans and performance   Investors should closely scrutinize and monitor whether the company's bonus plans are designed to actually reward good performance or only for name's sake. Bebchuk and Fried advise that investors should refrain from according their assent for the executive's accomplishments such as acquiring other companies or taking lead in merging the company with another as such actions do not warrant any special incentives.

Limiting and regulating the unwinding of equity incentives   Many a time the executives enjoy the freedom of unwinding the equity-based incentives included in their compensation plans. The vesting and unwinding of options should be seen as two separate issues. Executives should also be prohibited from engaging in any hedging or derivative transactions to reduce their exposure to the fluctuations that can happen to the company's stock price as this could be a way to circumvent the limits of unwinding.

Executives must also be asked to disclose in advance their intention to sell shares. They should be asked to provide information about the intended trade and the numbers to be sold. Such actions can help in reducing the ability of managers to profit from short-term gains.

Avoid soft landing in case of failure   Investors should be concerned about the practices and arrangements whereby failing managers get rewarded. When the company rewards failing managers, the board is in effect diluting the incentives that enhance shareholder value. On the contrary, the board is encouraging the destruction of shareholder value. Investors should be wary of generous severance payments and also about gratuitous payments beyond the contract.

Scrutinize the magnitude of non-performance pay   The magnitude of non-performance pay that is doled out to executives shall be scrutinized. A number of companies pay generous retiral benefits by using a multiple in counting the number of years of service for the reward of retiral benefits (Dimma 2006). When that is done, the company is actually rewarding managers for non-performance. Investors must take care to ensure that the total compensation is more sensitive to performance.

Executive Compensation and Market Forces

There have also been arguments as to why there is so much concern over the board's role or shareholders' interests as markets for managers, corporate control, capital, etc., will take their actions to align the interests of managers and shareholders. But Bebchuk and Fried (2004) feel that the assumption that any reduction in shareholder value decreases the value of shares and options granted as part of the CEO compensation is wrong because 'the direct benefits that managers reap from increasing their pay, however, might well be larger than any resulting reduction in the value of their shares.' Bebchuk and Fried refer to various studies conducted to prove this. According to these studies, the shares and options owned by the average CEO increase the CEO's personal wealth by approximately one per cent of any increase in the stock market capitalization of the firm's equity. If an 'average' CEO seeks an extra $10 million in compensation, it results in a reduction of firm value by $100 million (because of the poor incentive generated by the arrangement). Thus, the CEO gets an extra $10 million while reducing the value of the CEO's existing shares and options by $1 million, still leaving a net gain of $9 million.

The market for corporate control again has been proved futile in controlling the executive pay. Most of the time, the executives are able to block hostile bids with the help of directors and/or investors. If at all a takeover bid becomes successful, payouts such as golden or platinum parachutes usually get triggered, thereby weakening the takeover (corporate control) as a disciplinary force. The other market that can be expected to discipline the CEO/executive pay is the market for additional capital. Bebchuk and Fried (2004) state that the option of external equity financing is only a distant third behind retained earnings and debt. Even otherwise, Bebchuk and Fried feel that 'excessive executive compensation does not make equity unavailable, it only raises the cost of equity financing: inefficient compensation arrangements reduce firm value and thus cause investors to pay less for the firm's shares in a secondary offering than they would otherwise.'

Decision-making on CEO Compensation

Charan (2009) is of the opinion that 'mechanical formulas and quantitative absolutes simply do not work, because by generalizing across businesses and industries at a fixed moment in time, they freeze management's incentives. A "set and forget" approach to compensation ignores the fact that conditions will change.' Hence he advocates that the board scrap the static absolutes and use the board's collective judgements during the course of the year about the accomplishments of the CEO and his team. According to him, this job needs to be handled by the board and not left to any compensation consultant. While financial objectives for the short-term and long-term are necessary factors in incentive compensation fixation, they alone are not sufficient. Non-financial aspects like efforts and successes at building brands, an innovation mindset, efforts at the development of future leadership repository, efforts and outcomes of developing an organizational culture that encourages the sustenance of the above-mentioned factors must be kept in mind. A balanced scorecard (BSC) approach may be better suited to evaluate performance.

Charan (2009) suggests a compensation framework that translates the board's philosophy of quantitative as well as qualitative factors.

Management performance relative to direct competition   Compensation shall not be on the basis of the performance of the executives and the company as standalone. It shall be relative to direct competition. Charan suggests that the board ask questions like: Did management achieve better margins and/or better revenue growth through its initiatives like marketing or product launches compared with direct competitors? Did it continue to increase the gap between itself and the competition in productivity as in the case of companies like Toyota? It is important that the board uses judgement in a given year or even in a quarter to be in line with the environment.

Management performance in the context of uncontrollable macro factors   The board should include a methodology for taking factors beyond the control of the CEO or the company in the assessment of performance against targets. The board should again make a judgement on management performance relative to the competition in the context of such factors as politics, acts of god (hurricanes, tsunamis, earthquakes, etc.), terrorism, irrational behaviour of capital markets, or a sudden shift in the economy itself (from a boom almost till 2007 to almost a recession in 2008 from which the world is yet to recover) affecting every aspect of business.

Point target versus a range   Rather than fixing a point target, performance targets may be fixed in a range in collaboration with the management based on shared assumptions about future economic and market factors. Some of these factors might be complex and uncontrollable in the short-term; the board should have a range of targets to be evaluated based on these ever-volatile factors.

Compensation Issue Is Back in Limelight

The compensation issue is back in limelight because of the recent global economic meltdown. As Charan (2009) says, 'When it comes to CEO compensation, the game has changed permanently. The ground rules are being completely re-written: the validity of the stock prices has driven some option-based incentive pay to zero, competitive shifts are re-mapping the global economy, and the idea of rigidly comparing performance against traditional competitors is null and void when a significant number of your peers have disappeared or are on the verge of going out of business.'

Table 5.5 gives a discussion on how much shall a director be paid.

TABLE 5.5   Compensation paid to the directors of Infosys in the year 2008–09 (all figures in Rs crores)

Name of the director	Basic salary	Fixed perquisites/ allowances	Salary retiral benefits	Total fixed salary	Bonus/ incentives	Commission	Total
Founder and non-executive director							
N.R. Narayana Murthy	–	–	–	–	–	0.63	0.63
Founders and whole-time directors							
Nandan M. Nilakeni	0.30	0.10	0.07	0.47	0.44	–	0.91
S. Gopalakrishnan	0.30	0.11	0.07	0.48	0.44	–	0.92
S.D. Shibulal	0.28	0.09	0.07	0.44	0.43	–	0.87
K. Dinesh	0.30	0.10	0.07	0.47	0.44	–	0.91
Whole-time directors							
T.V. Mohandas Pai	0.36	0.14	0.09	0.59	2.00	–	2.59
Srinath Batni	0.35	0.12	0.09	0.56	1.31	–	1.87
Independent directors							
Deepak M.Satwalekar	–	–	–	–	–	0.68	0.68
Prof. Marti G. Subrahmanyam	–	–	–	–	–	0.71	0.71
Dr Omkar Goswami	–	–	–	–	–	0.58	0.58
Rama Bijapurkar	–	–	–	–	–	0.56	0.56
Claude Smajda	–	–	–	–	–	0.67	0.67
Sridar A. Iyengar	–	–	–	–	–	0.70	0.70
David L. Boyles	–	–	–	–	–	0.69	0.69
Prof. Jeffrey S. Lehman	–	–	–	–	–	0.63	0.63

Notes: None of the above directors are eligible for any severance pay.
None of the above directors hold any options as on 31 March 2009

On the director compensation policy of Infosys, Kumar (2008) opined: 'Infosys has always been able to attract talented experts from various fields as IDs with its well-intentioned policies of corporate governance and compensation practices which beat industry averages by a large margin. And in future, with all companies scouting around for talent, which is very much in short supply, to adorn their boards as independent directors, a company would have to reward them better than its peers to enthuse them to come on board. Infosys's policy of paying its independent directors high must once again be hailed as forward-looking and it has been one company trying to improve the very stature of independent directors on corporate boards in India by attributing lot of importance to the selection, compensation, and their review.' But according to him, 'Any independent director along with other NEDs will have to only attend the board meetings and the committee meetings. Estimates by experts like Jay W. Lorsch and Colin B. Carter (in their book *Back to the Drawing Board*, published 2004 by HBS Press) puts the time to be devoted by any NED for a company from about 80 hours (for a stable and satisfactory company situation and industry complexity and where the board plays a watchdog role) to 320 hours (for a challenging company situation and industry complexity where the board plays a pilot role). Even if we assume that at Infosys the board's role may be that of pilot, it may not be anything beyond 320 hours. And one can be sure that none of the IDs on the board of Infosys will be able to devote anything beyond this considering their full-time engagements, directorships on other companies, etc. So, what is the incentive for Mr Nilekani, Mr Gopalakrishnan and other WTDs to toil 24×7×52 for the company?'

COMPENSATION OF OTHER DIRECTORS

While the CEO and other executive compensation catches all the attention and hence is a very critical issue for all boards, the compensation level of other directors who are non-executive members on the board is also one that requires close attention of the board. Even though these directors are part-time, they have a huge responsibility on their shoulders and their jobs entail a lot of risks in the post-Enron and post-Satyam scenario. Since the risk factor has been discouraging potential candidates from accepting seats on boards, boards have been forced to rethink the compensation for directors. While the US companies have been paying not-so-small compensation, the Indian scenario was pathetically different till recently. Despite the fact that directors are accountable to shareholders and will be liable to being sued for lack of diligence in their duties, pays of directors other than those in the executive capacity used to be abysmally low. Companies in the earlier era, before Clause 49 came into being, used to pay only sitting fees in the range of Rs 250 to Rs 500 per meeting. Of course, people accepted directors' positions generally for the status and prestige associated with the position rather than for the financial benefits that were available. Also, their role in practice was rather limited to attending board meetings and according assent to decisions made by the management even though statutorily the board as a whole was accountable for everything under the statute. Call it ignorance about the roles and the liabilities that they could be subjected to in the event of something going wrong or the practice where board was considered just a compliance requirement, the boards and the individual directors rarely assumed the real roles they were expected to play. Consequently, the directors were not only not demanding but also subservient.

But, the post-Enron, post-WorldCom scenario changed everything. Non-executive and independent directors were brought into sharp focus and their roles became subjects of hot discussion and debate. In India, however, despite the introduction of Clause 49 guidelines in the company's listing agreements with stock exchanges and the high integration of Indian economy and the corporate to the global context and especially the western world, the need was not felt very seriously as there was no major corporate failure that could be ascribed to governance failure.

But the Satyam episode has changed all that. Boards, independent directors, their roles, the conflicts of interest, the involvement of the independent directors, etc., have been brought under the lens. Of course, post-Clause 49 stipulations mandating that the boards have a minimum percentage of independent directors depending on whether the chairman is executive or non-executive had propelled the demand for independent directors and companies have been scouting around for talents to their boardrooms. This has definitely resulted in pushing up the prices for the directors. Corporate laws were also relaxed and companies have availed such relaxations to compensate the NEDs reasonably well. Today directors can be paid as sitting fees up to Rs 20,000 per sitting for attending board meetings. Additionally, they can be compensated for attending committee meetings if they happen to be members of the committees with the chairman of the committee getting paid even more than committee members, or as lead independent director, etc. These directors may also get paid by way of commission subject to a maximum of one per cent of the net profits to be distributed among the NEDs. The percentage of commission (subject to the statutory limits) will be fixed by the board of directors and will need approval of shareholders. While a number of companies do not pay commission to NEDs even today, more and more companies have been joining the bandwagon. For example, while Infosys has been paying commission to the NEDs from very early on, Reliance Industries started only from the year 2005–06. Till then the NEDs of RIL were paid only sitting fees. HDFC still does not pay commission to NEDs and sitting fees at HDFC is only Rs 10,000 per meeting as against the limit of Rs 20,000. Infosys shows the total amount paid as commission with maximum amounts allocated for attendance and positions on the board.

Components of Non-Executive Director Pay

Different companies follow different methods of computing and compensating their NEDs. But the most common components are:

Sitting fees for attending board meetings   This is paid at a fixed amount subject to a maximum (Rs 20,000 in India) for meetings attended. For example, Infosys pays an attendance fee of $5000 per annum while RIL pays Rs 20,000 per board meeting. HDFC pays only Rs 10,000 per meeting.

Sitting fees for committee meetings   Committees are required to meet differently than the board. Many companies today make separate payment for attending committee meetings. Infosys pays Rs 0.5 million or $10,000 per annum for attending audit committee meetings whereas members of other committees are paid only Rs 0.1 million or $2,500 per annum. RIL pays Rs 20,000 per committee meeting. HDFC pays Rs 10,000 per committee meeting.

Chairing the board   Some companies pay extra to the NED who handles the role of the chairman. At Infosys, the non-executive chairperson gets a fee of Rs 1.3 million or $25,000 per annum. This is not a common practice and Infosys can be considered an exception.

Chairing the committee meetings   Chairmen of committees, considering their higher responsibilities, are sometimes paid a higher compensation than a committee member. For example, Infosys pays different compensations to different committee chairs. Audit committee chair at Infosys is paid Rs one million or $20,000 per annum whereas chairpersons of other committees get paid only Rs 0.3 million or $5000 per annum. RIL does not pay anything extra for chairing the committees.

Being the lead independent director   Many companies again do not pay specifically for the position whereas at Infosys, the lead independent director gets an extra Rs 0.8 million or $15,000 per annum. RIL does not pay anything extra to the lead independent director.

Commission   This is the major component in the compensation of the NEDs/independent directors. Some companies like Infosys treat this as a fixed component while it also calls the total payment by the same name. In some companies as in the case of Infosys, the commission is fixed and not variable according to attendance, while in some companies like Bajaj Auto, the payment is variable and related to attendance of board and/or committee meetings. At Infosys, the fixed part of the commission (presumably not related to attendance) is Rs 3.8 million or $75,000 per annum. At RIL, the commission was fixed at Rs 2.1 million during 2007–08. At times, it may even be difficult to ascertain how the commission payments to individual directors have been arrived at as such details are usually missing in the annual reports.

Stock option   NEDs are also paid by way of stock options in some companies. Infosys used to reward NEDs with stock options till sometime back and has since discontinued as there was not enough clarity regarding the expensing of options as also the tax treatment of them. Very few companies resort to this. Many big companies like RIL do not use options to compensate the NEDs. The options have usually been used by the new generation companies, especially in the high technology areas.

Others   The NEDs have also been reimbursed actual expenses incurred in connection with attending the board/committee or annual general meetings. Infosys pays its overseas directors an additional $5,000 per meeting considering that they have to spend two additional days in travel for attending board meetings in India.

Challenges and Concerns about Director Compensation

A suitable level—The 'how much' of director pay

The major challenge is to arrive at a suitable level. Very low levels will not help a company and its board to attract talents. In today's corporate scenario, the demand for good independent directors is high consequent to the changes in the regulatory regime. The demand in India is said to be in the vicinity of about 18,000 numbers according to IOD, India,[7] which has helped to raise the prices for good directors. But, while it is true that any pay has market factors acting on it, among many others, 'board compensation has its own special peculiarities. Even though director pay varies from industry to industry; directors on the same board are all paid the same, regardless of their performance and contribution. And reputation means nothing when it comes to the dollars', say Carter and Lorsch (2004). The differences in compensation between two directors on a specific board will be either due to additional responsibilities in the form of committee memberships/chairmanships or due to the number of meetings (board/committee) attended. Directors of bigger companies usually get paid more as these have better paying capacities. Directors of IT or Pharma companies in India are paid much higher than directors in the regular manufacturing sector (the outside NEDs of Infosys or Dr Reddy's Laboratories get paid more than those of RIL, Grasim, or Hero Honda). The actual role the board has to play (whether a watchdog or a pilot role) is usually ignored while deciding on the compensation package. According to Carter and Lorsch, all boards seem to feel that they should be in the upper half of the director pay surveys conducted by compensation consultants. 'Differences in the amounts of time the directors of different companies must devote to board business are ignored. Certainly, the performance of the board is not taken into account, and the legal and reputation risks a director assumes are rarely considered either. It all depends on the survey' (Carter and Lorsch). James Kristie, Editor and Associate Publisher of *Directors and Boards*, opines that 'directors are one of the great bargains. They are underpaid for the work they do and the responsibility they assume' (Shultz 2001). Getting the right balance has been difficult because companies, boards, and the so-called market for board talents tended to ignore the great responsibility and risks boards take. Shultz says 'The value of a single idea, of strategic succession planning, of risk avoidance, the value of one mistake prevented—is invaluable. These are the stories that rarely get told. Or measured.'

But the typical issue remains one of balance. Too small will not enthuse talents to come on board and too big will tempt them to act like insiders. Too big a pay for outsiders will also act as a disincentive for insiders. Carter and Lorsch (2004) say that 'a sensible discussion about directors' pay can only take place after the board has discussed its role. The level of compensation should reflect the time that directors have to commit to their board duties. It might also reflect the extent to which the board is engaged in value adding activities such as enhancing business strategy and delivering valued networks to the firm, as opposed to concentrating on a watchdog role. It is harder to justify premium levels of compensation if the board contributes little to the growth of the business or if the directors carry out a very limited role.' Thus, compensation has to be in line with the extent of involvement that a director and the board must have in the affairs of governing the company.

The suitable components of compensation—The 'how should it be paid'

In the earlier days of director compensation, most companies used to pay only in cash. But the thinking changed over a period of time. It was felt that directors must also be paid in the form of

---

[7] www.iodonline.com

stocks so that their interests get well aligned with shareholders. But there are people who strongly oppose this view. They feel that stock market behavior and firm performance may not necessarily have a one-to-one correlation. If we look into history, there have been many periods during which markets were not necessarily performing well even though the firms were reporting sterling performances. And, even according to modern financial theory, the current prices of stocks do not reflect the current performance of the company. It has more to do with the future performance as the current stock price is nothing but the present value of the future streams of returns which the shareholder will enjoy in the future. Can we predict the future streams of returns with certainty? Certainly not. But that is the risk the investors have to take while investing in a company's stock. And the returns could be phenomenal too! But should directors be subjected to such vagaries of the market? Are the employees' pay packets related to stock prices? Why should directors and senior executives be singled out and be subjected to the vagaries of the market? A director may serve a company for an initial term of say three Years and thereafter gets it renewed every year, which itself suggests that the future element is rather absent in his appointment. Then why should he take a risky job at a company's board if he is rather uncertain about the compensation he is entitled to. It would be better to have fixed compensation even if it is slightly on the lower side. Also, this can eliminate a large amount of 'outrage costs' by way of bad reputation and publicity. During a period when markets perform extremely well, directors may sometimes get windfall gains, which could attract a lot of attention. Also as Carter and Lorsch (2004) say, 'If all or a large part of directors' remuneration is at risk, and in equity, only wealthy people are likely to be able to serve on boards. Others may not be able to afford the initial investment or to forgo cash income. If one seeks diversity of experience on boards, this could be a problem.' One of the allegations against the use of options for rewarding managers is that this usually tends them to drive for short-term results (rather than the long-term intended or embedded in the concept). How can boards escape such allegations when they are also paid by the same method?

Of course, there is another line of argument. According to Shultz (2001), directors should hold shares (received via options or grants) as 'directors should believe in the company. If she does not think the company is worth investing in, how can she represent those who do?' But, then there is no evidence that those directors who held shares in the company performed better than those directors who did not own even a single stock of the company. It may also affect the issue of independence in the case of independent directors.

A best-practice in director compensation could be to compensate them by way of say sitting fees (the payment of which then depends on attendance and will motivate the director to attend board/committee meetings), remuneration for additional responsibilities (like chairing the committee, lead independent director, etc.), and a fixed component which will become payable only if the director attends a certain minimum percentage of board as well as committee meetings. Fixed payment without attending board meetings will invite flak from investors. Mr Kumar Mangalam Birla who did not attend any board meeting, committee meeting, or AGM during his three year stint at Maruti Udyog (Maruti Suzuki India, now) as an independent director was reported to have earned Rs 100,000 in each of the year, in the annual reports of Maruti. This is outrageous and is likely to invite investor flak. 'The remuneration must be in line with the efforts put in by them. Assuming that the average CEO puts in at least 14 hours a day, the independent director shall be compensated for the approximate number of hours he is expected to be involved for the preparation and attendance in the board/committee meetings at the same hourly rate of the chief executive' (Kumar 2005). And of course, one may not subscribe to Infosys's practice of paying very high to the NEDs (almost 85 per cent of the executive directors' remuneration in the year 2003–04 and about 60 per cent in 2007–08 and nearly 80 per cent in 2008–09), in which case it could be said that the non-executive directors may develop vested interests, but decent compensation to restrict their number of directorships so as to devote attention and get involved wherever they have memberships need to be worked out.

ROLE OF COMPENSATION COMMITTEE

In this era when CEO and director compensation gather a lot of public and media attention and even make headlines (ostensibly for the wrong reasons), the role of the compensation committee assumes enormous importance. While it helps in a big way, the responsibility of evolving the terms of reference for the committee to act lies, however, with the board. While compensation committees are mandatory in the US, under current regulations they are not mandatory in India under Clause 49. However, a number of forward looking companies (or might be because its presence makes them forward looking and creates a confidence among investors and public that at least a committee monitors the performance of the CEO and other directors) have embarked on constituting them. Charan (2009) says that 'compensation committees will have to take lead. Their members need to think through how the targets will be determined in the context of the global financial crisis and beyond, what the ideal balance of the short-term and long-term targets will be, and what forms of compensation are best to use.' Immediately after the Enron debacle, audit committees were the cynosure of all attention. But, of late there has been a gradual shift of attention to other committees, especially the compensation and nomination committees. As Ken Hugessen says: 'Much of the initial focus was on accounting and audit, but attention is now turning to the governance of executive compensation' (Dimma 2006). Since the power enjoyed by the CEO as head of management which has monopoly over information and in the use of firm's resources is very high and the board is at the mercy of management and/or CEO with regard to the availability of information. The ability of the board and the compensation committee to evaluate the performance of the CEO and other executives is rather limited. This has to be overcome by implementing an information architecture as suggested by Charan (refer to Chapter 6). As Hugessen says, 'Central to more balanced pay decisions is enhancement of the role and performance of the compensation committee and the board, including redressing the imbalance of information and resources between management and the directors' (Dimma). Hugessen suggests the following measures in order to enable compensation committees and boards to take balanced decisions in such conflicting environments (Dimma):

Strengthening the independence of both the compensation committee members and the processes they follow   A lot of attention on the structural independence of the committee has actually been given. But structural independence alone is not enough. What is required is an independent mindset and also processes that are independent. The committee has to collect and analyse data independently from management and if necessary 'compare and reconcile the data provided by management' (Dimma 2006).

Steps in improving committee's performance
- Review the committee charter once a year by the board. Committee can also ask for inputs from management. In case the committee has been in touch with major shareholders, their feedback also must be considered. If the committee has not drawn up a charter for itself, it must be done urgently. Many companies in India do not report the existence of any charter, except for a handful. Infosys has a charter describing the purpose, membership, organization and responsibility, and authority of the committee. It's major rivals in the IT sector namely, TCS and Wipro while having compensation committees, do not mention about a charter in their report to the shareholders.
- Set the year's specific meeting schedule and agendas in consultation with board, lead director and management.
- Any significant change in the executive compensation policy in view of the changes implemented by competitors or generally in the industry should be considered separately and analysis, diligence, and discussion of award shall not be done in the same meeting. This is to give significant time for members to reflect on the proposals.

Building the competence of the compensation committee and its members   All members of the committee shall be prepared to acquire knowledge and learn continuously about the trends in executive compensation. Since executive compensation has been accused of a lot of camouflage, members shall see that they understand the components well and are able to explain the intricacies of the various components to the shareholders. The chair should make the members take an annual self-assessment of their competence in the subject and their ability to independently discharge the responsibility assigned to them by the committee charter. The chair should then identify the development needs if any, in the committee members. The development needs then shall be addressed by roping in specialists in the subject.

Ensuring that the committee completes adequate amounts of research and analysis independent of management   The committee shall continuously be monitoring and collecting information about the changes and trends in the compensation policies due to changing conditions in the market for talent. They must also review and analyse not only pay but also performance on an on-going basis. They should then establish a pay-for-performance philosophy and policy and also the disclosure norms. The committee must disclose almost everything regarding the compensation packages and also the performance criteria arrived at to the shareholders. The committee must also interact with the shareholders to apprise them of the details and also to obtain their feedback on the compensation scheme. In case the committee needs support from a compensation consultant, they should engage the consultant with direct control over them.

Enhancing disclosure to and communication with shareholders   There have always been allegations that boards are more biased to management priorities than the priorities of shareholders. Shareholders always are of the view that boards are not responsive to their concerns and needs. The committee can take proactive steps to interact and solicit inputs from at least major shareholders, especially the institutional shareholders. In the US, governance-conscious institutions like CalPERS and TIAA-CREF regularly interact with the board and other committees to raise their concerns.

BOARD DEVELOPMENT—THE WAY AHEAD

Boards and directors have been under the lens for a variety of reasons. It could be the failure to identify and develop successors for the positions of CEO and other members and then roping in somebody from outside at outrageous pay levels; it could be the poor performance of the boards as a whole leading to loss of company's position in the market; it could be the atrocious compensation packages that the company doles out when the company itself shows decline in performance or fares poorly on a peer comparison; or it could even be due to not being able to attract and retain talent due to compensation policies that are not necessarily competitive. But one thing is certain: companies will be watched more closely by shareholders, the media, and the public. With shareholder activism catching up coupled with imminent entry of governance-conscious institutions into the country, corporate governance scenario in India is likely to undergo drastic changes and Indian companies will be required to spruce their practices up.

So, the board has to start with the right recruitment of both the CEO and other directors, based not only on their expertise and experience but also on how each of them will fit into the dynamics that the board wants to create. Once set up, the board has a responsibility to create and develop various mandatory as well as non-mandatory committees to facilitate better governance. Right people, passionate about their roles and jobs, shall be chosen. The directors and boards shall be appraised to identify the development needs at the individual level and the board level. Having identified the developmental needs, initiatives must be taken for providing necessary inputs for improving their performances. Finally, the board has to set clear terms for the compensation committee to establish policies and a philosophy for CEO and director compensation. With the ever-changing availability of the compensation components, the committee and the board must keep themselves abreast with the compensation-related trends that are current. The board should engage itself in continuous learning about changes that are happening in the environment and necessarily incorporate the demands for change in its agenda. Shareholders and other stakeholders have already been watching these developments with keen interest and are likely to be even more watchful in the future. Boards also have to rise to their expectations.

SUMMARY

Today the board is considered to be a competitive weapon for a company. For this the board must have competence. Board competence depends on the competencies of the individual directors and how they get along together to become a formidable force. The board should be able to attract the best talent suitable for the job, and best governance means best people. The kind of rigour in the form of time, energy, and effort usually observed to get the right people down the line is not usually seen in the recruitment of directors. Even though the requirement for independent directors is large (rough estimates put it in the range of 18,000 to 50,000), the Satyam fallout and the allegation that the IDs did not play their roles right, and the possible liabilities of those independent directors in the event they are held responsible, is forcing potential candidates to think twice before they accept an invitation to become directors.

While recruiting new directors, the board has to keep in mind the right mix appropriate not only for the present but also for the future. Since a director's job today involves lot of time commitment, the board has to widen the talent pool beyond the normal sources like existing CEOs or directors who sit on other companies. The board should then decide on the competencies and qualities that directors should possess. Having recruited the directors, they should be developed in view of the changes in the environment. And experts concur that the chairman has to take the responsibility of development of other directors in consultation with the CEO. Directors should also be evaluated for their performance. The board should also have clear succession planning policies. This is very essential as a CEO may have to be replaced suddenly when the company faces a crisis.

The executive compensation has been attracting lot of attention in the recent past. Most of these problems arise because of the lethargic or lacklustre performance of the board in this area. The board should have a clear idea as to what constitutes good performance. Goals of performance should not be strictly formulaic or quantitative. It should reflect what the CEO has to do in terms of management development, customer satisfaction, changing the organization's culture, or building competence for the future. As far as possible, windfalls in the equity-based compensation plans shall be avoided. The compensation of non-executive directors has also been on the increase as there has been heavy demand for good independent directors.

The compensation committee can play a major role in this era of attacks on executive compensation. While the committee can be of great help, the responsibility of evolving the terms of reference for the committee to act lies with the board. While compensation committees are mandatory in the US, under current regulations they are not mandatory in India under Clause 49. The board and director development, appraisal, and compensation policies are very important in making the boards an effective competitive weapon.

KEY TERMS

Arm's-length bargaining   Bargaining by board with executives whereby executives as well as the shareholders who represent the board get the best deal

Black-Scholes formula   An option pricing formula

Board dynamics   The way the board interacts and arrives at important decisions

Broadening the search   To go beyond the normally narrow focus areas for potential director material

Coaching and mentoring   Experienced person helping others to exploit potential and achieve goals

Commission   Component of compensation paid to executives for acting as agent for shareholders

Compensation framework   Broad outline about how to arrive at the total compensation

Compensation philosophy   Wisdom-generated decision on compensation policy that tries to balance various aspects

Corporate myopia   Short-sightedness about the talent needs

Cross fertilize   Providing diverse opinions that lead to better decisions

Director development   Imparting necessary education and skills to directors to perform duties better

Financials   Facts and figures which describe the financial position of the company

Fringe benefits   Additional benefits which usually accompany an employment contract for a position

Golden goodbye   Very high compensation offered when executives exit

Golden handcuff   Compensation that is so attractive that the CEO finds it difficult to exit

Golden hello   Bonus offered to the potential CEO recruits to join a firm

Golden parachute   Enables the company executive to safely land with high compensation in case of an exit from the company

Gratuitous payments   Payments offered as a gratitude for having served the company (not necessarily performance-related)

Harmony   State of peaceful existence and agreement

Head hunter   Individuals/firms searching for the right person to fit into a job

Human capital   Specific inventory of expertise and skills that a person has developed

Metamorphose   Transform from one kind to another

Nomination committee   Committee of the board which has the responsibility of identifying new directors and replacement for retiring directors

Outrage costs   Costs that give rise to an outrage (shareholder and other stakeholder attention)

Pay-for-performance   Compensation plan aligned with pre-determined performance yardsticks

Platinum parachute   Compensation even better than the golden parachute

Remuneration committee   Committee of the board that looks into CEO and other executive compensation

Severance pay   Compensation that is doled out when luring executives from other companies where he has not become eligible for long-term incentives or that is given to those who have been forced out

Soft landing   Ensure that the executive lands safely even in the face of failure

Stock grants   Grant of stocks themselves than a right to purchase stocks

Stock options   Rewards in the form of a right to buy the stock of the company at a pre-determined price

Succession   Process of appointing successors to take over organizational positions

Vagaries   Unpredictable and uncontrollable variations

CONCEPT REVIEW QUESTIONS

1. Why is it felt that director and board development is very important in aiming for a better governed corporation?
2. What are the essential qualities that should be kept in mind when the company needs to nominate a director?
3. What are the different steps towards better recruiting of directors?
4. How will a company assess the development needs of individual directors and the board as a whole?
5. Explain the tools that are available for evaluation of individual directors and the board itself.

6. How should a company plan senior executive succession well?
7. What is a compensation philosophy? Explain.
8. What are the major concerns about CEO compensation?
9. Stock-related compensation plans are well-suited to align the interests of the executives with those of the shareholders. Do you agree? Substantiate with arguments.
10. What all needs to be done to set the executive compensation right and get the issue away from public attention and flak?

CRITICAL THINKING QUESTIONS

Should there be external regulations on executive compensation or should it be left for self-regulation by the boards and shareholders? Support your answer with arguments in favour of your position.

PROJECT WORK

Study the changes in the compensation for the NEDs since the introduction of Clause 49 guidelines.

REFERENCES

Ashby, Meredith D. and Stephen A. Miles (2002), *Leaders Talk Leadership*, Oxford University Press, New York.

Bebchuk, Lucian and Jessee Fried (2004), *Pay without Performance: The Unfulfilled Promise of Executive Compensation*, HBS Press, Boston.

Bloomberg.com, 3 January 2007.

Carter, Colin B. and Jay W. Lorsch (2004), *Back to the Drawing Board*, HBS Press, Boston.

Charan, Ram (1998), *Boards at Work*, Jossey-Bass, San Francisco.

Charan, Ram (2005), *Boards that Deliver*, Jossey-Bass, San Francisco.

Charan, Ram (2009), *Owning Up*, Jossey-Bass, San Francisco.

Coley Jr., L. John, Jaqueline L. Doyle, George W. Logan, and Wallace Stettinius (2003), *Corporate Governance*, Tata McGraw Hill, Delhi.

Dimma, William A. (2006), *Tougher Boards for Tougher Times: Corporate Governance in the Post-Enron Era*, Wiley-India, New Delhi.

Gillan, Stewart L., 'Has pay for performance gone awry? Views from a corporate governance forum', in *Corporate Governance at the Crossroads*, Chew Jr, H. Donald and Stewart L. Gillan (eds) (2005), Tata-McGraw Hill, Delhi.

Hamel, Gary and C.K. Prahalad (1994), *Competing for the Future*, HBS Press, Boston.

Harper, John (2005), *Chairing the Board*, Kogan Page, London.

Jensen, Michael C. and Kevin J. Murphy, 'CEO incentives—It's not how much you pay, but how', in *Corporate Governance at the Crossroads*, Chew Jr, H. Donald and Stewart L. Gillan (eds) (2005), Tata-McGraw Hill, Delhi.

Kumar T.N., Satheesh (2005), 'Indian Family Managed Companies: The Corporate Governance Conundrum', Paper presented at International Conference on Business and Finance, at IBS Hyderabad on 22 and 23 December 2005.

Kumar T.N., Satheesh, 'The Compensation Conundrum', *Economic Times*, 18 February 2008.

Phan, Philip H. (2000), *Taking Back the Boardroom*, McGraw-Hill, Singapore.

Prasuna, D.G., 'Out of sync?', *Chartered Financial Analyst*, November 2002.

Ratna, C.V., 'Frankenstein phenomenon!', *Chartered Financial Analyst*, July 2003.

Shultz, Susan F. (2001), *The Board Book*, East-West Books, Chennai.

Smith, Roy C. and Ingo Walter (2006), *Governing the Modern Corporation*, Oxford University Press, New York.

Tricker, Bob (2004), *Essential Director*, The Economist/Profile Books, London.

Ward, Ralph, D. (1997), *21st Century Corporate Board*, John Wiley & Sons, New York.

Other resources

Annual Report of Infosys Technologies Ltd for the year 2007–08.

Annual Report of Maruti Udyog Ltd (presently Maruti Suzuki India Ltd) for the years 2003–04 to 2006–07.

Annual Report of Reliance Industries Ltd for the year 2007–08.

Annual Report of Tata Consultancy Services Ltd for the year 2008–09.

The Directors and Boards Survey: CEO and Executive Compensation 2009, Directors and Boards, Spring 2009. www.directorsandboards.com/DBFarientSurveyExecutiveCompensation.pdf

Closing Case

Pay for Performance or Pay without Performance?

GE Reports Highest Revenues, the Third Highest Earnings in History. But CEO Jeff Immelt Declines the Entire $11.7 million Earned under his Long-term Performance Award.

The economic meltdown that gripped the US in the middle of 2007 starting with the sub-prime crisis took its toll by bringing the once-highly regarded Lehman Brothers down and necessitating other Wall Street giants like Goldman Sachs and Merrill Lynch to be bailed out. The slowdown that ensued led to a number of bankruptcy filings including once-highly respected giants like GM, Chrysler, and AIG. The US government led by the newly elected President Barrack Obama stepped in immediately to initiate the rescue operations, by pumping hundreds of billions of dollars. Even the highly respected GE needed to turn to investors like Warren Buffet for fund assistance to stay afloat. The leadership of a number of companies came in the line of criticism and some were even on the firing line for their spending spree, improper risk management, and even for their greed for more power and money. While the government led rescue operations have been showing encouraging results, the US economy is yet to recover from the meltdown impact.

Compensation for CEO in a tough year at GE

GE is one of the most respected companies in the US. It has always been known for its innovative approaches to management practices and leadership and also respected for its governance practices. It had exemplary leaders like Reginald Jones and Jack Welch in its recent history with Jeff Immelt getting the mandate to lead the company from 2001. The difference between GE and many Indian companies is that GE does not have any family or dominant promoter shareholder controlling it. It is considered to be a typical example of a modern corporation where the shareholding is widely distributed with no dominant shareholder with controlling interests.

A few performance parameters of GE in the year 2008 compared to that of 2007 are given below:

	2007	2008	Change (per cent)
Consolidated revenues ($ billion)	172	183	6
Net Earnings ($ billion)	22.5	18	−19
EPS ($)	2.2	1.78	−19
Return on Total Capital Employed (ROTC)	18.9	14.8	−22
Stock price ($)			−56
Compensation ($ million)	19.59	14.09	−28

GE's Annual Proxy Statement for 2008 states: 'In one of the most difficult operating environments in memory, GE's leadership delivered more than $18 billion in earnings in 2008, and our industrial and financial earnings compared very favourably to the S&P 500.

This was the third best earnings year in GE's history. At the same time, however, our 2008 earnings from continuing operations were down 19 per cent compared to 2007. To align compensation with our financial performance, we reduced the size of our 2008 average bonus awards by 19 per cent from 2007.

Notwithstanding their decisive leadership during this time of external crisis, we adjusted 2008 executive compensation as follows:

- Mr Immelt proposed, and the MDCC agreed, that he would receive no bonus for 2008 and that he would decline the entire $11.7 million earned under his long-term performance award. The MDCC accepted Mr Immelt's proposal as appropriate recognizing that, although the company delivered a strong operational performance in 2008, this performance was not reflected in GE's stock price. The aggregate effect of these actions reduced the amount of cash compensation paid to Mr Immelt 64 per cent versus 2007.
- In light of the performance of our financial services businesses, Messrs. Sherin and Neal received bonuses for 2008 that were 15 per cent and 25 per cent lower than their 2007 bonuses, respectively. In addition, with the agreement of the MDCC, each declined half of the amount earned under his long-term performance award, which, if paid out according to formula, would have entitled each of them to an additional $2.6 million and $2.9 million, respectively. Mr Rice, who led Technology Infrastructure to a solid performance in 2008, received a 10 per cent lower bonus than awarded in 2007'.

In an interview with The *Wall Street Journal* in February 2009, Mr Immelt was reported to have said: 'My compensation is never going to be an embarrassment to GE… It's going to be responsible; it's going to be appropriate; it's going to be transparent; and it's going to reflect the financial performance of the company.'[8, 9]

Compensation in a Tough Year in a Sample of Indian Companies

Having been following a path of liberalizing and reforming the economic policies in pursuit of a globalization policy framed by the post-1991 governments, Indian economy could not be expected to be decoupled from the rest of the world. The economy in India too slowed down, albeit not hitting hard, with sectors like real estate, infrastructure industries suffering the worst. Many prominent and respected companies like Bajaj Auto in two wheelers, Dr Reddy's and Piramal Healthcare in pharma, Reliance Capital in financial services, Indian Hotels Company in hospitality, ITC in cigarettes, paper and food products faced stagnating or declining profits with some having been pushed into the loss-making zone for the financial year ending on 31 March 2009. The share prices of these companies took a severe beating during the year. Most financial ratios showed a downward tendency while the Debt-Equity ratio jumped for many, resulting in increased risk profile of the company. The details of six companies are provided in the table below.

It could be seen that barring ITC, the percentage changes in PBT, PAT, EPS, ROCE and share prices were negative for all of them. The Debt-Equity ratio of all except ITC, Indian Hotels Company, and Bajaj Auto worsened. But, as could be observed, the CEO as well as the total managerial compensation increased for all companies except RCL, where it remained at the same level as of 2007 while financial performance deteriorated.

---

[8] Leading by example: GE CEO Jeffrey Immelt Turns Down 2008 Bonus and Long-term Compensation www.rightattitudes.com/.../jeffrey-immelt-turns-down-bonus/, 28 February 2009.

[9] Those other executives who have been mentioned in the proxy statement are not board members.

Parameter (per cent change)	Company					
	BAL	PHC	DRL	RCL	ITC	IHC
Revenue	−6.6	14.4	39	45	8.4	−6.3
PBT	−15.57	−5.26	−220	−8.07	5.6	−37.6
PAT	−13.14	−5.26	−309	−5.58	4.6	−38.0
EPS	−16.60	−5.04	−234	−5.41	4.6	−48.4
ROCE	−26.00	−21.9	−255	−30.00	−8.5	−58.5
D/E Ratio	0	54.5	25	40	50	−19
Share Price	−34.56	−64.07	−17.3	−71	−10.45	−65.45
Promoter holding +	61.65	49.58	25.14	53.39	32.01	29.59
CEO Compensation	64.7	20	21.8	0	58	18.5
Total Managerial Compensation	48.5	20.6	2.4	0	20.4	53.2

+ This is the current holding of the promoters (as on 31 March 2009)

Legends:

BAL   Bajaj Auto Ltd
PHC   Piramal Healthcare Ltd
DRL   Dr Reddy's Laboratories Ltd
RCL   Reliance Capital Ltd
ITC   ITC Ltd
IHC   Indian Hotels Company Ltd
PBT   Profit Before Tax
PAT   Profit After Tax
EPS   Earning Per Share
ROCE   Return On Capital Employed
D/E   Debt-Equity

Sources: Annual report of GE for the year 2008; Annual reports of Bajaj Auto Ltd, Piramal Healthcare Ltd, Dr Reddy's Laboratories Ltd, Reliance Capital Ltd, ITC Ltd, and Indian Hotels Company Ltd for the years 2007–08 and 2008–09.

Discussion Questions

1. Does compensation policies enable the shareholders to differentiate leadership of the CEO and the board between companies?
2. Critically look at the compensation policies and comment on the possible rationale of each of the companies.

CHAPTER 6

BOARDS AND LEADERSHIP

A vital characteristic seldom cited is courage. No matter how many other requisite skills and values corporate directors possess, if they do not have courage, the board will fall short of making the level of contribution that shareholders expect.

– B. Kenneth West, Chairman, National Association of Corporate Directors, and Senior
Consultant for Corporate Governance, TIAA-CREF
(quoted in *Leaders Talk Leadership* by Meredith A. Ashby and Stephen A. Miles)

LEARNING OBJECTIVES

After studying this chapter, you will be able to
- Define the best practices of boards
- Describe the strategic role of boards
- Explain the surveillance role of boards
- Define learning boards
- Define board empowerment
- Explain the importance of developing a culture of good governance
- Understand governance as a competitive advantage
- Elucidate the relationship between governance and corporate citizenship

Opening Case

De-risking Strategy of Ramalinga Raju

Satyam Computer Services Ltd announced the takeover of Maytas Infra and Maytas Properties in a deal valued at approximately Rs 79 billion. Barely twelve hours later, after investors expressed their displeasure, Mr Ramalinga Raju, the chairman, called it off.

Background
Mr Ramalinga Raju promoted Satyam with his brother Mr Rama Raju in 1987 as a private limited company and converted it has into a public limited company in 1991. The company went public in 1992. Over the years, it built a large clientele and has become the fourth largest IT services provider and exporter, after TCS, Infosys, and Wipro. It also set up operations in most parts of the world with prestigious companies as clients.

16 December 2008

After the stock trading hours, Chairman Mr Raju announced the board's decision to invest up to Rs 79 billion (approximately $1.6 billion) in companies promoted by his family members. The distribution of investments would be Rs 64.35 billion (approx $1.3 billion) in Maytas Properties for a 100 per cent stake and about Rs 14.85 billion (approximately $300 million) in Maytas Infra for a 51 per cent stake. Mr Raju said the acquisition would 'pave the way for accelerated growth in new geographies and market segments, such as transportation, energy, and infrastructure, for the core IT business'. According to him, 'the buyout will de-risk the core business by bootstrapping a new business vertical in infrastructure. This market segment can mitigate the risks attributed to developed markets and traditional verticals that are likely to be impacted by the recessionary economy.'

Maytas Properties was run by one of Mr Raju's sons, Mr Rama Raju, and Maytas Infra was run by the other son, Mr Teja Raju.

Maytas Properties is a scale player in development of urban space infrastructure such as integrated townships, special economic zones, hospitality, retail, and entertainment spaces in tier-one and tier-two cities across India.

The twenty-three-year-old Maytas Infra is engaged in the business of infrastructure construction and asset development, spanning core areas of economic growth such as highways, metro railways, ports, transport management systems, airports, power, oil and gas, irrigation, and water treatment.

Other Data

Holding of Mr Raju and associates in Satyam on 16 December 2008: 8.74 per cent

Public holding:	72.5 per cent
Of which FII holding:	48 per cent
Indian public financial institutions (FIs):	12.9 per cent

Discussion Questions

1. Do you subscribe to the contentions of Mr Raju in support of the acquisitions?
2. Discuss whether the board of Satyam played its role, including the strategic role, in its decision to acquire the two companies promoted by the family members of the chairman.

STAKEHOLDERS DEMAND PERFORMANCE

Gone are the days when the board of directors was a body with the sole purpose of meeting the legal requirements of the corporate form of a business entity. While conformance to regulations is still an essential requirement, shareholders and other stakeholders expect boards to perform in terms of better returns and lesser risk to shareholders; better and innovative products to customers to meet their existing as well as potential needs; compete strongly in the market, adhering to ethical principles and values; adequately share the rewards of better performance with employees; comply with the laws and regulations of government and regulatory bodies who expect them to conform as well as adopt the best and next practices; and take care of the society in which they operate. Hence, the conventional laid-back attitude of promoters of companies that stacked the boards with their close associates to support them on board resolutions and of directors who enrolled for prestige and 'easy money' will not work anymore. Stakeholders expect them to be proactive in a cut-throat competitive scenario, where the market will not spare any wrongdoing. Hence, the onus to act as real leaders of change by bringing in talent, bearing in mind the competitiveness and well-being of the corporate entity, lies with the promoters. The directors thus nominated influence and drive the changes forward, meeting and delivering the value enhancement expected of the company and the board by all the stakeholders, relegating the prestige and money associated with directorships to the back.

Despite all efforts at improving governance by establishing a governance charter, insistence on having independent directors, including diversity on boards, and recruiting the most talented and brilliant people, one fact still remains deep-rooted: that it is the CEO who shapes the culture in the boardroom. This could be because the most developed economy of the world where a great deal of new thinking has been incorporated in the area of corporate governance, namely the US, has not considered leadership other than by a CEO in the boardroom, as they could never imagine that the roles of the chairman and CEO could be separated. According to Carter and Lorsch (2004), 'Most Americans can't imagine how a company can operate with shared leadership.' The position of CEO has always been dominant and will continue to be so, whether in a family-owned or professionally managed enterprise.

Earlier, the main reason may have been that directors owed their positions to the CEO and he was therefore a highly influencing factor. Even today, despite the nomination committees taking over the responsibility of nominating directors from the CEO and the remuneration committee fixing the remunerations of all directors including the CEO, the CEO has an overwhelming influence on the board and its culture as he/she is the head of the management function, which is expected to provide the necessary information inputs to the board. So, the board is by and large dependent on the CEO for the inputs they need to make informed decisions for and on behalf of the company. 'Too many CEOs believe that the boards in their companies exist to serve their needs and not those of their shareholders. They see the board as their personal perk', (Shultz 2001). But board observers and watchers such as Ram Charan cite examples of Citicorp and KeraVision to emphasize that changes are taking place. In Citicorp, director Roger Smith told the then chairman, CEO John S. Reed, that he believed the bank was accepting lower level audits than it should. Reed immediately acted to improve the audit function, which improved considerably. Charan quotes Reed as saying, 'We probably wouldn't have seen it from inside. Smith raised the bar.' Similarly, in 1995, the KeraVision board urged CEO Tom Loarie to take the company public. Loarie did not think the company was ready, but the board believed the market conditions were right. Charan (1998) quotes Loarie as saying, 'We did it and I've never looked back. It was the right decision.' Shultz also see that 'the best CEOs prioritize strategic boards.' She quotes Gary Lutin, consultant to the NYSE Security Analysts and chairman of the Shareholder Forum: 'Long-term adaptation to change is entirely dependent on the board as the CEO tends to be too involved in the operation to have the needed objectivity over the long term' (Shultz 2001).

The board leadership here is discussed not only from a point of view as to who takes lead in the boardroom but also how the board practices leadership as a process in guiding, directing, and controlling the management and the organization as an independent corporate entity in the interest of all stakeholders. The board leadership has also to be looked at from an angle of how the board considers itself as a competitive weapon that will enable the company to be ahead of competition and achieve responsible growth while keeping in mind the betterment and well-being of all stakeholders.

The board as a body must also be led towards achieving its goals and objectives. While many people will agree that the roles of the chairman and the CEO should be separated, with well laid-out reasoning that the chairman has to lead the board and the CEO the management and the company, there has not been any clear evidence to prove that this separation is better. While it makes real sense not to concentrate power in the same person and it is desirable that there be two separate, well-defined roles, there have been many instances of success stories of governance when the two jobs were combined and also failures when the two jobs were separated. For example, in GE the roles of the chairman and CEO are combined in one person and it is often considered to be an example of a high performing, well-governed company. On the other hand, British Telecom had very early separated the two roles but their performance was nothing spectacular or worth mentioning. Carter and Lorsch (2004) quote an unnamed CEO of a US company who said, 'So it is not a panacea to have the separation of the two roles. It all depends on the relationship of the people. It can work either way.'

Medtronic Inc. is another US-based company that is oft-quoted for its governance but has the two jobs combined in one person. In India, Hindustan Lever (now rechristened Hindustan Unilever) is an example of both the jobs combined in one until the recent switch over to a non-executive chairman and a CEO. There are other examples such as ITC, L&T, SBI, ONGC, etc., where the jobs of the chairman and CEO have been combined and these have been highly satisfactory from the governance and performance point of view.

BEST PRACTICES

At the heart of striving for best practices is the empowerment of the board—empowerment that will result in the best governance possible under the existing context. Even the laws and regulations try to achieve that intention—to empower the board so that the most important economic assets created, nurtured, and grown under the corporate form are put to an efficient and effective use in order to create value addition for the concerned stakeholders. It is believed that the best way to achieve empowerment is to ensure that boards are controlled by directors who are independent of company management and that directors' incentives are closely aligned to those of shareholders, according to Carter and Lorsch (2004).

Starting with the Cadbury Committee report, the first-ever organized attempt to provide a code for improving the governance of corporates, every initiative to improve governance was an exercise aimed at codifying and recommending best practices. Subsequently, acts such as SOX in the US adopted many of these best practice recommendations as laws. The commonly observed and recommended best practices include a good independent element on the board, splitting of the chairman and CEO positions, selection of directors by a nomination/governance committee constituted of only independent directors, formation of at least two more committees, namely audit and compensation also constituted of only IDs, that the IDs meet independent of management and a lead director be appointed to chair such meetings, that directors be generalists focused on the company as a whole rather than on any particular expertise, making boards as small as possible, clearly delineating the roles of the board and management, that independent directors be compensated decently while keeping in mind that the compensation is aligned to motivate them to keep their focus on the interests of the shareholders, approving the strategies developed by the CEO and management team, continuously evaluating the performance of the CEO and the management team, evaluation of the board and individual directors at least once a year, etc.

Best Practices Conundrum

Despite the availability and adoption of such best practices, there has been no assurance that corporates will excel on the governance front. The recently unveiled failure at Satyam is a case in point. Satyam had apparently adopted many of the best practices commonly highlighted and that must have been the reason behind the IOD India and the World Council for Corporate Governance (WCCG) deciding to honour the company with the Golden Peacock Award for the Best Governed Company in India in the year 2008, a few months before the whole Satyam issue became public. Best practices on paper (the corporate governance report as part of annual reports of every company that states that they are concerned about substance rather than form) or structure will not necessarily ensure that a company becomes well-governed. Good governance requires real implementation or practice of the so-called best practices. While it is good and may be essential to have an independent component of the board as it enables independent judgement of the company's broad strategy and its implementation, financial resources, their use and reporting, etc., do IDs get involved enough in order to have that kind of independent judgement? Do they find time to get involved to that extent? Even if they intend to make a difference, can they get so involved and committed to the company where they occupy independent directorships while being fully engaged as CEOs of other companies? Structures, which most laws mandate, do not guarantee good governance. What is more important is 'what happens behind the boardroom door through the interacting dynamics of those powerful egos who are charged with the fundamental dilemma of directing—how to drive their enterprise forward while keeping it under prudent control'(Garratt 2003).

This is very important. Mere structures mandated by laws and regulations will not necessarily result in better governance unless the board and directors show deep involvement. Many corporate failures such as Enron, WorldCom, Global Crossing, etc., in the early 2000s, and the recent ones such as Lehman Brothers, AIG, or Satyam, could have been avoided had the board shown greater involvement and the courage to challenge the management. As Ken West, former chairman of the National Association of Corporate Directors said: 'No matter what else a director brings to the boardroom table, it takes courage to be a fully competent, effective board member' (Ashby and Miles 2002). It may look a little ironic now that J. Stuart Francis, former vice-chairman, Lehman Brothers, had opined that 'increasingly important role of an involved, knowledgeable board that has the courage to challenge management decisions, could have been hugely important in preventing some of the major negative surprises that confronted companies such as Enron in

2001' (Ashby and Miles). The structural reforms of the board will definitely help the company on the compliance or conformance front.

Most of the laws governing corporations clearly state that the managing director (MD) (or the designated manager) of the company shall be subordinate to the BOD. For example, the Companies Act 1956 in India makes it clear that the MD of a company shall exercise his/her powers subject to the superintendence, control, and direction of the BOD (Section 2(26)). Section 2(24) makes similar provisions with respect to managers. Thus, in whatever way the powers are conferred on the MD/manager, these powers are subject to the control of the board. So, even if the powers of the MD/manager are prescribed in the general meeting or in the articles, he/she is still subordinate to the board. No provision in the articles of association or resolutions in a general meeting can override the provisions of the Act. This being so, the board has enormous power and some of the suggestions regarding best practices such as separating the positions of CEO and chairman for better governance look redundant if the boards take their governance roles seriously and diligently.

Best Practices Contradictions

Carter and Lorsch (2004) have identified a number of embedded contradictions in the so-called best practices, which every company and board aspire for. Their arguments about how the so-called best practices themselves become contradictions are given in Table 6.1.

TABLE 6.1   Best practices and contradictions

Best practices	Likely contradictions
1. Most of the directors are independent—'the more, the better.'	1. Board independence comes at a cost. Directors who have no other relationships with the company are unlikely to know much about its business and will have a lot to learn. What is more, they will be very reliant on management in doing so.
2. Directors should be financially aligned with shareholders through stock ownership and incentive compensation.	2. Aligning director interest with those of shareholders, by making them shareholders, can erode directors' independence and even act as a catalyst for actions that are not in the interests of all the shareholders. Directors who own stock could think about their personal interests as shareholders and not think broadly about all shareholders.
3. Directors should vigorously monitor management's activities and performance.	3. While good boards monitor and judge management's performance, they must also participate in key decisions and offer advice. Directors sit in judgement on management decisions to which they have contributed. This muddies accountabilities and makes the working relationship between board and management a difficult juggling act.

Contd

Table 6.1 contd

Best practices	Likely contradictions
4. Directors should be 'generalists'—all focused on their company as a whole (the only exception being the use of committees).	4. 'Generalist' directors, with only limited time to oversee complex companies, are likely to have a superficial understanding of their businesses. As the challenges of directors grow, directors may find that the key to getting their jobs done is to divide their efforts and focus on specific issues.
5. The primary task of a board is to create shareholder value.	5. Shareholder value is of course an important goal, but in reality boards are responsible to a diverse set of shareholders who may have widely varying investment objectives and time horizons. Further, achieving long-term shareholder value involves meeting the expectations of others who contribute to company success—employees, suppliers, customers, and so on. It would be easy if all parties could be satisfied in the same way, but invariably trade-offs among them are required.

Source: Carter and Lorsch (2004), *Back to the Drawing Board*, Boston, HBS Press.

Best Practices Frameworks

Notwithstanding the contradictions, experts have suggested best practices for the board to be more effective. Corporate governance experts, regulators, or even shareholders recommend that boards adopt and put into practice a set of practices which they consider as 'best practices' that will enable boards to improve their functioning. For example, Susan Shultz suggests the Strategic Board Continuum (SBC), John Pound provides a framework which distinguishes the Governed-Corporation Paradigm from the Managed-Corporation Paradigm, and Garratt suggests the Learning Board Model (explained in Chapter 4). Ram Charan is an ardent critic of the so-called best practices at the structural level. He is more concerned about the board dynamics than the structural aspects of the board. Let us first take a look at the Susan Shultz framework (Shultz 2001).

According to Shultz, there are ten most critical mistakes in corporate governance: 'Companies who make all or most critical mistakes in corporate governance are at the low end of the strategic board continuum and are characterized by weak, passive boards. The great boards are at the high end of the continuum and avoid those mistakes. Great boards mean great companies.'

Strategic board continuum

The list of the ten most critical mistakes include:
1. Failure to recruit strategically
2. Too many insiders
3. Too many paid consultants
4. Too much family
5. Too many cronies

6. Getting the money wrong
7. Fear of diversity
8. Information block
9. Passive directors
10. Failed leadership

At the lower end of the continuum, we have what is called a captive board and at the higher end we have the strategic board. See Fig. 6.1.

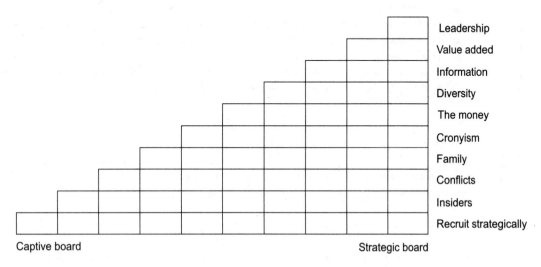

Captive board   Strategic board

FIG. 6.1 Strategic board continuum

Managed vs governed corporations—Boardroom paradigms and practices

John Pound, visiting professor at Harvard Law School, distinguishes between the managed-corporation paradigm and the governed-corporation paradigm to highlight the desirable best practices for boards (Pound 2000) (see Table 6.2).

Committee structure

Most experts and regulators also push for a committee mechanism to speed up the board processes. A committee structure is also considered to be a best practice almost everywhere in the world. The committee structure, its advantages, and the different types, have been discussed in detail in Chapter 4.

Contrarian views on best practices

Experts such as Ram Charan feel that best practices in the form of structural reforms of boards will not give the desired results. Regulators all over the world are preoccupied with insisting on structural solutions at the board level to improve governance practices. According to Charan (1998), 'Overemphasis on specific mechanisms can distract a board from the real issue, namely, how directors behave and interact.' He continues: 'Boards should choose only those committee

TABLE 6.2 The managed corporation vs the governed corporation:
Boardroom paradigms and practices

The managed–corporation paradigm	The governed–corporation paradigm
The board's role is to hire, monitor, and, when necessary, replace management.	*The board's role is to foster effective decisions and reverse failed policies.*
Board characteristics	
Power sufficient to control the CEO and the evaluation process	Expertise sufficient to allow the board to add value to the decision-making process
Independence to ensure that the CEO is honestly evaluated and that directors are not compromised by conflicts or co-opted by management	Incentives to ensure that the board is committed to creating corporate value
Board procedures that allow outside directors to evaluate managers dispassionately and effectively	Procedures that foster open debate and keep board members informed and attuned to the shareholders' concerns
Policies	
Separate the CEO and chair (or lead outside director)	Required areas and expertise that must be represented on the board such as core industry and finance
Board meetings without CEO present	Minimum commitment of 25 days
Committee of independent directors to evaluate the CEO	Large option packages for directors
Independent financial and legal advisors to outside directors	Designated critique to question new policy proposals
Explicit yardsticks for judging the CEO's performance	Regular meetings with large shareholders
	Board members free to request information from any employees

Source: Pound, John (2000), The Promise of the Governed Corporation, in *HBR On Corporate Governance*, pp. 79–103, Boston, HBS Press.

structures and leadership designations that clear the path for an open exchange of information and ideas among all directors, and between the directors and the CEO. The goal should be to avoid any mechanisms that inadvertently create pockets of power and to select those that streamline communication and enhance ability to work together.'

While history, including the recent past, points to the fact that simply having independent directors in requisite numbers or percentages, constituting audit, nomination, or remuneration committees entirely of independent directors, or encouraging IDs to hold separate meetings under a lead director, etc., do not ensure that there is better governance. Satyam from India, which has been in the news for all the bad governance that took place in the company, had all the so-called structural mechanisms but ended up in the garbage of poorly governed companies.

For Charan (1998), the catch phrases are 'less is more' and 'function, not form'. With the necessity for having a majority of outside directors and the formation of various committees, boards will usually be under pressure to have a larger size. Charan advocates that 'the size of the board be determined with the need for dialogue in mind.' He also opines that 'meetings without the CEO are okay but should not substitute for a direct communication with the CEO' and 'boards that function well have a minimal number of committees, each with a very clear mandate, and each in a role that supports, not replaces, the work of the full board.... These boards tend to resist the notion of a "lead director" or "outside chairman" not because the CEO has a stranglehold on the board but because the roles are extraneous and, worse, potentially destructive to the board dynamics.' Bill Adams, former chairman of Armstrong, supports the views of Charan: 'Boards need to be close-in-teams—large enough to represent a diversity of views—so the team doesn't get locked into something solely out of the past experience of one or two people but small enough for everyone to be involved.'

Thus, there are people who differ from the contention that the so-called best practices at the structural level will lead to better governance. Structures help many companies to score on a conformance level, which enables the company to meet the requirements in a box-ticking exercise to satisfy the demands of the regulators, and even shareholders, as it gives a perception about apparent good governance, but it doesn't guarantee real good governance. For the critics, best practices within the boardroom is what matters.

BOARD'S STRATEGIC ROLE

In Chapter 4 we discussed the varying roles that a board could assume. These could vary from that of a *watchdog* to that of a *pilot* (Carter and Lorsch 2004). As we have seen, watchdog boards only act when something goes wrong; pilot boards are more proactive and take a lot of interest in the company's direction. Pilot boards may get very involved with the management in making many decisions and probing performance. Whatever be the nature of the role (watchdog or pilot) that the board assumes, the board has a role to play in the strategy plane of the execution of the business. While a watchdog board may restrict itself to a body of approving (or disapproving, or advising to modify) the strategy map or strategic course for the company prepared by the management, a pilot board will even get involved in the preparation of strategy. The question that arises here is whether the board should confine itself to strategic issues at the corporate level or get involved in the company's major businesses, or all businesses?

Colley et al. (2003) feel that 'the board can't be content to endorse automatically the strategy devised by the CEO and senior management. The directors must ensure that operational plans are in place to carry out the strategic intent effectively. After the strategy has been adopted and the journey has begun, the board should systematically monitor the progress of the execution of strategy.' Thus, they put the board's role in strategy as one of deep involvement.

Garratt (2003) has identified four stages of strategy development and has clearly delineated authorities between the board and management. He has also identified areas where authorities are unclearly or jointly assigned to the board and the management (refer to Table 6.3).

Again, it can be seen that the board has to play a more or less exhaustive role in the strategy development stages. Carter and Lorsch (2004) advise boards to address five issues before engaging themselves in the strategy development process (see Exhibit 6.1).

TABLE 6.3   Stages of strategy development

Stage of strategy development	Board authorities	Managerial authorities	Clarifying joint or unclearly assigned authorities
Developing strategy	• Understand the external environment /changes • Main forum for debate and discussion of vision, values, goals and key issues • Develop and agree vision, values and culture • Provide advice and support to executives during the development of the plan • Comment on executives' drafts • Check compliance accountabilities • Agree final structure of strategy	• Undertake research to provide information for the development of the strategy • Embed the learning organization culture throughout the organization • Provide feedback on environmental scanning rapidly to the board	• Who will write drafts of strategy and implementation plans • Who will agree the use of consultants and advisors • Who will control the budget for strategy development
Ratifying the strategy	• Approve strategy implementation and feedback process • Delegate to senior management/executives	• Present implementation plan to board • Develop implementation plan • Allocate resources to implementation	• Who will disseminate the strategy • Who will complete the details of the strategy
Monitoring implementation	• Monitor overall progress of strategy implementation • Help executives in problem solving and trouble shooting • Communicate with shareholders/stakeholders	• Manage implementation process • Measure progress • Manage resource committed • Sign off completed tasks • Report frequently to the board	• Who is responsible for speed and frequency of feedback
Developing partnerships and alliances	• Identify and approach potential partners • Use board networks • Communicate with existing partners • Approve formal partnerships and alliances	• Help identify potential partners • Help approach potential partners • Negotiate detailed agreements • Manage partnerships and alliances	• Who will finalize partnership agreements

According to Charan (2005), 'directors don't develop the strategy, but their input is vital in making sure management has fully thought through its opportunities and options and has a realistic sense of the available resources, external factors, competitive threats, and risks.' He

Exhibit 6.1
The Five Issues Boards Must Address before Engaging in Strategy Development

- The board must define the scope of its strategic involvement by relating to its chosen role (*watchdog* or *pilot*).
- Is it interested primarily in 'corporate' level strategy or strategies in each or some of the major businesses? Information and knowledge needs will depend on the choice made.
- Does the board want to be involved at the start of the management's planning process and occasionally during it or is it content to review the plan when management has largely completed it?
- The board must clarify whether its expectations for engagement are congruent with the philosophy of the executives who lead the corporation, especially the CEO.
- Boards need to understand that developing strategy is a repetitive process and not a one-shot affair. It requires continuous board involvement. Strategic issues addressed at the annual strategic retreat at the beginning must be picked up during the rest of the year and progressively discussed until sufficient clarity is achieved. Unless this is recognized, directors will become frustrated as their experience will be seen as superficial.

adds that 'one challenge is for all the directors to have the same understanding of the company's strategy. This is often lacking; different directors on the same board at times articulate vastly different versions of the company's strategy.' According to him, for the directors to have a clear understanding of 'how a company, a division, or a major product category makes money is crucial.'

Harper (2005) is of the opinion that the board has a very definite role to play in the company's strategy. According to him, 'What has happened has already happened and the company is where it is—only future prosperity really matters. This requires the board to form some idea of what the company will be like in the future and how it will perform in its future environment. And yet, too many boards spend too much of their time looking in the rear view mirror instead of looking ahead and trying to anticipate what is around the next bend and how to negotiate it.' He says that the board must be equipped to formulate strategies that will be the basis for achieving the corporation's goals. 'The formulation requires a process (thinking) leading to the content (strategic plans). The board's main input will be the thinking process.' Thus, almost everybody suggests that the board has to play a fundamental role in the development, monitoring, and evaluation of strategy for the company.

Strategy Processes

Experts suggest a number of processes for the board to follow in order to get involved in the strategy process and several handy tools can assist their strategy development, assessment, monitoring, and evaluation process.

Harper suggests that the board must address six questions before embarking on its role in strategy development (Exhibit 6.2).

Once the board answers these questions, it will have a clear vision of where it wants the organization to be in the future.

Exhibit 6.2
Six Questions the Board Should Ask on Its Strategic Role

1. What must we do to ensure that the company is relevant in the future?
2. What will the company's future purpose be?
3. How will we sustain our position in the changing business environment that lies ahead?
4. What are these changes likely to be and what opportunities and threats might they pose?

5. How could we exploit those opportunities by moving into new areas on a sufficient scale?
6. What resources will we need and should we develop them or acquire them?

Source: Harper, John (2005), *Chairing the Board*, Kogan Page, London.

Garratt (2003) suggests the strategic decision-taking cycle. The framework helps the board while playing their strategic and surveillance roles (refer Fig. 6.2).

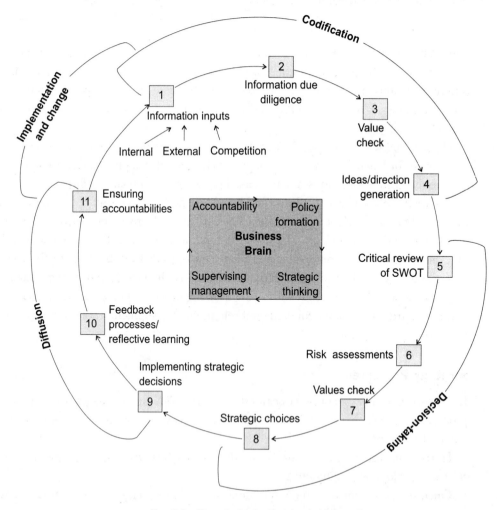

Fɪɢ. 6.2   The strategic decision-taking cycle

As can be seen, there are eleven elements that are sequential and closely related to the strategic decision-taking cycle.

Information inputs   Sieve data in order to gather information that will provide cues and ask discerning questions backed by an intelligent approach for taking decisions aimed at problem-solving. The board shall use the PPESTT (political and legislative, physical, economic, social, technological, and trade environment) framework to gather information about the external world. Information about the competitive environment as well as the internal environment also needs to be gathered from the management. Both have to be collected by probing questions.

Information due diligence   The board has to carry out a due diligence on the information gathered by posing questions such as:

- What is the source of data?
- Is this source reliable?
- How do we know that this data is valid?
- How can we cross-check this data?

Values check of due diligence   The board has to check whether the information gathered is legitimately and ethically acceptable and secure within the three values of corporate governance namely, accountability, probity, and transparency. This is necessary because today the intangible assets of a company such as intellectual property rights (IPR), business reputation, and brand equity account for a great percentage of a firm's net worth. Any adverse reputation arising from not adhering to ethics and values will directly affect the board and the individual directors.

Idea generation and critique   The board has to position the company in the changing market scenario by monitoring the external environment. Actually, this is the basic source of business strategy. This has to be done because of two reasons: one, the board has a responsibility to allocate scarce resources to the opportunities unveiled in the outside environment and two, protecting the company's strategic interests aimed at sustainability rather than meeting the ends of one or two dominant individuals on the board. For this, the board should initiate and install a thinking and debating process. The governance failure at Satyam happened because the idea generation (like that of merging the two associate companies with itself) and the subsequent decision-making was carried out by a few dominant board members. Apparently, there was no healthy dialogue or debate on the issue.

Comparison with SWOT analysis   While advanced tools of strategic analysis are available, the board can still use the time-tested, simple SWOT analysis for putting the firm on a comparative framework with competitors (see Fig. 6.3).

Risk assessment   Risk taking is the basis of capitalism and all factors or events that reduce the possibility of achieving the business goals and increase the probability of losses can be considered to be risks. At the board level, risk is the probability and the consequences of such factors and events affecting the desired outcome, and its management reduces the impact of uncertainties in the ever-changing environments. As is crystal clear, the exact assessment of

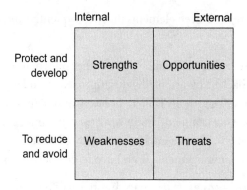

FIG. 6.3   SWOT analysis

risk is next to impossible; judgement on the part of directors is what matters. After assessing risks, they have to evolve ways to evaluate and manage risks. The board has to examine the internal control measures in order to determine whether they are sufficient to mitigate the effects of risks.

Major risks fall into the following categories (Garratt 2003):

- Reputation risk
- Financial risk
- Political risk
- Country risk
- Terrorism risk
- Legislative risk
- Regulatory risk
- Health and safety risk
- Physical environmental risk
- Human rights risk
- Information security risk
- Supply chain risk
- Intellectual property risk

The board has to see that there is a robust internal audit that can act as a 'worthy whistle-blower'.

Value check of risk assessment   The board has to consider the risk assessment from the values aspect. On the one hand, there is a set of values of governance—accountability, probity, and transparency—and on the other hand, there are the values which the organization and every member of it subscribes to, which may or may not be available in the form of a list. Assume that the value list contains an item 'Integrity: We deliver what we commit. With honesty, fairness, reliability, and uprightness, in whatever we do' (from the value list of Wipro Ltd, a major IT company in India). Now, the board has to anticipate risks of reputation if Wipro deviates from any of these espoused values in its business dealings.

Strategic choices   According to Garratt, strategic choices could be:

- Advance
- Retreat
- Hold our ground
- Make alliance
- Withdraw

In addition, the board should also have contingency plans which will be embraced when unexpected happenings occur. For example, the case of Boehringer Mannheim Ltd, which had operations in India. When administration of one of the drugs manufactured by the company resulted in the death of a few patients, the board had to take a contingent decision to salvage the situation: they decided to sell the company to Nicholas Piramal Ltd (rechristened Piramal Healthcare), who was on the prowl for acquisitions with the purpose of growth.

Implementing strategic decisions   Choice of the best strategy is only part of the job; the directors have to ensure that it gets implemented. This is where the organization's capabilities matter. The following matrix depicts the organizational capabilities with respect to four dimensions: task focus and process focus versus internal focus and external focus (refer Fig. 6.4).

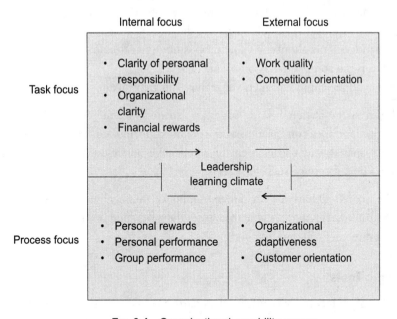

FIG. 6.4   Organizational capability survey

Feedback and board learning   When the board initiates changes in line with strategy, it is likely that many employees will have a tendency to resist and the board has to take steps to unblock such resistance to change. To do this, it will have to start a dialogue with the unions or other interest groups in order to impress upon them the necessity for such changes. Also, they can create action learning groups to communicate the strategy to them and also to make them comfortable with the likely changes that are expected once the chosen strategy is implemented.

Checking accountability   As a final step the board has to do an accountability check. It has to ensure that it complies with the laws and regulations, as well as with the agreements with the other stakeholder groups such as the company itself as a separate legal entity, the owners, the law makers, regulators, customers, staff, suppliers, local communities, and also the physical environment

According to Charan (2005), a differing view on strategy is that while boards need to understand strategy, it is not their job to create it. They may challenge the management's ideas for strategy, but it is not up to them to define alternatives. The board's real value comes by helping management to test whether the strategy is grounded in reality. Charan feels that the boards have to dig deeper and ask questions such as:

- How will money be made with this strategy?
- Does the company have the resources, not only financial but also human, to execute the strategy, and are they allocated appropriately?
- Is management devoting sufficient resources to the growth areas and pulling the plug on others?
- Has management considered the full range of external factors?
- Are key assumptions about business valid?
- Will judgements about the value proposition to customers hold up?
- What is the competitive reaction likely to be?
- How will the capital markets value the strategic moves?

Charan suggests that boards organize 'strategy immersion sessions' to gather relevant information and ideas on business and its context, formulate their questions and thoughts, and work with management to deepen their collective understanding of management's proposed strategy. The purpose of such sessions is:

- The board will have a clear understanding of management's view of the external context
- The top management is able to present their thinking on the content of strategy
- The directors will question and probe.

Strategic Tools

A number of tools come in handy for the board. SWOT analysis, the time-tested tool, has already been discussed earlier (see Fig. 6.3). A few more are described below.

Ansoff's product-market matrix (growth vector)

This tool tells the board what kind of strategy they should follow with respect to the market and product. One of the earliest tools in strategic management, this matrix is most suitable for companies in the early years of growth (refer Fig. 6.5).

Product / Market	Present	New
Present	Penetration	Product development
New	Market development	Diversification

FIG. 6.5   Product-market matrix

2×2 customer-need matrix

Charan and Tichy (1998) propose a simple tool for achieving strategic growth. They call it 'strategy from outside-in' because according to them, in the outside-in company the key aspect is need, not product. Its people are not focusing on getting half-a-point market share; they are totally immersed in the minds of customer, looking for ways to expand demand. A company can think of growing its business by moving across the quadrants (from A to B to D and finally to C). The 2×2 matrix could be a handy tool for boards and managers alike (refer Fig. 6.6).

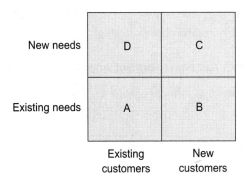

	Existing customers	New customers
New needs	D	C
Existing needs	A	B

FIG. 6.6   Customer–need matrix

Value chain analysis

It helps to analyse strategically relevant internal activities in the competitive advantage. It is a systematic way to examine all the activities a company performs and how they interact among themselves to identify sources of competitive advantage. According to Porter (1985), every company's value chain is composed of nine categories of activities (value addition steps) that can be classified under two major headings: primary and support activities.

Primary activities   These are connected with the physical creation of the firm's product or services, its marketing, delivery, and after sales service.

- Inbound logistics
- Operations
- Outbound logistics
- Marketing and sales
- Service

Support activities   These provide inputs for infrastructure for primary activities.

- Firm infrastructure
- HRM
- Technology development
- Procurement

Importance of value chain analysis

- Provides two pieces of competitive intelligence
  - Where in the chain is (which activities) the greatest value added?
  - In which segments of the chain do the competitors have an edge?
- Management concerns of such analysis: To take advantage of the distinctive competencies of the firm by way of:
  - Following a course of action that is different from that of rivals
  - Developing a strategy which will provide different and better outcomes than those of competitors
  - Adopting a strategy that is distinct and difficult to duplicate; and exploit the opportunity by suitably adapting the chosen strategy

PESTEL framework for environment analysis

It categorizes environmental influences into six main types:

1. Political
2. Economic
3. Social
4. Technological
5. Environmental, and
6. Legal

Portfolio analysis

For companies with a diversified portfolio of businesses, strategic tools such as the BCG matrix or GE nine-cell grid can come in handy to streamline the portfolio of businesses (Pearce II and Robinson Jr. 2005) (refer Figs 6.7 and 6.8). In the BCG matrix, all the businesses are plotted onto a 2×2 matrix with the relative market share of each business versus its potential market growth rate. Then, businesses are categorized into *dogs* (businesses that have low relative market share and whose growth potential is low), *cash cows* (currently enjoys good relative market share even though the growth potential is limited), *question marks* (whose relative market share is low but offers good potential for growth), and *stars* (where both relative market share and growth potential is high). The dogs have to be divested, cash cows have to be retained as they generate a lot of cash currently and even support other businesses, the board has to critically look at question marks as, with investment and management support, some of them could be pushed to become stars, and others have to be divested, and stars need to be supported with investment and other resources.

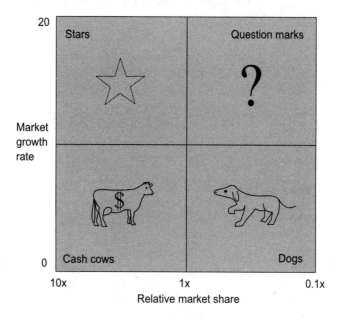

Fig. 6.7 The BCG matrix

Limitations the BCG matrix

1. Clearly defining a market and accurate measurement of share and growth rate are often difficult.
2. Division into four cells on low/high classification is simplistic in nature. Markets with average growth rates or businesses with average market shares are usually neglected.
3. Assumes that profitability will be proportional to market share. It may vary across industries and market segments. There need not be any direct relation between market share and profitability.
4. Not helpful in relative investment opportunities across different business units in the corporate portfolio.
5. Strategic evaluation of a set of businesses requires examination of more than relative market share and market growth. Attractiveness may increase based on technical, seasonal, competitive, or other considerations.
6. It doesn't reflect the diversity of options available since the classification is very simplistic.

The GE nine-cell grid or GE business screen tries to eliminate the limitations of the BCG matrix. Businesses are classified based on a number of factors, basically categorized into two: business strength factors and industry attractiveness factors. Business strength factors include market share, profit margin, ability to compete, customer and market knowledge, competitive position, technology and management calibre, etc. Industry attractiveness factors include market growth, size and industry profitability, competition, seasonality and cyclical qualities, economies of scale, technology and social/environmental/legal/human factors, etc.

The position of a business within the grid is calculated by subjectively quantifying the two dimensions of the grid by assigning weights for various factors under the industry attractiveness and business strength factors (refer Fig. 6.8).

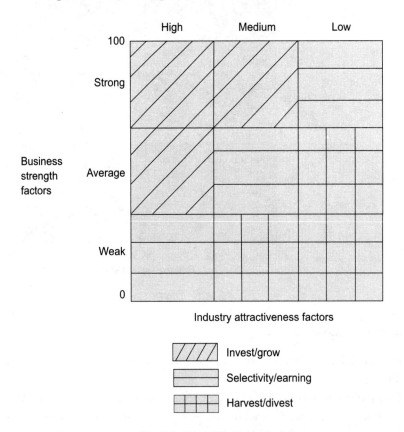

Fig. 6.8 The GE nine-cell grid

Decision-making

Invest/grow Businesses where industry attractiveness is high, and where the company has strength, shall be nurtured for growth by investing heavily.

Selectivity/earning In businesses which have medium industry attractiveness and where the company's strength falls in the medium category, the board has to take discernible actions based on the earning potential of the business.

Harvest/divest   These are businesses who fall into industries which are declining or not attractive, and the company doesn't have strengths in those areas, and hence, either such businesses shall be permitted to continue so long as they make money, or they be divested, and the resources freed shall be allocated to those businesses which look attractive and where the company has strengths.

For each of the businesses, a rating score can be arrived at based on the weightage of a particular industry, attractiveness factors, and where the company sees itself with respect to that particular factor. A similar rating score can be obtained for the business strength factors. Both these ratings will together show the position of a business on the grid., The board has to take/advise management to take decisions based on this.

Shell matrix, a variant of the GE grid, is also applied for portfolio analysis and decisions (refer Fig. 6.9).

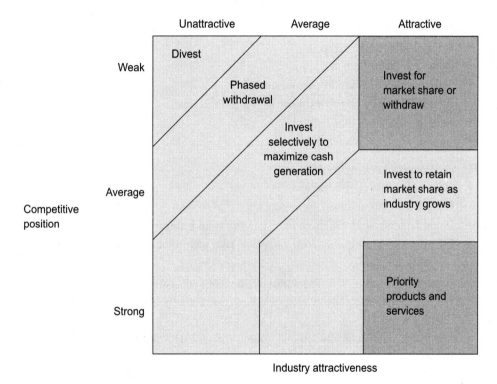

Fig. 6.9   The shell matrix

Core competence theory   In 1994, Gary Hamel and C.K. Prahald stated that companies must identify their core competencies in order to pursue their growth opportunities. They defined core competence as a 'bundle of skills and technology rather than a single discrete skill or technology'. Thus, core competence is any bundle of skills that yield a significant cost advantage in the delivery of a particular customer benefit. For example, Motorola's core competency is in fast cycle time production; at Sony it is miniaturization; at Federal Express it is logistics management; and at EDS it is system integration. Thus, a core competency is 'an area of specialized expertise that is the result of harmonizing complex streams of technology and work activity' (Hamel and Prahlad 1994).

Characteristics of core competencies
- Potential access to a wide variety of markets
- A core competency must make a significant contribution to the perceived benefits of the end product
- Core competencies should be difficult for competitors to imitate

Core competency perspective
- Identifying existing core competency
- Establishing a core competency acquisition agenda
- Building core competency
- Deploying core competency
- Protecting and defending core competency leadership

Identifying core competency
- Define core competency
- Build inventory
- Team works on defining core competency
- Identify elements that contribute to core competency
- Benchmark with other firms
- Involve senior managers

Benefits of core competencies
- It provides customer benefits
- It is hard for competitors to imitate
- It can be leveraged widely to many products and markets
- It leads to better organization of special skills, technologies, processes, knowledge, expertise, or abilities
- It establishes long-term development processes and experiences
- It creates customer value because is considered by your customers to be unique and distinguishable.
- It is not equally accessible to all competitors and is extremely difficult for other companies to imitate.

Other examples
- Honda has core competence in small engine design and manufacturing
- Microsoft has the core competence of designing office software products that are user-friendly
- PepsiCo has a core competence of mass production and distribution of bottled drinks
- Ernst & Young has the core competence of performing audit functions for Fortune 500 corporations
- One of Wal-Mart's core competencies is their massive real-time information system.

Ways of protecting core competencies
- Establishing a deeply involving process

- Defining a clear set of corporate growth
- Establishing explicit stewardship roles
- Setting up an explicit mechanism for allocating critical core competence resources
- Benchmarking competence building efforts against rivals
- Reviewing the status of existing and nascent core competencies
- Building a community of people within the organization

Industry analysis tools   There are basically two models available—Porter's Five Forces Model and Arthur D. Little's Life Cycle Approach.

Porter's model for structural analysis of industry is a framework on which one can identify the attractiveness of an industry (Porter 1980). According to Porter, five forces determine the ultimate profit potential of the industry. The impact of these forces may vary from intense, where no firm can expect to earn spectacular returns, to relatively mild, in which case returns are quite high. These five forces are:

- Threat of entry
- Intensity of rivalry among existing competitors
- Pressure from substitute products
- Bargaining power of buyers
- Bargaining power of suppliers

Force I   Threat of entry depends on (a) *barriers to entry and* (b) *reaction from existing competitors.*

(a) Major sources of barriers
    1. Economies of scale—can be present or help in many functions
    2. Product differentiation—established firms have brand identification and customer loyalties arising from many factors
    3. Capital needs—requirements of large investments in order to compete
    4. Switching costs—one-time costs facing the buyer for switching from one supplier's products to another
    5. Access to distribution channels
    6. Cost disadvantages independent of scale—proprietary product technology through patents or secrecy
    7. Access to raw materials
    8. Favourable locations
    9. Government subsidies—preferential subsidies to established firms
    10. Learning or experience curve—lesser unit costs as the firm gains experience—methods improvement, layout improvements, balancing equipment
    11. Government policy—policies can change over a period of time, e.g. pollution control

(b) Expected retaliation—conditions that signal strong retaliation are:
    - A history of vigorous retaliation to entrants
    - Established firms with substantial resources to fight back such as creating additional capacity to meet all future needs, or leverage with distribution channels or customers

- Established firms with great commitment to the industry with highly illiquid assets employed in it
- Slow industry growth, which limits the ability of the industry to absorb a new firm

Force II   Intensity of rivalry among existing competitors. Rivalry can be either 'warlike', 'bitter', 'cut-throat', 'polite', or 'gentlemanly'. Rivalry is the result of interacting structural factors such as:

- Numerous or equally balanced competitors
- Slow industry growth
- High fixed or storage costs— when there is excess capacity leading to price cutting
- Lack of differentiation or switching costs—with undifferentiated products such as commodities, customers put pressure for better prices or services.
- Capacity augmentation in large increments—large capacity additions for attaining economies of scale can disrupt the industry supply/demand balance especially in periods of overcapacity and price cutting.
- Diverse competitors—when competitors are diverse in terms of origins and strategies, personalities will have diverse ways of competing; one may find it difficult to 'read' others.
- High strategic stakes—rivalry becomes more volatile if a number of firms have high stakes in achieving success. For example, Toyota may perceive a strong need to establish a solid position in the US market in order to build global prestige.
- High exit barriers—sources of exit barriers can be:
  ○ Specialized assets having low liquidation values, or high costs transfer, or conversion
  ○ Fixed costs of exit such as labour agreements, resettlement costs, maintaining capabilities for spare parts, etc.
  ○ Strategic interrelationships of the business with other units of the company in terms of its image, marketing ability, access to financial markets, shared facilities, etc.
  ○ Emotional barriers such as management's identification with the particular business, loyalty to employees, pride, fear for own career, etc., not based on any economic reasons
  ○ Government and social restrictions—government may deny or discourage exits due to concerns of job loss and regional economic effects (mostly seen in developing countries)

Force III   Pressure from substitute products. In a broad sense, all firms in an industry are competing with industries producing substitute products. Substitutes put a limit to how far prices can be increased, and when the price performance alternative is offered by the substitutes, the pressure on industry profits is stronger.

Force IV   Bargaining power of buyers. Buyer groups will be powerful under following conditions:

- Concentrated purchase or purchases of a large volume of seller's sale results in the ability to extract better prices
- What gets bought forms a significant fraction of the buyer's costs or purchases
- What gets purchased are standard or undifferentiated
- Few switching costs, enabling the buyer to switch if necessary
- Buyer earning low profits as pressure on profits forces them to be more price sensitive

- Buyer has potential for backward integration
- The quality of the industry's product do not put any pressure on the buyer product quality and hence, price sensitive to buying
- When buyer has all the information about the demand, market prices, and even supplier costs

Force V Bargaining power of suppliers. Supplier groups will be powerful under following conditions:

- When supplier group is more concentrated than the industry or dominated by a few companies, can exert considerable influence in prices, quality, and even terms
- When substitutes are not competing
- Industry is not an important customer for the supplier group
- Suppliers' product is an important input to the buyer's business
- Supplier group's products are differentiated or it has built up switching costs
- The supplier group poses a threat of forward integration

Consulting firm Arthur D. Little has developed what is known as the life-cycle approach (Pearce II and Robinson Jr. 2005), which enables a company to identify suitable strategies depending on the stage of the life cycle that the industry is in, and the strength of the company in its business.

According to this approach, business environment indicates the four stages of the life cycle of the industry, namely embryonic, growth, mature, and aging.

Business strength measures the competitive position of a firm's business units, namely dominant, strong, favourable, weak, or non-viable (refer Fig. 6.10).

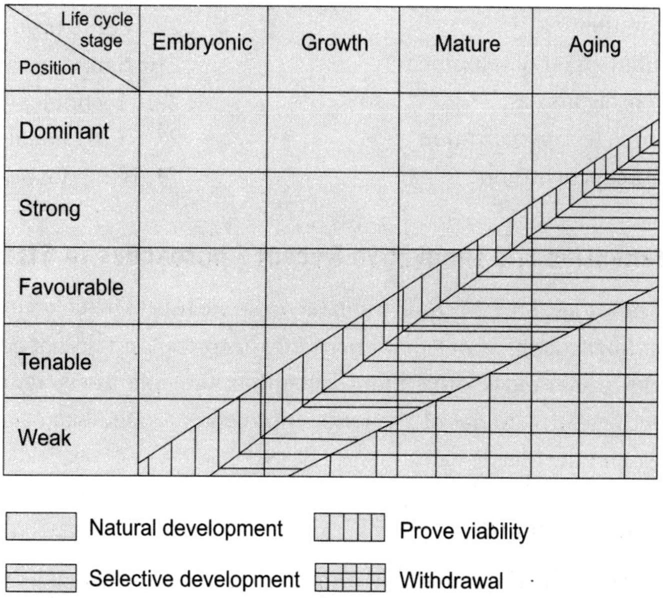

Fig. 6.10 Arthur D. Little's industry life-cycle matrix

Six steps to the approach

1. Identifying each line of business based on commonalities such as common rivals, customers, sustainability, prices, quality/style, divestments, liquidation, etc.
2. Assessing the life-cycle stage of each business based on market share, investments, profitability, or cash flow.
3. Identifying the competitive position of the firm as being dominant, strong, favourable, tenable, or weak.
4. Identifying strategy for the business based on its life-cycle stage and competition.
5. Assigning a natural thrust to the natural strategy detailing the set of specific actions that support the general direction defined in Step 4. For example, the actions can be start-up for a business with strong competitive potential, or growth with industry for a strong or dominant business in a mature industry seeking to maintain its position or gain position gradually by increasing market share incrementally, or defend in the early stages of industry maturity, or harvest in the aging stage enabling freeing of resources and reallocation to strong businesses.
6. Selection of one of the twenty-four generic strategies identified below keeping the strategic thrust of Step 5 in mind.

24 generic strategies

1. Backward integration
2. Develop business overseas
3. Develop overseas facilities
4. Distribution rationalization
5. Excess capacity
6. Export same product
7. Forward integration
8. Hesitation
9. Initial market development
10. Licensing abroad
11. Complete rationalization
12. Market penetration
13. Market rationalization
14. Method/functions efficiency
15. New products/new markets
16. New products/same markets
17. Production rationalization
18. Product line rationalization
19. Pure survival
20. Same products/new markets
21. Same products/same markets
22. Technological efficiency
23. Traditional cost-cutting
24. Unit abandonment

Comprehensive and Innovative Recent Approaches to Strategy

Of late, new tools have become available to strategists. The conventional approach was largely based on financial measures that are mostly historical and do not consider the development of intangibles which today drive more value than tangible assets, ignoring the factors that drive future performance. Some of the latest approaches are the balanced scorecard (BSC), strategy mapping, and the blue ocean strategy (BOS).

Balanced scorecard

BSC, developed by Kaplan and Norton (1996), provides managers with an instrument that can help them to navigate to future competitive success. Today, all organizations compete in complex environments; they vitally need an understanding of their goals and the methods for attaining them. BSC helps an organization to translate its mission and strategy into a comprehensive set of performance measures that provide a framework for strategic measurement and management system from four balanced perspectives: financial, customers, internal business processes, and learning and growth (refer Fig. 6.11). BSC thus enables companies not only to track financial results but to monitor the progress of building non-financial capabilities and intangible assets required for future growth.

The essential difference or advantage is that while traditional financial measures tell the story of past events or history, BSC includes, in addition to financial measures, measures that will monitor the progress of developing or acquisition of non-financial capabilities or intangible assets, which will add or deliver value to the organization in future. It helps to capture the critical value-creation activities by the organizational participants, thereby revealing the value drivers for superior long-term financial and competitive performance.

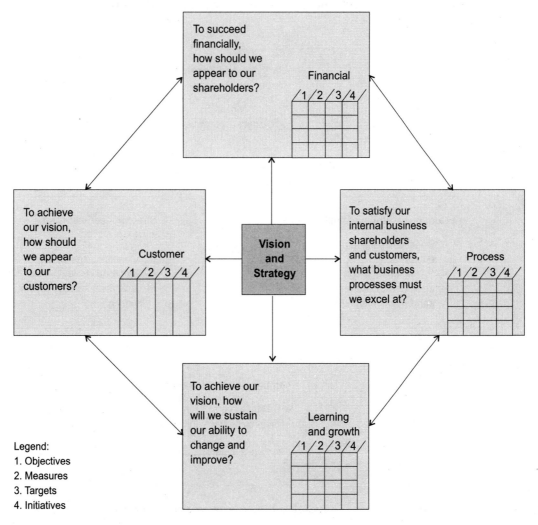

FIG. 6.11 The BSC framework

BSC emphasizes that financial and non-financial measures must be part of the information system for employees at all levels of the organization. It should translate a business unit's mission and strategy into tangible objectives and measures. The measures represent a balance between external measures for shareholders and customers, and internal measures of critical business processes, innovation, and learning and growth. The measures are balanced between the outcome measures—the results from past efforts—and the measures that drive future performance.

Innovative companies use the scorecard as a strategic management tool, to manage strategy over the long run. They use the scorecard to accomplish critical management processes of:

1. Clarifying and translating vision and strategy
2. Communicating and linking strategic objectives and measures
3. Planning, setting targets, and aligning strategic initiatives
4. Enhancing strategic feedback and learning

Fig. 6.12 details how the BSC can be used as a framework for strategy.

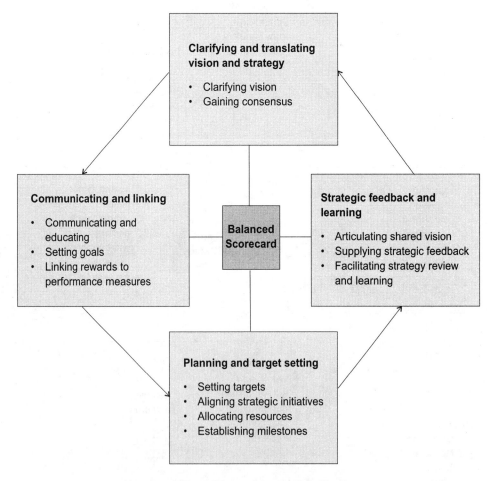

Fig. 6.12   BSC as a framework for strategy

Strategy mapping

A strategy map is a visual presentation of the cause-and-effect relationships among the components of an organization's strategy. It has evolved from the BSC and illustrates the time-based dynamics of a strategy by adding a second layer of detail, thus giving improved clarity and focus. Regardless of the type of strategic approach, the strategy map provides a uniform and consistent way to describe the strategy enabling us to establish and manage objectives and measures.

A strategy map is based on five principles

1. Strategy balances contradictory forces. The dominant objective of the firm is the sustained growth in shareholder value, which implies and necessitates a commitment to the long-term. All the same, the firm must show improved results in the short-term. Better short-term results can always be achieved by sacrificing long-term investments. Also, investing in intangible assets for long-term growth (such as brand building, etc.), usually conflicts with cutting costs for short-term financial performance. Thus, the starting point in describing any strategy is to balance and articulate the ST financial objective of cost reduction and productivity improvements with the LT objectives of revenue growth.

2. Strategy is based on a differentiated customer value proposition. Strategy requires a clear articulation of targeted customer segments and the value proposition to satisfy them. Clarity of this is the single most important dimension of strategy. Common value propositions found in practice are: (1) low total cost (2) product leadership (3) complete customer solutions, and (4) system lock-in. Each of these value propositions clearly defines the attributes that must be delivered if the customer is to be satisfied.

3. Value is created through internal business processes. What the firm wants to achieve through strategy as creation and sustenance of values are driven by the internal business processes such as (a) operations management (producing and delivering products/services to customers) (b) customer management (establishing and leveraging relationships with customers) (c) Innovation (developing new products/services/processes/relationships) (d) regulatory and social (conforming to regulations and societal expectations).

4. Strategy consists of simultaneous, complementary themes. The outcomes derived from the processes mentioned under 3 above may be in confrontation with each other and hence, attempts should be made to arrive at a balance.

5. Strategic alignment determines the value of intangible assets such as human capital, information capital, and organization capital. None of these intangible assets has value considered in isolation. But all of these derive value from their ability to help the organization implement its strategy.

Blue ocean strategy

Companies have for long engaged in head-to-head competition in search of sustained, profitable growth. They have always fought for competitive advantage, battled over market share, and struggled for differentiation. All strategic thrusts were aimed at the above. Professors Chan Kim and Renee Mauborgne (2005) say that in today's overcrowded industries the strategy of competing head-on results in nothing but a bloody 'red ocean' of rivals fighting over a shrinking profit pool, and is increasingly unlikely to create profitable growth in the future. They argue that tomorrow's winners will succeed not by battling competitors, but by creating 'blue oceans' of uncontested market space that is ripe for growth.

Such strategic moves, termed 'value innovation', create powerful leaps in value for both the firm and its buyers, rendering rivals obsolete and unleashing new demand. It is a systematic approach towards making the competition irrelevant. In the earlier context, the overriding focus of strategic thinking has been on competition-based red ocean strategies, which had its roots in military strategy. Described in military terms, strategy is about confronting an opponent and fighting over a given piece of land that is both limited and constant. But the authors argue that unlike war, industrial history points to a market universe that has never been constant, or that blue oceans have continuously been created over a period of time.

A focus on red ocean strategy is akin to accepting the constraining factors of war—limited terrain and the need to beat the enemy in order to succeed—and to deny the distinctive strength of business, namely the capacity to create new market space that is uncontested.

Value innovation

The cornerstone of BOS, the strategic approach consistently separated the winners from the losers in the creation of BOS. While companies caught in the red ocean followed a conventional approach of beating the competition by building a defensible position within the existing industry order, creators of blue oceans did not benchmark on competition but followed a different strategic logic, value innovation. The term was coined because BOS focuses on making competition irrelevant by creating a leap in value for buyers and the company, opening up new and uncontested market space. The value innovation by BOS defies the value-cost-trade-off dogma of the competition-based strategy. In the earlier context, the choice was between creating greater value at higher cost, or reasonable value at low cost, or looking at strategy as making a choice between differentiation and low cost, whereas BOS pursues differentiation and low cost simultaneously.

The four actions framework for creating a new value proposition (refer Fig. 6.13):

Eliminate   There are certain factors that companies in one's industry have long competed on. These factors are often taken for granted even though they no longer have value or may even detract from value. There may also be fundamental changes in what buyers value, but companies determined to benchmark one another do not act or even sense the change.

Reduce   One has to determine whether products or services have been over-designed in the race to match and beat the competition. Frequently, companies over-serve at a higher cost which the customer does not value.

Raise   One uncovers or eliminates the compromises one's industry forces customers to make and sets new standards that are well above those of competitors'.

Create   One discovers entirely new sources of value for buyers and creates new demand, and shifts the strategic pricing of the industry.

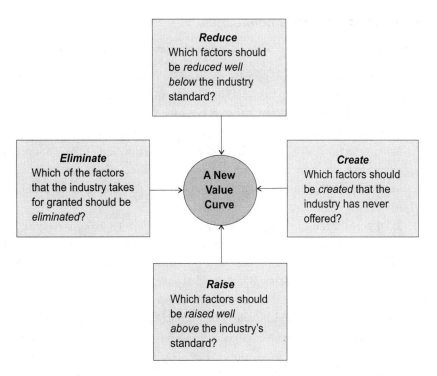

Fɪɢ. 6.13   The four actions framework for creating a new value proposition

According to BOS, there are three characteristics of a good strategy, namely focus, divergence, and compelling tagline.

Focus   Do not diffuse efforts across all key factors of competition. The company's strategic profile will clearly show focus. South West Airlines (SWA), for example, emphasizes only three factors: friendly service, speed, and frequent point-to-point departures. By focusing in this manner, SWA has been able to price against car transportation by not investing in meals, lounges, and seating choices. By contrast, SWA's traditional competitors invest in all the airline industry's competitive factors, making it very difficult for them to match SWA's prices.

Divergence   Don't benchmark competitors, instead look across alternatives. When a firm's strategy is the result of reaction as it tries to take on competition, it loses its uniqueness. On the strategy canvas, conventional airlines share the same strategic profile by having similarities in meals, lounges, etc., making their value curve more or less identical. By applying the four principles of elimination, reduction, raise, and creation, SWA differentiated their profile from the conventional ones by going for point-to-point travel as against the hub-and-spoke system of others.

Compelling tagline   Make the strategic profile clear. A good strategy must have a clear-cut and compelling tagline. It must not only deliver a clear message but also advertise an offering truthfully; otherwise customers will lose interest and trust. For example, SWA uses the tagline, 'The speed of a plane at the price of a car—whenever you need it.'

Reconstructing market boundaries

The six path framework for reconstructing market boundaries includes:

1. Look across alternative industries   Broadly speaking, a company competes not only with other firms in its industry but also with companies in other industries that produce alternative products or services. Alternatives are broader than substitutes. While substitutes are products or services that have different forms but offer the same functionality or core utility, alternatives are products or services that have different functions and forms but the same purpose, for example, restaurants and cinemas. Because of differences in form and function, they are not substitutes but are alternatives to choose from. In making every purchase decision buyers implicitly weigh alternatives, often unconsciously.

2. Look across strategic groups within industries   Strategic groups refer to a group of companies within an industry that pursue a similar strategy. In most industries, the fundamental strategic differences among industry players are captured by a small number of strategic groups. For example, Mercedes Benz, BMW, and Jaguar focus on out-competing one another in the luxury segment within the auto industry as economy car makers focus on excelling over one another in their strategic group. Pursuing BOS requires a firm to break out of this narrow tunnel vision by understanding which factors determine customers' decisions to move from one group to another, for example, Lexus by Toyota or Sony's Walkman.

3. Look across the chain of buyers   There are different buyer groups. There are buyers who are users too and there are buyers who are different from users; and there may also be a group of influencers for example, a corporate purchase person may be more concerned about the costs than a corporate user, who may be concerned with the ease of use. Challenging an industry's conventional wisdom about which buyer group to target can lead to the discovery of a new blue ocean, for example, the purchase decision on insulin, where the traditional focus was on doctors and manufacturers produced vials of insulin. The focus shifted to the users (patients) which resulted in user-friendly insulin pens, which Novo Nordisk identified and successfully exploited.

4. Look across complementary product and service offerings   Products and services are not used in a vacuum. In most cases, other products and services affect their values. But in most industries, competitors converge within the bounds of their industry's product and service offerings, for example movie theatres. The availability and cost of complementary services such as baby sitting facilities and car parks can affect the perceived value. But few theatres are ready to break the traditional definition of the product offering.

5. Look across a functional or emotional appeal to buyers   Some industries compete on price and function focusing on utility while others compete largely on feelings or their appeal is emotional. BOS strategy will require companies to challenge the functional—emotional orientation of their industry. For example, Swatch transformed the functionally-driven budget watch industry into an emotionally-driven fashion statement, whereas The Body Shop transformed the emotionally-driven industry of cosmetics into a functional one.

6. Look across time   This means looking at the value a market delivers today to the value it might deliver tomorrow. It is not an easy proposition and does not mean predicting the future;

it is about developing insights based on the trends of today. For example, Apple observed the rampant illegal music file sharing that happened in the late 1990s. The recording industry was the worst sufferer. Nobody wanted to buy a CD at a given price. But the trend was clearly towards digital music. So, Apple offered a very economically viable solution in agreement with five major music companies, namely Sony, BMG, EMI, Universal Music Group, and Warner Brothers—records in the form of iTunes which offered legal, easy-to-use, and flexible song downloads.

Business model innovation

Directors should always know that business models may require changes as the company moves ahead implementing strategies in pursuit of growth. A business model depicts how a firm delivers value to the customers. Every business exists because of its ability to meet certain needs of the customer. In the process of meeting these needs, the firm indulges itself in the transformation of certain inputs into certain outputs that satisfy the customer. Depending on the activities the firm undertakes, the business model can vary. For example, the firm may do everything internally or outsource part of the processes; they may add products or services which results in enhancement of value to the customer. For example, a textile company can think of making everything from yarn to finished textiles after weaving. Or, it may outsource the yarn, bleaching, and dyeing; reach the customer through wholesale/retail chain without necessarily owning them; decide to offer more value to the customers by entering into apparel making, design services, special event-related need satisfaction (of not only textile and related items), etc.

The foundation stone of the business model is business definition; it gives a firm the scope to meet a variety of customer needs.

Business models have to be dynamic and not static. As the environment changes, changes have to be incorporated in the business model too. They also have to be innovated to meet the ever-increasing needs of the customers (not always articulated). For example, Procter & Gamble, under what they call the Living It programme, makes its innovation team members stay with consumers for days together to find out what customer needs they can meet in order to make the consumers' lives better. Similarly, under the Working It programme, they also spend time with customers and retailers to find out how consumers shop and then work with retailers such as Wal-Mart to create better shopping experiences for the consumers (Lafley and Charan 2008).

Thus, business models need to be reconsidered at definite intervals. Otherwise, competition will move ahead of the company on the value curve.

STRATEGY AS STRETCH AND LEVERAGE

Just having a strategy isn't enough. One has to achieve more with less. One has to leverage the resources better. According to Hamel and Prahalad (1994), it does not have much to do with resource constraints but is the result of aspirations. It is this aspiration, the stretch which outpaces resources, that fuels the engine of advantage creation. Exploiting every possible opportunity for resource leverage takes creativity and persistence. A firm with outsized ambition but underdeveloped capacity for resource leverage will be just a dreamer. Alternatively, a firm with the capacity for resource leverage but with no galvanizing ambition will be a sleeper. A firm with neither aspiration nor capacity for resource leverage will be a loser and those with both will be winners.

Hamel and Prahalad (1994) cite Japanese companies as good examples. The Japanese companies that topped the US Patent Awards for the seventh consecutive year in 1992 are:

1. Canon
2. Toshiba
3. Mitsubishi
4. Hitachi

The statistics provided in Exhibit 6.3 show how Japanese companies were able to better leverage the resources at their disposal by applying stretch principles. Notwithstanding the fact that the US companies were spending more resources, in absolute and relative terms, it was not reflected in terms of better outputs.

'Stretch essentially means using dreams to set (business) targets—with no real idea as to how to get there. If you know how to get there, it is not a stretch target. It requires one to break out of both conventional thinking and conventional performance expectations. Stretch allows organizations

Exhibit 6.3
Japanese Companies Score over US or European Companies

Manufacturing labour productivity (per hour)

	1988	1989	1990	1991
US	118	119	120	122
Germany	115	118	122	124
Japan	125	135	143	150

Overhead costs (1991):

US	26%
Germany	21%
Japan	17%

R&D spending in absolute terms ($ millions, 1993)

Siemens	5322	Philips	2079
Hitachi	3907	Sony	1809
GM	5917	Xerox	922
Honda	1447	Canon	794
AT&T	2911	IBM	5083
NTT	2157	NEC	2274

R&D spending in relative terms (R&D as per cent of Sales, Fiscal 1993)			
Siemens	10	Hitachi	6.7
ABB	8.1	Mitsubishi	4.6
Thomson	8.3	Sharp	6.5
Philips	6.8	Sony	6.1
IBM	7.9	Matsushita	5.6
NTT	11.1	NEC	8.0
Bayer	7.5	Toray	3.4
Kodak	7.9	Fuji	6.6
Xerox	5.4	Canon	5.2

Source: Hamel and Prahalad (1994), *Competing for the Future*, Tata-McGraw Hill, New Delhi.

to set the bar higher than they ever dreamed possible', says Jack Welch, former Chairman and CEO of GE (Welch 2001). 'Stretch means really challenging yourself and believing there is infinite capacity to improve upon everything you do', says Robert L. Nardelli, CEO, Chrysler and Home Depot, and former Head, GE Power Systems (Slater 1999).

Strategic intent

Incumbent players usually tend to dismiss or ignore competitors with meagre resources. Hamel and Prahalad conclude that starting resource positions are a very poor predictor of future industry leadership. The basic problem in strategic management is that too often competitors are judged in terms of resources rather than resourcefulness. According to them, getting to the future is more a function of resourcefulness than resources; do not sprout from an elegantly structured architecture, but from a deeply felt sense of purpose, a broadly shared dream, a truly seductive vision of future opportunities. Such a dream energizes the company, and is more sophisticated and more positive than a simple mission or vision. Hamel and Prahalad call this dream the strategic intent. While strategic architecture may point the way to the future, it is the ambitious and compelling strategic intent that provides emotional and intellectual energy for the journey. If strategic architecture is the brain, strategic intent is the heart.

According to Hamel and Prahalad, strategic intent implies a significant stretch for the organization. Current capabilities and resources are not sufficient for the task. While the traditional view of strategy focuses on the 'fit' between existing resources and emerging opportunities, the strategic intent, by design, creates a substantial 'gap' between resources and aspirations.

Direction, discovery, and destiny—The attributes of strategic intent

A strategic intent implies a particular point of view about the long-term market or competitive position that a firm hopes to build over the future or it conveys a sense of direction.

A strategic intent is differentiated or implies a competitively unique position about the future. It offers employees the promise of exploration of new competitive territory or it conveys a *sense of discovery.*

A strategic intent also has an emotional edge to it; employees perceive it as a goal inherently worthwhile or it implies a *sense of destiny.*

Hamel and Prahalad cite examples of companies that attained leadership with strategic intent as shown in Table 6.4.

TABLE 6.4   Attaining leadership with strategic intent

Yesteryears' winners	Current winners
Volkswagen	Honda
Xerox	Canon
RCA	Sony
Pan Am	British Airways
Sears	Wal-Mart

Monitoring Strategic Pursuits

While the board's role in the development of strategy may vary depending on the role it assumes in a company, the board definitely has a role in monitoring the chosen strategy. While strategy chosen might be for a longer term, say five years, monitoring has to be done at frequent intervals. The board has to devise metrics which will enable them to understand the progress of strategy. The board has to pose probing questions to management in order to understand how the company's actions enable customers to find solutions to their problems, ascertain that the firm has operational efficiencies to make it competitive in the marketplace, etc. The board has to get the management to explain the causes for variances if milestones in the strategic plan are not met.

SURVEILLANCE ROLE OF THE BOARD

As seen earlier, one of the key tasks of the board is to delegate proper authority to managers, leaving the directors with sufficient time to design the destiny of the company, do things that will enhance the reputation of the organization, or at least control the management from indulging in acts that will affect the reputation of the company, and also protect the interests of the company as a separate legal entity. The board has to keep a vigilant eye on the acts of management while enabling it to carry out those actions which will help the company not only to sustain but move forward. The surveillance role of the board includes monitoring the financial health and operating performance, and risk assessment (Charan 2005).

Monitoring Financial Health

Charan (2005) feels that 'looking at earnings reports alone is not good enough for governance. The board must be forward-looking and anticipatory in making sure that the company stays financially viable at all times.... Many companies' grand visions dissolved because of inordinate amounts of debt taken during good economic times.' The board has to clearly understand that looking at net income and earnings alone could be misleading. They must look at the cash position and cash flow—the availability of cash or the liquidity of the company. They should understand where the cash is coming from and where it is going. The board needs to keep a watch on the company's long-term obligations and must be alert on how to tackle adverse scenarios. Often, boards leave the financial health monitoring to the management but may suddenly be taken by surprise in a downturn. That may lead to a downgrading by rating agencies, which may in turn, affect the company's ability to mobilize resources in tough times.

Monitoring Operating Performance

Financial statements are a manifestation of how the business has performed in the past. The board should actually be concerned about those operational activities that bring in financial results or cash, and must develop suitable metrics to ascertain their performance. Market share, the relation of market share and price points, customer satisfaction, market share/revenue share/ profit share of new products introduced by the company, say in the last two/three years, etc., need to be examined. Please note that these parameters need be looked at not in isolation but in comparison to competitors.

Monitoring Risk

As is common knowledge, every company is exposed to risks other than financial risks. Risks can be spread across the various aspects of business, right from the internal execution, supply chain, customers, labour issues, competition, environmental issues, economy, to natural disasters and outbreak of wars, all with their effect on the financial health of the company. There may also be specific risks such as geographical concentration of customers, political, legal, and regulatory. Charan suggests the formation of risk committees by boards to assure themselves that they understand the major risks the company faces. The committee can work on identifying early warning signals so that the management can develop plans to mitigate these risks.

Well-governed companies spend a good amount of time assessing risk and finding ways of mitigating their effects. For example, Infosys has formed a risk management committee which has adopted the following terms of reference.

The purpose of the risk management committee shall be to assist the board in fulfilling its corporate governance in overseeing the responsibilities with regard to the identification, evaluation, and mitigation of operational, strategic, and external environment risks. The committee has overall responsibility for monitoring and approving the risk policies and associated practices of the company. The risk management committee is also responsible for reviewing and approving risk disclosure statements in any public documents or disclosure.

Big companies such as Infosys and smaller companies such as Carborundum Universal detail the risks they may be subjected to as also the steps or initiatives taken to mitigate the impact of such risks. However, many of the bigger companies, such as RIL, have not formed any committees for risk assessment and management. Even though such companies could be subjected to much larger risks and on a wider spectrum their steps to identify and take action to mitigate them do not find any detailed treatment if one goes by what their boards state in their annual reports.

Information Needs of the Board and Supply Mechanism

Boards need a lot of information for decision-making and surveillance. Most of the boards get a routine MIS (management information systems) report, which is a very structured form of periodical information about various routine performance aspects of the organization. While boards may use them, the information needed by the BOD has to match its responsibilities (Gupta 1997). According to Charan (2005), the information needs to vary depending on the different stages of board evolution. He refers to the creation of an information architecture in the company so that the board gets the right information at the right time (Exhibit 6.4). Everybody knows that most of the information that the board needs comes from management. He says that directors are uniformly frustrated by the low quality of information they get. According to him, 'progressive boards work with management to design in advance what information they need. Directors put their hands together with the CEO not only on what information is provided but also when it is provided. This way the board knows what to expect and when to expect it.'

Exhibit 6.4
Charan Suggests Establishment of a Five-Channel Information Architecture

- Channel 1. Board Briefing: A comprehensive report that captures the current state of affairs without any jargon, enabling the BOD to prepare before each board meeting.
- Channel 2. Management Letter: A short topical letter from the CEO that keeps the board abreast of current conditions within and outside the company, between meetings.
- Channel 3. Employee Survey: A periodic instrument the board can request from management to monitor a specific set of issues.
- Channel 4. Director Outreach: The commitment of time to visit stores or plants, speak directly with line managers, attend conferences, and otherwise experience the business firsthand.
- Channel 5. Reports from Committees: Recommendations and relevant background information presented to the full board.

Source: Charan, Ram (2005), *Boards that Deliver*, Jossey-Bass, San Francisco.

Gupta (1997) has narrated some of the perennial problems with which boards concern themselves. Table 6.5 gives a list of such concerns along with the information needed to address these concerns.

TABLE 6.5   Board's concerns and related information

Concerns	Information
How well is the company performing? In particular, is it performing to its full potential?	Monthly/quarterly performance reports; Capacity utilization; interfirm comparison, plant visits, informal chats with senior managers at lunch, etc.
Are performance targets being set reasonably high and are they being met?	Annual operating budget, periodical performance reports, changes in market shares
Is the board being told the whole truth, or are problems being swept under the carpet?	Non-formal information sources; plant visits; oral presentations by divisional managers to the board
Does the company have a satisfactory budgetary planning and control system?	Budgets and performance reports
Are ethical standards being observed?	Internal audit reports; complaints from any sources
Does internal audit reveal any serious weaknesses in the internal control system?	Internal audit reports and discussions with auditor
Are the trouble spots which may endanger the company's future and what is being done about them?	Divisional/product group performance
How does the future look for the company?	Trend information; long-term plans covering 3–5 years.
Is it heading for trouble?	Performance reports and trend analysis
Are any of the major divisions not performing well? If so what is being done about it?	Divisional reports and oral presentations by divisional managers
Is there good planning and control system for new capital projects?	Memorandum for board on capital expenditure proposals and discussions with concerned executives; capital expenditure budget and progress reports
How good are divisional managers; are they fully seized of the problems in respective divisions?	Oral presentations by divisional managers about their charge
What trends are discernible in the company's business?	Trend analysis for the company together with industry-wide trend data

Boardroom Harmony not at the Expense of Truth

The board is a body of directors who should gel into a cohesive group showing enormous collegiality. Its aim must be to arrive at a consensus, but not at consensus at any cost.

Whenever a director feels uncomfortable about any issue, he/she must have the courage to raise the issue. Most of the boards and directors themselves consider dissent as bad. If there is dissent about the company's well-being from any of the angles, the board should encourage different and even dissenting viewpoints in order to arrive at better decisions. Board meetings should become a forum where discussion and debate takes place rather than endorsing the views and decisions of an influential CEO/chairman. Harmony in the boardroom is highly desirable but that should not come at a cost. As Cohen and Bradford say about leading cross-functional teams, and this is equally applicable to boards, 'You don't have to create a team where everyone loves working with everyone else, but you want people to feel open and direct because that is what gets the best results' (Cohen and Bradford 2006). Bad news, if any shall also be brought on the table and discussed from all angles.

THE BOARD AS A LEARNING ORGANIZATION

Revan's proposition $L \geq C$ states that if organizations want to survive and grow, their rate of learning has to be equal to or greater than the rate of change in their environment (Garratt 1996). Since environments undergo many changes, some of them dramatic and even punishing, organizations have to be in a continuous learning mode and failure to do so will lead to their demise. In this context, organizations have to be adaptive organisms.

Look at great organizations such as GE, DuPont, or Harley Davidson. They have been able to achieve sustained success because they were always one up in learning and adapting vis-à-vis the environment. 'Changes in the environment will force the organization to face 'moments of truth' with respect to customers, competitors, employees, regulators, shareholders, or any or all of the stakeholders (Garratt 1996). For example, answers to questions such as Who is your customer? Why do they buy from you? How many of them come for repeat purchases? Who are your competitors? Why do customers buy from them rather than from you? Do your customers perceive 'value for money'? How do you create such a perception in the customers' minds? and similar questions with respect to other stakeholders will lead to exposing the company to the various moments of truth. The board must also have reasonable depth of knowledge about such moments of truth. While much of this information has to come from management, it is unlikely that management will provide this information unsolicited. The board has to be in a continuous learning mode if it has to solicit and use such information. A board which functions as a learning organization will be actively and fully involved and committed to the causes of the organization. The chances of such boards being taken by surprise by changes in the environment are less as they may have developed a great deal of insights. They will also be able to weather many a storm. Most boards are taken by surprise, as in the case of Satyam. Had the directors been on a continuous learning mode, they would have sensed the moments of truth about the various developments that ultimately led to the downfall of the organization. In a matter of days, the reputation of the board as leaders of a well-governed corporate entity, as well as its erudite and eminent members, came to nought. So, every board must act as a learning organization and must take leadership in making the organization a learning one (Garratt 2003).

EMPOWERED BOARDS

Experts on corporate governance concur on the empowerment of the board as a necessary prerequisite for good governance. A sign of empowerment is whether the board acts independently of the management. When we talk about acting 'independently of the management', it means acting in an objective manner in the best interests of the company and its entire stakeholders rather than acting parochially to protect the interests of the promoters, or families, or the shareholders/groups who have a significant holding in the company (Kumar 2006). The word 'empowerment' in this sense is not used in the conventional sense.

In the current context, it is assumed that nobody can empower anybody (Spreitzer and Quinn 2001) and empowerment at the individual director level and at the collective board level has to happen out of volition (Bruch and Ghoshal 2004).

Empowerment and Board Leadership

Usually the CEO determines the culture of the board and many boards become captive to the CEO as he controls information, meetings, and even the management, and through this, the debates and dialogues in the boardroom. But good CEOs will consider the board as a competitive weapon and advantage. They will persuade the board to be involved in setting a vision and a set of core values for the company, strategic direction, and allocation of resources, in addition to its routine goals in governance.

What Hampers Empowerment?

Issues relating to both structure and process can hamper empowerment. The major pitfalls that affect empowerment are (Kumar 2006):

Failure to deal with paradoxes of corporate governance

According to Phan (2000), there are three paradoxes of governance:

1. The board is the highest authority in a company yet has to face the reality that it is the management that controls the information required to exercise oversight
2. Board members are expected to provide critical judgement on the performance of the corporation, which requires members to get personally close to the management and yet remain objective observers of managerial behaviour.
3. While individual board members rely on each other to make good decisions, they have to be individually as well as collectively accountable for these decisions.

These paradoxes create an implicit tension in the boardroom. Empowered boards accept these paradoxes as given and do not seek to eliminate them, but try to use them advantageously by adopting a structure that is essentially independent of managerial influence, yet sensitive and responsive to managerial concerns. Boards enjoy and exercise power de jure or by virtue of the legal authority they possess, whereas managements have de facto authority, by virtue of their control over resources and information, essential for decision-making by the boards. Empowerment is not about transferring power and using such transferred power but acting out of willpower or volition.

Lack of independence for real

Empowerment in the real sense happens when the board shows the willpower to think independently of the management and to act in the overall interest of the corporation and all its stakeholders rather than in the interests of a group of stakeholders, management, or themselves. The structural initiatives at independence will not result in real independence and empowerment. Only empowered behaviour of directors will ensure real independence. As James Kristie, editor, *Directors and Boards* said, 'Independence is a state of mind. You could have seemingly the most conflicted director turn out to be the most independent person on the board' (Shultz 2001).

Failing to recruit the right people

Most director recruitments take place from a point of view of comfort for the CEO in particular and other directors in general. Good governance essentially measures good people and little else matters. While in principle, directors are elected by shareholders, in practice they are just nominated by the nominations committee at the suggestion of the CEO. The policy seemingly used to be 'you scratch my back, I'll scratch yours'. Failure to recruit strategically can thwart any attempt towards empowerment.

Conflicts of interest

Often, directors who get nominated are from the company's investment banks, venture capital firms, commercial banks, solicitors, partners of the management consulting firm the company hires for restructuring, or the tax consultant, each giving rise to conflicts of interest. Since their professional association with the company depends largely on the closeness and loyalty towards the CEO and the top management, it is very unlikely that they may take an independent view that is different from that of theirs. While laws for disclosure of such conflicts of interest exist, they can never alleviate the existence of them. Even SOX permits such conflicts of interest.

Lack of/prevention of adequate information flow to the board

Any board, however famous it may be for its membership and structure, cannot do its job if it lacks information—information that is appropriate, intelligent, and comprehensive. Most managements either give the board information that is too little to take meaningful decisions or flood it with too much information so that it becomes difficult to separate the wheat from the chaff, and at times, even resort to handing over information at the last minute. There is no agreed format or frequency and guarantee of correctness as far as information to the board is concerned. Constricted information flow was a practice of many a controlling CEO.

Lack of clarity of roles

Many boards do not have clarity about their roles. According to Carter and Lorsch (2004), 'Boards rarely discuss their roles explicitly. Nor do they change their roles when circumstances change.' Boards usually do not determine their role within the strategic, legal, as well as social context, even when they enjoy a great deal of freedom in doing this. Many boards relegate themselves to a role of legitimizing, which is substantially different from the role of policy maker and guardian of shareholders' and public interest as contemplated in the very framework of joint stock companies. While the essential role of the board is overseeing the management, each board must explicitly choose the role it will play and the choice must be founded on the good understanding about the company's specific situation and needs. Lack of clear definition of the board's role hampers empowerment to a very large extent and results in lack of focus, failure to prioritize on ethics and values, being away from business realities, lack of preparation, poor listening, and even absenteeism.

Myths about best practices

We saw a list of best practices such as:

- Director independence, 'the more, the better'
- Financial alignment of the directors with shareholders through stock ownership
- Vigorous monitoring of management's activities and performance
- Director 'generalism' rather than specialization (except for committee memberships)
- The shareholder–value overemphasis

While apparently all these sound very sensible, encouraging, and even worthwhile, these assumptions are also beset with self-defeating flaws, as we saw earlier in the 'best practice contradictions' (refer p. 269).

Failure to learn and change

Most of the directors of boards simply do their duties to conform to the essential requirements rather than improve the performance of the board and the company. Since the board has the ultimate accountability for any organizational activity, it should keep itself informed about everything that happens within the organization and in the environment (refer to 'Board as a learning organization', page 304).

Lack of enthusiasm and commitment due to poor compensation levels for NEDs

According to James Kristie, editor of *Directors and Boards*, 'Directors are one of the last great bargains. They are underpaid for the work they do and the responsibility they assume' (Shultz 2001). While of late, a positive change has been visible, NED compensation can still be considered to be miniscule even in many large companies in India, for example, Hero Honda. While the CEO and the WTDs take about Rs 154 million as compensation, the NEDs of the company get paid approximately Rs 1 million (2007–08) resulting in a ratio of approximately 150:1 between the salaries of WTDs and NEDs. In the previous two years (2006–07 and 2005–06), the ratio was even bigger at 488:1 and 587:1, respectively. The improvement in 2007–08 happened because the company decided to reward the NEDs with commission for their services, in addition to sitting fees. See Exhibit 6.5 for more information.

Lack of mechanism for evaluating the performance of the board and the individual directors

Very rarely is a formal mechanism reported to exist for the self appraisal of the board or peer review of directors at an individual level. Without a mechanism, it becomes difficult to evaluate performance. It is essential to install such a mechanism since it is necessary to evaluate the performance with respect to the governance charter (if one exists) and the goals set by the board.

Exhibit 6.5
India Inc. Needs a Large Number of Independent Directors. How Well Are They Remunerated?

Progressive boards are responsible for millions to be added to the bottom line through active participation in strategic direction, right CEO appointment, risk management, succession planning, etc. In India, while the CEO and other whole-time directors are paid hundreds of millions of rupees as compensation, the NED pay levels are usually in thousands, exceptionally in lakhs, and rarely in millions. Take the case of the biggest private sector company in India, Reliance Industries Ltd, with revenues of nearly Rs 750,000 million and a net income of Rs 75,720 million, which pays its CEO Rs 217.2 million. But, the highest paid NED gets only Rs 0.58 million. Hero Honda, the biggest two-wheeler maker in India and motorcycle maker in the world, pays around Rs 130 million to each of its four whole-time directors, whereas the highest an NED gets is Rs 0.28 million. How do we expect the NEDs to be fully committed to their jobs? Since, they were also top-level executives (most of the NEDs are retired top management people) and are accustomed to a certain lifestyle fitting to their position, they would definitely be on the look-out for more directorships in order to make good money, resulting in dilution of attention in every company. Of course, there are examples of much smaller companies such as Ucal Fuel Systems, Godrej Consumer Products (with respective revenues of Rs 2,714 million and Rs 5,630 million, and respective net incomes of Rs 258 million and Rs 900 million), etc., which pay their NEDs well (minimum for Ucal Fuel and Godrej Consumer Products were respectively Rs 1.395 million and Rs 0.885 million) (all figures are for the year 2004–05).

Discussion Questions
1. Do you think that independent directors in India should be remunerated decently to motivate them to contribute?
2. Can there be a recommended formula for compensating independent directors and other non-executive directors?

Source: Annual reports of RIL, Hero Honda, Ucal Fuel Systems, and Godrej Consumer Products.

'The height of a good board is its willingness to evaluate itself', says Lois D Juliber, Director, DuPont and former Vice-Chairman, Colgate–Palmolive (Charan 1998).

GOVERNANCE AS A CULTURE—THE NEED FOR STRATEGIC INTENTION

Post 2000, consequent to the high profile corporate failure of companies such as Enron, WorldCom, Tyco, Parmalat, etc., and liquidation of the large, reputed accounting firm Arthur Andersen, many developed nations have made their corporate governance regulations more stringent. The US has even chosen to create a specific law (the Public Accounting Reform and Investor Protection Act 2002, popularly known as Sarbanes–Oxley Act, after Paul Sarbanes and Michael Oxley, senators who drafted the law and SOX for short) as a result of the pressure on the policy makers to act to mitigate the concerns of investors, politicians, and the public. A majority of the other developed and developing countries, including India, have chosen more moderate paths in the form of listing agreements or guidelines. The market regulator in India, SEBI, has initiated steps to strengthen corporate governance by incorporating

Clause 49, by and large inspired by Cadbury Report and SOX, making it mandatory as part of the listing agreement.

The question that troubles the minds of governance watchers is how far these external regulations or even laws will be successful in permeating good governance. While regulations are necessary, they alone will not guarantee good governance. Many companies conform to most or all of the regulatory requirements. Satyam, from India, is a very good example. Simply having IDs will not result in better governance.

While individuals as IDs exhibit an independent mindset or thinking, they have to remember that the board has to function as a group. The board has to collectively view corporate governance from a strategic perspective. They should be able to visualize together the strategic benefits of good governance in a competitive scenario. This requires the board to have a solid, well-founded intention when it comes to governance. This, in turn, necessitates that it subscribe to a set of values and principles of governance, and also communicates to the entire organization.

A culture of good governance involving performance on all fronts, discipline, strict conformance to regulations, openness, transparency, ethical values, trust, customer orientation, care for society, etc. has to be created for it to sustain beyond the current board and management, and for ever.

Good governance is not accidental. It has to be intentional. The board and the company have to make it happen.[1]

LEVERAGING GOOD GOVERNANCE FOR COMPETITIVE ADVANTAGE

The role of the board also includes protection and creation of enterprise value. In a competitive market scenario, the value of a company's stock is considered to be proxy for the enterprise value. Stock prices rise in comparison with others when the company's competitive position is better than that of others. And today, everybody concurs that the board can play a very decisive role in sharpening the company's competitiveness. Such boards and directors 'listen probe, debate, and become engaged in the company's most pressing issues. Directors share their experience and wisdom as a matter of course. As they do, management and the board learn together, a collective wisdom emerges, and managerial judgement improves. The on-site coaching and counselling expand the mental capacity of the CEO and the top management team, and give the company a competitive edge out there in the marketplace', according to Charan (1998).

Regulations and penalties for non-compliance may force companies on compliance and prevention of small frauds (and in some companies such as Satyam, which apparently was complying with all the corporate governance requirements, the CEO had to make an admission to an ongoing fraud of massive dimension for many years, catching even the regulators by surprise and forcing the government to supercede its board and appoint its own nominees). By and large, such regulations or penalties have not resulted in better governance and competitive advantage. The competitive advantage will arise from the judgement of directors and not from the structures imposed by regulators. The collective judgement and wisdom of directors will help management

---

[1] Adapted from Satheesh Kumar T.N., *Beyond Balance Sheet Good Looks: Corporate Governance Needs Passionate Commitment to Make It Work in Any Organization*, *Hindustan Times*, Mumbai, 16 January 2007.

and enable the company to have a competitive advantage. The active participation of the board in company matters, such as, strategy development and monitoring, continuous learning, risk assessment and management, evaluating the performance of the CEO and top management, etc., will enable it to create a competitive advantage for the company.

ETHICS, VALUES, AND BEING A GOOD CORPORATE CITIZEN

While any discussion on ethics deals with the moral standards the company has set for itself, post scandals such as Enron, WorldCom, or Parmalat, highlight expectations not only about adherence to such standards but also about the standards themselves. While 'it is strongly agreed by some philosophers that the West live in a "post-ethical" society where everything is relative and there are no firm guiding values other than self-interest' (Garratt 2003), the Satyam episode has proved that such actions of self-interest have started their journey in the East too.

'This is especially true if the basic relationship between people ceases to be tolerance, thoughtfulness to others, civility, and obeying fair law, and instead becomes anything goes provided I don't get caught', according to Garratt (2003).

Most enterprises work on an ethical foundation. Without such a foundation, it will be impossible to create and sustain long-term relationships with shareholders, customers, employees, and legislators. Johnson & Johnson could handle the Tylenol issue wonderfully well because of the solid foundation of ethics it had built. This ethical foundation helped Johnson & Johnson not only to manage the issue, which theoretically speaking was not created by it, but also to salvage its reputation. Had it dismissed the issue as being not one of it creations and hence, not responsible for the same, it would have suffered public wrath. The actions helped the company being viewed with great respect. Please remember that the company decided to suffer the consequences of the withdrawal of the product, estimated at more than $100 million, during an era when maximization of shareholders' wealth was considered to be the overriding goal of the enterprise.

Michael L Sherman, CEO of AIG Europe, once said: 'A company's ability to meet the expectations of the important stakeholders associated with it—particularly its customers, business partners, investors, staff, and suppliers—has a significant impact on its profitability, its capacity to grow, and indeed its overall viability. This is why reputation has moved out of the public relations area and into the boardroom. In markets where companies are having to strive harder in order to secure increasingly scarce resources and more demanding customers, reputation has the potential to be the single differentiating factor between a company and its competitors' (Harper 2005). Thus, it can be seen that reputation is a major intangible asset for any organization. If the company indulges in anything that causes ire and angst to its stakeholders, it can lead to a bad reputation for the organization and consequent loss of competitiveness in the marketplace. Sherman says that this intangible reputation asset can result in tangible benefits for the company such as:

- Create barriers to competition and inhibit the mobility of rival companies
- Attract the best recruits and therefore, help avert skill shortages
- Attract the best supply chain and business partners
- Enhance access to capital and attract investors

- Open doors to new markets
- Create a 'premium' value for a company's products and services, and
- Protect the business in times of crisis

As most experts agree, one of the important roles that a BOD needs to fulfil is to provide exemplary leadership to the organization. Leadership, in this sense, includes giving direction in the values and ethos that will define its culture. And, the leadership behaviour should demonstrate exemplary integrity embedded in it. It is only with this integrity that boards and directors can execute the fiduciary duty to the company they serve. Harper (2005) says that this fiduciary duty 'requires that they do not place themselves in a position where there is an actual or potential conflict between their duties to the company and their personal interests, or duties to third parties.' According to him, these obligations are met in various ways, in particular:

- Boards should ensure that their company complies with relevant laws, regulations, and codes of practices, refrains from any anti-competitive practices, and honours obligations and commitments.
- Individual directors should, at all times, comply with the law and set an example to help ensure that their company complies with laws and regulations governing its operations.
- Although not a legal obligation, each director should at all times respect the truth and act honestly in business dealings and in the exercise of all responsibilities as a director.
- Integrity should be the hallmark of each board member's conduct in decision-making, uninfluenced by shareholding or by business, political or personal commitments, and relationships external to his or her company duties.

As we have seen, most companies today feel that the expectations of the stakeholders about ethical standards are increasing. Companies must look at these standards as a source of competitive advantage as was proved by Johnson & Johnson almost a quarter century earlier. As Harper (2005) says, 'This approach considers good corporate citizenship as making good business sense, so that every one wins.'

Many companies have drawn statements that will act as guidelines for the board, as well as employees, to follow. Named as statement on policies/code of conduct/ethical code of conduct/ principles/values, etc., most of them attempt to clearly direct employees towards certain behaviour or conduct that they are expected to adhere to. Institutes of business ethics recommend that the following areas be considered while such a document is drawn up:

- General principles to be adopted
- Relation with customer
- Relation with shareholders
- Relation with employees
- Relation with suppliers
- Relation with government and the local community
- Relation with competitors
- Issues relating to international business

- Behaviour during merger and takeover
- Compliance and verification

For example, Infosys has a code of ethics for principal executives and senior financial officers which is applicable to all members of the board, the executive council, and senior financial officers. This code is in addition to the code of business conduct applicable to all employees and the company expects directors to adhere to it. There are two instances where the company enforced its code of conduct on its directors who deviated from the code. In one case, Mr Srinath Batni, wholetime director, was fined Rs 0.5 million in September 2006 for not informing the board that he had sold his holding within the stipulated timeframe (twenty-four hours). Only last year its CEO, Mr Gopalakrishnan was asked to pay a fine of Rs 0.5 million for not informing his board of a transaction in the company's shares between him and one of his family members. And, yet another independent director, Prof. Jeffrey S. Lehman was fined $2000 for failing to make timely disclosures regarding transactions (*The Economic Times* 2008).

Here the board has installed not only a code for every employee, including directors, to adhere to but also behaved in an exemplary manner for the employees. This type of behaviour from the higher echelons of the company results in communication of the good intentions to all stakeholders who admire the company, and hence its reputation among the stakeholders increases.

Thus, the board and the directors can initiate and sustain action directed at furthering the ethical behaviour of the organization as a whole in its environment, which will enable it to improve its reputation among all stakeholders.

In today's world, corporations also have to show good citizenship. As Charan (2007) said, 'Every business today operates in a complex societal and political milieu that demands more of it than just profits. Gone are the days when Milton Friedman could proclaim that 'the business of business is business'. It is a foregone conclusion that business leaders have to be able to deal with market forces, and over the years they have learned to live with them. In the twenty-first century, business leaders will be required to deal with issues that go beyond the market.' Thus, companies have to worry not only about the financial performance but also about the physical environment performance as well as the members of society. Shell has propagated the whole idea in the term, 'triple bottom line—profits, people, and planet (www.shell.com). While companies have a tendency to ignore the two Ps other than profits, a company will suddenly be taken by surprise when members of society retaliate by declaring a moratorium on its products. Hence, directors have to see that the company behaves like a good citizen, taking care to improve the living standards of the members of society.

SUMMARY

While boards continue to be a legal requirement and compliance is a necessity, stakeholders expect more from boards beyond just compliance. They expect them to guide the company in a constructive manner, so as to take it forward to meet the expectations and the value enhancement of all stakeholders. Despite attempts to make the board the ultimate authority of a company (which it legitimately is), it is generally the CEO who controls the board and shapes its culture. While best practices have been proposed, each of them has contradictions embedded in it. Despite such contradictions, attempts have been made in the form of structural changes on the board such as composition, number of meetings, splitting of chair and CEO positions, etc. Many feel that such structural changes have their own limitations as is demonstrated by the way some companies have been grounded on account of poor governance.

Many companies failed because the boards did not play their necessary roles. Boards have a definite role to be played in the strategic arena of the company. While they may not get involved hands on in strategy development in all companies, it has to definitely assume the oversight role. There must be clear delineation of authorities between board and management in strategic aspects. The extent of involvement of the board depends on whether the board wants to adopt a pilot role or a watchdog role. Experts have clearly identified the areas to be taken on by boards in the strategy process. A number of tools are available today for boards (as well as for managements) to check which strategy is suitable for the company in the given circumstances. It would help them to make better decisions if they are conversant with the tools of strategy. The tools that boards consider may vary from conventional and simple ones such as SWOT analysis to some of the latest trends such as balanced scorecard, strategy mapping, or the blue ocean strategy. Many businesses have failed because they stuck to the old business model in spite of overwhelming changes in the environment. Business models have to be innovated in view of the dramatic changes that take place. Boards have to monitor the strategy as it gets implemented, and must be concerned about and continuously monitor the financial health of the company, its operating performance, the risks it is exposed to, etc. In order to do this, boards need a great deal of information and most of these information inputs have to come from management. With managements controlling most of the information the boards need for decision-making, a clearly defined mechanism or architecture for provision of these inputs needs to be established. Boards must consider themselves as learning organizations and be in a continuous learning mode, not only using the information supplied by managements, but also gathering data on their own. While harmony in the boardroom is highly desirable, the attempt must be to bring the truth even if it is bad. Boards have to become empowered in order to enter into a meaningful dialogue, debate, and even encourage dissent. Empowerment is determined by the culture of the board. Every attempt shall be made to eliminate those factors which hamper empowerment. The leadership has to see that the company develops a culture for better governance throughout and consider better governance as a competitive advantage. Boards also have to ensure that companies adopt definite ethical standards and imbibe those values which will enable them not only to be better governed but also become responsible corporate citizens. These factors can become a set of intangible assets to the company which can create a competitive advantage.

KEY TERMS

Best practice contradictions   In-built opposite forces within best practices

Business model   Building blocks of business which bring money

Code of conduct   Expectations about dos and don'ts

Conformance   Compliance with laws and regulations

Contrarian views   Views which are different from the rest or mass

Corporate citizen   Corporate showing responsibility towards society

Diversification   Entering into diverse areas (of business)

Due diligence   Examining details to ascertain facts

Empowerment   Given power to act

Harmony   Pleasing combination resulting in agreement

Information architecture   Framework for information flow to and from the board

Leveraging   Using as a source of strength

Life cycle   Duration of the life of a product or industry

Monitoring   Following up to see whether things go as planned

Pilot   One who directs the object forward

Portfolio   Set of assets

Risk assessment   Estimating the impact of risk factors

Strategic intention   Strong feeling about strategy and the outcomes

Strategy mapping   Visual presentation of the cause and effect of strategy components

Surveillance   Keeping vigil

SWOT analysis   Analysis of strengths, weaknesses, opportunities, and threats

Triple bottomline   Performance measures to include societal welfare and environmental concerns beyond profits

Value chain   Different stages in business which add value to the raw material

Value innovation   Offer value which has not been perceived by the customer

Watchdog   One who is on constant vigil

CONCEPT REVIEW QUESTIONS

1. Why is it said that the so-called best practices have contradictions embedded in themselves?
2. Why do some experts express a dissenting note on best practices which are by and large universally accepted?
3. What is the role of the board of directors in risk assessment and management?
4. Diversified Ventures Ltd is a highly diversified company. Which strategic tools may come in handy for the board of this company?
5. How is the balanced scorecard different from other strategic tools available to the board?
6. Explain the surveillance role of the board.
7. Boards require information for all decision-making and management has the control on this. How can boards ensure that they get the right information at the right point in time?

CRITICAL THINKING QUESTIONS

1. Critically examine the role of the board in strategy making and monitoring in a company.

PROJECT WORK

Identify five publicly listed companies in your locality. Talk to the chairman/CEO/other directors about the steps taken by their boards for risk assessment and management. Comment on the initiatives of the boards.

REFERENCES

Ashby, Meredith D. and Stephen A. Miles (2002), *Leaders Talk Leadership*, Oxford University Press, New York.

Bruch, Heike and Sumantra Ghoshal (2004), *A Bias for Action: How Effective Managers Harness Their Willpower, Achieve Results and Stop Wasting Time*, Viking, Delhi.

Carter, Colin B. and Jay W. Lorsch (2004), *Back to the Drawing Board*, HBS Press, Boston.

Charan, Ram (1998), *Boards at Work*, Jossey-Bass, San Francisco.

Charan, Ram (2005), *Boards that Deliver*, Jossey-Bass, San Francisco.

Charan, Ram and Noel M. Tichy (1998), *Every business is a growth business*, Times Business, New York.

Cohen, Allan R. and David L. Bradford (2006), *Influence without Authority*, Wiley-India, New Delhi.

Colley Jr, John L., Jaqueline L. Doyle, George Wand Logan, Wallace Stettinius (2003), *Corporate Governance*, Tata McGraw Hill, New Delhi.

Garratt, Bob (2003), *Thin on Top*, Nicholas Brealey, London.

Garratt, Bob (2003), *The Learning Organization*, Profile Books, London.

Garratt, Bob (1996), *The Fish Rots from the Head*, Profile Books, London.

Hamel, Gary S. and C.K. Prahalad (1994), *Competing for the Future*, Tata-McGraw Hill, New Delhi.

Harper, John (2005), *Chairing the Board*, Kogan Page, London.

Kaplan, Robert S. and David P. Norton (1996), *The Balanced Scorecard*, HBS Press, Boston.

Kim Chan, W. and Renee Mauborgne (2005), *Blue Ocean Strategy*, HBS Press, Boston.

Kumar T.N., Satheesh, 'Empowered boards: Are we moving in the right direction?' Paper presented at *National Conference 2006 on Management Innovations for Growth* at ICFAI Business School, Ahmedabad (24 and 25 February 2006).

Lafley, Alan G. and Ram Charan (2008), *The Game Changer*, Crown Business, New York.

Pearce II, John A. and Richard B. Robinson Jr (2005), *Strategic Management*, Tata McGraw Hill, Delhi.

Phan, Philip H. (2000), *Taking Back the Board Room*, McGraw Hill, Singapore.

Porter, Michael E. (1980), *Competitive Strategy*, Free Press, New York.

Porter, Michael E. (1985), *Competitive Advantage*, Free Press, New York.

Pound, John (2000), 'The promise of governed corporation', *Harvard Business Review on Corporate Governance*, HBS Press, Boston.

Shultz, Susan F. (2001), *The Board Book*, East-West Books, Chennai.

Slater, Robert (1999), *Jack Welch and the GE Way*, McGraw Hill, New York.

Spreitzer, Gretchen M. and Robert E. Quinn (2001), *Company of Leaders*, Jossey-Bass, San Francisco.

The Economic Times, 'Infosys fines its CEO for violating insider trading rules', 23 January 2008.

Welch, John F. (2001), *Straight from the Gut*, Warner Books, New York.

www.shell.com.

Closing Case

Strategic Pursuits of Family-Managed Companies—Bajaj Auto Ltd vs Reliance Industries Ltd

Background Information

Bajaj Auto Ltd

Year went public:	1960
Revenue in 1960:	Rs 72 million
Rahul Bajaj became CEO:	1968
Product (1968):	Scooters
Revenue (1991):	Rs 12,199 million
Products (1991):	Scooters (major), Motor cycles (minor), Three-wheelers
Market position:	No. 1 in India and No. 3 in scooters in the world
Revenue in 2000:	Rs 42,155 million
Products:	Motor cycles (nearly 50 per cent of two-wheelers), Scooters (nearly 50 per cent of two-wheelers), Three-wheelers
Market position:	No. 1 but threatened by nearest competitor Hero Honda

Revenue in 2008:   Rs 30,973 million
Products: Motor cycles only in two-wheelers, three-wheelers
Market position: No. 2 in India behind Hero Honda
Current chairman (executive):   Rahul Bajaj
Current CEO: Rajiv Bajaj (son of Rahul Bajaj)

Reliance Industries Ltd
Year went public: 1977
Revenue 1977:   Rs 670 million
Dhirubhai Ambani became CEO: Right from inception
Products: Textiles
Revenue 1991:   Rs 21,050 million
Products: Textiles, Yarn, Petrochemicals
Market position: No. 1 in India in most areas
Revenue in 2000:   Rs 203,010 million
Products: Textiles (minor), Petrochemicals (major)
Position: Market leader in most of the products
Revenue in 2008:   Rs 13,92,690 million
Products: Almost the entire value chain from textiles back to petroleum and oil-drilling
Market position: No. 1 in India in almost every area and within No. 5 in the world in most of the product categories.
Current chairman and CEO: Mukesh D Ambani (became chairman in 2002 after the demise of D H Ambani)

Other information

Bajaj Auto
Founder: Jamnalal Bajaj, freedom fighter and Congressman, said to have been very close to Mahatma Gandhi

Rahul Bajaj: One of the first Indians to have an MBA from Harvard

Year 1994: The company collected funds equivalent to almost Rs 3,600 million from abroad through a GDR issue in order to enter into car manufacturing. However, it never ventured into cars because it felt that it would not be able to compete with Maruti on volumes as Maruti had already established itself as a major player. Later entrants such as Hyundai and Tata were successful with their cars. Recently, they seem to have plans for making small cars in a joint venture with Nissan.

Other areas where the company has entered into are: finance and insurance (both life and general).

In the post-liberalization period, Rahul Bajaj has been harping on the *Swadeshi* mantra and has vociferously supported the 'Bombay Club', a forum of Indian industrialists fighting for level playing ground vis-à-vis foreign competitors.

Expert opinion on strategy making of Baja Auto Ltd
To Rahul, nationalism is more than consumer sovereignty. It goes beyond saying, 'Given a choice of two equally good brands of an item, I will pick the Indian one.' Instead, it means, 'Even if the Indian item is (slightly?) worse, I should choose it', because, as Rahul will often

tell you, 'The colour of money is important.'.... The saffron squad who may soon anoint Rahul as their industrial icon, justifies this stance by referring to the old US slogan, 'Be American, buy American'.... The 'Be American, buy American' and 'colour of money' arguments can be illustrated by looking at Rahul's scooters.

Starting in the 1960s, Rahul has built a huge production, marketing, and delivery complex. Bajaj scooters dominate the domestic market; they are rugged and last a lifetime; the scooter plants have a very high level of cost efficiency; the company has no shortage of funds; and a Bajaj Auto scrip is a prize possession. If Rahul's products are so good, then why can't *Hamara Bajaj* penetrate the international market for scooters and become a world class Indian multinational? The answer, according to Rahul, can be found in the absence of a distribution network abroad, a limited range of products, and a very long time to develop new models compared to international competition. So, why didn't he address these issues until recently? He will of course, spew fire and brimstone, about four decades of socialism. I, for one, find it very difficult to believe that Bajaj Auto—with its huge cash surplus, in excess of Rs 1,500 crore—couldn't have used the 'breathing space' since 1985 to establish a distribution network, create snazzier products, and advertise in *Time*, *Newsweek*, and auto magazines, to build brand equity. If anyone could, Rahul could.

But he didn't. Why? Because it was not worth the bother. The domestic market was far too juicy for Rahul to slog and capture the competitive markets of East Asia and Europe.

Protect and prosper

Industrialists who today decry command economies and socialism were the real beneficiaries of the control *raj*. By pre-empting licenses, they prevented other competitors from entering the fray. Exports were largely for the plebians. The industrial patricians minted off the hugely protected domestic market. Today, Rahul needs 'breathing space' to put his international distribution network in place, improve R&D capabilities, and build brand equity. Fellow members of the *Mumbai Samiti* (*swadeshi* for Bombay Club) air equally noble objectives. Yet, it isn't credible. If he couldn't use a relatively protective regime to gear up to international levels from 1985 to 1997, why should we believe that he will do so in the next five years? The 'breathing space' that Rahul got, but didn't use since 1985, has much to do with the 'colour of money' in a protected regime. The breathing space that we haven't got can be seen in the colour of our children's lungs.

(Excerpts from Goswami, Omkar, 'Rahul's *Swadeshi*', *Business India*, 20 April–3 May 1998.)

Reliance Industries

Founder : Dhirubhai Ambani

Dhirubhai Ambani: Son of a teacher from Gujarat.

Was a clerk at a petrol station in Aden
Came back to India in 1958 and started trading in polyester yarn
Established Reliance Textile Industries Pvt Ltd in 1964
First Indian company to issue GDR
First Indian company to issue 50-year and 100-year bonds abroad

Expert opinion on strategy making of Reliance Industries Ltd

Business history relating to early Indian entrepreneurs clearly tells us that their approach to managing the future was entirely different from the forecasting-based planning models currently used by many large Indian companies. Jamshedji Tata's ability to seize and act on the strategic opportunity of setting up steel and textile mills was based on deep insights into the future direction of economic and industrial development of the country, matched by a similar understanding of the kinds of resources available to Indian industrialists in terms of raw material and markets. Walchand Hirachand was another such entrepreneur who saw the future not in terms of problems but opportunities, and built an industrial empire by acting upon his strategic insights and thinking.

Western influence

The post-independence expansion and growth of Indian industry was greatly influenced by western management styles and systems, which also dictated how to plan for growth and cope with the future. Essentially, these were systems-based techniques which tried to forecast the likely developments in the future and help the organization to adapt to this perception of the future. Budgeting was the beginning of system-based management, and by the early seventies, formal strategic (or long range) planning had become an accepted model for dealing with the future.

The intrinsic philosophy underpinning such a system was that there must be 'no surprises'. In other words, the attempt was to try and foresee what the future is likely to be in relation to our industry or activity, and take steps now to adapt ourselves to the change that is anticipated.

Change became a dirty word because it upset the apple cart and forced companies to depart from the 'way we do business here'. The result has been that the whole approach to managing the future has been based on a pessimistic adaptation to a future which bristled with all kinds of impediments in terms of control, regulation, tax levies, and so forth. A random selection of the statements of chairpersons of the top 50 private sector companies would indicate that most such companies feel deeply frustrated by government policies and environmental trends, such as, recession, international competition, imports, infrastructural problems, industrial relations, availability of credit and long-term funds, etc.

Unconventional success

In this scene appeared a remarkable strategic manager—Dhirubhai Ambani of Reliance Textiles. It is interesting to observe that everything that he has done seems to be very different from the conventional wisdom which forms the core philosophy and faith of Indian industry. Perhaps this is why most people do not quite know what to make of him, and explain away the outstanding and continued success of Reliance Textiles by rationalizing it either as a fluke, or worse still, manipulative in its content. Yet to everybody's consternation and amazement, Reliance continues to grow and is increasingly more successful, confounding the most ardent doomsayers. Like the sphinx, it refuses to disappear.

Tops in strategy

What explains this outstanding and continued success? The answer is that Ambani and his top managers represent some of the very best practitioners of insightful, perceptive, and courageous (or if you like, gutsy) strategic management. The distinction between Reliance and others is that it creates the future for itself rather than wasting time sobbing over governmental control and insensitivity of government policies. Simultaneously, it identifies the opportunities offered by the marketplace and the environment, and goes about with great vigour and purpose, developing distinctive capabilities which would lead to business success in its chosen fields. It refuses to accept adaptation to the projected future as the right strategic mode and typifies the basic strategic management approach of acting to seize opportunities which are emerging, as against adapting and reacting to anticipated changes in its existing business operations.

Gutsy approach

Two final issues need to be addressed. One is whether there is any assurance that such success, even if it was due to strategic management capabilities, will continue into the future. The answer of course, is that no assurance can be given. The probability however, is that Reliance Textiles and Dhirubhai Ambani will continue to move forward with their strategic management vision, a fine understanding of the marketplace and gutsy proactiveness to create new 'futures' for themselves. The real question to ask is whether courage and innovation are managerial 'commodities' which are susceptible to arithmetical measurements.

Creating the future

The second issue that needs to be addressed relates to the lessons to be learnt from the Reliance experience. Clearly, in our approach to dealing with the future we must move away from adaptation and forecasting, and see the future not as something messy which only complicates our lives. We must welcome it as an abiding source of new opportunities provided of course, we have the insights to relate such opportunities to our mission of growth and continuously increasing profitability, and the guts and courage to act in true entrepreneurial fashion, seizing new opportunities, and if necessary, getting out of current product-market postures, even though we might be very comfortable with them.

This would mean lesser emphasis on quantitative analysis beyond a point and putting an end to endless projections to convince ourselves that the future can be made risk-free by adapting to the projected change. On the other hand, it would require an external orientation, constantly finding out what is happening in the marketplace, what technologies are coming up, what are the new requirements of customers, and most importantly, how all these can be put together synergistically to forge a new strategy for the future and act upon it.

(Excerpts from Bhattacharya, S K, 'Strategic management: Reliance shows the way', *Business India*, 9–22 April 1984.)

Discussion Questions

1. Reliance Industries Ltd as well as Bajaj Auto Ltd are Indian family promoted and managed companies. But the growth of Reliance has been phenomenal compared to that of Bajaj Auto. RIL has grown in size as well as clout while Bajaj Auto has been pushed down from its *numero uno* position in two-wheelers. Do you think that the reason can be attributed to flawed strategic thinking? Good governance is expected to provide a competitive advantage to companies. Substantiate your reasoning.

PART III

THE STAKEHOLDER PERSPECTIVE

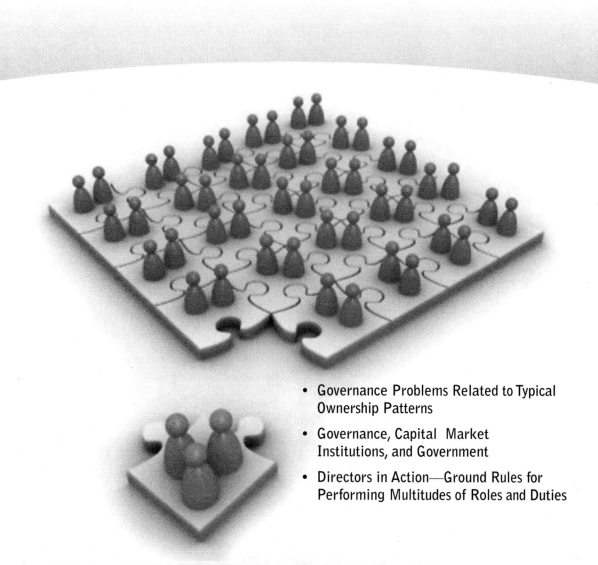

- Governance Problems Related to Typical Ownership Patterns
- Governance, Capital Market Institutions, and Government
- Directors in Action—Ground Rules for Performing Multitudes of Roles and Duties

CHAPTER 7

GOVERNANCE PROBLEMS RELATED TO TYPICAL OWNERSHIP PATTERNS

*Although most CEOs and directors understand and agree with the logic of the argument,
they still believe, often incorrectly, that they are accountable only to shareholders.*

— Jay Lorsch and Elizabeth MacIver in
Pawns or Potentates: The Reality of America's Corporate Boards

LEARNING OBJECTIVES

After studying this chapter, you will be able to

- List the different types of ownership structures of corporates
- Describe the typical governance issues that exist in family promoted and/or managed companies
- Define the best practices for governance in family-managed firms
- Understand governance-related concerns in companies where institutions hold major chunks of shares
- Describe governance of state-owned enterprises
- Explain conflicts of interest in various ownership structures
- Discuss remedial actions against conflicts of interest

Opening Case

Too Much Family on the Board—Comparison of Two Family-Managed Companies

A. Bajaj Auto Ltd

I. The annual report of Bajaj Auto Ltd for the year 2008–09 lists the board of directors as under:

Rahul Bajaj, Executive Chairman	D.J. Balaji Rao, Non-executive, Independent Director
Madhur Bajaj, Executive Vice-chairman	J.N. Godrej, Independent Director
	S.H. Khan, Non-executive, Independent Director

Rajiv Bajaj, Managing Director	Ms Suman Kirloskar, Non-executive,Independent Director
Sanjiv Bajaj, Executive Director	Naresh Chandra, Non-executive, Independent Director
D.S. Mehta, Non-executive, Independent Director	Nanoo Pamnani, Non-Excecutive, Independent Director
Kanti Kumar Podar, Non-executive Independent Director	Manish Kejriwal, Non-executive Director
Shekhar Bajaj, Non-executive Director	P. Murari, Non-executive,Independent Director
Niraj Bajaj, Non-executive Director	

There are a total of sixteen directors, of which seven are family members and hence, insiders. The designation of D.S. Mehta as a non-executive, independent director is questionable as he was a whole-time director of Bajaj Auto Ltd before the demerger in 2007–08.

II. Financials for the year 2008–09 (Rs million)

Sales	89,322.6
PBIDT	12,995.7
Interest	210.1
PBT	9,580.9
PAT	6,565.0

III. Compensation details of directors (Rs million)

Total remuneration: executive directors	146.10
Total remuneration: non-executive directors	5.95
Total remuneration to directors	152.05
Executive directors' compensation as a percentage of PAT	2.22%
Non-executive directors' copmpensation as a percentage of PAT	0.09%
Total compensation as a percentage of PAT	2.31%

IV. Ownership and control
Family: 50.28 per cent
Friends and associates: 11.37 per cent

B. Mahindra and Mahindra Ltd

I. The annual report of Mahindra and Mahindra for 2008–09 lists the board of directors as under:

Keshub Mahindra, Chairman, Promoter	R.K. Kulkarni, Independent Director
Deepak S. Parekh, Independent Director	Anupam Puri, Independent Director
N.B. Godrej Independent Director	A.K. Das Gupta, Independent Director
M.M. Murugappan, Independent Director	Anand Mahindra,Vice-chairman and Managing Director

| N. Vaghul, Independent Director | Bharat Doshi, Executive Director |
| A.S. Ganguly, Independent Director | A.K. Nanda, Executive Director |

The total number of directors in this company are twelve, of which two are family members. There are four insiders (including executive directors) and the remaining eight are independent.

II. Financials for the year 2008–09 (Rs million)

Sales	149,830
PBIDT	13,630
Interest	450
PBT	10,360
PAT	8,370

III. Compensation details of directors (Rs million)

Total remuneration: executive directors	51.57
Total remuneration: non-executive directors	10.46
Total remuneration to directors	62.03
Executive directors' compensation as a percentage of PAT	0.62
Non-executive directors' compensation as a percentage of PAT	0.12
Total compensation as a percentage of PAT	0.74

IV. Ownership and control
Family/promoters: 29.20%

Discussion Questions
1. Critically comment on the size of the boards of Bajaj Auto Ltd and Mahindra and Mahindra Ltd.
2. Do you think that the compensation paid to the different classes of directors have a bearing on the ownership pattern of the companies?

GOVERNANCE AND TYPICAL OWNERSHIP PATTERNS

Over a period of time since the incorporation of an organization, there may be a wider dispersion of ownership, whereby the original owners/promoters do not have physical control over the company. One of the compelling reasons for the concept of governance of the corporation was that the owners had to leave the control to a handful of professional managers. The varying ownership patterns themselves pose a challenge to governance. Even though the concerns of Berle and Means were not necessarily restricted to the US, typical ownership patterns exist in different economies, and each of these pose a different set of challenges to the governance of corporations. Of course, Berle and Means (1932) did say that 'while discussing problems of enterprise it is possible to distinguish between three functions: that of having interests in an enterprise, that of having power over it, and that of acting with respect to it. Single individuals may fulfill in varying degrees, any one, or more of these functions.' Also, economies are in different stages of development and have their own emphasis on the types and styles of ownership. For example, in the US, the original promoters of companies may have reduced their holding in favour of the public, making them typical proxies of what Berle and Means perceived, but a different picture of ownership emerges in India.

India followed the managing agency system, where the management of a firm rested with an industrial group who showed entrepreneurship and an agency's stakes in the companies they had managed. Ownership was not the only criterion for becoming a managing agent; it was the demonstrated managerial capability. On the concept and system, Tripathi and Jumani (2007) wrote: 'It is somewhat strange that expatriate firms like Birds and Andrew Yule in Calcutta, or Parry and Binny in Madras, function within the rubric of a managerial system perfected by the Indians. There was, however, a crucial difference between the functioning of the managing agency system in the Indian-controlled concerns and expatriate firms. While in the firms, the managing agencies continued to remain with promoters' families, in the latter, the partnerships controlling the managing agencies went on changing hands as the older generations continued to return home after relinquishing their holdings. There was one more difference: no Indian managing agency firm was ever placed in charge of the management of companies it did not control, while the expatriate managing agencies very often assumed a responsibility to manage the affairs of sterling companies operating in India.'

While the management of Indian-controlled concerns rested with the promoters' families, the ownership in such companies was not necessarily high. For example, the Tatas were rumoured to have held only a stake of about 4 per cent in Tata Steel, which was promoted and managed by them as agents. At times, there were outside investors (industrial families) who held higher stakes than the promoter families but the management and control rested with the promoter families, which nobody disputed. For example, Birlas had a stake of about 7 per cent in Tata Steel. Thus, management control without being a dominant shareholder was very much in vogue in India. A number of earlier corporations could have been well-governed by the promoters without the promoters having a significant stake in the company, which even today people such as Warren Buffet, consider as a desirable thing for better governance (Bebchuk and Fried 2004).

Infosys is considered to be among the better-governed companies in India even though the founders/promoters (non-family) hold only a total of 16.49 per cent (Infosys annual report 2008–09). While the size of the largest holding declined over a period of time in the US, as is confirmed by the analysis of Berle and Means, it is seen to be increasing in India, especially after the economy underwent a reform process after 1991 by making use of the new prescriptions in the capital market regulations. Even in Tata Steel, the Tatas today control about 33.95 per cent. This has also been true of some other big companies in India. The promoter family shored up their holdings because of the fear of threat from the consequence of some other company taking over. Table 7.1 shows the promoters' holding in the NSE fifty companies (Nifty) for the year 2008–09. 'F' indicates the family involvement as promoter and 'O' indicates the other category of promoters. 'NA' indicates that there are no identifiable promoters today.

TABLE 7.1 Promoter's holding in NSE fifty (nifty) companies
(as on 31 March 2009 and constituents as on 30 October 2009)

S. No.	Company	Promoter's holding (%)	Family/other (F/O)
1	RIL	49.03	F
2.	Infosys Technologies	16.49	O
3.	L&T	NA	NA
4.	ICICI Bank	NA	NA
5.	HDFC	15.03	O
6.	ITC	32.01	O
7.	SBI	59.41	O
8.	HDFC Bank	24.41	O
9.	ONGC	74.14	O
10.	Bharti Airtel	45.3 + 21.85	F + O
11.	BHEL	67.72	O
12.	HUL	52.06	O
13.	TCS	76.21	F
14.	Jindal Steel	58.75	F
15.	Sterlite Industries	61.71	F
16.	Axis Bank	27.08	O
17.	Tata Steel	33.95	F
18.	Tata Power	33.26	F
19.	Wipro	79.26	F
20.	IDFC	NA	NA
21.	M&M	29.2	F
22.	Maruti Suzuki	54.21	O
23.	NTPC	89.5	O
24.	JP Associates	45.24	F
25.	Reliance Infra.	35.95	F
26.	GAIL	57.35	O
27.	Tata Motors	33.42	F
28.	Grasim	25.2	F
29.	Cipla	39.38	F
30.	Hero Honda	28.96 + 26	F + O
31.	DLF	88.16	F
32.	Hindalco	31.42	F
33.	Reliance Communications	66.12	F

Contd

Table 7.1 contd

S. No.	Company	Promoter's holding (%)	Family/other (F/O)
34.	Cairn	64.68	O
35.	Unitech	64.52	F
36.	Punjab National Bank	57.8	O
37.	Sun Pharma	63.71	F
38.	SAIL	85.82	O
39.	Idea Cellular	57.69	F
40.	Reliance Capital	53.39	F
41.	Siemens	55.18	O
42.	ABB	52.11	O
43.	ACC	46.21	O
44.	Ambuja Cement	46.46	O
45.	HCL Technologies	67.54	F
46.	BPCL	55.79	O
47.	Power Grid	86.36	O
48.	Ranbaxy Laboratories	63.92	O
49.	Reliance Power	89.92	F
50.	Suzlon Energy	65.83	F

As we saw in Chapter 3, the problems related to governance in India are different from those in the US, where ownership and management are separate and distinct. In the US, governance can be described in terms of the agency problem whereas in the Indian context, the agent and owner are usually combined in one and issues can get very complicated if the governance issues are not handled properly. 'Ownership is the most important factor shaping the corporate governance in any country. The dynamics of agency conflicts inherent in a firm's structure influences all the decisions taken by the managers. Accordingly, the decision-making of owner-managers affects the market value of outstanding equity and the movement of the prices, as decision are determined in part by optimizations of management interests, which may not always be in the best interest of outside shareholders' (Som 2006). While privately promoted and publicly listed firms pose a typical set of challenges, the challenges posed by the governance of companies promoted by the government are different. They might be partly owned (as part of their share of the equity capital has been divested in favour of the public through a divestment process) making them just like other listed companies or fully owned by the government (and hence without any public participation), but corporate governance cannot be given any less importance. Compounding these may be the challenges posed by the subsidiary structures, cross-holding, etc.

Most theories of governance even today, rest on the premise that governance is required because there can be conflicts of interest between owners and managers in the running of the enterprise. As Wallace and Zinkin (2005) said: 'In the days when companies were owned and run by the same person in the family, there were no conflicts of interests between what the owner wanted to achieve and what the manager wanted to do. They were one and the same, so clearly their objectives were identical, and hence there were no problems.' Of course, the stakeholders got embedded as the proponents of the stakeholder theory, and in addition to the shareholders, it also brought in the different stakeholders into the whole perspective. While both these were right and are even today, the one thing that gets conveniently ignored or sidelined is the corporation itself. When we decide to establish or convert the economic entity into a form which is considered to have a life and existence, even though it may be artificial, why is it that nobody talks about corporate governance in the interest of the corporations from totally a shareholders perspective?

Corporate governance is the governance of a corporation in the best interests of a corporation—an effort to strengthen its very characteristics of unlimited life, ability to raise funds, and taxability of its profits—all related to the well-being and the sustainability of the corporation. Hence isn't it time to strengthen this view of corporate governance by strengthening the economic entity that it is, from a broad stakeholder perspective? Any issue related to corporate governance has to be viewed from the angle of whether it is in the best interest of the organization. Once this approach sets in, many of the so-called issues related to the specific ownership patterns will become meaningless. And the board of directors, the custodian of corporate governance under the corporate form, would take care of the interests of all stakeholders, including the owners. But this approach requires one (any stakeholder) to draw a clear line of demarcation between two things—the interests of the corporation and the interests of the shareholder group to which one belongs. The governance of the corporation would see a quantum jump if we approach it from a broader, what is best for the corporate view, rather than a narrow shareholder or even stakeholder perspective. This concept will invariably set in and then it will become very difficult to trace the original ownership/owners in the affairs of the company. A typical example could be GE, where no original owners or their successors are seen or considered to be interested in the conduct of the company.

Also, as Berle and Means proved in early 1932, as shareholding becomes widely dispersed, the relevance of the promoter owner gets lost. While our wish about a transition to 'what is best for the company' focus, as the corporate governance discipline evolves, let us try to understand the various governance issues that exist today in the context of different ownership patterns.

The ownership context of governance is the approach that is prevalent even today, even though the total stakeholder context is gathering steam. When it comes to the ownership context, the issue gets narrowed down to the lien on profits, the 'cash flow rights' as Das (2008) puts it as against the 'control' aspects over the assets of the corporation.

MOST COMMONLY OBSERVED OWNERSHIP PATTERNS

While there are different types of ownership structures and patterns for carrying out business, there are structures and patterns commonly observed from a corporate governance angle. The most commonly observed are as follows.

Widely distributed ownership with no one having dominant shareholding   This is typical of what Berle and Means had foreseen for the US. And even today, most of the companies in the US do not have any particular category of investors that are dominant. According to the US Federal Reserve Statistics, in June 2003 the ownership of US shares was as shown in Table 7.2 (Waring and Pierce 2005).

TABLE 7.2   Widely distributed ownership

Category	Shareholding (%)
Individuals	37
Mutual funds	18.9
(Corporate and Union Private)	
Pension funds	12
Foreign	10
State and local pension funds	8.4
Life and general insurance	7
Other	6.7

The above statistics show that ownership is widely distributed and hence no category can have a dominant holding. This pattern poses the greatest challenge in the corporate governance context. Typical agency problems are more prevalent in such companies. No shareholder will show any particular interest in furthering governance of the company. Every shareholder will assume that there are others who will take an interest in the affairs of the company unless some untoward incident happens, as in the case of Satyam. Satyam could be considered to be a typical example of this type of a company in India, which is very rarely the case.

Dominant shareholders with large block ownership   The large block holders could be promoters and their families, institutions such as investment banks, mutual funds, insurance companies, private equity or venture capital funds, etc. While promoters can be individuals or their families, they can also be companies from the home country or abroad. In India, the original promoters, their families, and associates, usually hold dominant stakes, sometimes even majority stakes or close to majority. For example, in RIL, the holding of Mukesh Ambani, his family, and associates, is 49.03 per cent according to the 2008–09 annual report. The promoter holding in the IT behemoth Infosys Technologies is put at 16.49 per cent in 2008–09; in Tata Steel it is at 33.95 per cent, while in Mahindra and Mahindra it is 29.2 per cent. Companies where individual institutions hold a dominant stake are rather rare in India; whereas in Germany there are companies that are controlled by a shareholder holding large block of shares or by banks through proxy vote on behalf of other investors; while in the UK, the percentage of ownership in the hands of individuals has fallen from about 54 per cent in 1963 to 14.3 in 2002. Consequently, the institutions have now increased their holdings to a level of 49.4 per cent (Waring and Pierce 2005).

Companies in which the government holds a majority stake   Such companies usually come into existence because of the divestment process initiated by the government which had earlier promoted these companies entirely in the public sector. Of course, there can also be instances where the government may form joint ventures with companies in the private sector. There are a number of companies in India such as BHEL, ONGC, SBI, and NTPC where the government has stakes varying from 67 to 89.5 per cent. France is another country where the government still has a wide degree of control despite several bouts of disinvestment initiatives. Such companies also pose a great challenge to corporate governance in India because they tend to be treated on par with any other publicly listed, privately promoted companies.

Companies that are fully state-owned   Since these companies have not issued any shares to the public, they may not come under the purview of the market regulator such as SEBI, but they have to be concerned about governance from a stakeholder perspective. Many companies in India which are fully owned by the government have also started serious deliberations into corporate governance.

Family-owned Firms

When family-owned businesses are relatively small, the family members themselves are able to direct and manage the enterprise and there are lesser issues of governance arising from the agency problems. This is because the ownership and control rests with the same group. This combining of ownership with management negates any issue of trust and the need for monitoring the activities of management. While many people advocate that those who manage the company should also own a reasonable amount of shareholding on the assumption that the manager's interests will be aligned with those of other shareholders, there can also be a downside to this. If the family owns a major chunk of shares and is also part of the management, the interests of minority shareholders in the company may get neglected. The managers may act to protect the interests of the family and not those of the shareholders in general.

The governance issues of family-owned enterprises deserve attention because about 80 to 90 per cent of all businesses in the world are family-owned, according to Paul Karofskey (Jain 2006) and according to Shalini Singh, globally, about 60 to to 70 per cent of GDP is generated by family businesses (Jain). Also, they generate huge employment, as depicted by the testimony of Richard Forrestel Jr, on behalf of the Association of General Contractors of America on 28 January 1998, which estimated the employment generation by family-owned businesses (FOBs) between 1977 and 1990 at 70 per cent of all jobs generated. The above-mentioned statistics clearly depicts the importance of family-owned enterprises in the business horizon.

In businesses owned by families but managed by professionals, conventional agency issues dominate and governance issues assume a typical dimension when the owners themselves manage the corporations. The biggest private corporate entity in India, namely Reliance Industries Ltd is still 49.03 per cent owned by the Ambani family and their associates acting in concert. Family management can have a lot of advantages for business as the family members meet informally and information dissemination can frequently happen voluntarily; and different members have different ideas, approaches, and strategies for businesses as in the case of Reliance Industries Ltd in India. There can also be issues related to the power equations within the family members, as well as between family members and the outside world.

In the formative years, business may run as a closed private affair but as the business grows, family members might not have all the expertise to handle different functions or may face paucity of members to handle various functions. When the family feels that they should have expert advice at the top level, they appoint outside experts as the board of directors. But Phan (2000) says that 'The role of the director on the board of a family-controlled business is advisory in nature. He is to act as a sounding board for the owner–manager and assert the strong council of an expert.' Shultz (2001) opines that 'just as with other small and midsize corporate boards, the board at a family company is an after thought. It is there because it is required when a company incorporates to do business.' And according to Richard Narva, principal at Genus Resources and consultant to family businesses, 'Commonplace wisdom has it that family businesses range from secret to hermetically sealed, and that both fiduciary and non-fiduciary governance bodies are merely rubber stamps' (Shultz). The governance issues are complicated in family-controlled businesses because, according to Phan, the type of relationship a director has 'is that of a trustee without the requisite fiduciary duty.' And, according to Phan, 'political issues belonging to the dining room table are often aired on the boardroom table.' According to him, political issues inherent in the family relationships manifest under three circumstances:

- During asset acquisition and disposal decisions as they can complicate the asset allocation among family members who take an active interest in the business
- During CEO succession since such issues are often viewed as birthrights, and
- During board appointments as these can affect the allocation of resources to family members managing the business.

All the above political issues were reflected in some of the high profile family splits in recent times.

The much publicized split between the Ambani brothers and the rivalry within the Bajaj group between Rahul and his brother Shishir were instances which showed how issues arise in family-owned and managed companies. Every family group has one or two highly performing companies in the one or two fast growing industries. Examples could be Hero Honda in the Munjal group, Bajaj Auto in the Bajaj group, or Ballarpur industries and Crompton Greaves in the Thapar group.

According to Kumar (2005), 'Better performing companies provide the members associated with them with opportunities for making more wealth in terms of better salaries, better dividends, and even better opportunities to increase the stake in their companies with the higher disposable income, and enter into new ventures rather easily on the strength of their wealth, while other members, managing less spectacular entities with lesser opportunities for making or acquiring wealth, might be deprived of such opportunities. Going by the conventional wisdom, such high performing entities are likely to be inherited by the member's sons/daughters, irrespective of their capabilities.'

Some members of the family might feel that they were deprived of such opportunities and this can lead to splits within the family as was the case in the Reliance and Bajaj groups. About the Bajaj family, Satheesh Kumar wrote: 'Mr Rahul Bajaj has been running Bajaj Auto since 1968 (till recently when he retired and became a part-time chairman), and the company performed well in the protected market till the nineties.... Why was it assumed that Mr Rahul Bajaj could manage Bajaj Auto better than his younger brother Shishir (or any other Bajaj) and gave him the mandate to hold on to the control over the blue chip for more than 35 years? And to top it all, why should children of Shishir (and/or other Bajajs) be deprived of the opportunities that the children of Rahul are exposed to? True, capabilities may differ; but who sits on the judgement of these capabilities? Questions such as these (even when labelled as hypothetical) and many more, when posed, may prove embarrassing and are extremely difficult to answer' (Kumar 2005). Issues such as these can arise in any family-managed company and the outside directors on the board of such companies are tested for their roles, actions, and decisions. Phan (2000) says that 'The effective director of such a board is one who is able to spot potential problems in the business–family link before they can erupt into crises, and is willing to warn the owner of the impending problem.'

Outside directors on the board of RIL were criticized by many experts and the media for the lethargy they showed and the passive role they played during the sibling feud, which culminated in the two-way split of the group. The rivalry within the Bajaj group took many years of litigation before the brothers amicably settled it in 2008. The boards have a very important role to play in the case of family-controlled companies which are public in nature, but where families control a major chunk of shareholding. For effective governance to happen in a family-controlled and managed company, Phan (2000) suggests that 'The role of senior family members who are also executive directors should be confined to that of an informational one and they should attend board meetings only to provide the managerial and family perspective. The task of the chairman on such a board is to ensure that interested party lobbying by family members are kept to the minimum to elicit the best contributions from the experts.'

It is the duty of the outside directors on the board to ensure that the interests of shareholders other than the family owners are protected and taken care of. Shultz (2000) quotes Richards Narva of Genus Resources thus: 'If there is even one shareholder who is not in management, then that owner deserves the same level of fiduciary care as all the stockholders of General Motors.'

Rajesh Jain provides a comparative analysis of family and business systems (see Table 7.3). The paradoxes in the family-controlled and managed companies are shown in Table 7.4.

TABLE 7.3 Comparative analysis of family and business systems

S. No.	Issues	Family system	Business system
1.	Ratoinale	Emotion-based	Accomplishment or task based
2.	Mission	Family harmony and mutual growth	Maximization of shareholders' returns
3.	Values	Loyalty, relationship, and protection	Competence and productivity
4.	Motivating factors	Love, share and care, parental approval	Stature, positions, remuneration, recognition
5.	Focus	Inwardly	Outwardly
6.	Approach	Resists change	Embrace change
7.	Membership	Event-based like birth, marriage, and so on	Need-based

Contd

Table 7.3 contd

S. No.	Issues	Family system	Business system
8.	Leadership	Generally undefined	Clearly defined
9.	Decision-making	Informal and gut-feel	Hierarchical and structured
10.	Evaluation	Generally none	Must
11.	Rewards	Tend to be equal	Competence-based
12.	Environment	Local social	Global

TABLE 7.4 Paradoxes of family controlled and managed companies

S. No.	Situation	Paradox
1.	Compensation	Family fosters equality; business needs to reward performance.
2.	Ownership	Family passes ownership to all, irrespective of the degree of involvement. But, business needs powerful managers. Hence, the most involved family member needs to have more ownership rights.
3.	Choosing successor	Family treats the eldest male heir as the leader; business requires the most competent to be the leader.
4.	Retirement	Families have leaders for life; business needs leaders who are tuned with the present realities and are suitable for the future.
5.	Professionalizing	Family tries to provide career opportunity to all members; business needs the fittest for the job.
6.	Control	Family needs to protect its investments by having control and direct supervision; business needs competent professionals who in turn need adequate freedom and hate micro-management
7.	Communication	Family members find it difficult not to carry over family experiences to business or vice versa. The way family members address one another in the business premises also reflects this carry over.
8.	Relationships	Family members find it difficult to act in an unbiased manner even in business settings. Many conflict of interest situations arise as a result. Sibling rivalry and generational conflicts cross over from one system to another.
9.	Speed of actions	Family reacts slow and takes time to adapt to new situations. Business requires fast decisions and reactions. When actions are dragged due to family influence, business suffers.
10	Values	Most family businesses adopt the value system followed by the owning families. For example, many families expect total obedience from juniors. When carried over to business, this may deprive the business from freshness and creativity. Businesses need to adapt fast to changing environments. Business today has a global context. In the process, many new values get picked up, which go against the values which the family strongly adheres to. For example, in marketing efforts, the business may require to indulge in partying to entertain customers or use cheer-girls to promote an important campaign or event.

Source: Adapted from *Chains that Liberate: Governance of Family Firms*.

According to Wallace and Zinkin (2005), 'Once owner-entrepreneurs or partners have decided to go to the market to access capital, divergence between the objectives of the dominant shareholder (the former owners or the owner's family) and those of the other shareholders, minority shareholders—often arise… In these circumstances, some former owner-entrepreneurs, at times continued operating as if nothing had changed. On occasion, owners undertook transactions that the other investors had no knowledge of; sometimes, those transactions were simply not what the new investors had put their money into the enterprise for.'

According to Phan (2000), 'The key success factors of a family business board are the seperation of business from family financial matters, and the creation of a non-family dominated board that is focused on the business decisions. Often, a family council may be constituted to focus on the family financial and political issues, and such a council may have an informal link with the business board to deal with the more sensitive issues.' Since family businesses play an important role in the economy of a nation, and also taking into account that they have social relevance and importance, an effective governance mechanism for family businesses is essential.

Family managed firms progress through four stages of development in the perspective of corporate governance, as shown in Fig. 7.1 (Mallin 2007).

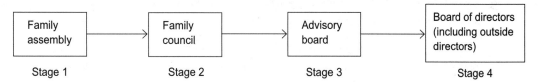

Fig. 7.1   Four stages of development in the perspective of corporate governance

Stage 1: The family assembly   In the early stages of the firm, the family will be small and the entire family can assemble and discuss the business.

Stage 2: The family council   As time passes, the family expands as does the business, and more members of the family may be involved in the affairs of the business. At that stage, a family council, drawn from representatives of different branches of the family must be constituted. According to Nenbaur and Lank, once the family strength goes beyond 30 to 40, a family council is advisable (Mallin 2007).

Stage 3: The advisory board stage   The growth in business may outgrow the family and family relationships themselves may affect its efficient running and development, or they may not realize that they are not managing the business as effectively as they can. They may seek the help of an advisory board constituted from experts in the business and organization contexts.

Stage 4: Board of directors   The final stage in the journey of governance of a family firm is the establishment of a board of directors which will include members from outside the family as directors. According to Adrian Cadbury, establishment of a board of directors in a family firm is a means of progressing from an organization based on family relationships to one that is based primarily on business relationships. The structure of a family firm in its formative years is likely to be informal and owes more to its past than to present needs. Once the firm has moved beyond the stage where an authority is vested in the founders, it becomes necessary to clarify responsibilities and the process for taking decisions (Cadbury 2000).

Jain (2006) suggests a three-pronged approach to enable family businesses to be better governed: setting up a family council, annual retreat, and family constitution.

Setting up a family council   When families are small, all members of the family can participate in the discussions about the business. But when they are large, not only does the participation by every member become next to impossible, but one also has to worry about the very relevance of it. Decision-making may be affected when a large number of members participate in the business proceedings. Hence, it is suggested that a family council be set up when the families are large. 'Family council is to the family what the board of directors is to the business' (Jain 2006).

Constitution of the council   The council should have representation from each family branch. They should also have representation from different generations having adult members. Female members should be included. All family members working in the business full time and also those senior members who may be non-executive directors, should be present in the council. If the family is spread over different locations due to the establishment of businesses in such areas, such locations should be properly represented in the council.

Meeting frequency   Jain suggests that the council should meet a few times every year for one or two days each time. The author feels that with the requirements on quarterly declaration of financial results, the council should meet at least four times a year. In addition to these meetings, the council should meet to discuss the strategic pursuit of business at least once a year, preferably before the beginning of new financial year. The council should also meet to discuss proposals of acquisitions or threats of accquisitions, in addition to the regular meetings. It should be prepared to face any emergency arising in the business or in the organization. The duration of one to two days is only indicative and should not become a limiting factor on fruitful discussions taking place. Issues which require more time should not suffer because of the paucity of meeting and discussion time.

Meeting process   The senior representatives of the family should take a lead in initiating the proceedings . They should also make it clear to the council that while every branch has a right to protect their interests, the interest of the business should be at the top of their minds. Transparency, openness, and candour are prerequisites for family councils to be effective and successful.

Deliberation on issues   According to Jain, issues listed below are dealt with in all family council meetings:

- All business-related relevant facts, decisions, and developments that have a bearing on financial performance and auditor's report on periodical financial performance
- Changes in family ownership and other significant changes in the non-family shareholding pattern
- Matters affecting the business such as alliances and collaborations, raising money from public, mergers and acquisitions, sale of any business, liquidation of the firm, etc.

- Entry and exit of key managers
- Restructuring, hiving off or diversification of the business portfolio, or changes related to business locations
- Changes in business environment that have a significant influence on the business
- Major capital expenditure plans
- Business liabilities and the solvency position
- Report of the board of directors
- CEO report on the strategic direction and future scenario
- Plans of family members to pursue any new venture or career outside the family
- Conflicts of interests affecting family relationships or business growth
- Issues such as marriage, higher education, medical problems, etc., of family members
- Succession related issues
- Achievements of individual family members
- Mentoring plans for the younger generation

Functions of a family council

According to Jain, a family council performs the following functions:

- Defining the family vision/mission
- Ensuring continuity of the family values not only by defining them, but also devising methods to transmit them to future generations
- Developing family creed, beliefs, and philosophies
- Drafting and implementing the family constitution/policies
- Defining roles, rights, and responsibilities of family members
- Managing the family business, family ownership, family–individual, and family–social dynamics
- Helping to strengthen the learning institutions through a structured mentoring process
- Developing an agenda for community service and philanthropy
- Providing for the security of family members
- Rejuvenating the members through interaction and fun
- Attending to issues, such as:
  - Suppressed individuality
  - Poor communication among members
  - Nepotism and favouritism
  - Conflicts
  - Conflicts of interest situations
  - Demotivated talent
  - Patriarchal dominance
  - Gender bias
  - Rigid culture
  - Youngsters drifting from family values

While operational frameworks such as assemblies and councils can help resolve many issues and problems, it is for the founders or the family patriarch to decide and create a clear division of assets. No issues may arise as long as the founder(s) or the patriarch lives, but rivalry and heartburn may arise later among the new generation family members. For example, both the Ambani brothers—Mukesh and Anil—were given equal status by Dhirubhai. Their salaries and perks were the same even when Mukesh was vice-chairman and managing director, and Anil was managing director. Also, there was a lot of clarity (or at least no confusion) regarding the allocation of responsibilities and power. But the whole scenario suddenly changed after Dhirubhai's death when Mukesh was named the chairman of RIL, the flagship company of the group. Conventionally, the chairman of RIL assumed extensive powers, including the power to control other subsidiaries, associates, and the investment companies of the group. So, as chairman, Mukesh became all-powerful and the sole decision-maker compared to the earlier scenario of two equal decision-makers under the patriarch. As chairman of RIL, Mukesh had the authority to control RIL's stake in all subsidiary/associate companies, including those which were headed by Anil. Or, in short, Anil owed his position of chairman in some of the subsidiary companies to RIL and Mukesh. He was theoretically reduced to the position of a professional manager who could be fired by the chairman of RIL (Mukesh) with the support of the RIL board. Also, Mukesh enjoyed the enviable position of controlling a company, which at that time, was generating cash to the order of Rs 120,000 million, which could enable him to pursue bigger projects.

In such situations, many family members, in order to retain control over their companies, create a cobweb of ownership structures in an effort to create ambiguity, and at times to circumvent the attention from the group's holding in the companies. At the time of the feud in the Reliance group, nobody was able to give a clear picture of the family's holding in RIL or other group companies. While the unofficial figure of the family control in RIL was 34 per cent, it still remains unclear as to why the RIL board did not move proactively to protect the interests of the outside shareholders whose stakes were as high as 66 per cent.

In recent times, SEBI has made it mandatory for the company to detail the promoter holding in the annual reports to shareholders. Some of the industrial groups in India had already done a clear bifurcation of assets among the second generation family members. The Birlas, Goenkas, and the TVS group in the South belong to this category.

Post the siblings split in RIL, many groups have started clearly defining the boundary lines and allocation of assets among family members. It has also been reported that family members are writing MOUs among them to prevent unsavoury happenings from disturbing family relationships. For example, 'Ashok Shah and his three brothers—Mahendra, Rajesh, and Hasmukh—who run a closely held logistics firm in Mumbai, use the same car model (Toyota Corrolla) and mobile handsets (LG). Any departure from this would be tantamount to a breach of trust that has been laid down in a memorandum of understanding the brothers signed when they set up the firm.'[1] According to *The Economic Times*, 'A big advantage of having such provisions in the MOU, according to the Shahs, is that they help keep at bay the usual grudge of 'one partner enjoyng more luxury' seen among family members which otherwise could pile up rather dangerously for the business.'

---

[1] Reported in 'Biz families sign formal MOUs to remain united', *The Economic Times*, 4 February 2006.

The intriguing situation in the RIL feud was that the board (consisting of very eminent and respected personalities) did not do anything during the time of the fued. What is unfortunate is that even today, the board seems to be playing a passive role in the ongoing tussle between the brothers on the issue of selling gas from the KG Basin to the Anil Ambani-controlled company, Reliance Natural Resources Ltd. This is a typical problem in many family-managed companies. Many of them do not use the boards effectively.

Annual retreat/family assembly

Many business families hold annual retreats or family assemblies where issues that are of primary concern to the family are discussed. Every member celebrates the occasion and uses it as an opportunity to strengthen the bonding. These retreats are also used as forums to discuss the business issues that are related to ownership and succession. Jain compares these retreats with the annual general meetings of shareholders and suggests that the retreats should have four components built into it.

Fun   Family members get an opportunity to meet and interact with other members, exchange pleasantries, and enjoy time together

Inculcation and articulation of vision and values   Elders get an opportunity to communicate to the younger generation, the vision of the family as far as the business is concerned and also the potential opportunities for the family members to participate in making the vision a reality. It also gives the opportunity to emphasize the need for strict adherence to the values propagated by the family. Elders also get an opportunity to listen to the next generations' views on vision and values. As such retreats are informal in nature, it is more likely that members will freely express their views on all issues related, as well as unrelated, to business.

Decision-making on critical issues   Issues that require the attention of the family such as entry into new businesses, threats or risks in the current business area, plans for acquisition, amalgamations, takeover, mergers, CEO succession, induction of new members into business, broad policies regarding recruitments and compensation, assessment of the economic and political environment, etc., can be looked into.

Learning and education   All members serious about business get an opportunity to participate in all the discussions, raise queries on issues they would like to be enlightened about, etc. This becomes a great learning opportunity for all, especially the younger generation. If the discussions are deep and broad, it can generate a lot of knowledge and education in everyone.

The operational process of family retreats

- Every member of the family, including the in-laws, should be invited.
- There shall be a well-laid-out agenda such as analysis of business performance, election of family council members, a detailed report of the last council, communications from the board of directors, if any, etc. In addition, the agenda may include any item the family members want to discuss.

- It should start with issues that are simple, so that a feeling of success will be created, before moving on to tougher ones where success will be achieved after a lot of deliberations.
- There shall be some consensus regarding the age of the children to participate in the serious business discussions.
- Assemblies should preferably be held over a period of two to three days in order to create a feeling of togetherness.
- Thanksgiving and forgiveness sessions should be included as these help to emphasize the unifying spirit in the family.
- They should provide occasions to laugh and cry together.
- Elderly people should tell the younger generation about the challenges they faced while establishing the business in the initial days.
- Younger members may interview the patriarch and/or the elderly members and present the story in the assembly as some of the elderly may generally be reticent.
- Leaders should explain the service that the business organization renders to the community and society.
- Practices followed by the business in the areas of quality, cost reduction, process improvement, innovation, information assimilation and sharing, leadership development, employee development, and customer services shall be explained to the family members.
- Information about any awards won and recognitions received should be shared with everybody to create a sense of pride among the members.
- Youngsters should be encouraged to organize and conduct special sessions during the retreat to showcase their ideas about business, both existing and new.

Family constitution

Just as a constitution helps a nation to conduct itself in an orderly manner, so also a constitution for the family enables it to have clarity in its relationship to the business. This can act as a frame of reference to help one prevent or resolve future family and business problems. 'It is a sign of maturity and signifies the commitment of the family towards a unified future' (Jain 2006).

According to Ivan Lansberg, 'A family constitution expresses the will of the family for future generations. Most important, it creates a foundation for maintaining trust within the family and for guiding the distribution of resources.... While it leaves many uncertainties, such as who will be allowed to enter the business and who will lead it, the document sets out guidelines for making such decisions' (Jain 2006). A constitution helps when families grow beyond the current generation, when the new generation may have a different perception about the business itself or the way it is conducted as of now. The constitution provides a common lens to see through reality, common measures to judge behaviour, common theme to relate to, and common value system to abide by, according to Jain. It helps to nurture cohesion within the family.

The process of constitution crafting   There are seven steps according to Jain (2006):

1. Discussion on goals, scope, and values
2. Fact finding
3. Preparing the draft

4. Discussion on the draft
5. Final draft
6. Adoption
7. Implementation

Jain (2006) says that it takes about two to three months to create a 20 to 30 page constitution, with bi-weekly meetings and take-home assignments. Alternatively, a constitution can be drafted in about three to four days if the process is done as a retreat. A retreat initiative can help as constitution drafters will not be disturbed by routine business chores. Exhibit 7.1 gives the basic contents of a typical family constitution (Jain).

Exhibit 7.1
General Contents of a Family Constitution

Introduction
- Preamble
- Importance of family and business continuity

Principles
- Values
- Beliefs
- Guiding principles

Vision and mission
- Directions, goals, and commitments

Systemic relationships (within legal boundaries)
- Family and business
- Family and ownership
- Ownership and business

Interpersonal relationships
- Categories and roles
- Defining expectations and responsibilities
- Establishing accountability
- Outlining authority and limitations
- Rights and duties of family members

Ownership and membership issues
- Pattern of ownership
- Issues related to transfer of ownership
- Provisions related to birth, adoption, marriage, and divorce
- Issues related to seperation or exit from family business

Action plan
- Governing bodies—procedures, rights, and obligations
- Communication and dispute resolution process
- Leadership and succession issues
- Policy for entry and exit in business
- Provisions related to compensation and other expenses
- Provisions related to non-family directors, managers, workers, in the business
- Other policies, rules, and guidelines
- Methods for monitoring and amendment
- Provision for arbitration

While a family constitution evolves over a period of time, any need for modification can be minimized if adequate care is taken while drafting it. While a constitution is not etched in stone, it should be driven by values that will endure and which have extreme appeal and relevance. Jain also suggests that constitutions be set as guidelines rather than rules because rules may require frequent amendments, whereas guidelines may not. Volatile and unpredictable situations should be kept out of the purview of the constitution and should be seperately dealt with as policies and guidelines.

Jain suggests that families can draw details of policies from Table 7.5 in their pursuit for better governance.

TABLE 7.5   Family policies

Policy	Content
Vision and mission statement	• Recognition of the stewardship role of the founders • Acceptance of the importance of business continuity for family unity • Prescription for playing supportive role to the management • Mentoring and education of future generations • Development and inculcation of family values • Recognition of individual identity • Commitment to social welfare
Conflct resolution policy	• Outline the process by which all conflicts and disputes will be resolved
Decision-making procedure	• Define the way all critical issues will be decided
Communication policy	• Dos and don'ts of communication • Directives regarding voicing disagreements and disclosures • Attempts to lay down platforms, occasions, and frequency of structured communication
Family council rules	• Lay down the process of organizing and running a family council
Mentoring policy for youngsters	• The age when mentors will be appointed • Who will act as mentors • The agenda for mentoring • The minimum knowledge and skill level expected from youngsters who wll become eligible for mentoring
Charity and philanthropy	• Resource allocation, limits, authorities, and eligible areas of activity • Guided by the bye-laws of the Trust, if organized as a Trust • View this as an opportunity to repay the society which has been instrumental in the family's growth and progress
Non-participating family members	• Rights and responsibilities applicable to family members pursuing outside careers, including issues, such as, rights of ownership; provision for residence; expectations regarding the conduct, such as, participation in family retreats; maintaining connection with family; etc.
Expenditure on marriage and education	• Clear guidelines and limits to ensure consistency and fairness

Contd

Table 7.5 contd

Policy	Content
Other issues	• Guidelines regarding family archives, family trophies, antique collection if any, important photographs and other memoirs, any other family legacy and heritage items • Performance of family rituals and celebration of festivals (in the Indian context)

Source: Jain, *Chains That Liberate: Governance of Family Firms*, Macmillan, New Delhi, 2006.

The family creed

Jain suggests that family businesses draft a family creed, a family philosophy, or a family code of conduct for the business. These act as guideposts in times of confusion and crisis that are based on family values. Jain feels that while drafting a creed, the family should never compromise. When the goals are set high, members and the family as a whole have to match up with corresponding better processes and methods. Such a document will nurture the commitment to the family through sharing, caring, sacrifice, understanding, mutual respect, and love. The creed should be treated with utmost reverence and revisited at suitable intervals to assess its relevance in the new context. While it must match with the family culture and core beliefs, it must also create an environment of positive tensions and stretch enabling the members to push for achieving excellence while maintaining excellent relationships.

Exhibit 7.2 provides a sample of a family creed.

Such a detailed family creed can act as a guide in creating a healthy environment within a family with respect to the business. Such family creeds could avoid many of the problems in the business families we observed earlier.

The Journey Towards Better Governance in Family-Managed Companies

While Christine Mallin feels that the final stage of development in corporate governance of a family-controlled firm is the establishment of a board of directors with outside directors present, Cadbury is of the opinion that establishing a board of directors indicates the progress from an organization based on family relationships to one based primarily on business relationships. However, it is better to have or continue with the family retreats and family councils even after the establishment of a board with outside directors as it may still help to resolve many issues which arise in the family's relationships within and with respect to the business.

Whatever be the advantages of a professional board of directors and professional management, delineation to the extent of 100 per cent between ownership and management is not only impossible but also not desirable. This is because the family may want to pursue its value systems in the conduct of the business, and may be more concerned about long-term sustainability of the business rather than short-term achievement of its objectives. While establishment of a board with outside directors is a move in the right direction, Phan feels that 'non-executives should dominate the board of a family-controlled business. For a family business to survive beyond the first stage of organic growth, it has to have in place a cadre of professional managers who may

Exhibit 7.2
A Sample Family Creed

We the members of--------------family, do hereby solemnly pledge ourselves to the growth and prosperity of our family, our business, the community, and the country we live in, and to the growth of each member of the family and say that:

- We strive to strengthen our family and our business
- We drive our identity from our business and are committed to its growth and continuity
- We treat our business as a responsibility and not as a privilege
- We understand that our business is constantly under threat from external factors beyond our control
- We also understand that over-indulgence of family in business may result in irreparable damage to business. We, as a family, are committed to be a strength to our business and not its weakness.
- We have confidence in our relationships as family members, and we believe that there is enough resilience to withstand the sacrifices made by the family in favour of business. In times of conflict between family interest and business interest, we commit to go by business interest.
- We are committed to the values of our family and to all human values and will always lead a life by living these values through exemplary behaviour
- We, as a family, are committed to the growth of each individual; we as individuals are committed to our personal growth
- We hold ourselves jointly and severally responsible for creating a healthy physical and emotional environment for others
- We will subject ourselves to governance measures as decided from time to time
- We will be an enterprising family, always investing in new products and businesses. Adaptability, learning, and entrepreneurship, are the rejuvenating features of our culture. But we will avoid taking undue risks without first making deep logical enquiry and investigation.
- We are committed to providing able and dynamic leaders to our business and to society
- We will judge business employees not by blood but by competence
- We will balance independence and commitment to ensure individual growth and family harmony
- We will ensure that we enjoy being a family and enjoy owning and managing the business together
- We take pride in our family name and commit to bring more glory to it
- We treat all family members equal, as human beings. Ownership and employment rights in family business will be governed by family policies.
- We allow each other opportunities to inform openly the feelings and creativity, and refrain from criticizing unless such expressions cross the limits of decency.
- We are committed to not discuss family matters with outsiders without the consent and knowledge of the family
- We consider different views. We focus on the whole while operating as a part of the whole. We learn to see many sides of any experience.
- We respect the need for privacy and provide each person with a designated private area, private time, and safe space
- We will be responsible citizens of the community we live in
- We will work for alleviation of poverty and eradication of illiteracy through our family foundation

Sources: Jain, Rajesh (2006), *Chains that Liberate: Governance of Family Firms*, Macmillan, New Delhi.

not be family members' (Phan 2000). But according to Shultz, the structure of the board has the greatest impact and she quotes Pascal N. Levensohn who says, 'By their very nature, families are closed systems and are therefore insular and exclusionary... As a result they often lead to emotionally rooted business positions that create deadlocks with disastrous consequences for competitive success in a dynamic business environment' (Shultz 2001).

While Shultz considers too much of family as one of the ten most critical mistakes that prevent companies from strategizing governance through a board of directors, Charan (2005) does not consider it as a disadvantage. He quotes in a *Business Week* report published in 2003 which found that S&P 500 companies with families involved in management had outperformed the remainder of the S&P 500 over the preceding decade. 'This, despite the fact that the boards of family companies tend to have a higher percentage of non-independent directors' (Charan). As *Business Week* said: 'With their intimate knowledge of the company gleaned from years of dinner-time conversations, many [family directors] are as knowledgeable as management about [the company's] inner workings' (Charan 2005). A study of the BSE 100 companies, conducted by *The Economic Times* between 2001 and 2006, showed that 'family-owned companies have reported higher growth in net sales, net profits, and market cap, as compared to professionally managed companies.'[2]

According to the *ET* report, family-owned companies in the BSE 100 sample have reported a five-year net sales CAGR of 22 per cent, net profit CAGR of 36 per cent, and market cap CAGR of 44 per cent. In contrast, professionally-managed companies, including MNC arms, have registered a sales growth of 19 per cent, net profit growth of 28 per cent, and a market cap growth of 41 per cent. But the ET report concludes that the relatively small gap in the growth rates between the two categories appears to show that the differences in the virtues of family-owned companies and professionally-managed companies are over-exaggerated.

T.R. Rajan, a management consultant, says that 'quarrels in family-run business often have their roots in a general unwillingness to address the issues related to ownership and management and nip them in the bud.' He says that there is a reluctance on the part of the family members and the different branches of the families to formalize the approach to business, and also to write and leave a will, that is at the root of the family squabbles. According to him, when the business is small, 'The founders work hard trying to make a success of their venture and would hardly have the time to argue about sharing the 'spoils' or dwell on the foibles of one another. At this stage, there is seldom any documentation of relative roles or sharing of profits except for an oral, or at best, a badly drafted agreement among the partners.' However, as the business prospers, 'the need to define roles and rights is keenly felt, and since this is not necessarily a pleasant task, it is postponed to another day. Or, it gets done in a most perfunctory way. It is seldom realized that the more prosperous the business becomes, the more quarrelsome a discussion on sharing can become' (Rajan 2006).

Glitches on the road

While corporate India in general (with its majority of family-controlled companies), and advocates of better governance in particular, feel that we need to address the issue of corporate governance

---

[2] This sentence and the following paragraph are from *The Economic Times*, 22 September 2006.

more seriously, there are a number of hitches or bumps along the journey towards a better governance regime. The major glitches are as follows.

The opaqueness in the Indian corporates   'Most of the corporations promoted by families have a 'pyramidal' structure and cross-holdings which enable the promoter family to control firms within the group without necessarily having a significant equity stake. In pyramids, the company at the top, usually the family/founder company, controls companies lower than theirs', according to Marisetty, Chalmers, and Vedpuriswar (Marisetty et al. 2005). While the holding company structure has been favoured by people, such as, Krishna Palepu and Tarun Khanna, as being 'effective in developing countries where many of the institutional mechanisms which facilitate market transactions are absent', Marisetty et al. say that 'instances of the structure being misused are widely reported in the media.' Marisetty et al. suggest that in order to promote effective governance and transparency of Indian companies, a dismantling of the pyramidal structure is needed.

Succession related issues   *The Economic Times* on 20 December 2006 reported that in an interview with a news agency, Mukesh Ambani, chairman of Reliance Industries Ltd, claimed that the ownership structure of RIL obviated the need for a will. This is because most Indian family businesses are held through a pyramidal structure of multi-layered investment companies. The family holding is typically concentrated at the tip of this structure. Also, usually, the capital of these investment companies acting as the tip of an iceberg does not need to be very large. The patriarch of an Indian family normally gets his son or sons to join the family business. The sons are placed somewhere in the corporate hierarchy, they work on the business, and earn a salary. The patriarch then gets the sons to use part of their salary to finance the acquisition of the controlling stake in the tip of the iceberg .The advantage of this complex route 'is to ring-fence the family from outside challengers. Any property that is willed can be challenged in a court of law and any such dispute can tie up the family business in legal knots for prolonged periods.'[3] Writing on the issue, Bhatt (2005) said: 'Big business family successions have relevance much beyond the family. The performance of an economy ultimately depends on how its assets are utilized by those who control them. If the assets of large firms are in the hands of underperforming managers for long periods of time, economic growth would suffer.'

Yet another complexity that is usually seen in the succession issue in family-managed companies is that 'it tends to favour the system of primogeniture, by which the elder son inherits (or legally, self-earns) his parents' property' (Bhat 2005). In fact, this was the crux of the issue in many of the family squabbles in the recent past.

Role of independent directors in family-managed companies   Families understand that too much of family on the board can dilute objectivity and result in lop-sided thinking. Hence, families do bring independent directors from outside on to the board. But who should they give allegiance to? There is a hierarchy of constituencies: the family shareholders, the outside shareholders, the CEO and management, or the entire stakeholders. This puts the independent director in a dilemma and limits his/her ability to act forcefully. In the US, where management

---

[3] 'Indian family business ownership structures—a ready reckoner', *ET in the Classroom*, 20 December 2004.

of publicly listed family-owned companies is usually different from family, he/she may owe his/her position mostly to the CEO, whereas in India, he/she may owe his position to the family; he/she is most likely to be a family loyal. With the position, prestige, and money that an independent director's position offers, it is quite natural that his/her independence could severely be limited. Also, in crucial decisions such as succession, he will have to simply go by the wishes of his family. While in the US, the independent director cannot be forced out easily by the family because their shareholding may not be high enough, in India it is rather easy, as the families usually command a majority ownership. Wallace and Zinkin (2005) say that this is true for many countries in Asia: 'In Asia, a particular fact that the family firms or family interests are so important—more so than in UK and the US—makes it difficult to argue that what is right in highly liquid markets with extremely dispersed ownership is correct for relatively illiquid markets with highly concentrated ownership structures and a great dependence on family or bank finance, rather than equity.' Shultz (2001) narrates a situation that arose in Scripps Inc where a question came up: 'We are outside board members, but the family has all the voting power. Do we really serve a purpose?' The answer, according to CEO William Burleigh, was that 'the family looks to outsiders for direction and leadership, and the outsiders look to the family for the anchor and the values they represent. There is excellent chemistry.' John Carver, whose approach 'policy governance' has identified that one of the tasks of the board is 'agreeing the purpose of the corporation' which he calls 'ends issues' (Wallace and Zinkin 2005). And, according to Wallace and Zinkin, 'It is important to recognize that the ends will reflect the type of ownership structure and it's priorities, and that therefore, 'Ends' that are suitable for a publicly held company may not be so appropriate for a family-owned firm or a non-profit organization.' Jain (2006) cautions: 'When business grows, the knowledge needs increase—not only in terms of depth, but also in terms of width. It is not possible for a single person to know all and to be an expert at that. When outsiders are added to the board or to the family councils, they bring in their diverse experience and knowledge to the table. What is needed is the awareness of the needs of the firm and the ability to pick up the right men who possess relevant expertise. Independent directors should be picked from diverse fields consisting of other business owners, consultants, attorneys, and accountants, etc.'

The compensation conundrum   By and large, family owners try to promote equity in the way the children are remunerated. Competence and hard work may get overlooked in this process. It may get into a situation where one of the nominee managers is overburdened while another may take things easily and lightly. Or, both could neglect work assuming that the other will take care of it.

The pressure from different family factions for representation on the board   The promoter family will be under pressure to include representations from various branches of the family. For example, Bajaj Auto Ltd has seven members from the family out of a total of 16 board members. Since regulations in force in India (under Clause 49) require that at least 50 per cent of the directors shall be independent when the chairman is executive, or when he is a family member, or belongs to the promoter family, such large number of family members on the board will force the company to have a board size beyond the necessary, resulting not only in increased compensation costs but also complicating the decision-making process.

The biggest private sector company in India, Reliance Industries, till a short time ago had only 13 directors. Only recently have they added members on the board in an executive capacity, taking the total to 15 members. According to Shultz, having too many insiders on the board is one of the ten mistakes preventing the company from achieving a strategic board. According to her, 'The essence of strategic boards is independence. When you see a board loaded with insiders, it's a sign certain of indifference to and perhaps disdain for governance' (Shultz 2001). Too many insiders can also hamper the functioning of the CEO, especially when the CEO is not one of the promoters, or from the family. Too many insiders will also render a board evaluation process ineffective. While companies in the US usually have only one insider (usually the CEO), the scenario in Indian companies is largely different. For example, GE has only one insider on its board, the CEO Mr Jeffrey Immelt.

Wallace and Zinkin (2005) say that 'it is not surprising that many firms that started out as family firms have chairmen and CEOs from the same family—indeed, often father and son. In such circumstances, it is difficult for the chair to be regarded as being independent, or for the CEO to be able to exercise effective authority without being undermined by the presence of the patriarch. It is doubly problematic because the board may well not know who to listen to if there is a disagreement on how best to pursue the interests of all shareholders . This is made even more poignant if the family is still in control of a commanding bloc of shares.'

Advantages of family control and ownership

While we narrated the downsides of the family-owned and controlled business above, when it comes to governance, we should not be under any impression that it is all bad; there are upsides too.

They are committed to a long haul   Having established the enterprise with a wealth creation motive, the family would expect the enterprise to continue to generate wealth for future generations. Thus, the family must theoretically be interested in the sustenance of the enterprise rather than any other shareholder who might be investing for the sake of a quick return. Even institutional investors, which every governance pundit highlights as a measure of development, and in that way of governance too, may not have the kind of long-term perspective of the enterprise that the family holds. Institutions would be interested in governance of a company only as long as they hold on to it. There may be institutions in the pension field who may be keen to keep themselves invested for a long-term such as CalPERS or TIAA-CREF. But other institutional investors such as mutual funds or investment banks are committed to a company to the extent they can offer good returns to their portfolio of assets under management.

The family owners and directors can be more objective than others because they might be financially content than others   For example, Bennett Dorrance, family leader on the board of Campbell Soup representing 12 per cent of the stock which the family owns, is of the opinion that since 'the family has made so much money, they can be more objective than others for whom the outcomes are financially important' (Shultz 2001).

The family owners try to preserve the value system they strictly adhere to   The family may have created a value system for the business aimed at future generations. It may be keen to preserve these values as the company progresses. These values could become strong in the company's pursuit of better governance. The family philosophy, the ethos, and the creed can enable the business and the company in their pursuit of growth and size.

Advantages of good governance in family-owned and controlled enterprises

Jain says that performance of a governance-based system is better than that of the traditional patriarchal system, for the leaders as well as for the subordinates (see Tables 7.6 and 7.7).

TABLE 7.6   Effect of governance on leaders

	Patriarchal system	Governance-based system
Attitude	'I have all the powers'	'I am accountable'
Behaviour	'I will do what I like'	'I'll combine the judgement and expertise available'
Outcome	Meet expectations	Exceed expectations

TABLE 7.7   Effect of governance on subordinates

	Patriarchal system	Governance-based system
Attitude	'I have no powers'	'My opinion counts'
Behaviour	'I'll do what I'm told'	'I'll stretch myself'
Outcome	Meet expectations	Exceed expectations

Family business and corporate governance: Best practices

As we have seen, family businesses have a predominant position in all countries and economies. They play such an important part that their well-being must be assured. Regulators should also appreciate this fact. While all encouragement is offered to them to adopt better governance practices, no action that curbs their initiatives and entreprenuership should be taken. While 'going public' has been the yardstick adopted by SEBI in India and regulators in other parts of the world, for market related governance regime to apply, one has to seriously look at the efficacy of this criterion. Going public should not be considered a crime calling for punishment, but be viewed as an opportunity for investors and other stakeholders to participate in the opportunities of growth and wealth creation of the firm. There is no question about the role played by companies such as Tata Steel and Reliance Industries in creating an interest in investments in corporate securities. Many other companies have also joined the bandwagon of creating investor enthusiasm in stock markets. Regulators must hence think of creating a threshold level, either for the promoter-family holding below, or for the public holding (non-family holding) above.

With delisting norms available, family-promoted enterprises may buy-back the outstanding equity as soon as they generate sufficient cash reserve and delist, and thus come out of the corporate governance regulatory framework. At the other extreme, companies would continue to remain as private ones in a way that an action would enable them to keep away from capital market regulators, investment bankers, analysts, and institutional investors, who are all interested in the the price of the stock (and related aspects) rather than in the business itself.

Jain has recommended a number of best practices to be adopted by family businesses (Exhibit 7.3).

Exhibit 7.3
Best Practices for Family Business

1. Conduct verification of the validity of your assumptions and business logic. Establish mechanisms to provoke the firm out of its comfort zone and disturb any sense of complacency that might have crept in.
2. Induct competent independent directors on your board . The strength of independent directors should exceed the inside directors.
3. Separate the chairman and the CEO positions.
4. Establish a clear process for the entry of family members into the business and an evaluation process after their entry, for progressing through the ranks.
5. Organize an advisory board consisting of family members, family friends, experts from the company, etc., depending on the objective.
6. Regularly organize family council meetings. Sustaining the practice is more important than the quality of the agenda.
7. Draft policies covering all major aspects, so that there is enough clarity to deal with issues as and when they arise.
8. Install a learning programme which will be continued as a routine practice. CEOs should join peer groups to fill gaps in skills. A mentoring programme for youngsters and reverse mentoring for seniors should be put in place.
9. Decide on a policy of sharing wealth with society. Future generations should feel proud about the role it plays in empowering and improving society and also continue with the good work.
10. Allow youngsters to work outside the family for a few years before they join the business.
11. Develop a policy regarding the succession plan and let it be known to all interested parties.
12. Be highly transparent.
13. Be as keenly concerned with family as you are about business. Let the family be a source of strength, as business can be constantly under threat.
14. Appoint the best person for the job—family or non-family.
15. Locate insecurity within the family and take steps to correct it, if not eliminate it altogether.
16. Take all the help you need and can get. Don't try to shoulder all the burden yourself.
17. Make communication seamless and take all opportunities to communicate.
18. Be accountable and demand accountability.
19. Confront a negative behaviour the first time you face it. Remember that 'you get the behaviour you tolerate'.
20. Be loyal to your values, not products, policies, and processes.
21. Set aside 25 per cent of your profits as the risk capital to be reinvested in new products, new businesses, and new technology.
22. Keep family at the top of the agenda; remember that 'families that eat and play together, stay together'.

INSTITUTIONAL INVESTORS AND DEVELOPED MARKET CONUNDRUM IN CORPORATE GOVERNANCE

Nearly 60 per cent of the outstanding equity shares of US listed companies are owned by institutional investors such as investment bankers, pension funds, mutual funds, etc. According to Smith and Walter (2006), 'The vast majority of the funds are actively managed, and their managers participate in far more trading than average individual investors. Consequently, institutionally managed funds account for the vast bulk of all equity trading in the United States, and have by far the greatest influence in price-setting among all investors. In some important ways, the institutions are the market.'

Very early, Berle and Means had foreseen that as the corporations become large, shareholders would be reduced to passive investors, giving the managers (the agents) full control of the company. So, according to Franklin Edwards and Glenn Hubbard, 'The growth of institutional stock ownership that has occurred during the last two decades—institutions now hold nearly 56 per cent of outstanding stock in US—is a hopeful development that promises to change the face of American capitalism in the next century' (Chew and Gillan 2005).

According to Phan (2000), 'Pressures from international institutional investors who only care about making their quarterly profitability targets have increased sharply. Global capital markets that demand an unprecedented degree of transparency in corporate reporting have fueled these pressures.' But Smith and Walter feel differently. According to them, 'During the latter years of the 1990s, it was clear that institutions on the whole were falling well short of their obligations to keep their investors out of trouble, as the asset management institutions themselves were seen to be major investors in all parts of the stock market that were subject to fraud or overvaluation. Consequently, much of the blame for the bubble and the episode of corporate governance failures that accompanied it, can be left on the doorsteps of the institutional investors who failed to see the dangers of the period, and failed to protect their clients from them' (Smith and Walter 2006). By and large, institutional investors, being large shareholders, must behave in a proactive manner and monitor the managers (agents) more closely than small shareholders.

According to Edwards and Hubbard, 'Institutions are better able to overcome the agency costs and information asymmetries associated with diffuse stock ownership' (Chew and Gillan 2005). So, according to Chew and Gillan, 'In principle therefore, institutional stock ownership should result in improved corporate governance generally and the accompanying increase in corporate efficiency and shareholder wealth.' Smith and Walter (2006) say that 'Institutions clearly have had the power to make a difference to companies such as Enron, WorldCom, and Tyco, either by not buying the stock, or selling it, or by voting shares against management when it was overreaching or engaging in practices that were not seen to be in the interests of long-term investors. Yet, investors whose money they manage have entrusted their voting powers to them and, it would seem that they ought to be entitled to see these powers utilized in their own best interests.'

Institutional investors can theoretically exert a lot of influence considering the size of their shareholding. As already seen, their holding in companies have been steadily increasing over the last twenty years or so. Hirschman identified two options at the disposal of the institution namely, the 'voice option' (expressing dissatisfaction directly to the management) or the 'exit option' (selling the shareholding) (Mallin 2007). According to Mallin, the latter choice is not available to many considering the size of their holdings or the policy of holding a balanced portfolio. According to Shultz (2001), 'Investment funds represent thousands, sometimes millions, of shareholders, and they are investing billions. They know that great boards mean great companies and they are the real drivers of governance reform.' The Cadbury Committee had clearly identified the responsibility of institutional investors ensuring that its recommendations were adopted by companies 'we look at institutions in particular, …to use their influence as owners to ensure that the companies in which they have invested, comply with the code' (Cadbury 1992). The Greenbury Report of 1995 also opined that 'The investor institutions should use their power and influence to ensure the implementation of best practices as set out in the code' (Greenbury 1995). Thanks to the influence of such governance guidelines, public outcry against executive excesses and also the general acceptance that it pays to be better governed, many institutions took serious steps towards making the companies imbibe better governance practices. For example, California Public Employees' Retirement System (CalPERS) suggested a set of guidelines for the companies to follow. This was titled Corporate Governance Core Principles and Guidelines and was published on 13 April 1998.[4] The recommendations stressed the importance of board independence and independent leadership, a board charter detailing the board processes and performance evaluation, competence and functioning of individual directors, effective CEO succession plan, and also the rights of shareowners in deciding on matters relating to board and governance.

According to Ashby and Miles (2002), institutions in general have a shorter term perspective. According to them, 'The tenure of CEOs has shrunk from an average of over 10 years in the latter part of the last century to about half that today…the norm is closer to fewer than three years at the helm. While ten years might be too long, given the fast pace of global business, three years is barely long enough even for the most gifted leader of a complex organization to make his or her impact evident. One of the main reasons for increased leadership turnover is the growing impatience of institutional investors for immediate results.'

However, Phan (2002) takes a different view. According to him, 'Large institutional funds, such as, CalPERS and Lens are leading the way by making it a policy not to use nominees even though they have the right to do so. The institutional investors are also lobbying for such fundamental reforms as the elimination of poison pills, the imposition of director term limits, and the use of performance-based compensation for directors and officers. In short, they are attempting to create a higher level of accountability by reducing incentives for directors to engage in nest feathering.'

We have earlier seen that the Cadbury and Greenbury reports emphasized the important role the institutions had to play in the implementation and monitoring of best practices. Other codes in the UK such as the Combined Code and the Bosch Guidelines in Australia also stress the importance of the role of institutional investors in improving corporate governance practices. Michael Useem described 'the rise of investor capitalism in the US and how the concentration of shares, and hence power , into a relatively small number of hands, has enabled institutional investors to challenge management directly on issues of concern' (Mallin 2007). In principle,

[4] www.calpers.ca.gov

'institutional stock ownership should result in improved corporate governance generally, and an accompanying increase in corporate efficiency and shareholder wealth', say Edwards and Hubbard (Chew and Gillan 2005). But they list four reasons why 'such optimism about the prospects of a corporate governance revolution led by a growth in 'institutional investor capitalism' may be premature' (Chew and Gillan).

1. While institutional stock ownership has indeed increased since 1980, it is generally still quite low.
2. There are good reasons to believe that unless significant changes are made in the legal and cultural environment of institutional fund management, ownership concentration in the US is unlikely to reach the level at which institutional investors will have a powerful voice in corporate boardrooms.
3. Institutional fund managers face significant legal and institutional constraints that deter them from both accumulating large ownership positions and attempting to use those positions to control corporate managers, and
4. Notwithstanding journalistic accounts of the rise of institutional shareholder activism, empirical studies suggest that such activism has had, at best, a modest effect on the performance of targeted firms.

But institutions such as Teachers Insurance and Annuity Association–College Retirement Equities Fund (TIAA–CREF) has been actively associating with International Corporate Governance Network (ICGN) and has made some significant strides in this direction. For example, they were able to inspire countries such as Brazil, which 'has welcomed recommendations on corporate governance that would lead to greater likelihood of "patient money" investments in their markets by establishing "Novo Mercado", a segment of the main stock exchange which would be reserved for companies with good corporate governance practices', according to John H. Biggs, chairman, president, and CEO, TIAA–CREF (Ashby and Miles 2002). Institutional investors have also started demanding an annual review of the effectiveness of the corporate boards, according to Jay Conger, David Finegold, and Edward Lawler III (Conger et al. 2000). According to Conger et al. (2000), 'A 1997 survey commissioned by Russel Reynolds Associates found that the quality of a company's board has now become an important evaluation factor for institutional investors.' But, according to Smith and Walter (2006), 'During the latter years of the 1990s, it was clear that institutions on the whole were falling well short of their obligations to keep their investors out of trouble. The fiduciary duties of asset managers are clear in both US state and federal law, and have been for some time…. The principal idea is that managers of other people's money must always put the interests of their clients first—ahead of their own interests—and act prudently.' John Pound, visiting professor at Harvard Law School, feels that the rise of institutional investors creates a unique opportunity for active shareholders to influence corporate policy. According to him, 'A heavy concentration of institutional investors greatly lowers the costs of pressing an alternative agenda. Thirty years ago, appealing to a majority of shareholders meant circulating materials to tens or even hundreds of thousands of poorly informed individual owners. Now a dissident investor can reach the fiduciaries in charge of voting a majority of outstanding shares through a series of quiet phone conversations and private meetings with 25 informed investment professionals, all of whom understand the issues and can devote a significant amount of resources to analyze them' (Pound 2000).

While ownership concentration can be a great boom in itself, there are a lot of regulations restricting institutions' ownership in companies. According to the Investment Company Act of 1940 in the US, mutual funds can invest only upto 5 per cent of the total value of the assets in the equity of a company and only upto 10 per cent of the total value of assets in all the outstanding securities of a company. SEBI regulations in India concerning investment by mutual funds are equally stringent, if not more. They also stipulate that no individual scheme of mutual fund should invest more than 5 per cent of its corpus in any one company's shares, no mutual fund under all its schemes taken together should invest more than 10 per cent of its funds in the shares or debentures or other securities of a single company, and no mutual fund under all its schemes taken together should invest more than 15 per cent of its funds in the shares and debentures of any specific industry (other than those which are specific industry or sector funds). The investment regulations in India are more stringent since there is a limit to the percentage of fund assets that can be invested across an industry, whereas US regulations do not provide for such industry strictures on investments by mutual funds. According to Edwards and Hubbard, 'Indirectly, the five per cent rule also is an important ownership constraint. It prevents all but the very largest mutual funds from taking sizable ownership positions in a company's stock' (Chew and Gillan 2005). Yet another major group of institutions which have increased their stakes in equities of companies is pension funds. But, according to Edwards and Hubbard, in the US, 'both corporate culture and law combine to discourage private pension funds from owning sizable blocks of stock, or from adopting an active corporate policy' (Chew and Gillan).

Culture   Corporate managers effectively control their own pension funds and few of them may meddle in the affairs of some other companies for fear of provoking similar reactions on the part of the pension funds controlled by those companies.

Laws   Laws such as the Employee Retirement Income Security Act (ERISA) pose significant legal risks to pension fund managers who acquire large blocks of stock or are active in corporate governance. The generally accepted practice in pension fund management is to hold a diversified portfolio consisting mostly of small ownership positions. A manager who deviates from this practice can run into a serious risk of liability in the event the fund loses a substantial amount of money in any position. Also, if there are benefits from concentrated ownerships, they primarily go to the beneficiaries and not to the fund managers leaving little incentive for them to take concentrated positions.

Pound disagrees and asserts that 'at no time has corporate America had a more natural long-term constituency in the area of institutional investors. All the characteristics of institutional investors—their concern about substance, their astute judgement, their political visibility, their intrinsic conservatism—make them open to overtures from corporations. By taking a systematic, indeed a scientific, approach to divining the concerns of their major institutional investors, corporations can create a governance process which begins to approach the ideal articulated for over a century by legal and economic theorists' (Pound 2000).

Edwards and Hubbard conclude that while 'much of the growth of institutional ownership since 1980 has been accounted for by the growth of mutual funds and private pension funds, there continue to be strong deterrents to these institutions using large ownership positions to influence corporate managers' and recommend that 'current legal restrictions on mutual funds be relaxed so that the mutual funds have a greater incentive to hold large ownership positions in companies, and to use those positions to more effectively monitor corporate managers' (Chew and Gillan 2005). In India, pension funds are conspicuous by their absence as the laws still prevent flow of pension money to equity markets.

How Institutional Investors Improve Governance of Companies

Institutional inventors can play a vital role in improving the governance of companies in which they have invested. According to Mallin (2007), corporate governance may be used as a tool for extracting value for shareholders in underperforming and undervalued companies. According to him, 'By targeting companies that are underperforming in one of the main market indices and analyzing those companies' corporate governance practices, improvements can be made which unlock the hidden value. These improvements often include replacing poorly performing directors and ensuring that the companies comply with perceived best practice in corporate governance.'

According to Mallin, there are four tools that come handy for institutional investors in their pursuit of better governance, which are discussed below.

One-to-one meetings

Considering that institutions have clout, they can force one-to-one meetings with companies which individual investors may find difficult to enforce. Companies which are keen to improve their governance practices will be proactive and will invite institutions on a regular basis. They usually look forward to meeting them in order to understand their concerns and suggestions for improving the practices. Issues such as strategy, plan for achieving objectives, quality of management, board level changes, succession plans for CEO and other senior executives, and also concerns on environment, employee care, etc. could be discussed during such meetings.

Voting

Shareholders' right to vote is an important element in the exercise of control over the affairs of corporations. While this right is available with every type of shareholder who holds voting shares, institutions, with their significant holdings, will be in a better position to influence the board and management through the exercise of their votes. While the voting pattern will be determined by the outcome of meetings between the company and the institutional investors, such voting could become crucial when there are vital issues yet to be resolved.

According to Mallin (2007), 'Generally, an institutional investor will try to sort out any contentious issues with management 'behind the scenes'; however, if this fails, then they may abstain from voting on a particular issue (rather than voting with incumbent management as they generally would) or they may actually vote against a resolution. In this case, they would generally inform the firm of their intention to vote against.' Smith and Walter (2006) say that while institutions vote on all of the shares entrusted to them, 'it seems unlikely that many mutual fund management companies or their financial advisors put a lot of expense and effort into careful monitoring of management conduct and governance issues in corporations whose stocks they hold, or into more proactively pressuring boards to avoid actions that harm investor interests. Why? Because most of the time it simply is not economically reasonable for them to do so.'

Focus lists

Institutional investors establish a 'focus list' whereby they target underperforming companies and include them on a list of companies that have underperformed on the main index, those companies who do not respond appropriately to the institutional investors' queries regarding underperformance and those who tend to ignore the institutional investors' views.

Corporate governance rating systems

With the thrust on corporate governance in recent times, a number of agencies such as Standard and Poor's, Governance Matrix International, etc., in a global scenario and CRISIL, CARE, and ICRA in India have developed corporate governance rating systems. This is perceived as benefiting investors in making decisions regarding investments based on the value added by the companies, both current and potential. Such ratings can come in handy for institutional investors. The corporate governance rating will be dealt with in greater detail in Chapter 8.

Other Concerns

Bebchuk and Fried (2004) say that 'the significance of outside shareholders as a check on managerial power may depend not only on the presence of a large shareholder but also on the percentage of shares held by institutional investors. Although institutional investors are often reluctant to fight management about pay issues, they are generally more vigilant than are the individual investors, who have little at stake in any given firm.' Also, many institutional investors such as banks, mutual funds, investment banks, and insurance companies have or plan to have business dealings with the firm and hence, have an interest in being on good terms with the management. Bebchuk and Fried say that 'Indeed, there is evidence that the tighter the business ties between a firm and its institutional shareholders, the higher is its CEO's compensation.'

PROBLEMS OF GOVERNANCE IN COMPANIES WHERE GOVERNMENT HAS A STAKE VARYING FROM MINORITY TO DOMINANT

Most of the industrialization in developing countries was initiated by governments due to the inherent problems associated with the mobilization of capital for the purpose of industrialization. Also, the pursuit of economic systems and ideologies such as socialism or communism required such countries either to wholly depend on or at least sustain with the initiatives of the public sector. While many countries initiated steps to gradually do away with the whole concept of the public sector except in strategically important areas such as defence or space research like the US or UK, the Government of India has been following a policy where the public sector co-exists with the private sector even though a great deal of effort has been taken at privatization of government-owned enterprises or part divestment of government stakes in the public sector companies.

While the UK government has been highly successful in divesting public sector corporations, generally as a one-time effort, India has been very slow in the divestment and privatization process. Even after eighteen years of economic reforms and liberalization, the country has not shown the political will and courage to exit the public sector fully. Most of our divestment processes are initiated when there is a genuine requirement of funds for meeting the plan expenditures. This has resulted in the continuing existence of firms with varying ownership by the government, leading to concerns and confusion about their governance. India is not the only nation having a huge network of public sector enterprises. According to Dewan (2006), 'After the Great Depression of 1929, the British economist, John Maynard Keynes suggested that governments should actively intervene in economies and spend money in order to create public sector enterprises, and generate employment and income.' But having embraced economic reforms in the year 1991 impending an economic crisis, the Indian government was forced to shift from a closed socialist economic system to an open free market economic system. Such market-oriented economic principles forced the dismantling of public sector units on the premise that government run businesses were less efficient and were not always run with a profit motive, and that they were a huge drain on the exchequer. Thus, after the initiation of economic reforms and liberalization, there has been a different approach to the concept of public enterprises and their very goals have undergone dramatic change. While they are still expected to fulfil the usual social obligations that go with the public sector, they are also expected to earn enough economic surplus in order to survive and grow. They may be forced to identify their own sources of funds for survival and growth rather than turn to government for funds. Corporate governance has become applicable to many of the public sector enterprises (PSEs) as they have chosen to raise funds from the capital markets, either through public offers of equity capital or through a process of divestment of equity in favour of private corporate bodies or institutional investors.

Features of Indian PSUs

Conventionally, the assumption about PSUs was that they were closely held by the government and its agencies; there was no public participation in equity as they were inaccessible to the public and they usually operated in monopolistic markets. Such assumptions were true in India too. For example, major Indian PSUs such as IOC, ONGC, or NTPC were entirely owned by the government and there was no public participation in their equity. All of them enjoyed monopolistic positions till very recently. But economic liberalization has changed all that. According to YRK Reddy, Indian PSUs have the following distinct features today (Reddy 2006).

Publicly listed and actively traded

While the government continues to hold dominant ownership in most PSUs, many of them are publicly listed and actively traded on the floors of the stock exchanges, and there are thousands of investors owning shares in PSUs today. For example, PSUS such as SBI, ONGC, and NTPC appear at the 7th, 9th, and 21st positions, respectively in terms of market capitalization (based on free-float market capitalization) in the BSE Sensex companies (on 14 October 2009).[5]

Government ownership of assets dominates both in the manufacturing and in the banking sector

In most of the developed countries, government ownership of assets in manufacturing and banking will be minimal.

The market capitalization of public enterprises

As a proportion of the total market capitalization this is among the highest in the world at about 32 per cent of the BSE.

Global presence

Many of the PSUs not only dominate the Indian industry scenario but have made their presence global in oil refining, oil exploration, banking, etc. For example, IOC today has been ranked at the 105th posiition in the Fortune 500 global companies list, while SBI has been ranked at the 363rd position.[6] ONGC has been acquiring oil and energy assets in different parts of the world through its subsidiary, ONGC Videsh Ltd.

DIFFICULTIES ENCOUNTERED IN GOVERNANCE

While routine governance regulations become applicable for public sector companies formed under the Companies Act, 1956 and come under the purview of SEBI regulations the moment they mobilize funds from the public, the typical organizational structure of PSUs makes it difficult for the implementation of corporate governance practices as applicable to other publicly-listed private enterprises. The typical difficulties faced are:

- The board of directors will comprise essentially of bureaucrats drawn from various ministries which are interested in the PSU. In addition, there may be nominee directors from banks or financial institutions who have loan or equity exposures to the unit. The effect will be to have a board much beyond the required size, rendering decision-making a difficult process.
- The chief executive or managing director (or chairman and managing director) and other functional directors are likely to be bureaucrats and not necessarily professionals with the required expertise. This can affect the efficient running of the enterprise.

[5] *The Economic Times*, 15 October 2009.
[6] *Fortune*, 20 July 2009.

- Difficult to attract expert professionals as independent directors. The laws and regulations may necessitate a percentage of independent component on the board; but many professionals may not be enthused as there are serious limitations on the impact they can make.
- The lower pay levels applicable to public sector executives also act as a deterrent to professional executives taking up public sector executive positions. For example, the CEO of SBI, the county's largest commercial bank, is paid only Rs 1.99 million, while his private sector counterparts in ICICI Bank and HDFC Bank earn Rs 26.5 million and Rs 25.3 million, respectively. The highest compensation received by a non-executive independent director at SBI is Rs 165,000 for board meetings, whereas his counterparts in ICICI and HDFC Bank are paid upto Rs 840,000 and Rs 620,000, respectively for attending board/committee meetings. While ICICI pays Rs 20,000 per board as well as committee meetings and HDFC Bank pays Rs 20,000 per board and committee meeting, except for investor grievance committee for which only Rs 10,000 is paid, SBI can pay only upto Rs 5,000 for attendance at central board meetings and Rs 2,500 for attending a board level committee.
- Due to their very nature, there are difficulties in implementing better governance practices. Many public sector corporations are managed and governed according to the whims and fancies of politicians and bureaucrats. Many of them view PSUs as a means to their ends. A lot of them have turned sick due to overdoses of political interference, even when their areas of operations offered enormous opportunities for advancement and growth. And when the economy was opened up, many of them lacked the competitiveness to fight it out with their counterparts from the private sector.

It may be worthwhile to evaluate the main objectives for setting up PSUs as stated in the Industrial Policy Resolution of 1956. The main objectives at the time are as shown in Exhibit 7.4.

One can easily find that some of these objectives are no longer valid or are better taken care of by the private sector due to the policy shifts in later years, and especially in the post-reforms era.

Exhibit 7.4
Outdated Objectives?

(a) To help in rapid economic growth and industrialization of the country and create the necessary infrastructure for economic development
(b) To earn a return on investment and thus generate resources for development
(c) To promote distribution of income and wealth
(d) To create employment opportunities
(e) To promote balanced regional development
(f) To assist the development of small-scale and ancillary industries
(g) To promote import substitutions, and save and earn foreign exchange for the economy.

Source: Bhattacharya, Ashish R, 'Role of Government', in *Corporate Governance in Public Sector Enterprises*, ed. S.M. Dewan, 2006, Dorling-Kindersely, New Delhi.

THEORETICAL FRAMEWORK FOR GOVERNANCE IN PSUS

The first requirement while studying governance of any type of firm (private or state-owned) is to establish the objective functions of the firm, in order to ascertain at individual firm level what the firm is trying to accomplish, and how managers should measure better versus worse (Bhattacharya 2006). According to Jensen, the objective function of a firm should be to maximize the value of the firm. And, value of the firm is the total of the market value of equity and the market value of debt (Bhattacharya). According to Bhattacharya, Jensen and many others disapprove the stakeholder theory of corporate governance as it aims at the welfare of stakeholders, which, according to them, forces managers to achieve a variety of objectives diluting the accountability of managers. They are of the opinion that 'maximization of firm value' is the appropriate objective function of the firm, because the product market determines the legitimacy of the existence of the firm. If a firm fails in the product market, its very existence is threatened. On the other hand, if it succeeds in the product market, every element in the value chain from the suppliers of raw materials to the ultimate consumers benefit, and even the objective of social welfare is achieved provided the firm doesn't create any negative 'externalities' (Bhattacharya).

Now, the question is whether the standard objective function of a firm can be replicated in the case of state-owned enterprises or PSUs? Mihir Rakshit feels that 'performance of enterprises should be judged on the basis of their profitability, and they must not be called upon to bear the cost of attaining other goals, such as, support to special sectors or groups, however deserving they may be. But Bhattacharya disagrees and says that 'maximization of firm value cannot be the objective function of all firms operating in the public sector. Unlike a firm in the private sector, a public sector firm is not simply a vehicle for creating wealth for investors. PSUs, particularly those that are operating in areas of strategic importance, are expected to create "positive externalities"' (Bhattacharya 2006).

For example, ONGC cannot decide 'maximization of firm value' as its objective function. The government would like to use ONGC as a vehicle for implementing its strategy for achieving energy security (Bhattacharya 2006). It is felt that the objective function of the PSUs should be reflected in the vision and mission statements for the PSUs by the government. In a publicly-listed PSU, the government, by way of its dominant shareholding, becomes accountable to other shareholders too. Hence, it is essential that the government acts highly transparently in all its acts with respect to the PSU. The boards of PSUs should be empowered in order for the PSU to enjoy managerial and commercial autonomy. And autonomy should not be construed as the autonomy of the CEO, but that of the board of directors.

The Board Constitution and Independent Directors

The government being the dominant holder of equity will have overwhelming rights to nominate members to the board of PSUs. Other investors will also be able to nominate their representatives depending on their holdings, and the terms and conditions of the prospectus through which the PSU raised funds from the public. The independent directors nominated shall not only be independent of the executive management, but be independent of the government, as also of political parties. This is one area where government usually falters. Normally, there is pressure from political parties that are members of the coalition to nominate their nominees to positions of power.

According to the government guidelines, the 'Navratna' PSUs namely, BHEL, BPCL, GAIL, HPCL, IOC, MTNL, NTPC, ONGC, and SAIL had competitive advantages and could emerge as global giants. They were given enhanced autonomy and delegation of powers in the areas of capital expenditure, technology, or other strategic alliances, mobilization of capital from domestic and international markets, etc. But, such enhanced autonomy would be available only when the boards of these companies were restructured to include at least four non-official professional independent directors. In case of 'Mininavratnas', which included 42 companies, there shall be at least three non-official, professional, independent directors. The idea is to bring a third-person view to the management of the company's affairs, and also act as a check and balance on acts of the interested directors. This becomes very important, as part of the ownership lies outside the government after a disinvestment process. Independent directors are expected to fill the knowledge gap that exists in the boardroom. Most of the PSUs, even today, have the position of chairman and managing director combined to render the person very powerful. This necessitates a very strong independent component on the board. According to SEBI guidelines, the presence of a full-time chairman necessitates that at least 50 per cent of the directors be independent. This is one guideline which the public sector companies contest because they do not have a free hand in constituting and nominating members to the board.

Another concern is about the role that the board has to play in the PSU. Should it assume a strategic role by actively participating in the strategic direction aspect or simply be there to rubber stamp the decisions of the government conveyed through their representatives in the management such as chairman, managing direcor, or other operating directors or their nominees on the board? Many of the PSUs enter into a memorandum of understanding (MOU) with the government, detailing their strategic pursuits for the near-term future. Also, investment allocations for them are made by the government through budgets and five year plans, virtually reducing the role to be played by the board in the strategic arena. While Clause 49 guidelines provided under the listing agreements between companies and the stock exchanges where their shares have been listed, do not distinguish PSUs from any other companies, the chairman and managing directors of many of the 'Navratnas' feel that this lack of distinction is not correct.

One of the critical areas they find problems with is the percentage of independent directors on the board. In September 2007, SEBI had initiated adjudication proceedings against 20 companies for non-compliance with the Clause 49 guidelines, with five PSUs among the twenty. These PSUs were pulled up for non-compliance with the provisions related to board composition, with regard to the number of independent directors, At the time the government had asked all the PSUs to stall the appointments of independent directors in the face of flak about the appointment of political nominees as independent directors.[7] ONGC was one of the five PSUs and adjudication proceedings were initiated against it for non-compliance with

---

[7] 'Clause 49 fears', *Business India*, 2 December 2007.

respect to the percentage of independent directors. 'Non-compliance with listing agreement can invite a fine upto Rs 2.5 billion. Besides, stock exchanges can suspend the dealing or trading of the securities of the company'. According to R.S. Sharma, chairman of ONGC, 'Unlike the private sector, accountability is higher in PSUs as they are highly regulated and thus there is no need for 50 per cent independent directors on the board.' His argument is that a PSU not only has government nominees on the board, but it is also answerable to authorities such as Comptroller and Auditor General (CAG), Chief Vigilance Commissioner (CVC), Right to Information Act (RTI), and Committee on Public Undertaking. Besides, a PSU also faces parliamentary accountability ('Clause 49 fears'). Notwithstanding the pleas from the PSU head honchos, SEBI has decided not to dilute the requirements. The new Companies Bill may give them some reprieve as it is likely to peg the independent component required at one-third rather than one-half.

OECD Guidelines for Corporate Governance of State-owned Enterprises

Many of the developing countries still continue to have a dominant presence of state-owned enterprises. Hence, OECD thought it appropriate to evolve a set of governance guidelines for the state-owned enterprises as it did for the private enterprises in member countries. According to OECD, 'A major challenge is to find a balance between the state's responsibility for actively exercising its ownership functions, such as, the nomination and election of the board, while at the same time refraining from imposing undue political interference in the management of the company. Another important challenge is to ensure that there is a level playing field in markets where private sector companies can compete with the state-owned enterprises, and that governments do not distort competition in the way they use their regulatory or supervisory powers.'

According to OECD, the guidelines 'suggest that the state should exercize its ownership functions through a centralized ownership entity, or effectively co-ordinated entities, which should act independently and in accordance with a publicly disclosed ownership policy. The guidelines also suggest the strict seperation of the state's ownership and regulatory functions. If properly implemented, these and other recommended reforms would go a long way to ensure that state ownership is exercised in a professional and accountable manner, and that the state plays a positive role in improving corporate governance across all sectors of our economies. The result would be healthier, more competitive, and transparent enterprises'. The major rcommendations in OECD guidelines are as discussed below.

Ensuring an effective legal and regulatory framework for state-owned enterprises

- There should be a clear separation between the state's ownership function and other state functions that may influence the conditions for state-owned enterprises, particularly with regard to market regulation.
- SOEs should not be exempt from the application of general laws and regulations. Stakeholders, including competitors, should have access to efficient redress and an even-handed ruling when they believe that their rights have been violated.

- SOEs should face competitive conditions regarding access to finance. Their relations with state-owned banks, state-owned financial institutions, and other state-owned companies, should be based on purely commercial grounds.

State acting as an owner

The state should act as an informed and active owner, and establish a clear and consistent ownership policy, ensuring that governance of state-owned enterprises is carried out in a transparent and accountable manner with the necessary degree of professionalism and effectiveness.

- The government should develop and issue an ownership policy that defines the overall objectives of state ownership, the state's role in corporate governance of SOEs, and how it will implement its ownership policy.
- The government should not be involved in the day-to-day management of SOEs and allow them full operational autonomy to achieve their defined objectives.
- The state should let SOE boards exercise their responsibilities and respect their independence.
- The state should exercise its ownership rights according to the legal structure of each company. Keeping this in mind, it should ensure that remuneration schemes for SOE board members foster the long-term interest of the company, and can attract and motivate qualified professionals.

Equitable treatment of shareholders

The SOEs should recognize the rights of all shareholders and in accordance with the OECD principles of corporate governance, ensure their equitable treatment and equal access to corporate information.

- SOEs should observe a high degree of transparency towards all shareholders.
- The co-ordinating or ownership entity and SOEs should ensure that all shareholders are treated equally.
- The participation of minority shareholders in shareholder meetings should be facilitated in order to allow them to take part in fundamental corporate decisions, such as board election.

Relations with stakeholders

The state ownership policy should fully recognize the state-owned enterprises' responsibilities towards stakeholders and report their relations with them.

- Listed on large SOEs, as well as SOEs pursuing important public policy objectives, should report on stakeholder relations.

Transparency and disclosure

State-owned enterprises should observe high standards of transparency in accordance with the OECD Principles of Corporate Governance.

- SOEs should develop efficient internal audit procedures and establish an internal audit function that is monitored by and reports directly to the board and to the audit committee or the equivalent company organ.
- SOEs, especially large ones, should be subject to an annual independent external audit based on international standards. The existence of specific state control procedures does not substitute for an independent external audit.

Responsibilities of the boards of state-owned enterprises

The boards of state-owned enterprises should have the necessary authority, competencies, and objectivity to carry out their function of strategic guidance and monitoring of management. They should act with integrity and be held accountable for their actions.

- The boards of SOEs should be assigned a clear mandate and ultimate responsibility for the company's performance. The board should be fully accountable to the owners, act in the best interest of the company, and treat all shareholders equally.
- SOE boards should carry out their functions of monitoring of management and strategic guidance, subject to the objectives set by the government and the ownership entity. They should have the power to appoint and remove the CEO.
- The boards of SOEs should be so composed that they can exercise objective and independent judgement. Good practice calls for the chair to be separate from the CEO.
- SOE boards should carry out an annual evaluation to appraise their performance.

The Public Definition Dilemma

There is also a debate as to whether a company partly divested in favour of public, institutions, private investors, or a company still fully-owned by the government is more public? According to conventional knowledge, any company that has chosen to mobilize funds from the public is considered as public, whereas companies which are 100 per cent owned by the government are not considered public. Thus, companies which have chosen to raise money from the public, or where the government has divested part of its stake in favour of a private entrepreneur, come under the purview of SEBI regulations as far as governance is concerned. The puzzling question is, which is more public in nature? When the government divests part of its stake in favour of a private entrepreneur, it has actually become more private than it was when it was 100 per cent owned by the government. This is because, when a company is 100 per cent owned by the government, it is doing so on behalf of all the public who support it by way of their payment of various taxes and levies. Thus, a company owned 100 per cent by the government is more accountable to the public, and hence should follow governance practices more stringently than a company where the government has divested part of its stake in favour of a private promoter and/or the public.

CONFLICTS OF INTEREST

Conflicts of interest are a major challenge to the establishment and maintenance of good governance practices, and can occur and exist irrespective of the ownership structures. While some of the conflicts may be similar in nature, others may be typical to the type of ownership structure. Let us look into the conflicts of interest in typical ownership structures which we discussed in the previous sections. Exhibit 7.5 has examples from the Indian context.

Exhibit 7.5
Conflicts of Interest—Just Disclose and Go Forward?

Often directors are nominated from the company's investment bankers, venture capitalists, commercial bankers, solicitors, partners of the management consulting firms whom the company hires for restructuring, partners of auditing firms which audit other companies in the in the group, tax-consultants, etc., giving rise to conflicts of interests. Since their professional association with the company depends largely on their loyalty towards the CEO and the top management, it is very unlikely that they will take an independent view that is different from that of the CEO/top management. While the law for disclosure of such conflicts of interest exists, it can never alleviate their existence. Even the very stringent Sarbanes–Oxley permits such conflicts of interest. Most companies appoint directors in this manner because then one does not need to pay them very highly since the consultant, the solicitor, or the investment banker get paid well by the company for the professional services they offer to it. Given below are a few examples from the Indian context:

- Y.H. Malegam has been an independent director of Tata Tea for many years now. He was a partner of the auditing firm SB Billimoria and Company, which was an independent, external auditor for many other companies in the Tata group.
- Mr Shailesh Haribhakti of Haribhakti and Company, was an independent director of IPCL while his audit firm was an independent auditor for Reliance Energy (now Reliance Infrastructure), both companies belonging to the Reliance Group (in the pre-demerger scenario).
- Prof. Krishna Palepu was an independent director of Satyam Computer Services Ltd while also offering consultancy services to the company. He received Rs 7.95 million for the consultancy work and Rs 1.24 million for his directorship (annual report of Satyam Computer Services Ltd for 2008–09).
- M.L. Bhakta, lead independent director at RIL, is a senior partner of Kanga and Company, solicitors and advocates for the company. The compensation of Mr Bhakta as an independent director during the year 2008–09 was Rs 2.34 million while M/s Kanga and Company were paid Rs 15.2 million as professional fees.
- Mr R.K. Kulkarni, non-executive independent director at Mahindra and Mahindra, is a partner of the firm M/s Khaitan and Company, advocate and solicitors for the company. Mr Kulkarni received Rs 0.97 million as compensation for his directorship while his firm M/s Khaitan and Company was paid Rs 8.56 million (annual reports of RIL and Mahindra and Mahindra, respectively, for 2008–09).

Questions:
1. Do you think that the instances mentioned above are examples of conflicts of interest?
2. Critically comment on the practice of disclosures of instances of inherent conflicts of interest?
3. Can you suggest some remedies beyond just declaration of conflicts of interest?

Conflicts of Interest in Family-owned and Managed Companies

While the earlier allegations of family-managed partnerships or private limited companies flourishing at the expense of publicly-listed companies managed by the same families may no longer be valid, thanks to the transfer pricing norms to be followed by them, a number of conflicts of interest continue to exist. The most commonly observed conflicts are:

- Delineating ownership from management becomes difficult. Governance has to be distinct from management. Managers might embrace risks which at times could affect the very existence and/or goodwill of the organization and business. The board's job is to have a hold on risks in order to ensure a sustained well-being of the business and the organization. When owners are also in management, there can be serious conflicts of interest. The issue becomes more complicated when owners handling management have an overwhelmingly dominant shareholding.
- Another issue relating to conflicts is when the publicly-listed family companies enter into dealings or transactions with other publicly-listed or other entities belonging to family members or their relatives. The expression, 'Blood is thicker than water', could be used to justify such transactions. Today, SEBI insists that all such related party transactions be disclosed in the corporate governance report. For example, the annual report of Bajaj Auto Ltd details the 'pecuniary relationship or transactions of non-executive directors' who belong to the family under the heading 'Remuneration of directors' as follows.
  - Shekhar Bajaj is a director of Bajaj Electricals Ltd. During the year under review, the total value of services availed by Bajaj Auto from Bajaj Electricals Ltd amounted to Rs 22.8 million.
  - Shekhar Bajaj is a director of Hind Musafir Agency Ltd, an accredited travel agency. During the year under review, the total value of services availed by Bajaj Auto from Hind Musafir Agency Limited amounted to Rs 79.1 million.

Loopholes in the Company Law

The company law also has loopholes in this regard. Under Sub-clause (5) of Clause 132, independent directors can have transactions with the company up to a value of 10 per cent of the turnover of the company. 'Many companies have an annual turnover in excess of Rs 100 billion, (Rs in crores in the article) and if a director transacts with such a company for Rs 9.9 billion (Rs in crores in the article), he would still be an independent director, in law. Such a provision throws all canons of corporate governance to the winds', according to LVV Iyer, a corporate lawyer.[8]

- The issue could be relating to the nomination of independent directors itself. The loopholes in the Companies Act enable companies and/or promoters to nominate persons known to them. Prithvi Haldea calls such directors 'Home Directors' ('Independent Directors: The Bare Truth', *The Economic Times*, 14 May 2009). This is because, according to the Companies Act, persons from the wife's side (such as, brother/sister-in-law or father-in-law) or mother's side

[8] Companies Bill, 2009—A desultory exercise, *The Hindu*, 17 August 2009.

(mother's brother) are not considered as relatives. Thus, relatives can be on boards, giving rise to conflicts of interest, but they do not catch the attention as they could be classified as independent. Promoters could thus muster enough support from boards where independence could be only on paper.

- Another issue could be squeezing the public limited company for private gain. This was evident in the case of the Satyam affair. The Rajus, who held a minority stake of 8.6 per cent in the flag-ship company, publicly listed Satyam and tried to use the cash from Satyam to invest in two family-promoted companies—unlisted Maytas Properties and listed Maytas Infrastructure (where the stake of Rajus were reported to be 35 and 36 per cent, respectively).

Conflicts of Interest where Institutions Hold Major Stakes
Variety of financial interests

Most of the institutional investors, such as pension funds, mutual funds, or insurance companies are part of a financial conglomerate offering a variety of financial services, such as advisory, restructuring, investment banking, venture capital, cross-border deals, and some even commercial banking services. While the individual entities offer these services, they would be subsidiaries or associates of an umbrella company offering a gamut of financial services. One mutual fund arm of a financial service conglomerate may have invested their funds in the company's equity and the pension fund arm may manage the pension fund contributions of the company's employees on behalf of the company. The mutual fund as well the pension fund would aim for the total net benefits for the two arms together. They may also keep in mind the potential business interests. While the mutual fund has a responsibility to act in a fiduciary capacity for the investors who have put their hard-earned savings in the units of the mutual fund, which might force the mutual fund to take a hard look at governance of the company, they may relax on this if they stand to gain in the form of additional businesses for the conglomerate as a whole.

According to Smith and Walter (2006), individuals who have invested funds in the company's equity through the mutual fund vehicle 'are exposed to both agency conflicts of corporate managers as well as agency conflicts of investment managers.' When institutions, such as mutual funds or investment bankers not only act as agents on behalf of their clients (investors) but also invest their own funds generated over a period of time, there can be conflicts of interest. According to Smith and Walter, 'They are often very active principals investing their own money (in underwriting, trading positions, and bridge loans), and facilitating transactions (new issues of securities, mergers, restructuring, and off-balance-sheet financial vehicles) on the interface between buying and selling clients, for which their fees and returns on their investments can be considerable.'

Cross directorships

Cross directorships can also result in conflicts of interest. Many bank nominees may occupy board seats on client companies. These banks, or their investment banking arms, or mutual funds promoted by them, could also be investors in the client company's shares. Such cross directorships may prevent the right information from reaching investors. Smith and Walter talk about a high profile example: 'A member of the AT&T board, Citigroup chairman and CEO Sanford Weil, allegedly urged the firm's telecom analyst, Jack Grubman, to rethink his negative views on the company's stock. AT&T's CEO, Michael Armstrong, also served on the Citigroup board. AT&T shares were subsequently up-rated by Grubman and Citigroup coincidentally was mandated to co-manage a major issue of AT&T mobile tracking stock.'

Use of lending power

A financial conglomerate may use its lending power to influence a client to employ its securities or advisory services, or on the other hand, deny credit to clients that refuse to use their other services.

Smith and Walter (2006) identified eight basic conflicts of interest in the fund management industry:

1. Fund managers prefer independent directors who comply with the rules but are cooperative, supportive, and not difficult to work with . Investors prefer directors who will robustly perform their fiduciary duties to the mutual fund shareholders.

    Mutual fund directors are expected to represent the interests of their shareholders in the selection of the fund management company, and in negotiating fees and expense reimbursements. If the directors are not satisfied with the fund manager, they can fetch another. But in practice, this very rarely happens (of course, individual portfolio managers are frequently fired for failing to meet return criteria) even when the fund manager's performance is very poor or fees are very high.

2. Fund managers want maximum fees and expense reimbursements. Investors want their fund directors to negotiate minimum total costs and fully disclose these costs. But very rarely do boards try to reduce the expenses. In fact, expenses have increased from about 0.91 per cent in 1978, when the assets under management were only about $56 billion, to 1.36 per cent in 2004, when the assets under management have grown many fold, to $7,500 billion (Smith and Walter 2006). Mutual fund directors get fat pay cheques so that they never even try to question the fund managers, forget about replacing the fund manager. According to Warren Buffet, the state of affairs of mutual fund directorships is 'a sombie-like process that makes a mockery of stewardship.... A monkey will type-out Shakespeare before an 'independent' board will vote to replace management.'

3. Fund managers want to ensure that they are re-appointed . Investors want boards that act vigorously in selecting the best managers they can find who are capable of top-flight, risk-adjusted performance.

4. Fund managers want to increase assets under management. Investors want optimum investment returns, after expenses and taxes. In reality, while funds under management have increased considerably, the fees and other expenses have also gone up. Smith and Walter say that even fund managers such as John Bogle are critical of the high fees and high portfolio turnover resulting in increased costs. According to him, in 2003, 'the stock market returned

an average of 11.1 per cent to investors, but the average equity mutual fund has delivered just 8.6 per cent—a 2.5 per cent shortfall that was roughly equal to the drain of heavy sales charges, management fees, and operating expenses, and the portfolio turnover cost incurred.'

5. Managers want to push their funds through brokers and financial advisers who need to be compensated by charging fees for distributing the funds to the investors who buy them. Investors do not want to pay these fees if they receive no benefit from them. These fees appear to benefit management companies at the expense of fund investors .

6. Managers want to lower unreimbursed costs through soft dollar commissions from broker-dealers. Investors want the best-price execution of trades and lowest commissions. Brokerages usually reimburse the various costs incurred by fund management companies in return for volume of business. When this is done, the fund managers may not get the best-price execution of trades and lowest commissions.

7. Managers want to favour their own funds by obtaining a 'shelf space' in distribution channels, while investors want access through brokers, to the best and most appropriate funds for their own needs. For example, SEC investigators found that Morgan Stanley was pushing its own in-house mutual funds over third-party funds, and fined them $ 20 million, in 2003.

8. Managers want to be able to organize funds to assist other business interests of the firm, such as investment banking and promoting investments in particular stocks. Investors want all investment decisions by managers to be at arm's length and objective. For example, in 2004, Merrill Lynch was alleged to have failed to disclose investment banking services offered to more than one-third of the companies whose stocks its fund had invested in. Notwithstanding all the stringent regulatory framework for maintaining arm's length criteria for different financial services offered by a financial services conglomerate, conflicts of issues continued to appear in the governance arena with respect to institutional investors.

CONFLICTS OF INTEREST IN PSUS

Most of the conflicts of interest in PSUs occur because of the roles played by bureaucrats and politicians in the running and management of the enterprise. For example, polticians or bureaucrats may try to have their candidate as the chairman and/or managing director in order to push through their private agendas rather than getting the best professional to run the PSU. There have also been many instances where the chairman and/or managing director, or other senior executives of the PSU has placed orders or awarded contracts at rates higher than the best prices, and earned hefty commissions on these. Orders or contracts may also be given to those who do not have the necessary capabilities to execute them. What is best for the PSU usually gets neglected. There may also be issues such as ministers or politicians yielding to recommendations of their cadre and sometimes even creating positions or designations that are not at all needed, leading the PSU to have a bloated workforce and driving it into the sick category. Politicians or bureaucrats may even harp on the flimsy reason that PSUs have employment generation as one of their aims. Most of the conflicts of interest with regret to PSUs dwell on the area of decision-making, which is very often not founded on merit.

OTHER CONFLICTS OF INTEREST IN GENERAL

While the conflicts of interest discussed above are typical of the type of ownership, there are a number of other kinds of conflict of interests which are general in nature and observed across all enterprises irrespective of the ownership criteria. The commonly observed conflicts of interest are:

- A director keeps or adheres to a narrow agenda reflecting the interests of the sponsoring shareholders rather than representing the entire shareholders as a group, as the law mandates.

- The auditor in one company is an independent director in another company belonging to the same group. While we debated about the very independence of such directors, this can also result in conflicts of interest. Anybody who earns compensation from one company for services as a director may lose his/her effectiveness as auditor as he/she may bring down the rigour of audit.

- An independent director acting as a consultant. Shultz (2001) quotes David Bays, a corporate lawyer, thus, 'One board member only accepts directorships if he is assured a minimum number of hours of consulting contracts with the company. He makes considerably more money than before he is "retired".' Shultz also mentions Henry Kissinger, former Secretary of State in the US, who had a huge consultancy with American Express while he sat on their board.

- Another situation which could cause conflict of interest is when the CEO's colleague on another board is appointed a director on the board, and is also given the responsibility of chairing or being a member of important committees such as audit, compensation, or nomination committees.

- The CEO of a company may also appoint a college friend, a batchmate, or a room mate as director and also as members or chairmen of important committees. The law is ineffective in curbing such practices as it is very difficult to identify such earlier associations.

- An independent director of the company may also be a partner of the firm of solicitors and advocates which offer legal advisory services to the company. While we have discussed this earlier from a real independence point of view, conflict of interest is another fall out.

- Directors may have pecuniary interests beyond compensation such as J.N. Godrej, director at Bajaj Auto, who is also a director and shareholder of Godrej & Boyce Manufacturing Company Ltd, which is a vendor to Bajaj Auto. Bajaj Auto purchased goods worth Rs 7.1 million from Godrej & Boyce as on 31 March 2009.

REMEDIAL ACTIONS

While it may be extremely difficult to totally eliminate the conflicts of interest, conscious effort should be made to reduce the instances of such conflicts occurring. Many companies and boards have adopted a 'disclose and go forward' policy, but it should be noted that disclosure of a conflict of interest does not remove the conflict of interest; it continues to exist. As far as possible, any issue such as buying materials from companies under the management of independent directors or being an independent director while also being a partner of the firm offering solicitor's services, must be declared as in the best interests of the company by the CEO/CFO and auditors, and must be put before the shareholders for approval. Companies must bring out details of any type of relationship that exists between the CEO and promoter directors with the existing/potential independent directors. Any kind of MOU between promoters should also be brought to the board and before the shareholders if the company is publicly listed.

In the case of PSUs, the government has to take meticulous care in constituting the board consisting of a majority of really independent directors and the chances of political interferences should be reduced to the minimum. All transactions should be certified by the external independent auditors, as well as the comptroller and auditor general (CAG). The vigilance officers should function under totally independent authority.

In cases where conflicts of interests exist among institutions which hold major stakes in companies, the scenario is very complex and mitigation of conflicts of interest is very difficult considering the structure under which the institutions have been constituted. We have already seen that institutionalizing arm's length practices have not yielded the desired results. The only solution could be not to have more than one kind of service from the umbrella institution. It may sometimes increase the cost but will definitely reduce hidden costs as well as conflicts of interest.

Also, the company should not engage the institution which has invested in the company for any services. In a typical corporate scenario in India, where promoters/promoter families promote a number of companies, measures have to be taken to prevent instances of conflicts of interest across the entire group. This might not be easy as the two companies belonging to the same group are treated as two independent economic entities under the law. Boards, as well as directors, have to remember that their reputations are at stake, and that they are accountable. Hence, it is better for the board to avoid nominating or continuing with directors who are vulnerable to conflicts of interest and also for directors not to get involved in acts or actions that will result in conflicts of interest. When directors have conflicts of interest, it will be extremely difficult for them to handle their fiduciary roles and be accountable to the shareholders as a whole.

DOES SIZE OF THE BOARD MATTER IN GOVERNANCE?

What should be the right size of a board? This has been a puzzling factor for many boards. According to Ram Charan (1998), 'Although the precise number of directors may vary, the rationale for having a relatively small board is consistent.' He says that the median size of large-company boards dropped from 14 in 1972 to 12 in 1989, with experts driving for even fewer members. But there has not been much correlation between company size and board size, at least in India. The biggest and highly diversified company in India, namely, Reliance Industries Ltd, has a board size of 15 (including two executive directors appointed very recently), according to the RIL annual report for 2008–09. Reliance achieved a revenue of about Rs 1463.3 billion (approximately $28.85 billion) and a profit after tax of Rs 153.1 billion (approximately $3.02 billion) during the year. Out of the 15 directors, six are whole-time and the balance nine are non-executive directors. There are only four directors from the family.

Bajaj Auto Ltd, a Rs 90 billion (approx. $2 billion) and PAT of Rs 6.565 billion (approx $146 million) has 16 members on its board with seven representations from the family. There are four directors in an executive capacity and all of them belong to the family..

'The smaller the board, the greater the director involvement' (Shultz 2001). Carter and Lorsch (2004) concur: 'Boards should be as small as feasible. A smaller group of directors will find it easier to interact and reach decisions subject to the need for enough directors to do the work of the board and its committees.' According to Charan (1998), 'To truly work, the board must be able to engage in substantive dialogue. Managing the dialogue to ensure balanced participation among sixteen or more people is a Herculean task for any individual.' When boards are large, there will not be enough time for every director to explain fully his opinions. Another problem which Shultz (2001) has identified is that 'because a large board is cumbersome, deliberation, and decision-making tend to get pushed down to the committee level, with the result that the full board evolves into an increasingly passive forum.'

But Carter and Lorsch caution: 'While smaller boards have definite advantages over large boards, an individual board's circumstances should determine the appropriate number of directors. What factors should influence board size? A primary one is the skill set the board needs in order to do its job. Each board needs a specific range of skills and experience around the table. The more categories of expertise directors feel they need, the larger the board will have to be' (Carter and Lorsch 2004).

In professionally-managed companies, the number of directors could be smaller or just adequate, while in family-managed companies, the members could be larger as there may be compulsions from various family factions to have their nominees on the board. The numbers would have been even higher had the practice of 'nominee directors' from institutional investors continued. Dimma (2006) says that 'best practice dictates that a dominant shareholder ought to be able to appoint directors in proportion to its shareholdings upto a maximum of 50 per cent, plus one. One such shareholder can and should be satisfied with less than such proportionate entitlement.' According to him, 'the ideal board should consist of seven to thirteen members. The precise number will vary with company size, as well as, with the nature of the business, and with idiosyncratic preferences of the board chairman and directors.' One major contributor to the increase in numbers is the insistence on forming committees, some of which may be mandatory.

While Clause 49 requires that audit committees and investor grievance committees should be mandatory, US regulations make it mandatory to have audit committees, remuneration committees, and nomination/governance committees, all made up of independent directors. Thus, those Indian companies which have sought to raise money abroad and list on stock exchanges, such as the New York Stock Exchange (NYSE) or NASDAQ, will also have to follow the US regulations. It also depends on the logistics that the board and directors have to deal with. As Carter and Lorsch (2004) say, 'Given the time limits boards face, it is generally more efficient for all of the board's committees to meet simultaneously just prior to the full board's meetings. This means a board needs enough members so that there isn't any overlap among committee rosters.'

Dimma (2006) cautions about large numbers: 'With boards bigger than perhaps fifteen members, speech-making tends to replace serious discussion. And the locus of decision shifts from the full board to an executive committee along with a generous assortment of functional committees.' While Carter and Lorsch (2004) felt that the requirement of committees and their meeting logistics tended to make boards larger, 'but we remain strongly committed to the proposition that boards should drive to be as small as they can be. What do we mean by small? If pushed to offer a number, we would suggest a maximum of ten directors.'

Charan (1998) quotes Bill Adams, former Chairman of Armstrong, who believes that boards can function very effectively with just six outside directors and one inside director. According to Adams, 'Beyond that you are not adding any new perspectives, and the larger number diminishes the board's ability to have long, intensive, discussions either across the top, or drilling down into the issues. If you take a board of, say, twelve directors, you usually have about six who are pulling the weight anyway.'

While family dynamics may result in an increase in the size of boards in family-managed companies in India, PSUs also face the problem of larger boards. This is largely because a number of ministries are involved in the setting up of a typical PSU in India. There will be nominees from the particular ministry under which the PSU comes, there may also be representatives from the ministries of industry and commerce, nominees from the state government where the unit is located, and representatives from ministries such as environment, tourism, etc., if it has a bearing on these aspects. Then there will be full-time professional directors heading each of the functions, such as, finance, production/operations, marketing, HR, technical, etc. There can also be nominees from financial institutions. According to SEBI guidelines in force, independent directors up to 50 per cent may also be required as in most of the PSUs, the chairman is full-time. This tends to make the boards of PSUs unusually large and unwieldy. Some head honchos of PSUs have been bargaining and lobbying for a lesser percentage of independent directors as they feel that there are a number of checks and balances conducted by various government agencies which reduce the need for a higher percentage of independent directors.

SUMMARY

What essentially led to the necessity of corporate governance was the wide dispersion of ownership as corporations grew and control over the assets was left to professional managers. As early as the 1930s, Berle and Means had established this concern, and management control, without being in dominant control of ownership, was in vogue in India too. But post-economic liberalization in India, initiated in the early nineties, most promoters have increased their stakes in their companies to much larger levels.

Even though there has been a gradual shift from a shareholder approach to a stakeholder approach with respect to the firm, most of the theories of corporate governance revolve around the premise that governance is essential because there can be conflicts of interests between owners and managers. There may also be typical governance issues depending on the type of ownership structure that exists—the family-owned and managed firm, the institutional investors holding dominant positions, and the government owning major chunks of shares.

The governance of family-owned enterprises deserve attention because 80 to 90 per cent of all businesses across the globe are family-owned. But there can be a number of issues among family members that complicate the entire governance mechanisms of such companies. Also, there can be a number of paradoxes which the family-owned and managed companies have to deal with. Families try to deal with governance issues through mechanisms such as a family council, advisory boards, and a board of directors with outside directors present. Keeping the potential conflicts in mind, some family-managed businesses have started creating MOUs between the members of the family, whereby they agree on various things so as to prevent such issues from cropping up. At times families also create a family constitution which will act as a guideline for all the members and glue the family together. There may also be a set of family policies detailing how the family can deal with issues as and when they arise. Some even go to the extent of creating a family creed or philosophy. The family-managed companies have to deal with ownership related issues, the role of independent directors on their boards, compensation-related issues, the commitment to the long term, etc.

In most developed markets, institutions hold major chunks of shares in publicly-listed companies. While it is expected that institutional investors show more interest in governance, they often get mired in conflicts of interest. But one can witness the rise of governance-conscious institutions and some of them such as CalPERS, have created their own corporate governance guidelines. While institutions have been proactive, their ability to influence the governance procedures is severely limited due to the stringent restrictions on their holdings in companies where they invest.

Another kind of ownership that is commonly observed is where the government is a dominant shareholder. This is usually typical of lesser developed or developing countries, which have or hitherto had,

lesser opportunities for private entrepreneurship. These pose great problems to governance as governmental or bureaucratic interferences are common. Also, there can be a serious issue concerning the goals and objectives of the companies. While regulators such as SEBI insist that PSUs which choose to raise money from the public follow the same set of guidelines as other publicly-listed companies, the chief executives of these companies have been pleading for less stringent norms for them, as there are numerous additional checks and balances for PSUs. Bodies such as OECD, have evolved specific corporate governance guidelines for state-owned enterprises (SOEs) considering that they continue to exist and operate in many countries.

One puzzle the governance mechanisms have to deal with is the conflict of interest of directors and boards. While a number of companies adopt a 'disclose and go-forward' policy, on closer scrutiny several of them seem to be beset with such conflicts. Disclosure of conflicts of interest do not remove them. There can be a variety of conflicts of interests depending on the types of ownership. A number of alternative remedial actions have been discussed.

The debate on the size of the board has been ongoing. While experts feel that the smaller the board, the better, the size may also be determined by the diversity of operations, type of ownership, the regulatory requirements regarding constitution of committees, etc. The general agreement is that very large boards will fail to encourage participation from everybody, and will thus curtail discussion and debate in the boardroom.

KEY TERMS

Adjudication   Sit in judgement

Advisory board   Body of experts who advise

Cobweb of ownership   Deliberate effort to create lack of clarity about ownership

Conflict of interest   Engaging in transactions that may raise questions about objectivity

Creed   Philosophy

Deterrents   Discouraging factors

Family assembly   Coming together of all family members.

Family council   Representative body of different family factions

Fostering equality   Encouraging to be fair

Hermetically sealed   Totally closed from outside view

Inculcations   Fix through repetitive effort

Incumbent management   Management in position today

Intrinsic conservatism   Inbuilt conservative approach

Nepotism   Showing partisan attitude

Nest feathering   Make things comfortable for enriching oneself

Objective function   What a firm wants to accomplish

Ownership constraint   Limiting the ability of the owner to influence

Patient money   Investments aimed at long-term sustainability

Philanthropy   Helping those sections of society who are in need of help

Poison pill   Defence technique used by a firm under threat of a takeover (such as stripping assets to reduce the value of the firm)

Privatization   Change the ownership from public to private sector

Solvency   Liquidity ensuring financial commitments

Umbrella company   Holding company that offers a variety of products (services through its individual, separate entities)

CONCEPT REVIEW QUESTIONS

1. What are the different forms of ownership structures commonly observed?
2. What are the problems faced in family-managed firms in the area of corporate governance?
3. What are the different stages of evolution of family-promoted and managed enterprises with respect to corporate governance?
4. What are the problems faced by PSUs in implementing corporate governance?
5. Critically examine the role of institutional investors in corporate governance.
6. Narrate the difficulties of implementing a good corporate governance process in PSUs?
7. What are conflicts of interest? Is there any relationship between the nature of ownership and conflicts of interest?

CRITICAL THINKING QUESTIONS

What steps should family leaders take to prevent squabbles in family businesses?

PROJECT WORK

Compare the presence of insiders (promoter nominees, executive directors, etc.) on the boards of major Indian and US companies, using constituent companies in a bechmark index in the two countries as samples.

REFERENCES

Ashby, Meredith D. and Stephen A. Miles (2002), *Leaders Talk Leadership: Top Executives Speak Their Minds*, Oxford University Press, New York.

Bebchuk, Lucian and Jesse Fried (2004), *Pay without Performance: The Unfulfilled Promise of Executive Compensation*, Harvard University Press, Cambridge, Massachusetts.

Berle, Adolf A. and Gardiner C. Means (1932), *The Modern Corporation and Private Property*, Transaction Publishers, New Brunswick.

Bhat, U.R. (2005), 'The business of inherited control', *The Economic Times*, 13 July 2005.

Bhattacharya, Ashish K. (2006), 'Role of Government', in *Corporate Governance in Public Sector Enterprises*, S.M. Dewan (ed.), Dorling Kindersley, New Delhi.

Cadbury, Sir Adrian (1992), *Report of the Committee on the Financial Aspects of Corporate Governance*, Gee & Co Ltd, London.

Cadbury, Sir Adrian (2000), *Family Firms and Their Governance: Creating Tomorrow's Company from Today's*, Egon Zehnder International, London.

Carter, Colin B. and Jay W. Lorsch (2004), *Back to the Drawing Board*, Harvard Business School Press, Boston.

Charan, Ram (1998), *Boards at Work: How Corporate Boards Create Competitive Advantage*, Jossy-Bass, San Francisco.

Charan, Ram (2005), *Boards that Deliver: Advancing Corporate Governance from Compliance to Competitive Advantage*, Jossey-Bass, San Francisco.

Chew Jr, Donald H. and Stuart L. Gillan (2005), *Corporate Governance at the Crossroads*, Tata McGraw-Hill, New Delhi.

'Clause 49 Fears' (2007), *Business India*, 2 December 2007.

Conger, Jay A., David Finegold, and Edward E. Lawler III (2000), 'Appraising Boardroom Performance', *Harvard Business Review on Corporate Governance*, Harvard Business School Press, Boston.

Das, Subhash Chandra (2008), *Corporate Governance in India: An Evaluation*, Prentice-Hall of India, New Delhi.

Dewan S.M. (2006), 'Public Sector Overview', in *Corporate Governance in Public Sector Enterprises*, S.M. Dewan (ed.), Dorling Kindersley, New Delhi.

Dimma, William A. (2006), *Tougher Boards for Tougher Times: Corporate Governance in the Post-Enron Era*, Wiley-India, New Delhi.

Edwards, Franklin R. and Glen R. Hubbard (2005), 'The growth of institutional stock ownership: A promise unfulfilled', in *Corporate Governance at the Crossroads*, Donald H. Chew Jr and Stuart C. Gillan (eds), Tata McGraw-Hill, New Delhi.

'Family biz beats professional cos fair and square' (2006), *The Economic Times*, 22 September 2006.

Greenbury, Sir Richard (1995), *Director Remuneration*, Report of a study group chaired by Sir Richard Greenbury, Gee & Co Ltd, London.

'Indian family business ownership structure—A ready reckoner' (2004), ET in the Classroom, *The Economic Times*, 20 December 2004.

Infosys annual report 2008–09.

Jain, Rajesh (2006), *Chains that Liberate: Governance of Family Firms*, Macmillan, New Delhi.

Kumar T.N., Satheesh (2005), 'Anil Ambani Ko Gussa Kyon Aaya?' *Effective Executive*, November.

Mallin, Christine A. (2007), *Corporate Governance*, Oxford University Press, New Delhi.

Marisetty, Vijay B., Keryn Chalmers, and A.V. Vedpuriswar (2005), 'Confounding Corporate Governance', *Business Line*, 20 May.

Phan, Philip H. (2000), *Taking Back the Boardroom*, McGraw-Hill, Singapore.

Pound, John (2000), 'Beyond Takeovers: Politics Comes to Corporate Control', *Harvard Business Review on Corporate Governance*, Harvard Business School Press, Boston.

Rajan, T.R. (2001), 'How quarrels in family-run businesses begin', *Business Line*, 18 September 2001.

Reddy Y.R.K. (2006), Issues in public sector governance in *Corporate Governance in Public Sector Enterprises*, S.M. Dewan (ed.), Dorling Kindersley, New Delhi.

Shultz, Susan F. (2001), *The Board Book*, East West Books, Chennai.

Smith, Roy C. and Ingo Walter (2006), *Governing the Modern Corporation: Capital Markets, Corporate Control, and Economic Performance*, Oxford University Press, New York.

Som, Lalita (2006), *Stock Market Capitalization and Corporate Governance*, Oxford University Press, New Delhi.

Tripathi, Dwijendra and Jyoti Jumani (2007), *The Concise Oxford History of Indian Business*, Oxford University Press, New Delhi.

Wallace, Peter and John Zinkin (2005), *Mastering Business in Asia: Corporate Governance*, Wiley-India, New Delhi.

Waring, Kerrie and Chris Pierce (2005), *The Handbook of International Corporate Governance: A Definitive Guide*, Kogan Page, London.

www.calpers.ca.gov.

www.oecd.org/document/33/0,3343,en_2649_3484 7_34046561_1_1_1_37439,00.html, 19 October 2009.

Closing Case

Should RIL Board Sack the CEO or Shareholders Express No Confidence in the Board?

Ambani brothers, Mukesh and Anil, Chairman and CEO of RIL and Chairman of RNRL, respectively have been locked in a battle about the supply of gas from the KG Basin–D6 Block developed by RIL to RNRL at a price of $2.34 per mmbtu, for 17 years. The suit is being heard by a division bench of the Supreme Court starting from 20 October 2009. RIL has filed the appeal in the Supreme Court praying for nullifying the Mumbai High Court judgement on the issue of pricing of the gas supplied by RIL, managed by Mukesh, to RNRL, managed by Anil. The judgement delivered by the Mumbai High Court ordered RIL to honour the 2005 family agreement to supply gas to RNRL at the previously agreed price.

Business Line dated 21 October 2009 reported that Mr Harish Salve, senior counsel for RIL, told a bench headed by the Chief Justice K.G. Balakrishnan that if Mr Anil Ambani has any grievances regarding the family agreement with his elder brother as part of the de-merger pact of the business, then he should sue Mr Mukesh Ambani as an individual, rather than indulging in 'shadow boxing', using RNRL. Mr Salve also pointed out that RIL and RNRL have more or less a common shareholder base and there were no issues between the shareholders of the companies. 'You have to deal with private disputes and personal losses, if any, separately. You cannot bring private remedy to the shareholder level', Mr Salve is reported to have said.

According to the report that appeared in *The Economic Times* on 21 October 2009, the court is reported to have said: 'There is no fight among the shareholders of RIL and RNRL'. It compared the dispute between the Ambanis to a war between two nations: 'It is like a fight between two nations, the conflict is between the heads of nations and not the people', Justice Raveendran is reported to have remarked. The Mumbai High Court, while delivering judgement on the issue had said, 'Parties should enter into suitable agreement on the basis of quantity, tenure, and price, as specified under the MOU either by renegotiating the terms…or reverting to Smt Kokilaben Dhirubhai Ambani, who has reserved her ability to intervene again if the parties fail to act upon the MOU' ('RNRL wins rights for RIL gas, 44 per cent cheaper', *ET*, 16 June 2009).

On 18 June 2009, *ET* further reported that two directors of RIL told *ET Now* that they will talk to the chairman, Mukesh Ambani and will also call for an urgent board meeting of the company to discuss the fallout of the High Court judgement since it had mentioned RIL's board meeting which had endorsed the family MOU soon after the brothers split in 2005, and that the corporate governance panel of India's largest company would study the judgement to understand its implications on shareholders. *ET* also said that both the directors spoke on condition of anonymity.

But, before the Supreme Court, Harish Salve, counsel for RIL, maintained that the board of directors of RIL were not aware of the MOU which was signed after the mediation of Kokilaben, mother of the Ambani brothers. According to him, the MOU was never placed before the board of directors of the company and its content was not known to them.

In 2008, a gas utilization policy was drawn up by the government according to which the government fixed the price of sale of gas by RIL to some power and fertilizer companies at $4.20 mmbtu.

Other facts:

- Mukesh Ambani controlled 49.03 per cent of RIL's equity capital as on 31 March 2009, while Anil Ambani controlled 54.84 per cent of RNRL's equity.
- At the time of de-merger in 2005, the Ambanis were said to be controlling only 46 per cent of the equity capital of RIL.
- Apparently, the board of RIL did not discuss the de-merger during the period of arriving at a formula for the settlement between the warring brothers even though the de-merger would change the very constitution of RIL as most of the other companies were subsidiaries of RIL or RIL had a major stake in them as promoter.
- Apparently, no shareholder or regulatory body raised any serious questions about the role of the boards of the various companies within the group.
- The Mumbai High Court never raised the issue of the role of the boards in the de-merger decisions.
- The de-merger scheme was approved by the Mumbai High Court in 2005.
- RIL signed a set of agreements with four companies—Reliance Communications Ventures, Reliance Energy Ventures, Reliance Capital Ventures, and Reliance Natural Resources—in January 2006. The agreements included the gas supply agreement and non-competition agreement with a right of first refusal, allowing either side to buy out the other in case the business was being sold. Thereafter, the company boards were reconstituted allowing Anil to take over and then list these companies. In November 2006, Reliance Anil Dhirubhai Ambani Group (R-ADAG) challenged the gas supply agreement in the Bombay High Court saying that the spirit of the June 2005 agreement had not been followed in the January 2006 agreements; and that these agreements were signed with the four companies before their management control was handed over to Anil.
- The Mumbai High Court verdict in favour of RNRL says that RIL's counsel, Harish Salve, was asked by the Bench whether the price of $2.34 per mmbtu has a component of profit, to which Salve made a very categorical statement, that even at that price RIL makes a profit (*Businessworld*, 29 June 2009).
- There is only one KG-D6 Block from which Mukesh had promised to supply gas to Anil's RNRL.

Discussion Questions

1. Critically comment on the role of boards of directors in family-promoted, controlled, and managed companies.
2. What actions must RIL take on Mukesh Ambani, Chairman and Managing Director of RIL, for entering into a private agreement with his brother concerning the assets and resources owned and operated by the company in which outside public and other shareholders held 54 per cent?
3. Should outside shareholders have expressed their lack of confidence in the current RIL board?
4. Do you think that legal bodies such as courts and regulatory bodies such as SEBI should act more in consonance with each other?

Note: At the time of this book going to print, a division bench of the Supreme Court has already given a verdict in favour of RIL on its appeal and the companies have started negotiations for the supply of gas to RNRL.

CHAPTER 8

GOVERNANCE, CAPITAL MARKET INSTITUTIONS, AND GOVERNMENT

And, perhaps most important of all, the shareowners themselves must learn to trust in the market over the longer term.

– William Dale Crist, President and Chairman of the Board of Administration, CalPERS
(quoted in *Leaders Talk Leadership*, by Meredith A. Ashby and Stephen A. Miles)

LEARNING OBJECTIVES

After studying this chapter, you will be able to
- Explain the role of shareholder activism in corporate governance
- Define the role played by institutions, institutional investors, investment bankers, asset management companies, banks, venture capitalists, stock exchanges, auditors, etc., in the governance of a firm
- Describe the developed market argument and list the flaws observed in the developed markets
- Elucidate whether it is better to have laws or codes of best practices
- Explain the role of the government, describe company laws and regulations, and list the provisions and deficiencies
- Explain governance ratings and list rating agencies
- Understand the importance of information in governance and the need for co-operation and collaboration

Opening Case

Can Auditors Act Independently?

According to company law everywhere, shareholders do not have the right to inspect the account books of the companies in which they have invested. This requires that a body independent of the company be appointed to inspect the accounts on their behalf, and keep the management on vigil about financial transactions. Alternatively, the auditors have to act in a fiduciary capacity to ensure that the management and the company use its finance prudently. They have to watch shareholders' money really closely. But can they be committed to protect shareholder interests, given that their remuneration is fixed and paid by the company management? Even though theoretically shareholders have no access to books of accounts, some shareholders who may be on the management do get the privilege of accessing books. Ramalinga Raju, the displaced executive chairman of the ertswhile Satyam Computers, owned only 8.61 per cent of the company's equity, but had access to all the books of accounts and other financial data, which enabled him to indulge in and commit fraud. In RIL, almost three million shareholders outside the company did not have any right to inspect the accounts, but Mukesh Ambani, who controlled 49.03 per cent had the authority to inspect the books, as he was also on the management. With his commanding position as the person who controlled an overwhelming block of shares, could he not influence the appointment of the so-called independent auditors? If Raju could do so with his minor holding, Mukesh could easily have done it too. While Raju could not get away with it because of his low shareholding, Mukesh could get out of the problem or defeat any move by other shareholders against him.

The issue is not one of promoter shareholders influencing auditors, but rather, of auditor independence. 'On 12 January, elected representatives of accountants and auditors debated the Satyam scam and PWC's role in it. Many among these 34 members of the council of the Institute of Chartered Accountants of India (ICAI), the sole regulator for statutory auditors, demanded at the meeting—as others have for years—greater independence from the companies they audit.

'Greater? How can the statutory auditors be independent if they are paid by the company they are supposed to audit? Big or small, the fees can influence the report card', wrote Puja Mehra (Mehra 2009). She continued: 'Who should pay the piper? Top office-bearers of ICAI council agree that the appointment of auditors—and also payments for services rendered—should not be left to the companies they audit. One solution is for listed companies to pool in money and hand it over to the stock exchanges who can then appoint auditors.This will make the auditors answerable to the bourses and not corporate executives.'

Business Today dated 8 February 2009 also carried an article titled 'Confessions of Auditors' and quoted confessions of three auditors. Confession 2 is reproduced here: 'I had taken up a plum position at one of the big four accounting firms. They had placed me at their office in a BRIC (Brazil, Russia, India, China) country. It was to be a new world, a new job, a new life. There was a lot of excitement. One of the first audits assigned to me was of the accounts of an auto major. Its operations in this country were sizable. The portfolio of investments ran into billions of rupees. At some point during the audit, I found that as much as a quarter of the advances this company had been extended were unsecured, meaning no securities backed them. This immediately raised a bright red flag in front of me. Unsecured advances remain harmless for as long as nothing happens. If there is a mishap, they lose value, causing catastrophes. The minimum stipulated disclosure requirements had not directed the balance sheet or the audit to reveal distinctly, the exposure to unsecured advances. A complete picture of the risk on the balance sheet however, was required, especially since the amount was huge. As auditors are free to raise the bar on disclosures above the stipulated minimum for the benefit of society at large, I decided to include the break-up in my notes in the audit. The company however, disagreed. Following lengthy discussions, my boss, who was the partner due to sign the audit report, overruled me.'

'Regulations of Audit', *Business Today,* dated 22 February 2009 compares the audit regulations in six countries, namely the US, the UK, Japan, France, Belgium, and India ('Inside The Secret World of Auditing: How It's Done Globally').

US

- The SEC regulates auditors in the US and appoints members of the Public Company Accounting Oversight Board under the Sarbanes–Oxley Act of 2002.
- CEOs and CFOs have to certify the financial statements they file with the SEC.
- A company cannot have certain types of consulting contracts with auditors.
- The Auditing Standards Board of the American Institute of Certified Public Accountants, a representative body issued a standard (SAS 99) in 2002 that has several requirements to help an auditor find frauds, not all of which are mandatory.

UK

- The government adopted Financial Reporting Council regulates auditors.
- One of it boards, the Accounting Standards Board, issues accounting standards.

Japan

- The government-appointed Accounting Standards Board regulates auditors. The certified Public Accountants and Audit Oversight Board is appointed by the prime minister with the consent of the Diet.

France

- Joint audit is mandatory and companies therefore have two auditors.

Belgium

- If an auditor provides any permitted non-audit services to a company it audits, the fees for such services cannot exceed the audit fees.

India

- Auditors regulate themselves through ICAI and there is no independent regulator.

Discussion Questions

1. Do you think that the independence of auditors is questionable because they are appointed and paid by companies?
2. Shareholders, as a rule, cannot inspect the books of accounts of the companies. But shareholders who are in the management have access to all books of accounts. Does this lead to ambiguity in regulation?
3. Do you think that Indian regulations on auditing need to be strengthened? If yes, suggest various steps.

GOVERNANCE—THE ROLE OF CAPITAL MARKET INSTITUTIONS AND GOVERNMENT

Governance of companies is taken care of by the boards of directors, who represent and are responsible to the shareholders through their fiduciary duties. In companies that are listed, the shares get exchanged or transacted between investors through a process facilitated by institutions that constitute the capital market. As we have seen in Chapter 7, institutional investors have become dominant shareholders in most of the developed markets such as the US and UK. In addition to institutional investors, capital markets include intermediaries and even experts, who continuously acquire and disseminate information on a timely basis, enabling fair and efficient execution of financial transactions. According to Smith and Walter (2006), these elements—the investors and the intermediaries—represent 'external' factors affecting modern corporate governance that are as important to the enduring health of the system as the 'internal' factors such as the very formation of corporations. The fiduciary duty of the board of directors is exercised on behalf of the shareholders, and the efficient utilization of assets and other resources by its management team led by the CEO.

In this chapter, we will discuss the roles played by the various capital market institutions such as stock exchanges, brokers, investment bankers, financial institutions and banks, and venture capital and private equity companies. We will also discuss mutual funds, pension funds, and foreign institutional investors (FIIs); audit firms; regulatory agencies such as SEBI, RBI, IRDA, PFRDA, etc., and institutions that cater to specific segments such as SIDBI, NSIC, state government industrial development corporations, etc. All these institutions play a very important role in bringing a platform for transactions in capital and the way capital markets function and establish norms for corporate governance. In addition, governments, both federal as well as state, create a framework of laws for the establishment of a corporate entity and constitution of the board of directors and norms for compensating the managing director and other directors, submission of returns to the governments on the financial structure and performance of the entity, the size of the board, raising capital, closure or winding up, etc. Thus, governments or its bodies also play a definite role in establishing a framework for corporate governance. The institutions in the capital market, through their interventions, enable companies to establish and nurture a process of governance in them. One of the most important and effective ways of ensuring good governance is through the active involvement of shareholders in ensuring that the right questions are asked at appropriate times so that wide variations from a desired set of practices do not ever happen.

Shareholder Activism

While boards have, theoretically, been appointed or at least the nomination of directors to the board has been approved or ratified by shareholders, the shareholders' involvement usually stops there. And according to conventional wisdom, directors and boards are fiduciaries for shareholders, and hence shareholders expect them to act in their interests. While joint-stock companies have many positive sides to it, as Berle and Means found, the shareholding becomes highly dispersed putting the onus of taking care of the interests of such widely distributed shareholding on the board.

However, what if the board ignores its fiduciary responsibilities and breaches the trust vested in it by the shareholders? The very advantage or benefits derived from the joint stock corporate concept itself could become self-defeating. When the number of shareholders were small, they could be brought together and such bodies could easily influence the board if it were deviating from its fiduciary responsibilities. As the numbers became large, this union of shareholders became rather difficult, and hence the chances of influencing the board also became weaker. Also, a large number of investors are not really interested in or aware of the role of board of directors as fiduciaries. They do not become shareholders viewing the ownership of shares as ownership of business. They may invest their hard-earned money in a company's voting share with the idea of making good returns on their investments. If they have not been rewarded with the returns expected, they will exit from the investment in a particular company's shares and invest elsewhere with the help of various institutions that enable the capital market to survive and prosper.

For example, Reliance Industries Ltd has a total number of 2,158,238 shareholders according to the annual report for the year 2008–09. Of this, 2,109,191 hold shares in the range 1-500. These shareholders together hold 114,696,426 shares amounting to 7.29 per cent of the outstanding equity shares of the company. About 89 per cent of the shares are held by 2863 shareholders, holding in excess of 5000 shares. And, of this, 44 shareholders control 49.03 per cent of the outstanding shares. These 44 shareholders form part of the promoter group. Thus, about 40 per cent of the shareholding is spread among 2819 shareholders. Even though this number dwarfs in comparison to the number of shareholders in the category 1-500, this number is still high, in the sense that the average holding per shareholder (outside shareholder) is only roughly 0.01 per cent making it very difficult to influence the board, unless all of them come together. These shareholders generally belong to the category of Indian institutional investors, foreign institutional investors (FIIs), other corporate bodies, custodians of depository receipts, etc., who may be more interested in getting a good return on their investments in the near term, rather than in the long-term. It is seen that those who are really interested in good corporate governance cannot have a short-term outlook. Those who have a short-term outlook will usually be looking for quicker returns in the near term rather than worry about corporate governance. Very few of the institutional investors have genuine incentives in terms of rocking the boat in pursuit of good governance. While, in general, the intervention from shareholders has been rather low, according to Colley et al. (2003), boards and directors have been under pressure because 'recent years have seen a rise in the number of organizations engaged in shareholder activism and the intensity of their attempts to interfere with the normal processes of board oversight.' Ward (1997) has opined that 'Investor activism, though quieter, has grown more popular, in part because it seems to work. A growing body of evidence suggests that shareholder activism raises share prices, even if a takeover is not in the air.'

According to a study conducted by Gompers, Ishii, and Metrick (2003), of 1500 publicly-listed companies, there is a strong correlation between good corporate governance and superior shareholder value. The study also pointed out that those companies which are 'democracies', granting great powers to the voters (shareholders), have outperformed the 'dictatorships', those trying to protect the management from being accountable to voters (shareholders). According to Shultz (2001), 'There are millions of individual shareholders who invest in good faith and who deserve to be fairly represented by the directors. Often individual shareholders are dismissed as gadflies, misdirected, and microfocused.' This puts the responsibility on the shoulders of institutional investors.

But institutions, as a common practice, do not interfere with the decisions of management or promoter owners unless there is a serious issue which necessitates their intervention, as happened in the Satyam case. For example, institutions hold about 25.22 per cent in RIL, but they have never questioned any of the RIL decisions such as the de-merger of various businesses or the board's passive attitude towards the ongoing tussle between the company and Anil Ambani regarding supply of gas from KG-D6 Block. But Colley et al. feel that 'Activists representing shareholders and other pressure groups have increasingly come to question the activities of boards and the companies they oversee in areas related to shareholder fraud, legally required disclosure of appropriate facts and figures, conflicts of interest on the part of directors, and the carrying out of other duties of directors.' But shareholder democracy has its own limitations. Like any other scenario of democracy, shareholder democracy also must mean 'one-share, one-vote'. In many companies in the US, the promoter's holding is usually not very high, whereas in India it is usually very high.

In the thirty-seventh convention of the Institute of Company Secretaries of India, a senior member, Mr J. Krishna Murthy, is reported to have stated: 'When a promoter puts up his hand (in the annual general meetings), the resolution is passed and when he puts it down, the resolution gets turned down.'[1] Also, at present, we do not have any major institutional investors or other categories of investors who show active interest in the affairs of governance of the company. Even proxy fights rarely occur or succeed in a majority of Indian companies. While shareholders of US companies have different avenues such as open voting, proxy fights, or class-action suits, apart from selling their holdings, the Indian counterpart is usually left with the last two options. And, the last alternative, namely the class-action suit is very unlikely to happen, keeping in mind the power of promoter shareholders and also because the process is costly and time-consuming. Also, courts usually do not interfere with the actions of the board of directors as it is felt that directors must have the discretion and freedom in managing the affairs of the company.

Notwithstanding the obstacles and dissuading aspects, institutional investors such as CalPERS, TIAA-CREF, LENS, etc., have been trying relentlessly to make a difference by targeting underperforming companies. *Journal of Applied Corporate Finance*, a study by Stephen Nesbitt published in 1994 provides data that establishes 'a real, beneficial CalPERS effect' from institutional input. Studying 42 companies targeted by CalPERS as underperformers, Nesbitt found that in the five years after CalPERS came knocking, 'these targeted companies outperformed the Standard & Poor index by 41 per cent' (Ward 1997).

According to Shultz (2001), CalPERS 'reminds its shareholders that stock ownership is an ongoing event with ongoing oversight responsibilities.' She says that 'CalPERS, holder of 10.2 million shares, withheld votes for senator George J. Mitchell and for Robert A.M. Stern, an architect who has designed buildings for Disney and its chairman, Michael Eisner, because Disney pays them consulting fees.' Smith and Walter (2006) narrate how TIAA-CREF acted in the case of Disney: 'During the shareholder meeting, TIAA-CREF withheld its support for Michael D Eisner and the entire board of directors of Walt Disney. This vote reflects TIAA-CREF's view that corporate boards must be independent and fully accountable to meet their fiduciary obligations to shareholders. At present, there is a considerable question as to whether this is the case at Walt Disney. Boards of Directors must play their required oversight role. To enhance shareholder value over the long-term, we believe the board of Walt Disney needs to meaningfully examine

---

[1] 'Shareholder democracy has long way to go in India', *Business Line*, 8 November 2009.

and analyze its structure and board leadership to give the company the credibility it needs on issues, such as, CEO succession, company strategy, and executive compensation. We think our vote, together with the votes of other concerned investors, sends the right message.' Nesbitt's study also revealed an interesting development: 'It found that CalPERS's efforts from 1987–89 were much less successful than those launched after 1990, Why? Before 1990, CalPERS had concentrated on putting out anti-takeover fires. But starting with the new decade, their strategy shifted to a greater concentration on building value and share price 'through more aggressive pressure on management and board directors' (Ward 1997). This shift has found favour with all major institutions and Robert Pozen of Fidelity Investments wrote in 1994 that 'activism could be an effective technique for raising stock prices, but only if the right tools were used' (Ward). Even while people such as Phan (2000), writing on the shareholder activism in the Asian region, feel that as 'foreign investors increased their holdings in the region, the ability for boards to ignore the minority shareholders, many of whom are now powerful institutional investors, has decreased. These institutional investors bring with them a brand of activism heretofore only seen in the US and the UK.' Very rarely have institutions raised issues with management in India. The Satyam Computers incident is a glaring exception. But, of late, it is felt that there has been a gradual change.

Business India dated 8 February 2009 cites two instances of increasing shareholder activism. It says, 'Investors have become more demanding after the Satyam Computers debacle. Corporate deals and announcements are being probed minutely and there is demand for more disclosures'.[2] *Business India's* first example is with respect to Larsen & Toubro Ltd. Shares of L&T met with a selling pressure after it was revealed that Larsen Capital had acquired nearly four per cent stake in Satyam, making it one of the biggest stakeholders outside the company. It was also reported that L&T was interested in taking over the company, Satyam. The share price of L&T dropped from a high of Rs 860 to a low of Rs 661 on 9 January 2009. Even the volume of shares traded increased to 1.18 billion shares as against an average volume of 686 million since January 2009.

Another example that the magazine cites is of Siemens Ltd, which announced the transfer of 100 per cent of its stake in Siemens Information Systems Ltd to a subsidiary of its parent company, Siemens AG. Investors expressed their displeasure on the lack of details about valuations and other financial aspects by offloading the company's shares on the stock market. The shares dropped from Rs 290 to about Rs 260 on 9 January 2009. Subsequently, the shares fell to a low of Rs 211 before the company management came up with full disclosure on 14 January 2009. *Business India* asserts that 'There is more awarness and investors are demonstrating their activism to the fullest possible extent'.[3] *Business India* quotes D.R. Dogra, deputy managing director, Care: 'Had it been before, nobody would have bothered to ask for so much disclosure. All these years, most companies have taken these announcements as a formality and just stuck to the minimum statutory disclosure norms. But now they will have to satisfy the ever-demanding investors'.[4] While these developments are really encouraging, in how many companies, out of a total number of 4000 and odd companies listed on Indian stock exchanges, do shareholders act decisively on decisions

---

[2] 'Activism to the fore'.

[3] *Business India*, 8 February 2009.

[4] *Business India*, 8 February 2009.

and steps taken by the board and management? Very rarely do shareholders raise any questions regarding the actions of the board and management in the general meetings of shareholders. According to Sanchety (2005), 'It is common experience across the board that Indian shareholders do not take interest in AGMs. Though the Companies Act allows postal ballot facility, shareholders have not been seen to be using this privilege. Most AGMs and EGMs are convened and conducted simply to comply with the form of legal requirements.' Recently, the Bombay Stock Exchange has started a website where investors can vote electronically. Let's hope that the facility will be used by investors and will make changes in the way investors exert their rights. Regarding this, Ward (1997) writes that 'because of the hard evidence that the shareholder activism can bring positive results, the traditional activists are gaining reinforcements.' According to him, 'Major commercial funds are increasingly willing to make their voices heard. In 1993, Campbell Soup Company, for long an innovator on corporate governance matters, directed the managers of its pension funds to take an activist role in voting their proxies. Companies with more than three inside directors, or which tried to reprice underwater stock options, would receive 'no confidence' votes, and the Campbell fund managers were told to support measures tying executive pay to shareholder value.' While shareholder activism is very much desirable in the context of better governance of corporates, the progress in India has been rather slow while developed markets such as the US and UK have shown advancement in this respect.

Post-Satyam, investors in India seem to have become more alert, active, and cautious. At the twenty-eighth annual general meeting of Infosys Technologies held on 20 June 2009, a number of investors were concerned about the role of the auditors. 'Shareholders asked if auditors have physically verified the bank balance of the company.... The auditors confirmed they have checked Infosys' bank balance independently' reported *Business Line*.[5]

THE DEVELOPED MARKET ARGUMENT

As economies develop, it is reflected through the increased level of activity in the product or service areas indicated by measures such as GDP and a variety of products and services expanding into different sectors, some of which did not even exist earlier. Pressure on markets and even governments by consumers and customers to facilitate availability of the latest and best, either products or services, establishes a new set of market behaviour. This transformation could at times be initiated by a sudden crisis (as it happened in India) or a gradual progress (as has been happening in China). Further changes in the economy, happening gradually or in sudden steps, take the economy from an underdeveloped or developing to a developed one. While this transformation could be normal for some, for others it could even be painful. But as economies migrate to the developed category, certain characteristics manifest. The main characteristics of developed markets are:

Development of capital markets   One of the first factors that gets attention during the development of the economy is freeing of capital markets. Entrepreneurship, which hitherto has been tightly controlled, forces this change for loosening controls on capital mobilization. There may also

---

[5] 'Quizzing on auditors at Infosys AGM', *Business Line*, 21 June 2009.

be pressures from international development organizations to reduce controls and lessen the involvement of governments in the establishment of industrial undertakings. There could also be pressure from foreign countries and investors, especially when they find that the country has huge reserves of natural resources and other potential which could be tapped by them. The government gradually relaxes its controls and establishes different institutions that will in turn ensure the establishment of other institutions and processes for the good conduct of the so-called capital market. The government further relaxes various controls vested with them and expects the institutions to act in good faith. Gradually, such institutions become the pillars of the capital market.

Development of institutions   As the capital markets develop, it necessitates the establishment of a variety of institutions that facilitate the smooth functioning of the capital markets. For example, after the establishment of SEBI as a capital market regulating institution scrapping the earlier controller of capital issues (CCI), it enabled the orderly establishment of a number of institutions such as merchant bankers, brokers, underwriters, investment banks, registrars and transfer agents, trustee institutions, etc., which helped in the process of mobilization of capital by companies. Later on mutual funds, insurance companies, venture capital institutions, private equity providers, and foreign institutional investors came into being. Some of the institutions such as rating agencies, expanded their activities. Government expected SEBI and other SEBI initiated institutions to play an active role in not only the mobilization of capital for entrepreneurs but also for bringing about a change in the way capital was mobilized. These institutions were also expected to function on the basis of strong market principles.

Availability of a variety of financial products, services, and instruments   Once institutions are permitted to be established, a variety of them come into being. Investment banks offer a whole range of services; mutual funds start offering a variety of schemes; banks, which hitherto confined their operations to lending only, offer a range of services; rating agencies offer a number of new services; investment banking institutions design new financial instruments and use innovative approaches to financing takeovers and acquisitions; companies are enabled to raise money from abroad through ingeniuous methods, etc. Conventional commercial banks whose operations were restricted to only collection of deposits and lend to businesses, now become universal banks offering a wide variety of financial services. Specific institutions offering information services appear in various areas. They continuously monitor and review the various aspects of the economy, business, firms, market moves, new and innovative things that happen in every area, etc., and supply it to the needy.

Availability of and access to information   We saw that institutions that collect, monitor, and disseminate information get established as an economy grows and institutionalization takes place. Market players, be it other institutions, foreign institutional investors, brokers, investment bankers, or even investors, now have not only the availability of information but also accessibility to it. By and large, information which was either not available or available only in haphazard form, is now available in a ready-to-use form. While some institutions charge for this kind of information, a large amount of information is now available for free. This enables investors to use the right information at the right time to make their decisions. It also enables other market players to use the available information for their specific purposes. Advances in communication mechanisms help information to be exchanged so that everybody becomes equally informed. When everybody becomes equally informed, there are very limited chances of anybody making big gains because they have privileged information.

Transparency in the processes and transactions   The extensive search for availability and accessibility of information and the latest communication mechanisms force a minimum level of transparency about the processes and transactions in the capital and other markets. This necessitates disclosure of a variety of information and thus, conflict of interest if any, becomes apparent. The threat of being exposed and grilled force every player, institutions as well as individuals, to be as transparent as possible.

The market for corporate control   With the information explosion, availability, and accessibility coupled with other factors such as communication, easy accessibility of capital, and institutional advisory services, the market for corporate control opens up and flourishes. In most developed markets, the shareholding pattern of companies is likely to be highly dispersed with no owner having a dominant holding. This makes any company vulnerable to takeover acquisition. This developed market condition for corporate control is expected to put restraints on management and board actions.

Delineation between ownership and management   It has also been observed that in developed markets, there is usually a clear distinction between ownership and management. Owners are content to enjoy the fruits of ownership leaving the running of the business to professional managers. This enables the management and board to initiate actions in the best interests of the corporation. When owners are themselves managers, whatever actions they take as managers will have a direct bearing on their ownership. They may try to protect their capital and wealth rather than betting on the future, which could be in the best interests of the corporation.

More of self-regulations than external regulation   As institutionalization takes place, as information becomes available and accessible freely, as transparency in the processes and transactions increases, as the market for corporate control develops, and as management becomes delineated from ownership, the expectation is that the various players or elements in the economy and the market assume more self-regulation than external regulations. For example, since the market for corporate control is very active, there is a responsibility and incentive for an incumbent management and board to self-regulate through better management and better governance.

Increased shareholder/management/board activism   All the above factors lead to a very activist attitude among shareholders, boards of directors, and management. This necessitates very high interactions not only within each of the constituents but also among the constituents. This is the kind of situation that is expected to exist in the developed market context.

Flaws in the Developed Market Argument

Going by the developed market argument, failures in corporate governance are unlikely to occur in developed markets such as the US, UK, etc. But as everybody knows, some of the most high profile corporate governance failures have occured in what is considered to be the most developed market in the world, namely the US. The US is home to some of the best known institutions, its society is said to be one of the most transparent, coupled with freedom of expression, and highly individualistic oriented and respected legal and regulatory systems. But have these been enough to prevent governance and company failures from occurring? Not necessarily. This is because there are a number of flaws in the developed market argument. Let us look at some of the major flaws:

Flaws on the institutional front   Most of the institutions of the developed markets choose to offer a variety of services in their strategic thrust for growth, often resulting in conflicts of interest situations. Since such conglomerates look at the overall benefits for the conglomerate as a whole, there may be instances of compromise, rather than rightful action. For example, if one arm of a financial services conglomerate offers advisory services to a targeted mergers and aquisitions (M&A), another unit may provide analyst's service tracking the company's equity shares. Since the money involved in advising M&A could be high, the conglomerate is likely to be very positive on the company's outlook from the analyst's perspective, rather than being highly objective about it. These types of conflicts of interest are usually embedded in the institutional set-up.

Cross-relationships leading to collusions   Often there exists a cross-relationship especially at the director level, leading to a 'you scratch my back, I'll scratch yours' situation. The director of a company may sit on the board of a financial institution whose nominee will be on the board of the company. In some cases, they may both be on the board of a third company or a non-profit organization. Cross-directorships can get extended to committee level where the committee may be persuaded to increase the remuneration package of the CEO or nominate a candidate who is expected to support the CEO unquestionably.

Pressure to produce quick results   There is enormous pressure on companies and their executives to produce better results every time and stay ahead of competition. This has forced companies and executives to cut corners or adopt shortcuts. With the CEO pay packet linked to the performance of the company's stock on the markets, there is a lot of pressure on the CEO to indulge in acts that perk up the stock prices. Sustainability over the long-term has been given a go by everybody except a few interested groups.

Money and wealth has become the yardstick of success and power   Leading an organization to success and in the process getting rewarded adequately has been replaced by a change in the thinking. Money has became the basis for power and an indicator of success. Because of information explosion and seamless communication, the opportunities for talent have become widely known. By talent, we mean those who are skilled with specific capabilities. Such talents today know that they can demand their price through hard bargaining. During bargaining for better compensation, they demand components which were not part of conventional compensation packages. For example, some CEOs demand that their wife or even in-laws get certain benefits on their being sacked or on retirement. Those who are very successful at hard bargaining adopt their own ingenious ways of making more money and wealth.

The haphazard system of rewarding for non-performance   There have been many cases in the recent past in the so-called developed markets, especially in the US, where compensation used to move north (increases) while performance moved south (decreases).While pay for performance has become the norm, and rightly so, in reality though this has not been the case. There have been wide variations between performance and compensation levels. A number of CEOs, in their anxiety to preside over a bigger company, entered into M&A deals, which if successful, would catapult them into the big league and earn them a fat bonus, without waiting to see whether the merger was actually beneficial for the company and its shareholders or not.

Agency conflicts   Agency conflicts have continued to exist, and in fact, have been extended to other parts of the system. For example, agency conflicts exist between the owners and managers of a company; similar kinds of agency conflicts exist between the investors and managers of the mutual fund which has chosen to invest in the company. Now, let us look at how some of these flaws affect the pillars of the developed market, the so-called capital market institutions.

CAPITAL MARKET INSTITUTIONS

As discussed earlier, as the capital markets develop, market-related institutions also get established. These institutions became facilitators such as stock exchanges, or investment banks, or brokers; regulators such as SEC in the US or SEBI in India; corporate watchdogs and scorekeepers such as auditors; funds mobilizing savings from the public and the employed such as mutual funds or pension funds; and banks which provide short-term as well as long-term finance for corporates. These institutions have genuine reasons for being interested in the well-being of the firms with which they are associated. Even while conflicts of interest arise in many cases, these institutions have become pillars of the capital markets in any modern economy. Let us now see how each of these institutions plays its role in the capital markets and in the establishment of better corporate governance practices.

Institutional Investors

In Chapter 7 we have seen how institutional investors have become major shareholders in developed countries, especially the US. While this has pushed them into the region of power of control, our aim is to ascertain whether they have lived up to their promises in the developed market argument, especially when it comes to corporate governance. In a typical developed market environment, information flow is high and leads to high levels of transparency. Everybody has access to the same information and hence can act upon it. Thus, information advantages are rather limited. So, institutions with their power and clout, aided with the kind of funds available with them, usually, engage exclusive personnel to study, monitor, and make judgements on companies and their future.This, in fact, enables them to avoid making wrong investments and make only good investments. These institutions are supposed to follow the concept of a 'prudent man rule' as a test of satisfactory fiduciary concept. A prudent man will manage the money of others just as he would manage his own, that is, carefully and wisely. The principal idea is that managers of other people's money must always put the interests of their clients first—ahead of their own interests—and act prudently, according to Smith and Walter (2006). But this does not always happen. Investment managers act in their own interests, when they increase the assets under management in order to earn better fees, or ignore the interests of the investors who may be looking for the best risk-adjusted return from their investments. Managers may look for quick gains in order to be rewarded while investors' interests may be sustainable of better than market returns over the long-term. Let us see how such problems arise and exist in different categories of institutional investors.

Investment Bankers

Their ploy with companies usually starts with Initial Public Offers (IPOs) of companies. In order 'to gain mandate for IPOs, the banks had to promise the new companies that they would wholeheartedly sponsor the IPO, by making an extra effort to distribute the shares to investors all over the world, by following the company in research after the issue, and by making a secondary market (for block trades) in the stock for institutional investors' (Smith and Walter 2006).

During the mid-1990s, when internet companies were mushrooming, the demand for IPOs was very high. There was a huge potential for a good gain on selling it immediately on listing. Smith and Walter (2006) say that 'realizing the premium available to investors favoured by generous IPO allocations became a way to lock-in solid investment profits, and as a result, most large institutional investors began to demand IPO allocations from the investment bankers handling the sales.' Such was the nexus between investment bankers and institutional investors. Investment bankers and institutional investors offering a variety of financial and other services often acted in connivance with the companies, not acting in the best interests of their clients and/or investors. The 'prudent man' approach was very often missing. Most of the investment banks who employed analysts to ascertain the future prospects of a potential client, advised on possible mergers and acquisitions, and also in identifying potential IPO candidates. According to Smith and Walter, 'Such analysts, however, to get the jump on other analysts and on the company's own announcements, had to be plugged in to the company's chief executive officer (CEO) and chief financial officer (CFO) closely, so as to receive information that not everyone was getting. Many CEOs believed that such close information sharing with star analysts would be to their advantage.'

This nexus between the investment bankers was evident in the case of Enron. 'Chung Wu, a broker with UBS Paine Webber, a subsidiary of UBS, a Swiss bank, e-mailed his clients to sell Enron shares. He was sacked and escorted out of his office…. Other UBS analysts were still recommending a strong buy on Enron. UBS Paine Webber received substantial brokerage fees from administering the Enron employee stock option programmes' (Tricker 2004).

Asset Management Companies

Trillions of dollars have been under the management of different types of asset management companies all over the world. In the 1970s and 1980s in the US, the asset management business was handled by individual trustees, banks, insurance companies, and even corporations managing assets on behalf of their own employees or for other clients. In the US, the Employee Retirement

Income Security Act (ERISA) 1974 made the regulations for management of assets stringent, necessitating appointment of professional experts to provide the best risk-adjusted performance. But by 1990s, almost every type of financial services firm was involved in asset management. This has been the case even in India. In the beginning, many of the local industrial houses joined hands with foreign asset management companies to start mutual funds. Stringent regulations and capital adequacy requirements restricted the entry and growth. But as time passed by, the asset management industry (restricted to mutual funds as India was yet to open the doors to pension funds) gained growth and became attractive. A number of brokers have also established mutual funds ever since. For example, Edelweiss Mutual Funds, Benchmark Mutual Funds, Religare Mutual Funds, etc. have been launched by stockbrokers.

While the mutual fund business has grown considerably over the years, it has also added many other banking and non-banking services such as commercial banking, credit cards, broking, off-balance sheet financing, etc. Also, pure commercial banks, sensing that mutual funds could be a threat to their deposit mobilization efforts, have also started their own mutual fund schemes. Such extension of services by mutual funds (and vice versa) have given rise to many avenues for conflicts of interest. Also, fund managers try to maximize the assets under management since their rewards essentially are decided by the size of assets under their management while investors want the best risk-adjusted returns on their investments. These two aims need not go together.

According to Smith and Walter (2006), these asset management companies 'are powerful players in exercising (or failing to exercise) control rights. As an industry, they can make the difference between governance successes and failures. But many of the agency conflicts among professional fund managers have become embedded in the system itself, and appear to have weakened the overall ability of the market to defend against value-destroying behaviour on the part of the corporations.' During the later part of 1990s, overnight gains from high-tech or internet IPOs and mutual funds, who hitherto feared or disliked them on the premise that they were overvalued, forced fund managers to look at the tech and internet sectors seriously as ignoring them would have meant investor backlash. According to Smith and Walter, many mutual funds 'became "momentum investors" or they bought what everyone else was buying, hoping to be able to get out before the others when they had to.' But the internet bubble burst soon after and many funds suffered heavy losses. Also, the funds entered into trading activity in the hope of making quick returns. Smith and Walter say that the median holding period of investors in mutual funds came down to 11 months in 1990s from about 6 years in 1950s. The turnover in the equity fund portfolio jumped to 108 per cent in 2000 from 17 per cent in 1950s. 'Such high turnover generated problems for investors. One was that the tax burden of fund investing rose sharply (high turnover generated regular income, not capital gains), and the other was that investment managers, expecting to hold on to the stocks for only a few months, had no incentive to consider corporate governance issues of the companies they invested in' (Smith and Walter). The conflicts of interest in mutual fund management have been discussed in detail in Chapter 7.

Some of the funds, however, are governance conscious. For example, Shultz (2001) says, 'Sherwood "Woody" Small, senior partner at ER Taylor Investments, says their mutual fund examines the board of directors before purchasing a company of any size.' Shultz has also listed six instances where CalPERS' influence has been recognized:

- Cummins will adopt an independent audit committee, appoint a lead outside director, consider EVA as a performance measure, and add strong independent directors.
- National Semiconductor agreed to add independent directors.
- Pacific Century Financial agreed to adopt CalPERS' definition of independence and restructure its board so that it has a majority of independent directors, to identify a lead independent director, and to diversify its board geographically.
- Pioneer Resources will have a majority of independent directors.
- Sierra Health will add two independent directors.
- St Jude Medical will have a majority of independent directors and restructure so that the audit, compensation, nominating, and governance committees, are exclusively composed of independent directors.

TIAA-CREF also has been able to make some inroads into governance reforms in companies where they have invested. Their process of improving governance involves three steps (Shultz 2001).

1. Write to the target company citing concerns
2. Meet them
3. Publicize concerns if a company refuses to respond and the issue is put to shareholders' vote.

Shultz (2001) says that 'TIAA-CREF filed seven resolutions on independence and withdrew them all after the targeted companies agreed to take action. They filed ten resolutions against 'dead hand poison pills', an oppressive takeover defence, and withdrew all but three, against Lubrizol, Bergen, Brunswig Corporation, and Mylan Laboratories. Brunswig and Lubrizol recinded their 'dead hand poison pills', but the Mylan action is still pending.'

Insurance Companies

Insurance companies also invest heavily in equity assets. According to Smith and Walter, life insurance companies owned 5.4 per cent of all equities outstanding in the US. Some schemes of insurance companies such as ULIPs (unit linked insurance plans) are more like mutual funds rather than insurance products. Similarly, they have also launched pension schemes which are similar to pension funds. Most of the insurance companies have also floated mutual funds. Many of these are issues that were earlier applicable to the two other types, namely investment bankers and asset management companies, but most insurance companies have also entered into many other areas of financial services.

Venture Capitalists/Private Equity

Venture capitalists (VCs) usually enter a company at the time of start up. Since they invest in or acquire a reasonable holding in equity, they are usually given a seat on the board. While the presence of a dominant shareholder is desirable for better governance, they are mostly concerned about the financial success of the company, and their commitment to any company is only as long as they get the right price to exit. Hence, one cannot expect any long-term commitment for the better governance of the company. The company also may have to compromise when it comes to the choice of director. They have no choice but to be content with the choice offered by the venture capital. When more than one VC invests in a company, the choice may be further limited.

Rob Dunaway, attorney and a venture capitalist himself, warns: 'Remember the hat the VC wears. Me and my investors first. Because his fiduciary responsibility to his fund is to exit that investment with as much money as possible, even if at the expense of someone else. It's a direct conflict with other shareholders' (Shultz 2001). Tom Emerson, former CEO of several venture-supported companies, feels that 'if investors become nervous about their investment, either because the company is slow on the upswing or because of inexperience or pressure on the investor director, he will often make demands that may not be in the best interest of the company' (Shultz). Of course, some of the VCs or private equity funds enter a company after it has grown to reasonable size. There, they may not get a seat on the board and would remain just like other institutional investors, but with an important difference. Once the valuations reach their target, they may exit. Hence, even in such cases, it is rare that they take any specific interest in the governance aspects of the company. But there are venture capitalists such as James Breyer, Bruce Golden, and Eli Cohen, partners at Accel Partners, who feel that 'too often, corporate venture programmes have become separated from the corporation's core business and have focused on returns. While the public market initially rewarded this behaviour, the party is now over, and a hangover has set in for many. The knee-jerk reaction may be to drastically reduce or eliminate the programmes' (Ashby and Miles 2002).

Institutional investors have been applying pressure on corporates to improve board structure and achieve board independence. According to Millstein and MacAvoy (2004), 'Many observers see such activism as ultimately improving investor returns; nonetheless, Roberta Romano concludes that such activities have had little or no effect on targeted firm's performance and that investors would be well served if they moved their attention elsewhere.' According to Romano (2000), 'For a large portion of the governance structures that are the focus of shareholder activism, such as independent boards of directors, limits on executive compensation, and confidential proxy voting, there is a paucity or utter absence of data which demonstrates that such devices improve performance.' Bernard Black also feels negatively about the impact of shareholder activism on firm performance and concludes that 'American shareholder activism to date has had little impact on performance' (Millstein and MacAvoy 2004).

Auditors

Transparency, availability, and accessibility of information are key tenets of free market economies and hence developed markets. Developed markets exist in free economies. So, all the free market characteristics will be reflected in developed markets. Lack of this can result in a distorted functioning of the capital market, leading to investment decisions that could end up in trouble. According to Smith and Walter (2006), 'Distorted information can allow capital to flow to the real underperformers that ought to be subject to market discipline and forced to adjust. Equally, healthy corporations under such circumstances can find access to capital more difficult and expensive than it should be.' Accounting and auditing firms play a big role in eliminating this problem by bringing transparency in the processes and transactions enabling better investment allocation decisions involving publicly-listed corporate entities. Company laws and/or securities laws in almost every country necessitate that publicly listed companies have to engage an independent accounting firm to audit and examine its financial accounts and certify: 'In our opinion and to the best of our information and according to the explanations given to us, the said accounts read together with the significant accounting policies and notes thereon give the information required, by the Companies Act, 1956 in the manner so required and give a true and fair view in conformity with the accounting principles generally accepted in India.'[6]

This way the auditors in an effort to plug the information deficit ensure that investors receive information that is accurate and to the best of their knowledge. Institutions such as auditors, make the concept of the modern corporation, identified by widely dispersed shareholders, work and make them sustainable. There may have been a number of instances such as Enron or WorldCom in US, or Satyam in India, where auditors colluded with management and deprived the investors of right information, causing miseries not only to the investors but also to many other stakeholders. The Companies Act 1956 even provides for the appointment of auditors for a publicly-listed company by the central government under Sections 224(3) and 224 (4). Section 224(3) requires that where no auditors have been appointed at the AGM, the company shall intimate the fact to the central government within 7 days of the meeting, and thereupon the central government will make the appointment. Section 224(4) is enforced where the company was responsible for making the appointment of auditors by passing a special resolution as per Section 224 A(1) but the company has failed to do so. The law, in their insistence that the auditors do the job with rigour, even restricts the number of auditorships to twenty companies per auditor, of whom not more than ten shall be the companies having paid up capital of Rs 1 million or more. In case of a firm of auditors, the ceiling shall be twenty companies per partner, while excluding the branch audit of foreign companies from the number. Private companies are also excluded from the maximum limit.

Berle and Means (1932) had very early stressed on the importance of accounting as a basis for a joint stock company to sustain. According to them, 'Accountancy plays a great part at this point, as indeed elsewhere, in the market career of the security. It is customary for bankers to rely in making up their statements on accountant's reports, and the integrity of the accountant and the soundness of his method are the greatest single safeguard to the public investor and to the market in general.' And, talking about the control the board and management will have over the various types of assets and resources in a joint stock company with a widely dispersed ownership, Berle and Means said, 'The directors have another powerful weapon which may be combined with any or all of the foregoing. They have a large measure of control over the company's income account. So long as accounting standards are not hardened and the law doesn't impose any specific canons, directors and their accountants may frame their figures, within

---

[6] Auditor's report, accompanying the annual report of any company in India.

limits, much as they choose.' Thus, the role that accounting and auditing plays in disseminating correct information not only to investors and potential investors in the company, but also to other interested parties, is very clear.

An auditor, who is appointed by the shareholders, is an agency that comes into being when shareholders are not empowered to examine the books of accounts of the company. Thus, an auditor is intended to be a shareholders' man, to report to them about the state of affairs of the company. The audit function and auditors ensure that the directors do not misuse their fiduciary position. While appointment by shareholders is to ensure independence of auditors, independence must also mean that the auditor is capable of rendering an opinion that is not compromised by conflicts of interest. While theoretically, auditors can be independent and even fearless in reporting to shareholders, under Indian conditions promoters are also directors, with a management role, and they are able to appoint auditors of their choice. And, antagonizing the management, who also happen to control the shareholding, makes the execution of auditors' duties extremely difficult. The auditor's report contains a statement from the auditors: 'We conducted our audit in accordance with the auditing standards generally accepted in India. Those standards require that we plan and perform the audit to obtain reasonable assurance about whether the financial statements are free of material misstatement. An audit includes examining, on a test basis, evidence supporting the amounts and disclosures in the financial statements. An audit also includes assessing the accounting principles used and significant estimates made by management, as well as evaluating the overall financial statement presentation. We believe that our audit provides a reasonable basis for our opinion.' Thus, while auditors and audit reports try to give a true and fair view it is done in the context of:

- Best of information and according to the explanations given to the auditors (by the management and board).
- It is based on accounting principles and audit standards generally accepted in India. Indian accounting standards have been framed by the Institute of Chartered Accountants of India, which is not necessarily fully aligned with the best practices elsewhere in the world.
- The auditors plan and perform the audit to obtain reasonable assurance about whether the financial statements are free of material misstatement. So, it is only a reasonable assurance to investors that the statements given by the company and certified by the auditor is correct.

Auditing as an industry

Till the 1980s, there were several audit firms in the US with a number of them such as Arthur Andersen and Arthur Young having their offices in many parts of the world. But the later part of 1980s and early part of 1990s saw a wave of consolidation within the auditing industry. The 'big eight', namely Arthur Young, Pricewaterhouse, Coopers & Lybrand, Arthur Andersen, Deloitte, Haskins & Sells, Peat Marwick Mitchell, and Ernst & Whinney in the 1980s became the 'big five' after a number of consolidations, namely KPMG, Pricewaterhouse Coopers, Arthur Andersen, Deloitte & Touche, and Ernst & Young. According to Smith and Walter (2006), 'The consolidation drive was the result of multiple factors that can be broadly divided into economies of scale and economies of scope. Economies of scale refer to the notion that average cost of production decreases as a result of increasing production volume. Economies of scope refers to the notion that average total cost of production decreases as a result of increasing the number of different products or services, and that cross-selling these products or services generates higher volumes or prices.' This is how the transformation in the auditing firms happened. Most of these firms identified opportunities in providing consultancy services to the companies where they were auditors. Most of the accounting firms started to offer management consultancy services in specific areas, which later became their expertise. And soon after, the consulting business often became more important than the audit business. According to Smith and Walter, 'The combinations of auditing and consulting revenues was growing rapidly, and the associated profits available to accounting professionals became very tempting. The firms themselves began to feel the need for greater scale and scope, as well as better management to take advantage of these developments' (Smith and Walter).

This development made the essential attribute of the auditor, namely his independence questionable. A study of more than 4000 proxy statements on the EDGAR database filed to the SEC between February and June 2001 revealed that non-audit fees averaged two-thirds of the total fees billed by the 'big five' auditors, according to Smith and Walter (2006). And, Micklethwait and Wooldridge (2003), writing on the dramatic weakening of the proper checks and balances in the corporate system say, 'Above all, auditors had come to see themselves as corporate advisors, not the shareholders' scorekeepers.'

Limitations of auditor and audit process

As we have already seen, the audit process relies on information provided by management. It is usually based on random tests and not on a review of every transaction. Auditing of every transaction would be prohibitively costly. 'Because of the limitations in audit tests and in all systems of internal control, there is always a limited risk that some misstatement will remain undiscovered' (Wallace and Zinkin 2005). While auditors are expected to maintain an attitude of professional skepticism throughout their work and international accounting standards prescribe the performing of fraud-related procedures by the auditors, the primary responsibility of prevention and detection of fraud rests with management who should encourage success through whistle-blower mechanisms.

The independence issue

The external auditors are expected to be independent and to make an independent judgement of the financial position of the company. While the independence itself is in question, how can they provide an independent judgement? According to the SEC in the US, independence is not only 'independence in fact'—the state of mind that permits performing of an audit service without being affected by external influences—but also 'independence in appearance'—the avoidance of circumstances that would cause a reasonable third-party to conclude that the firm's integrity or independence has been compromised (Smith and Walter 2006). Audit quality is usually defined in terms of the probability that (the audited) financial statements are free of material errors. Thus, if they are free of material errors, then the issue of independence doesn't warrant any attention and importance, whatever be the appearance. According to Smith and Walter, 'Although it would seem that auditors have an economic incentive to accede to their client's wishes by not reporting errors, there is a counterincentive for auditors to maintain high levels of quality—a lower quality audit may be discovered and this could drive away clients who value higher quality.' However, a number of studies in accounting literature 'suggested that provision of non-audit services increased the auditors' incentive to acquiesce to client pressure....seemed to indicate that the more the firms paid their auditors for non-audit services, the more likely they were to engage in "earnings management", that is, in meeting or beating Wall Street analysts' forecasted earnings per share' (Smith and Walter). The independence question right from the time of appointment is, should there be auditors or independent directors? The independent auditor or the independent director get paid by the same firm that they are auditing or overseeing. When auditors or independent directors get into a dispute, they are under the threat of losing the account or their directorships. The assumption here is that it is for the betterment of the firm that both are working; both of them are accountable to shareholders because they appoint the auditors and directors (at least on paper). The resources with the company, including the cash generated by it, belongs to shareholders and hence, the payments can be said to be made by the management or board on behalf of shareholders. This money is being paid for delivering transparency. Garratt (2003) finds fault with the UK and Commonwealth countries where 'the auditors, not directors, take the responsibility for stating publicly that the company's finances are "a true and accurate account" and so allow investors to conclude that they must be investing in a going concern', whereas in the US, 'directors make this statement and are held personally and criminally liable for it.'

The author feels that there is nothing wrong in this because auditors also have been appointed by shareholders (theoretically), as are the directors, and hence both have fiduciary responsibilities, though different in nature. Despite all the stringent requirements of independence and rigour expected of them, auditors have been alleged to go along with their clients in their report, leaving transparency to nought. Pricewaterhouse Coopers' involvement in the Satyam Computer fraud is only one of many such instances. According to a *Business Today* report, 'The US arm of BDO International, the world's number five accounting firm (which in India has an affiliation with Haribhakti & Company), had to pony up damages of $521 million awarded against it for a negligent audit. A month ago, three of the big four—PWC, KPMG, and EY—were dragged into Bernard Madoff's alleged $50 billion fraud—they were all auditors of the feeder funds that channelled money into the accounts of Madoff's New York brokerage.... Deloitte stood accused of falsely certifying GM's accounts—the Detroit major had apparently accelerated the booking of income between 2002 and 2006.'[7] Yet, it is hoped that the auditing profession will regain the respectful position it had and will function as an important institution of responsibility, enabling companies to be better governed.

---

[7] 'Inside the Secret World of Auditing', *Business Today*, 22 February 2009.

BANKS

Banks play a very important role in the development of entrepreneurship and the economy. They help mobilize savings of the people of a country and lend it to entrepreneurs to meet their capital investment needs, as well as working capital needs. Banks play a very important role in the early stages of development of an economy since the capital markets are likely to be less active and entrepreneurs have to resort to borrowing resources to meet their capital needs. Less developed countries have less developed capital markets (and therefore the possibility of raising funds through issues of securities) and hence, have to resort to borrowings from banks in order to meet their fund requirements. Even when the capital markets are developed, banks can play a major role as borrowing enables a company to avail of tax benefits on interest payable, reducing the cost of capital as cost of capital on debt compared to that of equity is low. Thus, while there is no doubt about the role played by banks in the development, growth, and sustainability of the corporate sector, let us see how they influence the various factors affecting the corporate governance of a company .

According to Mallin (2007), 'A corporate governance system may also be termed "bank-oriented" or "market-oriented".' The other terms are 'insider' and 'outsider' systems to denote concentrated ownership with holding companies or families and widely dispersed ownership among a large number of outside investors. According to her, a *bank-oriented* system implies that banks play a very important role in the funding of companies and hence, will be able to increase control through their nominees on the board, whereas a *market-oriented* system doesn't enable banks to exert similar control. While a market-oriented system may be more prevalent in countries such as the US or UK, the bank-oriented system prevails in many continental European nations and Japan. One of the reasons could be that holding companies or families with whom ownership has been concentrated would like to retain their control over the firm by restricting the public participation and rather resort to borrowing in order to meet their funding needs. Charkham (2000) identifies four reasons why banks play an important role in Germany:

- There is a direct ownership of company shares by banks.
- German shareholders generally lodge their shares with banks authorized to carry out their voting instructions (deposited share voting rights on DSVR).
- Banks tend to lend for the long-term and hence develop a longer term relationship with the company (relationship lending).
- Banks offer a wide range of services that the company finds it useful to draw upon. Because of all these, banks play a major role in the corporate governance of German companies through their representation on supervisory boards or other links. According to Das (2008), bankers 'frequently hold the chairmanship or deputy chairmanship of the "supervisory board" of major companies.'
- Japan is one country where banks and other financials institutions hold major chunks of the equity capital of companies. According to Charkham, they held 25.2 per cent of total outstanding common shares in 1990. But in later studies this has been shown to be coming down. A Standard & Poor's study reveals that cumulative 'shareholdings of banks fell to 8.7 per cent of the total market capitalization of Japan's five exchanges as of

31 March 2002 compared with a level of roughly 15 per cent until the mid-1990s' (Waring and Pierce 2005).

The role played by banks in an economy where a market-oriented system prevails such as the US presents a different picture. Pre-1933, banks offered a variety of intermediary services such as underwriting new public offers, broking, and also engaged themselves in trading in securities. Banks were competing with specialist investment banks that hesitated to enter the regular banking business as it required heavy capital investments, depending on the banking regulations. This is because they were mobilizing public money and there was a need to protect depositors from risk. But, the crash of 1929 revealed the exposure of banks to risky avenues leading to bank failures. In 1933, Congress passed the Banking Act that included the Glass-Steagall provisions, necessitating banks to exit their securities related to operations in order to avoid risk and conflicts of interest.

The Glass-Steagall provisions introduced fine distinctions between capital market-related activities and banking. The period till the early 1980s saw a boom in capital market activities and a decline or even collapses in the banking industry arising from mismatch of assets and liabilities. The banking system was rescued through a nearly $300 billion intervention by the federal government or the coverage offered by the Federal Deposit Insurance Corporation. Even big banking entities such as Citibank and Bank of America were lacklustre in their performance and were even faced with a crunch in deposit mobilization as savings in large quantum found their way to mutual funds and or short-term securities such as commercial papers by corporates which put pressure on the banks' general ability to lend with a greater effect on the short-term working capital loans, usually a less risky and more profitable avenue for banks. In simpler terms, when mutual funds or other companies offer better returns to investors by way of investments in MF units, or companies offer better returns on their securities such as commercial paper, the funds from depositors will go to MFs or such companies and not necessarily to banks.

As Smith and Walter (2006) say, 'Term loans were replaced by lower cost bond issues or medium term notes in the markets. Lucrative merger and restructuring transactions had little room for banks, except as providers of lines of credit and high-risk leveraged buyout loans. Hemmed in by government restrictions on their activities, banks watched helplessly as much of their business disappeared into the capital markets.' Because of the severe restrictions on their growth opportunities, banks were challenging the Glass-Steagall provisions and looking for loopholes to circumvent such restrictions.

According to Smith and Walter (2006), 'Most important was Section 20 of the provisions of the 1933 Banking Act, which allowed the Federal Reserve to permit a limited amount of otherwise prohibited transactions to occur. The Federal Reserve gradually opened the doors to banking participation in the capital markets in the early 1990s, and several banks set up special Section 20 subsidiaries to function as investment banks.' Banks started setting up their own investment banking arms or acquiring them. The path-breaking change happened when Travelers Group acquired Citicorp in 1998, which combined banking, insurance, asset management, and broker–dealer businesses under one roof. This 'transaction turned out to be a catalyst for the ultimate repeal in 1999 of Glass-Steagall and the Bank Holding Company

Act' (Smith and Walter). This led to a flurry of acquisitions leading to integration of normal banking business with investment banking operations . Thus, banks started offering multiple services to their clients. Since the competition among such entities was cut-throat, companies started demanding association according to their terms. According to Smith and Walter, 'Some insisted that if the banks and investment banks wanted their fee business, they should extend credit to them, and in addition should be shown favourable treatment by banks' research analysts and stock traders, and by its most creative finance thinkers.... In the process, the banks lost whatever ability they once had to discipline their clients. Someone else would do the deal if they criticized too much' (Smith and Walter 2006). In this way, banking as an institution that could enable good governance in companies was rendered powerless. The failures of companies such as Enron, Global Crossing, WorldCom, etc., exposed the corporates–banking nexus. The intense competition among banks led them to take highly risky adventures such as sub-prime lending and creation and transaction of derivatives. This culminated in the 2007–08 sub-prime crisis, which led to a global recession from which countries have yet to emerge fully. In the process, the position of banks as institutions capable of disciplining and instilling better governance practice got weakened, especially in the US.

Banks in the Indian Corporate Governance Scenario

Till the capital market received a development push in the early nineties, thanks to the new economic policy initiatives taken by the then government under Narasimha Rao, investment requirements of companies were mostly met by development financial institutions and banks. According to L.C. Gupta, 'It was not a general practice of Indian financial institutions before 1970 to nominate representatives on the boards of assisted companies except in problem cases' (Gupta 1989). The Dutt Committee Report of 1969 (Report of the Industrial Licensing Policy Enquiry Committee 1969) recommended that public financial institutions should participate actively in the control and management of assisted enterprises. Most of the development financial institutions (which were expected to extend credit to meet the long-term capital requirements of firms) and banks, which were expected to provide working capital to industry, included loan covenants while extending financial assistance. Given the thrust of active involvement in the control of firms, banks and financial institutions included nomination of directors by them on the boards of companies to which they lent funds. This practice continued till recently when the Kumar Mangalam Birla Committee, constituted by SEBI, recommended that institutions shall appoint nominees on the boards of companies on a selective basis, where such appointment is considered necessary to protect the interests of the institution.

Thus, most of the institutions and banks, which hitherto had nominees on the boards of assisted companies, did not seek re-election of them once their existing tenures ended. According to Gupta (1989), 'Even before the nominee director system was introduced in India, term financing institutions had required assisted companies, and still require them, to broad-base their boards as a condition for providing assistance.' The basic idea behind this requirement was to prevent companies from packing the boards with family members and associates of promoters. The basic role of the nominee director was to 'facilitate effective functioning of the board of directors', according IDBI's guidelines for nominee directors (Gupta). Government guidelines required nominee directors to be particularly vigilant about the following (Gupta):

- Financial performance of the company
- Payment of dues to institutions
- Payment of government dues, including excise and customs duty, and statutory dues. Where the company feels that a particular tax demand is unjustified, nominee directors should satisfy themselves about the prima facie reasonableness of the company's case
- Intercorporate investments in, and loans to or from associated concerns in which the promoter group has significant interest
- All transactions in shares
- Expenditure being incurred by the company on management group, and
- Policies relating to the award of contracts, and purchase and sale of raw materials, finished goods, machinery, etc.

The nominee director can be instrumental in the board's awakening and attitude with respect to practices that may fall outside the purview of independent audit. These practices may include things such as extravagant perquisites enjoyed by top management, maintaining luxury apartments as guest houses when the company has been losing money, or inter-company transactions of a questionable nature within a business group, etc. (Gupta 1989).

While banks and financial institutions can play a very important role in governance, the recent track record has not been very encouraging. Universal banking (banks offering a variety of products or services under the same umbrella) is good for banks as they can on the whole make money; but the same bank offering different services can result in conflicts of interest. For example, the bank may lend or arrange a M&A advisory, and at the same offer analysts' services. If the company buys the M&A advisory from the bank, they may give a 'buy' recommendation on the company's shares to their clients. 'Citigroup was identified as having had many roles and relationships with the company. It was serving simultaneously as research analyst recommending purchase of the stock, it advised WorldCom management on strategic and financial matters, it maintained an active lending and underwriting relationship (including making large loans to the CEO), and it also served as exclusive pension fund advisor to WorldCom. It executed significant stock option trades for WorldCom executives as the options vested, while at the same time conducting proprietary trading for its own account in WorldCom stock', which was revealed in the $103 billion bankruptcy of the company, according to Smith and Walter (2006).

Big banking groups such as Citigroup and JPMorgan Chase were said to have played roles in the bankruptcies that happened in the early 2000. Both Citigroup and JPMorgan Chase had made write-offs of $1.3 billion each in the year 2002. Citi again announced a write-off of $5 billion in 2004, while JPMorgan set aside $2.3 billion for litigation reserves in the same year (Smith and Walter 2006). While JPMorgan had come out safe in the recent economic meltdown, Citigroup once again had a tough time. Writing about the 2007-08 meltdown, Bill George, professor of management practices at Harvard Business School says: 'With notable exceptions, Wall Street leaders failed to learn from these earlier events. Their high-risk strategies and excessive leverage continued to escalate along with their compensation, reaching a crescendo in 2007' (George 2009).

Merrill Lynch was taken over by Bank of America, the Obama government bailed out AIG by buying 79.9 per cent of the company's equity, Goldman Sachs got a timely infusion of capital from Warren Buffet, but a number of others such as Bear Stearns, Lehman Brothers, etc., went into bankruptcy following the meltdown. Goldman Sachs CEO, Lloyd Blankfein, while addressing the council of institutional investors said: 'Financial institutions have an obligation to the broader financial system; we depend on a healthy, well-functioning system, but we collectively neglected to raise enough questions about whether some of the trends and practices that became commonplace really served the public's long-term interests', acknowledging the financial community's responsibility for the events that precipitated the economic meltdown (George 2009).

STOCK EXCHANGES

Stock exchanges play a vital role in the capital market of any country. The joint stock company concept needs an exchange mechanism enabling investors to transact their holdings. In addition to this, stock exchanges try to bring in a discipline in the firms by insisting on many disclosure requirements keeping the investors in mind. The first set of corporate governance guidelines in the US was actually evolved by the New York stock exchange (NYSE). In fact in the US, the NYSE acts as a subordinate capital market regulator even though it is a private body. Many countries have incorporated the governance mechanism for companies by incorporating necessary guidelines through listing agreements between the company and stock exchange/s. In India also, SEBI regulates corporate governance through a clause (Clause 49) forming part of the listing agreements.

CAN INSTITUTIONS PLAY A MORE MEANINGFUL ROLE?

As seen earlier, institutions have become a major force in most of the developed countries, holding close to, or over a majority of voting shares in most of the companies. In most developing economies, institutions have been the target market in the divestment processes of PSUs initiated by their governments. Efforts at increasing globalization is likely to witness the rise of global institutional investors, holding voting shares of companies in different parts of the world. Institutions are also on the look out not only for higher returns offered by emerging markets, but also diversification opportunities for their portfolios. Hence, it is felt that institutions will be a major force in the capital markets of most countries. This puts them in an enviable position capable of influencing governance practices of companies across the spectrum. The question here is whether institutions assume the responsibility of influencing governance practices by enforcing this responsibility because of their widely varying interests (usually short-term). It would be worthwhile, only if enforced keeping in mind the long-term interests. While everybody thought or assumed that institutional investors, in general, would look at the long-term prospects of the companies, the assumption or thinking was proved wrong when they started trading in the securities in which they had invested. In their anxiety, and also because of the pressure for quarterly performances, they started indulging in activities which they were essentially not supposed to do. Except for a few such as CalPERS, TIAA-CREF, LENS, Vanguard, etc., institutions in general forgot about or ignored the fact that they have fiduciary responsibilities to their investors. It has been documented that active investors such as CalPERS and TIAA-CREF have been able to make a difference in the way companies have been governed. MacAvoy and Millstein (2004) even report better financial performance in companies which have been actively monitored by CalPERS: 'For those with weak governance, reform promised financial gain. According to our calculations, at least companies could gain more than 200 basis points of annual EVA^{TM}'. This has actually proved that there is a genuine incentive for institutions to enforce and monitor good governance practices in companies. 'The voting rights should be viewed as an asset, the use of which is of legitimate interest to those on whose behalf the institutional investors invest' (Das 2008). But very few institutions, other than pension funds, have tried to initiate reforms of governance of companies. This says a lot about their outlook on investments—many of them have only a near-term outlook. So, why disturb the status quo and harmony? Notwithstanding the financial gains of governance reforms, there is a genuine responsibility on them to make the companies sustain for a longer term as institutions have a responsibility to the economy and society at large. Of course, they are not expected to advise boards or managements on how to run their business, nor are they expected to micromanage the companies; they are only expected to voice their expectations and concerns to boards of directors.

While institutions, as fiduciaries for their clients, have to seek governance reforms in companies where they invest, the benefits of such efforts and reforms will accrue to all investors. But many institutions take a very narrow view as costs of enforcing such reforms will ultimately have to be borne by their clients in the form of reduced returns to them. This could be one of the reasons why institutions, especially mutual funds, do not put serious effort into pushing for reforms. 'Individual portfolio managers are expected to make the key asset allocation choices and live or die by the results. Investors can buy or redeem funds and select others at any time. Everything is marked to market, everything is out in the open, and investors get what they see' (Smith and Walter 2006). Even institutions such as banks usually have a tendency to align with the management even though they do not have a short-term outlook like mutual funds, which are under compulsion to generate better returns for their investors and better fees for investment managers. For example, Deutsche Bank cast its votes in favour of the management in the HP–Compaq merger because of its other business interests with the company (Bebchuk and Fried 2004). But on the whole, institutional investors seem to be making some encouraging advances in the right direction. 'Institutional investors are becoming even more effective, as they hone their skills, tamp down their aggressiveness, and refine the nuances of working with target companies…. No one can deny that institutional investors are a force in establishing the platform essential to good governance' (Shultz 2001).

India lacks powerful institutional investors such as CalPERS or TIAA-CREF. We also don't have institutions such as Institutional Shareholder Services (ISS) or Corporate Library which provide updated information about corporate governance matters. With the pension fund regulator in place, it is expected that pension funds will start operating in India too, which may usher in a new era in corporate governance.

REGULATORS AND THEIR ROLES

Corporate governance, as of now, encompasses only companies or corporate entities which have chosen to raise money from the public. Even though the stakeholder theory or approach has been considered as good for the running of an enterprise, the underlying premise of corporate governance continues to be the shareholder theory or approach, as the assumption that continues to pervade even today is that corporate governance is required because (or only because) there is a possibility for agency conflict to exist between owners and managers. Most of the regulations in the area of corporate governance in most parts of the world have been drawn up on this fundamental premise. While arguments against it are plenty, let us also try to explore the roles played by regulator(s) for companies to be better governed from this fundamental perspective.

There are definite expectations about corporates from the economy and society. Companies use a lot of resources in the economy and hence are accountable to them. They also depend on a number of stakeholders for their success—other service providers, customers, government, and of course, the shareholders. They have a responsibility to ensure that the interests of all these stakeholders are taken care of. While it is expected that the corporate entity takes care of the interests of the different stakeholders voluntarily, there may arise situations which may affect the stakeholders, since the corporate entity may act in ways that will try to achieve one of its objectives—making more money for the business and increasing the wealth of the providers of capital (the shareholders). This is where some kind of external regulation makes sense. 'To the extent corporations don't meet implicit and explicit expectations, regulation looms' (Shultz 2001).

According to convention, developed markets and countries have lesser external regulations, and the institutions created by the market regime are expected to make the necessary checks and balances, while lesser developed markets and countries have in many ways prohibitive external regulations. India has been, till the eighties, a shining example of the latter. Productivity was not encouraged and the freedom of entreprenuers restricted (there was a time when companies would be penalized if they produced anything beyond 125 per cent of the installed capacity, licenses were required for producing anything, better performance of managers could not be rewarded, dividends could be paid only subject to lenders' clearance, etc.), which only acted to curtail entrepreneurship. Regulations were, to a very large extent, anti-entrepreneurship and anti-development. At the other extreme, the regulatory regime was gradually relaxed to such an extent that it resulted in a situation of chaos, as was the case in the US. Relaxations of regulations led to exploitation by market players leading to conflicts of interest situations culminating in crises such as Enron, WorldCom, etc., with the US government giving a knee-jerk response in the form of the Sarbanes–Oxley Act to discipline the corporates. 'Capital markets failed in developing or developed countries not because they were inherently flawed and fundamentally dangerous in their design. They failed because their structural weaknesses (and every society, economy, or market, has some) were systematically exploited and abused (in the same way as a knife can be used to cut onions, or to kill). Regulatory and governance mechanisms designed to prevent such outcomes failed to do what they were supposed to' (Som 2006) . This was revealed again in 2007–08 in the US and India in the form of failures of Bear Stearns, Lehman Brothers, AIG, Merrill Lynch in the US, and Satyam in India, despite the very stringent governance norms in these countries. Boards failed to curtail the risks through self-regulation, and regulators failed by encouraging firms and boards to take unfettered risks and not enforcing the checks and balances which they have to perform. The unfortunate part is that the fortunes of even better-managed and better-governed corporations have been badly affected. A few bad apples have made the entire lot rotten.

Limits of Regulation

We have seen and experienced that governance failures occur despite stringent regulations. Is it that the regulations in position are not enough or adequate? Or, is it that the regulations are enough but have not been enforced in the required manner so as to prevent a crisis from recurring? Or, is it that there is a limit to which regulations can help, or that self-regulation by boards and companies is what is required and regulators have to be there just to offer guidelines? There are no definite answers to these questions. But, one thing is very clear. Despite stringent regulations, failure of corporations due to corporate governance shortcomings recur. Also, there were extremely well-governed companies in the US and India before the Sarbanes–Oxley Act and Clause 49 guidelines.

Failures of the likes of Enron and WorldCom in the US, Satyam in India, or Parmalat in Italy happened because of a few people who were enjoying a great deal of power and nurturing unfettered financial ambitions. Can regulators make a few people sit around a table in the boardroom, behind closed doors, and behave in the right manner? Should they make the regulations even more stringent or should they encourage and take steps to develop more activism among institutions such as institutional investors, auditors, banks, etc., and within boards? Some of the regulations themselves have to be seriously looked into. Most of the capital market regulators require corporates to announce quarterly performance. This essentially puts pressure on corporates to show better performance every quarter. Prices of company stocks are very much linked to such announcements. When executive compensation is linked to the company's stock performance, there could be incentives for executives to do some dressing of the financial performance or cut a few corners here and there. 'Abolish reliance on quarterly reporting of financial results. Reliance on quarterly results assumes the possibility of ever-increasing performance in a complex and discontinuous world. It is based on an artificial model of uninterrupted growth', said Bob Garratt[8] while addressing a workshop on 'directing board performance' in India, organized by the National Foundation for Corporate Governance (NFCG) and the Confederation of Indian Industry (CII). 'Over-reliance on quarterly performance had resulted from pressures exerted by venture capitalists and equity funds. However, a study done by the Boston Consulting Group showed that over the long-term, companies which showed a steadily rising curve of profit had collapsed, while those whose results curve showed ups and downs, survived and flourished. This is because the unsteady curves represented the 'learning curve' of the companies concerned and their adjustment to the ever-changing environment' said *The Hindu* report, quoting Garratt.

Notwithstanding the limitations of regulation on corporate governance and firm behaviour, regulations are necessary even in the most free market oriented economies. This is because even

---

[8] 'Dependance on quarterly performance "not advisable"', *The Hindu*, 7 February 2006.

they will be constrained by the economic and social policies which are directly determined by the political processes. Such involvement of the political processes on the economic policies may result in, and at times even significant, deviations from total free market conditions. Enron benefited from such political processes which decided to deregulate the power generation industry in many of the states in the US. Had it been a free market, as perceived by Adam Smith, such a thing would not have happened as consumers and even stakeholders would have objected to the de-regulation.

According to Dimma (2006), 'Laws and regulations influence both structures and processes, which in turn can influence behaviour, but only to a degree. Just as the death penalty does not prevent murder, laws and regulations fail to deal effectively with the aberrant behaviour of some CEOS and other executives.' Shultz is of the opinion that 'government regulation should aid, not harm or hinder. Its role should be to define and enforce the ground rules that make the playing field level and keep the system open. When change is the barometer, government regulation, which looks backwards instead of forward, can be stifling if not crippling. It smothers the very creativity and innovation that has allowed business to flourish' (Shultz 2001).

Smith and Walter (2006) opine that 'regulators constantly face the possibility that inadequate regulation will result in costly failures, as against the possibility that over-regulation will result in opportunity costs in the form of economic efficiencies which are not achieved, or in the relocation of firms to other, more friendly regulatory regimes .... Consequently, there are no definitive answers with respect to optimum regulatory structures with respect to corporate governance.'

J.R. Varma, professor at IIM, Ahmedabad and former member, SEBI, feels that there is a view that corporate governance 'too, is an area where market discipline is more valuable than regulation. The threat of hostile takeovers disciplines incumbent managements to a far greater degree than all the corporate governance codes put together' and, 'in the market discipline approach, disclosure is the only thing that needs to be ensured, because once the disclosures are there, market forces respond to the information and impose pressure on the company to shape up' (Basu 2005).

While governance experts and critics put the blame for all the failures at the doors of the entire board, citing conflicts of interest, passive attitudes of the independent directors, lack of expertise of or diligence or rigour by the audit committee, and other innumerable reasons, analysis of failures mostly leads to a general conclusion: most of the failures have occurred due to the selfish interests nurtured by a few powerful individuals—be it Enron, WorldCom, or Satyam. The search for the reasons for the ills end at one thing: glaring deficiencies in the quality of leadership—a lack of values, integrity, humility, the knowledge that you are there to serve others, a sense that you are being looked up to for inspiration by associates within and outside your organization, concern for those whose lives depend on the organization you lead, the responsibility of leaving a rich legacy, and the moral character and courage to desist temptation. Can laws such as the Sarbanes–Oxley, or guidelines like Clause 49, or regulators such as SEC or SEBI influence leaders of corporates to bring about perceptible changes in the above aspects? It is very doubtful. Governance is not a 'hardware' in the sense that changes in the structure of the board by including a majority of independent directors or by having a non-executive, independent chairman or by having audit, compensation, and nomination committees constituted only of independent directors, whereas it must become a 'software' that runs through the entire organizational system like processes, culture, and value systems.

It has also been the experience of many countries that when laws and regulations are too stringent, the propensity to break them, or at least find loop holes in them, becomes higher. Hence, it is felt that the law-makers and regulators have to adopt a 'normative' approach of development rather than a 'coercive' approach of making the corporates and leaders behave by forcing laws. Before they embark on a development mode in full force, they can introduce an incentive system, whereby the best performers based on certain yardsticks are rewarded.

Regulators should also understand that rules cannot substitute for character. Initially, the regulators can think of creating a group such as A0 for companies that excel in governance and offer them incentives in the form of reduced listing renewal charges, tax exemptions, etc. Such a system prevails in Brazil where, in 2000 the Sao Paulo stock exchange (BOVESPA) created a new listing agreement called the 'novo mercado' (new market). Participation in the 'novo mercado' is voluntary, but companies willing to have their shares traded in this segment must undertake to comply with corporate governance standards, and disclosure requirements are more stringent than those applicable to the traditional segment.

The 'novo mercado' segment has two entry levels. Level one basically concerns disclosure rules and a free float of 25 per cent, whereas level two requires level one disclosure conditions plus annual reports conforming to US GAAP or international accounting standards (IAS), and a unified term of one year for board members. Out of about 400 companies listed on BOVESPA, only 26 companies are listed in level one, only 3 are listed in level two, and only 2 in 'novo mercado' (Waring and Pierce 2005).

Laws or Codes?

A debate is also on as to whether the area of corporate governance should be regulated through specific laws passed in a particular direction (for example, in the US the Sarbanes–Oxley Act 2002) or in the form of guidelines or codes of best practices for the companies to follow. The supporters of specific laws argue that disciplining corporates doing businesses with a profit motive through codes is difficult because there can be agency conflicts and other types of conflicts of interest that are difficult to deal with. According to Varma, 'The fact that the governance requirements are being enforced primarily through the listing agreement is an important weakness. And, the threat of de-listing is too weak to deter companies that are not in compliance' (Basu 2005). The supporters of the other view—guidelines or codes are better—argue that governance is a subject which is taken care of by the shareholders and stakeholders in a well-functioning market mechanism for which rules and regulations are already in place. If the market mechanism functions well, it will reward good governance or punish bad governance. And under such codes of practices, governance is voluntary in nature and uses a 'comply or explain' approach, which is expected to provide information on the state of compliance, explaining the reasons for non-compliance. According to those who support the code of practices approach, it is for the market to take decisions based on the information provided by the companies. Supporters of this view point to the continuing failures of corporates which are due to poor corporate governance in the US. While the laws do not necessarily improve the governance of corporates per se, how can a system book culprits to some kind of a punishment without any laws available? Performance differs from compliance. The laws help to create a certain standard of 'form' which most companies usually comply with. One can, apparently, say that performance of the company over a long-term is the indicator of good governance performance, but anybody who leads the company to trouble shall be punished.

Guidelines or codes of best practices may not be enough for this purpose. The opponents of the specific law regime say that these laws increase the costs to the exchequer, implying increased costs to stakeholders. In Chapter 3, we have seen how the Sarbanes–Oxley Act 2002 resulted in higher costs for companies. 'According to the British Government's own regulatory impact assessments, the European working-time directive alone, which is set at a maximum of forty-eight hours a week, was costing the country's business more than £2 billion a year by 2001. According to the same figures, Tony Blair's Labour government added £15 billion worth of regulatory costs in its first five years' (Micklethwaite and Wooldridge 2003). While statistics may provide evidence that structural reforms have improved corporate governance in many companies, it is for the board to decide whether they want to be perceived as a strong, proactive board or a weak, reactive board. Weak boards and their directors will face a reputation risk which will render the director's positions on other boards also weak. In this respect, self-regulation by boards and companies augur better for them, while external regulations (through laws or listing agreements) enable them to conform to compliance requirements. This reputation factor is very important. For example, Prof. Krishna Palepu, Director on Satyam's board, had to relinquish his independent directorship at Dr Reddy's Laboratories soon after the Satyam story became public.

Who Should Regulate?

Since a company has to go through different steps for carrying out its business, it becomes mandatory for it to deal with different types of regulators whose regulatory frameworks very often overlap. For example, for the incorporation of a corporate entity, the company law provisions of the country (or state of the country as in the case of the US) become applicable and there are a number of requirements to be met by the entity in its conduct of business. A number of rules become applicable to all types of companies (private limited or public limited). But there are also differences in laws that vary between private limited or public limited companies. As the company expands its operations (or grows), the promoters or their associates who had earlier contributed funds to meet the fixed as well as working capital requirements (of course, they may also have resorted to borrowing to meet their fund requirements), may find it difficult to raise funds from among themselves and will be forced to raise funds from the public. Once the company decides to this, it will be subjected to a new set of regulations by the capital market regulator.

Since corporate governance is an area which involves boards, shareholders, auditors, financial reporting, disclosures, transparency, etc., drawing a fine line separating the regulations proposed by company law provisions and those proposed by provisions in the capital market regulatory framework is extremey difficult.

In addition to the common regulators whose controls are mostly macro in nature, affect or apply to all the companies across industries, there are industry specific regulators such as the Reserve Bank of India (RBI) for banking companies and non-banking financial entities (NBFCs, Nidhi/benefit companies, etc.), Insurance Regulatory and Development Authority (IRDA) to regulate insurance companies (both life as well as non-life or general), Pension Fund Regulatory and Development Authority (PFRDA) to regulate pension funds (we are yet to open up the market for pension funds), etc. While these specific regulators usually restrict their regulatory powers and reach to matters related to specific industries that fall under them, there have been a lot of overlaps between the regulatory mechanisms and processes by the department of company affairs (DCA, under the Ministry of Finance and Company Affairs) and SEBI, when applied to corporate governance. Within the area of corporate governance, considerable overlap exists when it comes to the structural part. While discussing the controversy on regulatory framework, in the background of the Irani Committee (constituted by DCA) recommendations, which were different from Clause 49 guidelines by SEBI, Kumar (2005) wrote, 'While SEBI has a bigger role to play in the practices and processes of governance, the structure for governance shall be vested with DCA. Since SEBI has actually nothing to do with structure, or formation, or composition of the board, such aspects shall rest with DCA, since all incorporation regulations are monitored and controlled by DCA. Hence, any recommendation or guideline regarding the structure part, such as formation of the board, independent component, committees, etc., shall come under the purview of the DCA and not SEBI.'

While SEBI constituted a number of committees to study the corporate governance practices and make their recommendations (Kumar Mangalam Birla commiittee, Narayanana Murthy committee, etc.), the department of company affairs has also set up a number of committees (Naresh Chandra committee, Irani committee, etc.). While the committees took reasonable care not to step on each other's brief, both the DCA and SEBI appointed committees had made their recommendations pertaining to more or less the same areas. Even regulators revealed that there were overlaps. In fact, this made the Naresh Chandra committee on corporate audit and governance to make the following observations in its other recommendations under Chapter 5 of the report. In its general observation, the report said: 'The committee was repeatedly reminded to be careful not to increase compliance costs to companies, as ultimately, not only is this against the interest of shareholders but also has the danger of making Indian industry uncompetitive. In this connection, a serious unnecessary cost noticed by the committee was the overlap and duplication between the SEBI and DCA. The committee has recommended removal of this overlap, keeping in mind two other principles. First, subordinate legislation cannot override provisions enacted by Parliament. Second, the doctrine of 'occupied space' needs to be respected and complied with'. And specifically as recommendations in 5-I:

- 'Wherever possible, SEBI may refrain from exercising powers of subordinate legislation in areas where specific legislation exists in the Companies Act 1956, and
- If any additional requirements are sought to be prescribed for listed companies, then, in areas where specific provision exist in the Companies Act, it would be appropriate for SEBI to have the requirements prescribed in the Companies Act itself through a suitable amendment.'

Balakrishnan (2005), in an article wrote that 'the Securities and Exchange Board of India seems to have a penchant for blatantly overstepping its authority.' The percentage of independent directors shall be 50 per cent or more in the case of companies where the chairman is full-time or promoter-nominee, and it shall be one-third when the chairman is independent, according to Clause 49 of SEBI listing regulations. The Irani committee had recommended one-third independent directors irrespective of whether the chairman is full-time, promoter-nominee, or independent. Of course, the exact proportion of requirements of independent directors on a board will be known only when the Companies Bill Amendments 2009 is passed by the Parliament. Such overlaps in regulations will only confuse companies. There must be absolute clarity regarding guidelines or laws on corporate governance for companies to follow.

GOVERNMENT'S ROLE IN CORPORATE GOVERNANCE—THE COMPANY LAW PROVISIONS

In Chapter 2 we have seen the characteristics of a modern corporation. The modern corporation has its origin in England and almost all the countries follow this concept as perceived by the English law. According to the Anglican legal system, 'A body corporate is a collection of individuals united into one body under a special denomination, having perpetual succession under an artificial form, and vested by policy of law the capacity of acting in several aspects as an individual.' Thus, it could be noticed that a body corporate is an identity, separate and independent of its members, created by law or under authority of law, or it is a legal personality. This is why the government has a role in the establishment and overseeing the running of such corporate bodies. In India, the law under which body corporates are formed is the company law. The company law in India made its first appearance in 1857 as Joint Stock Companies Act. Thereafter the Companies Act 1866 was passed which was changed in 1882. Then it was replaced by the Indian Companies Act 1913, which was later replaced by the Companies Act 1956, which is in force even today, though a number of amendments have been incorporated from time to time (Taxman's Company Law Ready Reckoner 2008). Since a company is an artificial person, it cannot sign as a natural person. Hence, the company must use a common seal in place of a signature, or the common seal should become the signature of the company. A company can empower any person to execute deeds under the common seal and it becomes binding on the company. While there are a large number of provisions in the company law relating to governance, we will limit our discussion to those with direct impact on the governance of a company.

Memorandum of Association (MOA)   It is the constitution of the company and hence its foundation.

Articles of Association (AOA)   This prescribes rules regarding internal management of the company. It describes the authorities and responsibilities of members (shareholders), directors, managing director, manager, etc. It also contains provisions regarding raising funds through issue of shares, borrowing, etc.

Body of members   They are real owners of the company but have no authority to look after the day-to-day affairs of the company, or enter into contracts on behalf of the company. They must meet at least once a year at the AGM. They have powers to (1) adopt directors' report (2) adopt auditors' report (3) elect directors (4) appoint auditors and fix their remuneration (5) declare dividend. They can also exercise powers to approve the proposed actions of the company at the AGM or specially called meeting of members, namely the EGM.

Board of directors   Directors elected by members form the board of directors, who has the authority to supervise and regulate the activities of the company. It has the overall control over the affairs of the company. The board must meet at least once every quarter and as often as necessary for the purpose of business. A director has no authority individually and decisions must be taken by the board as a body.

Managing director/manager/director   Since the board cannot look after the day-to-day affairs of the company, they appoint a manager, managing director, or a whole-time director, who work under the overall supervision and control of the board.

IMPLICATIONS OF COMPANY BEING A SEPARATE LEGAL ENTITY
General

Perpetual succession   The company continues to exist even if members change.

Can hold property in its own name   The company can own property and the property of the company is not the property of its members.

Liability of the company is not liability of its members.

Members can enter into contract with the company.

Legal   Common directors or common shareholders does not mean that one company has interest in another company. This provision enables a person to be on the boards of more than one company of an industrial group, without being liable to be questioned on his/her independence.

Company cannot be penalized for the actions of promoters   This is what RIL counsel Mr Harish Salve argued in the RIL vs RNRL case involving the allocation of gas from KB-D6 block according to a family agreement on division of assets among promoters.

Government company is not government   Even though the government owns the shares in most of the PSUs (in the name of the president and other designated officers as nominees of the government) the company is not 'government' and employees of the company are not public servants.

Wholly-owned subsidiary and holding company are not single economic units   According to law, they are also two separate legal entities.

Liability of company is not liability of directors   Since the company has a legal identity independent of its directors, directors cannot be held liable for liabilities of the company.

Director/secretary cannot file suit on behalf of the company   Only a person authorized by the board can file a suit on behalf of the company.

Act beyond powers   Act beyond powers can be ratified by the board. While nobody other than the board has powers to act on behalf of the company, the board can ratify the actions if it deems fit, according to the Supreme Court judgement. This is essentially to bring in practicality to the issues, as it may not be possible every time to wait for approval from the board, especially when the suit is likely to be time-barred.

Number of directors   Minimum three and maximum twelve which can be increased with the permission of the central government.

Shareholder democracy   In addition to the AGM and EGM called by the board of directors, members may themselves ask the board to hold EGMs if such members individually or together hold at least 10 per cent of the paid-up equity having voting rights. EGM must be held within 45 days from the date of requisition. In case the board fails to call the meeting, the members themselves hold the meeting at the company's expense. It is not necessary that the requisitionists disclose the reason. A minimum of 21 days notice is required for convening a general meeting (except for Section 25 companies, in which case the notice required is 14 days).

Election of directors   Elections is by simple majority. Only one director should be appointed by one resolution. One-third of the retiring directors (as against permanent, who need not retire by rotation) must retire every year and if the number of directors is not in multiples of three, the number nearest to one-third shall retire. Disclosure about relationships between directors should be made in the annual report. Every director should submit a declaration to the board regarding his shareholding in the company as well as his interest in other companies/firms directly or through relatives.

Related to Directors

Restrictions on number of directorships   According to Section 275, a person cannot be a director in more than 15 companies. While counting directorships, directorship of a private limited company, which is not a subsidiary or holding company; unlimited companies; directorship in associations not carrying on business for profit or which prohibits payment of dividend; and alternate directorships are not taken into account.

Duties of director
- Duties to the company
  1. Obedience—No engagement in ultra vires activities
  2. Diligence—Exercise degree of care as a prudent man does
  3. Loyalty—Must refrain from engaging in personal activities that will injure or take advantage of the corporation
- Duties to the members in fiduciary capacity
  1. Duty of reasonable care—He/she should not be negligent, must act honestly and reasonably

2. Apply business judgement—Make honest, unbiased business judgement, comply with laws, perform duties as fiduciary
3. Duty to disclose his/her interest

Rights of director
1. Right to inspect books of accounts and other books and papers (Section 209 (4))
2. Right to receive notices of board meetings (Section 286 (i))
3. Right to receive draft circular resolution for approval (Section 289)
4. Right to attend board meetings and receive sitting fees (Section 309 (2))
5. Right to be heard at the general meeting if notice for his/her removal has been received. He/she can also make a representation in writing, which the company is expected to send to every member, except in some cases (Sections 284 (3))
6. Right to record his/her dissent to any proposed resolution in board meeting (Section 193(4))
7. Right to participate and vote at board meetings, unless he/she is interested in a particular resolution (Section 300)
8. Right to claim travel, hotel, and other expenses, for attending board and committee meetings, and also in connection with the business of the company
9. Right to summon board meetings
10. Right to compensation for loss of office (if he/she is managing director, whole-time director, or manager).

Liabilities of a director
Officers in default are liable. According to Section 2 (30), 'officer' includes any director, manager, or secretary, or any person in accordance with whose instructions the board of directors, or any one or more of the directors are accustomed to act. Thus, a director is an officer of the company. Legally, there is no distinction between executive and non-executive directors, or inside directors or independent, outside directors. But some courts have felt that a distinction be made between independent, outside directors, and directors who are in effective control of the management of the company (Bombay HC, 1983, 54 Compo Case 197 in respect of Trisure India Ltd). However, in case of default in respect of repayment of deposits of small depositors (who have kept deposits of Rs 20,000 or less with the company), every officer including ordinary directors are held liable.

- Offences under the act which will attract personal liability for directors if active part in violation:
  ○ Failure to pay interest/principal amount to small depositors (Section 58AA)
  ○ Civil liability for misstatement in prospectus (Section 62)
  ○ Allotment of shares without minimum subscription (due to misconduct or negligence) (Section 69 (5))
  ○ Irregular allotment—allotment without filing statement in lieu of prospectus in case of private placement or allotment without receiving minimum subscription in case of first issue

- Failure to refund application money if shares not listed on stock exchange (Section 73(2))
- Non-payment of dividend within 30 days after declaration (Section 207)
- Non-maintenance of account books in case company does not have managing director or manager (Section 209)
- Contravening provision of Section 295 regarding loans to directors or firm/private company in which such director is partner/director.
- Personal fine for the following:
    § Failure to disclose his/her interest in contract or arrangement
    § Participating in any board meeting relating to contract in which he/she is interested
- Managing director cannot be made personally liable for recovery of dues against the company. Individual director is not liable for payment of wages under Payment of Wages Act. Directors are not liable for breach of trust for non-payment of ESIC dues as they are not 'employers'. Directors are not personally liable for payment of taxes in case of default by the company, unless specifically provided for.
- Personally liable if they act dishonestly and fraudulently. Negligence, even though no personal involvement, can attract liability.
- Director becomes liable for contempt of court by company according to Section12(5).
- Company cannot indemnify a director against any liability which the officer may incur on account of negligence, default, misfeasance, breach of duty or trust.
- In case the director gives personal guarantee for loans taken by the company from a bank, the director becomes personally liable.
- Company can take directors and officers (D&O) policy for directors to give them insurance cover against liabilities, except those arising from professional negligence, personal body injury, sickness, bad faith, damages arising out of frauds and dishonest or fraudulent acts of directors, criminal behaviour, wilful infringement of law, libel, defamation, etc.

Remuneration to non-whole-time directors

Sitting fees for attending board/committee/general meetings   Maximum Rs 20,000 in case of companies with paid-up capital plus free reserves of Rs 1 billion or more, or turnover is Rs 5 billion or more; Rs 10,000 in other cases. The limit was Rs 5000 upto July 2003 and Rs 2000 till March 2000. Approval for the sitting fee shall be required by the AOA. Sitting fees can be paid even if the company is making losses. No sitting fees for attending AGMs.

Reimbursement of expenses in connection with board meetings   Directors can be reimbursed all reasonable expenses incurred in connection with attending board/committee/general meetings.

Sitting fees and expenses for adjourned meeting   Sitting fee must be paid for adjourned meetings.

Ceiling on total managerial remuneration   The total managerial remuneration payable by a public limited company shall not exceed 11 per cent of the net profits of the company, computed in accordance with Sections 349 and 350.

The ceiling on remuneration to non-executive directors, by way of share of profits, is 1 per cent of the net profit when the company has a managing director, whole-time director, or manager.

When the company does not have an MD, WTD, or manager, the maximum limit is 3 per cent. Any remuneration in excess of 1/3 per cent shall be paid subject to the approval of the central government (refer to Table 8.1).

TABLE 8.1   Summary of managerial remuneration

S. No.	Person entitled to remuneration	Maximum % of net profit
1.	Non-executive directors where the company has managing director(s)/whole-time directors/manager	1
2.	Non-executive directors where there is no managing director/whole-time director/manager	3
3.	Managing director when there is only one	5
4.	Whole-time director where there is only one	5
5.	All managing directors/whole-time directors put together, when more than one	10
6.	Manager (only one permitted)	5
7.	Total managerial remuneration to all directors, managing directors/whole-time directors/manager put together	11

Source: Taxman's Company Law Ready Reckoner 2009.

Related to Board Meetings

Board meetings
- Board is in supreme position in the management of a company, according to Section 291 (1)
- Board can ratify the actions of a director/manager, post action
- Court should not interfere in commercial decisions of the board. Courts do not determine business judgement but will determine only questions of law.
- Restrictions on powers of the board
  - Restrictions under Companies Act
  - Restrictions under MOA
  - Restrictions under AOA
  - Restrictions placed by resolution in GMs
  - Prohibitions under any other act or regulation

Residuary powers vest with the board   All residuary powers to rest with the board and shareholders can exercise only those powers vested in them by the Companies Act or by the AOA.

Decisions at board meetings
- Collective decisions
- 'Meeting' should mean personal attendance. There is no provision for telephonic meetings or video conferencing and there is no prohibition either.

- No provision for proxy. A director cannot appoint a proxy or nominee to attend the meeting in his/her place.
- Act of board valid even if a director's appointment is found invalid. Even if it has been discovered that a director's appointment was invalid after the meeting, acts and decisions by the board and the director will be valid.
- Frequency, venue, and timings of board meetings
  - At least one meeting every quarter
  - Adjournment due to lack of quorum will not become violation
  - Meeting can be held at any time including outside business hours or on public holidays
- Board decisions on resolutions
  - Usually all decisions by the board are by simple majority
  - In the case of resolutions dealing with appointment of MD/manager in two companies (public limited or private limited, which is a subsidiary of a public limited company) and giving loans, making investments, or giving security or guarantee by the company, needs unanimous voting by the board.

Board committees

The board can delegate powers to committees if AOA provide for it. The decisions of the committee become the decisions of the board. Notwithstanding the constitution of committees, the board must exercise supervision and control.

- Powers that can be delegated to the committees:
  - Approval of quarterly results
  - Power to borrow money other than through debentures
  - Power to invest funds subject to the limit prescribed by the board
  - Power to make loans provided that the delegation is through a unanimous resolution of the board

Table 8.2 shows the differences between general meetings and the board meetings.

TABLE 8.2   Differences between general meetings and board meetings

General meeting	Board meeting
Minimum one meeting a year	Minimum one meeting per quarter
Chairman of the board, if any, chairs the meeting	Chairman of the board, if any, chairs the meeting
Quorum: Public company 5; Pvt company 2	Quorum: One-third strength; min 2
No quorum reqd for adjourned meeting	Quorum reqd for adjourned meeting too
Minimum 21 days clear notice required	No period of notice prescribed, but required
Notice must specify agenda	Notice need not specify agenda
Accidental omission to give notice does not vitiate the meeting	Even accidental omission to give notice vitiates the meeting
Item not on agenda cannot be taken	Item not on agenda can be taken (except in case of appointing a person as MD/manager of Pub ltd company if he is already MD/manager of another public company, which requires notice)

Contd

Table 8.2 contd

General meeting	Board meeting
AGM only in city where registered office is situated	Meeting anywhere in world possible
No AGM on public holiday (EGM can be held on public holiday too)	Can be held on public holidays too
Directors' interest must be disclosed	Directors' interest must be disclosed
Interested director can participate and vote	Interested director cannot participate and/or vote
Resolution by circulation not permissible	Circular resolutions can be passed except where circular resolution not permitted
Chiarman has casting vote	Chiarman has casting vote
Proxy can be appointed	No provision for proxy
Committes cannot be formed	Committees can be formed
Some resolutions require 75 per cent voting	Almost all resolutions by simple majority (except those that specifically require all directors present must vote in favour)
Special notice required for some resolutions	No provisions for special notice
Meeting can be called by board of directors or by requisition	Meeting can be called by any one of the directors
Provision for requisition meeting by members	No provision for requisition as any one director can call a meeting
Minutes to be written in 30 days (however, need not be signed within 30 days)	Minutes to be written in 30 days (however, need not be signed within 30 days)
Authentication of minutes by chairman of same meeting	Authentication of minutes by same chairman or chairman of next meeting
Members can inspect minute book	Members cannot inspect minute book
Confirmation of minutes of earlier meeting not required	Confirmation of minutes of earlier meeting not required (but usually done as it is a good secretarial practice)

Source: Taxman's Company Law Ready Reckoner 2009.

Procedures relating to board meetings

Chairing the board meeting   Usually by the chairman of the board. But if the chairman is not present within five minutes of the appointed time, the members present can appoint a chairman from the directors present.

Casting vote to chairman   In case of a voting on the board and if votes are equally divided, an additional or casting vote is given to the chairman (in addition to his vote as a member). But, if casting vote is not mentioned in the AOA, the company cannot follow this practice.

Removal of chairman   Chairman can be removed only as per provisions of statute. A vote of no confidence and a majority is not enough to remove him/her.

Calling a board meeting   Meeting of the board can be called by any director. None other than director or chairman can call a meeting of the board.

Notice of board meeting   There is no period prescribed for notice. The notice should be sent in writing to every director and should be signed by secretary, chairman, or any other person authorised by the board. Proof of sending notice shall be kept. If the AOA does not specify a particular mode of serving notice, it can be sent by post, courier, fax, or e-mail. Adequate time shall be given to the directors to receive notice and attend, failing which the notice will be declared invalid. Notice must be given to all directors. Failure to send notice even to one director makes meeting null and void. It may also be noted that if the AOA specify the date of meeting, informing the directors about this provision is enough and separate notices need not be sent.

Agenda for the board meeting   Normally, the agenda for the meeting shall accompany the notice but any item can be taken on agenda for discussion with the permission of the chairman. The agenda should contain notes to explain the proposal and its relevant statutory provision. Agenda should be divided into two parts: (a) Routine items, and (b) other items. The explanatory note should include:

- Background
- Proposal
- Provisions of law
- Decisions required
- Interest of directors, if any.

Quorum for the board meeting   Quorum is one-third of total strength of the board or two directors, whichever is higher. Any fraction of one-third should be rounded-off as one. For example, if the board strength is three, four, five, or six, the quorum is two directors. If the strength is seven, eight, or nine, the quorum is three. If the strength in ten, eleven, or twelve, the quorum is four. Vacant positions shall be ignored while taking the strength for determining the quorum. For discussions and voting of item on agenda where a director is interested, his/her presence cannot be considered as meeting the quorum. The minimum requirement of two (uninterested) directors must be met in such cases. When all the directors are interested, the resolution should be passed at the general meeting. Any meeting without the necessary quorum will be rendered invalid. The quorum should be present throughout the meeting. Exemptions regarding quorum requirement are permitted only for the purpose of (a) increasing the number of directors to that fixed for the quorum, or (b) calling EGM of the company, if sufficient number of directors to form the quorum are not available in India.

Filing of board resolutions with ROC   The resolution of the board of directors for appointment and terms of appointment of MD, and copies of terms of appointment of a sole selling agent shall be filed with ROC within 30 days.

Minutes of board meeting   Under Section 193(1), minutes of the board meeting have to be maintained. Minutes should be written and the pages shall be consecutively numbered. Default of maintaining a minute book will attract a fine of up to Rs 500. Minutes should be written within 30 days. It may be signed during the next board meeting. Minutes should contain details, such as, (1) Name of directors present at the meeting (2) Names of directors who dissent. The chairman has the freedom to delete any material that is irrelevant, defamatory, or detrimental to the interests of the company. He/she has absolute discretion about the contents of the minutes. The minutes shall be kept as per the legal provisions as evidence of the proceedings recorded. Unless otherwise proved, it is presumed that the meeting was held and the proceedings have been recorded. Auditors, directors, and a registrar, or inspector appointed by the central government have powers to inspect the minutes.

Amendment of resolution   A resolution previously passed can be rescinded or amended at a later meeting. But old minutes should not be deleted or crossed out at the subsequent meeting.

Report of board of directors to members   A report of the board of directors should be attached to the balance sheet laid before the AGM. Such a report shall contain:

- State of the company's affairs
- Appropriations of profits to reserves
- Amount recommended to be paid as dividend to shareholders
- Material changes and comments, if any, affecting the financial position of the company after the close of financial year, till the date of the report
- Conservation of energy, technology absorption, foreign exchange earnings, and outgoings in the prescribed format
- Changes during the financial year in the nature of business of the company, changes in the companies' subsidiaries or nature of business carried out by them, and the changes in the class of business in which the company has an interest
- Statement giving details of employees whose salaries are beyond prescribed limit (presently Rs 200,000 per month or Rs 2.4 million per annum)
- Complete information and explanations about every reservation, qualification, or adverse remarks, in the auditor's report
- Directors' responsibility statement
- Reasons for not accepting report of audit committee, if applicable
- Secretarial compliance report to be attached
- Number of meetings of board and committees held during the year and attendance record of each director
- Statement of holding company's interest in the subsidiary
- Reasons, if any, for the non-completion of 'buy-back' of shares approved by members within a specified time
- Details of shares issued under sweat equity, ESOP, and ESPS

The report of the directors shall be approved by the meeting of the board signed by any director authorized by the board.

Related to Restrictions on the Board

Restrictions on powers of the board

- Any sale, lease, or other kind of disposal of whole or substantially whole of the undertaking, or of other undertakings owned by the company, shall be done only after approval of members in a general meeting.

- Company cannot remit or give time for repayment of any debt due from a director without a resolution in the general meeting.
- Investment of compensation received after compulsory acquisition in other than trust securities can be made only with approval of members in the general meeting.
- Any borrowing of money in excess of paid capital and free reserves, and short- term loans to meet the working capital requirements, must be approved in the general meeting.
- Any contribution by the company to charitable funds beyond the limits (Rs 50,000 or 5 per cent of average net profits during the preceding three years calculated according to Section 349 and 350, whichever in greater) shall be approved through a resolution in the general meeting.

Restrictions on political contributions

Government companies cannot make any contribution to political parties. In other companies, a resolution must be passed in the meeting of the board of directors. Advertisements in a souvenir published by a political party will be treated as political contribution. Donations so made shall be disclosed in the annual accounts, mentioning the name of the party or the person. Donations are deductible from the income of the company for the computation of income tax (Section 80GGB). Violation of the guidelines will attract penalty of upto three times the amount contributed.

Related to Managerial Personnel

Appointment of managerial personnel

- A company with a paid-up share capital of Rs 5 million or more must appoint a managerial person (managing director/whole-time director/manager).
- Powers of the managerial person.
  Powers have to be conferred on him by a resolution or through agreement as per the provision in the articles. A managerial person acquires powers through (a) agreement with the company, which must be approved by either the board of directors or general meeting (b) resolution passed by a company in the general meeting (c) resolution passed by the board of directors, or (d) through the powers provided for in AOA.
- A company can appoint more than one MD. The board will decide how the powers shall be divided between them.
- A director who exercises substantial powers will be deemed as MD even if he/she is called by other names.
- MD/manager is subordinate to the board of directors.
- MD is not an owner. The company liabilities cannot be recovered from him/her. Even if the MD is declared as principal employer for statutory purposes, he/she is still an employee
- MD acts in a dual capacity. He/she is an agent of the company as director and at the same time he/she is an employee.

Eligibility to become MD/WTD/manager

- Age limits
  Having attained 25 years and less than 70 years. Persons above 18 but below 25 and persons above 70 years can be appointed by a special resolution passed by the general meeting.

- Residential status
  Normal resident of India; person who has been staying in India for a continuous period of at least 12 months immediately preceding his appointment. Approval of the central government is required in the case of those who do not meet the criteria. For appointment as MD/WTD in a special economic zone (SEZ) the above criteria is not applicable.
- Appointment of foreign national as MD/ WTD requires approval of the central government. Permission/work permit from the home ministry also is required.

Disqualification as MD/WTD

MD/WTD is a director first. So, any disqualification as director will automatically disqualify him as MD /WTD. Thus, if an additional director or director retiring by rotation is appointed as MD/WTD, he/she ceases to be MD/WTD if he/she ceases to be a director of the company. A person (a) who is an undischarged insolvent or has at any time been adjudged as insolvent (b) suspends or has at any time suspended payment to creditors, or has made any time composition with creditors, or (c) who has been convicted by a court for an offence involving moral turpitude, cannot be appointed or continued as MD/WTD. For a 'manager' also, these criteria for disqualification are applicable but only for a period of five years. While the central government has been empowered to remove the disqualification of a manager by notifying this in the gazette, such power is not available in the case of MD/WTD. A person is also disqualified if he/she has been sentenced to imprisonment for any period on account of economic offence or has been fined more than Rs1000. Economic offences include offences under Indian Stamp Act, Central Excise Act, Prevention of Food Adulteration Act, Essential Commodities Act, Companies Act, Securities Contracts (Regulation) Act, Customs Act, MRTP, SICA, FEMA, SEBI, FTDR, COFEPOSA, etc.

Appointment of MD/WTD is subject to approval in general meeting by ordinary resolution. If such approval is not accorded in the first general meeting after his appointment, he ceases to act as MD/WID/manager. Appointment of MD/WTD/ manager is only for five years at a time. He/she can be reappointed, or his/her term may be extended only for five years at a time.

Remuneration to managerial person

If the company is making profits, remuneration payable is 5 per cent of the net profits calculated for the purpose when there is only one MD/WTD/manager. When there are more than one managerial persons, the limit is increased to 10 per cent as above. Remuneration includes salary, DA, perquisites, commission, and other allowances. The minimum remuneration payable when profit is inadequate or the company is in loss is determined by the effective capital of the company. Effective capital is the sum of paid-up capital, amount in share premium account, long-term loans and deposits repayable after one year minus investments (in shares, debentures, securities), accumulated losses and preliminary expenses not written off, and will be calculated as on the last date of the financial year preceding the financial year in which the appointment is made.

Table 8.3 gives the minimum remuneration that can be paid corresponding to different slabs of effective capital.

TABLE 8.3   Minimum remuneration for various slabs of effective capital

S. No.	Effective capital	Minimum remuneration payable
1.	< Rs 10 million	Max. Rs 75,000 p.m.
2.	≥ Rs 10 millionand < Rs 50.00 million	Max. Rs 1,00,000 p.m.
3.	≥ Rs 50 million and < Rs 250 million	Max. Rs 1,25,000 p.m.
4.	≥ Rs 250 million and < Rs 500 million	Max. Rs 1,50,000 p.m.
5.	≥ Rs 500 million and < Rs 1 billion	Max. Rs 1,75,000 p.m.
6.	≥ Rs1 billion	Max. Rs 2,00,000 p.m.

If the remuneration exceeds the above prescribed limits, approval of the central government is required.

Restrictions with respect to managerial remuneration have been relaxed for companies in SEZs. The remuneration can be upto Rs 2 million p.m. or Rs 24 million p.a. without approval of the central government, provided (a) the company has not raised any money by public issue of shares or debentures in India (b) the company has not made any defaults in India in repayment of any of its debts (including public deposits) or interest thereon for a continuous period of thirty days in any financial year.

- Maximum remuneration when a person is appointed in more than one company—if a person is appointed as a managerial person in more than one company, the total remuneration shall not exceed the higher maximum limit from any one of the companies.
- Compensation for loss of office—MD/WTD/manager must be paid compensation if his/her services are terminated before the due date when he/she was not involved in any negligence, default, fraud, or breach of trust. In such a case, what the MD/WTD manager can be paid is the remuneration he would have earned if he/she had been in the office for the unexpired part of his term or three years, whichever is less. The compensation should be calculated on the basis of the average remuneration actually earned by him during a period of three years immediately preceding the date on which he/she ceased to hold office. If the company is under a winding up process, or plans for winding up in 12 months, such compensation will be payable only after the share capital (including premium, if any) is repaid to shareholders.

Related to Appointment and Role of Company Secretary

A company secretary is a key person in the functioning of the board of a company. Company secretaries are expected to guide management in legal matters, especially relating to company laws. They coordinate the activities of the board chairman and other directors. They organize board and general meetings, keep the minutes of the meeting, record approved share transfers, corresponds with directors and shareholders, maintain statutory records, files necessary returns with ROC, etc. They also coordinate between various departments and the board, act as the secretary of the audit committee and also as the compliance officer in a listed company, as necessitated by SEBI.

Statutory duties and authorities of a company secretary include:

- Signing declaration that all the requirements of the Companies Act and rules have been complied with
- Authenticating a document on behalf of the company
- Signing of the share certificates along with two directors (one of which shall be MD/WTD, if appointed)
- Making statutory declaration for obtaining certificate for commencement of business
- Signing the annual return to be filed with ROC
- Authenticating balance sheet and P&L account to be filed with ROC along with two directors (one of which shall be MD/WTD, if appointed)
- Certifying a copy of the balance sheet and P&L account to be filed with ROC
- Certifying and submitting the statement of affairs regarding assets, debts, and liabilities, of the company to the official liquidator
- Signing applications, particulars, notices, and returns to be submitted to ROC under various provisions of the Companies Act as a 'responsible officer' of the company
- Appearing before Company Law Board (CLB) on behalf of the company
- Signing any pleading in a suit by or against the company according to Order 29, Rule 1 of the Civil Procedure Code.

Related to Accounts of the Company

Every company must maintain proper books of accounts at its registered office in respect of (a) All sums of money received and expended by the company and the matters in respect of which receipt and expenditure take place (b) All sales and purchase of goods by the company (c) All assets and liabilities of the company (d) Cost records in case of companies specified by the central government.

All accounts shall be maintained according to double entry system of accounting. While the Companies Act requires accounts to be kept at the registered office of the company, they can be kept at any other place in India as may be decided by the board of directors. If the board decides so, electronic return in the Form e-23 AA has to be filed within seven days to ROC. Other aspects relating to accounts are as follows:

- Accounts should reflect a true and fair view of the state of affairs of the company
- Accounts shall be maintained on accrual basis
- Accounts shall be prepared as per the accounting standards. In case, it is not prepared accordingly, the company shall disclose the deviations from accounting standards, reasons for such deviations, and the financial effect, if any, of such deviation. The auditor has to state whether, in his opinion, the accounts are prepared as per accounting standards or will have to qualify the report. Accounting standards in India are prescribed by the central government in consultation with National Advisory Committee on Accounting

Standards (NACAS) on recommendations of the Institute of Chartered Accountants of India (ICAI)

- Default in maintenance of accounts will attract penalty of imprisonment upto 6 months or fine upto Rs10,000 or both. When the company has an MD/manager, punishment can be imposed on him. Where an MD/manager is not available, punishment can be imposed on all directors

Inspection of books of accounts

Any director, ROC, officer of the central government authorized by the central government, or officer of SEBI authorized by SEBI can do the inspection.

- Every company must prepare a balance sheet at the end of the financial year and profit and loss account for the period of the financial year. In case the company is non-profit making, it has to prepare an income and expenditure account instead of a P&L account. Annual accounts should be presented at the AGM of members, normally to be held within six months from the close of the financial year, extendable by three months with permission from ROC. In the case of the first AGM of a company, it should be held within nine months of the close of the financial year. Failure to prepare the annual accounts can attract a penalty of imprisonment upto 6 months and fine upto Rs 10,000 for the directors. Imprisonment is applicable only when the offence was committed wilfully
- The balance sheet and P&L account have to be prepared as per the requirements of Schedule VI to the Companies Act
- The financial year can be less than or more than 12 months, but cannot be more than 15 months. It can be extended to 18 months with special permission from ROC
- While ROC permits any period of 12 months for the financial year, the IT Act requires that all companies must submit their IT returns on the basis of a uniform financial year, closing on 31 March every year
- Authentication of the balance sheet and P&L account
  Every balance sheet and P&L account shall be signed by the secretary or manager on behalf of the board, with due authentication by the board and at least two directors, one of them being the MD, if the company has one. The balance sheet and P&L account must be accompanied by the directors' report.
- A copy of the balance sheet with all accompanying documents must be sent to members. Members have a right to receive this. Since most of the annual reports are bulky with all its accompanying documents which investors are not necessarily interested in or not in a position to understand the details, the Companies Act has made a provision for sending an abridged balance sheet containing the important details. If investors need the full balance sheet, they can request for it from the company
- The balance sheet must be filed with ROC within 30 days from the date of laying it at the AGM, with all the accompanying documents. In the case of limited banking, insurance, and deposit/provident/benefit companies, the audited balance sheets have to be filed on the first Monday in February and August, every year

- Failure to comply with the requirements mentioned above will attract penalty of Rs 500 per day for the defaulted period. Also, if a company fails to file annual accounts continuously for three financial years, a director on the company is disqualified to become a director of any other public limited company for a period of five years
- Audited accounts can be revised only to comply with the requirements of any other law to achieve the object of exhibiting a true and fair view. The revised accounts shall be adopted either in the EGM or AGM
- Balance sheet of the holding company should include the following details of each subsidiary company:
    - Balance sheet, P&L account, report of the board of directors, and auditors' report of the subsidiary company. If the financial years are different, accounts and reports in respect of the latest financial year of subsidiary prior to closing of the financial year of the holding company should be given, but the maximum gap between the financial year of the holding company and the subsidiary company can be six months
    - Statement of the holding company's interest in the subsidiary at the end of the financial year
    - Non-compliance will attract imprisonment of upto 6 months and a fine of up to Rs 10,000 for directors.

Related to Audit of Accounts

Since shareholders are not empowered to examine books of accounts of a company, they need to ensure that the affairs of the company are being carried out properly. So, they appoint an independent auditor to ensure that the directors do not misuse their fiduciary position. The auditor is appointed for a year and his/her term is renewed every year at the AGM.

Auditors

Number of auditors   A company can appoint one or more auditors.

Qualification   He/she must be a chartered accountant. A firm of chartered accountants can also be appointed but all partners of the firms must be chartered accountants.

Information of appointment to ROC   The auditor appointed must inform his/her appointment to ROC within 30 days of such appointment by the company, along with the intimation letter from the company.

Disqualification of auditors

The following persons cannot be appointed as auditor/s, even if he/she/they are chartered accountants:

- A body corporate
- An officer or employee of the company
- A person who is in employment of an officer or employee of the company
- A person who is a partner of an officer or employee of the company
- A person who has given any guarantee or security in connection with indebtedness of any

third person to the company for amount exceeding Rs10,000

- A person who holds any security of the company which carries voting rights
- A person is disqualified to be auditor under any of the aforesaid clauses; he will also be disqualified to be an auditor of a subsidiary or holding company of that company, or subsidiary of that company's holding company. Once a person is disqualified, he/she shall be deemed to have vacated his/her office. As per the Chartered Accountants Act, a member is disqualified if (a) he/she ceases to be a member of the institute (b) his/her certificate of practice is cancelled (c) he/she is adjudged to have unsound mind, or (d) he/she is declared insolvent.

Auditor appointments

- Appointment of the first auditor shall be made by the board of directors within one month after registration. This automatically gets terminated at the conclusion of the first EGM/AGM after incorporation
- Reappointments of auditors is not automatic. A resolution for his/her appointment is required. While in the normal course, an ordinary resolution would be sufficient, in the case of companies where public financial institutions, government companies/central government/state governments/state financial institutions where the government holds at least 25 per cent of equity/nationalized banks/nationalized general insurance company either singly or jointly hold 25 per cent or more equity, a special resolution is required
- Appointment of auditors in a government company is not made by shareholders but by the comptroller and auditor general of India (C&AG)
- Remuneration of auditors is fixed by the AGM except in cases where the central government appoints the auditors, the company having failed to do so

Auditor removal

- An auditor automatically retires at the next AGM. He/she can be removed before the AGM only with the previous approval of the central government

Powers of the auditor

- Right to access at all times to the books and accounts and vouchers of the company kept at any of its offices
- Can seek information and explanations he/she thinks necessary for the performance of duties from all officers in the company
- An auditor can attend meetings of the audit committee of the board
- He/she can make adverse comments on the accounts prepared by the company in the form of qualifications and reservations

Duties and liabilities of an auditor   An auditor is only a 'watch dog' and not a 'hunter dog'. While scepticism is their forte, they have to only make their observations on accounts prepared by the company, certify them in the light of information provided to them, and make comments on deviations, if any, from the standards or reservations about things which they are sceptical about. In the light of this, their major duties are:

- Evaluation of financial statements to see whether they reflect the true and fair state of affairs
- Act as fiduciary for shareholders
- Apply reasonable care and skill in accordance with professional standards expected of them, and act in good faith
- Verify rather than detect, but can look deep if suspicious
- Certify that in their opinion and to the best of their knowledge, the balance sheet and P&L account give a true and fair view
- They must act as whistle-blowers if they detect fraud committed by the employees/ management
- Certify the report on corporate governance, which is a mandatory part of the directors' report.

Here we have discussed only those parts of company law in India which have a direct bearing on the governance of companies. There are other provisions in the law which can affect the conduct of companies indirectly.

DEFICIENCIES AND LOOPHOLES IN THE LAWS

While the company law in India is very exhaustive, a number of deficiencies or loopholes exist, and there have been wide variations in their interpretations by the courts. The following list highlights some of the major deficiencies/loopholes:

- Directors who sit on many group companies can be independent in all because the group companies are considered to be independent entities (for example, Nusli Wadia on the boards of Tata Steel, Tata Motors, and Tata Chemicals).
- Inside directors (formerly WTDs) can become independent directors on the board of one company which is incorporated afresh after a restructuring process (for example, DS Mehta on the board of Bajaj Auto).
- A company cannot be penalized for the actions of the promoters. Family promoted and managed companies in India, where family members are actively involved in management while being major shareholders, pose serious challenges to law and its implementation (for example, the ongoing tussle between Mukesh Ambani of RIL and Anil Ambani of RNRL and their family agreement for demerger of the group companies has already posed a great challenge to the law-makers and the judiciary).
- Act beyond powers can be ratified by the board. This is what Mukesh Ambani did as chairman of the board of RIL in order to enter into a family agreement regarding the demerger within the group which was later approved by the board of RIL. Whether such an important decision, involving an array of big corporate entities, could be left to one person was never questioned (or nobody dared to question). While practicality must be appreciated, in some cases prudence must override practicality.
- The maximum limit of 15 directorships in publicly-listed companies is too high considering the involvement and rigour expected of directors today. In addition, they may also have

directorships in private limited companies and non-profit organizations. This is likely to affect a director's effectiveness in diligently attending to the duties as a director.

- All directors are equally liable for damages. Should independent directors who spend limited time with the companies in the execution of their duties, be held equally liable as the whole-time directors or promoter directors who are in full-time management of the company?

- There is no specific notice period prescribed for calling a board meeting; this can be misused by some directors, especially the promoter directors or inside directors. Subject to the availability of a quorum (which is supportive), an interested director can push resolutions through in the absence of directors who are likely to dissent. Of course, companies can pre-announce the dates in the AOA or clearly mention the notice required in the company governance charter, if existing.

- The time given for writing minutes of meeting (30 days) seems to be very high. Directors, especially those who are part-time, may even forget what transpired during the meeting after some time. Hence, if they receive the minutes after such a delay, they may have no cross-check on what is written in the MOM with what they have in memory.

- The fine of Rs 500 for default of maintaining a minute book appears to be too little to incentivise writing of the minute. Please note that while it is not available for shareholders for inspection, this is an important document during litigations.

- The absolute discretion that the chairman has about the contents of the minutes is questionable. Using this discretion, the chairman (especially the one who is full-time or is a promoter nominee) can change the minutes to suit or protect his/her interests.

- Even though auditors are prevented from holding shares in the company they audit, there is no law against their family members holding such shares. The auditor, having access to all financial statements and data of the company, has a lot of inside information which enables passing on this information to family members who may hold shares in the company.

The list given above is not an exhaustive list of deficiencies in the law. These are only some of the major lacunae which can hinder effective governance of corporations and hence need the attention of law-makers.

GOVERNANCE RATINGS—MERITS AND DEMERITS

In Chapter 7 we identified that institutional investors use the corporate governance rating system as a tool to ascertain the quality of governance systems in a company where they propose to invest or where they have invested. 'A corporate governance rating can be a powerful indicator of the extent to which a company is currently adding, or has the potential to add in the future, the shareholder value. This is because a company with good corporate governance is generally perceived as more attractive to investors than one without' (Mallin 2007). Post Enron, WorldCom, etc., in the US and post-Satyam in India, investors have begun to be seriously concerned about governance practices of companies where they plan to invest their hard-earned savings (see Exhibit 8.1). 'With this increasing level of awareness of corporate governance, there is a role for global benchmarks to help a company's stakeholders to assess and compare corporate governance

Exhibit 8.1
Governance Ratings—A Saviour for Investors?

Post Enron, WorldCom, Tyco and similar scandals, a number of corporate governance institutions have come into being as self-proclaimed standard-bearers for protecting shareholder rights. In addition to acting as quote machines, the firms which include the Corporate Library and Risk Metrics Group's ISS Governance Services—are also big businesses that sell, among other things, ratings that say whether a company is well-governed or not (Bandler and Burke 2008). Bandler and Burke reproduce the data from a study conducted by Stanford University's Rock Center for Corporate Governance. The governance ratings awarded by four rating firms, namely ISS, the Corporate Library, GovernanceMetrics International (GMI), and Audit Integrity, with respect to three companies, Walt Disney, General Motors and Xerox, vary widely from one rater to another (see table below):

Governance rating firms	Scale	Overall governance ratings		
		Disney	GM	Xerox
Audit Integrity	1 to 100	69	48	64
Institutional Shareholder Services	1 to 100	100	100	99.46
Governance Metrics International	1 to 10	8	9	10
The Corporate Library	A to F	C	D	D

Some of the ratings for other companies are as follows:

- Pfizer earned 100 on a scale of 1 to l00 (1 being the lowest and 100 the highest) from ISS while Corporate Library awarded it D on a scale of A to F (A being the highest and F the lowest).
- Lockheed Martin scored a 9.5 out of 10 (10 highest) from GMI, but Corporate Library gave Lockheed its worst possible F grade.

Research finding
- 'The Stanford team found very little or no statistical evidence of links between the ratings and the company performance, undermining the firm's very reason for being', according to Bandler and Burke.

Comments from the rating firms (Bandler and Burke 2008)
- 'The fact that our primary customers are investment managers suggests they are finding value in what we deliver' (Howard Sherman, CEO, GMI).
- 'The study used the wrong kinds of metrics and should have looked at more than one year of ratings data, and points out that the ratings are "a tool, not a talisman" and not meant to act as a predictor of performance' (Patrick McGurn, special counsel at ISS).
- The Corporate Library declined to comment.
- The CEO of Audit Integrity praised the study.

Other comments (Bandler and Burke 2008)
- 'It points out that there is no grand unified theory of corporate governance' (Cary Klafter, VP, legal and corporate affairs, Intel Corp).
- '[Good] governance is a little bit like porn, I can spot it when I see it, but it is hard to say what it is' (Robert Daines, co-director of Stanford's Rock Center for Corporate Governance and one of the authors of the study).

Questions

1. How do you explain the differences in ratings assigned to the same companies by different raters?
2. Do you think that corporate governance ratings enable companies to attract investors to them and reduce their cost of capital?
3. Corporate governance ratings are awarded only when a firm volunteers. Should it be made mandatory?

practices from one firm to another, and from one county to another. The concept of corporate governance rating or scoring is a way to address this gap' (Adilabadkar 2005).

A number of rating agencies from all over the world have developed their models for evaluating corporates from a governance point of view, and assigning them corporate governance scores. Institutions/firms, such as Standard and Poor's (S&P), Governance Metrics International (GMI), Institutional Shareholder Services (ISS), the Corporate Library, and Audit Integrity in the US; Credit Rating Information Services of India Ltd (CRISIL), an affiliate of S&P, Investment Information and Credit Rating Agency Ltd (ICRA), and Credit Analysis and Research Ltd (CARE) in India; and Deminor in Brussels, Belgium, etc., have been in the practice of rating governance of publicly-listed corporates for many years now. While the Indian outfits have restricted their operations to Indian publicly-listed companies, S&P has been using its governance rating system in widely different markets. GMI ratings extend beyond the US to countries in the Asia-Pacific region and Europe. Deminor has been concentrating on European companies while ISS, Corporate Library, etc. have concentrated mainly on the US. With the acquisition of the corporate governance practice of Deminor, ISS has been extending its presence in Europe.

Since corporate governance depends greatly on the levels of transparency and the reporting practices in a county in general, 'an appropriate approach for a corporate governance rating system is first to have a rating of the corporate governance in a given country' (Mallin 2007). This necessitates finding out whether the country is enlightened on the need for better corporate governance, are there established guidelines, laws, or codes of best practices, and are the corporates following these. After establishing the scenario present in a country, the rating companies can set about assigning governance ratings for individual companies. The rating agencies collect a variety of information from companies but do not depend only on them. They also try to cross-check and verify such information through other channels. Different rating agencies follow different rating models, but the underlying fundamental principles are rather similar—fairness, transparency, accountability, and responsibility.

According to Adilabadkar (2005), a corporate governance score is based upon the assessment of four key areas of corporate performance:

- Ownership structure, which asks who owns and controls the company and what conflicts are likely to arise from the ownership structure;
- Financial stakeholder rights and relations, which look into ownership rights; minority shareholder protection, voting procedures and takeover defences;

- Transparency and disclosure, which look at the quality and accessibility of financial and operational disclosure, including transparency of accounting methods, the integrity of the audit process, and how the audit committee oversees and maintains auditor independence;
- Board structure and process, which looks at board independence, effectiveness, succession policies, and the process of setting executive pay and aligning it with the interests of shareholders.

S&P, which started its corporate governance score (CGS) services in 2002, is based on four company characteristics (Adilabadkar 2005):

- Ownership structure and concentration
- Financial stakeholders' rights and relations
- Transparency and disclosure, and
- Board structure and process.

For S&P to determine a CGS for a company, the company has to request S&P for it. S&P reviews the client company's documents both publicly available and confidential, and has discussions with executive management, directors, shareholders, analysts, bankers, etc. After the process is completed, S&P awards a score on a scale of 1 to 10 within each of the four areas mentioned above. The client company can decide whether to make the rating public.

GMI on the other hand, examines a company's website, statutory filings, press coverage, etc., gathers data on each of the 600 metrics, and checks with the company for verification of facts. After getting feedback from the company, it puts the details into the database which comes out with the governance score on a scale of 1 to 10. In addition to an overall score, it provides scores in seven discrete categories.

CRISIL uses the following rating criteria:

- Equitable treatment of shareholders
- Ownership rights of shareholders
- Transparency and disclosure
- Composition of board
- Management assessment
- Value creation for various stakeholders.

CARE, on the other hand, uses the following seven criteria:

- Board composition and functioning
- Ownership structure
- Organization structure and management information system
- Shareholder relationship
- Disclosure and transparency
- Financial prudence, and
- Statutory and regulatory Compliance.

Merits of Corporate Governance Ratings

Investors have become highly demanding and discerning after the high profile corporate collapses at the beginning of the century. This has put pressure on corporates to be better governed. Evidence from various studies on corporates, with emphasis on the governance processes and practices, point to the fact that those with less meaningful governance practices have been required to pay a significant risk premium in their competition for garnering funds from capital markets. While legislation and regulations can mostly enforce a 'form' thorough insistence on the structure of the board, formation of committees, separating chairman and CEO positions, etc., the 'substance' of governance will eventually determine the credibility of the firm among all the stakeholders. Hence, the onus falls on the firm to be better governed and also to project it as being better governed to the stakeholders. The governance rating process enables a company to achieve this and, in turn, enables investors to make informed choices from among a large range of options available. This can be of great help to investors in countries such as India where more than 4000 companies are listed on the stock exchanges. The major advantages of governance ratings can be listed as follows:

For firms

- Enables firms to obtain an independent and reliable assessment about their quality of governance
- Firms can understand their relative positioning in the national and international scenario
- Firms with better ratings can expect to lower the risk premium placed on them by capital markets, and thereby reduce cost of capital
- Firms can use the ratings (their own and those of competitors) as references and set benchmarks for further improvements
- Firms get to understand whether they add value to the stakeholders of the company
- It enables firms to improve their image/visibility/credibility in society
- Enables the company to attract talent to the board and management.

For investors/other stakeholders

- Enables investors to make informed decisions
- Information availability brings in institutional interest in the company resulting in better price efficiency
- Banks and other financial institutions can make informed decisions to lend and fund the company
- Employees, customers, suppliers, and other stakeholders will be keen to associate with a well-governed firm
- Increases the confidence of the capital markets in firms.

Limitations and Demerits of Corporate Governance Ratings

While apparently governance ratings have a number of merits as described above, there are also de-merits and limitations:

- The rating agencies have to rely heavily on information provided by the firms.
- Different institutions offering governance ratings stress on different parameters to ascertain governance performance. Thus, the ratings of a firm may vary from one rater to another. This can send confusing signals to the ordinary investors who do not know or who do not have the time to learn about the differences in parameters.
- It is voluntary in nature; hence, if a company does not volunteer it need not necessarily mean that they are low on governance performance compared to other firms with a high rating.
- The methodology relies heavily on structural aspects rather than on the process of governance. This, once again, brings back the criticism on general governance reforms which has been more structural with consequent in-built deficiencies.
- Governance scores may not be able to prevent many maladies such as insider trading, false reporting, intentional fraudulent practices of the CEO and other members of the board, or misuse of resources by the management, etc. This was evident in the case of Satyam Computers which had a high governance rating.
- The decision on making the rating public, by and large, rests with the company.
- Since rating is not compulsory and involves a lot of costs for the firm (S&P is said to be charging a fee in the range of $18,000 to $150,000, according to Adilabadkar (2005)), only a very small percentage have volunteered, making it difficult for an investor to use them as a yardstick.
- Ratings have been assigned based on data and information about current working of the firm. They do not necessarily look at the historical behaviour of a firm with regard to governance matters and cannot assure that the good/bad practices of the current will be carried over to the future. This once again puts the responsibility on to the investors to make their own judgements.

Notwithstanding the deficiencies, the number of institutions that are entering the governance rating business and the number of firms volunteering to be rated have been on the rise.

INFORMATION IS THE KEY—COOPERATE AND COLLABORATE FOR INFORMATION

While shareholders are the owners of the corporation, managers enjoy not only unlimited control over the assets of the corporation, but also information about everything that is happening within the company. Since the shareholders do not have the privilege of having information about what is happening, this puts managers in an enviable position. According to Phan, 'This information asymmetry inevitably leads to the under specification of performance standards for the managers' (Phan 2000). This information asymmetry may exist even in the boardroom. Directors who are also involved full-time in the management have the privilege of having all the information, compared to the outside directors. 'When a considerable disparity occurs, which happens frequently, discussions become one-sided' (Colley et al. 2003).

Such information gaps can lead to poor decisions leading to flawed governance. Rigorous efforts must be taken to see that the management does not conceal information from the board, preventing them from taking informed decisions. Efforts shall be made to close the information gap and to provide all directors with the right, necessary, and same amount of information. In Chapter 6 we saw how establishing an information architecture can help. The board has a responsibility, as a single body, to take decisions that are in the best interest of the firm, its shareholders, and other stakeholders. Without having the right kind of information at the right time, it is not possible to do the job. There must be a seamless flow of information between the management and board for the corporation to embark on better governance practices. Information is the fundamental resource with which the board can execute its duties and responsibilities. The board and management should not consider each other adversaries but should cooperate and collaborate with each other to get the best information, to enable the board and ensure that right decisions are made. The management should have systems in place to capture information from all employees. And similarly, the board should have a system (such as the information architecture we referred to earlier) to capture all needed information from management. Information being the raw material for decision-making by the board, they must evolve a well-functioning system.

MATURE MARKET FOR CORPORATE CONTROL

When shareholders, by and large, are not interested in the well-being of the firm, as there are easy exit options available, boards do not necessarily take steps to enforce good governance and it has also been proved that there are serious limitations to what regulators can do. Who then will bring in the necessary disciplinary behaviour in firms? The only alternative seems to be a well-developed market for corporate control. Poor governance usually leads to poor performance, leading to rejection by product and capital markets, driving down the value of the company in the markets. When such a downward push of share prices happens, the firm may become vulnerable and attractive to many investors. But are there enough investors and the market mechanisms to support them in enabling them to threaten the poorly governed companies with takeover attempts? In developed markets, corporate control threats are very commonly seen but there is very little evidence of the existence of a market for corporate control in emerging markets such as India. When boards, shareholders, and regulators fail in disciplining companies, the market for corporate control can effectively instill a governance process which will force the boards and shareholders to see that their firm is not under threat, and improve the governance processes in their companies.

Many developing countries such as India do not have legal systems conducive to such establishment of a market for corporate control. Till recently, takeover regulations were absent in India. Even though the regulations are in place now, the market for competitive corporate control is by and large absent. All developing countries should encourage such a market for corporate control, which will act as a disciplining mechanism on corporates.

SUMMARY

Boards have fiduciary responsibilities towards shareholders and are expected to act in such prudent manner that will protect the interests of the corporates according to the fundamental concept of the corporations. And had boards functioned in such a self-regulatory manner, corporate failures would not have occured on account of corporate governance failures. But, we have seen that a number of failures have happened, starting from the turn of the century, which put the blame squarely at the feet of the boards of those corporates who failed to play the role assigned to them and failed miserably in their duties. If boards themselves do not do their duties diligently in the normal course, are there other agencies who can think of disciplining boards and companies?

In a developed market, there are a number of institutions who can play meaningful roles in disciplining the corporations. Institutions that are characteristic of developed markets, such as institutional investors, investment banks, banks, stock exchanges, auditors, and rating agencies have been taking active roles in the establishment and running of corporations. Hence, these institutions can play a major role in the governance processes of corporations. Many of them have high stakes in modern corporations. Thus, if these institutions play an active role, governance processes can be improved considerably. Institutional investors, who over a period of time have become major investors in corporates, can discipline corporates if they play an active role as shareholders. While in developed markets such as the US institutional investors like pension funds take active interest in the governance focus, that kind of shareholder activism is usually absent in developing economies.

Auditing is another institution that can play a definite role in improving governance. Auditors are supposed to be the scorekeepers for the shareholders. But questions have very often been raised about their integrity and conflicts of interest. In many of the failures, auditors, who are expected to act as fiduciaries for investors, have chosen to collude with management and take the investor for a ride.

Through enacting laws for corporates to follow—right from incorporation to winding up, governments also play a very important role in the way the corporations conduct themselves. But, usually there are overlaps between the laws established by the government and the capital market regulators. It is very often felt that there should be a fine line dividing the regulatory framework between the two.

Post-Enron, WorldCom, and Tyco failures, rating agencies have added corporate governance practices to their regular rating business. Institutions such as S&P, the Corporate Library, Audit Integrity, etc., in the US and CRISIL, ICRA, and CARE in India have started offering corporate governance scores for corporates. But, the effectiveness is still questionable, not only because the rating process is voluntary in nature but also because the rating parameters vary widely among raters. Any governance process is based on information. There has to be a well-laid out information flow from management to board and vice versa, between employees and management, between different shareholders and company, and among shareholders and stakeholders in order for better governance to happen.

KEY TERMS

Aberrant   Straying away from normal

Bail out   Enable to escape harsh action

Canon   Heavy gun

Casting vote   Vote given to the chairman to break an impasse aring out of equality in votes

Collusion   Secret agreement or understanding for deceitful or fraudulent purpose

Cripple   Unable to move

Dead hand poison pills   Anti-takeover defense mechanism stipulating that only persons who were members of the board of directors at the time the anti-takeover measure was put into place have the power to rescind the anti-takeover measure

EDGAR   Electronic data gathering, analysis, and retrieval system

EVA™   Economic Value Added—computed as net operating profit after taxes (NOPAT) less cost of capital (a registered trade mark of Stern Stewart Co)

Information asymmetry   Lack of balance in information availability

Knee-jerk reaction   Unprepared and sudden reaction

Misfeasance   Wrongful performance of a normally lawful act

Momentum investors   Investors who buy and sell, watching the movements of shares in the markets

Mushroom   Grow fast in numbers

Perpetual succession   Existence beyond current members

Quorum   Minimum number of persons to be present for proceedings to have authority

Rating   Position awarded to an economic entity on a scale

Residuary powers   Legal or legitimate powers or powers entrusted by law

Shareholder activism   Shareholder taking active interest in the affairs of the company (to protect their and the company's interests)

Shareholder democracy   Equal treatment to all shareholders

Stiffle   Struggle for breath

Subordinate legislation   Legislation dependent on another legislation

Ultra vires   Beyond power or authority granted by law

CONCEPT REVIEW QUESTIONS

1. Explain the concept of shareholder activism.
2. What are the characteristics of developed markets?
3. Explain the pitfalls of the developed market argument.
4. Too many regulators confuse the firms. Do you feel that governance matters should be assigned to only one regulator? Explian the rationale behind your arguments.
5. Why are auditors required? Explain the roles and duties expected of them.
6. Comment on the statement, 'Corporate Governance Ratings: A Saviour for Investors'.
7. What is a market for corporate control? How can it help to further the cause of corporate governance?

CRITICAL THINKING QUESTIONS

Auditors getting paid by the companies whose accounts they audit can lead to dilution of the rigour expected of them. Do you think that this allegation is worth the attention? Give your suggestions to overcome this problem.

PROJECT WORK

Study the instances of the same auditor performing the audit of different companies belonging to the same industry/family group of companies for at least five major industrial groups in India.

REFERENCES

'Activism to the fore', *Business India*, 8 February 2009.

Adilabadkar, Suhani, 'Corporate Governance Ratings: Savior of the Stakeholders?' in *Corporate Governance: The Current Crisis and The way Out*, Suryanarayana, A. (ed) (2005), Icfai University Press, Hyderabad.

Annual report of Satyam Computer Services Ltd for 2007–08.

Annual report of Reliance Industries Ltd, 2008–09.

Ashby, Meredith D. and Stephen A. Miles (2002), *Leaders Talk Leadership*, Oxford University Press, New York.

Balakrishnan, S., 'SEBI, a law unto itself', *The Hindu*, 10 October 2005.

Bandler, James and Doris Burke, 'Who is watching the watchdogs?', *Fortune*, 7 July 2008.

Bebchuk, Lucian and Jesse Fried (2004), *Pay without Performance: The Unfulfilled Promise of Executive Compensation*, Harvard University Press, Cambridge.

Berle, Adolf A. and Gardiner C. Means (1932), *The Modern Corporation and Private Property*, Transaction Publishers, New Jersey.

Charkham, Jonathan (2000), *Keeping Good Company: A Study of Corporate Governance in Five Countries*, Oxford University Press, Oxford.

Colley Jr, John L., Jacqueline L. Doyle, George W. Logan, and Wallace Stettinus (2003), *Corporate Governance*, Tata McGraw-Hill, New Delhi.

'Confessions of auditors', *Business Today*, 8 February 2009.

Das, Subhash Chandra (2008), *Corporate Governance in India: An Evaluation*, Prentice Hall of India, New Delhi.

'Dependance on quarterly performance "not advisable"', *The Hindu*, 7 February 2006.

Dimma, William A. (2006), *Tougher Boards for Tougher Times: Corporate Governance in the Post-Enron Era*, Wiley-India, New Delhi.

Garratt, Bob (2003), *Thin on Top*, Nicholas Brealey, London.

George, Bill (2009), *Seven Lessons for Leading in Crisis*, Jossey-Bass, San Francisco.

Gompers, Paul A., Joy Ishii, and Andrew Metrick, 'Corporate governance and equity prices', *Quarterly Journal of Economics*, 118(1), February 2003, pp. 107–155.

Gupta, L.C. (1989), *Corporate Boards and Nominee Directors: Making the Board Work*, Oxford University Press, New Delhi.

'Inside the secret world of auditing: How it's done globally', *Business Today*, 22 February 2009.

Khoppikar, Rachna M., 'Unravelling the Fraud', *Business Today*, 19 April 2009.

Kumar T.N., Satheesh (2008), 'Indian family-managed companies: The corporate governance conundrum', http//:papers. ssrn.com.

MacAvoy, Paul W. and Ira M. Millstein (2004), *The Recurrent Crisis in Corporate Governance*, Stanford Business Books, California.

Mallin, Christine A. (2007), *Corporate Governance*, Oxford University Press, New Delhi.

Mehra, Puja, 'Audit: Elusive independence' *Business Today*, 8 February 2009.

Micklethwait, John and Adrian Wooldridge (2003), *The Company: A Short History of a Revolutionary Idea*, Phoenix, London.

Phan, Philip H. (2000), *Taking Back the Boardroom*, McGraw-Hill, Press India, Singapore.

'Quizzing on Auditors at Infosys AGM', *Business Line*, 2 June 2009.

Report of the Naresh Chandra Committee on Corporate Audit and Governance, Department of Company Affairs, 2002.

Romano, Roberta, 'Less is more: Making institutional activism a valuable mechanism of corporate governance', http//: papers.ssrn.com (2000).

Sanchety, Deepak, 'Good corporate governance: Chasing a mirage', *Business Line*, 23 January 2005.

'Shareholder democracy has a long way to go in India', *Business Line*, 8 November 2009.

Shultz, Susan F. (2001), *The Board Book*, East-West Books, Chennai.

Smith, Roy C., and Ingo Walter (2006), *Governing the Modern Corporation*, Oxford University Press, New York.

Som, Lalita (2006), *Stock Market Capitalization and Corporate Governance*, Oxford University Press, New Delhi.

Taxman's Company Law Ready Reckoner, 2009.

Tricker, Bob (2004), *Essential Director*, Profile Books, London.

Varma, Jayanth R. (2005), 'Selected issues in the regulation of firms and capital markets', in *India's Finance Sector: Recent Reforms, Future Challenges*, Basu, Priya (ed.), Macmillan, New Delhi.

Wallace, Peter and John Zinkin (2005), *Mastering Business in Asia: Corporate Governance*, Wiley India, New Delhi.

Ward, Ralph D. (1997), *21st Century Corporate Board*, Wiley, New York.

Closing Case

Gatekeeper Integrity Becomes Questionable

'A Collusive Management Fraud Is Extremely Hard To Detect And An Audit Is Not Planned Or Performed With That Objective', Vishesh Chandiok, Managing Partner, Grant Thornton in India

Business Today, 22 February 2009 ('Inside The Secret World of Auditing') quoted Mr Vishesh Chandiok as having made this statement.

BT also quoted Tridibes Basu, partner, SR Batliboi, an E&Y affiliate in India, as having said, 'Fraud is particularly difficult to detect in cases where there is management override of set processes'.

Ved Jain, former president of ICAI, acknowledged that 'The biggest challenge for the professionals today is the huge gap between society's expectation of what auditors must do and what auditors actually can do' (*BT*, 22 February 2009).

According to the letter written by the erstwhile chairman of the board of directors of Satyam on 7 January 2009, addressed to the board of directors of Satyam, the following revelations were made:

1. The balance sheet carries as of 30 September 2008
   (a) Inflated (non-existent) cash and bank balances of Rs 50.4 billion (as against Rs 53.61 billion reflected in the books)
   (b) An accrued interest of Rs 3.76 billion which is non-existent
   (c) An understated liability of Rs12.30 billion on account of funds arranged by me
   (d) An over stated debtors position of Rs 4.90 billion (as against Rs 26.51 billion reflected in the books)
2. For the September quarter (Q2) we reported a revenue of Rs 27 billion and an operating margin of as Rs 6.49 billion (24 per cent of revenues) as against the actual revenues of Rs 21.12 billion and an actual operating margin of Rs 0.61 billion (3 per cent of revenues). This has resulted in artificial cash and bank balances going up by Rs 5.88 billion in Q2 alone

The gap in the balance sheet has arisen purely on account of inflated profits over a period of the last several years (limited only to Satyam standalone, books of subsidiaries reflecting true performance). What started as a marginal gap between actual operating profit and the one reflected in the books of accounts continued to grow over the years'.

'Every attempt made to eliminate the gap failed. As the promoters held a small percentage of equity, the concern was that poor performance would result in a takeover, thereby exposing the gap. It was like riding a tiger, not knowing how to get off without being eaten'. According to a *BT* report (Khoppikar 2009), 'Initial investigations have revealed that an in-house team of Satyam developed software to generate fake invoices. The fake invoice would include a genuine name of the client, genuine name of the project manager for the client, but the invoice amount was overstated' and 'during the interrogation session, Raju is believed to have said that he never did anything wrong as everyone else in the industry does it.

'The fictitious cash balance of Rs 50.40 billion was introduced in the balance sheet through fake fixed deposit receipts worth Rs 33 billion, and a current account balance of Rs17 billion. The accounts department had to accept the receipts shown by Raju and his team, whereas the actual receipts from the banks showed a much lower figure. Simultaneously, another fictitious entry of accrued interests on fixed deposits had to be shown and that is how Rs 3.76 billion was introduced in the books.

'For every fictitious transaction, another one had to be created to hide it. The actual liability of Rs12.30 billion was the amount lent by private companies of Raju to Salmon. Had this liability been shown in the books, it would have raised eyebrows. After all, why should a company incur this liability when it has so much cash on its books? So, to keep analysts and investors at bay, this amount was not shown in the books.'

BT dated 22 February 2009 states that the US accounting standard, SAS 99, that came into existence after Enron went bust, 'requires auditors—amongst other things—to gather information necessary to identify risks of material misstatement due to the fraud by a series of measures (like making surprise inventory checks)'.

Other information
- Satyam prepared accounts not only on Indian GAAP but also on US GAAP as their ADS were listed on NYSE.
- Satyam made four acquisitions in 2007–08 worth more than $40.5 million.
- The audit committee consisted of 100 per cent independent directors.
- Satyam provided consolidated financial statements in accordance with international financial reporting standards (IFRS) issued by International Accounting Standards Board (IASB) in their annual report for 2007–08.
- According to Investor Relations Global Rankings (IRGR) for the Asia-Pacific and Africa regions, Satyam was ranked as below:
  ○ IR website: Top 2 in the region
  ○ Corporate governance practices: Top 5 in the region
  ○ Financial disclosure procedures: Top 5 in the region
  ○ First in technology
  ○ First in India

Discussion Questions
1. Do you think that the auditors of Satyam were negligent of their fiduciary responsibilities?
2. Should there be two or more independent auditors for every company or at least in the case of companies above a minimum size?
3. Comment on the statement: 'A collusive management fraud is extremely hard to detect and an audit is not planned with that objective'.

DIRECTORS IN ACTION

GROUND RULES FOR PERFORMING MULTITUDES OF ROLES AND DUTIES

The prevailing sentiment favoured a kind of reciprocal back-scratching: you sit on my board but I'll run my company; I will sit on your board and you will run your company.

— William A. Dimma in *Tougher Boards for Tougher Times*

LEARNING OBJECTIVES

After studying this chapter, you will be able to
- Describe how directors in general have to conduct themselves in practice
- List the specific conducts that are applicable to different classes of directors
- Enumerate the personal codes of principles that the directors have to observe
- Explain how the directors can be more committed to their directoral duties
- Enumerate the precautions the directors should take to avoid conflicts of interest
- Explain how to choose directorships so that the directors can be fully involved and committed
- List the leadership qualities required to be shown by the directors

Opening Case

How Many Directorships

'I sit only on 13 boards, Company Law permits up to 15!'
Deepak S. Parekh who has been the full-time chairman of Housing Development Finance Corporation (HDFC) Ltd, since 1993 seems to be saying. According to the annual report of HDFC, the chairman is the chief executive of the company. Mr Parekh is a highly respected professional and has been in great demand as an independent director and as chairman or member of various committees constituted by the government. The details of independent or

other directorships of Mr Parekh in public limited and other companies (as on 9 December 2009) are given in the table below.

Directorship of Deepak Parekh in public limited companies

S. No.	Company	Position
1.	GlaxoSmithKline Pharma	Chairman (Ind)
2.	IDFC	Chairman (Ind)
3.	Siemens	Chairman (Ind)
4.	Castrol India	Director (Ind)
5.	Mahindra & Mahindra	Director (Ind)
6.	Indian Hotels Company	Director (Ind)
7.	Hindustan Unilever	Director (Ind)
8.	HDFC Asset Management	Chairman (Ind)
9.	HDFC Standard Life	Chairman (Ind)
10.	HDFC Ergo General	Chairman (Ind)
11.	HOEC	Director (Non-ind)
12.	HDFC	Executive Chairman

Source: bseindia.com

He also sits on the board of Mahindra Satyam as a government nominee. This is a consequence of the government replacing the former Satyam Computer board in the aftermath of the scandal involving the promoters of Satyam (taken over by the Mahindra group and rechristened Mahindra Satyam)

In addition to this, Mr Parekh is also on the board of a number of companies as alternate director and on the boards of private limited companies as given in the table below.

Mr Parekh's directorship in other companies

S. No.	Company	Position
1.	Bharat Bijlee	Alternate Director
2.	Borax Morarjee	Alternate Director
3.	Exide Industries	Alternate Director
4.	Zodiac Clothing	Alternate Director
5.	Lafarge India Pvt Ltd	Chairman
6.	WNS Global Holdings Ltd	Director

Over and above these, Mr Parekh has been nominated to sit on or chair many committees constituted by the government and is a nominee of the Civil Aviation Ministry on the board of Airports Authority of India.

Jay Lorsch and Elizabeth MacIver on Time Commitment by Directors
'The Martin Marietta board met 12 times during the 30-day crisis, an obvious disruption of, and pressure on, directors' normal schedules. Some of the meetings were as long as nine hours,

yet all accepted the commitment as part of their job', write Lorsch and MacIver, while describing a case involving the situation in Martin Marietta Corporation in the face of a takeover attempt by Bendix Corporation (Lorsch and MacIver 1989).

Comments from the Press

'In India, senior executives are attracted to boards, primarily to lend their name and credibility. This is not as structured and bulleted in both role or the accountability as in the West', says Deepak Gupta, managing director of executive search firm Korn/Ferry.[1]

'The country's highest paid independent directors who sit on the board of companies, such as Infosys Technologies and Tata Steel, among others went home with an average 13 per cent hike in their remuneration last year, higher than the 9 per cent pay hike that the country's top ten CEOs pocketed in the same period', according to an *Economic Times* study.[1]

'...top paid independent directors last year include former global chief of HSBC Aman Mehta, banker Deepak Parekh, former head of HDFC Standard Life Insurance Deepak Satwalekar, and market strategist and consumer behaviour expert Rama Bijapurkar.'[1]

Discussion Questions

1. Critically comment on the number of directorships a person can handle in today's context looking at it from all angles. What is your perception of Mr Parekh handling the director's duty with care considering that he is in full-time employment at HDFC?
2. Both HDFC and IDFC have promoted asset management companies. Can Mr Parekh's directorships on both companies lead to a conflict of interest?
3. Find out whether Mr Parekh has been able to honour all his commitments to all the companies, using secondary data. This can be done by checking the attendance record of Mr Parekh at the companies where he is a director.

[1] Independent directors take home 13 per cent hike, economictimes.com, 9 November 2009.

GROUND RULES FOR PERFORMING MULTITUDES OF ROLES AND DUTIES

There has been a lot of bad publicity arising out of myriad stories of corporate scandals, corporate and executive greed, and corporate failures due to inaction or frenzied action by corporate captains. This has led to contemptuous treatment of CEOs, corporate directors, and boards. According to Dimma (2006), 'To say that in the sixties, directors as a class constituted an old boys' club perpetuates a cliché but on the whole, an accurate one' but 'it seems to me that corporate leaders were held in higher regard in the sixties than they are today....This decline in societal regard has been intensified greatly by the recent epidemic of scandals and malfeasance' (Dimma 2006). According to Finkelstein (2003), 'Some organizations are ungovernable simply because of fundamental breakdowns in their boards of directors, the group most responsible for vital information and the ultimate governance mechanism in a company.'

In the earlier chapters we saw that the regulators have been initiating and/or enforcing laws and regulations that detail how the board should be constituted, how many committees are mandatory, that the chair and CEO positions be separated, committees be constituted only of independent directors, etc. But such structural reforms have, by and large, failed to control corporations from going under. Finkelstein (2003) opines that 'What really counts for board effectiveness is something that is not easily captured in statistics and averages, yet is inherently understood by many directors. How boards function as a group—the nature of their interactions among themselves and with the CEO, and what they consider important to look into, and what they don't—plays a huge part in board effectiveness.' While structural reforms give an apparent comfort to investors, shareholders, and the public, what goes on behind the closed doors of the boardroom is all that matters, but is anybody's guess. A director's job requires him or her to gather, study, analyse, and frame his/her points of view of what is expected to be discussed in the meeting. But how many directors, especially those who are full-time with another company as chairman, or CEO, or a whole-time director do justice to this requirement? If somebody is a director on 10 or 15 companies, the writing on the wall is clear: he/she cannot do justice to any. How can a director be expected to actively participate in the proceedings of the board meetings without having acquired, analysed, and learnt the information?

Kevin Roberts of Saatchi and Saatchi describes directors on many boards as: 'Their average age is ten years off the pace, experience is pretty similar. Generally speaking, they are don't-rock-the-boat guys at the end of their careers who have been there, done that ... aren't driven or hungry anymore and ... haven't seen a cutomer for so long that they are totally out of sync with what the company is trying to sell' (Finkelstein 2003). Many legal systems demand that directors show 'business judgement' and ignorance cannot be taken as an an excuse.

A survey conducted by the Institute of Directors in UK revealed the lack of knowledge about legislation among directors. Fifty-eight per cent of those surveyed were not aware of the Director Disqualification Act of 1986. Of the 42 per cent who said they were aware of it, about 63 per cent felt that it was not relevant to the business and 90 per cent thought it was not relevant to them personally. And, the said law does not distinguish between the types of companies, according to Martin (2000). Hence any person who assumes the position of a director on a company or anybody who plans or aspires to join a company as a director, must have a reasonable depth of knowledge about the rules and regulations binding on them. Also, there are many things to be kept in mind or taken care of beyond rules if the person wants to excel as a direcor in today's context. This chapter discusses the various roles that have to be played and the duties and responsibilities directors have to assume, in general, for all directors and those with regard to specific director categories. Please note that these are not a reproduction of the directoral best practices available in all published literature on corporate governance, but are practices that many will consider unnecessary or difficult to implement but which will definitely make their job more meaningful and purposeful. Let us first look into the matter from a general point of view applicable to all directors.

APPLICABLE TO ALL DIRECTORS

All directors must have reasonable depth of awareness about the company laws relating to the company formation, various statutes the company has to observe, the various provisions regarding the constitution and functioning of the board, the functions of the directors, etc. While directors can take the initiative for such an effort, the company secretary and the chairman of the board can also take the initiative as they must know that ignorance on the part of one director can create problems for everybody, and for the company. They must also know the corporate governance guidelines in force in their countries. For example, in India, companies have to follow regulations by a number of regulatory agencies, including those that look after specific industrial groups. The distinction between different types of companies such as private limited companies, public limited companies, government companies, etc., must be known to the director. Please note that Clause 49 in India or SOX in the US are applicable only to publicly-listed companies. Rules and regulations about holding companies and subsidiary companies also must be known to them if the company has a holding company as a shareholder or has promoted subsidiaries. The directors and the board derive their power and authority from the law, which very clearly explains the rights and liabilities of directors. It does not mention any specific competencies in directors other than business judgement. This has nothing to do with qualifications or financial background; it comes from experience as well as learning about business. Directors should know that according to Anglo-American company laws, which most countries of the world follow, there is no distinction between different types or classes of directors. Or, the law does not differentiate between executive, non-executive, or independent directors.

All directors must have detailed knowledge about the memorandum of association and articles of association. These may contain many important provisions which will become binding on all directors. It should be remembered that MOA and AOA form the constitution of the company. For example, as we have seen in Chapter 8, the number of meetings of the board and even the dates of the meetings can be included in the AOA. Once such provisions are included, it is not binding on the company, the chairman, or the company secretary to inform the directors about the meetings before every meeting. The AOA may also contain provisions regarding directors' retirement. Listed companies require directors to retire by rotation after an initial period of, usually, three years. The AOA may also specify those directors or class of directors who need not retire by rotation. Most of companies require that one-third of the directors retire by rotation every year.

- They should have reasonable knowledge about business, its products, customers, markets, major shareholders, the promoter stake, and influence on the company.
- They should develop knowledge about how the board of directors embark on governance—which are the committees constituted, what are their specific roles, etc.

Other things that directors must know/do are:

- Should know if there are any litigations against or involving the company. Do they involve moderate or serious risks?
- Identify the risks that the company faces and whether they will result in liabilities for directors.
- Should know whether the promoter shareholder or dominant shareholder influences the decisions of the board.
- Is the board active or is it passive? (Does it play a pilot's role or simply a watchdog's role?)
- Does the board take an active role in the the creation of the company's strategy? According to Thomas Whisler, ' We [directors] don't set strategy'. But the board should cast a 'critical eye' on it and 'bear the responsibility for insisting that the CEO develop sound and explicit strategy for the company….' (Lorsch and MacIver 1989). On the other hand, Kenneth R.

Andrews 'has argued vigorously for more board involvement in strategy formulation and his several *Harvard Business Review* articles, in the early 1980s drew heated criticism from many CEOs and others, who felt the board's involvement in strategy formulation would usurp prerogatives reserved for management' (Lorsch and MacIver).

- What is the culture in the boardroom—open and straightforward, permitting discussion, debates, and even dissent, or is it that all the decisions are taken by the CEO and one has to only rubber-stamp them? Is there a pressure 'don't rock the boat', 'peace at any price' or 'let the game go on as it is'? (Lorsch and MacIver).
- Is there a review process for the board as a whole and directors at individual levels?
- Was the company the target of public outrage in the recent past and what were the reasons for the same?
- Is the policy for compensating executive/non-executive directors adequate?
- What has been the director turnover in the past and specific reasons if the turnover has been high?
- Do I have the competence to meet the requirements expected of me as a director?
- Do I have the courage and character to meet the challenges of the office of the director, the boardroom, and the company?
- Does it fit into my leadership style and my life's goals?
- Do I get all the information that I require to carry out my duties as a director? Is the information architecture in place and/or sufficient to meet the requirements of the board and directors?
- Do I get sufficient time to prepare for board meetings? Does the agenda reach me sufficiently in advance?
- Does the CEO keep the directors informed of the important events/developments between board meetings?
- Does the CEO encourage discussions in the boardroom?
- Does the CEO seek advice from directors?
- Do I get the minutes of the last board meeting within reasonable time for me to think of and initiate future course of action on any issue?
- Is the company conducting committee meetings on the same day as board meetings under the premise of austerity? If the board members feel that austerity measures are necessary, they should try to reduce the costs of attending the meetings, rather than clubbing board and committee meetings on the same day.
- Is there a governance charter? If yes, understand the contents thoroughly.
- Is the board balanced in terms of size so that individual directors get enough air-time?
- Are the directors provided insurance cover by the company in the eventuality of legal actions against them?
- What is the perception among investors, other stakeholders, and the general public, about the company?
- Does the company have a track record of meeting its objectives?
- Does the company command respect from its lenders?
- Is the company financially sound? Or is it always a hand-to-month situation?

- Is the company solvent or is it facing liquidity problems?
- Is the board taking an active role in risk containment?
- What can I contribute to the board and the company?
- Is there a whistle-blowing system in place?
- Have the auditors been making serious reservations and/or comments on accounting practices of the company?
- Does the board organize refresher programmes for directors?
- Is there an ethical code of conduct applicable to directors?
- Can I devote sufficient time to my directorial duties or have I been under time pressure due to the high number of directorships?
- Is there any conflict of interest in my being a director of the company?
- Is the board diversified enough to have diverse viewpoints?

This is not an exhaustive list of things to be done or actions to be taken by all directors generally, but an attempt has been made to cover a majority of them. Now let us discuss the things to be taken care of by other categories of directors.

THE NON-EXECUTIVE DIRECTOR

A non-executive director is a nominee of the promoters (sometimes more than one). According to the AOA, promoters will usually have a right to nominate a certain number of directors. These directors are nominated in addition to the chairman and/or managing director or CEO. Non-executive means promoter nominees who function in a non-executive capacity. Even though the laws do not distinguish between any classes of directors, non- executive directors are nominated with the express purpose of protecting the promoters' interests. In addition to the general points discussed earlier, they may have to take specific actions. Some of these are:

- Protect the interests of the promoters while keeping in mind the interests of the outside shareholders.
- Apprise the chairman or CEO, if they are not nominees of the promoter, about the larger interests of the promoter/family, their vision, their goals, and objectives of running the business.
- Push for items that will take care of the interests of the promoters.
- Exercise their rights in case it is found that the professional chairman and/or CEO is not acting in the larger interests of the corporation.
- Act as a mediator between the CEO if he/she is a promoter nominee and outside directors when their ideas and plans for the company do not match.
- Advise the CEO who is a promoter nominee if it is felt that his/her actions are not in line with the family's values, vision, and goal for the company.
- Guide younger directors, especially the other promoter nominees, to mature into good directors.
- They can play a very crucial role in mitigating the differences of opinions among the whole-time directors, who are nominees of the promoters.
- Act as the buffer between the promoters/families and the board and the company.

THE NON-EXECUTIVE INDEPENDENT DIRECTOR

In today's context of corporate governance, one term that is widely applied is 'independent director'. The institution of independent directors has turned out to be highly established and essential. Corporate governance laws, regulations, or guidelines, irrespective of the nature and country of origin, recommend that independent directors must generally form a majority of the board. Also, many of the regulators stipulate that certain types of committees be formed exclusively of independent directors.

Most of the current thinking and regulations are overwhelmingly skewed towards independent directors and hence, it would appear that this institution is here to stay and gain in strength. Board independence is considered to be a practice of which the more there is, the better. When independent directors form a majority, it is expected that many of the ills of the agency conflicts can be mitigated. The expectation of independent directors is that as they provide an independent view of all the managerial transactions, they are in a better position to act as a check and balance system. Hence, the expectation of the independent directors from shareholders is high and they therefore have to conduct themselves properly and act responsibly. With this background, let us try to fix independent directors' actions.

- Understand very clearly the meaning of independence. One should see to it that independence not only happens in appearance and form, but also in spirit.
- Understand very clearly the expectations placed on him/her in the current context of corporate governance.
- As independent directorship today is financially rewarding, one has to devote reasonably sufficient time even when it is part-time.
- Never accept the position if there is even a remote possibility of conflict of interests. Some of the conflicts of interests become acceptable under the law or regulatory framework (by declaring the material interests). Never succumb to such practices to circumvent the issues.
- Resist the temptation to join boards of a number of companies. Consider the huge responsibilities on your shoulders, especially when you take up one in addition to your full-time job/occupation. The commitment expected of independent directors today is very high. There is no point in having independent directors if they are not able to attend board/committee meetings. Choose only a few so that you can meet the expected requirements. Independent directors are in great demand, and supply is said to be deficient to meet the demand. But one can very easily comprehend the justice an independent director can do to any company if he/she is on the board of, say, 15 companies, in addition to being full-time CEO of a company (the Indian company law permits up to 15, excluding private limited companies or alternate directorships).
- Resist the compensations by way of stock options or other stock-related items. One doesn't have to become a shareholder in order to keep the company's interests in mind. When independent directors get paid by way of options or other stock-related items, the assumptions about them become highly skewed; they should also be concerned mainly about financial

performance of the firm which will be reflected in the stock prices. Independent directors may also be tempted to take a short-term view if they get paid through stocks or stock-related rewards. Exhibit 9.1 depicts stock options enjoyed by independent directors at two prominent Indian companies.

Exhibit 9.1
Independent Directors or Interested Shareholders?

Ever since the regulator permitted the issue of stock options, many companies have started rewarding their employees and directors, including independent directors, through stock options. While some companies have stopped or decided to suspend this, as there has been some confusion on the issue of expensing stock options, some others have continued with the issue of these. While opinions differ about whether independent directors should be rewarded at all by way of stock options or restricted stocks, etc., some of the companies in India have issued them even to independent directors. Of course, some of the directors may already own shares other than those received via options. The stocks held by independent directors in two major Indian companies are detailed in the tables below.

Shareholding of independent directors at Mahindra & Mahindra Ltd

S. No.	Name of independent director	Shares held as on 31 March 2009
1.	Deepak S Parekh	52,754
2.	NB Godrej	1,81,421
3.	MM Murugappan	46,664
4.	N Vaghul	46,664
5.	AS Ganguly	46,664
6.	RK Kulkarni	45,452
7.	Anupam Puri	43,332

Shareholding of independent directors at Infosys Technologies Ltd

S. No.	Name of independent director	Equity shares held as on 31 March 2009	ADS held as on 31 March 2009
1.	Deepak M. Satwalekar	56,000	–
2.	Marti G. Subrahmanyam	8,000	37,300
3.	Omkar Goswami	12,300	–
4.	Rama Bijapurkar	20,000	–
5.	Claude Smadja	3,900	–
6.	Sridar A. Iyengar	4,000	–
7.	David L. Boyles	–	2,000
8.	Jeffrey S. Lehman	–	–

Audit Committee at Mahindra & Mahindra

Deepak S. Parekh (Chairman)

R.K. Kulkarni

N.B. Godrej

M.M. Murugappan

Audit Committee at Infosys Technologies

Deepak M. Satwalekar

Marti G. Subrahmanyam

Omkar Goswami

Sridar A. Iyengar

Rama Bijapurkar (Ceased to be member with effect from 1 August 2008)

David L. Boyles (Ceased to be member with effect from 1 August 2008)

Questions

1. Should independent directors be rewarded by way stock options? Substantiate your answer with arguments.
2. There has been a call on putting a cap on director tenures. How will you view the issue of options to independent directors from this perspective?
3. The audit committee members of Mahindra & Mahindra and Infosys Technologies as on 31 March 2009 are holding shares in the company Do you think that the shareholding of the committee members cloud the objectivity?

Source: Annual Reports of Infosys Technologies Ltd and Mahindra & Mahindra Ltd for the year 2008–09.

- Never accept the directorship if it will result in cross-directorships.
- Never accept the directorship if you had ever been an employee of the company (the law permits one to join after a cooling-off period of three years).
- Never accept a position in more than one company belonging to the same group.
- Never accept a position in one company if you are part of the auditor of another company in the group.
- Never hold any shares in the company other than what is mandatory, according to AOA, to qualify to become a director.
- Observe absolute confidentiality about the financial details of the company.
- Prevent any family member from owning shares in the company.
- Apprise the board regarding the establishment of an information architecture in order to enable regular access to important information from management. In case of any specific information, speak to the chairman/CEO to get the same.
- Never indulge in micromanaging or providing unsolicited advice to the CEO directly. Encourage more discussions to take place in the boardroom. Request the chairman not to keep meetings of various committees on the same day as board meetings.
- Take an independent view of any situation. This does not mean that will always dissent with the CEO/management. The basic idea in the boardroom must be to support the CEO after all the detailed deliberations.

- Encourage dissenting opinions from other directors to understand their view points.
- Encourage candour in the boardroom.
- Be ready to serve on committees, if necessary.
- Undergo refresher training and development programmes to be better equipped for the job.
- Always remember that the most important asset one possesses, namely one's reputation could be at stake if one does not take the responsibility seriously.
- Attend all board meetings and committee meetings, if possible.

DIRECTOR AS A COMMITTEE MEMBER

Since the assembly of the full board becomes unwieldy for a number of aspects of board functioning, a committee structure has become the norm and practice in most companies. Some of the committees have also been made mandatory. US laws require that the audit, remuneration, and nomination committees are mandatory. Clause 49 regulation in India requires the audit and investor grievance committees as mandatory. Since board sizes are, as a norm, becoming smaller, many of the directors—executive, non-executive, and independent—will be required to become members in several committees. Delegation of authority to committees is for specific purposes, and some of the committees may require specific skills. For example, the audit committee should have at least one person who has expertise in accounting matters. Other members should also be financially literate to effectively participate in the proceedings of the committee. Let us consider some of the things which a director, as a committee member, is expected to do.

- Have a clear understanding of the duties of the committee member (from the committee charter, if any).
- How often the committee shall meet? (This may depend on the extent of complexity. For example, the audit committee may meet more frequently in a company that is a conglomerate, whereas the remuneration committee may be required to meet only once or twice a year. The investor grievance committee may be required to meet more frequently if the company has undertaken some issue of securities during the year).
- Ensure that committee meetings are not held on the same day as the board meeting so that more attention can be given to the committee duties.
- What can I contribute to the committee?
- Is everybody participating well?
- Is there a deficiency in understanding among members necessitating the hiring of external experts?
- Does the expert hand in the committee (in the case of audit and compensation) take initiative in disseminating the necessary knowledge among other members?
- Is there sufficient time to thoroughly discuss and debate all the matters?
- Are internal and external auditors asked to brief when required? (For audit committee members)

- Is the process of selecting the external auditor based on merit? (For audit committee members).
- Does the auditor mention deficiencies in the accounting processes or the standards followed by the company, and make comments or express reservations about accounts? (For audit committee members).
- Are there any conflicts of interest in the case of the external auditor? (For audit committee members).
- Does the committee act in an independent manner or is it influenced by management representatives? (In India, while audit committees are mandatory, only a majority of members need to be independent).
- Has the audit committee given very clear instructions to the external auditor about physical verification of important items such as cash, bank deposits, inventories, etc.?
- Is the remuneration committee clear about the implications of the various components of compensation, especially by way of stock options?
- Does the nomination committee regularly identify potential independent director candidates so that appointments can be made at short notice?

There may be many other committees depending on the nature of the business. For example, many companies today have a risk management committee, banking companies have credit monitoring committees, and some companies constitute project management committees if a major project is under implementation, etc. Members of such committees will have to take necessary actions and/or ask the right questions about the way the committee functions.

DIRECTOR AS A COMMITTEE CHAIR

One of the committee members will have to assume the responsibility of being the chairman of the committee. The chairman has to coordinate all the activities of the committee and also apprise the full board about these and functioning of the committee. Some of the essentials for the chairman of the committee are:

- Should have good leadership qualities. The chairman has to engage the members in such a way as to get full participation and support from all the members.
- Fix the general meeting schedule for the year in advance in consultation with the chairman of the board and the company secretary.
- Draw the agenda for the meeting ahead of it and circulate this among the members. Request members to suggest any other points to be added to the agenda.
- In times of emergency, coordinate to arrange the meetings at short notice.
- Apprise the board about the outcomes of the committee meetings.
- Give every member an opportunity to contribute to the deliberations of the committee.
- Encourage members to openly express their opinions. Chairmen of important committees such as audit must apprise the committee members of the expectations from stakeholders about its performance, especially from a risk management perspective.
- Initate action to create a charter for the committee, if it does not already exist.

- If the need arises, the chair should take a decision to engage an outside expert to advise the committee, with permission from the board.
- Administer training and development programmes for members to become aware about the latest developments in their specific areas.
- In the case of the audit committee, the chair has to decide on the auditor/s and their remuneration after consultation with the members and then recommend to the board who will, in turn, put it up for shareholder approval.
- Take a decision on approval of non-audit services provided by the external auditor, in the case of audit committees.
- Take a lead in monitoring compliance with statutes and regulations.
- Take a lead in the formulation and review of the company's code of ethics, in the case of the audit committee.
- Take a lead in the committee's role in the appointment of the CFO and other key financial executives, in the case of the audit committee.
- Review the expenses of the CEO and other senior executives, and in case of excesses, inform the concerns to the board, when chairing the audit committee.
- Take a lead in reviewing major contracts in the case of the audit committee.
- Take a lead in fixing the remunerations of the CEO, WTDs, and other senior executives, in the case of the remuneration committee.
- Review related party transactions, in the case of audit committees.
- Ensure that the committee has the necessary competence, in the case of audit and remuneration committees.
- If the nominations committee also has the additional responsibility to oversee the governance function, then the chairman has to lead the committee to draft a charter (if it doesn't exist), and/or oversee the corporate governance policies and procedures of the company (if the charter already exists).
- The chair of the nomination committee can take a lead in getting the new directors inducted with the help of other senior members of the board.
- Get the committee to review the unaudited/audited quarterly and annual financial statements, in the case of the audit committee.
- Lead the committee to conduct a post-audit review of the financial statements and audit findings in the case of the audit committee.
- Get the committee to review, along with the legal counsel, legal matters that could have a significant impact on the financial statements, in the case of the audit committee.

AS LEAD INDEPENDENT DIRECTOR

The appointment of a lead independent director to lead the class of independent directors and coordinate governance activities among the independent directors and between independent directors and inside directors has been considered as a best practice in today's context. While some people such as William A. Dimma still feel that separating the chair and the CEO positions is better than having a lead independent director, Ram Charan who was vocal in his opposition both to the concept of splitting the CEO and chairman positions and appointing a lead director[2] seems to have mellowed. In his latest book on corporate governance (Charan 2009) he has devoted an entire chapter[3] to lead directors and how to make them effective. Let us see some of the actions that lead directors need to perform.

- Preside over the executive session of the board's independent directors.
- Coordinate with the chairman and CEO to formalize the information flow, fix meeting agendas, and meeting schedules.
- Act as liaison between independent directors, and the chairman and/or CEO.
- Take an active role, along with the chairman, in the board evaluation process.
- Help the board to reach a concensus, especially when discussions meet a roadblock.
- Facilitate the expression of opinions by independent directors, particularly outside the boardroom.
- Facilitate in the boardroom to enable the board to bring issues to the table, rather than finding who is at fault.
- Work with the chairman and CEO to prioritize issues and set the agenda accordingly and guide discussions to prevent them from going off-track.
- Work towards establishing a rapport between the CEO/inside directors, with outside directors.
- Ensure the diverse points among directors but at the same time enable the board to function better by showing courage when required.
- Shed individual egos for a better board functioning.
- In typical family-controlled and managed companies, which have the chairman and managing director posts either combined in one family member or when both are family/promoter nominees, the lead director can preside over board meetings or meeting of shareholders when the chairman and/or managing director is not present, or whenever they are interested parties.
- Take leadership in organizing training and development programmes for all directors to make them aware of the latest developments in the area of corporate governance.

The role of the lead independent director will vary from company to company. In countries such as the UK and Canada, where there has been a separation of the chairman and CEO positions in a majority of companies, the lead independent director, if any, will have a rather limited role, whereas in counties such as the US where the positions are usually combined or in India where either the positions are combined or both the chairman and CEO are family/promoter nominees, the lead independent director has a genuine and meaningful role to play. Notwithstanding the allegations from a few corners that the creation of a lead director will establish another power centre in the board which is not necessarily healthy, the concept seems to be gaining momentum and acceptance.

---

[2] 'No Lead Director', *Boards at Work*, Jossey-Bass, 1997, p. 49.
[3] 'Why do You Need a Lead Director Anyway?' *Owning Up*, Jossey-Bass, 2009, pp. 101–116.

AS THE CHAIR OF THE BOARD

Conventionally, the chairman is the leader of the board, while the CEO is the leader of the management. Hence, there is a definite role to be played by the chairman. This includes monitoring and evaluating management, and that is why it is recommended that the two roles be separated. Now, let us see what are the specific duties of the chairman.

- Lead the board in establishing values and standards for the board and the company.
- Play a pivotal role in promoting the highest standards of corporate governance, and comply with all laws and regulations.
- Create a sense of teamwork among the colleagues on the board.
- Have a clear understanding of the provisions of the law and in the company constitution with respect to the board, the chairman, and management.
- Delegate power and responsibilities suitably.
- Draw clear lines demarcating the authority of the board and the management. If ambiguity arises, he should deal with it in such a way that there is a clear idea about responsibilities.
- While conforming to the requirements of law and regulations, understand and make the board understand, that performance beyond conformance is all that matters.
- Organize board meetings, prepare agendas after talking to the CEO and other top management, circulate the agenda for the meeting among members of the board, etc., with the help of the company secretary.
- Conduct board meetings in the most effective manner. Allocate time appropriately for various issues.
- Take a lead in establishing an information architecture to enable the board to take informed decisions.
- Ensure that:
  o No member steals a majority of air-time
  o An exhaustive discussion takes place
  o Encourage a constructive debate
  o Encourage participant to reach a consensus and use casting vote only when there is an impasse
- Take a lead in identifying the development needs of the individual directors and the board as a whole, and organize for the same.
- Take a lead in evaluating the CEO, whole-time directors, and other top management personnel.
- Take a lead in approving the compensation package for CEOs, whole-time directors, and top management, recommended by the compensation/remuneration committee.
- Take a lead in evaluating individual directors and the board as a whole.
- Take a lead in the evaluation of the functioning of the various committees of the board.
- Chair the annual general meetings and extraordinary general meetings, and lead the board team to give responses to shareholder queries.
- Ensure that systematic contacts and communications happen with the shareholders, to apprise them of the various developments in the company at frequent intervals.

- Take a lead in unifying the board as a group that gels well together.
- Take a lead in the board putting in place a succession plan for the CEO and other top management personnel.
- Take a lead in replacing the CEO if there has been a crisis due to violation of ethical code of conduct, laws and regulations, or sustained poor performance for a definite period.

The chairman is the ultimate leader in the organization. The position requires enormous leadership qualities. One has to continuously develop and nurture these leadership traits in order to be an effective chairman.

DIRECTOR AS INSTITUTIONAL NOMINEE

Most of the literature on corporate governance puts a huge responsibility of overseeing governance at the gate of institutional investors who have chosen to invest in the company, either on their own or on behalf of other investors who have invested their savings with them. The expectation is high because the institutional investors normally hold reasonable chunks of stocks compared to individual investors. Also, institutional investors would like to have the company generate better returns for their clients and at the same time not take too many risks which would alter the risk of investments by the clients. Of course, there have been allegations that many of the institutional investors also look only at short-term, and not necessarily at the longer-term outlook of the corporate. Let us consider some of the things that institutional nominee directors have to do.

- Have a long-term view about the health of the company. Sustainability over a long-term must be emphasized over and above the short-term gain of stock market prices.
- Be concerned about the risky ventures the corporate undertakes as it might topple the risk profile of the company and may negatively affect the risk of the institution's portfolio of which the company forms a part.
- Advise the CEO and the board on specific matters.
- Act as a watchdog against the occurrence of any managerial abuse.
- Apprise the board of the institution's concerns.
- Put pressure on management to increase the effort.
- Since institutional investors act as fiduciaries for their clients, close monitoring becomes essential.
- While, as shareholders they can vote with their feet (by selling the company's shares), such actions should be resorted to only as a last resort. The purpose should not be to exit at the earliest but make the management and company perform consistently well so that exit is not contemplated.
- Take care to see that conflicts of interest do not exist.
- Advise the institution not to enter into dealings with the company that will result in conflicts of interest which may weaken the position of the directorship.
- Since nominee directorships get changed from one person to another, adequate information must be passed on to the next person so that seamless takeover can occur.
- Care should be taken to see that they do not get associated with a competitor in any manner.

THE EXECUTIVE DIRECTOR

These directors are in full-time employment with the company. Hence they have access to all the information, including books of accounts, at any time. While they may be looking after specific functions or operations in the company, when they sit on the board, they are just like other directors. They may report to the managing director or CEO in the management hierarchy, but they cannot absolve themselves from the responsibilities assigned to them as directors. In the boardroom and in front of the law, they are just like other directors. Let us see how an executive or whole-time director should conduct in his/her duties.

- Be conversant with all the laws and regulations applicable to all directors, and also to directors who are full- time.
- Do not act like a subordinate of the MD in the boardroom.
- Must have thorough knowledge about his/her functional areas. Must offer insights to the board with respect to specific knowledge related to his/her functional areas.
- Be reasonably conversant with all the matters about the company, even those that are beyond his/her specific areas.
- Never indulge in any activity that may lead to questions about his/her integrity.
- Should not accept any director positions outside if that will require more than reasonable attention.
- Strictly follow the code of conduct for directors/employees of the company.
- Be a role model for the employers and nurture ethical behaviour among employees.
- Communicate to the lower levels in hierarchy about the importance of good governance.
- Work with other whole-time directors/CEO to create a culture of corporate governance.
- Never indulge in any activity that will result in conflicts of interest with the company.
- Maintain absolute confidentiality about the financial matters of the company.
- Never indulge in stock market deals in the company's shares other than disposing of stock options received.
- Advise close family members not to indulge in transactions in the company's shares.
- Shed all those existing factors that can get entangled in the conflicts of interest issue, irrespective of the monetary value.
- In case EDs/WTDs are members of the promoter family, they should not indulge in any activity based on any privileged information. In case their holding decreases due to issue of additional shares via the options or restricted stock issue, they should inform the board and the stock exchange about their intention to top up in order to maintain their percentage of holding.
- In case there is more than one member from the promoter family as executive director, there shall be clear understanding among them about their positions, and all such matters be known to the board. Failure can lead to problems similar to those happened in the case of the Ambani brothers in Reliance.
- The director should abstain from any meeting which concerns him/her or matters in which he/she is deemed to be interested.

- Never show the authority of control over the management and also the power of being a representative of the major shareholder.

AS MANAGING DIRECTOR OR CEO

While the managing director or CEO is another whole-time director, his treatment under the law is different. A managing director or CEO is the leader of the management and is supposed to be representing the company on many forums and places. Legally, a CEO or managing director runs the company under the supervision of the board of directors. While the MD/CEO is subordinate to the board, he/she is virtually the public face of the company. Because he/she controls the management, he/she has access to all the privileged information, which makes him/her extremely powerful. In fact, the board has to depend on the CEO for all the information it requires for decision-making. Thus, in the practice of governance by the board, the CEO plays an important part. While we use the term CEO in general, it applies to the full-time chairmen of companies who are virtually the CEOs even when another person is designated as CEO/MD. In HDFC, Deepak Parekh is the executive chairman. While someone else is the MD, for all practical purposes and also according to their annual report, the chairman is the CEO. In Hero Honda, there is an MD and a CEO, but as the chairman is executive, he is the virtual CEO. Let us see certain things which CEOs/MDs have to invariably observe.

- Be conversant with all the laws and regulations applcable to the company, board, MD, etc. Ignorance is not an excuse.
- Act as one of the directors in the boardroom. Approve the power and authority of the chairman and other directors.
- Must have thorough knowledge about all aspects of the business. Must educate the board members if called for.
- Never indulge in any activity that might lead to questions about one's integrity.
- Should refuse to accept any outside director positions if that will require allocation of time leading to lesser involvement in the company. There have been cases where a full-time chairman sits on 15 other companies.
- Strictly follow the code of conduct for directors/employees of the company.
- Be a role model for all the employees, including other employees who are directors.
- Communicate the importance of good governance to everybody in the company.
- Work with other whole-time directors to create a culture of corporate governance.
- Never indulge in any activity that will result in conflicts of interest with the company.
- Maintain absolute confidentiality about the financial matters of the company.
- Never indulge in stock market deals in the company's shares other than disposing of stock rewards received.
- Advise close family members not to indulge in transactions in the company's shares.
- Shed all those existing factors that can get entangled in conflict of interest issues, irrespective of the monetary value.

- Members of the promoter family should not indulge in any activity based on any privileged information. If their holding decreases due to issue of options/restricted stocks, they should intimate the board and the stock exchanges about their intention to top this up in order to maintain the percentage.
- There shall be clear delineation of power and authority, and responsibility between the MD/CEO and other whole-time directors, approved by the board.
- The MD/CEO should abstain from any meeting which concerns him/her or matters in which is he/she is deemed to be interested.
- Never show the authority of control over the management and also the power of being representative of the major shareholder.

SUMMARY

Consequent to the multitude of corporate governance failures, regulators, investors and many other stakeholders, including the public, have turned their attention to boards for their inaction in times of need. A close look at boards would reveal the reasons for such inaction. Many of them, especially those who are CEOs or other busy executives do not find sufficient time to prepare for board meetings. In certain other cases, independent directors were members on too many boards limiting their effectiveness in all. In some other cases, they were having a number of conflicts of interest, forcing them to be in no position to question the management for its deeds. So, directors have to take specific steps to make themselves more effective in the boardroom, as well as to further the cause of corporate governance. Since there are different classes of directors, each with a different set of roles, the actions to be taken by each of them will vary in the context of corporate governance. There are many actions to be taken by all directors irrespective of the class to which they belong.

There are specific actions to be taken by directors when they have specific roles as promoter nominees who are non-executive directors, independent directors, as a committee member, as chair of a committee, as lead independent director, as chairman of the board, as an institutional nominee, as a whole-time director or as a managing director/CEO. Such actions by them will help them to become better directors leading to better governance of companies.

KEY TERMS

Austerity   Simplicity and plain in style of living
Buffer   Act as a softening medium between two parties
Cliché   Expression that has been used too much but is now outdated
Containment   Preventing something to affect
Exhaustive   Complete
Hand-to-mouth   Just sufficient to meet the essential requirement

Mantle   Wearing the coat
Micromanage   Getting too involved even to the extent of minor details
Mitigate   Make less severe, reduce the impact
Rechristen   Rename
Rock-the-boat   Upsetting the smooth progress of
Unsolicited   Not asked for

CONCEPT REVIEW QUESTIONS

1. Why is it felt that directors who were held in high regard earlier are not getting that respect today?
2. Company laws permit one to have upto 15 directorships on public limited companies. Do you think this number is justified or is it too high from a business judgement angle? Substantiate your arguments.
3. The law does not mention any specific competencies for directors other than business judgement. What other essential competences make a good director?
4. What are the specific responsibilities of the chairman?
5. The board of directors is a group that has to gel well to deliver the performance expected of them. What are the essentials for them to gel well?
6. An independent director spends only part of his time with the company. What are the specific actions that he should take to make his position meaningful?

CRITICAL THINKING QUESTIONS

An independent director needs to be on one or more committees as companies feel that the smaller the board, the better. Estimate the minimum time an independent director has to devote to a company if he/she is a member of two important committees such as audit and remuneration.

PROJECT WORK

A director's job requires rigour and depth in order to achieve better governance of companies. Find out with the help of data collected from a sample of companies (say, Nifty companies) whether that kind of rigour and attention is given on the basis of board and various committee meetings.

REFERENCES

Annual Report for 2008–09, Mahindra & Mahindra Ltd.

Annual Report, 2008–09, Infosys Technologies Ltd.

Charan, Ram (1997), *Boards at Work*, Jossey-Bass, San Francisco.

Charan, Ram (2009), *Owning Up*, Jossey-Bass, San Francisco.

Dimma, William A. (2006), *Tougher Boards for Tougher Times*, Wiley-India, New Delhi.

Finkelstein, Sydney (2003), *Why Smart Executives Fail*, Portfolio/Penguin, New York.

'Independent directors take home 13 per cent hike', economictimes.com, 9 November 2009.

Lorsch, Jay W., and Elizabeth MacIver (1989), *Pawns or Potentates: The Reality of America's Corporate Boards*, HBS Press, Boston.

Martin, David (2000), *One Stop Director*, ICSA Publishing, London.

Closing Case

The Clause 49 Millionaires—Boardroom Becomes Financially Rewarding

In the backdrop of the initiatives in the UK in the form of Cadbury Committee Report, the Indian industry, in general, and regulator SEBI, in particular, took initiatives to improve the corporate governance practices in India. The Confederation of Indian Industry (CII) was the first to go off the block in 1998. Later, SEBI took the mantle as the responsible body for monitoring corporate governance and the capital market regulator in India.

SEBI formed a number of committees to study the governance practices in India and make recommendations for further improvements. One of the major recommendations for governance reforms starting with the Cadbury Report was to have more independent directors on the board. SEBI accepted most of the recommendations of the Kumar Mangalam Birla Committee and instituted a clause covering the corporate governance aspects of a company in the listing agreement between the company and the stock exchanges where the company's shares are listed. SEBI inserted a new Clause 49, covering the guidelines for corporate governance, famous today as Clause 49 guidelines. Clause 49 guidelines also stipulate that all listed corporates must have a certain minimum number of independent directors. To be more precise, Clause 49 prescribes one-third of the board be independent if the chairman is part-time and not a nominee of the promoters, and 50 per cent otherwise. SEBI had taken a decision to implement Clause 49 in stages, based on the net worth of the companies. And all companies had to meet the Clause 49 stipulations by 31 December 2005. This forced boards to search for and fill the posts for the requisite number of independent directors. There was a scramble for independent directors and this pushed up the demand for reputed professionals who could be appointed as independent directors.

The demand coupled with the short supply of good quality directors (this paucity of supply not finding adequate support in a country of more than one billion population) resulted in the class of independent directors being priced high. The company law provisions were also suitably amended to permit upto Rs 20,000 per board meeting and committee meetings for companies with a networth of Rs 1 billion or more, or a turnover of Rs 5 billion or more, and Rs 10,000 in other cases, as against Rs 2,000 upto March 2000, and Rs 5000 from April 2000 to July 2003. Many companies have been making provisions for making payment of commissions up to 1 per cent of the net profits to non-executive directors. The opportunity opened up new vistas for not only existing CEOs or other existing directors, but also, for retired bureaucrats, scientists, economists, and other professionals. The good directors receive recognition from the corporate world. Most of the companies pay Rs 20,000 for attending board meetings and committee meetings. In some companies, chairmen of different committees, especially of audit committees, are paid more. But it should also be remembered that responsibilities have increased and the directors' reputations could be seriously at stake if they fail to deliver.

The table below provides the details of the remuneration package of some of the priciest independent directors in India.

The priciest independent directors in India

S. No.	Name	Directorships considered	Companies	Remuneration received in 2008–09 (Rs in millions)
1	Naresh Chandra	7	ACC	1.46
			Balrampur Chini	0.353
			Bajaj Auto	0.84
			Electrosteel Castings	1.36
			Hindustan Motors	0.12
			TCS	7.17
			Crompton Greaves	0.48
			Total	11.883
2.	Deepak Satwalekar	6	Infosys	6.8
			HDFC	0.05
			Asian Paints	1.055
			Nicholas Piramal Ltd	1.3
			Tata Power	0.287
			Entertainment Network (I)	0.12
			Total	9.612
3.	Aman Mehta	5	Jet Airways	0.18
			TCS	7.64
			Wockhardt	0.1
			Godrej Cons. Products	1.115
			Cairn India	0.44
			Total	9.475
4.	Omkar Goswami	8	Dr Reddy's	3.174
			IDFC	0.5
			Crompton Greaves	1.82
			Sona Koyo Steering	0.02 (1 meeting)
			Ambuja Cements	0.7
			Cairn India	0.4
			Infosys	5.8
			Godrej Cons.Products	0.886
			Total	13.3
5.	Rama Bijapurkar	5	Infosys	5.6
			CRISIL	1.684
			Axis Bank	0.42
			Godrej Cons.Products	1.135
			M&M Fin.Services	0.035
			Total	8.874
6.	RA Mashelkar	5	Reliance Ind.	2.2
			Tata Motors	0.34
			Hind.Unilever	0.648
			Thermax	0.94
			KPIT Cummins	0.713
			Total	4.841

Source: Annual reports of the companies in the list for the latest financial year (31 March 2009, 30 September 2008, or 31 December 2008, as the case may be)

Notes:

1. This is not an exhaustive list of directorships of the professionals mentioned above. Many of them are directors on other public/private limited companies but the remuneration packages from those companies are not publicly available.

2. This list is only a sample to impress upon the development post-Clause 49. There are many other professionals who are in great demand.

3. During the year 2008–09, companies such as Wockhardt and Tata Motors did not pay any commission as financial performance was not adequate.

4. People like Dr Mashelkar have only recently joined the corporate boards. Most of the others have been directors for more than ten years, even before Clause 49 came into being.

Discussion Questions

1. Do you feel that there is a genuine shortage of good quality independent director candidates in India? Is the high compensation paid to independent directors indicative of the demand-supply situation for them in India?

2. Do you think that there is a correlation between the remuneration of independent directors and the effort they put in as director of a company?

3. High remunerations to independent directors will make them behave like insiders rather than independent directors. Critically comment on the statement.

PART IV

THE ROAD AHEAD—
THE FUTURE OF
CORPORATE GOVERNANCE

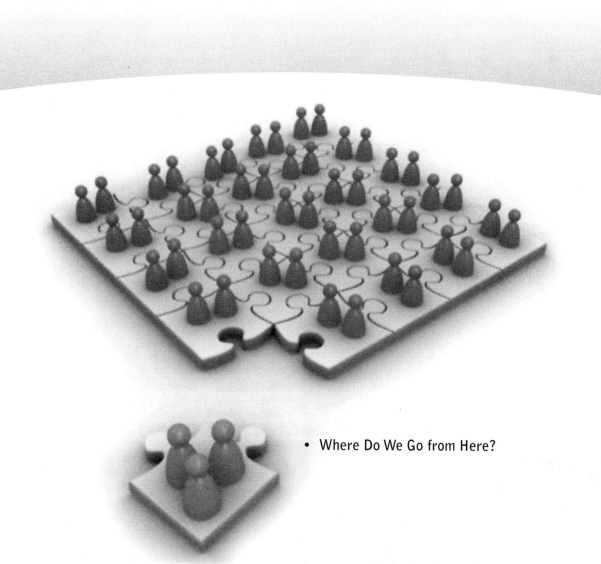

- Where Do We Go from Here?

CHAPTER 10

WHERE DO WE GO FROM HERE?

The biggest problem with corporate boards is not who is on the board, but what transpires there.

– Ram Charan, in *Boards at Work*

LEARNING OBJECTIVES

After studying this chapter, you will be able to
- Define the best practices of corporate governance
- Discuss the criticisms and pitfalls of the current best practices
- List the suggestions regarding next or innovative practices
- Explain whether a political approach works better
- Describe the boards of the future
- Explain whether to conform to the requirements or approach from a performance angle
- Discuss the issues that have no straight solutions but need to be dealt with

Opening Case

Evidence of Rigour in Board and Committee Meetings

Committee structure has become a common format in corporate governance throughout the world. Audit committees constituted of majority independent directors have become mandatory in India too. It is assumed that audit committees need reasonable time if they want to do their job meticulously. Full boards also require reasonable time to discuss the matters concerning the corporations. Given below are the details of the board meetings and audit committee meetings of BSE Sensex companies.

Details of board meetings and audit committee meetings of BSE Sensex companies

S. No.	Company	Year	No. of BMs	BM Dates (Y/N)	No. of ACMs	ACM Dates (Y/N)	No. of ACMs on the same date as BMs
1	RIL	2008–09	7	Y	5	N	NA
2	Infosys	2008–09	6	Y	4	Y	0/4
3	L&T	2008–09	10	Y	7	Y	4/7
4	ICICI Bank	2008–09	8	Y	6	N	NA
5	ITC	2008–09	5	Y	9	Y	4/9
6	HDFC	2008–09	5	Y	%	Y	5/5
7	Bharti Airtel	2008–09	10	Y	9	N	NA
8	HDFC Bank	2008–09	10	Y	9	N	NA
9	SBI	2008–09	9	Y	9	Y	0/9
10	ONGC	2008–09	13	Y	11	Y	8/11
11	BHEL	2008–09	10	Y	3	Y	3/3
12	HUL	2008–09	8	Y	7	Y	6/7
13	TCS	2008–09	7	Y	8	Y	7/8
14	Tata Steel	2008–09	10	Y	9	Y	4/9
15	Tata Power	2008–09	7	Y	13	Y	2/13
16	Grasim	2008–09	5	Y	6	N	NA
17	NTPC	2008–09	17	Y	6	Y	4/6
18	Stelite Ind.	2007–08	7	Y	4	Y	4/4
19	Maruti Suzuki	2008–09	6	Y	6	Y	5/6
20	Rel. Comm.	2008–09	4	Y	6	Y	2/6
21	Rel. Infra.	2008–09	5	Y	5	Y	2/5
22	JP Assoc.	2008–09	6	Y	4	Y	3/4
23	Wipro	2008–09	4	Y	5	Y	1/5
24	M&M	2008–09	7	Y	5	N	NA
25	DLF	2008–09	8	Y	10	Y	3/10
26	Hero Honda	2008–09	4	Y	7	Y	4/7
27	Hindalco	2008–09	7	Y	6	N	NA
28	Tata Motors	2008–09	9	Y	10	Y	1/10
29	Sun Pharma	2008–09	4	Y	5	Y	4/5
30	ACC	2008–09	5	Y	5	Y	0/5

Legend:
BM: Board meeting; ACM: Audit committee meeting; Y: Yes; N: No; NA: Not applicable

Source: Annual report of Sensex companies for the year 2008–09, except for Sterlite Industries.

Discussion Questions
1. Companies follow the governance regulations more from a compliance point of view than in spirit Comment.
2. Do you think that boards and audit committees do justice to the rigour expected of them?
3. Make critical comments on the state of affairs in corporate governance in India based on the data given above.

GOVERNANCE SO FAR

We have seen in the earlier chapters: how the concept of the corporate form took its birth, enabled entrepreneurs to grow their firms to greater sizes, and economies to depend on them for their own growth and industrialization; how the modern corporations saw wide dispersal of shareholding compared to the earlier concentrated ownership; and how this puts the responsibility of looking after the shareholders on to the boards. We have also discussed the constitution of boards, election of the directors, their roles, duties and responsibilities, how and why committees get formed for better administration of the governance processes, how directors undergo the development process, how they get compensated, and how their performance is reviewed, etc. We have also learnt about the guidelines, codes, or laws that deal with or cover the multitude aspects of governance, how governance happens in different types of firms where ownership structures differ, the roles played by the different institutions that have become the hallmarks of the modern market economies, and also the conflicts of interest of the various capital market institutions, and how shareholder activism and/or a well-developed market for corporate control can discipline corporations and boards, leading to better governance. We have also seen that notwithstanding the codes, guidelines, laws, and regulations, and the reforms that have been taking place, failures of corporates and businesses continue to occur. In this chapter, we will see how we can think of having better practices (or what management gurus call next practices) that will guide the governance of firms in the future. This chapter will also try to address some of the paradoxes for which there are no straight and easy solutions, but a pressing need to address them.

GOVERNANCE PRACTICES FOR THE TWENTY-FIRST CENTURY

From the earlier days since the concept came into being, experts have been suggesting best practices such as having a majority of independent directors, separating the chairman and CEO positions, having a lead director, having certain committees made up of only independent directors, reviewing the performances of individual directors and the board as a whole, directors owning stocks in order for them to better align with the interests of shareholders, etc. Some countries have chosen to be content with guidelines or codes (such as the UK), while others have chosen subordinate laws in the form of listing agreements between companies and stock exchanges where their shares have been listed as required by the market regulator (such as SEBI in India), and still others have chosen to have exclusive laws to deal with corporate governance (such as the Sarbanes–Oxley in the US). It may be a little premature to make a final verdict on the efficacy of the different initiatives as even the first initiative in the form of the Cadbury Code in the UK is only seventeen years old. Considering that many new thoughts in management will take not only years but decades to sink in and become widely practised despite the availability of ample evidence about the dramatic improvements resulting from such new thoughts/practices, it is not surprising that many countries, even the so-called developed ones, have not implemented some of the so-called best practices. For example, Peter Drucker made a passionate plea for GM to treat workers as a 'resource rather than just a cost' through his book, which was essentially the result of his study of GM, *The Concept of the Corporation*, according to Micklethwait and Wooldridge (2005). At the conclusion of his study of GM, Drucker (1946) wrote, 'Unfortunately, the 'assembly-line mentality' among modern management which believes that a worker is the more efficient, the more machine-like and the less human he is and '… to enlist the active participation of the worker in improving the efficiency of production and organization would strengthen the corporate noticeably. As a matter of fact, any other policy would be harmful to the large corporation. Faced with an ever-growing need for executives and engaged in a technological and efficiency competition, which is becoming fiercer all the time, the corporation simply cannot afford to deprive itself of the intelligence, imagination, and initiative, of 90 per cent of the people who work for it, that is, the workers.' And evidence of the result of application of this idea has been available from some of the great organizations such as General Electric, Toyota, and many others. But these organizations, even today, form only a small percentage of the total number of corporations in the world. Why is it that such a wonderful and useful idea is not sinking in the corporate system as a whole even after sixty-three long years? But that is the fate of many a good ideas/thoughts. And if such an idea of best practice (or a next practice at the time he wrote it), which can have very clear, tangible outcomes, has not been implemented by a very large number of firms even today, how can one expect the so-called best practices or the next practices in governance to take root so fast, especially when there are not many tangible benefits to prove it (very few studies have been conducted and still very few prove that better governed companies are valued better by the market). Notwithstanding the absence of clear evidence to prove that a well-governed company will be valued better by market forces, and also what parameters or aspects of governance lead to better valuation, the so-called best practices have been recommended by practising chairmen, directors, and corporate governance experts. Let us now look into some of the best practices that are in place now, and the pitfalls or criticisms against some of them, before we embark on a journey towards the best and next practices for the future.

General Criticisms on the Best Practices Today

- Most of the reforms recommended (by way of laws, guidelines, or codes) are structural, such as separating the chairman and CEO positions, insisting on a definite percentage of independent directors, having certain committees made up only of independent directors, appointing a lead director, exclusive meetings of independent directors, etc. The attempt has so far been to look at governance as a 'hardware' or looking at the structure such as having a definite proportion of independent directors, separating the chairman and CEO positions, or having a lead independent director, etc. Whereas some kind of 'hardware' is essential, it is the 'software' or the spirit behind such structural changes that determines the performance of governance.

- Regulators and regulations incentivise or encourage companies to go mostly on a compliance mode rather than a performance mode. The whole effort usually gets reduced to more or less a box-ticking exercise and does not help or enable the board or the company to improve upon other governance processes. Of course, Sarbanes–Oxley could be said to be different.
- While the Sarbanes–Oxley Act 2002 in the US is more process-oriented, it inevitably resulted in higher costs for companies, which means lesser profits for the company and lesser returns for shareholders. Unless this cost is compensated by the reduction of risks of the shareholders, this again, though process-oriented, cannot be considered to be efficient.

In the earlier chapters, we have studied the so-called best practices that have been adopted by a number of boards ever since the first ever, organized attempt happened in the UK in the form of the Cadbury Report. According to Carter and Lorsch (2004), these best practices 'all intended in one way or another to enhance board power and foster "independent" thinking with shareholders' interests in mind.' To reiterate the best practices:

- Boards should have a majority of independent directors and many countries, including India, have made the definition of independence very stringent.
- The chairman and CEO positions shall be separated to prevent concentration of power in one position and also to achieve delineation of roles. By definition, the chairman is the leader of the board while the CEO is the leader of the management. In many countries, if the chairman and CEO are combined in one person, there is a practice of designating an independent director as lead director who chairs the meetings of independent directors without management directors and promoter directors and their nominees.
- All boards essentially have three committees, namely audit, compensation, and nomination committees, all constituted fully of independent directors. While Sarbanes–Oxley of US insists on independent members on all three committees, Clause 49 in India is less stringent. It requires that only the audit committee is mandatory and that too constituted of a majority of independent directors. The compensation and nomination committees are non-mandatory but are recommended and need to be reported under the non-mandatory provisions.
- The smaller the board the better. Bigger boards will reduce interactions or make it difficult to interact freely, affecting decision-making. While experts concur that it is difficult to precisely fix a number, it should be as small as possible subject to the constraint of constituting a sufficient number of committees.
- The compensation paid to the directors should be designed in such a way that their interests get aligned with the interests of the shareholders. In effect, this means that a major part of the compensation should be in the form of stock options or restricted stocks, etc.
- Independent directors can have access to external professional advice if they require, paid by the company.
- Declaration of related party transactions and the interests of directors in firms that deal with the company to avoid conflicts of interest.
- Stringent independence criteria for auditors restraining them from offering any other services to the company.

- Restricting the number of directorships in publicly-listed companies (a maximum of 15 directorships in India) to ensure that the directors are committed to those companies in which they are directors and can allot quality time to carry out the duties.
- Independent directors must meet without the chairman/whole-time and management/inside directors at least once a year.
- Use of a single indicator such as EVA™ to ascertain the financial performance of the company (MacAvoy and Millstein 2004). According to MacAvoy and Millstein, this is a very apt metric to measure corporate performance when we discuss corporate governance because of the following reasons:
  - It relies on the basic assumption (in most corporate governance theories) that the most important financial objective of any company is to maximize the wealth of the shareholders.
  - It is simple and straightforward, and can be applied to all firms allaying the need to rely on multiple financial measures.
  - It can be used at all stages of business and for all types businesses.
  - It takes into account the investment as it is arrived at after deducting the cost of investments and the cost of capital.
  - It also takes care of the cost of equity capital, as measured by shareholders' expected returns.

    The EVA™ based performance measure has merits and is recommended by institutional investors such as CalPERS and also experts like MacAvoy and Millstein, though some of the contentions are questionable. In their anxiety to report better EVA™, managers may resort to off-balance sheet financing such as lease financing, which may change the risk complexion of the company, which in turn, will lead to increased cost of capital that is not usually taken into account in the computations of EVA™. It depends on the industries in which the companies operate. Companies with higher costs of capital may be able to report positive or higher EVA™ if they are able to price their products high. Thus, a company in the IT-related business or FMCG may be able to price its products high and thereby earn a positive EVA despite the fact that their cost of capital is high compared to a commodity firm which may not be able to price their products high despite having a lower cost of capital (due to better and efficient use of capital) when compared to the IT or FMCG firm. Also, in certain areas such as IT/FMCG/Pharma, etc., the companies can have more flexibility to change the product mix and produce those with the highest margins. This flexibility may not be available for a cement company or a petrochemical company, the machinery and processes of which are usually designed to produce only one product. Also, since other incomes are included in the computation of NOPAT, EVA™ would be positive in a year in which the other incomes were high. Since other income may arise out of sale of assets also, managers may be motivated to strip assets to report a positive EVA™ (Kumar 2000).

While some of these have contributed to the better governance of some companies, many of these changes are primarily structural and one cannot take it for granted that structural initiatives will invariably lead to better governance. And even when boards may meet the structural requirements, there are many loopholes in the laws and regulations that put a limit on the structural changes alone bringing out initiatives towards better governance.

For example, consider the requirement of independent directors in India. The law defines relationships in such a way that it is very easy to appoint some of your close relatives as independent directors. Also, one director sitting on the boards of many companies belonging to the same industrial/family group have been considered independent according to law because each of the companies are considered to be separate entities. Interpreting the law in the same way, the same external, independent auditor can audit the accounts of many companies belonging to the same group without any questions being raised on their independence. For example, all the four major companies from the Tata group that are constituents of Sensex as on 30 November 2009 have Deloitte, Haskins, and Sells as their auditors. While Tatas may, as a group, gain cost advantages by engaging the same auditor in many companies, and the auditors may be doing a very stringent and excellent job as score keepers, it seems cloudy from its appearance. The law also permits a former executive director (an outsider) of a company to be designated as non-executive, independent director after a de-merger process as the entities arising out of a de-merger are considered to be independent. While independence per se is not only desirable but essential for better governance to happen, such loopholes or deficiencies in the law, coupled with the 'compliance at any cost' attitude by companies and boards, can defeat the very idea and meaning behind independence.

The recommendation that the chairman and CEO positions be separated has genuine merit if certain deficiencies in the practice are eliminated. This is because, according to most of the company laws, the CEO is subordinate to the board, and when the positions are combined, the adherence to this law becomes difficult. Also, the contention that the chairman is the leader of the board and the CEO of the management becomes legitimized. But, this becomes a complicated issue in many companies in India. While the positions have been separated, the chairman is full-time, effectively making him the de facto CEO (for example, HDFC, Hero Honda, Bajaj Auto, Wipro, etc.). In such cases, the separation does not mean much from the governance angle.

The recommendation regarding the formation of committees only with independent directors is also worth a serious consideration as it may bring objectivity into the whole process, and also because these processes necessitate independence from promoters or family in order to ensure better governance. But the issue and processes get diluted because the very independence of the independent directors is under a cloud. As we have seen in earlier chapters, the independence of many of the so-called independent directors is questionable. And also regulations such as permitting a director to have or enter into transactions with the company (such as consulting or supplying materials) within a certain limit enables companies and processes to compromise on independence. The suggestion that the boards be as small as possible is again laudable as it is very likely that very active discussions and debates might occur. When board sizes are larger, everybody fights for air-time, every one is under compulsion to complete the proceedings, and many may not get chances to express their views. But boards shall be as big as required not only to meet the committee requirements but also to have diverse opinions and viewpoints. While smaller size may also reduce costs, the requirement of diversity cannot be overlooked. The more or less general acceptance of the recommendation that the compensation for director shall be in the form of stock options or other equity-related items does not find the support of some. Those who oppose the idea feel that while alignment with shareholders is ok, when it comes to inside directors, such as managing or executive directors, compensating outside directors, especially the independent directors with stock related items, will only make them behave like some shareholders who have a short-term outlook, as director tenures are not necessarily long-term. Also, he may align with other directors (those inside and/or promoters) defeating the very purpose of having them. Hence, this best practice has certain built-in flaws.

The idea that independent directors should have access to outside professional help, while good, will find opposition even from shareholders as it increases the cost to the company, thereby affecting the returns to them. Also, there maybe arguments that directors be chosen with the necessary expertise.

Regarding the disclosure of related party transactions, mere disclosure will not remove the malady of conflicts of interest. Also, the limits permitted by law in terms of percentage of revenues of the related party could be quite considerable as we have seen in Chapter 8. The independence of auditors, at times, becomes questionable as laws permit them to offer such services as long as the billing from these are lower than the audit billing.

While the law restricts the number of directorship to 15, the number seems to be very much on the higher side, considering the role and responsibilities directors and boards have to play and undertake. The expectations of investors, regulators, and even good boards from directors are very high today. Boards are no longer an old boys' club or a country club. No director can take the job lightly. No independent director can do justice to such high numbers of directorship even if he does not hold any full-time position in any company. If an independent director is also a CEO, or a whole-time director, or employee of another company, the time he can devote to other companies, in addition to his full-time responsibilities in his company, will be severely limited.

Deepak Parekh, a highly respected professional is the full-time chairman of Housing Development Finance Corporation Ltd (HDFC). He sits on the boards of nine publicly-listed companies and in three of them he is also chairman. In addition, he is an alternate director in four companies and a director in two other public limited companies (not listed), and chairman of one private limited company. The law mentions only the limit of directorships on public limited companies. It is high time that this limit is reduced to more reasonable levels. As early as 1989, Jay Lorsch and Elizabeth MacIver found that 'the active CEOs of *Fortune* 1000 companies would each have to serve on almost six boards to meet the demand. In the past, active CEOs may have joined six or more boards, but the increasing complexity of both a CEO's and directors' job has made such a heavy commitment impossible and unwise' (Lorsch and MacIver 1989). Lorsch and MacIver present the Heidrick and Struggles Study report of 1987 which details the reasons for people refusing board membership (refer to Table 10.1).

This very clearly shows how directors were concerned about the time they have to devote even though the demands on them were to join only six boards. How can anybody, especially

TABLE 10.1   Reasons for refusing board membership

(Scale: 1= Very influential, 5 = Not influential)

Lack of time	1.72
Meeting conflicts	2.19
Conflict of interest	2.30
Could not play useful role	2.68
No interest in firm industry	2.78
Uncertainty about firm's future	2.97
Personal liability	2.97

Source: Lorsch, Jay W and MacIver, Elizabeth, *Pawns or Potentates: The Reality of America's Corporate Boards*, Boston, HBS Press, 1989.

full-time CEOs today, find time to join and serve fifteen companies when the demands on their rigour and oversight are very high?

Most governance experts recommend that independent directors should meet independent of management. One fails to understand the very logic behind this. Is there anything governing the company that needs to be discussed by independent directors privately? Board members are professionals with expertise in specific areas. They can always exchange ideas as professionals in the boardroom. By suggesting that independent directors meet without management is encouraging the formation of a group within the board. It will affect the total board dynamics. What is expected of the board is to gel together into a homogenous, decision-making group based on diverse ideas from people of diverse expertise. This is different from the interested directors leaving the boardroom when certain matters concerning them are discussed.

INNOVATIVE PRACTICES FOR THE FUTURE

While thinking of establishing a new set of best/next practices for the boards, directors, auditors, regulators, etc., the following can be thought of.

A re-look at the very purpose of corporate governance   One should move away from the conventional approach that governance is essential because shareholders' interests have to be protected. While this is true, there are other stakeholders such as customers, without whom the business of the corporation cannot even exist, employees who have chosen to invest a lifetime for the company, suppliers whose fortunes may depend entirely on the survival and progress of the organization, the community surrounding the corporation which looks up to the corporation for the betterment of their well-being, etc. Investors, on the other hand, may not be interested for long, except for a handful of them. They will look for quick returns on their investments. It is high time we move away from the agency theory of corporate governance as we did with strategy, where strategies were once thought to be required only in a competitive environment, but today we feel that strategies are essentially required to meet the firm's goals and purposes of the firm and will be required even when firms are operating in monopolistic environments. It is better to move away from the hitherto popular shareholder and stakeholder approaches to a firm approach. A firm or a corporation is an artificial person and that is the essential reason why shareholders have to give it money, entrepreneurs have to provide it with entrepreneurial capabilities, managers have to to lend their managerial capabilities, employees have to offer their skills, and suppliers have to supply their products. If it had the capability to do all these, it would not depend on anybody. So, considering that everybody contributes what is required for the corporation and what is best for it, it will grow and flourish, and every stakeholder including shareholders will stand to gain. This point can also be explained with an extreme and hypothetical point. Shareholders get importance because they exist. What will happen if the company grows to such an extent that it builds up reserves sufficient to buy back all the shares outstanding? In such a case, the company will continue to exist even though the shareholder will not be necessary. The company still needs to be governed even though in such a hypothetical situation the conventional agency conflicts don't exist. This thinking, though radical, can bring dramatic improvements in governance.

Governance should become a culture   Everybody in the organizations should know how good governance will lead to reduction in risks, how it will enable the firm to grow and perform better, and result in better rewards for employees, as well as shareholders. Day-to-day activities that will lead to good governance will become part of the value system. Governance should be approached strategically as it will add not only competitive value but also enable the firm to achieve its goals better. Delivering the fourth Palkhivala Memorial Lecture on 9 January 2004, under the auspices of the Nani Palkhivala Foundation, YH Malegam, managing partner at SR Batliboi who headed a number of SEBI committees on capital market regulation, said: '....corporate governance ought not to be considered involving mere compliance with the letter of the law but should be adopted as a way of life' (*The Hindu*, 11 January 2004).

Develop social capital within the boardroom   Within the board, there should be social capital development, facilitated preferably by outside expert, so that the board as a group interacts, debates, dissents, and ultimately reaches an outcome that is far better than earlier outcomes. The chairman and CEO should learn to take an impassionate view of what is best for the organization. While they have leadership responsibilities within their sphere of activities, boards have to gel well as a cohesive group.

Give importance to values   While evaluating the performance of the CEO/other whole-time directors/top management personnel, a 2×2 matrix should be drawn between the performance and value systems of the personnel; such a method is used by GE to evaluate its managers. See Fig. 10.1.

Those who are high both on values and performance (quadrant H), must be given better rewards and/or responsibility and opportunities for growth. Those who are low on performance and values (quadrant L) should be removed. For both these cases, the decision is easy. The issue of decision-making arises when a manager falls in quadrants P or V.

GE has created a system where managers whose values are good but performance needs improvement are given a second chance. Those managers who show good performance but are low on the value parameters are removed. This can be applied to the board level too, with required

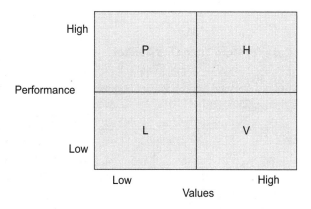

Fɪɢ. 10.1   Performance–value matrix for directors

modifications. For example, if somebody is either in quadrant L or P, the nomination committee should not recommend their names for re-election when it is due. The board, of course has to explain to the shareholders why somebody's name has not been recommended for re-election. True, to implement the same, very high objectivity is required. And the expected behaviour of directors when it comes to values should be known to every director and board as a whole.

The director talent-pool shall be expanded   There should be a definite retirement age for directors, not necessarily because they are bad or non-functional, but because you have to encourage entry of youngsters to the boardrooms to meet the ever-increasing demand for directors. If somebody will be there till he/she attains 85 or 90, no new director, especially younger ones, can replace him/her. Also, the articles of association must clearly mention the need to leave one or two additional director slots which will be filled a year or so before an incumbent director retires. The newly inducted director gets an opportunity to learn the ropes of the game before he/she is expected to fill the slot when the person currently in the slot retires.

Number of directorships   The cap on the number of directorships shall be reduced to around 5 from the current 15 to enable the directors to devote quality time to each company. This decision has to come from the directors rather than law makers/regulators.

Auditing   There must be at least two auditors over and above a threshold size. Only eight companies of the 30 companies in the Sensex have more than one auditor, and of these, three are PSUs. Please note that these companies are some of the biggest in India and auditors have to be changed after a fixed period, say five years. This will bring in more credibility to auditing as an institution.

Auditor independence and indulgence   Different auditors must audit the companies belonging to the same group. Also, auditors must verify a few important items which will have an impact on the bottom line and where there are possibilities of fraud in every company. Exhibit 10.1 shows the number of auditors in the BSE Sensex companies, and how the same auditors serve a number of companies in a group.

Exhibit 10.1
Satyam Failure—A Case for More Than One Auditor?

S. No.	Company	Revenue (Rs in millions) (2008–09)	Number of auditors	Auditor firms
1.	RIL	14,63,280	3	Chaturvedi & Shah Deloitte Haskins & Sells Rajendra & Co
2.	Infosys	2,16,930	1	BSR & Co
3.	ICICI	3,18,180	1	BSR & Co
4.	L&T	4,06,080	1	Sharp & Tannan
5.	HDFC	1,10,176.6	1	Deloitte Haskins & Sells
6.	ITC	2,36,784.6	1	AF Ferguson & Co
7.	HDFC Bank	1,97,505.4	1	Haribhakti & Co
8.	SBI	7,64,790	14	(See below)
9.	ONGC	6,50,494.0	5	(See below)
10.	Bharti Airtel	3,73,521.0	1+1 (for US GAAP)	SR Batliboi & Co Earnst & Young
11.	BHEL	2,80,330	1	ML Puri & Co
12.	TCS	2,19,477.6	1	Deloitte Haskins & Sells
13.	HUL	2,05,171.0	1	Lowelock & Lewis
14.	Sterlite Ind.	2,84,380	2	Chaturvedi & Shah Das & Prasad
15.	Tata Steel	2,43,157.7	1	Deloitte Haskins & Sells
16.	Maruti Suzuki	2,03,583	1	Pricewaterhouse Coopers
17.	M&M	1,49,830	1	Deloitte Haskins & Sells
18.	Tata Power	72,360	1	Deloitte Haskins & Sells
19.	Wipro	2,16,128	1	BSR & Co
20.	NTPC		6	(See below)
21.	Tata Motors	2,85,992.7	1	Deloitte Haskins & Sells
22.	J P Assoc.	62,479.3	1	MP Associates
23.	Grasim	1,84,040	2	Kapadia & Co Deloitte Haskins & Sells
24.	Hindalco	1,97,183.4	1	Singhi & Co
25.	Hero Honda	1,25,400	1	AF Ferguson & Co
26.	Rel.Infra.	1,09,590	2	Pricewaterhouse Coopers Chaturvedi & Shah
27.	DLF	38,390.4	1	Walker & Chandiok
28.	Rel. Comm.	1,36,946.6	2	BSR & Co
29.	Sun Pharma	43,750.6	1	Deloitte Haskins & Sells
30.	ACC	85,484.8	1	SR Batliboi & Co

SBI	DP Sen & Co (Kolkota Circle)
	GM Kapadia & Co (Mumbai)
	RGN Price & Co (Chennai)
	SK Mittal & Co (Delhi)
	Vardhman & Co (Hyderabad)
	VK Jindal & Co (Patna)
	Jain Kapila Associates (Bhopal)
	AK Sabat & Co (Bhubaneswar)
	Datta Singla & Co (Chandigarh)
	Dutta Sarkar & Co (North Eastern)
	Gupta & Shah (Lucknow)
	Guha & Nandi & Co (Ahmedabad)
	AR Viswanathan & Co (Bangalore)
	Chokshi & Chokshi (Kerala)
ONGC	Padmanabhan Ramani & Ramanujam (Chennai)
	Singhi & Co (Kolkata)
	PSD & Associates (Jaipur)
	Arun K Agarwal & Associates (New Delhi)
	Kalyaniwala & Mistry (Mumbai)
NTPC	Varma& Varma
	BC Jain & Co
	Prakash & Co
	SK.Mittal & Co.
	Das Gupta & Associates
	S.K. Mehta & Co.

Source: Annual Reports of Companies for the year 2008–09 (except for Sterlite Industries which is for 2007–08).

Questions
1. Do you think that there is a need for more than one auditor to audit companies above a minimum size?
2. Many companies belonging to the same indstrial group have the same auditors. Does it affect objectivity?
3. The same auditor firm has been found to be auditing competing companies. Does it lead to any conflicts of interest?

Audit of corporate governance practices   The current practice in India is that the auditor (same auditor who audits the financial statements) gives a certificate stating that they have examined the compliance of conditions of corporate governance of a company as stipulated in Clause 49. This is not an audit. It is also not clear why auditors have been entrusted with the job as they need not be equipped for it. A process of auditing corporate governance practices by an expert body constituted by SEBI/CLB or other recognized private organizations such as IOD should be developed.

Verification by regulators and certain institutions   Regulators and institutions such as ICAI must randomly verify the accounts from a research point of view. They should also publish their findings so that other companies will be on their toes.

Regulators to play a development role   Regulators such as SEBI should play a more development role of educating the investors and other market intermediaries, and participants, than just monitoring. The basic ideology shall not be to punish the crimes as and when they occur but to prevent crimes from occurring.

Have a governance charter   There should be a well thought-out governance charter for every company clearly detailing not only the roles, duties, and responsibilities expected of them but also mentioning the values that the company expects the director and board to follow.

Take an oath of office   Last but not the least: directors should take an oath before assuming the position and role to administer the duty of diligence, care, and oversight of the company, and its assets and resources. A director is a professional in the same category as a doctor. The patient approaches the doctor with symptoms or discomfort. The doctor uses a process to diagnose the disease or illness and decides on the treatment. The patient does not know what is to be done. He/she submits to the doctor for his/her decision and the doctor, after a diligent process, takes his/her decision and administers the treatment. The patient has trust in the 'care' of the doctor. Is a director's job any different? Before they enter into the profession, doctors take an oath, called the Hippocratic oath. Why do directors, on whom a number of stakeholders depend for their dutiful care, not take an oath before they enter into a professional responsibility of care?

CAN POLITICAL APPROACH BE BETTER?

Political approach does not mean any involvement of politicians in the process. It means that some of the tools of politics will be used in dealing with corporate governance issues. Here we will see whether the tools of politics such as debates (as the American presidential candidates indulge in during a presidential campaign), or negotiations (different parties sit together and arrive at a consensus regarding what is the best course of action for future), or bargaining between any two parties (as unions do with management) will result in better outcomes as far as governance is concerned.

Political approach adopts 'give and take' policies. For example, if shareholders want decisions to be made regarding the distribution of profits, the company must require the investors to be there for a minimum period. Please note that the discussion here does not only aim at adopting a political framework while negotiating with investors, as suggested by John Pound, visiting professor at Harvard Law School. According to Pound (2000), 'In the new marketplace for ideas, debate will replace debt, as active shareholders press specific operating policies for their target corporations in a new politicized market for corporate control' and 'this political approach to governance gives the management a chance to embrace a bargain that is in its long-term interest. By promoting politically based tactics, managers can generate political capital with the major investors.'

Pound's views are based on the conventional approach to corporate governance, which is that governance is necessary because the board and management have a fiduciary responsibility only to shareholders. Here, we take a broader view of political approach, that businesses and corporations are necessary for the well-being of the different stakeholders, including the economy and country. Hence, nothing that dissuades entrepreneurship should be done.

At the same time, businesses have to take adequate care of all the interested stakeholders and the best way to meet these aims is through a process of negotiations and bargaining. This will increase predictability, and by and large, can eliminate surprises. Everybody, including regulators and government, has to participate in the process and arrive at a general consensus about the firm. This approach becomes relevant as other approaches, including stringent external regulations, have failed to bring discipline among the corporations. If a political approach and solution are possible, it may score over other approaches. The only hitch is to bring all the interested parties together on the table to start negotiations. The strengths or the advantages of a political approach is that the stakeholders have to be better informed about the corporate and make realistic demands on them, and corporations can understand the expectations of all the classes of stakeholders and discuss what kind of conduct is expected of them.

THE BOARD FOR THE FUTURE

In Chapter 4 we saw the different types of boards according to governance experts like Bob Tricker, Ram Charan, etc. We have also seen the best practices at the board level and that boards have to determine the specific roles they have to play in their respective companies. Considering that the board is being looked up to by all the stakeholders as a key constituent in the corporation, who will protect their interests by guiding the corporation and its management with adequate care, the board of the future will have the following characteristics or meet the following criteria:

- Will have a broader view that they have a responsibility to all the stakeholders, including shareholders. They will fit into the definition of 'broad constructionists' coined by Lorsch and MacIver. According to Lorsch and MacIver (1989), this 'group of directors openly recognizes that their responsibilities encompass more than shareholders. If this attitude produces conflicts, they recognize and deal with them, without assuming that every decision must be in the shareholders' interests.'
- The sizes of the boards will be decided by the need for expertise. But every effort will be made to make it as small as possible, subject to the minimum size required to meet the regulatory requirements.
- The chairman and CEO positions will be separate. The chairman will be independent, an outsider. While some experts such as Ram Charan feel that this separation is not essential and even undesirable for better governance, there is a general agreement that the separation makes sense. This is because:
  - The board should have a leader different from management because the roles of the chairman and CEO are different
  - The evaluation of the CEO should be carried out by the board under the leadership of the chairman.

  Please note that the necessity of separation of the positions does not arise because combining them can result in concentration of power as the board can put in position systems to overcome this problem.

- An overwhelming majority of boards will be independent. While the experience does not necessarily provide evidence that the governance will be better if the percentage of independent directors is more than the insiders, there really is a meaning behind the requirement. Independence can really help provided it is for real or the independent director applies an independent mindset. The decision regarding the percentage should be taken by the board, rather than thrust upon the company by the regulators.

- All new directors would have undergone a development process. New recruits would also have undergone some training from bodies such as NACD, IOD, etc., who provide certification as chartered directors. Such training programmes enable director aspirants to have a broad idea about the roles, duties, and responsibilities of individual directors and boards.

- Directors would be recruited/nominated for their professional expertise and not because they are known to the chairman/CEO/other directors.

- The board will widen the talent pool for directors beyond CEOs and other current directors to one or two rungs below the CEO level. Since a strategic business unit (SBU) or a profit centre head of a larger company will be managing an even bigger business compared to many other companies, they can definitely be included in the search for new talent for directorships. This will enable corporates to create a new pool of talent who can gain good experience and develop into better directors, who could assume responsibilities in bigger corporations as time passes.

- They will establish a governance charter for the board detailing what kind of role, duties, and responsibilities the board has to play, perform, and take. Please note that this charter will not be etched in stone. It will be reviewed at pre-determined intervals but at least once a year or when some emergent situation demands it.

- They will be actively involved in the formulation of strategy. After formulation, they will only monitor the progress through monitoring the management deeds. They will keep themselves updated with knowledge about the various changes in the environment that may affect implementation of the strategy.

- They will meet more often as they would like to ascertain the progress of strategy and monitor management.

- Directors will be on a fewer number of boards. Because of the expectations from directors to devote quality time to each of the companies where one is a director, one will try to restrict the number of directorship to manageable limits.

- There will be more discussions, dialogues, and debates in the boardroom and directors will eagerly participate in them. Dissents will not be looked down upon and will be treated as an opportunity to learn different perspectives about a particular subject under discussion.

- Directors and boards will seek more information from management. They will decide on an information architecture for capturing information from various sources.

- Directors and boards will get actively involved in the selection of CEOs, other whole-time directors, and non-executive directors, and in their succession plan.

- Will have clearly laid out evaluation process for individual directors, as well as for the board as a whole.

- The boards will be actively involved in setting the compensation packages for the CEO and other top executives, and also for non-executive directors based on performance. They will not indulge in anything that will invite outrage from shareholders or the public.
- Will take all necessary steps to reduce the impact of risks on the enterprise and will intervene whenever they see or get information regarding actions or non-actions on the part of the management to mitigate the risk to the enterprise.
- They will be more concerned about the performance of the board than mere compliance with laws and regulations.
- Take meticulous care to avoid falling prey to the loopholes and ambiguity that invariably exist in any legal/regulatory framework.
- Boards will try to avoid any existence of conflicts of interest rather than adopt the 'disclose and move forward' principle.
- Boards will be more self-regulatory and will have clearly laid-out directions for board processes and also yardsticks for measuring performance.
- Directors will take an oath of office. It will become part of the corporate constitution or article of association of the company. It need not be the same for every company, but will clearly contain the expectations from the directors and board as a whole in the execution of its roles, duties, and responsibilities.

CONFORMANCE VS PERFORMANCE

While discussing corporate governance, two concerns confront everyone. This has to do with whether corporates and boards should take efforts to conform to the statutory requirements (legal as well as regulatory) in every possible way while not really worrying about whether these have actually resulted in any concrete improvements in the way the corporation is governed. Or, the changes happen in 'form' rather than 'substance'. The other is about improvements or better performance rather than just compliance. Merely complying with or conforming to the statutory requirements does not assure better governance. Examples such as Enron earlier, or Satyam in the immediate recent past, very clearly indicate this. Both had independent directors meeting the statutory requirements, audit committees, compensation committees, and nomination committees, made up of only independent directors. The audit committee included members with financial expertise, any related party transactions were declared, but ultimately both failed. Such governance debacles occurred in these companies despite both companies meeting, or complying, or conforming to all the statutory requirements. This shows very clearly that mere compliance will not necessarily lead to better real governance.

For example, the purpose of having an independent director is to take an independent view of the decisions the company management or CEO takes. While independence is really essential in order to take an independent view, it is not necessary that independent directors take a really independent view. Even though apparently everything looks fine and well on paper, things do not improve on the governance front. While there are many flaws in the criterion for independence from the legal and regulatory side, even those independent directors who are really independent need not take their roles as directors seriously and execute their duties and responsibilities. Although defined as independent, many independent directors owe their positions to the CEO or chairman of the board and would not usually express their dissent on any issue under discussion. While every company claims to be concerned about 'substance', rather than 'form', it is usually on paper and is rhetoric in nature. Most of the companies consider it another box-ticking exercise.

According to Garratt (2003), 'Good corporate governance is not just complying with the rules in a formulaic way, but is about the board's performance contributing to the direction, health, and wealth of the organization.' And most laws and regulations are largely concerned about conformance. As we have seen in Chapter 8, the laws in most parts of the world are stringent on form. The debate is usually based on the agency theory, which in essence says that people cannot be trusted, and in order to avoid problems of agency (and that agent according to them has to only worry about the shareholders), they recommend drafting more regulatory legislation or changing the existing ones. According to Garratt, these are aimed at 'improvising the "hard" (and easily debated) issues of board conformance/compliance, rather than the crucial "soft" (and difficult to debate generically) aspects of the specific mix of human vision, values, and behaviour, that lead to performance for a particular board.' When boards are on a conformance mode, focus is mostly internal on the performance of pre-set goals of accountability to its shareholders and other stakeholders, whereas a performance mode forces them to focus on external factors over which the corporation has much less control, but on which depends the success of the firm through competitive positioning and allocation of the vital resources (Garratt, 1996).

The external focus in the performance mode forces the firm to set their sight on long-term performance by constantly monitoring the environment for its changes and finding out the various threats and opportunities that it offers, and thereby insisting that the board, as well as the company are on a learning mode. For corporate governance to move from a conformance to a performance mode, a lot of initiatives and actions from boards, as well as regulators are required. It is for the board to decide whether it wants to pursue performance or only conformance. According to Garratt (2003), 'Board *conformance* is necessary but not sufficient. Sufficiency comes from wealth generation through effective board *performance* within the law, for the propagation of sustainable civil societies.' Regulators should also encourage performance, rather than only enforcing strict conformance. The existence of laws and their enforcement forces every company to meet the legal or regulatory requirements, irrespective of whether it is good or bad. This is where the question of whether laws or guidelines are better for corporate governance arises.

The US has enacted a specific law (SOX) to discipline corporates, whereas the UK has continued with a code of best practices for the corporates to follow. SOX was a knee-jerk reaction to governance failures such as Enron, WorldCom, or Tyco. Despite the stringency of the law, governance failures continue to happen in the US, whereas in the UK the governance failures are far less. In fact, this prompted Paul Volcker, ex-chairman of the Federal Reserve to make 'a plea to the Bush administration that it should immediately adopt the UK's accounting practices and study its corporate governance procedures' (Garratt 2003). According to Garratt, 'The bigger picture shows that in the last ten years, the UK has developed a robust national structure and process for both the board conformance and board performance aspects of corporate governance.'

Thus, UK guidelines are seen to be more enabling than the stringent US laws in corporates driving for both corporate governance conformance and performance. The leadership of the board and the board as a whole has to think differently from a narrow perspective of fiduciary duty to shareholders to a larger perspective of the company as not only an economic entity but also as a human and social organization.

Drucker (1946) wrote that 'As the representative social institution of our society, the corporation, in addition to being an economic tool, is a political and social body; its social functions as a community are as important as its economic function as an efficient producer.' But, he cautions: 'This does not mean that the economic purpose of the corporation, efficient production, is to be subordinated to its social function, or that the fulfilment of society's basic belief is to be subordinated to the profit and survival interest of the individual business' (Drucker 1946). When corporations want good governance, they should understand the meaning behind the requirements, including structural requirements. For example, the purpose of having independent directors is to take an independent view of the performance of the company and not to meet the regulatory (Clause 49 in India or SOX in US) requirement regarding the numbers or percentage of independent directors. If this is not internalized and companies nominate the independent directors in the required percentage, it does not automatically result in any improvement in governance. Similarly, there is a reason why regulation or codes demand corporations to adhere to certain standards. If these standards show only on paper, it becomes mere compliance. It does not necessarily lead to any improvement in governance.

JOURNEY TO THE GOVERNED CORPORATION

The fundamental assumption about corporate governance is that governance is required to ensure effective decision-making. But, most of the current thinking about governance is about power relationships and how to effectively control the power enjoyed by the CEO. This is true in many countries and especially in the US. According to Garratt (2003), 'Part of the US corporate folklore is the belief in the paramount importance of the rough, tough, all-powerful, chief executive, who creates new markets, cuts costs ruthlessly, sees trade unions as for wimps, and is paid hugely.' When we discussed the managed corporation versus the governed corporation in Chapter 6 (as explained by John Pound), we learned that the boards of the managed corporations will be characterized by:

- Power sufficient to control the CEO and the evaluation process
- Independence to ensure that the CEO is honestly evaluated and that directors are not compromised by conflicts or co-opted by management, and
- Board procedures that allow outside directors to evaluate managers dispassionately and effectively.

As can be seen, the board characteristics revolve around the concept of reining in the power enjoyed by the CEO. All characteristics have been brought in to control the CEO as he/she enjoys unlimited power. It is not clear how this thinking was developed as most of the laws, including those of India, very clearly say that the board has the ultimate responsibility as far as a corporation is concerned, not the chairman or the CEO. The Indian Companies Act very clearly makes the point that the managing director (as CEOs are called in India) is a subordinate of the board. Or, has this been created by the laws prevailing in the state of Delaware in US, which encourages companies to register in that state? Delaware has been considered to be very accommodating with respect to the registration of companies. This encouraged companies to go and register their companies in Delaware and approximately 50 per cent of the *Fortune* 500 companies are registered in Delaware (Garratt 2003).

In addition to the ease of registration of companies, Delaware courts were also said to be 'business-friendly' (Garratt 2003). Garratt says that 'if they [CEOs] are successful, many minor infringements of good governance and the law, and holding some debatable personal values, are not only forgiven but celebrated publicly. This is usually measured only by rising share prices' and 'Delaware became an international byword for an over-comfortable relationship between the state and corporations at the expense of the shareholder' (Garratt). Thus, corporate governance, as we it see today, has been necessitated by a basic requirement to control the CEO, who had over a period of time become more powerful than the board which appointed him. The suggestion relating to governance such as separating the CEO and chair positions, board meetings without CEO being present, independent directors meeting without management/inside directors, the provision to use external financial legal experts by independent, outside directors, have all been included in the current corporate governance provisions because of the lack of trust on the CEO, who has become so powerful. As Pound (2000) says, 'The board's role is to his hire, monitor and, when necessary, replace management in a managed corporation context.'

As against this, the corporations should become governed ones. A governed corporation, is characterized by a board whose 'role is to foster effective decisions and reverse failed policies' (Pound 2000). According to Pound, the board will have the following characteristics:

- Expertise sufficient to allow the board to add value to the decision-making process.
- Incentives to ensure that the board is committed to creating corporate value.
- Procedures that foster open debate, and keep board members informed and attuned to the shareholders' concerns.

This will necessitate a change in policies too. Directors must be willing to commit a minimum number of days to a company (25 according to Pound), regular meetings with large shareholders such as institutional investors, recruiting/nominating directors with necessary expertise, etc. The governed corporation will look at what is good for the corporation. The boards will try to make it bigger, stronger, and sustainable. They will not necessarily worry about the short-term performance and will never put management under pressure to put up better performance quarter after quarter. They understand very clearly that they are required because the firm is an artificial entity. Of course, they will comply with and conform to all legal requirements and regulations, but go much beyond this to ensure the real well-being of the corporation. They understand the importance of the role a corporation has to play in the economy and society. Thus, the job of the board changes from one of monitoring the management to one of enabling managers to make improved and effective decisions.

In its journey towards a governed corporation, a firm would have adopted most of the next practices we discussed earlier. Governed corporations will be on a continuous learning mode and their boards will conform to the learning board conceived by Garratt (1996). In the process, every constituent is considered to be a partner in a co-operative and collaborative governance process, and shareholders would willingly offer suggestions for improving governance rather than exit when governance becomes questionable. Leaders of such companies will be guided by a value system which will result in positives for everybody, including the artificial entity, the corporation.

THE GOVERNANCE CONUNDRUM—NO STRAIGHT SOLUTIONS

There are many issues and concerns in the area of corporate governance which are tricky in nature and nobody can give a solution straightaway. But, these are issues and concerns that need to be addressed anyway. Such issues and concerns pose great challenges to the boards themselves, to regulators, and government and governance experts. We may already have seen or discussed some of them in the earlier chapters, but here we try to consolidate all such issues and concerns.

- Should the functioning of the boards be regulated externally or are they better self-regulated? This issue becomes difficult to resolve or at least perceived to be difficult to resolve as despite the availability of stringent external regulations, corporate failures continue to happen on account of poor corporate governance in many parts of the world. Does this mean that regulations have failed miserably? Or are they of not much use? Do boards consider that when external regulations are present, they just have to comply with them and not worry about anything beyond that?
- Shareholders who are also part of management pose a great challenge to the corporate governance pundits. By being on management, they have a great deal of privileged information which outside shareholders are deprived of. The concern is whether they will utilize this information to further their own interests. We have not been able to find any easy solution to this problem.
- Should independent directors hold shares in the company? If they hold shares, how will they be different from promoter nominees who are also shareholders? Will insisting on a limit, such as 2 per cent, as in India, not affect their independence?
- How many directors are required on the board of a company? Can there be a number related to company size? This is very difficult to prescribe. Certain bigger companies have smaller boards, whereas smaller companies have bigger boards.
- Should there be a lead director and should independent directors meet separately under the leadership of the lead director? There is no evidence that this helps. None of the annual reports of major companies in India have reported separate meetings of independent directors. The question is: does it help? Or does it lead to the creation of another group within the board?
- Should outside, independent directors be generalists or specialists with expertise in certain areas? Generalists can have a broader view compared to specialists. Should boards be homogenous or heterogeneous in terms of composition?

- Should independent directors be compensated with stock-related items such as stock options, or restricted stocks, etc., in order to align their interests with other shareholders? Is such alignment necessary?
- How much time shall an outside director devote to a company? Does it relate to the complexity of the business?
- Can directors who meet once every quarter (as per the Indian regulations) perform the duty of diligence and care expected of them?
- Can we expect that the directors who are part of the promoters will take care of the interests of all the shareholders alike?
- Can we expect a director who represents a significant outside shareholder (such as institutional investors) be taking care of the interests of other shareholders as well ?
- How can independent directors monitor the chairman/CEO who represents the promoter or family who has significant shareholding?
- How can the board ensure that it gets all information so that it is able to monitor management, and prevent it and the company from entering into risky actions or areas?
- How can each director be made to understand that a director is a director with responsibilities like all others, irrespective of the class to which he belongs?
- Who is interested in corporate governance? Apparently nobody is interested in the governance of a company, or every stakeholder is only interested in bettering his/her outcome of association with a corporate and that too till as long as he/she is associated with it, be it as a director, a shareholder, customer, supplier, or any other stakeholder. The question is: is there a tangible difference in the perception about a corporate body in the minds of different stakeholders, including the general public, because the corporate body is well-governed? We fail to observe any perceptible evidence to this. Then the next question is: why go through all the trouble?

We have listed most of the concerns that pose challenges to the process of corporate governance today. More concerns may emerge as we progress and some of the existing concerns may get resolved by the boards themselves/regulators/legal systems.

SUMMARY

While the concept of corporate governance and the regulatory frameworks vary from country to country, there are certain best practices which every country advocates and follows. These enable companies and regulatory frameworks achieve better governance than previously by bringing in more objectivity within the legal or regulatory framework prevalent. Or, to put it in another way, regulators and legal systems have evolved based on some of these best practices. Of course, there have been criticisms of some of the best practices currently followed. The most important of these is that the best practices are mostly structural and hence force corporations to go on a compliance or conformance mode, rather than performance mode. Despite the pitfalls, some of these practices are considered to be essential for better performance too. These best practices are essential, but companies have to constantly look for reforms in the governance related areas.

A few suggestions regarding the 'next' practice have been discussed. The recommendations for future practices include a re-look at the very purpose of governance, the need for governance to become a part of the corporate culture, better social capital development in the boardroom, a value-based approach to leadership, directors voluntarily restricting directorships to manageable numbers, better audit practices, regulators playing more of a development role than monitoring and control roles, every company to establish a governance charter, and even directors taking an oath of office. How the boards of the future would look and perform will depend on how the company perceives corporate governance. The question is how many corporations want to go beyond the conformance requirements and shift into a performance gear. Apparently, very few constituents of the corporate structure are really interested in taking further steps as there has not been much evidence to support the fact that good governance necessarily leads to better outcomes. Bad governance may lead to failures, such as Satyam, but will good governance, as perceived today, lead to all-round improvements in the corporation? One is not necessarily sure. And, there are a number of issues or concerns which have to be addressed but straight solutions are not easy to find.

KEY TERMS

Best practice   Practice which can deliver better outcomes

Conformance   Conform to the statutory requirements

Conundrum   Puzzling question

Defacto   For all practical purposes

Governance charter   Comprehensive set of processes and procedures for governing the firm

Hippocratic oath   Oath to observe the medical code of ethical andprofessional behaviour

Improvising   Creating or performing spontaneously

NOPAT   Net operating profit after taxes

Oath   Solemn undertaking

Off-balance sheet financing   Acquiring assets which will not be reflected in the balance sheet

Political approach   Approach of give and take, with an idea of arriving at an agreeable position.

Pundit   Authority, expert

Social capital   Wealth of experience of working together as a group

Social institution   Institution where people work together in relationships

Talent pool   Source from where one can get talented people

Untenable   That cannot last

CONCEPT REVIEW QUESTIONS

1. What are the general criticisms on the current best practices in corporate governance?
2. What are the benefits of splitting the chairman and CEO positions?
3. What is a political approach in corporate governance?
4. Comment on the statement: 'Good corporate governance is not just complying with the rules in a formulaic way, but is about the board's performance contributing to the direction, health, and wealth, of the organization.'
5. What will be the major characteristics of the board of the future?
6. Describe those issues that are essential in governance but finding solutions is very difficult.

CRITICAL THINKING QUESTION

Do you think that self-regulation by boards will be better than external regulations for the betterment of governance practices?

PROJECT WORK

Study the corporate governance practices of the Nifty companies based on secondary data and critically comment on whether they have adopted some innovative practices.

REFERENCES

Carter, Colin B. and Jay W. Lorsch (2004), *Back to the Drawing Board*, HBS Press, Boston.

Charan, Ram (1997), *Boards at Work*, Jossey-Bass, San Francisco.

Charan, Ram (2005), *Boards that Deliver*, Jossey-Bass, San Francisco.

Charan, Ram (2009), *Owning Up*, Jossey-Bass, San Francisco. ·

Drucker, Peter F. (1946), *The Concept of the Corporation*, Transaction Publishers, New Brunswick.

Dimma, William A. (2006), *Tougher Boards for Tougher Times*, Wiley-India, New Delhi.

Garratt, Bob (1996), *Fish Rots from the Head*, Profile Books, London.

Garratt, Bob (2003), *Thin on Top: Why Corporate Governance Matters and How to Measure and Improve Board Performance*, Nicholas Burley, London.

Kumar T.N., Satheesh, 'Economic value added: A critique', *Indian Management*, March 2000, vol. 39, no. 3.

Lorsch, Jay W. and Elizabeth MacIver (1989), *Pawns or Potentates: The Reality of America's Corporate Boards*, HBS Press, Boston.

Mac Avoy, Paul W. and Ira M. Millstein (2004), *The Recurrent Crisis in Corporate Governance*, Stanford Business Books, California.

Malegam, Y.H., 'Adopt corporate governance as a way of life', *The Hindu*, 11 January 2004.

Micklethwait, John and Adrian Wooldridge (2005), *The Company*, Phoenix Books, London.

Myles Mace in *Directors: Myth and Reality*, quoted in Jay Lorsch and Elizabeth MacIver (1989), *Pawns or Potentates:, The Reality of America's Corporate Boards*, HBS Press, Boston.

Pound, John (2000), 'Beyond takeovers: Politics comes to corporate control', in *HBR on Corporate Governance*, HBS Press, Boston.

Pound, John (2000), 'The promise of the governed corporation', *HBR on Corporate Governance*, HBS Press, Boston.

Tichy, Noel M. and Eli Cohen (2002), *The Leadership Engine*, Harper Business, New York.

Closing Case

A Journey through the Changing Roles of the Board

The following are some of the comments or quotes from practicing directors and/or corporate governance experts about their perception of the roles of the board and directors and the transformations they underwent.

- 'Board membership is more of an accolade than an obligation and directors are 'ornaments on a Christmas tree' (Mace 1989).
- 'Directors were usually chosen from the corporate's executives, both retired and active, from more indirectly related sources, such as lawyers and bankers, and from successful friends and acquaintances of the CEO—a sort of "old boys' club", with the protection of shareholder interests and evaluation of top management secondary to the role of advising the CEO' (Lorsch and MacIver 1989).
- 'In the early years, being invited to join a board was a sign of respect … some people served on a lot of boards because the duties were minimum …. But now that the courts hold directors liable if they don't uphold the business judgement rule, directors have begun to ask for information so they can make informed decisions. They have to be more responsible now; they can't go on 18 boards now, because it is too dangerous'.[1]
- 'I'm on ten boards at the moment. It is not a big deal; it is like ten half-days a month. I wasn't on ten boards when I was CEO, though. I am a great believer that you cannot be on lot of boards and run a company at the same time. Once I stepped down as a CEO, at 60, and decided I didn't want to go to Washington, I decided that being a director was a good idea.'
- 'There are two reasons why I said 'yes' to these two boards and have said no to all the rest. One, you have so little time that you really can't take on more than two if you want to do the job properly. Two, these two are convenient to my office and my schedule.'
- A minimum time commitment of 25 days by directors is required, according John Pound, if the corporation has to become a governed corporation (Pound 2000).
- 'The two large-company boards I am on meet eight times per year. One of these meetings is for a multi-day offsite. So, it is roughly ten days for board and committee meetings each year or about eighty hours, plus preparation time and casual conversations with the CEO and other members of management. I think that the range is one hundred to one hundred twenty-five hours each year.'[2]
- 'The crisis in corporate governance in western democracies has occurred because the roles, tasks, and accountabilities, of the board of directors are not understood by politicians, business executives themselves, or the general public…. I argue that until we see the board director role being professionalized and the supremacy of the board being reasserted, we shall not restore full confidence in either our business or public leaders, or the markets. We

---

[1] This and the next two are statements of directors as quoted in Lorsch and MacIver, *Pawns or Potentates*, Boston, HBSPress, 1989.

[2] This is a statement of a director as quoted in Carter and Lorsch, *Back to The Drawing Board*, Boston, HBS Press, 2004.

need to ensure a system of board director selections, training, development, values, annual appraisal, and self-regulation, which will add the same type of rigour around the boardroom table as is often found further down the business' (Garratt 2003).

- 'The typical board is locked into a pattern that seems unbreakable. For them, board meetings are tightly scheduled, well- rehearsed presentations that leave little time for questions or reactions.The directors sit politely at the table, sometimes in order of seniority. Serious questions are considered bad form at best, and any discussion of issues outside the boardroom is viewed as an open threat to the CEO. The presentation seldom give directors the information they really want or need' (Charan 1997).

- 'The board of GM during Roger Smith's tenure shows how ineffective some boards have been. In their book *Comeback: The Fall and Rise of the American Automobile Industry* (Simon and Shuster 1994), Paul Ingrassia and Joseph B White paint a vivid picture of the GM board under Roger Smith. Non-executive members of the board sat on one side of the table while inside directors (those on the management team) sat on the other. Inside directors got information their counterparts across the table were not allowed to see. The typical GM board meeting consisted of well-rehearsed presentations by management during which the presenter would flip through dozens of slides in a darkened room, reading aloud every word. Roger Smith would not tolerate any deviations. According to Ingrassia and White, when Roger Smith heard that attorney Ira Millstein was talking to directors outside board meetings, he stormed into Millstein's office and berated him for meddling' (Charan 1997).

- Ram Charan described a ceremonial board as: 'A decade ago, when one non-executive director joined the board of a paragon of American industry, a long-serving colleague told him, in private, "New Directors shouldn't speak up during board meetings for the first year." That attitude is untenable today and, in fact, that board is much different now. But such comments are indicative of the culture of passivity that permeated the Dark Ages of corporate governance.... These boards perfunctorily performed a compliance role. Many directors served for the prestige and rarely spoke among themselves without the CEO present. They made sure to fulfil their explicit obligations, including attending the required board meetings and rubber-stamping resolutions proposed by management' (Charan 2005).

- Charan (2005) described liberated boards as: 'Most boards left their ceremonial status behind after the passage of Sarbanes-Oxley. A new generation CEO now expects boards to contribute. And candidates for directorship now expect active participation as a condition of their acceptance. There is a general sense of excitement as directors embrace an active mindset.'

- The transition to liberation had really begun about a decade earlier. In 1994, the General Motors board, advised by Ira Millstein, first published its 'Guidelines for Corporate Governance'. The document was widely praised as a model for corporate boards. *BusinessWeek* even called it a 'corporate Magna Carta', referring to the document signed in 1215 by King John that stipulated among other things, that no one, including the king, is above the law (Charan 2005).

- The comparison was fitting: 'GM's CEO and chair, Robert Stempel, stepped down late in 1992 after losing the confidence of GM's non-executive directors. When the non-executive directors named one of their own as chair, it signaled a distinct change in the general attitude of boards as passive bodies' (Charan 2005).

- The progressive board, according to Ram Charan, 'comply meticulously with the letter of the law, and they also embrace its spirit. Further; they aim, as Andy Grove, founder, former

CEO, and current chair of Intel, is quoted by *Fortune* magazine as having said, "to ensure that the success of the company is longer lasting than any CEO's reign, than any market opportunity, than any product cycle"' and 'Directors on a progressive board gel into a coherent and effective group. All directors contribute to a dialogue that has lively debates, sticks to key issues while dropping tangents, and leads to consensus and closure. They challenge each other directly, without breaking the harmony of the group and without going through the CEO. Directors find the give-and-take in board meetings energizing. They enjoy the intellectual exchange and they learn from each other' (Charan 2005).

- '1. A maximum term should be established for all directors. This should be ten years or age seventy, whichever comes first. (On the whole, I disagree. Continuity, experience, judgement, and wisdom, matter. A strong chairman terminates non-performers, regardless of age or length of service.)

  2. No board can have more than two insiders on it and preferably only one, the company's CEO. (A limit of two management members is fine. But a simple majority of independent directors, in relation to insiders, is sufficient.)

  3. The board chair and CEO should be two different persons. Failing that and as a minimum, a lead director must be appointed and given clear responsibilities in certain areas. (In my view, the separation of chair and CEO is much preferable to a lead director, But either is better than full role combination in one person.)' (Dimma 2006).

- 'Boards need to own up to their accountability for the performance of the corporate. In the past, employees, shareholders, and the press, looked to the CEO to ensure that the corporation performed well. Now they have also begun to look to you, the board, to be the leader. You need to own up to this accountability for the business' (Charan 2009).

- 'The role of the board has changed for ever, *"Governance", now means leadership*, not just over-the-shoulder monitoring and passive approvals. Boards must fiercely guard their companies against threats of rapid decline and sudden demise, while at the same time helping management seize the opportunities that tumultuous change presents but are hard to see in the daily fray of running the business. The board that does both turns governance into a competitive advantage' (Charan 2009).

Discussion Questions

1. Do you see any perceptible change in the way directors and boards viewed governance from the late 1980s up to the present? Explain with reasons.
2. Will the structural changes initiated by regulatory agencies encourage boards to transform their approach to governance?
3. Do you think that the responsibilities of the boards have considerably increased over a period of time? Do boards and directors appreciate this as a fact?

APPENDICES

- GRI Compliance Report of Jubilant Organosys Ltd
- EU Approach to Corporate Governance
- K.M. Birla Committee Report on Corporate Governance
- Narayana Murthy Committee Report on Corporate Governance

GRI COMPLIANCE REPORT OF JUBILANT ORGANOSYS LTD

At Jubilant, we believe that for long-term sustainability of business, the company needs to look at its performance in the social and environmental areas also along with the financial performance. The concept of sustainability in the company has been built on the foundation of:

- Corporate governance
- Environmental performance
- Social responsibilities
- Economic contributions to society

Jubilant has been publishing its sustainability report for the last five years covering the above issues. The above wholistic approach towards business has helped convincing its business partners on long-term sustainability of the company and the investing fraternity on the company being a reliable organization to invest in. It has also brought in many awards and recognitions to the company.

SUSTAINABILITY POLICY

Jubiliant Organosys Limited is an integrated pharmaceuticals industry player offering products and services to pharmaceuticals and life sciences industry. We are the country's leading CRAMS and API company, having business interests in pharmaceuticals and life science products, performance products and industrial products. We believe in sustainability of growth. Our approach to sustainable development focuses on the triple bottom lines of economics, environment, and people. As a business entity, we aim at improving stakeholder value through improved eco-efficient use of capital and natural resources.

The nature of our activities makes efficient utilisation of resources, environmental protection, operational and transportation safety, and employee's health, significant components for long-term sustainability of our business and we stand committed to these. Being responsible corporate citizens, we understand our role towards society. We encourage and practise open dialogue with all our stakeholders and value their esteemed opinion, reflecting them in our strategic plans. We also recognize that development and empowerment of our human resources are crucial to achieving our stated objectives. As in the past, we shall continue to adopt a structured approach for implementation of the policy and will regularly monitor the progress.

Shyam S. Bhartia
Chairman and Managing Director

Hari S. Bhartia
Co-Chairman and Managing Director

Corporate Sustainability Report

Jubilant Organosys Ltd has for the past three years prepared reports on its sustainability initiatives using the Global Reporting Initiative guidelines as the foundation.

The reports demonstrate how the Company meets its commitments and responsibilities. The reports attempt to present a balanced and reasonable presentation of our organization's economic, environmental, and social performance.

The Climate Change and Mitigation Policy is shown below.

CLIMATE CHANGE MITIGATION POLICY

Jubilant, committed to Sustainable Development, recognizes the risk of *Climate Change*. We shall initiate actions at all our manufacturing locations, R&D centres and offices to reduce carbon emission as a step towards climate change risk mitigation.

Our initiatives include:

o Creating awareness among employees, their families and community
o Continuous improvement for energy conservation measures
o Install energy efficient fixtures and metering systems in our buildings
o Reduce emission and promote renewable energy sources
o Optimize usage of all resources
o Use advancement of Information Technology to reduce travel related emission
o Plant trees for carbon sequestration
o Involve suppliers through Green Supply Chain Management to use energy efficient equipment

We shall endeavor to mitigate the impact of Climate Change by above initiatives.

Shyam Bang
Executive Director

5 June 2009

Environment, Occupational Health and Safety Policy

Jubilant Organosys Limited is an integrated pharmaceutical industry player, offering products and services to global life sciences industry through R&D, innovation, efficient manufacturing and cost leadership. The company's operations are diversified which also include industrial chemicals, performance polymers and fertilizers. Jubilant is committed to care for the environment and achieve high standards of occupational health and safety performance.

We shall achieve this by striving to:

➤ Comply with and go beyond relevant legislations and standards on environment, occupational health and safety.
➤ Prevent pollution and optimize utilization of resources through process improvements and R&D.
➤ Identify hazards at the design stage of the processes and services and build in appropriate measures for minimizing and controlling them.
➤ Ensure safe and healthy workplace by providing necessary systems and infrastructure.
➤ Promote awareness and learning amongst employees, suppliers, contractors and communities around our operation sites through training and communication.
➤ Monitor the performance in above areas for continual improvement.

The policy will be implemented, monitored and reviewed on regular basis. It shall be communicated to all employees and made available to the interested parties on request. This policy will be applicable to Jibilant Organosys Ltd, and its wholly owned subsidiaries in India.

Shyam Bang
Executive Director

June 5, 2008

Jubilant is a professionally managed company stressing on ethical and transparent governance. In the company's board of directors, 7 out of 12 members are independent directors.

The corporate governance principles of the company are:
- Caring for the environment which includes caring for the society around us.
- Enhancement of stakeholders value through pursuit of excellence, efficiency of operations, quest for growth, and continuous innovation.
- Transparency, promptness, and fairness in disclosures to any communication with all stakeholders including shareholders, government authorities, customers, suppliers, lenders, employees, and the community at large.
- Comply with laws in letter as well as in spirit.

Our vision is driven by our values, which are:
- teamwork to inspire confidence
- efficiency to create and provide best value to customers
- know-how to provide innovative solutions
- delivery to provide excellent quality of products and services

The highlights of Jubilant's Corporate Governance Regime are:
- Broad based and well-represented board with a fair representation of executive, non-executive, and independent directors with more than three-fourths of the board being non-promoters.
- Constitution of several committees, such as Audit Committee, Remuneration Committee, Investors Grievance Committee, etc. for more focused attention.
- Established codes of conduct for directors and senior management as also for other employees. Instituted whistle-blower policy and code of conduct for prevention of insider trading.
- Focus on hiring, retaining and nurturing best talent and to promote a culture of excellence across the organization. Exhaustive HRD policies cover succession planning, training and development, and employees' grievance handling.
- Organization wise 'velocity' initiatives taken, which include world-class improvement mythologies such as Six Sigma, Lean, and World Class manufacturing.
- Exhaustive and unique system of internal controls spanning over 1000 control points mentioned through especially designed software. The company has voluntarily completed the documentation required as per Sarbanes–Oxley Act.
- Robust risk management framework for identifying various risks, assessing their probability as well as likely impact and finalizing risk minimization plans.
- Regular communication with shareholders including through mailing of quarterly results along with chairman's message, e-mailing of quarterly results just after release to stock exchange, obtaining regular and also online feedback from shareholders.
- Comprehensive corporate sustainability management system focusing on triple bottom-line reporting on economic, environment, and social parameters as per global reporting initiatives standards with a stated policy on sustainability.

The corporate governance practices of the company are now being recognized by society. Jubilant was selected as one of the top 25 companies for Institute of Company Secretaries of India National Award for Excellence in Corporate Governance, 2006. Similarly, Institute of Directors selected the company as finalist in the Golden Peacock Award for Excellence in Corporate Governance, 2006.

Environment

At Jubilant we realise that we all share the same planet and are obligated to ensure that we use naturally available resources, responsibly, safely, and undertake conservation and preservation measures to ensure that we minimise the impact of our operations on the environment, employees, and surrounding communities.

The above goal is approached with in-depth identification of environmental issues involved in various activities of the company and their impact on the receiving environment. Environmental management has been integrated in the business and no investment in the company is approved till the proposal has been vetted from environmental angle and signed off by the Chief of Environment, Health, and Safety. Typically, environment management costs constitute 10 to 12 per cent of the total cost of the project.

During the operational phase, the environment management is established as a line function and the respective unit heads are responsible for meeting all environmental requirements at various locations, where company's manufacturing facilities are situated. Broadly speaking, environment management in the company encompasses the following:

Effluent Management

All new projects are approved only on the basis on zero discharge of effluent. For existing plants also, most of the facilities are in place to achieve zero discharge of effluent. Effluents are classified under the four heads:

- Biodegradable effluents—For which state-of-the-art two-stage activated sludge treatment followed by the polishing unit are installed. The treated effluents are recycled or used for horticulture purposes within the plant premises.
- Non-biodegradable effluents—These are normally concentrated in evaporators and while the concentrates are incinerated in captive incinerators, the condensates are recycled.
- Utility effluents—These are generally given physico-chemical treatment followed by reverse osmosis (RO). The permeate from the RO plants are recycled and the rejects are disposed off through the spray dryer attached to various incineration systems.
- Sewage—The company has provided both packaged as well as elaborate treatment plants based on activated sludge process at various plants and in its colonies. The treated effluents are normally used for horticulture purposes.

Thus, the company has built up facilities for effluent treatment across the board including physico-chemical treatment, biological treatment, evaporation, incineration, spry drying, and reverse osmosis. It has been proactively trying out new technologies. Setting up concentration and slop burning boiler systems for distillery effluent is the latest example in this direction.

Hazardous waste—Being a chemical and bulk drug industry, Jubilant has taken special care towards identification and management of hazardous wastes. The major plants at Gajraula and Nanjangud have captive incineration systems and secured land fills (SLF) to take care of the hazardous wastes generated from the processes. In fact, Jubilant is one of the few companies in India who have set up their own SLF with major capital investment as well as tough challenges of operational control. For management of Hazardous wastes at other major plants at Nira and Samlaya, the company has taken up membership of common TSDF available in the states.

Odour Management

This is another focus area of the company's environment management programme. Sources of odour in the industry are:

- Process equipment vents—The approach adopted is 'reduce, recovery, and treat'. Through in-house R&D, the process efficiencies are being continuously improved which automatically reduces waste generation including emissions. Recovery is done through use of condensers, chillers, etc. The residual and leftover emissions are treated by catalytic incineration and thermal oxidation.
- Storage tank vents—Vents of smaller storage tanks have been combined and passed through condensers for recovery or through scrubbers for control. For larger storage tanks with potential for higher VOC emissions, individual condenser systems are being installed.

- Fugitive emission—Efforts are continuously on to reduce fugitive emissions of VOCs causing odour problem by upgradation of equipment (pumps with double mechanical seals), regular auditing, and monitoring.
- Air pollution control.

In the area of air pollution control, requisite measures like cyclones, multiclones, bag filters, scrubbers, ESPs, etc. have been provided. While specifying the control equipment, the emission limits are kept lower than the national standards, for example 50 mg/Nm^3 in ESPs for coal fired boilers as against 150 mg/Nm^3.

The above approach of environment management is backed by systems and trained manpower to operate them. All facilities of the company are certified to ISO 14001. There are well-developed environment management groups both at Unit level and at Corporate level. There is a strong monitoring and review system–monthly, at the level of Chief of Manufacturing and Chief of Environment, Health and Safety and quarterly at director's level.

In the last 8–10 years, the company has taken major initiatives in improving its environmental performance by developing expertise, systems, and facilities. An investment of approx. Rs. 157 crores has been made on environmental management during this period.

Safety

The nature of processes and the chemicals/raw materials used in Jubilant plants makes safety an extremely important aspect of company's operations. The main objective of safety management in Jubilant is to protect the employees, assets, and the community around. Fire safety, process related safety, and chemical safety are the main aspects of hazards involved company's operations. Like environment management, safety is also a line function in Jubilant's plants. The approach adopted to handle various aspects of safety include:

- Identification of hazards and assessment of risk involved in various activities carried out at product development stage as well as on the manufacturing sites of the company.
- Comprehend and incorporate necessary safety measures at the design stage itself.
- Develop and implement effective systems such as work permits, mock drills, system of reporting incidents, identifying the root cause of the same and built-in preventive measures, etc.
- Fire being a major hazard in all its manufacturing locations, the company has developed elaborate fire fighting systems comprising alarm systems, manual call points, sprinkler systems, pressurized fire hydrant system, fire tenders, and well trained human resource to handle emergencies.
- Each of company's manufacturing sites has 'on site emergency' plans which are updated regularly, training imparted, mock drills organized to fine tune the emergency plans.
- Carrying out HAZOP/ HAZAN studies, developing safety data sheets, selection of suitable material of construction, developing standard operating procedures, carrying out hazardous area classification are some of the methods adopted to handle safety aspects of company's operations.
- Safety training are imparted to both employees as well as contract workers regularly.

Health

The company has fully equipped occupational health centres at two locations Gajraula and Nanjangud. The occupational health centres coordinate the following activities:

1. Medical examinations
   - Pre-employment
   - Periodic medical examination
   - Return to fitness
   - Separation medical examination
   - Contractual workers health examination
   - Food handlers check-up
2. Out-patient/family services—to the families and dependants of the employees
3. In-patient services—short-term admission facilities including IV administration and minor surgical procedure
4. Specialized services—gynaecology, cardiology, paediatrics, opthalmology, ENT, orthopaedics, physiotherapy
5. Immunization services and pulse polio services
6. Specialized investigations—pulmonary function test, audiometry, ECG
7. Industrial hygiene monitoring—noise monitoring, illumination monitoring
8. Trainings—first aid, CPR, diet counseling, ergonomics, hazard identification and risk assessment, hearing conservation program, sight conservation program
9. Lifestyle modification and yoga camps
10. Workplace program on HIV AIDS

The Occupational Health Centre focuses on prevention and health promotion. All employees as a part of their annual health check-ups get themselves examined. During the examination they are counseled on communicable and non-communicable disease control, balanced diet, healthy heart, and first aid. If any deviation is noticed in their medical records, specialist advice is sought and necessary treatment is given. An annual medical surveillance plan of such employees is maintained and they are followed up with necessary lifestyle modification measures.

At other locations, the health monitoring and counseling activities have been outsourced to selected medical agencies.

Corporate Social Responsibility

For variety of reasons, including incentives from the government, many industries are set up in India in economically backward and remote areas. Most of Jubilant's plants are also located in similar areas.

There are aspirations of the local community of gainful employment and general well-being in the area due to coming up of such industries.

While direct and indirect economic benefits do come through, the employment expectation cannot be always fulfilled in view of requirement of skilled manpower and generally non-availability of such skills in those areas. Moreover, the industry operates and uses local resources, which impact the population both positively, as well as sometime not so favorably. In view of the above, Jubilant always considered the surrounding community as an important group of stakeholders in its business and is committed to contribute towards improving their quality of life through various measures suiting local situations.

While there are many requirements in rural India, Jubilant decided to take a scientific approach of finding out the specific needs in the Gajraula area where its first plant came up in early 1980s. A reputed NGO, Development Alternatives, was retained way back in 1992 to carry out a need assessment study. The findings revealed urgent necessities of basic health care facilities in Gajraula area. Responding to this requirement, Jubilant set up a community health care centre namely Sarvajanik Medical Centre (SMC) at Gajraula in association with the Birla Trust. Later, it added two mobile dispensaries also to its medical services for the community. Together, these facilities cater to about 40 villages in the area with OPD services to almost 13,000 people in a year. The services provided include general health care, a DOTs Centre for diagnosis and treatment of TB, mother-child health care as well as day care facilities. The company also provides similar services in association with JSS medical college at Kalahalli village adjacent to its Nanjangud facilities. Specialists from the Hospital attend medical OPD services in the village. Subsidised in-patient treatment for the referred cases is also organized at the JSS hospital in Mysore, about 20 km from Kalahalli.

Apart from the above, company organizes various types of medical camps in association with different agencies and hospitals at all its locations. It also organizes veterinary camps for cattle whenever such needs are felt or requested by the villagers.

The company has also been active in creating awareness for prevention of HIV/AIDS. It has signed a memorandum of understanding (MoU) with the International Labour Organisation (ILO) for prevention and management of HIV at work place for its employees. It also works through various NGOs for its HIV/AIDS awareness programmes for contract workers, employee's families, nearby industries, and surrounding community. The company is now planning to go for the second stage of HIV/AIDS treatment and care by proposing to open an integrated counseling and testing centre (ICTC) at SMC, Gajraula, in association with the UP State AIDS Control Society.

The company recently initiated project MUSKAN for improving the quality of education in primary schools in rural areas adjacent to its manufacturing plants. This is brought about by active involvement of community including teachers and parents, which makes the effort a sustainable model. The community, teachers, and parents are engaged intensively by the company's development team through various schemes to motivate them to get involved in creating better learning atmosphere in the village school. The pilot scheme with the Government Upper Primary School at Sultander about 7 km from Gajraula plant has been highly successful and the district authorities have requested Jubilant to take up six more schools in the area under the Muskan project. The company has initiated activities in these schools in the current year. Other community activities of the company relate to income generation programme through creation of self-help groups organizing various training programmes to bring awareness about different government schemes, which the community can take advantage of to improve their lot. Training is on various aspects of agriculture to improve yield for the local farmers, contributing to improving infrastructural facilities in the local areas, etc.

The company also has several policies in the social area and partners with large number of national and international government and non-government agencies to implement its social agenda.

JUBILANT ORGANOSYS LTD
Corporate Sustainability Report 2008–09

All social interventions of the Company are now carried out through Jubilant Bhartia Foundation, a not-for-profit organisation created for the purpose.

One, precious fossil fuels are saved as the cement kiln uses the calorific value of the organic waste and secondly the waste is utilized properly. In the social arena, the Company has identified the following three areas for intervention to bring in long term impacts in the communities in areas where Company's manufacturing facilities are located in India:

1. Providing vocational training for the youth in the neighbourhood to enhance their employment opportunities.
2. Supporting primary education at the rural level, which is the bed block that would help build the future generation in the country.
3. Providing basic health care aimed at 'mother and child'. As committed last year, the Company has started Jubilant Bhartia Foundation, a not-for-profit Company to carry out social work. The focus areas of work are healthcare, primary education, and livelihood generation as mentioned above. These programmes target the rural population of the country with the aim of contributing to building a better nation. Last year, the Company had set a few targets to be implemented during this year. Progress on the same is as under: The recovery of ammonia from the raffinate was increased in the production of pyridine. The increased recovery of ammonia resulted in reduced consumption of ammonia, thereby conserving the raw material. Several initiatives have been taken to conserve energy in different forms through process improvements. The details of some of these initiatives are given in the report. Water conservation has been a major focus area for the Company. Reverse osmosis plants have been put up to treat waste water and recycle the treated water. Rain water harvesting has been implemented at Gajraula and is under implementation at Nira. As planned, the Company set up an integrated counselling and testing centre at Gajraula to strengthen its activities related to HIV/AIDS. A mobile dispensary has been started at Nanjangud to provide basic healthcare services in villages around the manufacturing location. The mobile dispensary has helped increase the coverage area beyond one village as healthcare services are now provided to three villages in the Nanjangud area. At Nira, the Company is continuing to provide services through the existing dispensary. As there are already many doctors in the neighbouring area, the Company decided against starting a mobile dispensary service at Nira.

- The success of pilot model Muskaan in Gajraula for supporting primary school education in rural areas encouraged the Company to implement the same in other schools. As committed, 12 more schools were adopted, not only at Gajraula, but at all major manufacturing locations. The Company is now working in 15 schools across the locations.
- To complement the Company's programme to support government primary schools, the Company had planned to initiate a school health programme 'Nirog Bachpan'. As a first step, the Company has started the activity in seven schools at Gajraula, which are also covered under the Muskaan project.
- The Company has launched a project for greening of supply chain. The initiative aims at creating awareness and improving the environmental performance of the business partners.

The Company would continue its focus on sustainability despite global challenges. Jubilant is committed to serve society at large through its products and services while maintaining harmony with the environment. As always, the Company has received support from its stakeholders and expects their continued cooperation to contribute to the cause of sustainable development. The report has been prepared in-house and feedback from all stakeholders will enable the Company to improve the report in future, both in terms of coverage and quality of information provided.

Best wishes and regards,

Shyam S. Bhartia   Hari S. Bhartia
Chairman and Managing Director   Co-Chairman and Managing Director

This corporate sustainability report is for Jubilant Organosys Limited for the year 2008–2009.

- Jubilant Organosys Ltd is an integrated pharmaceuticals industry player, one of the largest custom research and manufacturing services and drug discovery and development services companies in India.
- The Company has a presence across the pharmaceuticals value chain through a wide range of products and services such as proprietary products, exclusive synthesis, active pharmaceutical ingredients, contract manufacturing of sterile injectables (liquids and lyophilized) product, non-steriles (ointments, creams, and liquid) and radiopharmaceuticals, drug discovery services, medicinal chemistry services, clinical research services, generic dosage forms, and healthcare.
- Jubilant Organosys has geographically diversified manufacturing facilities at ten locations worldwide. Together, these help Jubilant cater to 150 customers across more than 50 countries around the world. The business is organized in two distinct segments—pharmaceuticals and life sciences products and services and industrial and performance products. Each business segment has independent growth units that cater to industries like pharmaceuticals, biotechnology, agrochemicals, construction, textiles, paper and packaging, and food and beverages. The Company has its corporate office at Noida (UP), India and the contact address is:

Jubilant Organosys Limited 1–A, Sector 16 A,
Noida-201301, Uttar Pradesh, India
Phone: +91-120-2516601-11
Fax: +91-120-2516628-30
email: support@jubl.com

Jubilant currently has manufacturing units in three different countries, which are specifically relevant to sustainability issues. Other than India the Company has presence in:

United States of America
Hollister-Stier Laboratories
LLC., Spokane, Washington

Cadista Pharmaceuticals Inc.,
Maryland
Canada

Draxis Specialty
Pharmaceuticals Inc.,
Montreal, Quebec

EU APPROACH TO CORPORATE GOVERNANCE

FOREWORD

Promoting the private sector as an engine of growth, reducing the vulnerability of developing and transition economies to financial crises, and providing incentives for corporations to invest and perform efficiently in a socially responsible manner—these are key priorities for the World Bank Group.

Strengthening corporate governance is essential in achieving these priorities because it creates the necessary climate for investment and economic development. Sound corporate governance practices inspire investor and lender confidence, spur both domestic and foreign investment, and improve corporate competitiveness.

Towards that end, the Global Corporate Governance Forum (the Forum) sponsors regional and local initiatives that address the corporate governance weaknesses of middle- and low-income countries in the context of broader national or regional economic reform programs. The Forum focuses on raising awareness, building consensus, sponsoring research, disseminating best practices, and rendering support and guidance for technical assistance and capacity-building of institutions leading corporate governance reforms.

In fulfillment of our mission, we are proud to sponsor this paper on the EU Approach to Corporate Governance. We believe this paper will be particularly useful for countries in the region developing corporate governance codes or in the process of revising such codes with the purpose of setting internationally recognized standards and practices of good corporate governance.

The European Union (EU) has achieved a great deal in terms of addressing disclosure, shareholder protection, and board structures and responsibilities since the adoption of its Action Plan for Modernizing European Company Law and Enhancing Corporate Governance in the EU (2003). Yet, candidate and potential candidate countries are not always conversant with EU corporate governance requirements and recommendations.

To facilitate access to current European best practices, this paper provides a brief review of the EU approach to corporate governance including recent developments. Its objective is to build understanding and awareness of the EU corporate governance directives, regulations, best practices, and guidelines and to help candidate and potential candidate countries better access relevant EU information. Beyond EU accession, it is important for countries of the Southeast European region to better comply with EU corporate governance standards to improve trade with EU partners, attract EU investors, and compete with EU companies.

We are grateful to the EU Commission (Company Law, Corporate Governance and Financial Crime, DG Internal Market and Services) for their support and for reviewing the content and accuracy of this paper.

We would like to especially thank Ken Rushton, former Director of Listings at the UK Financial Services Authority, for providing the first draft of this paper, the Forum's Marie-Laurence Guy and Desislava Radeva for their valuable input, and Marci Schneider for editing the document.

Philip Armstrong
Head: Global Corporate Governance Forum

This paper highlights EU corporate governance essentials that EU candidate and potential candidate countries, as well as countries seeking to increase trade with EU members or attract investors from the EU, should take into account when developing their own corporate governance code and reviewing their corporate governance framework.

BACKGROUND

The background to the current debate in the European Union (EU) on corporate governance begins with the report from the High Level Group of Company Law Experts in 2002. This report focused on corporate governance and the modernization of company law. Action Plan on Modernizing Company Law and Enhancing Corporate Governance in the EU (2003).

Moving forward, the European Commission issued in May 2003 a communication titled, 'Modernizing Company Law and Enhancing Corporate Governance in the European Union—A Plan to Move Forward.' This communication outlined the reasons why both company law and corporate governance needed to be updated: the impact of recent financial scandals; the trend of European countries to engage in cross-border operations in the internal market; the integration of European capital markets; the rapid development of new information and communication technologies; and, the increase of member states to the European Union.

Company Law and Corporate Governance

Harmonization of the rules relating to company law and corporate governance, as well as to accounting and auditing, is essential for creating a Single Market for Financial Services and products. In the fields of company law and corporate governance, objectives include: providing equivalent Company Law and Enhancing Corporate Governance protection for shareholders and other parties concerned with companies; ensuring freedom of establishment for companies throughout the EU; fostering efficiency and competitiveness of business; promoting cross-border cooperation between companies in different Member States; and stimulating discussions between Member States on the modernization of company law and corporate governance.

– EUROPEAN COMMISSION, DG Internal Market

At the time, EU Internal Market Commissioner Frits Bolkestein said, 'Company law and corporate governance are right at the heart of the political agenda, on both sides of the Atlantic. That's because economies only work if companies are run efficiently and transparently. We have seen vividly what happens if they are not: investment and jobs will be lost; and in the worst cases, of which there are too many, shareholders, employees, creditors, and the public are ripped off. Prompt action is needed to ensure sustainable public confidence in financial markets. The Action Plan provides a clear and considered framework combining new law where necessary with other solutions. It will help deliver the integrated and modern company law and corporate governance framework which businesses, markets and the public are calling for.'

'The Commission is shouldering its responsibilities: Corporate Europe must shape up and do the same. Working in partnership, we have a unique opportunity to strengthen European corporate governance and to be a model for the rest of the world.'

Other corporate governance initiatives proposed in the action plan cover: achieving better information on the role played by institutional investors in corporate governance; addressing the principle of proportionality between capital and control; offering to listed companies the choice between the one-tier and two-tier board structures; and, enhancing directors' responsibilities for financial and key nonfinancial statements.

The 2006 review of the Action Plan has prioritized the strengthening of shareholders' rights, but acknowledges that there was a growing sense of regulatory fatigue and the need to pause and allow both businesses and investors more time to digest recent legislation.

In 2007, the Commission published two reports that reviewed how well member states had implemented the recommendations on independent directors and directors' remuneration. The reports find that all member states have issued corporate governance codes and most codes apply on a comply-or-explain basis. However, the reports identify certain areas where the recommendations' principles have not been adequately followed.

The Action Plan's Initial Objectives

- Introduction of an annual corporate governance statement. Listed companies should be required to include in their annual documents a coherent, descriptive statement covering the key elements of their corporate governance structures and practices.
- Development of a legislative framework aiming at helping shareholders to exercise various rights (for example asking questions, tabling resolutions, voting in absentia, participating in general meeting via electronic means). These facilities should be offered to shareholders across the EU, and specific problems relating to cross-border voting should be solved urgently.
- Adoption of a recommendation aimed at promoting the role of (independent) non-executive or supervisory directors. Minimum standards on the creation, composition, and role of the nomination, remuneration, and audit committees should be defined at the EU level and enforced by member states at least on a 'comply or explain' basis.
- Adoption of a recommendation on directors' remuneration. Member states should be rapidly invited to put in place an appropriate regulatory regime, giving shareholders more transparency and influence, which includes detailed disclosures of individual remuneration.
- Creation of a European Governance Forum to help encourage coordination and convergence of national codes and of the way they are enforced and monitored.

Codes of Best Practice

With respect to corporate governance, the Commission in 2002 published a comparative study of the main codes produced by member states. This study concluded that the EU should not attempt to develop a pan-European code but rather consider 'a certain coordination' of corporate governance codes to encourage further convergence. Convergence should focus both on reducing barriers to cross-border voting by shareholders, and on barriers to information that affect shareholders' ability to evaluate the governance of companies. On 22 February, 2006, the European Union Corporate Governance Forum (EUCG Forum) strongly endorsed the view that national corporate governance codes should be implemented under the comply-or-explain principle.

But the EUCG Forum stressed the need for this principle to be underpinned by regulation and enforced by shareholders. It pointed out the need for companies to provide meaningful explanations for non-compliance. The 2006 Directive, amending the Fourth and Seventh Accounting Directives, requires that listed companies publish an annual corporate governance statement which refers to the corporate governance code that is applied by the company and explain whether, and to what extent, the company complies with that code.

BOARD OF DIRECTORS

Recommendation on the Role of Non-executive/Supervisory Directors and Supervisory Board Committees (2004)

The Commission formally invited member states, through a commission recommendation, to reinforce the presence and role of independent non-executive directors on listed companies' boards. Protecting shareholders, employees, and the public against potential conflicts of interest through an independent check on management decisions, constituted an important move to restore confidence in financial markets after a number of high-profile scandals. The non-binding recommendation concentrates on the role of non-executive or supervisory directors in key areas where executive or managing directors may have conflicts of interest. It includes minimum standards for the qualifications, commitment, and independence of non-executive or supervisory directors.

The main principles in the recommendation are:

- Boards should comprise a balance of executive and non-executive directors, so no individual or group of individuals can dominate decision making.
- The chairman and CEO roles should be separate and the CEO should not immediately become chairman of either a unitary or a supervisory board.
- Nomination, remuneration, and audit committees should be set up and they should make recommendations to the board. The board can delegate decision-making powers to these committees but the board itself must remain fully responsible for its decisions.
- The board should carry out an annual evaluation of its performance, including the competence and effectiveness of each board member and of the board committees.
- The board should report annually on its internal organization, procedures, and on its self-evaluation.
- The board should ensure shareholders are kept informed on the affairs of the company, its strategy, and on how risks and conflicts of interest are managed.
- The board should determine the knowledge, judgement, and experience required on the board. The audit committee, collectively, should have recent and relevant experience of finance and accounting.
- All new directors should receive an orientation program. A skills assessment should be made each year with updates recommended accordingly.
- Each director should devote sufficient time and limit the number of their other commitments.
- A list of criteria for determining the independence of a director was established. However, it is the board that should determine this issue and justify its conclusion in its disclosures.
- Detailed guidance is provided on the composition, role, and operation of board committees. The nomination committee should be comprised mainly of independent non-executive directors; the remuneration and audit committees should be comprised exclusively of non-executive directors with a majority being independent.

Board Director Criteria

- Cannot be an executive or managing director of company or have been in such a position within last five years.
- Cannot be an employee of company, or have been within last three years, unless legally elected as a worker director representative.
- Cannot receive significant additional remuneration to his non-executive director's fee, meaning no share options or other performance-related pay.
- Cannot be or represent controlling shareholder.
- Cannot have, or have had in the past year, a significant business relationship with a company, such as being a supplier or customer.
- Cannot be, or have been within last three years, an employee of auditor of company.
- Cannot have significant links with executive directors of company through involvement in other companies or bodies.
- Cannot have served on board of company for more than 3 terms (or more than 12 years).
- Cannot be a close family member of an executive or managing director of the company.

Recommendation on the Remuneration of Directors (2005)

Remuneration is one of the main areas of potential conflicts of interest for executive directors. This and the fact that excessive remuneration has emerged as a prominent feature in many corporate fraud scandals has led the Commission to adopt a recommendation on directors' remuneration. It recommends that member states should ensure that listed companies disclose their policy on directors' remuneration and tell shareholders how much individual directors are earning and in what form. Furthermore, listed companies should ensure that shareholders are given adequate control over these matters and share-based remuneration schemes. The Commission's 2004 Recommendations on directors' remuneration provides that:

- Each listed company should publish an annual statement of its remuneration policy and post it to its website.
- The statement should cover contract terms for executive directors, particularly notice periods and termination payments (if any).
- The remuneration policy should be voted on by shareholders. This vote may either be mandatory or advisory.
- The total remuneration and benefits granted to individual directors should be disclosed in the annual accounts or the remuneration report.
- Incentive share-based schemes for directors, such as share options, should be subject to prior shareholder approval.

EU Recommendations: 2007 Review on Implementation

The European Commission published two reports on member states' application of EU recommendations on company director's pay and independence. Both reports conclude that the application of corporate governance standards has improved, but some weaknesses remain.

The report on directors' remuneration shows that transparency standards are widely followed, but in some member states, it is still not recommended that shareholders vote on this issue.

The report on the role of independent directors finds that there is real progress in improving performance standards in this field, but some of the recommended standards have not been followed in all member states. For example, in some member states, a former chief executive officer of a company, can still become its chairman without any 'cooling off' period. This undermines the independence of non-executive supervision. Also, some member states do not recommend a sufficient number of independent board members in remuneration and audit committees.

The remuneration policy statement

- Explanation of importance of fixed and variable components of directors' remuneration
- Information on performance criteria for share incentives or variable components of remuneration
- Linkage between remuneration and performance
- Parameters and rationale for annual bonus and other non-cash schemes
- Description of supplementary pension or early retirement schemes for directors

Disclosure of individual directors' remuneration

- Total salary including any attendance fees
- Remuneration received from any company belonging to the same group
- Profit-sharing and/or other bonus payments
- Additional remuneration for special services outside normal functions
- Compensation paid to any former director paid in the same financial year
- Total value of non-cash benefits considered as being remuneration

As regards to share incentive payments or share options

- Number of share options offered or shares granted in the year
- Number of options exercised and exercise prices or value of interest in share incentive scheme at end of year
- Number of options unexercised at end of year, exercise prices, exercise dates and main conditions for exercise

As regards to directors' supplementary pension schemes

- Benefit schemes defined: changes in accrued benefits during the year
- Contribution schemes defined: contributions paid or payable by the company during the year

DISCLOSURE

Directive on Company Law, Accounting and Auditing Rules (2007)

A new directive on the statutory audit of annual and consolidated accounts was adopted in 2006 and must be implemented by June 2008. The new directive clarifies the duties of auditors and provides for their oversight, independence, and adherence to ethical standards. From a corporate governance perspective, a key provision is Article 41, which requires 'public interest entities' (essentially listed companies, credit institutions, and insurance companies) to have audit committees. Member states can determine how these committees should be comprised in terms of non-executive directors and how they are appointed. However, at least one member must be independent and be competent in accounting and/or auditing.

In certain public-interest entities, the audit committee functions can be performed by the entire board. If the chairman is an executive board member, he must not chair the audit committee. The audit committee's functions include reviewing: the financial reporting process; the effectiveness of internal control, internal audit (where applicable), and risk management systems; the audit of the accounts; and the independence of the auditor.

The Commission hopes that the amendments to the 4th and 7th Company Law Directives, which have to be transposed into national laws by 2008, will result in the needed improvements.

Fourth and Seventh Accounting Directives Amended (2006)

This 2006 Directive is designed to enhance confidence in financial statements and annual reports. Most of its provisions are related to accounting. However, there is a requirement for listed companies to publish a discrete corporate governance statement either in their annual report or separately, and for board members to be collectively responsible for the annual accounts and reports. The company will also have to: describe the main features of its internal control and risk management systems in relation to financial reporting; provide information on the composition and operation or the board; and, determine the procedures of shareholders' meetings and how shareholders' rights are to be exercised. These provisions must be implemented by September 2008.

The Transparency Directive (2005)

The Transparency Directive replaces and updates parts of the existing EU legislation (the Consolidated Admissions and Reporting Directive). The directive on transparency obligations of listed companies is designed to improve the quality of information available to investors on companies' performance, their financial position, and changes in major shareholdings.

The directive establishes minimum requirements on:

- Periodic financial reporting: The directive aims to ensure that the financial information provided by listed companies is standardized and provided frequently and quickly. A key part of this strategy is the requirement that an issuer of shares must issue either quarterly reports or an interim management statement that, broadly:
- gives a general description of its financial position and performance during the relevant period; and
- explains material events and transactions and their impact on the financial position.
- Disclosure of major shareholdings for issuers whose securities are admitted to trading on a regulated market in the EU. The notification requirement is triggered when the size of holdings reach, exceed, or move below certain thresholds stated in the directive (5%, 10%, 15%, 20%, 25%, 30%, 50%, and 75%). The shareholder will be required to inform the issuer, who, in turn, will inform the market.

The directive also deals with the mechanisms through which this information is to be stored and disseminated. The Directive came into force on 20 January 2005 and member states were due to write this measure into law by 20 January 2007. The directive is a minimum harmonization directive. It allows member states to impose more severe requirements on 'home' issuers, but does not allow member states to impose more severe requirements on issuers admitted to trading on a regulated market within the 'host' member state's territory, or on investors in relation to their major shareholding disclosure notification requirements.

Possible Implementation of the Directive at Member State Level

The new Transparency Directive requirements may increase the liability of a listed company and its directors and auditors for the accuracy of the company's financial reports.

The UK Financial Supervision Authority suggests that listed companies may be able to use 'Responsibility Statements': The persons responsible within the listed company—usually the directors—will be required to state publicly that:

To the best of their knowledge, the annual financial statements are prepared in accordance with the applicable set of accounting standards, and give a true and fair view of the company's consolidated assets, liabilities, financial position, and profit or loss;

The annual management report includes a fair review of the development and performance of the business and the company's position, with a description of the principal risks and uncertainties that it faces;

The half-year management report includes a fair review of the important events that have occurred in the first six months of the financial year and their impact on the financial statements, with a description of the principal risks and uncertainties for the remaining six months (there are additional requirements relating to related parties' transactions).

SHAREHOLDER RIGHTS

Directive on Takeover Bids (2004)

This directive was scheduled to be implemented by all Member States by 20 May 2006. Eddy Wymeersch, the chairman of the Committee for European Securities Regulators, welcomed the directive: 'It has achieved a very welcome harmonization of the securities regulatory provisions, especially by introducing a rather strict home rule regime along with mutual recognition, and leveling the conditions for bids (irrevocability, disclosure, equal treatment) although regretfully many concepts remain undefined (equitable price, concert action, etc.).'

The purpose of the Takeover Bids Directive is to create a favorable regulatory environment for takeovers and to boost corporate restructuring within the EU. The directive also increases the protection of minority shareholders. However, since the final directive was the result of a difficult compromise, some provisions related to the use of defensive measures by companies remain ambiguous.

The key minimum standards introduced by this directive include

- All shareholders of the same class must receive equal treatment;
- The target company's shareholders must have sufficient time and information to decide whether to accept an offer;
- The target company's board must give shareholders guidance on the bid's effects on the company;
- The board of the offer or company must act in the interest of the company as a whole and must not deny the holders of securities the opportunity to decide on the merits of the bid;
- False markets must not be created in the securities of the offer or company;
- The bidder may only make an offer if he is sure that he can pay the price; and
- The takeover process should not unreasonably hinder the target company's business.

Directive on the Exercise of Shareholders' Rights (2007)

To improve cross-border voting practices, a directive was adopted on the exercise of voting rights by shareholders across the EU in 2007. This directive has to be implemented by September 2009.

Under its provisions, minimum standards have been introduced to ensure that shareholders of companies, whose shares are traded on a regulated market, have timely access to relevant information in advance of general meetings and have the means to vote from a distance. In addition, there are provisions enabling shareholders to ask questions, place items on the general meeting agenda, and table resolutions.

The directive also abolishes a practice referred to as share blocking. This required shareholders to deposit shares at a designated institution for a certain period in advance of general meetings essentially blocking the shares from trading.

Key provisions of this directive include

- Minimum notice period of 21 days for most general meetings, which can be reduced to 14 days where shareholders can vote by electronic means and the general meeting agrees to the shortened convocation period;
- Internet publication of the convocation and of the documents to be submitted to the general meeting at least 21 days before it convenes;
- Abolition of share blocking and introduction of a record date in all Member States which may not be more than 30 days before the general meeting;
- Abolition of obstacles on electronic participation to the general meeting, including electronic voting;
- Right to ask questions and the company's obligation to answer questions;
- Abolition of existing constraints on the eligibility of people to act as proxy holder and of excessive formal requirements for the appointment of the proxy holder; and
- Disclosure of the voting results on the issuer's Internet site.

One-Share, One-Vote: Dropped

In 2006, a review of the action plan showed support for addressing the one-share, one-vote proposal through a Recommendation rather than by a directive. This review was conducted against the backdrop of the Commission's policy of 'Better Regulation', which sought to cut red tape for businesses and eliminate outdated requirements.

On October 3, 2007, in the follow-up to the public consultation held in 2006 on future priorities in EU company law Commissioner McCreevy introduced, in front of the European Parliament's Legal Committee, the DG Internal Market's new agenda for the forthcoming years. On the basis of the results of a study and the Commission's impact assessment on the matter, McCreevy announced that he did not envisage to propose any initiative on one-share, one-vote. The study showed that there is no sound causal link between the one-share, one-vote principle and the economic performance of companies. However, some evidence does exist to show that investors perceive these mechanisms negatively, requiring more transparency prior to making their investment decisions. As lots of EU measures had recently been introduced to increase transparency on disproportionate control structures, the Commissioner argued that it was necessary to wait and see what would be the effects of these measures before taking any further step.

The fact that there will be 'no action' on the issue of one-share, one-vote was also influenced by strong lobbying from large EU corporations and the general fear of hedge funds in Member States, as well as the appearance of sovereign wealth funds.

> **Further Recommendations in the Pipeline**
>
> In May 2007, the Commission launched a consultation on the need for further measures to supplement the recently adopted Directive on Shareholders' Rights. Initial feedback suggests that the following issues could be addressed through a recommendation (rather than another directive):
>
> - For depository receipts, should these be prohibited from voting without instructions given by the holder unless the holder has expressly given the depository such discretion?
> - Should stock-lending be addressed at the EU level? Pertaining to this issue, the Commission has indicated possible recommendations such as requiring that parties be informed about provisions of stock-lending agreements affecting voting rights attached to transferred, or lent, shares. The usual effect would be that the borrower has the right to vote.
> - Shares might only be lent by intermediaries where the investor has agreed to such lending.
> - Borrowed shares might not be voted except where the voting rights are exercised on instructions from the lender. Although stock-lending can be used to manipulate voting, this is not usually the main reason for borrowing stock. Arguably the onus should be on the lender to recall borrowed shares for voting purposes. Active investors are more likely to recall stock and vote as part of their ownership responsibilities.
> - Stock-lending agreements might require borrowers to return equivalent shares to those borrowed promptly when requested.

SETTING EU CORPORATE GOVERNANCE STANDARDS

Basic Glossary

The key players

The European Commission The European Commission(EC) is essentially the European Union's executive branch and has the sole right of legislative initiative. It is independent of national governments and represents the European (as opposed to individual member state) perspective. The Commission proposes legislation to the EU Parliament and the Council of the European Union. Proposed legislation must defend the interests of the Union and its citizens, not those of specific countries or industries. The Commission also seeks the opinions of national parliaments and governments. To get the technical details right, the Commission consults experts through its various committees and groups.

The European Parliament Since 1979, the European Parliament (EP) has been directly elected by the EU citizens under a system of population-based proportional representation, with each member serving a five-year term. The EP passes European laws—jointly with the Council of the EU in many policy areas. The EP can veto legislation in specific policy areas. The European Parliament has the power of 'co-decision' with the Council of the European Union, a power granted in 1993 and expanded in 1999. Parliament does not merely give its opinion in this procedure—it shares legislative power equally with the Council of the EU. The co-decision procedure requires the two bodies to agree on identical text before a proposal becomes law. If the Council and Parliament cannot agree, a special Conciliation Committee is formed. Even if the committee agrees to a joint text, the Parliament may still reject the proposed act by a majority vote of its members.

The European Council The Council is the EU main decision-making body and represents the member states. The Council adopts European laws—jointly with the European Parliament in many policy areas. The European Council comprises heads of states and/or governments and gives political impetus in the process of the construction of the EU.

Consultative Bodies in the field of Corporate Governance   The Commission has established two permanent consultative bodies to assist the development of corporate governance and company law policies. In addition, the Commission consults widely on individual proposals for legislation. The first standing body is the European Corporate Governance Forum.

The European Corporate Governance Forum was established in 2004 by the Commission 'to enhance the convergence of national codes of corporate governance and provide strategic advice to the Commission on policy issues in the field of corporate governance.' The Forum is comprised of 15 non-governmental experts including regulators, issuers, investors, market practitioners and academics. Commissioner Charlie McCreevy initially expected the Forum to identify priorities for convergence. Yet, more than focusing on convergence, the EU CG Forum developed and shared best practices on corporate governance. The Forum's early work produced papers on the functioning of boards including internal control, comply-or-explain, and barriers to the exercise of shareholder rights. In respect of internal control, the EU CG Forum stated that it saw no need to follow the United States' example of introducing a legal obligation for boards to certify the effectiveness of internal control.

Advisory Group on Corporate Governance and Company Law   In 2005, the Commission established a second consultative body, to provide detailed technical advice on preparing corporate governance and company law measures. Like the EU CG Forum, this advisory group comprises non-governmental experts with various professional backgrounds. The advisory group is consulted by the Commission on initiatives and its technical work is complementary to the more strategic role of the EU CG Forum. The group has tended to focus on company law measures.

The key outputs

Green Paper   A green paper is a discussion document released by the European Commission intended to stimulate debate and launch a process of consultation, at European level, on a particular topic. A green paper usually presents a range of ideas and is meant to invite interested individuals or organizations to contribute views and information. It may be followed by a white paper recommendation, an official set of proposals or lead to a new directive.

Position Papers   Position papers are views and information presented to the Commission in response to a consultation process.

Recommendation   A non-binding act of the EU which explains current EU policy and recommends further member state actions. Since differing approaches to corporate governance are deeply rooted in national traditions, particular care has been taken to provide for maximum flexibility in the ways member states can apply the principles in the recommendation. The recommendation takes account of efforts already made in member states and aims by identifying best practices to foster convergence on these issues in the EU. The Commission closely monitors the application of its recommendations to identify whether additional measures may be desirable in the medium term.

Regulation   An act of the Council or joint-act of the Council and the Parliament which has direct and general application in member states. The Commission may also issue regulations limited to certain sectors. The Commission considers regulations only when it believes an EU-level remedy is necessary for a problem that cannot be solved by national or local governments.

The EU Co-Decision Process

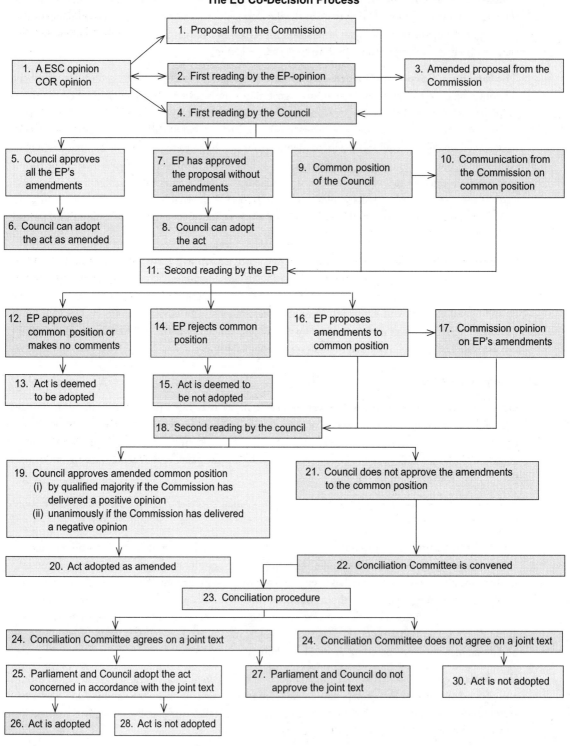

Source: EU Commission – February 2008, http://ec.europa.eu/codecision/stepbystep/diagram_en.htm.

Directive   The most common type of EU legislation, not directly applicable, but may have direct effect; binding upon Member States as to the objectives to be achieved but leaving to the member states the choice of form and method; preferred means of harmonization of laws; usually enacted by the Commission.

Decisions are binding in their entirety upon those to whom they are addressed—member states, companies, or persons.

The EU Legislative Co-decision Making Process

In the field of corporate governance most common type of legislation are directives, which provide the objectives to be achieved but allow member states to chose the form and method of achieving those objectives. Dealing with a growing sense of regulatory fatigue in member states, the Commission has been advancing a substantial part of the corporate governance agenda through non-legislative methods—mainly recommendations. The following chart explains the EU legislative co-decision making process which applies to regulations and directives.

REFERENCES

All Directives can be found on:

http://ec.europa.eu/internal_market/company/index-en.htm

January 2002   Comparative Study of Corporate Governance Codes by Holly Gregory, Weil, Gotshal & Manges

http://europa.eu.int/comm/internal_market/en/company/company/news/corp-gov-codes-rpt_en.htm

May 2003   Action Plan on Modernizing Company Law and Enhancing Corporate Governance in the EUCOM (2003) 284 final

http://europa.eu.int/comm/internal_market/en/company/company/modern/index.htm

December 2004   Recommendation on the remuneration of directors and July 2007 report on its application by Member States

http://ec.europa.eu/internal_market/company/directors-remun/index_en.htm

Transparency Directive 2004/109/EC

February 2005   Recommendation on the role of non-executive or supervisory directors and February 2007 report on its application by Member States

http://ec.europa.eu/internal_market/company/independence/index_en.htm

October 2005   Communication of the Commission: A strategy for the simplification of the regulatory environment

http://ec.europa.eu/enterprise/regulation/better_regulation/simplification.htm

July 2006   Report on consultations for future priorities for Action Plan

http://ec.europa.eu/internal_market/company/docs/consultation/final_report_en.pdf

Amendments to 4th and 7th Company Law Directives 2006/46/EC

Directive on statutory audit of annual and consolidated accounts 2006/43/EC

Directive on the exercise of shareholder rights 2007/36/EC

European Corporate Governance Forum

http://ec.europa.eu/internal_market/company/ecgforum/index_en.htm

http://ec.europa.eu/internal_market/company/directors-remun/index_en.htm

http://ec.europa.eu/internal_market/company/independence/index_en.htm

Global Corporate   **International**
Governance   **Finance**
Forum   **Corporation**

OUR MISSION

Established in 1999, the Global Corporate Governance Forum is an IFC multi-donor trust fund facility located in the Corporate Governance and Capital Markets Advisory Department. Through its activities, the Forum aims to promote the private sector as an engine of growth, reduce the vulnerability of developing and transition economies to financial crises, and provide incentives to corporations to invest and perform efficiently in a socially responsible manner.

The Forum sponsors regional and local initiatives that address the corporate governance weaknesses of middle- and low-income countries in the context of broader national or regional economic reform.

OUR FOCUS

- Raising awareness, building consensus
- Disseminating best practices
- Sponsoring research
- Funding technical assistance and capacity-building

OUR DONORS

- Canada
- France
- Luxembourg
- The Netherlands
- Norway
- Sweden
- Switzerland
- International Finance Corporation

OUR FOUNDERS

- World Bank
- Organiszation for Economic Co-operation and Development

Global Corporate Governance Forum | 2121 Pennsylvania Avenue, NW | Washington, DC 20433 USA
Telephone: +1 (202) 458 1857 | Facsimile: +1 (202) 522 7588 | cgsecretariat@ifc.org | www.gcgf.org

K.M. BIRLA COMMITTEE REPORT ON CORPORATE GOVERNANCE

PREFACE

1.1 It is almost a truism that the adequacy and the quality of corporate governance shape the growth and the future of any capital market and economy. The concept of corporate governance has been attracting public attention for quite some time in India. The topic is no longer confined to the halls of academia and is increasingly finding acceptance for its relevance and underlying importance in the industry and capital markets. Progressive firms in India have voluntarily put in place systems of good corporate governance. Internationally also, while this topic has been accepted for a long time, the financial crisis in emerging markets has led to renewed discussions and inevitably focussed them on the lack of corporate as well as governmental oversight. The same applies to recent high-profile financial reporting failures even among firms in the developed economies. Focus on corporate governance and related issues is an inevitable outcome of a process, which leads firms to increasingly shift to financial markets as the pre-eminent source for capital. In the process, more and more people are recognizing that corporate governance is indispensable to effective market discipline. This growing consensus is both an enlightened and a realistic view. In an age where capital flows worldwide, just as quickly as information, a company that does not promote a culture of strong, independent oversight, risks its very stability and future health. As a result, the link between a company's management, directors, and its financial reporting system has never been more crucial. As the boards provide stewardship of companies, they play a significant role in their efficient functioning.

1.2 Studies of firms in India and abroad have shown that markets and investors take notice of well-managed companies, respond positively to them, and reward such companies with higher valuations. A common feature of such companies is that they have systems in place, which allow sufficient freedom to the boards and management to take decisions towards the progress of their companies and to innovate, while remaining within a framework of effective accountability. In other words they have a system of good corporate governance.

1.3 Strong corporate governance is thus indispensable to resilient and vibrant capital markets and is an important instrument of investor protection. It is the blood that fills the veins of transparent corporate disclosure and high-quality accounting practices. It is the muscle that moves a viable and accessible financial reporting structure. Without financial reporting premised on sound, honest numbers, capital markets will collapse upon themselves.

1.4 Another important aspect of corporate governance relates to issues of insider trading. It is important that insiders do not use their position of knowledge and access to inside information about the company, and take unfair advantage of the resulting information asymmetry. To prevent this from happening, corporates are expected to disseminate the material price sensitive information in a timely and proper manner and also ensure that till such information is made public, insiders abstain from transacting in the securities of the company. The principle should be 'disclose or desist'. This therefore calls for companies to devise an internal procedure for adequate and timely disclosures, reporting requirements, confidentiality norms, code of conduct, and specific rules for the conduct of its directors and employees, and other insiders. For example, in many countries, there are rules for reporting of transactions by directors and other senior executives of companies, as well as for a report on their holdings, activity in their own shares and net year-to-year changes to these in the annual report. The rules also cover the dealing in the securities of their companies by the insiders, especially directors and other senior executives, during sensitive reporting seasons. However, the need for such procedures, reporting requirements, and rules also goes beyond corporates to other entities in the financial markets such as stock exchanges, intermediaries, financial institutions, mutual funds, and concerned professionals who may have access to inside information. This is being dealt with in a comprehensive manner, by a separate group appointed by SEBI, under the chairmanship of Shri Kumar Mangalam Birla.

1.5 The issue of corporate governance involves besides shareholders, all other stakeholders. The Committee's recommendations have looked at corporate governance from the point of view of the stakeholders and in particular that of the shareholders and investors, because they are the raison de etre for corporate governance and also the prime constituency of SEBI. The control and reporting functions of boards, the roles of the various committees of the board, the role of management, all assume special significance when viewed from this perspective. The other way of looking at corporate governance is from the contribution that good corporate governance makes to the efficiency of a business enterprise, to the creation of wealth, and to the country's economy. In a sense both these points of view are related and during the discussions at the meetings of the Committee, there was a clear convergence of both points of view.

1.6 At the heart of the Committee's report is the set of recommendations which distinguishes the responsibilities and obligations of the boards and the management in instituting the systems for good corporate governance and emphasises the rights of shareholders in demanding corporate governance. Many of the recommendations are mandatory. For reasons stated in the report, these recommendations are expected to be enforced on the listed companies for initial and continuing disclosures in a phased manner within specified dates, through the listing agreement. The companies will also be required to disclose separately in their annual reports, a report on corporate governance delineating the steps they have taken to comply with the recommendations of the Committee. This will enable shareholders to know, where the companies, in which they have invested, stand with respect to specific initiatives taken to ensure robust corporate governance. The implementation will be phased. Certain categories of companies will be required to comply with the mandatory recommendations of the report during the financial year 2000–2001, but not later than 31 March 2001, and others during the financial years 2001–2002 and 2002–2003. For the non-mandatory recommendations, the Committee hopes that companies would voluntarily implement these. It has been recommended that SEBI may write to the appropriate regulatory bodies and governmental authorities to incorporate where necessary, the recommendations in their respective regulatory or control framework.

1.7 The Committee recognised that India had in place a basic system of corporate governance and that SEBI has already taken a number of initiatives towards raising the existing standards. The Committee also recognised that the Confederation of Indian Industry had published a code entitled 'Desirable Code of Corporate Governance' and was encouraged to note that some of the forward looking companies have already reviewed or are in the process of reviewing their board structures and have also reported in their 1998–99 annual reports the extent to which they have complied with the Code. The Committee however felt that under Indian conditions a statutory rather than a voluntary code would be far more purposive and meaningful, at least in respect of essential features of corporate governance.

1.8 The Committee however recognized that a system of control should not so hamstring the companies so as to impede their ability to compete in the market place. The Committee believes that the recommendations made in this report mark an important step forward and if accepted and followed by the industry, they would raise the standards in corporate governance, strengthen the unitary board system, significantly increase its effectiveness, and ultimately serve the objective of maximizing shareholder value.

THE CONSTITUTION OF THE COMMITTEE AND THE SETTING FOR THE REPORT

2.1 There are some Indian companies, which have voluntarily established high standards of corporate governance, but there are many more, whose practices are a matter of concern. There is also an increasing concern about standards of financial reporting and accountability, especially after losses suffered by investors and lenders in the recent past, which could have been avoided, with better and more transparent reporting practices. Investors have suffered on account of unscrupulous management of the companies, which have raised capital from the market at high valuations and have performed much worse than the past reported figures, leave alone the future projections at the time of raising money. Another example of bad governance has been the allotment of promoter's shares, on preferential basis at preferential prices, disproportionate to market valuation of shares, leading to further dilution of wealth of minority shareholders. This practice has however since been contained.

2.2 There are also many companies, which are not paying adequate attention to the basic procedures for shareholders' service; for example, many of these companies do not pay adequate attention to redress investors' grievances such as delay in transfer of shares, delay in despatch of share certificates and dividend warrants and non-receipt of dividend warrants; companies also do not pay sufficient attention to timely dissemination of information to investors as also to the quality of such information. SEBI has been regularly receiving large number of investor complaints on these matters. While enough laws exist to take care of many of these investor grievances, the implementation and inadequacy of penal provisions have left a lot to be desired.

2.3 Corporate governance is considered an important instrument of investor protection, and it is therefore a priority on SEBI's agenda. To further improve the level of corporate governance, need was felt for a comprehensive approach at this stage of development of the capital market, to accelerate the adoption of globally acceptable practices of corporate governance. This would ensure that the Indian investors are in no way less informed and protected as compared to their counterparts in the best-developed capital markets and economies of the world.

2.4 Securities market regulators in almost all developed and emerging markets have for sometime been concerned about the importance of the subject and of the need to raise the standards of corporate governance. The financial crisis in the Asian markets in the recent past have highlighted the need for improved level of corporate governance and the lack of it in certain countries have been mentioned as one of the causes of the crisis. Indeed corporate governance has been a widely discussed topic at the recent meetings of the International Organisation of Securities Commissions (IOSCO). Besides in an environment in which emerging markets increasingly compete for global capital, it is evident that global capital will flow to markets which are better regulated and observe higher standards of transparency, efficiency, and integrity. Raising standards of corporate governance is therefore also extremely relevant in this context.

2.5 In the above mentioned context, the Securities and Exchange Board of India (SEBI) appointed the Committee on Corporate Governance on May 7, 1999 under the chairmanship of Shri Kumar Mangalam Birla, member SEBI Board, to promote and raise the standards of corporate governance. The Committee's membership is given in Annexure 1 and the detailed terms of the reference are as follows:

(a) to suggest suitable amendments to the listing agreement executed by the stock exchanges with the companies and any other measures to improve the standards of corporate governance in the listed companies, in areas such as continuous disclosure of material information, both financial and non-financial, manner and frequency of such disclosures, responsibilities of independent and outside directors;

(b) to draft a code of corporate best practices; and

(c) to suggest safeguards to be instituted within the companies to deal with insider information and insider trading.

2.6 A number of reports and codes on the subject have already been published internationally—notable among them are the report of the Cadbury Committee, the report of the Greenbury Committee, the Combined Code of the London Stock Exchange, the OECD Code on Corporate Governance, and The Blue Ribbon Committee on Corporate Governance in the US. In India, the CII has published a Code of Corporate Governance. In preparing this report, while the Committee drew upon these documents to the extent appropriate, the primary objective of the Committee was to view corporate governance from the perspective of the investors and shareholders and to prepare a code to suit the Indian corporate environment, as corporate governance frameworks are not exportable. The Committee also took note of the various steps already taken by SEBI for strengthening corporate governance, some of which are:

- strengthening of disclosure norms for initial public offers following the recommendations of the Committee set up by SEBI under the chairmanship of Shri Y. H. Malegam;
- providing information in directors' reports for utilisation of funds and variation between projected and actual use of funds according to the requirements of the Companies Act; inclusion of cash flow and funds flow statement in annual reports;
- declaration of quarterly results;
- mandatory appointment of compliance officer for monitoring the share transfer process and ensuring compliance with various rules and regulations;
- timely disclosure of material and price sensitive information including details of all material events having a bearing on the performance of the company;
- despatch of one copy of complete balance sheet to every household and abridged balance sheet to all shareholders;
- issue of guidelines for preferential allotment at market related prices; and
- issue of regulations providing for a fair and transparent framework for takeovers and substantial acquisitions.

2.7 The Committee has identified the three key constituents of corporate governance as the shareholders, the board of directors, and the management and has attempted to identify in respect of each of these constituents, their roles and responsibilities as also their rights in the context of good corporate governance. Fundamental to this examination and permeating throughout this exercise is the recognition of the three key aspects of corporate governance, namely; accountability, transparency, and equality of treatment for all stakeholders.

2.8 The pivotal role in any system of corporate governance is performed by the board of directors. It is accountable to the stakeholders and directs and controls the management. It stewards the company, sets its strategic aim and financial goals, and oversees their implementation, puts in place adequate internal controls, and periodically reports the activities and progress of the company in the company in a transparent manner to the stakeholders. The shareholders' role in corporate governance is to appoint the directors and the auditors and to hold the board accountable for the proper governance of the company by requiring the board to provide them periodically with the requisite information in a transparent fashion of the activities and progress of the company. The responsibility of the management is to undertake the management of the company in terms of the direction provided by the board, to put in place adequate control systems and to ensure their operation, and to provide information to the board on a timely basis and in a transparent manner to enable the board to monitor the accountability of management to it.

2.9 Crucial to good corporate governance are the existence and enforceability of regulations relating to insider information and insider trading. These matters are being currently examined separately by a group appointed by SEBI under the chairmanship of Shri Kumar Mangalam Birla.

2.10 Adequate financial reporting and disclosure are the corner stones of good corporate governance. These demand the existence and implementation of proper accounting standards and disclosure requirements. A separate committee appointed by SEBI under the chairmanship of Shri Y. H. Malegam (who is also a member of this Committee) is examining these issues on a continuing basis. This Committee has advised that while in most areas, accounting standards in India are comparable with international accounting standards both in terms of coverage and content, there are a few areas where additional standards need to be introduced in India on an urgent basis. These matters are discussed in greater detail in para 12.1 of this report.

2.11 The Committee's draft report was made public through the media and also put on the web site of SEBI for comments. The report was also sent to the Chambers of Commerce, financial institutions, stock exchanges, investor associations, the Association of Merchant Bankers of India, Association of Mutual Funds of India, The Institute of Chartered Accountants of India, Institute of Company Secretaries of India, academicians, experts and eminent personalities in the Indian capital market, foreign investors. A copy of the draft report was also sent to Sir Adrian Cadbury who had chaired the Cadbury Committee on corporate governance set up by the London Stock Exchange, the Financial Reporting Council, and the accountancy bodies in the UK in 1991.

2.12 The committee has received comments from most of the above groups. Besides, Sir Adrian Cadbury, and several eminent persons in the Indian capital market, have sent detailed comments on the draft report. Separately, the Committee held meetings with the representatives of the Chambers of Commerce, Chairmen of the Financial Institutions, stock exchanges, investor associations. Thus, the Committee had the benefit of the views of almost all concerned entities that have a role in corporate governance. The Committee has taken into account the views and comments of these respondents in this final report.

2.13 The Committee puts on record its appreciation of the valuable inputs and painstaking efforts of Shri Anup Srivastava, Vice-President Corporate Strategy and Business Development of the Aditya Birla Group, Shri P.K. Bindlish, Division Chief, SEBI, Shri Umesh Kumar, and other officers of the SMDRP department of SEBI, in the preparation of this report.

THE RECOMMENDATIONS OF THE COMMITTEE

3.1 This report is the first formal and comprehensive attempt to evolve a code of corporate governance, in the context of prevailing conditions of governance in Indian companies, as well as the state of capital markets. While making the recommendations the Committee has been mindful that any code of Corporate Governance must be dynamic, evolving and should change with changing context and times. It would therefore be necessary that this code also is reviewed from time to time, keeping pace with the changing expectations of the investors, shareholders, and other stakeholders and with increasing sophistication achieved in capital markets.

CORPORATE GOVERNANCE—THE OBJECTIVE

4.1 Corporate governance has several claimants—shareholders and other stakeholders—which include suppliers, customers, creditors, the bankers, the employees of the company, the government, and society at large. This report on corporate governance has been prepared by the Committee for SEBI, keeping in view primarily the interests of a particular class of stakeholders, namely, the shareholders, who together with the investors form the principal constituency of SEBI while not ignoring the needs of other stakeholders.

4.2 The Committee therefore agreed that the fundamental objective of corporate governance is the 'enhancement of shareholder value, keeping in view the interests of other stakeholder'. This definition harmonises the need for a company to strike a balance at all times between the need to enhance shareholders' wealth whilst not in any way being detrimental to the interests of the other stakeholders in the company.

4.3 In the opinion of the Committee, the imperative for corporate governance lies not merely in drafting a code of corporate governance, but in practising it. Even now, some companies are following exemplary practices, without the existence of formal guidelines on this subject. Structures and rules are important because they provide a framework, which will encourage and enforce good governance; but alone, these cannot raise the standards of corporate governance. What counts is the way in which these are put to use. The Committee is thus of the firm view, that the best results would be achieved when the companies begin to treat the code not as a mere structure, but as a way of life.

4.4 It follows that the real onus of achieving the desired level of corporate governance, lies in the proactive initiatives taken by the companies themselves and not in the external measures like breadth and depth of a code or stringency of enforcement of norms. The extent of discipline, transparency and fairness, and the willingness shown by the companies themselves in implementing the Code, will be the crucial factor in achieving the desired confidence of shareholders and other stakeholders and fulfilling the goals of the company.

APPLICABILITY OF THE RECOMMENDATIONS
Mandatory and Non-mandatory Recommendations

5.1 The Committee debated the question of voluntary versus mandatory compliance of its recommendations. The Committee was of the firm view that mandatory compliance of the recommendations at least in respect of the essential recommendations would be most appropriate in the Indian context for the present. The Committee also noted that in most of the countries where standards of corporate governance are high, the stock exchanges have enforced some form of compliance through their listing agreements.

5.2 The Committee felt that some of the recommendations are absolutely essential for the framework of corporate governance and virtually form its core, while others could be considered as desirable. Besides, some of the recommendations may also need change of statute, such as the Companies Act, for their enforcement. In the case of others, enforcement would be possible by amending the Securities Contracts (Regulation) Rules, 1957 and by amending the listing agreement of the stock exchanges under the direction of SEBI. The latter, would be less time consuming and would ensure speedier implementation of corporate governance. The Committee therefore felt that the recommendations should be divided into mandatory and non-mandatory categories and those recommendations which are absolutely essential for corporate governance, can be defined with precision and which can be enforced through the amendment of the listing agreement could be classified as mandatory. Others, which are either desirable or which may require change of laws, may, for the time being, be classified as non-mandatory.

Applicability

5.3 The Committee is of the opinion that the recommendations should be made applicable to the listed companies, their directors, management, employees, and professionals associated with such companies, in accordance with the time table proposed in the schedule given later in this section. Compliance with the code should be both in letter and spirit and should always be in a manner that gives precedence to substance over form. The ultimate responsibility for putting the recommendations into practice lies directly with the board of directors and the management of the company.

5.4 The recommendations will apply to all the listed private and public sector companies, in accordance with the schedule of implementation. As for listed entities, which are not companies, but body corporates (eg private and public sector banks, financial institutions, insurance companies, etc) incorporated under other statutes, the recommendations will apply to the extent that they do not violate their respective statutes, and guidelines or directives issued by the relevant regulatory authorities.

Schedule of Implementation

5.5 The Committee recognises that compliance with the recommendations would involve restructuring the existing boards of companies. It also recognises that some companies, especially the smaller ones, may have difficulty in immediately complying with these conditions.

5.6 The Committee recommends that while the recommendations should be applicable to all the listed companies or entities, there is a need for phasing out the implementation as follows:

- By all entities seeking listing for the first time, at the time of listing
- Within financial year 2000–2001, but not later than 31 March 2001 by all entities, which are included either in Group 'A' of the BSE or in S&P CNX Nifty index as on January 1, 2000. However to comply with the recommendations, these companies may have to begin the process of implementation as early as possible. These companies would cover more than 80% of the market capitalization.
- Within financial year 2001–2002, but not later than 31 March 2002 by all the entities which are presently listed, with paid-up share capital of Rs. 10 crore and above, or net worth of Rs. 25 crore or more any time in the history of the company

- Within financial year 2002–2003, but not later than 31 March 2003 by all the entities which are presently listed, with paid-up share capital of Rs. 3 crore and above
- This is a mandatory recommendation.

BOARD OF DIRECTORS

6.1 The board of a company provides leadership and strategic guidance, objective judgement independent of management to the company, and exercises control over the company, while remaining at all times accountable to the shareholders. The measure of the board is not simply whether it fulfils its legal requirements but more importantly, the board's attitude and the manner it translates its awareness and understanding of its responsibilities. An effective corporate governance system is one, which allows the board to perform these dual functions efficiently. The board of directors of a company thus directs and controls the management of a company and is accountable to the shareholders.

6.2 The board *directs* the company, by formulating and reviewing company's policies, strategies, major plans of action, risk policy, annual budgets, and business plans; setting performance objectives, monitoring implementation, and corporate performance; and overseeing major capital expenditures, acquisitions and divestitures, change in financial control and compliance with applicable laws, taking into account the interests of stakeholders. It *controls* the company and its management by laying down the *code of conduct*; overseeing the process of disclosure and communications, ensuring that appropriate systems for financial control and reporting, and monitoring risk are in place; evaluating the performance of management, chief executive, executive directors; and providing checks and balances to reduce potential conflict between the specific interests of management and the wider interests of the company and shareholders including misuse of corporate assets and abuse in related party transactions. It is *accountable* to the shareholders for creating, protecting and enhancing wealth and resources for the company, and reporting to them on the performance in a timely and transparent manner. However, it is not involved in day-to-day management of the company, which is the responsibility of the management.

Composition of the Board of Directors

6.3 The Committee is of the view that the composition of the board of directors is critical to the independent functioning of the board. There is a significant body of literature on corporate governance, which has guided the composition, structure, and responsibilities of the board. The Committee took note of this while framing its recommendations on the structure and composition of the board.

6.4 The composition of the board is important in as much as it determines the ability of the board to collectively provide the leadership and ensures that no one individual or a group is able to dominate the board. The executive directors (like director-finance, director-personnel) are involved in the day-to-day management of the companies; the non-executive directors bring external and wider perspective and independence to the decision making. Till recently, it has been the practice of most of the companies in India to fill the board with representatives of the promoters of the company, and independent directors if chosen were also handpicked thereby ceasing to be independent. This has undergone a change and increasingly the boards comprise of following groups of directors—promoter director, (promoters being defined by the erstwhile Malegam Committee), executive and non-executive directors, a part of whom are independent. A conscious distinction has been made by the Committee between two classes of non-executive directors, namely, those who are independent and those who are not.

Independent Directors and the Definition of Independence

6.5 Among the non-executive directors are independent directors, who have a key role in the entire mosaic of corporate governance. The Committee was of the view that it was important that independence be suitably, correctly, and pragmatically defined, so that the definition itself does not become a constraint in the choice of independent directors on the boards of companies. The definition should bring out what in the view of the Committee is the touchstone of independence, and which should be sufficiently broad and flexible. It was agreed that 'material pecuniary relationship which affects independence of a director' should be the litmus test of independence and the board of the company would exercise sufficient degree of maturity when left to itself, to determine whether a director is independent or not. The Committee therefore agreed on the following definition of 'independence'. Independent directors are directors who apart from receiving director's remuneration do not have any other material pecuniary relationship or transactions with the company, its promoters, its management or its subsidiaries, which in the judgement of the board may affect their independence of judgement. Further, all pecuniary relationships or transactions of the non-executive directors should be disclosed in the annual report.

6.6 The Blue Riband Committee of the USA and other Committee reports have laid considerable stress on the role of independent directors. The law however does not make any distinction between the different categories of directors and all directors are equally and collectively responsible in law for the board's actions and decisions. The Committee is of the view that the non-executive directors, i.e. those who are independent and those who are not, help bring an independent judgement to bear on board's deliberations especially on issues of strategy, performance, management of conflicts and standards of conduct. The Committee therefore lays emphasis on the calibre of the non-executive directors, especially of the independent directors.

6.7 Good corporate governance dictates that the board be comprised of individuals with certain personal characteristics and core competencies such as recognition of the importance of the board's tasks, integrity, a sense of accountability, track record of achievements, and the ability to ask tough questions. Besides, having financial literacy, experience, leadership qualities, and the ability to think strategically, the directors must show significant degree of commitment to the company and devote adequate time for meeting, preparation, and attendance. The Committee is also of the view that it is important that adequate compensation package be given to the non-executive independent directors so that these positions become sufficiently financially attractive to attract talent and that the non-executive directors are sufficiently compensated for undertaking this work.

6.8 Independence of the board is critical to ensuring that the board fulfils its oversight role objectively and holds the management accountable to the shareholders. The Committee has, therefore, suggested the above definition of independence, and the following structure and composition of the board and of the committees of the board.

6.9 The Committee recommends that the board of a company have an optimum combination of executive and non-executive directors with not less than fifty per cent of the board comprising the non-executive directors. The number of independent directors (independence being as defined in the foregoing paragraph) would depend on the nature of the chairman of the board. In case a company has a non-executive chairman, at least one-third of board should comprise of independent directors and in case a company has an executive chairman, at least half of board should be independent.

   This is a mandatory recommendation.

6.10 The tenure of office of the directors will be as prescribed in the Companies Act.

NOMINEE DIRECTORS

7.1 Besides the above categories of directors, there is another set of directors in Indian companies who are the nominees of the financial or investment institutions to safeguard their interest. The nominees of the institutions are often chosen from among the present or retired employees of the institutions or from outside. In the context of corporate governance, there could be arguments both for and against the continuation of this practice.

7.2 There are arguments both for and against the institution of nominee directors. Those who favour this practice argue that nominee directors are needed to protect the interest of the institutions who are custodians of public funds and who have high exposures in the projects of the companies both in the form of equity and loans. On the other hand those who oppose this practice, while conceding that financial institutions have played a significant role in the industrial development of the country as a sole purveyor of long-term credit, argue that there is an inherent conflict when institutions through their nominees participate in board decisions and in their role as shareholders demand accountability from the board. They also argue that there is a further conflict because the institutions are often major players in the stock market in respect of the shares of the companies on which they have nominees.

7.3 The Committee recognises the merit in both points of view. Clearly when companies are well managed and performing well, the need for protection of institutional interest is much less than when companies are badly managed or under-performing. The Committee would therefore recommend that institutions should appoint nominees on the boards of companies only on a selective basis where such appointment is pursuant to a right under loan agreements or where such appointment is considered necessary to protect the interest of the institution.

7.4 The Committee also recommends that when a nominee of the institutions is appointed as a director of the company, he should have the same responsibility, be subject to the same discipline, and be accountable to the shareholders in the same manner as any other director of the company. In particular, if he reports to any department of the institutions on the affairs of the company, the institution should ensure that there exist Chinese walls between such department and other departments which may be dealing in the shares of the company in the stock market.

CHAIRMAN OF THE BOARD

8.1 The Committee believes that the role of chairman is to ensure that the board meetings are conducted in a manner which secures the effective participation of all directors, executive and non-executive alike, and encourages all to make an effective contribution, maintain a balance of power in the board, make certain that all directors receive adequate information, well in time and that the executive directors look beyond their executive duties and accept full share of the responsibilities of governance. The Committee is of the view that the chairman's role should in principle be different from that of the chief executive, though the same individual may perform both roles.

8.2 Given the importance of Chairman's role, the Committee recommends that a non-executive chairman should be entitled to maintain a Chairman's office at the company's expense and also allowed reimbursement of expenses incurred in performance of his duties. This will enable him to discharge the responsibilities effectively.

This is a non-mandatory recommendation.

AUDIT COMMITTEE

9.1 There are few words more reassuring to the investors and shareholders than accountability. A system of good corporate governance promotes relationships of accountability between the principal actors of sound financial reporting–the board, the management, and the auditor. It holds the management accountable to the board and the board accountable to the shareholders. The audit committee's role flows directly from the board's oversight function. It acts as a catalyst for effective financial reporting.

9.2 The Committee is of the view that the need for having an audit committee grows from the recognition of the audit committee's position in the larger mosaic of the governance process, as it relates to the oversight of financial reporting.

9.3 A proper and well-functioning system exists therefore, when the three main groups responsible for financial reporting—the board, the internal auditor, and the outside auditors—form the three-legged stool that supports responsible financial disclosure and active and participatory oversight. The audit committee has an important role to play in this process, since the audit committee is a sub-group of the full board and hence the monitor of the process. Certainly, it is not the role of the audit committee to prepare financial statements or engage in the myriad of decisions relating to the preparation of those statements. The committee's job is clearly one of oversight and monitoring and in carrying out this job it relies on senior financial management and the outside auditors. However it is important to ensure that the boards function efficiently for if the boards are dysfunctional, the audit committees will do no better. The Committee believes that the progressive standards of governance applicable to the full board should also be applicable to the audit committee.

9.4 The Committee therefore recommends that a qualified and independent audit committee should be set up by the board of a company. This would go a long way in enhancing the credibility of the financial disclosures of a company and promoting transparency.

This is a mandatory recommendation.

9.5 The following recommendations of the Committee, regarding the constitution, functions, and procedures of audit committee would have to be viewed in the above context. But just as there is no 'one size fits all' for the board when it comes to corporate governance, same is true for audit committees. The Committee can thus only lay down some broad parameters, within which each audit committee has to evolve its own guidelines.

Composition

9.6 The composition of the audit committee is based on the fundamental premise of independence and expertise.

The Committee therefore recommends that

- the audit committee should have minimum three members, all being non-executive directors, with the majority being independent, and with at least one director having financial and accounting knowledge;

- the chairman of the committee should be an independent director;
- the chairman should be present at annual general meeting to answer shareholder queries;
- the audit committee should invite such of the executives, as it considers appropriate (and particularly the head of the finance function) to be present at the meetings of the Committee but on occasions it may also meet without the presence of any executives of the company. Finance director and head of internal audit and when required, a representative of the external auditor should be present as invitees for the meetings of the audit committee;
- the company secretary should act as the secretary to the committee.

These are mandatory recommendations.

Frequency of Meetings and Quorum

9.7 The Committee recommends that to begin with the audit committee should meet at least thrice a year. One meeting must be held before finalisation of annual accounts and one necessarily every six months.

   This is a mandatory recommendation.

9.8 The quorum should be either two members or one-third of the members of the audit committee, whichever is higher and there should be a minimum of two independent directors.

   This is a mandatory recommendation.

Powers of the Audit Committee

9.9 Being a committee of the board, the audit committee derives its powers from the authorisation of the board. The Committee recommends that such powers should include powers:

- To investigate any activity within its terms of reference
- To seek information from any employee
- To obtain outside legal or other professional advice
- To secure attendance of outsiders with relevant expertise, if it considers necessary.
- This is a mandatory recommendation.

Functions of the Audit Committee

9.10 As the audit committee acts as the bridge between the board, the statutory auditors, and internal auditors, the Committee recommends that its role should include the following:

- Oversight of the company's financial reporting process and the disclosure of its financial information to ensure that the financial statement is correct, sufficient, and credible
- Recommending the appointment and removal of external auditor, fixation of audit fee, and also approval for payment for any other services
- Reviewing with management the annual financial statements before submission to the board, focussing primarily on:
  » Any changes in accounting policies and practices
  » Major accounting entries based on exercise of judgement by management
  » Qualifications in draft audit report
  » Significant adjustments arising out of audit
  » The going concern assumption

>> Compliance with accounting standards

>> Compliance with stock exchange and legal requirements concerning financial statements

>> Any related party transactions, ie transactions of the company of material nature, with promoters or the management, their subsidiaries or relatives, etc that may have potential conflict with the interests of company at large.

- Reviewing with the management, external and internal auditors, the adequacy of internal control systems

- Reviewing the adequacy of internal audit function, including the structure of the internal audit department, staffing and seniority of the official heading the department, reporting structure, coverage, and frequency of internal audit

- Discussion with internal auditors of any significant findings and follow-up thereon

- Reviewing the findings of any internal investigations by the internal auditors into matters where there is suspected fraud or irregularity or a failure of internal control systems of a material nature and reporting the matter to the board

- Discussion with external auditors before the audit commences, of the nature and scope of audit. Also post-audit discussion to ascertain any area of concern

- Reviewing the company's financial and risk management policies

- Looking into the reasons for substantial defaults in the payments to the depositors, debenture holders, share holders (in case of non-payment of declared dividends), and creditors

This is a mandatory recommendation.

REMUNERATION COMMITTEE OF THE BOARD

10.1 The Committee was of the view that a company must have a credible and transparent policy in determining and accounting for the remuneration of the directors. The policy should avoid potential conflicts of interest between the shareholders, the directors, and the management. The overriding principle in respect of directors' remuneration is that of openness and shareholders are entitled to a full and clear statement of benefits available to the directors.

10.2 For this purpose the Committee recommends that the board should set up a remuneration committee to determine on their behalf and on behalf of the shareholders with agreed terms of reference, the company's policy on specific remuneration packages for executive directors including pension rights and any compensation payment.

This is a non-mandatory recommendation.

10.3 The Committee however recognised that the remuneration package should be good enough to attract, retain, and motivate the executive directors of the quality required, but not more than necessary for the purpose. The remuneration committee should be in a position to bring about objectivity in determining the remuneration package while striking a balance between the interest of the company and the shareholders.

Composition, Quorum, etc of the Remuneration Committee

10.4 The Committee recommends that to avoid conflicts of interest, the remuneration committee, which would determine the remuneration packages of the executive directors should comprise of at least three directors, all of whom should be non-executive directors, the chairman of committee being an independent director.

10.5 The Committee deliberated on the quorum for the meeting and was of the view that remuneration is mostly fixed annually or after specified periods. It would not be necessary for the committee to meet very often. The Committee was of the view that it should not be difficult to arrange for a date to suit the convenience of all the members of the committee. The Committee therefore recommends that all the members of the remuneration committee should be present at the meeting.

10.6 The Committee also recommends that the chairman of the remuneration committee should be present at the Annual General Meeting, to answer the shareholder queries. However, it would be up to the chairman to decide who should answer the queries.

All the above recommendations in paragraphs 10.4 to 10.6 are non-mandatory.

10.7 The Committee recommends that the board of directors should decide the remuneration of non-executive directors.

This is a mandatory recommendation.

Disclosures of Remuneration Package

10.8 It is important for the shareholders to be informed of the remuneration of the directors of the company. The Committee therefore recommends that the following disclosures should be made in the section on corporate governance of the annual report:

- All elements of remuneration package of all the directors, ie salary, benefits, bonuses, stock options, pension, etc.
- Details of fixed component and performance linked incentives, along with the performance criteria.
- Service contracts, notice period, severance fees.
- Stock option details, if any–and whether issued at a discount as well as the period over which accrued and over which exercisable.

This is a mandatory recommendation.

BOARD PROCEDURES

11.1 The measure of the board is buttressed by the structures and procedures of the board. The various committees of the board recommended in this report would enable the board to have an appropriate structure to assist it in the discharge of its responsibilities. These need to be supplemented by certain basic procedural requirements in terms of frequency of meetings, the availability of timely information, sufficient period of notice for the board meeting as well as circulation of agenda items well in advance, and more importantly, the commitment of the members of the board.

11.2 The Committee therefore recommends that board meetings should be held at least four times in a year, with a maximum time gap of four months between any two meetings. The minimum information as given in Annexure 2 should be available to the board.

This is a mandatory recommendation.

The Committee further recommends that to ensure that the members of the board give due importance and commitment to the meetings of the board and its committees, there should be a ceiling on the maximum number of committees across all companies in which a director could be a member or act as Chairman. The Committee recommends that a director should not be a member in more than 10 committees or act as chairman of more than five committees across all companies in which he is a director. Furthermore it should be a mandatory annual requirement for every director to inform the company about the committee positions he occupies in other companies and notify changes as and when they take place.

This is a mandatory recommendation.

ACCOUNTING STANDARDS AND FINANCIAL REPORTING

12.1 Over time the financial reporting and accounting standards in India have been upgraded. This however is an ongoing process and we have to move speedily towards the adoption of international standards. This is particularly important from the angle of corporate governance. The Committee took note of the discussions of the SEBI Committee on Accounting Standards referred to earlier and makes the following recommendations:

- Consolidation of Accounts of subsidiaries
  The companies should be required to give consolidated accounts in respect of all its subsidiaries in which they hold 51 per cent or more of the share capital. The Committee was informed that SEBI was already in dialogue with the Institute of Chartered Accountants of India to bring about the changes in the Accounting Standard on consolidated financial statements. The Institute of Chartered Accountants of India should be requested to issue the Accounting Standards for consolidation expeditiously.

- Segment reporting where a company has multiple lines of business
  Equally in cases of companies with several businesses, it is important that financial reporting in respect of each product segment should be available to shareholders and the market to obtain a complete financial picture of the company. The Committee was informed that SEBI was already in dialogue with the Institute of Chartered Accountants of India to introduce the Accounting Standard on segment reporting. The Institute of Chartered Accountants of India has already issued an Exposure Draft on the subject and should be requested to finalise this at an early date.

- Disclosure and treatment of related party transactions
  This again is an important disclosure. The Committee was informed that the Institute of Chartered Accountants of India had already issued an Exposure Draft on the subject. The Committee recommends that the Institute of Chartered Accountants of India should be requested to finalise this at the earliest. In the interim, the Committee recommends the disclosures set out in Clause 7 of Annexure-4.
- Treatment of deferred taxation
  The treatment of deferred taxation and its appropriate disclosure has an important bearing on the true and fair view of the financial status of the company. The Committee recommends that the Institute of Chartered Accountants of India be requested to issue a standard on deferred tax liability at an early date.

MANAGEMENT

13.1 In the view of the Committee, the overriding aim of management is to maximize shareholder value without being detrimental to the interests of other stakeholders. The management however, is subservient to the board of directors and must operate within the boundaries and the policy framework laid down by the board. While the board is responsible for ensuring that the principles of corporate governance are adhered to and enforced, the real onus of implementation lies with the management. It is responsible for translating into action, the policies and strategies of the board and implementing its directives to achieve corporate objectives of the company framed by the board. It is therefore essential that the board should clearly define the role of the management.

Functions of the Management

13.2 The management comprises the Chief Executive, Executive-directors, and the key managers of the company, involved in day-to-day activities of the company.

13.3 The Committee believes that the management should carry out the following functions:

- Assisting the board in its decision making process in respect of the company's strategy, policies, code of conduct, and performance targets, by providing necessary inputs.
- Implementing the policies and code of conduct of the board.
- Managing the day-to-day affairs of the company to best achieve the targets and goals set by the board, to maximize the shareholder value.
- Providing timely, accurate, substantive, and material information, including financial matters and exceptions, to the board, board-committees, and the shareholders.
- Ensuring compliance of all regulations and laws.
- Ensuring timely and efficient service to the shareholders and to protect shareholder's rights and interests.
- Setting up and implementing an effective internal control systems, commensurate with the business requirements.
- Implementing and comply with the code of conduct as laid down by the board.
- Co-operating and facilitating efficient working of board committees.

13.4 As a part of the disclosure related to management, the Committee recommends that as part of the directors' report or as an addition thereto, a management discussion and analysis report should form part of the annual report to the shareholders. This management discussion and analysis should include discussion on the following matters within the limits set by the company's competitive position:

- Industry structure and developments
- Opportunities and threats
- Segment-wise or product-wise performance
- Outlook
- Risks and concerns
- Internal control systems and their adequacy
- Discussion on financial performance with respect to operational performance
- Material developments in human resources/industrial relations front, including number of people employed

This is a mandatory recommendation.

13.5 Good corporate governance casts an obligation on the management in respect of disclosures. The Committee therefore recommends that disclosures must be made by the management to the board relating to all material, financial, and commercial transactions, where they have personal interest, that may have a potential conflict with the interest of the company at large (for e.g. dealing in company shares, commercial dealings with bodies, which have shareholding of management and their relatives, etc)

This is a mandatory recommendation.

SHAREHOLDERS

14.1 The shareholders are the owners of the company and as such they have certain rights and responsibilities. But in reality companies cannot be managed by shareholder referendum. The shareholders are not expected to assume responsibility for the management of corporate affairs. A company's management must be able to take business decisions rapidly. The shareholders have therefore to necessarily delegate many of their responsibilities as owners of the company to the directors who then become responsible for corporate strategy and operations. The implementation of this strategy is done by a management team. This relationship therefore brings in the accountability of the boards and the management to the shareholders of the company. A good corporate framework is one that provides adequate avenues to the shareholders for effective contribution in the governance of the company while insisting on a high standard of corporate behaviour without getting involved in the day-to-day functioning of the company.

Responsibilities of Shareholders

14.2 The Committee believes that the General Body Meetings provide an opportunity to the shareholders to address their concerns to the board of directors and comment on and demand any explanation on the annual report or on the overall functioning of the company. It is important that the shareholders use the forum of general body meetings for ensuring that the company is being properly stewarded for maximising the interests of the shareholders. This is important especially in the Indian context. It follows from the above that for effective participation shareholders must maintain decorum during the general body meetings.

14.3 The effectiveness of the board is determined by the quality of the directors and the quality of the financial information is dependent to an extent on the efficiency with which the auditors carry on their duties. The shareholders must therefore show a greater degree of interest and involvement in the appointment of the directors and the auditors. Indeed, they should demand complete information about the directors before approving their directorship.

14.4 The Committee recommends that in case of the appointment of a new director or re-appointment of a director the shareholders must be provided with the following information:

- A brief resume of the director;
- Nature of his expertise in specific functional areas; and
- Names of companies in which the person also holds the directorship and the membership of Committees of the board.

This is a mandatory recommendation.

Shareholders' Rights

14.5 The basic rights of the shareholders include right to transfer and registration of shares, obtaining relevant information on the company on a timely and regular basis, participating and voting in shareholder meetings, electing members of the board, and sharing in the residual profits of the corporation.

14.6 The Committee therefore recommends that as shareholders have a right to participate in, and be sufficiently informed on decisions concerning fundamental corporate changes, they should not only be provided information as under the Companies Act, but also in respect of other decisions relating to material changes such as takeovers, sale of assets or divisions of the company and changes in capital structure which will lead to change in control or may result in certain shareholders obtaining control disproportionate to the equity ownership.

14.7 The Committee recommends that information like quarterly results, presentation made by companies to analysts may be put on company's website or may be sent in such a form so as to enable the stock exchange on which the company is listed to put it on its own website.

This is a mandatory recommendation.

14.8 The Committee recommends that the half-yearly declaration of financial performance including summary of the significant events in last six-months, should be sent to each household of shareholders.

This is a non-mandatory recommendation.

14.9 A company must have appropriate systems in place which will enable the shareholders to participate effectively and vote in the shareholders' meetings. The company should also keep the shareholders informed of the rules and voting procedures, which govern the general shareholder meetings.

14.10 The annual general meetings of the company should not be deliberately held at venues or the timing should not be such which makes it difficult for most of the shareholders to attend. The company must also ensure that it is not inconvenient or expensive for shareholders to cast their vote.

14.11 Currently, although the formality of holding the general meeting is gone through, in actual practice only a small fraction of the shareholders of that company do or can really participate therein. This virtually makes the concept of corporate democracy illusory. It is imperative that this situation which has lasted too long needs an early correction. In this context, for shareholders who are unable to attend the meetings, there should be a requirement which will enable them to vote by postal ballot for key decisions. A detailed list of the matters which should require postal ballot is given in Annexure 3. This would require changes in the Companies Act. The Committee was informed that SEBI has already made recommendations in this regard to the Department of Company Affairs.

14.12 The Committee recommends that a board committee under the chairmanship of a non-executive director should be formed to specifically look into the redressing of shareholder complaints like transfer of shares, non-receipt of balance sheet, non-receipt of declared dividends, etc. The Committee believes that the formation of such a committee will help focus the attention of the company on shareholders' grievances and sensitise the management to redressal of their grievances.

This is a mandatory recommendation.

14.13 The Committee further recommends that to expedite the process of share transfers the board of the company should delegate the power of share transfer to an officer, or a committee, or to the registrar and share transfer agents. The delegated authority should attend to share transfer formalities at least once in a fortnight.

This is a mandatory recommendation.

Institutional Shareholders

14.14 Institutional shareholders have acquired large stakes in the equity share capital of listed Indian companies. They have or are in the process of becoming majority shareholders in many listed companies and own shares largely on behalf of the retail investors. They thus have a special responsibility, given the weightage of their votes and have a bigger role to play in corporate governance, as retail investors look upon them for positive use of their voting rights.

14.15 Given the weight of their votes, the institutional shareholders can effectively use their powers to influence the standards of corporate governance. Practices elsewhere in the world have indicated that institutional shareholders can sufficiently influence because of their collective stake, the policies of the company, so as to ensure that the company they have invested in, complies with the corporate governance code in order to maximise shareholder value. What is important in the view of the Committee is that, the institutional shareholders put to good use their voting power.

14.16 The Committee is of the view that the institutional shareholders:

• Take active interest in the composition of the Board of Directors
• Be vigilant
• Maintain regular and systematic contact at senior level for exchange of views on management, strategy, performance, and the quality of management
• Ensure that voting intentions are translated into practice
• Evaluate the corporate governance performance of the company

MANNER OF IMPLEMENTATION

15.1 The Committee recommends that SEBI writes to the Central Government to amend the Securities Contracts (Regulation) Rules, 1957 for incorporating the mandatory provisions of this report.

15.2 The Committee further recommends to SEBI, that as in other countries, the mandatory provisions of the recommendations may be implemented through the listing agreement of the stock exchanges.

15.3 The Committee recognises that the listing agreement is not a very powerful instrument and the penalties for violation are not sufficiently stringent to act as a deterrent. The Committee therefore recommends to SEBI, that the listing agreement of the stock exchanges be strengthened and the exchanges themselves be vested with more powers, so that they can ensure proper compliance of code of corporate governance. In this context the Committee further recommends that the Securities Contract (Regulation) Act, 1956 should be amended, so that in addition to the above, the concept of listing agreement be replaced by listing conditions.

15.4 The Committee recommends that the Securities Contracts (Regulation) Act, 1956 be amended to empower SEBI and stock exchanges to take deterrent and appropriate action in case of violation of the provisions of the listing agreement. These could include power of levying monetary penalty both on the company and the concerned officials of the company and filing of winding-up petition, etc.

15.5 The Committee also recommends that SEBI write to the Department of Company Affairs for suitable amendments to the Companies Act in respect of the recommendations which fall within their jurisdiction.

15.6 The Committee recommends that there should be a separate section on corporate governance in the annual reports of companies, with a detailed compliance report on corporate governance. Non-compliance of any mandatory recommendation with reasons thereof and the extent to which the non-mandatory recommendations have been adopted should be specifically highlighted. This will enable the shareholders and the securities market to assess for themselves the standards of corporate governance followed by a company. A suggested list of items to be included in the compliance report is enclosed in Annexure 4.

This is a mandatory recommendation.

15.7 The Committee also recommends that the company should arrange to obtain a certificate from the auditors of the company regarding compliance of mandatory recommendations and annex the certificate with the directors' report, which is sent annually to all the shareholders of the company. The same certificate should also be sent to the stock exchanges along with the annual returns filed by the company.

This is a mandatory recommendation.

END NOTE

There are several corporate governance structures available in the developed world but there is no one structure, which can be singled out as being better than the others. There is no 'one size fits all' structure for corporate governance. The Committee's recommendations are not therefore based on any one model but are designed for the Indian environment.

Corporate governance extends beyond corporate law. Its fundamental objective is not mere fulfillment of the requirements of law but in ensuring commitment of the board in managing the company in a transparent manner for maximising long-term shareholder value. The corporate governance has as many votaries as claimants. Among the latter, the Committee has primarily focussed its recommendations on investors and shareholders, as they are the prime constituencies of SEBI. Effectiveness of corporate governance system cannot merely be legislated by law, neither can any system of corporate governance be static. As competition increases, technology pronounces the death of distance and speeds up communication, the environment in which firms operate in India also changes. In this dynamic environment the systems of corporate governance also need to evolve. The Committee believes that its recommendations will go a long way in raising the standards of corporate governance in Indian firms and make them attractive destinations for local and global capital. These recommendations will also form the base for further evolution of the structure of corporate governance in consonance with the rapidly changing economic and industrial environment of the country in the new millenium.

NARAYANA MURTHY COMMITTEE
REPORT ON CORPORATE GOVERNANCE

8 February, 2003

PREAMBLE

Corporations pool capital from a large investor base both in the domestic and in the international capital markets. In this context, investment is ultimately an act of faith in the ability of a corporation's management. When an investor invests money in a corporation, he expects the board and the management to act as trustees and ensure the safety of the capital and also earn a rate of return that is higher than the cost of capital. In this regard, investors expect management to act in their best interests at all times and adopt good corporate governance practices.

Corporate governance is the acceptance by management of the inalienable rights of shareholders as the true owners of the corporation and of their own role as trustees on behalf of the shareholders. It is about commitment to values, about ethical business conduct, and about making a distinction between personal and corporate funds in the management of a company. It was the belief of the Securities and Exchange Board of India ('SEBI') that efforts to improve corporate governance standards in India must continue. This is because these standards themselves were evolving in keeping with market dynamics.

Accordingly, the Committee on corporate governance was constituted by SEBI, to evaluate the adequacy of existing corporate governance practices and further improve these practices. The Committee comprised members from various walks of public and professional life. This includes captains of industry, academicians, public accountants, and people from financial press and from industry forums. The issues discussed by the Committee primarily related to audit committees, audit reports, independent directors, related parties, risk management, directorships and director compensation, codes of conduct, and financial disclosures. The Committee's recommendations in the final report were selected based on parameters including their relative importance, fairness, accountability and transparency, ease of implementation, verifiability, and enforceability.

The key mandatory recommendations focus on strengthening the responsibilities of audit committees; improving the quality of financial disclosures, including those related to related party transactions and proceeds from initial public offerings (IPOs); requiring corporate executive boards to assess and disclose business risks in the annual reports of companies; introducing responsibilities on boards to adopt formal codes of conduct; the position of nominee directors; and stock holder approval and improved disclosures relating to compensation paid to non-executive directors.

Non-mandatory recommendations include moving to a regime where corporate financial statements are not qualified; instituting a system of training of board members; and the evaluation of performance of board members. The Committee believes that these recommendations codify certain standards of 'good' governance into specific requirements, since certain corporate responsibilities are too important to be left to loose (as in report) concepts of fiduciary responsibility. When implemented through SEBI's regulatory framework, they will strengthen existing governance practices and also provide a strong incentive to avoid corporate failures. Some people have legitimately asked whether the costs of governance reforms are too high. In this context, it should be noted that the failure to implement good governance procedures has a cost beyond mere regulatory problems. Companies that do not employ meaningful governance procedures will have to pay a significant risk premium when competing for scarce capital in today's public markets.

The Committee would like to thanks Mr G.N. Bajpai, Chairman of SEBI and Mr Pratip Kar, Executive Director, SEBI for their support. In addition, the Committee would like to thank Mr P.K. Bindlish, General Manager, Mr Manoj Kumar, Assistant General Manager and other staff at SEBI along with Mr Sumanth Cidambi of Progeon Limited, who assisted in the preparation of this report.

N. R. Narayana Murthy
Chairman
Committee on Corporate Governance, SEBI
Mumbai
February 8, 2003

1 INTRODUCTION
1.1 The need for Corporate Governance

1.1.1 A corporation is a congregation of various stakeholders, namely, customers, employees, investors, vendor partners, government, and society. A corporation should be fair and transparent to its stakeholders in all its transactions. This has become imperative in today's globalized business world where corporations need to access global pools of capital, need to attract and retain the best human capital from various parts of the world, need to partner with vendors on mega collaborations, and need to live in harmony with the community. Unless a corporation embraces and demonstrates ethical conduct, it will not be able to succeed.

1.1.2 Corporate governance is about ethical conduct in business. Ethics is concerned with the code of values and principles that enables a person to choose between right and wrong, and therefore, select from alternative courses of action. Further, ethical dilemmas arise from conflicting interests of the parties involved. In this regard, managers make decisions based on a set of principles influenced by the values, context, and culture of the organization. Ethical leadership is good for business as the organization is seen to conduct its business in line with the expectations of all stakeholders.

1.1.3 Corporate governance is beyond the realm of law. It stems from the culture and mindset of management, and cannot be regulated by legislation alone. Corporate governance deals with conducting the affairs of a company, such that there is fairness to all stakeholders and that its actions benefit the greatest number of stakeholders. It is about openness, integrity, and accountability. What legislation can and should do, is to lay down a common framework—the 'form' to ensure standards. The 'substance' will ultimately determine the credibility and integrity of the process. Substance is inexorably linked to the mindset and ethical standards of management.

1.1.4 Corporations need to recognize that their growth requires the cooperation of all the stakeholders; and such cooperation is enhanced by the corporation adhering to the best corporate governance practices. In this regard, the management needs to act as trustees of the shareholders at large and prevent asymmetry of benefits between various sections of shareholders, especially between the owner-managers and the rest of the shareholders.

1.1.5 Corporate governance is a key element in improving the economic efficiency of a firm. Good corporate governance also helps ensure that corporations take into account the interests of a wide range of constituencies, as well as of the communities within which they operate. Further, it ensures that their Boards are accountable to the shareholders. This, in turn, helps assure that corporations operate for the benefit of society as a whole. While large profits can be made taking advantage of the asymmetry between stakeholders in the short run, balancing the interests of all stakeholders alone will ensure survival and growth in the long run. This includes, for instance, taking into account societal concerns about labor and the environment.

1.1.6 The failure to implement good governance can have a heavy cost beyond regulatory problems. Evidence suggests that companies that do not employ meaningful governance procedures can pay a significant risk premium when competing for scarce capital in the public markets. In fact, recently, stock market analysts have acquired an increased appreciation for the correlation between governance and returns. In this regard, an increasing number of reports not only discuss governance in general terms, but also have explicitly altered investment recommendations based on the strength or weakness of a company's corporate governance infrastructure.

1.1.7 The credibility offered by good corporate governance procedures also helps maintain the confidence of investors—both foreign and domestic—to attract more 'patient', long-term capital, and will reduce the cost of capital. This will ultimately induce more stable sources of financing.

1.1.8 Often, increased attention on corporate governance is a result of financial crisis. For instance, the Asian financial crisis brought the subject of corporate governance to the surface in Asia. Further, recent scandals disturbed the otherwise placid and complacent corporate landscape in the US. These scandals, in a sense, proved to be serendipitous. They spawned a new set of initiatives in corporate governance in the US and triggered fresh debate in the European Union as well as in Asia. The many instances of corporate misdemeanors have also shifted the emphasis on compliance with substance, rather than form, and brought to sharper focus the need for intellectual honesty and integrity. This is because financial and non-financial disclosures made by any firm are only as good and honest as the people behind them. By this very principle, only those industrialists whose corporations are governed properly should be allowed to be a part of committees. This includes the Prime Minister and Finance Minister's advisory councils, committees set up by the Confederation of Indian Industry (CII), the Securities and Exchange Board of India (SEBI), the Department of Company Affairs, ministries, and the boards of large banks and financial institutions.

1.1.9 Corporate governance initiatives in India began in 1998 with the Desirable Code of Corporate Governance—a voluntary code published by the CII, and the first formal regulatory framework for listed companies specifically for corporate governance, established by the SEBI. The latter was made in February 2000, following the recommendations of the Kumarmangalam Birla Committee Report.

1.1.10 The term 'corporate governance' is susceptible to both broad and narrow definitions. In fact, many of the codes do not even attempt to articulate what is encompassed by the term. The motives for the several corporate governance postulates engaged in these definitions vary, depending on the participant concerned. The focal subjects also vary accordingly. The important point is that corporate governance is a concept, rather than an individual instrument. It includes debate on the appropriate management and control structures of a company. Further it includes the rules relating to the power relations between owners, the board of directors, management and, last but not least, the stakeholders such as employees, suppliers, customers, and the public at large.

1.1.11 The majority of the definitions articulated in the codes relate corporate governance to 'control'—of the company, of corporate management, or of company conduct or managerial conduct. Perhaps the simplest and most common definition of this sort is that provided by the Cadbury Report (UK), which is frequently quoted or paraphrased: 'Corporate governance is the system by which businesses are directed and controlled.'

1.1.12 The definition in the preamble of the OECD Principles is also all encompassing: 'Corporate governance...involves a set of relationships between a company's management, its board, its shareholders, and other stakeholders. Corporate governance also provides the structure through which the objectives of the company are set, and the means of attaining those objectives and monitoring performance are determined.'

1.1.13 The most common school of thought would have us believe that if management is about running businesses, governance is about ensuring that it is run properly. All companies need governing as well as managing. The aim of 'Good Corporate Governance' is to enhance the long-term value of the company for its shareholders and all other partners. The enormous significance of corporate governance is clearly evident in this definition, which encompasses all stakeholders. Corporate governance integrates all the participants involved in a process, which is economic, and at the same time social. This definition is deliberately broader than the frequently heard narrower interpretation that only takes account of the corporate governance postulates aimed at shareholder interests.

1.1.14 Studies of corporate governance practices across several countries conducted by the Asian Development Bank (2000), International Monetary Fund (1999), Organization for Economic Cooperation and Development (OECD) (1999) and the World Bank (1999) reveal that there is no single model of good corporate governance. This is recognized by the OECD Code. The OECD Code also recognizes that different legal systems, institutional frameworks, and traditions across countries have led to the development of a range of different approaches to corporate governance. Common to all good corporate governance regimes, however, is a high degree of priority placed on the interests of shareholders, who place their trust in corporations to use their investment funds wisely and effectively. In addition, best-managed corporations also recognize that business ethics and corporate awareness of the environmental and societal interest of the communities within which they operate, can have an impact on the reputation and long-term performance of corporations.

1.2 The Kumarmangalam Birla Committee on Corporate Governance

1.2.1 SEBI had constituted a Committee on 7 May, 1999 under the chairmanship of Shri Kumarmangalam Birla, then Member of the SEBI Board 'to promote and raise the standards of corporate governance'. Based on the recommendations of this Committee, a new clause 49 was incorporated in the Stock Exchange Listing Agreements ('Listing Agreements').

1.2.2 The recommendations of the Kumarmangalam Birla Committee on Corporate Governance are set out in Enclosure I to this report.

1.3 Financial Reporting and Disclosures

1.3.1 Financial disclosure is a critical component of effective corporate governance. SEBI set up an Accounting Standards Committee, as a Standing Committee, under the chairmanship of Shri Y.H. Malegam with the following objectives:

- To review the continuous disclosure requirements under the listing agreement for listed companies;
- To provide input to the Institute of Chartered Accountants of India (ICAI) for introducing new accounting standards in India; and
- To review existing Indian accounting standards, where required and to harmonize these accounting standards and financial disclosures on par with international practices.

1.3.2 SEBI has interacted with the ICAI on a continuous basis in the issuance of recent Indian accounting standards on areas including segment reporting, related party disclosures, consolidated financial statements, earnings per share, accounting for taxes on income, accounting for investments in associates in consolidated financial statements, discontinuing operations, interim financial reporting, intangible assets, financial reporting of interests in joint ventures, and impairment of assets.

1.3.3 With the introduction of these recent Indian accounting standards, financial reporting practices in India are almost on par with international accounting standards.

1.4 Implementation of Corporate Governance Requirements

1.4.1 The recommendations were implemented through Clause 49 of the Listing Agreements, in a phased manner by SEBI.

1.4.2 They were made applicable to all companies in the BSE 200 and S&P C&X Nifty indices, and all newly listed companies, as of 31 March 2001.

1.4.3 The applicability of the recommendations was extended to companies with a paid-up capital of Rs 100 million or with a net worth of Rs 250 million at any time in the past five years, as of 31 March 2002.

1.4.4 In respect of other listed companies with a paid-up capital of over Rs 30 million, the requirements were made applicable as of 31 March 2003.

1.4.5 The accounting standards issued by the ICAI, which are applicable to all companies under sub-section 3A of Section 211 of the Companies Act, 1956, were specifically made applicable to all listed companies for the financial year ended 31 March 2002, under the Listing Agreements.

1.5 Compliance with the Code and SEBI's Experience

1.5.1 In terms of SEBI's Circular No. SMD/Policy/CIR-03/2001 dated 22 January 2001:

All companies are required to submit a quarterly compliance report to the stock exchanges within 15 days from the end of a financial reporting quarter.

The report has to be submitted either by the compliance officer or by the chief executive officer of the company after obtaining due approvals. SEBI has prescribed a format in which the information shall be obtained by the stock exchanges from the companies. The companies have to submit compliance status on eight sub-clauses, namely:

- Board of directors;
- Audit committee;
- Shareholders/investors grievance committee;
- Remuneration of directors;
- Board procedures;
- Management;

- Shareholders; and
- Report on corporate governance.

Stock exchanges are required to set up a separate monitoring cell with identified personnel, to monitor compliance with the provisions of the Recommendations. Stock exchanges are also required to submit a quarterly compliance report from the companies as per the Schedule of Implementation. The stock exchanges are required to submit a consolidated compliance report within 30 days of the end of the quarter to SEBI.

1.5.2 Both the Mumbai and National Stock Exchanges have submitted a consolidated quarterly compliance report for the quarter ended 30 September 2002. It was observed that 1848 and 741 companies were required to comply with the requirements of the Code, for the Mumbai and National Stock Exchanges, respectively. Of these, compliance reports were submitted in respect of 1026 and 595 companies, for the Mumbai and National Stock Exchanges, respectively.

1.5.3 The status of compliance with respect to provisions of corporate governance analysed from data submitted by the Mumbai Stock Exchange for the quarter ended 30 September 2002 is set out below.

Board of directors	999
Audit committee	981
Shareholders' grievance committee	1005
Remuneration committee	677
Board procedures	575
Management	774
Shareholders	998
Report on corporate governance	786
Total	1026

* Applicable to 1848 companies

1.5.4 The key observations contained in the consolidated compliance report sent by the Mumbai and National Stock Exchanges are set out below.

- The compliance level in respect of requirements relating to board of directors, audit committee, shareholders grievance committee, and shareholders is very high;
- Many companies are yet to comply with the requirements relating to remuneration committee (which is not mandatory), board procedures, management and report on corporate governance; and
- Few companies have submitted that the provisions relating to management and board procedures are not applicable.

1.5.5 SEBI observed that the compliance with the requirements in clause 49 of the Listing Agreement is, by and large, satisfactory; however, an analysis of the financial statements of companies and the report on corporate governance discloses that their quality is not uniform. This is observed on parameters such as the nature of qualifications in audit reports, the quality of the corporate governance report itself (which is often perfunctory in nature), and the business transacted and the duration of audit committee meetings. Variations in the quality of annual reports, including disclosures, raises the question whether compliance is in form or in substance; and emphasise the need to ensure that the laws, rules, and regulations do not reduce corporate governance to a mere ritual. This question has come under close scrutiny in recent times.

1.5.6 SEBI has analysed a few recently published annual reports of companies to assess the quality of corporate governance. The directors' reports could be classified into the following categories:

- Reports where there is no mention about the compliance with corporate governance requirements;
- Reports that state that the company is fully compliant with clause 49 of the Listing Agreement, but where independent auditors have made qualifications in their audit reports;
- Reports that mention areas of non-compliance with clause 49 of the Listing Agreement and provide explanation for non-compliance; and
- Reports that mention areas of non-compliance with clause 49 of the Listing Agreement but provide no explanation for auditor's qualification or for reasons for non-compliance.

1.5.7 SEBI also observed that there is a considerable variance in the extent and quality of disclosures made by companies in their annual reports.

1.6 Rationale for a Review of the Code

1.6.1 SEBI believes that efforts to improve corporate governance standards in India must continue. This is because these standards are themselves evolving, in keeping with market dynamics. Recent events worldwide, primarily in the United States, have renewed the emphasis on corporate governance. These events have highlighted the need for ethical governance and management, and for the need to look beyond mere systems and procedures. This will ensure compliance with corporate governance codes, in substance and not merely in form.

1.6.2 Again, one of the goals of good corporate governance is investor protection. The individual investor is at the end of a chain of financial information, stretching from corporate accountants and management, through boards of directors and audit committees, to independent auditors and stock market analysts, to the investing public. Many of the links in this chain need to be strengthened or replaced to preserve its integrity.

1.6.3 SEBI, therefore, believed that a need to review the existing code on corporate governance arose from two perspectives, (a) to evaluate the adequacy of the existing practices, and (b) to further improve the existing practices.

2 THE COMMITTEE, TERMS OF REFERENCE, AND APPROACH
2.1 Constitution of the Committee

2.1.1 In the context of the rationale set out in Section 1.6 of this report, SEBI believed it necessary to form a committee on corporate governance, comprising representatives from the stock exchanges, chambers of commerce, investor associations, and professional bodies.

2.1.2 The SEBI Committee on Corporate Governance was constituted under the Chairmanship of Shri N.R. Narayana Murthy, chairman and chief mentor of Infosys Technologies Limited.

2.1.3 A list of names of the members of the Committee is set out in Enclosure II to this report.

2.1.4 The Committee met thrice on 7 December 2002, 7 January 2003 and 8 February 2003, to deliberate the issues related to corporate governance and finalize its recommendations to SEBI.

2.2 Terms of Reference

2.2.1 The terms of reference of the Committee are set out below.

- To review the performance of corporate governance; and
- To determine the role of companies in responding to rumour and other price sensitive information circulating in the market, in order to enhance the transparency and integrity of the market.

2.2.2 The recommendations of the Committee are presented in this report.

2.3 Approach

2.3.1 Members of the Committee met to deliberate the issues related to corporate governance, primarily relating to audit committees, audit reports, independent directors, related parties, risk management, directorships and director compensation, codes of conduct and financial disclosures.

2.3.2 The Committee felt that that the regulator should clearly define regulations and be able to effectively enforce the recommendations. The regulations should be as few as possible and the role of the regulator should primarily be that of a catalyst in enforcement.

2.3.3 The issues relating to corporate governance were discussed by the Committee.

Based on the responses/suggestions to the issues, draft recommendations were prepared. These recommendations were circulated to the members. Members were asked to rate the recommendations on a scale of 1 (least) through 10 (most) across the seven following parameters:

- Importance—How important is the recommendation to the member?
- Fairness—Does the recommendation enhance fairness to all stakeholders, by minimizing asymmetry of benefits?
- Accountability—Does the recommendation make corporate management more accountable?
- Transparency—Does the recommendation enhance transparency?
- Ease of implementation—Is the recommendation easy to implement?
- Verification—Is the recommendation objectively verifiable?
- Enforcement—Can the recommendation be effectively enforced?

2.3.4 The ratings received from members were first aggregated across recommendations and tabulated. Recommendations whose ratings were 7 and above were then aggregated, on each of the seven parameters set out above. The rating score for each such recommendation was aggregated.

2.3.5 The recommendations were then sorted in descending order of importance. The top 20 recommendations were presented to the Committee for their views. These recommendations were discussed in detail by the members and will form the basis of the final recommendations of the Committee.

2.3.6 Certain recommendations that were not part of the top 20 recommendations were also presented to the Committee. This was because of their important nature.

2.3.7 Certain recommendations that were already contained in the Report of the Naresh Chandra Committee on Corporate Audit and Governance (the 'Naresh Chandra Committee') were also discussed briefly. The members of the Committee agreed in principle with the recommendations set out by the Naresh Chandra Committee that are directly related to corporate governance.

2.3.8 It was therefore decided by the Committee, that in making the final recommendations to SEBI, the Committee would also recommend that the mandatory recommendations in the report of the Naresh Chandra Committee, insofar as they related to corporate governance, be mandatorily implemented by SEBI through an amendment to clause 49 of the Listing Agreement. These recommendations are contained in Section 4 of this report.

2.3.9 The Committee accepted that ratings were not received from all members. It was of the view that members who have not submitted their ratings should not raise objections to the Committee's recommendations at a later stage.

2.3.10 The Committee also acknowledged that the ratings methodology did not capture the qualitative comments of the members. Further, it was also accepted that a few recommendations could not be rated since they were more of a qualitative nature for which it was difficult to assign a numerical weight.

3 KEY ISSUES DISCUSSED AND RECOMMENDATIONS
3.1 Background
3.1.1 The key issues debated by the Committee and the related recommendations are discussed below.

3.2 Audit Committees
3.2.1 Review of information by audit committees
3.2.1.1 Suggestions were received from members that audit committees of publicly listed companies should be required to review the following information mandatorily:

- Financial statements;
- Management discussion and analysis of financial condition and results of operations;
- Reports relating to compliance with laws and to risk management;
- Management letters/letters of internal control weaknesses issued by statutory/internal auditors;
- Records of related party transactions.

3.2.1.2 The Committee noted that most of this information was already reviewed by audit committees during the audit committee meeting. Further, it was already contained as a recommendation in the Kumarmangalam Birla Committee on corporate governance.

3.2.1.3 The Committee also noted that the recommendation in the Birla Committee Report cast a responsibility on the audit committee vis-à-vis their duties and role. Further, the compliance report of the Mumbai Stock Exchange showed that approximately only 53 per cent of the companies complied with this requirement contained in the Birla Committee Report.

3.2.1.4 In view of the above deliberations, the Committee makes the following mandatory recommendation:

Mandatory recommendation
Audit committees of publicly listed companies should be required to review the following information mandatorily:

- Financial statements and draft audit report, including quarterly/half-yearly financial information;

- Management discussion and analysis of financial condition and results of operations;
- Reports relating to compliance with laws and to risk management; management letters/letters of internal control weaknesses issued by statutory internal auditors; and
- Records of related party transactions.

3.2.2 Financial literacy of members of the audit committee

3.2.2.1 Suggestions were received that all audit committee members should be 'financially literate' and at least one member should have accounting or related financial management expertise. It was also suggested that all audit committee members should be able to read and understand financial statements at the time of their appointment rather than within a reasonable period.

3.2.2.2 The Committee was of the view that the first recommendation was acceptable. It was also of the view that the definition of the phrase 'financially literate' should be explained further.

3.2.2.3 Based on the above discussions, the Committee accordingly makes the following mandatory recommendation:

Mandatory recommendation
All audit committee members should be 'financially literate' and at least one member should have accounting or related financial management expertise.

Explanation 1   The term 'financially literate' means the ability to read and understand basic financial statements, ie balance sheet, profit and loss account, and statement of cash flows.

Explanation 2   A member will be considered to have accounting or related financial management expertise if he or she possesses experience in finance or accounting, or requisite professional certification in accounting, or any other comparable experience or background which results in the individual's financial sophistication, including being or having been a chief executive officer, chief financial officer, or other senior officer with financial oversight responsibilities.

3.3 Audit Reports and Audit Qualifications

3.3.1 Disclosure of accounting treatment

3.3.1.1 It was suggested that in case a company has followed a treatment different from that prescribed in an accounting standard, independent/statutory auditors should justify why they believe such alternative treatment is more representative of the underlying business transaction. This should also be explained clearly in the footnotes to the financial statements.

3.3.1.2 The Committee noted that accounting policies and principles are selected by a company's management. Consequently, the onus should be on management to explain why they believe such alternative treatment is more representative of the underlying business transaction. The auditor's responsibility is to express a qualification in case he disagrees with the explanation given by the company's management. The responsibility should not be cast on the auditor to justify such departures from an accounting standard. The members were of the view that the auditor may either concur or disagree with management's viewpoint. The auditor may draw reference to this footnote without necessarily making it the subject matter of an audit qualification, unless he disagrees with the departure from the accounting standard, in which case he would be required to issue a qualification.

3.3.1.3 In light of the above deliberations, the Committee was of the view that the suggestion should be modified to reflect this. The Committee therefore makes the following mandatory recommendation:

Mandatory recommendation

In case a company has followed a treatment different from that prescribed in an accounting standard, management should justify why they believe such alternative treatment is more representative of the underlying business transaction. Management should also clearly explain the alternative accounting treatment in the footnotes to the financial statements.

3.3.2 Audit qualifications

3.3.2.1 Suggestions were received that where financial statements contain qualifications, companies should be given a reasonable period of time within which to cure the qualifications, by SEBI/stock exchanges. Mere explanations from companies may not be sufficient.

3.3.2.2 The Committee noted that the above recommendation be dropped since adequate safeguards already exist. It was also of the opinion that it may not be possible to cure a taint in some cases and this would lead to undue hardship on companies.

3.3.2.3 Based on this discussion, the Committee accordingly makes the following recommendation:

Non-mandatory recommendation

Companies should be encouraged to move towards a regime of unqualified financial statements. This recommendation should be reviewed at an appropriate juncture to determine whether the financial reporting climate is conducive towards a system of filing only unqualified financial statements.

3.4 Related Party Transactions

3.4.1 Basis for related party transactions

3.4.1.1 Suggestions were received that for each related party, a statement shall be recorded disclosing the basis/methodology for various types of transactions.

3.4.1.2 It was also suggested that the records of all transactions with related parties including their bases/ methodology should be placed before the independent audit committee at each board meeting for formal approval/ratification. This should include any exceptional transactions that are not on an arm's length principle together with reasons for such deviation.

3.4.1.3 The Committee noted that a statement disclosing the basis/methodology for various types of transactions entered into with related parties should be prepared and submitted for the information of the audit committee. It also opined that this statement should include transactions which are not on an arm's length principle. The company's management should explain to the audit committee the reasons for the non-arm's length nature of the transaction.

3.4.1.4 The Committee also noted that the definition of '*arm's length*' should be clarified in the recommendation. It noted that a reference may be made to the report of the Department of Company Affairs' Expert Group on Transfer Pricing Guidelines for a suitable definition.

3.4.1.5 Based on the above discussions, the Committee accordingly makes the following mandatory recommendation:

Mandatory recommendation

A statement of *all* transactions with related parties including their bases should be placed before the independent audit committee for formal approval/ratification. If any transaction is not on an arm's length basis, management should provide an explanation to the audit committee justifying the same.

3.4.2 Definition of 'related party'

3.4.2.1 It was suggested that SEBI should clarify the definition of the term 'related party'.

3.4.2.2 The Committee noted that Accounting Standard 18, Related Party Transactions (AS 18) issued by the ICAI contained the definition of this term.

3.4.2.3 Based on this discussion, the Committee adopted the definition of 'related party' as set out in AS 18 and makes the following mandatory recommendation:

Mandatory recommendation

The term 'related party' shall have the same meaning as contained in Accounting Standard 18, Related Party Transactions, issued by the Institute of Chartered Accountants of India.

3.5 Risk Management

3.5.1 Board disclosures

3.5.1.1 The Committee believes that it is important for corporate boards to be fully aware of the risks facing the business and that it is important for shareholders to know about the process by which companies manage their business risks.

3.5.1.2 In light of this, it was suggested that procedures should be in place to inform board members about the risk assessment and minimization procedures. These procedures should be periodically reviewed to ensure that executive management controls risk through means of a properly defined framework. These risks will include global risks; general, economic, and political risks; industry risks; and company specific risks.

3.5.1.3 It was also suggested that management should place a report before the board every quarter documenting any limitations to the risk-taking capacity of the corporation. This document should be formally approved by the Board.

3.5.1.4 The Committee believes that this recommendation is important. This is because the management discussion, and analysis of financial condition, and results of operations, are the responsibility of a company's management. It is therefore important that the audit committee be made aware of the risks faced by a company. It is management's responsibility to demonstrate to the audit committee the measures taken to address business risks. Further, it was added that the compliance officer of the company should certify the risk management report placed before the audit committee.

3.5.1.5 The Committee also noted that it was not practicable to put the responsibility of review of risk management only on the audit committee. It agreed that there must be a process by which key risks are reviewed by the entire board of directors and not just the audit committee. Further, there must be evidence demonstrating that this review process has actually taken place. Investors in a company would therefore know how the company has identified and addressed its business risks.

3.5.1.6 It was also mentioned that verifiability and enforceability of this recommendation was difficult. This was because companies could obtain a sign-off from the board members that such procedures were complied with.

3.5.1.7 Based on the above deliberations, the Committee makes the following mandatory recommendation:

Mandatory recommendation
Procedures should be in place to inform board members about the risk assessment and minimization procedures. These procedures should be periodically reviewed to ensure that executive management controls risk through means of a properly defined framework. Management should place a report before the entire Board of Directors every quarter documenting the business risks faced by the company, measures to address and minimize such risks, and any limitations to the risk taking capacity of the corporation. This document should be formally approved by the board.

3.5.2 Training of board members

3.5.2.1 It was also suggested that board members be trained in the business model of the company as well as the risk profile of the business parameters of the company.

3.5.2.2 The Committee noted that there is a real necessity for board members to understand the components of the business model and the accompanying risk parameters. However, the Committee also noted that board members can always ask for information relating to the business model of the company.

3.5.2.3 It also observed that the process of board review of business risks will be a mandatory recommendation of the Committee. Therefore, training of board members could be made recommendatory.

3.5.2.4 Based on the above deliberations, the Committee makes the following non-mandatory recommendation:

Non-mandatory recommendation
Companies should be encouraged to train their board members in the business model of the company as well as the risk profile of the business parameters of the company, their responsibilities as directors, and the best ways to discharge them.

3.6 Proceeds from IPOs

3.6.1 Use of proceeds

3.6.1.1 It was suggested that companies raising money through an IPOs should disclose the uses/ application of funds by major category (capital expenditure, sales and marketing, working capital, etc) on a quarterly basis as part of their quarterly declaration of (unaudited) financial results.

3.6.1.2 The Committee noted that that disclosure of unspecified uses of IPO proceeds would be a more transparent measure. A statement of funds utilsied for purposes other than those stated in the offer document/prospectus should be prepared by management. This statement should be certified by the independent auditors of the company and approved by the audit committee.

3.6.1.3 Based on the above discussion, the Committee makes the following mandatory recommendation:

Mandatory recommendation

Companies raising money through an IPO (as per report) should disclose to the audit committee, the uses/applications of funds by major category (capital expenditure, sales and marketing, working capital, etc), on a quarterly basis. On an annual basis, the company shall prepare a statement of funds utilized (as per report) for purposes other than those stated in the offer document/prospectus. This statement should be certified by the independent auditors of the company. The audit committee should make appropriate recommendations to the board to take up steps in this matter.

3.7 Code of Conduct

3.7.1 Written code for executive management

3.7.1.1 It was suggested that there should be a written code of conduct of for board members (by category of directors–executive directors, independent directors, nominee directors and, promoter directors). Further, there should be a written code of conduct for senior financial personnel including the chief financial officer, treasurer, and financial controller (or the officer who discharges these functions).

3.7.1.2 The Committee noted that the Birla Committee Report had defined the broad roles and responsibilities of management. It was obligatory on the part of the board of directors of a company to define a code of conduct for itself and the senior management of the company, not just senior financial personnel. Concerns were expressed on two main areas, (a) enforceability, and (b) definition of senior management. The Committee also noted that sample codes were available at www.choan.edu.

3.7.1.3 Based on the deliberations and views expressed by several members, the Committee makes the following mandatory recommendation:

Mandatory recommendation

It should be obligatory for the board of a company to lay down the code of conduct for all board members and senior management of a company. This code of conduct shall be posted on the website of the company. All board members and senior management personnel shall affirm compliance with the code on an annual basis. The annual report of the company shall contain a declaration to this effect signed off by the CEO and COO.

Explanation   For this purpose, the term 'senior management' shall mean personnel of the company who are members of its management/operating council (ie core management team excluding board of directors). Normally, this would comprise all members of management one level below the executive directors.

3.8 Nominee Directors

3.8.1 Exclusion of nominee directors from the definition of independent directors

3.8.1.1 It was suggested that nominee directors should be excluded from the definition of independent directors.

3.8.1.2 The Committee felt that the institution of nominee directors creates a conflict of interest that should be avoided. Such directors often claim that they are answerable only to the institutions they represent and take no responsibility for the company's management or fiduciary responsibility to other shareholders. It is necessary that all directors, whether representing institutions or otherwise, should have the same responsibilities and liabilities.

3.8.1.3 If the institution, whether as a lending institution or as investing institution, wishes to appoint its nominee on the board, such appointment should be made through the normal process of election by the shareholders.

3.8.1.4 The Committee noted a dissenting view that FI nominees should not be granted any board representation rights. Management should treat them on par with other investors and disseminate the same information that other shareholders would obtain. By virtue of their board seat, FIs are placed in an advantageous position over the other shareholders, in terms of company price-sensitive information.

3.8.1.5 Based on the above distinction, the Committee makes the following mandatory recommendation:

Mandatory recommendation
There shall be no nominee directors.

Where an institution wishes to appoint a director on the board, such appointment should be made by the shareholders.

An institutional director, so appointed, shall have the same responsibilities and shall be subject to the same liabilities as any other director.

Nominee of the government on public sector companies shall be similarly elected and shall be subject to the same responsibilities and liabilities as other directors.

3.9 Non-Executive Director Compensation

3.9.1 Limits on compensation paid to independent directors

3.9.1.1 The Committee discussed the following issues relating to compensation of independent directors:

- Whether limits should be set for compensation paid to independent directors and how should these limits be determined;
- What are the disclosures to be made to ensure transparency; and
- In case of stock-based compensation, the vesting timeframe of the options and the parameters that trigger vesting such as average return on capital employed, turnover criteria, etc.

3.9.1.2 Based on its deliberations, the Committee makes the following recommendation:

Mandatory recommendation
All compensation paid to non-executive directors may be fixed by the board of directors and should be approved by shareholders in general meeting. Limits should be set for the maximum number of stock options that can be granted to non-executive directors in any financial year and in aggregate. The stock options granted to the non-executive directors shall vest after a period of at least one year from the date such non-executive directors have retired from the board of the company.

Companies should publish their compensation philosophy and statement of entitled compensation in respect of non-executive directors in their annual report.

Alternatively, this may be put up on the company's website and reference drawn thereto in the annual report.

Companies should disclose on an annual basis, details of shares held by non-executive directors, including on an 'if-converted' basis.

Non-executive directors should be required to disclose their stock holding (both own or held by/for other persons on a beneficial basis) in the listed company in which they are proposed to be appointed as directors, prior to their appointment. These details should accompany their notice of appointment.

3.10 Independent Directors

3.10.1 Definition of independent directors

3.10.1.1 The Committee noted that the definition of independent directors should be clarified in the recommendations. It observed that the definition of independent directors as set out in the code of the International Corporate Governance Network may be referred to. The Committee also noted that the Naresh Chandra Committee report has attempted to define the term 'independent director'. The Committee was of the view that the same definition may be used to define independent directors.

3.10.1.2 An issue often raised in the context of independence is whether independent directors are entitled to any material benefits from the company other than sitting fees, remuneration, and travel and stay arrangements. Such benefits include stock options and performance bonuses that executive directors may be entitled to. The central issue is whether such benefits serve as incentives or hindrances to the objectivity of decision-making and hence, compromise its quality. It also needs to be considered that restrictions such as these could disenchant a person from accepting the position of independent director that carries onerous responsibilities without appropriate reward.

3.10.1.3 The Committee decided that the term 'independent director' shall have the same meaning as contained in paragraph 4.1 of the Naresh Chandra Committee Report.

3.10.1.4 Based on its deliberations, the Committee makes the following recommendation:

The term 'independent director' is defined as a non-executive director of the company who:

- apart from receiving director remuneration, does not have any material pecuniary relationships or transactions with the company, its promoters, its senior management or its holding company, its subsidiaries and associated companies;
- is not related to promoters or management at the board level or at one level below the board;
- has not been an executive of the company in the immediately preceding three financial years;
- is not a partner or an executive of the statutory audit firm or the internal audit firm that is associated with the company, and has not been a partner or an executive of any such firm for the last three years. This will also apply to legal firm(s) and consulting firm(s) that have a material association with the entity.
- is not a supplier, service provider, or customer of the company. This should include lessor-lessee type relationships also; and
- is not a substantial shareholder of the company, ie owning two percent or more of the block of voting shares.
- The considerations as regards remuneration paid to an independent director shall be the same as those applied to a non-executive director.

3.11 Whistle Blower Policy

3.11.1 Internal policy on access to audit committees

3.11.1.1 It was suggested that personnel who observe an unethical or improper practice should be able to approach the independent audit committee without necessarily informing the board. There should also be a mechanism for employees to be aware of this privilege.

3.11.1.2 The Committee agreed with this suggestion. It also noted that the suggestion may be accepted, with one modification i.e. the word 'board' be replaced with 'supervisor'.

3.11.1.3 Based on the above, the Committee makes the following recommendation:

Mandatory recommendation

Personnel who observe an unethical or improper practice (not necessarily a violation of law) should be able to approach the audit committee without necessarily informing their supervisors.

Companies shall take measures to ensure that this right of access is communicated to all employees through means of internal circulars, etc. The employment and other personnel policies of the company shall contain provisions protecting 'whistle blowers' from unfair termination and other unfair prejudicial employment practices.

3.11.2 Whistle blower policy

3.11.2.1 It was also suggested that SEBI should monitor compliance with the recommendation set out in Section 3.11.1 above.

3.11.2.2 The Committee noted that companies should affirm periodically (at least on an annual basis) that they have complied with this requirement.

3.11.2.3 The Committee also noted that it was necessary to provide protection to the internal auditor by enhancing his independence. This can be done by mandating that the appointment, removal, and terms of remuneration of the chief internal auditor must be subject to review by the audit committee.

3.11.2.4 Based on this discussion, the Committee makes the following mandatory recommendation:

Mandatory recommendation

Companies shall annually affirm that they have not denied any personnel access to the audit committee of the company (in respect of matters involving alleged misconduct) and that they have provided protection to 'whistle blowers' from unfair termination and other unfair or prejudicial employment practices.

The appointment, removal, and terms of remuneration of the chief internal auditor must be subject to review by the audit committee. Such affirmation shall form a part of the board report on corporate governance that is required to be prepared and submitted together with the annual report.

3.12 Subsidiary Companies

3.12.1 Audit committee requirements

3.12.1.1 It was suggested to the Committee that the requirements relating to non-executive independent directors and audit committees should be extended to subsidiaries of listed companies. Further, the scope of the audit committee should be enlarged to include review of investments made by subsidiaries and associates to ensure that Section 77 of Companies Act, 1956 is not violated.

3.12.1.2 The Committee noted the following additional suggestions:

- It may be difficult to monitor compliance with the suggestion, in the case of associate companies, insofar as it related to a review of investments. This requirement may, therefore, be made applicable to subsidiary companies only;
- It should be recommended to the Central Government that the Companies Act, 1956 should be amended to exclude common directorships in holding and subsidiary companies, in computing the limits on directorships that an individual may hold;

- The provisions relating to the composition of the board of directors of the holding company shall also be made applicable to the composition of the board of directors of subsidiary companies;
- At least one-third of the board of directors of the subsidiary company shall be non-executive directors of the parent company;
- The audit committee of the parent company shall also review the financial statements of the subsidiary company;
- The minutes of the board meeting of the subsidiary company shall be placed for review at the board meeting of the parent company; and
- The board report of the parent company should state that they have reviewed the affairs of the subsidiary company also.

3.12.1.3 Based on the deliberations, the Committee makes the following mandatory recommendation:

Mandatory recommendation

The provisions relating to the composition of the board of directors of the holding company should be made applicable to the composition of the board of directors of subsidiary companies.

At least one independent director on the board of directors of the parent company shall be a director on the board of directors of the subsidiary company.

The audit committee of the parent company shall also review the financial statements, in particular the investments made by the subsidiary company.

The minutes of the board meetings of the subsidiary company shall be placed for review at the board meeting of the parent company.

The board report of the parent company should state that they have reviewed the affairs of the subsidiary company also.

3.13 Real Time Disclosures

3.13.1 Disclosure of critical business events

3.13.1.1 It was suggested that SEBI should issue rules relating to real-time disclosures of certain events or transactions that may be of importance to investors, within 3–5 business days. These would include events such as (a) a change in the control of the company, (b) a company's acquisition/disposal of a significant amount of assets, (c) bankruptcy or receivership, (d) a change in the company's independent auditors, and (e) the resignation of a director.

3.13.1.2 The Committee noted that there are certain practical problems in ensuring timely disclosures. For example, a business transaction that is under negotiations may have an impact on the market price. However, its disclosure may prejudice the underlying business negotiations.

3.13.1.3 The Committee also noted the issue of rumor verification by stock exchanges. It noted a view that board decisions that were price sensitive should be disclosed to the markets within 15 minutes. Stock exchanges are currently responsible for rumor verification. The Committee however believed that this issue needs to be studied with much greater depth by SEBI and the stock exchanges, and should not be restricted to a corporate governance perspective alone.

3.13.1.4 The Committee was of the view that no recommendation would be made to SEBI in respect of this suggestion.

3.14 Evaluation of Board Performance

3.14.1 Mechanism for evaluating non-executive board members

3.14.1.1 The Committee received the following suggestions:

- The performance evaluation of non-executive directors should be done by a peer group comprising the entire board of directors, excluding the director being evaluated; and
- Peer group evaluation should be the mechanism to determine whether to extend/continue the terms of appointment of non-executive directors.

3.14.1.2 The Committee noted that evaluation of board members is in a germane stage in India. It is necessary to have a robust process in place for such evaluation. It is also necessary to ensure continuity of top leadership, including CEO succession planning. However, the Committee believes that this should be of a recommendatory nature at first, before becoming a mandatory requirement. This will help companies develop robust processes for board evaluation. This may be made mandatory after a period of 4–5 years.

3.14.1.3 Based on the above deliberations, the Committee makes the following non-mandatory recommendation:

Non-mandatory recommendation

The performance evaluation of non-executive directors should be by a peer group comprising the entire board of directors, excluding the director being evaluated; and

Peer group evaluation should be the mechanism to determine whether to extend/continue the terms of appointment of non-executive directors.

3.15 Analyst Reports

3.15.1 Disclosures in reports issued by security analysts

3.15.1.1 It was suggested that rules should be put in place by SEBI regarding reports issued by security analysts.

3.15.1.2 The Committee noted that the integrity and credibility of reports issued by security analysts could be compromised owing to pressures to which the security analyst may be subject. This is because of the conflict of interest that arises between the stock analysts and their employing brokerage/investment-banking firms, on the one hand and the listed companies that the stock analysts write reports about, on the other hand.

3.15.1.3 Based on the discussions, the Committee makes the following mandatory recommendation:

Mandatory recommendation

SEBI should make rules for the following:

- Disclosure in the report issued by a security analyst whether the company that is being written about is a client of the analyst's employer or an associate of the analyst's employer, and the nature of services rendered to such company, if any; and
- Disclosure in the report issued by a security analyst whether the analyst or the analyst's employer or an associate of the analyst's employer hold or held (in the 12 months immediately preceding the date of the report) or intend to hold any debt or equity instrument in the issuer company that is the subject matter of the report of the analyst.

4 RECOMMENDATIONS OF THE NARESH CHANDRA COMMITTEE

4.1 Background

4.1.1 Section 2.3.8 of this report states that the Committee would also recommend that the following mandatory recommendations in the report of the Naresh Chandra Committee, relating to corporate governance, be implemented by SEBI.

4.1.2 This section sets out such recommendations of the Naresh Chandra Committee that were considered by this Committee.

4.2 Disclosure of Contingent Liabilities (Section 2.5 of Naresh Chandra Committee Report)

4.2.1 The Committee makes the following mandatory recommendation:

Management should provide a clear description in plain English of each material contingent liability and its risks, which should be accompanied by the auditor's clearly worded comments on the management's view. This section should be highlighted in the significant accounting policies and notes on accounts, as well as in the auditor's report, where necessary. This is important because investors and shareholders should obtain a clear view of a company's contingent liabilities as these may be significant risk factors that could adversely affect the company's future financial condition and results of operations.

4.3 CEO/CFO Certification (Section 2.10 of Naresh Chandra Committee Report)

4.3.1 The Committee makes the following mandatory recommendation:

For all listed companies, there should be a certification by the CEO (either the executive chairman or the managing director) and the CFO (whole-time finance director or other person discharging this function) which should state that, to the best of their knowledge and belief:

- They have reviewed the balance sheet, and profit and loss account and all its schedules and notes on accounts, as well as the cash flow statements, and the directors' report;
- These statements do not contain any material untrue statement or omit any material fact, nor do they contain statements that might be misleading;
- These statements together present a true and fair view of the company, and are in compliance with the existing accounting standards and/or applicable laws/regulations;
- They are responsible for establishing and maintaining internal controls and have evaluated the effectiveness of internal control systems of the company; and they have also disclosed to the auditors and the audit committee, deficiencies in the design or operation of internal controls, if any, and what they have done or propose to do to rectify these;
- They have also disclosed to the auditors as well as the audit committee, instances of significant fraud, if any, that involves management or employees having a significant role in the company's internal control systems; and
- They have indicated to the auditors, the audit committee, and in the notes on accounts, whether or not there were significant changes in internal control and/or of accounting policies during the year.

4.4 Definition of Independent Director (Section 4.1 of Naresh Chandra Committee Report)

4.4.1 This has been incorporated in clause 3.10.1.4 of this report.

4.5 Independence of Audit Committee
(Section 4.7 of Naresh Chandra Committee Report)

4.5.1 The Committee makes the following mandatory recommendation:
   All audit committee members shall be non-executive directors.

4.6 Independent Director Exemptions
(Section 4.10 of Naresh Chandra Committee Report)

4.6.1 The Committee makes the following recommendation:

Legal provisions must specifically exempt non-executive and independent directors from criminal and civil liabilities under certain circumstances. SEBI should recommend that such exemptions need to be specifically spelt out for the relevant laws by the relevant departments of the government and independent regulators, as the case may be. However, independent directors should periodically review legal compliance reports prepared by the company as well as steps taken by the company to cure any taint. In the event of any proceedings against an independent director in connection with the affairs of the company, defense should not be permitted on the ground that the independent director was unaware of this responsibility.

5 OTHER SUGGESTIONS AND THE COMMITTEE'S RESPONSE

5.1 Background

5.1.1 The Committee also received certain other suggestions relating to corporate governance. These suggestions and the Committee's response/recommendation are set out in the following paragraphs.

5.2 Harmonization

5.2.1 It was suggested that SEBI should work towards harmonizing the provisions of clause 49 of the Listing Agreement and those of the Companies Act, 1956.

5.2.2 The Committee noted that major differences between the requirements under clause 49 and the provisions of the Companies Act, 1956 should be identified. SEBI should then recommend to the government that the provisions of the Companies Act, 1956 be changed to bring it in line with the requirements of the Listing Agreement.

5.3 Removal of Independent Directors

5.3.1 It was suggested that companies should inform SEBI/stock exchanges within five business days of the removal/resignation of an independent director, along with a statement certified by the managing director/director/company secretary about the circumstances of such removal/resignation (specifically whether there was any disagreement with the independent director that caused such removal/resignation). Any independent director sought to be removed or who has resigned because of a disagreement with management should have the opportunity to be heard in general meeting.

5.3.2 The Committee noted that under the existing provisions, companies are required to inform the stock exchanges of any changes in directors. The existing safeguards are adequate and hence no further action is required.

5.4 Disgorgement of Profits

5.4.1 It was suggested that CEOs/COOs/CFOs should disgorge equity- or incentive-based compensation, or profits arising from trading in company stock, if a restatement of financial statements is required or if there is any corporate misconduct leading to a financial liability.

5.4.2 The Committee noted that this was one of the recommendations of the Naresh Chandra Committee. Therefore, the Committee resolved that no further action is required at this stage.

5.5 Term of Office of Non-Executive Directors

5.5.1 It was suggested that there must be a cap on the term of office of a non-executive director.

5.5.2 The Committee noted that persons should be eligible for the office of non-executive director so long as the term of office did not exceed nine (as per report) years (in three terms of three [as per report] years each, running continuously). [Also refer to recommendation under Section 3.9 of this report.]

5.5.3 The Committee also noted that it would be a good practice for directors to retire after a particular age. Companies may fix the retirement age at either 65 or 70 years.

5.5.4 The Committee recommends that the age limit for directors to retire should be decided by companies themselves. Corporate boards should have an adequate mechanism of self-renewal, as part of corporate governance best practices.

5.6 Corporate Governance Ratings

5.6.1 It was suggested that corporate governance practices followed by companies should be rated using rating models. It was also suggested that companies should be rated based on parameters of wealth generation, maintenance and sharing, as well as on corporate governance.

5.6.2 The Committee deliberated and noted that corporate governance ratings are desirable, as this will provide a process of independent appraisal. Certain rating agencies have begun work in this area; however, the process is still in a development phase and may need to be evolved based on future experience.

5.6.3 The Committee is therefore of the view that for the time being, it should not be mandatory for companies to be rated on corporate governance parameters. However, it should be left to the management of companies to decide whether they want to be rated or not (as per report) on corporate governance .

5.7 Media Scrutiny

5.7.1 The Committee considered the views expressed by members on scrutiny of the media, especially the financial press. A code of conduct for the financial media is already prescribed by the Press Council of India. However, verifying adherence to this code of conduct is difficult in the current circumstances. The Committee suggests that it is desirable for SEBI to review this issue in greater detail, keeping in mind issues like transparency and disclosures, conflicts of interest, etc, before making any final rule.

5.7.2 The Committee noted that SEBI should consider discussing this issue with representatives of the media, especially the financial press.

6 IMPLEMENTATION AND WAY FORWARD

6.1 The Committee noted that the recommendations contained in this report can be implemented by means of an amendment to the Listing Agreement, with changes made to the existing clause 49.

6.2 A primary issue that arises with implementation is whether the recommendations should be made applicable to all companies immediately or in a phased manner since the costs of compliance may be large for certain companies. Another issue is whether to extend the applicability of these recommendations to companies that are registered with BIFR (no expansion as per report). In the case of such companies, there is likely to be almost little or no trading in their shares on the stock exchanges.

6.3 The Committee believes that the recommendations should be implemented for all companies to which clause 49 apply. This would also continue to apply to companies that have been registered with BIFR, subject to any directions that BIFR may provide in this regard.

6.4 There are several corporate governance structures available in the developed world, but there is no one structure, which can be singled out as being better than the others. There is no 'one size fits all' structure for corporate governance. The Committee's recommendations are not, therefore, based on any one model, but, are designed for the Indian environment. Corporate governance extends beyond corporate law. Its fundamental objective is not mere fulfillment of the requirements of law, but, in ensuring commitment of the Board in managing the company in a transparent manner for maximizing long-term shareholder value.

6.5 Corporate governance has as many votaries as claimants. Among the latter, the Committee has primarily focused its recommendations on investors and shareholders, as they are the prime constituencies of SEBI. Effectiveness of a system of corporate governance cannot be legislated by law nor can any system of corporate governance be static. In a dynamic environment, systems of corporate governance need to continually evolve. The Committee believes that its recommendations raise the standards of corporate governance in Indian firms and make them attractive for domestic and global capital. These recommendations will also form the base for further evolution of the structure of corporate governance in consonance with the rapidly changing economic and industrial environment of the country in the new millennium.

INDEX